THE EGYPT
OF NASSER
AND SADAT

Princeton Studies on the Near East

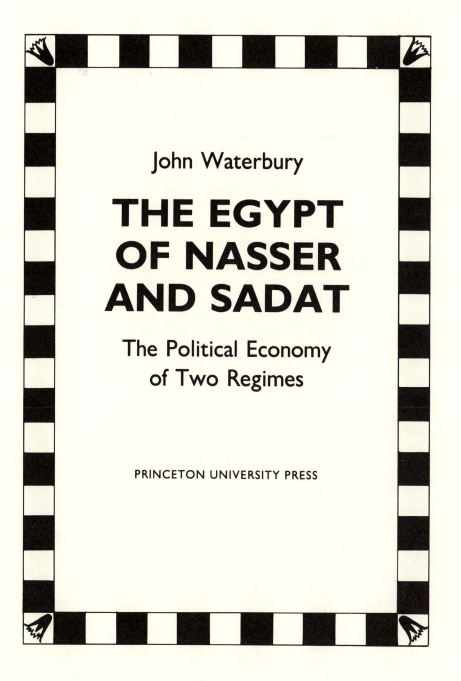

John Waterbury

THE EGYPT OF NASSER AND SADAT

The Political Economy of Two Regimes

PRINCETON UNIVERSITY PRESS

Copyright © 1983 by Princeton University Press

Published by Princeton University Press, 41 William Street, Princeton, New Jersey
In the United Kingdom: Princeton University Press, Guildford, Surrey

All Rights Reserved

Library of Congress Cataloging in Publication Data will be
found on the last printed page of this book

This book has been composed in Linotron Times Roman

Clothbound editions of Princeton University Press Books
are printed on acid-free paper, and binding materials are chosen for
strength and durability. Paperbacks, while satisfactory for personal collections,
are not usually suitable for library rebinding.

Printed in the United States of America by Princeton
University Press, Princeton, New Jersey

Second printing, with corrections, 1984

To all those Egyptians and *khawagas* whom I unashamedly cribbed, plundered, and cited out of context.

And to the memory of Dick Mitchell

You have retired to your island, with, as you think, all the data about us and our lives. No doubt you are bringing us to judgment on paper in the manner of writers. I wish I could see the result. It must fall very far short of *truth*: I mean such truths as I could tell you about us all—even perhaps about yourself.

Lawrence Durrell, Balthazar

Contents

CONTENTS

Part 5 Regional and International Dependency

Tables

TABLES

TABLES

Preface

The focus of this book is more often than not the "elite," "leadership," or the "regime." A word about these terms is in order. I do not have a fixed notion of the contours of the Egyptian elite; instead the term is used as a kind of shorthand for those occupying the most prominent posts in the state and military apparatus. Until recently there have been very few Egyptians outside this public apparatus who, in my view, enjoyed elite status. Relative power within the elite has shifted over time. During the 1960s Field Marshal 'Abd al-Hakim 'Amir was the second most powerful man in Egypt, but under Sadat neither the chief of staff nor the minister of defense attained equivalent power. Under Nasser the minister of planning was always a minor figure, but with the advent of 'Abd al-Razzaq 'Abd al-Magid (a civilian) under Sadat considerable power inhered in that position. Elite power has typically been more a function of personality and proximity to the "boss" than of institutional position.

The term regime normally connotes a political order of some kind; e.g., we speak of monarchical, totalitarian, or republican regimes. Indeed, in Arabic the word for order, *nizam*, may also mean regime. But like "elite," my use of the word regime is more a matter of convenience than of analysis. When I refer to the Nasserist regime I am implying something a good deal less than a formal system or a sophisticated ideology. It was, by definition, highly personalized, and thus the passing of the regime's founder meant the passing of the regime itself. After about 1974-75 it could be said that Sadat had elaborated his own regime. I see the regime as that nexus of alliances within and without the formal bureaucratic and public sectors that the leader forms in order to gain power and to keep it.

The manuscript for this book was in the hands of the publisher when President Anwar Sadat was assassinated by Muslim extremists on October 6, 1981, marking the end of his regime. His successor, Husni Mubarak, will, if given the chance, build his own regime, gradually forming a new nexus of alliances that will make his incumbency distinctive. He will share with Nasser and Sadat the fact that he is the nominally elected president of a republic, but he too, for a time at any rate, will build his order on his personality, his associates, and the policies they feel comfortable in espousing.

It is in more than definitional terms, however, that a new regime has been born in Egypt. Mubarak is almost a full decade younger than Sadat, Nasser, and all the other officers that contributed to the July Revolution of 1952. With Sadat's passing that generation, including the civilian wing, will be largely retired. Some figures may linger on—perhaps Mamduh Salim or Mustapha Khalil, the one Egypt's foremost politician under Sadat, the other a prominent technocrat in the regime of both Nasser and Sadat. But sooner rather than later Mubarak will call upon people of his own generation or younger. He may do so in the military more rapidly than among the civilians, for it is always difficult for a military man, even if he is president, to deal with officers who were his senior in rank and age. The task should be fairly easy. Most of those senior to Mubarak had already been retired or cashiered by Sadat, while several others died in a helicopter crash in the spring of 1981. Only General 'Abd al-Hamid Abu Ghazala, whom Mubarak kept as minister of defense, may stay on from a somewhat older group of peers.

The 1952 generation is thus going or gone. Mubarak and the people to whom he will turn played no role in the 1952 revolution. They do not share in its legitimacy; it is not the benchmark against which all they do in their adult lives must be measured. With few exceptions they fought none of its battles until 1967.

Husni Mubarak himself is in striking contrast to his two predecessors. In his teens in the late 1930s Nasser flitted from one political movement to another, tasting and testing them all. Politics and ultimately conspiracy were in his blood from adolescence. His military career was very nearly an after-thought. Sadat's military career ended in 1946, but his political career had begun long before and ended only with his death. Mubarak, however, if we take him at his word (interview with Ibrahim Sa'adah in *al-Mayo*, October 19, 1981), is the epitome of the professional officer. In his youth he studied hard and did well. In 1947 and 1948, at a time when Prime Minister Nu-qrashi was assassinated and then Hassan al-Banna, the leader of the Muslim Brethren; at a time when Egypt went to war with Israel and when nationalist fidayeen launched terrorist attacks on British troops ensconced in the Canal Zone, at a time, in short, when Egypt was in political ferment of such magnitude that only something like a military coup or a religious revolution could have put a cap on it; at such a time Mubarak plugged diligently away at his War College studies.

In 1950 he completed training as a pilot. From 1952 to 1959 he was an instructor in the Air College. He eventually became a commander and checked out on Soviet TU 16s. During 1964 and 1965 he underwent advanced training at the Frunz Academy in the USSR, learning to fly Ilyushin 28s. Upon his return to Egypt, he was made commander of Cairo West airbase. At the time of the June War of 1967 he was director of the Air College. Two years later, after the removal of his senior and thoroughly disgraced officers, he was made chief of staff of the air force. From that position he successfully deployed the Egyptian air force during the crossing of the Suez Canal in October 1973.

It came as a surprise to Mubarak as well as to most other observers when Sadat appointed him vice president in the spring of 1975 to replace Hussain Shafa'i, an original member of the 1952 conspiracy, who got on badly with Sadat. It was no surprise that Sadat chose someone from the military. For his own survival, Sadat had to reassure the senior officers that he would not ignore their interests in an era that was already being dubbed as one of peace. Mubarak was by no means the most prominent of those who could have been chosen, but it may have been easier to pick someone from the air force rather than undertake the invidious choice of a single person from among rival ground forces.

Whatever the explanation, it was only in 1975, at the age of forty-seven, that Mubarak began his political apprenticeship. By that age Nasser had thirty years of experience under his belt and over a decade as head of state. Still, Mubarak learned fast. Egyptians must count themselves lucky that Sadat was no workaholic. Increasingly he delegated the day-to-day supervision of the presidency and the cabinet to his vice president. He entrusted Mubarak with scores of sensitive missions to other Arab states, France, Britain, the US, and several African countries. Mubarak learned how to be a power broker in cabinet affairs, and he began to place his own favorites, such as Foreign Minister Kamal Hassan 'Ali (also an officer) in important positions. Finally, at the time of Sadat's death, Mubarak was in effective charge of the president's National Democratic Party and head of the Supreme National Security Council. The man was ready as few vice presidents have ever been for the job thrust upon him.

Taciturn, self-effacing, careful, tough, and when need be, ruthless are all adjectives regularly used to describe Mubarak. He is, despite six years as vice president, still a professional soldier who plays well a political game he fundamentally dislikes. After the crisis management and repression of Nasser and Sadat's half-blind leaps into the unknown, Egyptians may get what most want: *un bon gérant*. Moreover he is not personally bound to Sadat's most daring initiatives, such as the open-door policy and the Camp David accords. For Sadat to have changed or moved away from these policies in any major way would have been an admission of personal failure. Mubarak does not suffer from such personal involvement.

Like Nasser and Sadat, Mubarak will have little choice but to worry above all about his survival, and again like them he may come to equate his survival to the national good. There has been a successful transition of power in Egypt twice since 1952, but that is scarcely sufficient to declare such transfers as institutionalized. The stakes of the political game in Egypt remain very high, a fact to which Sadat's assassination attests. I want, therefore, to the greatest extent possible, to put my readers in the shoes of Egypt's leaders so that they can share in the primal concern of these men for their own self-preservation.

If one accepts my assumption about the elite's preoccupation with survival, some derivative points can be made. Policy may, and in Egypt has been, designed to enhance survival. It has frequently had a defensive and preemptive quality, anticipating or meeting imagined or real threats. But to reduce Egypt's policy process to a crude quest for power would do grave injustice to reality. Egypt's leaders, including Nasser and Sadat, have had strong ideological and programmatic predilections independent of their survival. They would have little leverage in promoting these predilections so long as they were distant from positions of real power. Hence survival becomes the necessary but not sufficient starting point for all else. There is no single optimal survival strategy and perhaps, once survival is assured, no single optimal strategy for translating predilections into policy. Much of this book will explore how Nasser and Sadat strove at a minimum for survival and, maximally, how they sought to remake Egyptian society in an image congenial to their own values. The Egyptian ''masses'' will become the focus of the analysis only insofar as by complying, resisting, or sabotaging the experiments they were being asked to live out for the greater good they caused policies to be adjusted or scrapped altogether.

It would be tedious to set forth here an annotated table of contents of the book; the unannotated one can do just as well. The five underlying themes of the book are embodied in the titles of each part. My major task is to describe a state or public apparatus put at the disposal of leaders determined to use it to remake the economic character of Egypt. This is not a question of the mere encouragement of economic development, but one of the state taking upon itself the full responsibility for allocating scarce resources and indeed for owning and supervising the assets that generate them; that story is at the heart of Part 2. The growth process—or frequently the stagnation process—creates new interests, tramples upon the old, and fosters new class alignments. It is upon the shifting class and interest alignments that Part 3 focuses.

State involvement in the economy evokes attempts by the regime to devise supportive political arrangements to contain those who are asked to pay part of the price of development and/or stagnation. In this sense both Nasser and Sadat tried to subordinate politics to economics and to propagate an illusion of political participation while demanding the reality of economic docility. The politics of containment are the subject of Part 4.

Egypt does not govern its affairs in a vacuum. Throughout the period under consideration foreign actors have had considerable influence on the policy-making process, not to mention on the question of war and peace. Survival has been determined by external actors as much as by domestic interests. In Part 5 the various sources of external influence are examined.

In Part 1 I want to situate the specifics of the Egyptian case in the context of a number of questions that preoccupy students of all lesser developed countries (LDCs). These revolve around two fundamental points of debate: 1) the degree to which a regime and the state at its service can divorce itself from domestic class interests and rebuild class alignments; and 2) the degree to which the regime is the captive, willing or otherwise, of the economic and geopolitical interests of the dominant industrial powers of the so-called Northern core. Egypt's answers to these questions will be outlined in the next two chapters.

There is, of course, no end to the story, and we shall have gotten on and off a moving train. We cannot be sure of destination, but I will offer some informed estimates as to possible resting places. It is my conviction that no matter how weak the value of prediction, it is of great importance to know where Egypt has been. I make no excuses for the amount of descriptive analysis served up. Further, my aim is not to generate new theories or paradigms but rather to test the utility of a few of the plethora that now exist with respect to a concrete case. This then is not a political history of Egypt since 1952; much is left out that has at any rate been covered elsewhere. Still, there are many voids in our factual knowledge of what transpired in Egypt in the 1960s. Where I feel I have new information or a new interpretation, I have brought it forward. The period since the death of Nasser, to which I was a direct witness, has understandably received even less scholarly coverage, and in consequence I place considerable emphasis upon it (see, however, Baker 1978).

A final word about structure—the major sections of the book center on basic public policy issues. Each policy is studied during that diachronic slice of the regime's life that seems most relevant. This structuring brutalizes reality, for all these policy domains interacted at any given point in time. I shall refer to such interactions when possible and where relevant, but were I to have organized the study so as to look at *all* policy issues at specific points in time, the result would have been no more than an annotated chronology of policy "happenings." The trade-off is not altogether satisfactory, and readers will have to contain their desire for more empiric evidence within any one policy treatment as well as their restlessness at a certain amount of factual reprise as we move from section to section. The big picture, to the extent it can be discerned, must await the end of the undertaking.

Acknowledgments

This book has gestated for a long period, and the cumulative debts I have incurred have been commensurate with the time spent in preparation. First and foremost it was the opportunity of six years residence in Egypt under the auspices of the American Universities Field Staff that enabled me to assemble the materials for the book. I was in Egypt from 1971 to 1977 and have been back four times since, the latest visit being in October 1981.

The Center for Research and Studies of Mediterranean Societies (CRESM) of the University of Aix-Marseille III gave me a year (1977-78) in which I was able to sort through and organize my documentation. The actual writing was made possible by the Woodrow Wilson School and its Research Program in Development Studies that supported me for two summers in connection with this study.

My greatest debt is to the many Egyptians, foreign experts, journalists, and academic colleagues who have guided me, reacted to my ideas, and plumbed their own memories and knowledge of Egypt for my benefit. I have a list of 137 people whom I interviewed at least once, and many several times, in the course of my study in Egypt. I have chosen throughout this book, with rare exceptions, to honor the confidentiality in which they talked to me. Still, I feel bound to mention a few friends whose patience, willingness to give up their time to me, and great knowledge of Egyptian society cannot go unrecognized: Rushdy Said, Tahsin Bashir, Lutfi 'Abd al-'Azim, Mohammed Sid Ahmad, Essam Montasser, Mustapha Gabali, Ahmad Baha al-Din, Louis Awad, Nazih Daif, 'Ali Salim, Mahmud Maraghi, and 'Ali Dessouki. Among the *khawagia* were Delwin Roy, Henry Bruton, Edward Peck, Tom Croley, Peter Nichols, Robert Armstrong, Jack Goodridge, Gordon McClean, and Henry Tanner. I will not absolve them totally from errors in fact and judgment that will occur in the following pages, but whatever merit this book contains is in large measure their responsibility.

The technical challenge of producing this book was daunting. To meet it I was ably assisted by three graduate students in the Woodrow Wilson School: Dani Rodrik, N. Ranjan Pal, and Shamsher Singh. They checked tables, Arabic transliterations, citations, and bibliographic entries. Jerri Kavanagh, Michael Padulo, Dee Wilson, Shirley Canty, and Jean Gallo typed the manuscript in its various versions with grace and precision. Finally the editing of

ACKNOWLEDGMENTS

the manuscript was skillfully carried out by Marilyn Campbell of Princeton University Press.

T. did not actually share in the work or even care much about it, but her presence during some difficult times made it go much more easily.

Princeton, New Jersey
November 1981

A Note on Transliteration

The system of rendering Arabic proper names in English has been kept as simple as possible. No diacritical marks have been used, and the only Arabic letter that has a distinctive rendering is the *'ayn*, represented by a single quotation mark. The *alif* has not been rendered except in the rare instances that it appears in the middle of a word. It is then represented by a single quotation mark, e.g., *fi'at*. The *qaf* is transliterated by a q and the *kaf* by a k. The *ya*, whether terminal or medial, is represented by i, e.g., 'Ali or Shaikh. If it is double, however, it will appear as yy as in Sayyid, or as y at the beginning of a word, e.g., Yazid. The *jim*, represented by g, is pronounced hard as in go: e.g., Gamal.

It has not been possible to maintain consistency in all spellings. Where names have acquired an accepted rendering in the English language press or have been transliterated in a certain manner by the bearers themselves, I have honored established usage. Thus Nasser and not Nāṣir or Naguib and not Najīb. Similarly, because it appears everywhere in company advertising, it will be Osman Ahmad Osman and not Uthman Ahmad Uthman. Some confusion is unavoidable in cases such as that of Khalid Muhy al-Din, who has not published in English, but whose cousin Amr has written extensively as Amr Mohie-Eldin. Both versions will appear according to the person involved.

A Note on Citations

I have tried to minimize the number of footnotes by including references in the text. These first indicate the author or the periodical from which the information is drawn, followed by the date and, where relevant, the page number. Citations from newspapers and periodicals are frequently self-contained. Otherwise the reader should refer to the bibliography arranged alphabetically according to the author's last name or the title of the periodical, followed by the year of publication.

Exchange Rates, Weights, and Measures

July 14, 1947 Egypt left the Sterling Zone, but in 1948 Egypt devalued its pound in concert with the pound sterling.

1948	£E 1 = $2.87	
1962	£E 1 = $2.30	
1975	Official rate £E 1 = $2.50	
	Incentive rate £E 1 = $1.70	
1976	Incentive rate £E 1 = $1.42	
1979	Unified rate £E 1 = $1.40	

1 *feddan* = 1.038 acres = .42 hectares = 24 *qayrots*
1 metric *qantar* (unginned cotton) = 157.5 kgs. = 346.5 lbs.
1 metric *qantar* (lint cotton) = 50 kgs. = 110 lbs.

Abbreviations

ACKNOWLEDGMENTS

MNC   Multinational Corporation
NDB   National Development Bank
NDP   National Democratic Party
NIB   National Investment Bank
NMC   New Middle Class
NPC   National Planning Commission
OPNUR   Organization of Progressive Nationalist Unionist Rassemblement
PCDNP   Permanent Council for the Development of National Production
RCC   Revolutionary Command Council
RMC   Rural Middle Class
SUMED   Suez-Mediterranean Pipeline
UAR   United Arab Republic

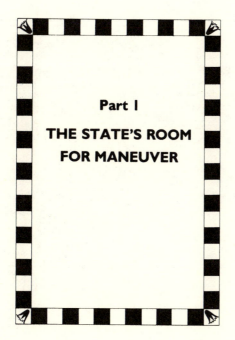

Part I

THE STATE'S ROOM
FOR MANEUVER

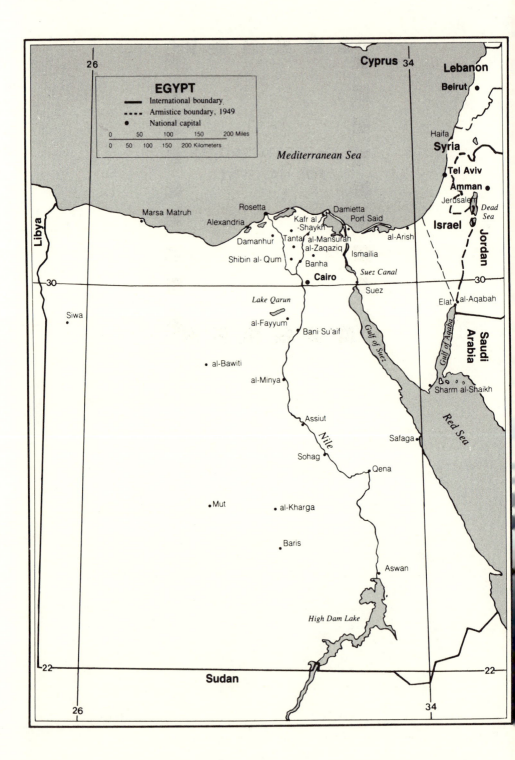

Chapter One

THE NATURE OF THE STATE
AND OF THE REGIME

The stage of revolutionary administrative measures is in fact outmoded. The time has come for us to rely upon the popular conscience of the people and not upon government intervention.... The only path that will allow us to meet the challenge of reaction and imperialism, the only way that will enable us to accomplish the transformation from capitalism to socialism is that of political and not governmental action.
[Gamal 'Abd al-Nasser, November 12, 1964, cited in Mahfouz 1972, p. 185.]

Egypt's geopolitical significance, its overall weight in the important Arab world, and the fact that it was one among a handful of Third World states to move in the 1950s toward a socialist transformation, would in themselves constitute adequate justification for a one-country case study. Much of this book can be considered just that. Where Egypt has been in the last quarter century, no less whither Egypt, are questions of intrinsic significance to experts and laymen alike. I cannot pretend to advance authoritative answers to these questions, but I shall certainly give my own best estimates.

The balance sheet of Egypt's "revolutionary" experiment, both in political and economic terms, is highly mixed. In the following chapters the reader will be barraged with assessments of what went wrong. This is not a pleasant task and it is one that legitimately draws the fire of policy-makers who cannot enjoy the luxury of carping on the sidelines. My carping is not intended, however, to show up Egyptians as hopeless bunglers. To the contrary, unsatisfactory as it may appear, they could have done much worse, and in many respects have done quite well. Still, because of my respect and affection for them as people, I know they deserve better, and perhaps they will get it.

Yet, more important, Egypt's problems are reflected with more or less acuity in dozens of other developing societies. Egypt is in some ways unique as a society but in ways that matter most to economic performance, the ordering of national politics, and the conduct of foreign affairs, it has no claims to separate categorization. Thus it is hoped that through a detailed assessment of the elaboration and implementation of development strategies and the political structuring of domestic interests, we may better grasp the dynamics of other like polities.

This is, of course, a two-way street, and I have learned much about Egypt from studies of other countries seemingly far afield. Egypt has made abundantly clear to me the commonalities linking Third World countries, commonalities that partially wash out the significance of cultural variations in general and those of political culture in particular. This is not an easy confession for one who devoted most of a book to the cultural determinants of political behavior in Morocco.[1] But in emphasizing the socio-economic characteristics that link developing countries regardless of their cultures, I incur a major risk of falling into crude and insensitive determinism. For instance, a recurrent analytic theme in this study will be the degree to which the policy-making elites of Egypt or of any other LDC can make sovereign, autonomous decisions with respect to domestic and foreign policy. In Marxian and *dependencia* analysis there has been a tendency to deny national elites meaningful scope for independent action. Each step of these polities in the implementation of their development strategies and in their dealing with the outside world is, so it has been argued, preprogrammed by the "world capitalist system." I do not believe that there is compelling evidence to support this proposition in its more extreme forms. By the same token one must discount the claims of leaders of LDCs who insist that they are not moved by nor will they tolerate external influence in the shaping of their policies. For its part, Egypt appears to be the prisoner of two kinds of situations that severely limit the range of policy responses it can reasonably contemplate (everything hinges, of course, on the definition of reasonable). One emerges from its socio-economic makeup and the other from its dependency upon external sources of finance capital, technology, markets, and arms.

Egypt is a large semi-agricultural country about half of whose population participates in one of the oldest and most intensive peasant-based societies in the world. It manifests a number of characteristics that one commonly associates with the societies of the underdeveloped world. The general standard of living is low, with per capita income at about $300 a year. The rate of private savings is commensurately low. Among the adult population a majority remains illiterate. Illiteracy is particularly marked among women. One major result of this situation is that it is very difficult to bring about broad technological changes in agriculture or the development of a skilled nonagricultural labor force. The cities themselves, rapidly approaching the

---

[1] *The Commander of the Faithful* (New York: Columbia University Press, 1970).

point where they will harbor more than half of the total population, survive not on the strength of a growing manufacturing sector, but on the private and public consumption of the sprawling civil service. Alongside this salariat are hundreds of thousands of urbanites in the ''informal'' sector who, at very low levels of capitalization and productivity, make up the private service sector.

Rising above, although sometimes just barely, the urban and rural ruck are the elite of industrialized labor, the vast civil service growing parasitically at exponential rates, the upper echelons of the public bureaucracies and their counterparts in the private sector, and, finally, the middle-level commercial farmers of the countryside. All of these groups will be described in much greater detail in the following chapters. My point here is that the roster I have just presented does not differ in any major respect from that of several developing societies. Consequently one may argue that the range of development strategies open to the elites of these countries is rather narrowly circumscribed and takes on a certain sameness.

The second situation of which Egypt is a prisoner arises from the search for great power patronage, arms supplies, external aid, and investment capital. Once again Egypt is not fundamentally different from other developing countries that experience chronic balance of payments difficulties and foreign exchange crises. To develop and grow these states rightly assert that they must live beyond their means until such time as their economies can pay their own way *and* service the debts incurred during the transition to self-sustaining growth. National elites find themselves in a continual scramble for external financing. If it comes, it does so either with political strings attached if bilateral public aid, or with financial strings if private commercial (banks) or multilateral (IMF). Meeting short-term obligations frequently propels such states into policies of expediency which nonetheless have long-term consequences limiting future options. Moreover, even the short-term expedients are greatly influenced by domestic concerns (e.g., should one allow peasants to grow produce for lucrative domestic urban markets or ''force'' them to produce for export when foreign exchange is in short supply?) and the grinding momentum of existing policies (e.g., continuation of the government as the employer of last resort whatever the cost in efficiency).

Reconciliation of these countervailing forces often proves impossible and the country limps from one external or domestic crisis to another. Salvage operations, austerity programs, reform packages and the like are invoked to deal with the immediate situation, but once the heat of the crisis subsides they dissipate or are forgotten. If one adds to this, as one must with respect to Egypt, the constant possibility and regular recurrence of war one has all the elements of a formula for transition without end.

There are some predictable patterns inherent in the process of transition, especially as they relate to both sequential and cyclical crises in the process of capital accumulation and growth. To get a grasp on these patterns, I shall examine some general propositions on the nature and functions of the state in the process of development. These propositions are grouped under three headings:

1) Authoritarianism and economic development—the paradigm of the bureaucratic-authoritarian (BA) state
2) State autonomy and state capitalism
3) External dependency and the peculiar characteristics of states in the semiperiphery

The Bureaucratic-Authoritarian State

Guillermo O'Donnell's original and revised formulations of what he calls the "bureaucratic-authoritarian state" (O'Donnell 1973, 1978, and 1979) have stimulated a useful debate that has for the most part been confined to Latin America. What he and others are dissecting is the domestic or internal end of a series of linked factors that lead to varying degrees of external dependency and "dependent development."

The crux of O'Donnell's argument is that import-substituting industrialization (ISI) proceeds through an easy phase of expansion into basic consumer goods (textiles, food processing, beverages, some consumer durables, vehicle assembly, etc.), and that this phase, as in Argentina (Peron) and Mexico (Cárdenas in the 1930s), is accompanied by political mobilization, populism, and welfare policies that bring about some redistribution of national income.

It has often been the case, however, that the initial stages of ISI provoke an upsurge in the imports of raw materials and capital goods needed to supply the new consumer goods industries. At the same time the latter are highly protected and have little incentive to become competitive in international markets. The ISI enterprises do not generate their own foreign exchange so that their expansion becomes contingent on external borrowing. Once they have satisfied middle and upper class demand in particular and domestic mass markets (for beverages and textiles) in general, the easy phase is over and the crisis or challenge of "deepening" begins (cf. Lewis 1978, pp. 31-32).

The final moments of the easy phase are typified by high rates of inflation, costly welfare programs, some degree of worker mobilization and/or political liberalism, and economic stagnation frequently exacerbated by a balance of payments crisis. As long as the country continues to operate within a capitalist framework, the situation calls for a number of painful remedies: a reduction in welfare outlays, a lowering of protective measures for local industry, and a concentrated effort by the state to capture and reinvest the surplus of the most productive sectors. There may or may not be an export drive, but almost certainly there will be a turn toward foreign investment. The goal is to promote backward linkages from existing enterprises so that intermediate and capital goods industries emerge. This is the process of deepening, but to meet its capital and raw materials needs requires increased efficiency, high rates of investment, and labor docility. Populist inclusivism is brought to an end, labor unions are decapitated and contained, and wages are allowed to lag behind inflation and production. The actual seizure of the state apparatus by authoritarian actors and the shift to exclusivism may be triggered by perceived threats of mass upheaval that threaten orderly capitalist growth.

The process of deepening calls forth an alliance of state technocrats, military, and less frequently, civilian political leaders, with foreign investors and select domestic entrepreneurs. Foreign creditors and the IMF may have a considerable voice in the process, as Pinochet's Chile indicates, but that is not an unavoidable ingredient. These then are the basic elements of the BA state, and, according to O'Donnell (1979, p. 298), the political and economic exclusion of the working and lower middle classes is reenforced by the regime's reliance upon "the upper fractions of the local bourgeoisie and of transnational capitalism." While still invoked, corporatist ideology, elaborated during the populist phase, can no longer contain divergent class interests, and police repression becomes the glue of the polity. Political parties and liberal institutions are tamed or abolished and interest expression becomes fragmented and channeled along access routes to the bureaucracy and the presidency. Even then, O'Donnell suggests (1973) internal cleavages take shape within the ruling coalition. Typically the status and well-being of the middle class shows no improvement, and the elimination, in the name of efficiency, of some public enterprises serves to alienate that part of the coalition with vested interests in parastatal activities.[2] Thus in an advanced stage of BA and of the process of deepening (Brazil of the late 1970s) the regime must strike new colors (O'Donnell 1978, p. 22):

> . . . the state must become less orthodox and more nationalist; it must be more protectionist . . . it must reserve for itself and for the national bourgeoisie hunting grounds forbidden to the direct access of international capital; and it has to be itself more entrepreneurial in directly productive activities. In other words the BA state must come to restrict international capital to a degree almost unthinkable during the initial orthodox stage . . .

[2] Chile is probably without rival in its divestment from and sale of public enterprise to private interests. Between 1973 and 1977 300 industries nationalized by Allende were returned to their former owners, and another 200 started by the state were sold to the private sector (Kaufman 1979, p. 180).

Failing this, the BA state may give way altogether, as has occurred in Turkey after 1946 (Okyar 1975) and in Peru after 1977 (Stepan 1978; Lowenthal 1975; Handelman 1980). But the eclipse of the BA state, which in itself is not inevitable, is not necessarily part of a sequence but rather part of a pattern of oscillation between accumulation and reform.

In fact this oscillation has been suggested by Albert Hirschman who, along with several others, has tried to test and refine O'Donnell's paradigm (Hirschman 1979). Hirschman sees the consolidation of authoritarianism not so much in terms of deepening as in terms of the political traumas of transition from reform to accumulation. This occurs in three stages (although there is nothing rigid about this: cf. Kaufman 1979). The years of "easy" ISI lead to a period of inflation, overvaluation of the national currency, import controls, and resort to foreign finance. This in turn provokes balance of payments difficulties, which require anti-inflationary policies, devaluation, and export promotion. In both the latter stages working class elements must be closely policed and repressed. Deepening may or may not be important in this process, and may or may not be a stated objective of the regime. Like the reform and redistribution stage, that of belt-tightening and accumulation cannot be sustained indefinitely and will give way to another period of reform.

For Hirschman the two kinds of processes alternate. What Nasser's Egypt of the 1960s and Nehru's India of the second Five-Year Plan (although India was clearly not a BA state) demonstrate is that reform and accumulation can be attempted simultaneously, albeit with disappointing results on both counts. One of Hirschman's most intriguing speculations offers an explanation of what happens next. During an initial period of accumulation what Hirschman (1973) calls the "tunnel effect" applies. The groups least favored by the process, like motorists stopped in one lane of a tunnel watching the other lane move ahead, will tolerate their condition so long as they expect their turn to move ahead is coming soon. If their expectations are disappointed, which they often are, then protest will follow. This will usher in a new period of reform which, under certain circumstances, "can act as a strong homogenizing influence on society so that . . . the stage is set for highly uneven development and prolonged tolerance thereof, even and perhaps particularly in countries where the reduction or elimination of inequalities was one of the principal aims of revolution or reform." Hirschman cites Mexico from Cárdenas to the riots of 1968 as an example (1979, p. 94).

It is not clear what psychological element spawns this "false tolerance" and acceptance of inequity. But whatever it is, it has been at work in Egypt since 1965 when the redistributional effects of an era of reform came to an end, when the wedding of accumulation and redistribution was annulled, and when an erratic course toward accumulation and growth that has benefited mainly the middle classes and working class elite has been pursued. Part of the explanation may lie in the phenomenon of massive worker migration to labor markets of developed countries. This factor has surely mitigated the resentment that might have undermined Mexico's political formula from 1940 to the present, and certainly bought time for Sadat after 1971.[3]

Very important questions lie unanswered in O'Donnell's propositions: to wit, is BA somehow objectively necessary, and do the leaders of BA regimes have a clear idea of what they are about? Robert Kaufman (1979) answers both questions in the negative. Looking at a group of Latin American nations, Kaufman concludes that civilian, nonauthoritarian elites have demonstrated as much capacity for deepening as BA regimes, and that the latter have not always been successful in their endeavors. Moreover, some BA elites came to power without any strategy of deepening and in some instances with no economic strategy at all (Kaufman 1979, p. 248). This is a fundamental point, for Kaufman at once argues that BA regimes are not objectively necessary to deal with a certain kind of economic crisis, nor, when on the scene, need they have a clear idea of their role. Nonetheless he sees in the proliferation of BA regimes a logic that by and large sustains O'Donnell's thesis.

In the same spirit I find O'Donnell's ideas useful in getting at some of the dynamics of Nasserist and post-Nasserist Egypt. The assertions I am about to make will have to be taken on a certain measure of faith until more detailed information is offered in future chapters. First, the advent of Nasser and military rule in Egypt can be seen as a response to the considerable political turmoil in the country after World War II. Militancy on the left (the Worker-Student Council of 1946) but especially on the right among the Muslim Brethren, political assassination, the first Arab-Israeli war, and the burning of Cairo in January 1952 may in part explain why the Free Officers acted.

At the same time it would be absurd to argue that the Free Officers came to power with blueprints for deepening in their attaché cases. That an easy phase of ISI was coming to an end and that the officers almost immediately plumped for heavy industrial projects is undeniable. But the industrialization drive was launched in the name of national independence and economic sovereignty. It was not until the rise to prominence of 'Aziz Sidqi and the First Industrial Plan in 1957 that an articulated strategy of deepening was adumbrated.

From then on Egypt was run by an alliance of the military and state technocrats (there was certainly no reliance upon the upper bourgeoisie) who were very much concerned with discipline, order, and production. Yet this alliance, while it repressed the labor force, did not have the will to exploit it, to extract from it through inflation and low wages an investable surplus.

---

[3] Hirschman does not mention this factor in his 1979 essay but certainly does in his *Exit, Voice and Loyalty* (1970).

Indeed, Nasser's authoritarianism was ostensibly inclusivist, both politically and economically, and populist at least in its rhetoric. There was a major effort at redistribution of wealth that, ultimately, derailed the process of accumulation. In picking up the pieces, Sadat was no more willing to exploit the working classes, but he put aside programs of income redistribution in favor of satisfying middle-class consumerism. Under Nasser accumulation took place primarily through nationalization; under Sadat it took place primarily through deficit financing and external borrowing. The recurrent tightening and relaxing of authoritarian controls was not a response to the challenge of deepening but to policies of redistribution and welfare. What changes is not the authoritarian soul of the regime—that may be a constant as in Algeria, 1962-1980 or Peru 1969-1980—but the expansion and contraction of state welfare in its broadest sense. A quick review of the major phases of ISI in Egypt will help focus some of these questions.

Egypt, I argue, has gone through two modes of accumulation and growth, and is now well into a third. The first mode includes the initial efforts at ISI beginning with the world depression and the introduction of protective tariffs in 1930 (Radwan 1974, p. 245). Other than easing some credit constraints through the Industrial Bank, the state played a minor role in this period. In political terms the period bore some superficial marks of inclusivist politics, but the dominant trait was exclusivist. The few relatively open elections were eclipsed by the authoritarian and repressive government of Isma'il Sidqi in the early thirties, the period of martial law during the Second World War, and in a general sense the continuing role of Great Britain as watchdog and final arbiter of Egyptian politics. Economically, the emphasis upon textiles, fertilizers, sugar, and food-processing makes this the "easy" phase of ISI.

The second mode was initiated almost immediately by the military regime that took over in 1952. This consisted in state-led ISI, which persisted until 1967. The state involved itself directly in designing a strategy of accumulation, mobilizing capital, and starting up or expanding enterprises. This was a period of deepening and of developing vertical linkages in the industrial sector. It was anything but easy and anything but successful. To bring it off at all, so Egypt's leaders judged, required the nationalization of the nonagricultural private sector. The strategy was in disarray by 1966, and the June War of 1967 delivered the *coup de grâce* to strategies of accumulation of *any* kind.

This more difficult ISI phase was inclusivist in economic terms with real progress in welfare programs and employment, and superficially inclusivist in political terms as mass-based corporatist structures were put in place (cf. Stepan 1978, p. 80). But, as Cardoso pointed out (1979, pp. 36-37) the rhetoric of populism in bureaucratic-authoritarian polities is no more than a gloss on political repression and demobilization.

After 1979 Egypt moved into a third mode of accumulation that has the potential at least for producing political and economic configurations similar to those in several contemporary Latin American states. The emphasis has been on export-led growth, with the state acting as catalyst to and partner in alliances with foreign private capital and technology, and, on occasion, with the Egyptian private sector. If this strategy eventually succeeds, *tri-pe* arrangements along the lines described by Peter Evans for Brazil (1979) may well emerge. Again, a surface political liberalism has accompanied the third mode, but it is a slender reed that could not withstand the policing of labor and the general belt-tightening that would be required if the regime ever summoned the resolve to make Egyptian manufactures competitive in international markets.

The stage is set, as it has been since 1965, for a government by technocrats under the aegis of a strong personalistic president (supported by but not necessarily from the military) with national goals defined as greater and more efficient production. Those who resist the reforms that must accompany the attainment of this goal will be treated as enemies of the public good. The range of permissible debate must therefore be strictly circumscribed. Thus while Sadat's good will may have moved him toward liberalism, his instincts for survival and his entourage drove him toward exclusivism and authoritarianism. It may be that Husni Mubarak, a taciturn *bon gérant*, may accentuate the move toward economic efficiency and controlled liberalism.

He may, in this respect, have the support of the public sector managerial elite and the private sector middle class. The first would come down strongly for efficiency at the expense of equity, while the second, reaping the benefits of speculative investment during a period of high inflation, would not want their activities publicized by a free press or genuinely popular politicians.

Concomitantly both public and private sector interests have entered into joint ventures with foreign investors who have been welcomed back to Egypt since 1973. Their presence was hoped to promote innovation, new managerial techniques, and the technological renovation of the overprotected and languishing public sector. It was also intended to bring in foreign exchange through direct investment and open access to foreign markets by mobilizing the know-how and names of MNCs.

On the whole Egypt's has been "soft-hearted" authoritarianism, producing neither Stalinists of the left nor of the right. This requires an explanation, and it lies, I believe, in the international arena. For several LDCs the historical moment in which they pursued strategies of ISI corresponded to a particularly accommodating international climate. For those who had to import petroleum for their industrial projects, energy in the 1950s and 1960s was very cheap. The Food for Peace Program in the same years made available US surplus grain on easy terms. Expanding international trade in the 1960s led to growing markets for LDC manufactures and some improvement in the terms of trade for raw materials. Finally, Soviet-American competition for influence in the Third World resulted in significant aid and arms flows from both powers. In other words countries like Egypt, India, Ghana, or Indonesia could try to combine accumulation and reform and seemingly get away with it.

The favorable moment came to an end somewhere around 1971. The weakening of the dollar, détente, widespread famine, and the OPEC price increases ushered in a new era, in which the non-oil-exporting LDCs could no longer afford reform and accumulation. Many resisted having to choose, but massive external borrowing on nonconcessional terms merely postponed the day of reckoning. Egypt held out, while Indonesia after 1965 and the Philippines after 1972 and Turkey after 1980 lapsed into modes that confirm nearly all O'Donnell's predictions. It could be that the rekindling of the Cold War atmosphere in the early 1980s will grant some LDCs of peculiar geopolitical significance (Egypt is one of them) a reprieve, as the superpowers increase their levels of aid and support to them, but I would contend that the era of "easy" ISI is gone forever.

The Autonomy of the State

Can the state loosen itself, however temporarily, from class domination? Can the state itself constitute or engender the creation of a new class? Despite a tendency for the terms of the debate surrounding these questions to be dictated by Marxian logic and preconceptions, they nonetheless address issues that are crucial to understanding the scope of policy action available to the Egyptian state. To put the matter as simply as possible, if the Egyptian state is the witting or unwitting captive of class interests (as argued by Riad 1964; Abdelmalek 1968; and Hussein 1971) then it is essential to understand the nature of these interests if one is to grasp the logic of state action. If, on the other hand, the Egyptian state has not been so captured, that fact itself must be explained and an effort made to determine the domestic and international constraints that *do* impinge upon the policy process.

There is surprising unanimity among most observers that the state in noncommunist societies and in the world capitalist order is, whatever outward appearances might suggest, in the final analysis an instrument of class domination. Non-Marxists are as convinced of that fact as Marxists (Hirschman 1979, p. 95).

. . . Both functions, entrepreneurial and reform, are essential for the successful achievement of development under capitalist auspices, even from the point of view of the longer run interests of this process itself. But at the same time, the reformers are unlikely ever to appear as "little helpers" of the entrepreneurial groups. When they enter the stage, they may well be full of invective against the latter, who will return the compliment.

12

So the invective is part of an unwitting charade; the self-styled revolutionaries are no more than reformers who, guided by an invisible hand, reorder the process of accumulation in a manner ultimately beneficial to the capitalist classes. Or, if the state is capable of destroying vested class interests, the outcome of its actions is foregone. ". . . autonomous bureaucrats who in a crisis situation become dynamically autonomous of class forces have the capacity only to constitute themselves as a new ruling class, which in a capitalist world economy, means a capitalist class" (Trimberger 1978, p. 174).

It is still the case that several analysts have insisted upon the empirical reality of state autonomy in a given set of *temporary* circumstances. Some, like Poulantzas (1978) argue from a tradition that finds its roots in the now hoary conception of the Bonapartist state as put forth in Marx's *Eighteenth Brumaire of Louis Bonaparte* (1898, pp. 70-71). Marx insisted that the second Bonaparte's regime, "This fearful body of parasites" as he called it,[4] was "independent" but not class-free. It in fact represented a class, the most numerous in France, that of the "allotment" peasants or those who received land in the course of the French Revolution. But, in his famous comparison of this class to potatoes in a sack, Marx stressed that this peasantry was a class only in its relation to the means of production but not in terms of consciousness or self-awareness; hence the state was and was not class-based and therefore quasi-autonomous.

Nicos Poulantzas has sought to refine the concept of state autonomy by emphasizing the distinction between the long- and short-term interests of the dominant classes. The state always acts in favor of the long-term interests of the several "fractions" that make up the bourgeois classes, but in the short-term it must manipulate, mediate, and occasionally thwart the divergent objectives of these same fractions. "The state can fulfill this organizational and unifying role insofar as it retains a *relative autonomy* in relation to one or

---

[4] This executive power, with its tremendous bureaucratic and military organization; with its wide-spreading and artificial machinery of government—an army of office holders, half a million strong, together with a military force of another million men—; this fearful body of parasites, that coils itself like a snake around French society, stopping all its pores, originated at the time of the absolute monarch, along with the decline of feudalism, which it helped to hasten. . . . The first French revolution, having as a mission to sweep away all local, territorial, urban and provincial special privileges, with the object of establishing the civic unity of the nation, was bound to develop what the absolute monarch had begun—the work of centralization, together with the range, the attributes and the menials of the government. Napoleon completed this governmental machinery. The legitimist and July Monarchy contributed nothing thereto, except a greater subdivision of labor. . . . Finally, the parliamentary republic found itself, in its struggle against the revolution, compelled, with its repressive measures, to strengthen the means and the centralization of the government. [Marx 1898, p. 70.]

another of its fractions or to one or another of its particular interests'' (Poulantzas 1978, p. 139; emphasis in the original).[5] In this manner Poulantzas tries to overcome the crudeness and empiric inaccuracy of standard Marxist assertions that the state is always and everywhere the instrument of the dominant class.

In most respects Poulantzas is concerned by the state in general or the state in relatively advanced capitalist societies. By contrast E.V.K. Fitzgerald focuses on the question of state autonomy in developing countries. In his view development consists in a process of restructuring capital accumulation at certain crucial junctures, such as the transition from agrarian-dominated, export-based growth to that of ISI. ". . . For the state to fulfill this 'historic task' it must possess a certain degree of autonomy relative to the dominant elite—particularly the traditional agrarian and financial groups on the one hand and foreign interests on the other—and seek support among other social classes because in restructuring capital it must inevitably prejudice the interests of those fractions of capital that benefit from the existing order of things *even though in the long run the effect is to allow capitalism to develop more effectively''* (Fitzgerald 1979, pp. 4-5; emphasis added). Such autonomy is accentuated during "atypical" periods of economic and political crisis, sometimes involving an external threat (Fitzgerald 1979, p. 36).

Cardoso and Falletto (1979, p. 212) put the matter somewhat differently. In their words "the entrepreneurial-repressive state *dissociates* itself from the nation" in order to extract, police, and deliver the human and material resources the MNCs require for local accumulation.

In more open defiance of Marxist orthodoxy are Alfred Stepan (1978) and Ellen Trimberger (1978): Stepan rests his case for the more or less prolonged autonomy of the state upon a cultural-legal explanation while Trimberger looks to the characteristics of military rule. One may presume, however, that Stepan shares Trimberger's assertion that ". . . the governing apparatus [is] a source of power independent of that held by class . . ." (p. 7). Stepan explains this for Latin America through certain predispositions and perceptions of the proper role of the state that are rooted in the combination of the Roman law tradition, the views of the Catholic Church on the uses of secular power, and Latin culture. This combination produces "organic statism," which imbues the state with a purposeful role of achieving the common good in the name of all of society but independent from any of its constituent parts. Overlaying this old, deep-seated cultural expectation is the contemporary phenomenon that no class in Latin American society is clearly dominant: the landed oligarchy has faded away while the bourgeoisie remains weak and

---

[5] Translated by the author. Unless otherwise indicated all translations from Arabic and French sources are my own.

parasitical, the peasantry dispersed and quiescent, and industrial labor isolated and co-opted. The state apparatus has no class master and no class rival. The state may in fact *create* class interests through its policies (Stepan 1978, p. 26).

I would only add to the above that the cultural referants invoked by Stepan are by no means unique to Catholic-cum-Latin American societies and are mirrored in the values of the Muslim *umma*, or community of believers, whose secular leaders God has charged with managing the collective interests of its members. Moreover, throughout Muslim dynastic history the state has retained title to vast amounts of property and real estate which it has granted in revocable praebends to its minions. Through periodic distribution and revocation of usufruct rights, dynasties have regularly made and broken propertied interests. In such situations political or state power has provided access to material assets (the means of production) rather than the latter determining access to political power as Marxists would have it.

Culture is not of much explanatory value as far as Trimberger is concerned. What links Meiji Japan, Attaturk's Turkey, Nasser's Egypt, and Velasco's Peru in her analysis is the common element of military rule and radical change. By definition the status of military elites is dependent upon the state, and for certain of them to promote "revolution from above" requires 1) that their links with the class owning the means of production be absent or severed; 2) that they be politicized around an ideology of nation-building; 3) that they feel threatened by popular movements from below; 4) and that they be able to exploit contradictions in the international power constellation that augment national autonomy. The class origins of officers will tell us relatively little and their positions in the state apparatus a great deal about how they will use their power (Trimberger 1978, pp. 156-57).

It may be countered that while cultural predispositions and military rule may enhance state autonomy, neither are requisite to produce it. Civilian leaders as diverse as Nehru, Cárdenas, and Nyerere have all struck at the heart of dominant class interests in their societies with as much or little success as the military. None were, or are, military leaders, although, at a minimum, the neutrality of their military establishments must be assured before they proceed with radical change. And only one had been exposed to the cultural traditions to which Stepan alludes.

Part of the explanation probably lies in the fact that the state which radical reformers capture was already autonomous because it was constructed by colonial powers. These may have chosen to rule through indigenous classes or interests, and in some instances created class-based clientele, but they were in no way dependent upon such interests. Second, as has already been argued, since the Second World War most developing societies have lacked a hegemonic class if, in fact, any ever had one. In turn class affiliation has been so weak and class lines so fluid that one's status by birth was of relatively little use in predicting values and behavior. Finally, in the great majority of LDCs, regardless of their ideologies and internal class alignments, there is a consensus that the state has the right and duty to intervene massively in the development process and to engage in socio-economic engineering.

All these factors amount to considerable state autonomy in some but not all LDCs. The influence of class upon state power is stronger in countries like Morocco, the Philippines, or the Ivory Coast than in military-authoritarian regimes like Egypt, Peru, or even Pakistan. Nonetheless, the state in all of them acts as an independent source of power—at least for a time.

Curiously, in the heated debate regarding both state autonomy and state capitalism reference is seldom made to Soviet views on the subject. It seems to be forgotten that during the early 1960s the official line put out by the Kremlin was that certain developing countries, without socialist leadership, were on the noncapitalist path to socialism. The leading theoretician of this school was G. I. Mirsky, who put forth arguments for state autonomy in developing societies not dissimilar to those presented above. He concluded that in some instances the "national bourgeoisie" led by the military could rise above class interests to such an extent that the foundation could be laid for true socialism (Mirsky 1964; Landa 1966; Carrière d'Encausse 1975; pp. 155-82). LDCs that received the accolades of this school were Burma, Mali, Algeria, Guinea, and the UAR. Khrushchev was won over by Mirsky's analysis and backed it diplomatically: in May 1964 in Aswan he said publicly to Nasser that Egypt was "building socialism" and, in the same month, Ahmad Ben Bella of Algeria was awarded the Order of Lenin.

Since Khrushchev's political demise this line lost favor, and it is worth summarizing the main lines of its revision (Valkenier 1980). First, the idea of stage-skipping has fallen into disrepute. The possibility or reality of state autonomy is not at issue, but rather forced-draft socialism and heavy industrialization imposed upon societies that have not undergone the class development requisite to support such policies.

According to Valkenier, Soviet institutes concerned with the study of LDCs, while disagreeing about the importance of cultural variations, are in accord that a phase of intensive interaction between LDCs and the capitalist world, including MNCs, is desirable.[6] They see a combination of free enterprise and foreign investment within a mixed economy as the proper catalyst to the evolution of society in a direction that would make socialism possible. For them Lenin's New Economic Policy of the 1920s rather than Stalin's industrialization drive of the 1930s is the model to be followed.

---

[6] The main protagonists are the Institute of World Economics and International Relations and the Institute of Oriental Studies.

Valkenier does not argue that these institutes have actually influenced policy, and Soviet interest in Ethiopia, South Yemen, and Vietnam indicates that isolation from the capitalist world is not always to be discouraged. Still, the opening to the West and the wooing of foreign capital that Sadat engineered after 1973 (see Chapter Seven) may be seen as a "necessary" stage in the maturation of Egypt's class configuration. Neither under the old or new schools of thought do Soviet scholars question the possibility of state autonomy. Instead they have argued that a strong autonomous state can drag a backward society into socialism, or, latterly, that there is no capitalist class sufficiently strong to capture the state and use it to drag the society into the unavoidable capitalist stage.

In sum, I do not believe that there were insurmountable class obstacles confronting Nasser that would have kept him from remaking Egypt's pattern of stratification even more than he did. Nor do I believe that he was constrained by his own class identity, whatever that might have been. On those occasions when Nasser moved against class interests—1952, 1961, 1966—he met little resistance. When he hesitated there is little evidence that he did so out of fear of class resistance, but rather because he needed to send different signals abroad or because what was proposed was administratively unworkable. What Nasser sought was a kind of humanitarian socialist order in which all the major means of production were owned or controlled by the state. What eventually held him in check was his reluctance to demand immediate unrequited social sacrifice, and a hostile international environment in which, at a crucial moment, even the USSR failed to offer him the political and economic backing he needed.

State Capitalism

Radical political economists are no less at odds with one another with respect to the idea of state capitalism. This idea comports two subthemes: 1) that the *dirigeants* and upper echelons of the personnel of the state come to constitute a class despite the fact that they do not *own* any means of production and hence cannot appropriate for themselves the surplus value so generated; and 2) that in its economic undertakings the state acts according to capitalist criteria, maximizing financial returns on investment and inevitably exploiting the work force in the process.

Many observers of developing countries have followed the lead of Milovan Djilas's *The New Class* (1957) which asserts that the state *and the party* in communist societies give rise to a new form of class identity and reality. No noncommunist developing countries can boast the equivalent of the party *apparatchiki* of the USSR and elsewhere, but they can boast a vast array of high-ranking administrators and technocrats, who, along with the military, share a common interest in the perpetuation of the state.

The state bourgeoisie, according to Charles Bettelheim (1974, p. 41; cited in Jacquemot and Raffinot 1977, pp. 119-20) is made up ''. . . of the agents of social reproduction, apart from the immediate producers, and who, by virtue of the existing system of social relations and dominant social practices, effectively dispose of the means of production and the products that formally belong to the state.'' The state bourgeoisie can become the dominant class in society, as Jacquemot and Raffinot argue is the case in Algeria, when it is able to exploit its privileged position in the economy and to separate the workers from any real control over the means of production.

Just as the president of the board of directors of a capitalist corporation seeks to maximize earnings for its shareholders, so too the state capitalist managers seek to maximize returns for the state. For the worker on the assembly line there may be no difference in his effective relation to the means of production and to his employers.

All of these propositions call into question fundamental axioms of Marxian understanding, and, not surprisingly, have elicited strong rebuttals. Alex Dupuy and Barry Truchil, for example, contend that the notion of state capitalism simply confuses the assessment of basic issues. State personnel, they assert, cannot, whatever their control over the means of production, accumulate wealth for their own private ends, nor can they purchase the means of production and labor power which are the ''prerequisites'' of a capitalist class (1979, p. 30). My only rejoinder to this is that rather than the idea of state capitalism being inadequate, it is in fact the Marxist idea of class that is deficient. For my purposes I will define class as any group within society sharing the same relationship to the means of production and the same level of material well-being, privilege, and power. The class position of its members need not be heritable, and it is in the quest for access to, maintenance of, or escape from status within that class that consciousness and self-aware-ness is forged. More specifically the state capitalist class has the potential power to change its relations, as well as those of all other classes, to the means of production. Through its own policies it may transform itself into a full-fledged capitalist class or foster the development of such a class. Public ownership of the means of production thus impedes neither the perdurance of class phenomena nor the exploitation of the laboring masses.

Let us turn to the second facet of the state capitalist thesis, the nature of the activity of the state itself. This brings us back to some of the themes examined with respect to state autonomy, e.g., whether or not the state is simply and over the long haul the handmaiden of capitalist interests. Dupuy and Truchil are convinced that that is the only way to view the matter. ''Thus the greater intervention of the state in these Third World societies can be explained in terms of the logic of capitalism and its specific forms of expression in those societies" (1979, p. 10). Implicit in their reductionism is the lumping together of states as diverse as those of Peru, India, Algeria, or Korea. In fact these authors dismiss Algeria as being a capitalist society with a relatively strong state sector (p. 13).

This will not do, for it does not permit any qualitative distinctions to be made among states that share only a propensity for significant intervention in their economies. Fortunately, E.V.K. Fitzgerald has been more discerning. A reformist, anti-imperialist bureaucratic class, linked to the military, and astride state-led programs of industrialization can give rise to state capitalism This

> . . . is not just equivalent to a large state-enterprise sector, for in many cases this merely assists the penetration of foreign capital. But when the domestic bourgeoisie is particularly weak and an industrial fraction incapable of dominating the state, the state itself can substitute for nonexistent capitalists, performing the function of "collective capitalism" . . . [Fitzgerald 1979, p. 37].

For such a state to go beyond a supportive role of both domestic and international private capital, it must take over ownership of surplus-generating sectors, secure adequate means of public finance, and undertake central planning of the major sectors of the economy. If the state merely socializes the capital costs of accumulation but not the profits, it cannot be said to have fully embarked upon state capitalism (Fitzgerald 1977, pp. 70, 86).

Both in terms of state personnel and state intervention in the economy, Egypt undeniably entered a state capitalist mode in 1957. Here the "state" is equivalent to the public sector and the tutelary ministries in production, the provision of power, water, and means of transport. The state sector that grew up after 1956 has engaged in three distinct types of capitalist activity. The first type consisted in the establishment of holding companies with diverse interests that were to compete with one another in production, sales, and profits. This approach was abandoned after 1961 and replaced by sectoral monopolies. Even the ideal of competition was eliminated, while the goals of job creation, planned production, and planned prices guided industrial strategy. In the first period, but particularly in the period 1961-1971, it would be hard to discern in state capitalist undertakings any supportive role for the private sector; more often suspicion and hostility typified the official attitude. It was during the second period that the state bourgeoisie took discernible shape. This segment is smaller than the upper echelons of the administration as a whole. It is made up of the upper managerial and technocratic stratum that directs the state capitalist sector.

From 1973 on a period of fragmented parastatal activity developed. Sectoral monopolies were broken up and individual companies urged to sink or swim on their own through the reintroduction of market mechanisms in determining levels of investment and profits. In terms of gross investment the public sector remains the dominant force in the economy, but with official legitimation of domestic and foreign private capital, it is rapidly moving toward a role that can only be described as supportive of private interests. The state bourgeoisie is, on an individual basis, moving into private sector activities or exploiting the growing links between the public and private sectors.

Although I have tried to demonstrate that the Egyptian state and its leaders enjoyed sufficient autonomy to put the country squarely on a noncapitalist path, is that demonstration vitiated by the outcome that so many others (except Mirsky et al.) would have predicted? Egypt has returned to something resembling capitalist economic orthodoxy, and many would claim that that outcome flowed from the dynamics of state autonomy and the structural goals of state capitalism. I cannot argue convincingly to the contrary, nor can I point to other LDCs that have sustained successfully noncapitalist strategies—Guinea appears to be only the most recent renegade to return to the fold. However, it does seem to me that until the June War of 1967 Nasser had the personal will and desire, sufficient albeit limited personnel, and the bureaucratic and economic instruments at his disposal, to push Egypt much further toward socialism. I do not believe that he was simply a closet capitalist of petty bourgeois origins whose radical rhetoric was only skin-deep.

He was, as I have already suggested, an advocate of far-reaching change; his failing was that he insisted on trying to combine reform and accumulation, growth and equity, social discipline and political mobilization. Since he was not a Stalinist, he could not bring this off because it simply cost too much and failed to lead to self-sustaining growth or to broad-based prosperity. To keep the quest alive, Nasser had to resort increasingly to the outside world where his room for maneuver was severely circumscribed.

Chapter Two

SOVEREIGN STATE OR LINK IN THE CHAIN OF DEPENDENCY?

It is as if poverty and wealth were independent phenomena that happened to exist side by side in a world where national independence automatically entailed equal opportunity for development.
[Emmanuel 1972, p. 263]

. . . We must place much more emphasis upon the internal dynamics of underdeveloped economies and see dependency as a 'conditioning situation' which constrains but does not determine entirely the pattern of accumulation . . .
[Fitzgerald 1979, p. 18]

While those who use the concept of *dependencia* in their analysis of LDCs can hardly be seen as a school there are some basic themes about which there is little disagreement. This view emphasizes that underdevelopment and development are not *successive* stages in the life of states and societies, but rather simultaneous conditions mutually linked and interdependent (P. J. O'Brien 1975, pp. 11-12). The dynamic of the global system is to keep the backward relatively backward and dependent upon the developed "core" (this core is or is not exclusively capitalist according to the analyst) whose dominance is thereby perpetuated. By debunking the notion of sequential development, *dependencia* insists upon the integration of nations into a near-universal system (*inter alia*, Samir Amin, 1976a; Gunder-Frank 1971; Wallerstein 1976; Furtado 1973; Dos Santos 1970). At the heart of this view is the notion of an international division of labor, although most authors fail to specify if they believe this division is somehow planned by the core states (Furtado 1973, p. 120, does so believe) or emerges spontaneously through the workings of the capitalist order.

A second linkage that is stressed in dependency analysis is that of joining national domestic interests in the core to those of the periphery. This is an important point for it moves us beyond two simplistic ideas concerning the possibility of autonomous action by elites in developing countries. The first, neo-Marxian, sees these class fractions and the internal constituency interests to which they respond as the helpless playthings of international capitalism and imperialism. Understanding or measuring their own room for maneuver thus becomes a matter of relatively minor importance in analyzing the overall dynamic of the international system. The second idea is somewhat the inverse. In it national elites are treated as operationally autonomous and able to make decisions affecting the course of their nations which may be shaped, but are not necessarily forced or dictated by external forces. It should be noted that some proponents of *dependencia* analysis stress the neo-Marxist view (e.g., Dos Santos, Amin, Gunder-Frank), but in general the school allows for patterns of interaction in which the dependent groups are by no means passive actors.

In a similar vein some authors have argued that developing countries lack an autonomous capacity for change and growth and are dependent for these upon the core. What economic expansion may take place in the periphery can occur only as a reflection of expansion in the core and not as a self-sustaining process. For example, Celso Furtado speaks of "peripheral capitalism . . . unable to generate innovations and dependent for transformation upon decisions coming from the outside" (1973, p. 120). More radical exponents of dependency theory, again typified by Gunder-Frank, are convinced that the workings of the international capitalist order lead to the absolute impoverishment of the periphery, thus recasting on a global scale the Marxist concept of pauperization. By implication there is little that developing countries can do about their plight short of dropping out of (decoupling) or assaulting the international system.

Good sense and empirical evidence suggest that reality is much more complex. Four studies dealing with different sets of developing countries demonstrate that the degree of external dependence is positively correlated with increased economic growth. It is less clear whether or not it is positively correlated to greater disparities in the distribution of land and wealth or to levels of authoritarian rule (Kaufman et al. 1975; Chase-Dunn 1975; Vengroff 1977; McGowan and Smith 1978).[1] What is probably at work here is that capital, credits, and the activities of MNCs, all derived from the core, are attracted to those developing countries with a combination of good resource endowment, relative political stability, and the capacity in terms of personnel and infrastructure to carry the developmental effort. This means in turn that it is countries like Brazil, Indonesia, Venezuela, Zaire, Pakistan, India, and Egypt—as opposed to Haiti, Chad, or Afghanistan—that attract the attention of the core and exhibit the highest levels of dependency. It is therefore not the case that dependency provokes pauperization; indeed, neglect by the core may contribute to that. Nor is it clear whether or not the expansion in de-

[1] The only attempt at analyzing the Arab states according to levels of dependency that I have seen is Brahimi 1977, pp. 132-43.

pendent countries is solely a function of the dynamism of the core. Here again, common sense would indicate that countries of the size and diversity of Brazil, Indonesia, India, Argentina, and Iran have considerable scope for autonomous development. Fifteen years ago, Egypt would have figured among such states, but its inclusion now is problematic. The conclusion that is emerging from the debate is that external dependency can and does lead to real growth in the periphery, that it can and does promote some forms of industrialization, and that local elites can and do enjoy some sovereign autonomy in shaping the links that bind them and their countries to the interests of the core.

Dependent Development

The belief that the core's capitalism is inherently inimical to development on the periphery is rooted in the Marxist position adopted after the 1928 International, when the original notion that international capitalism would inevitably create its own likeness in the periphery was muted if not rejected (Palma 1978, p. 885). The evidence alluded to above has rendered this position increasingly untenable and the analyses of some of its early exponents in dependency theory (e.g., Paul Baran 1957) sorely dated. Palma has in fact argued that Marx's earlier expectations about the growth of capitalism under the auspices of imperialism may be applicable, as the capitalist core actively seeks a certain kind of industrialization of the periphery.

Bill Warren in 1973 examined the record of industrialization for twenty-nine LDCs over the period 1950-1970. He found that manufacturing increased dramatically in terms of value added, contribution to GNP, rates of industrial growth, and the expansion of exports. The *dependencia* argument of the net transfer of assets from the periphery to the core, and the consequent pauperization of the former, appeared to him to be empirically bogus. He rightly noted that measurements of net transfer of capital, even when clearly in favor of core states, generally failed to take into account the uses to which that capital is put while it remains in the peripheral economy. Moreover he believed that the impact of political independence as a catalyst to industrialization among LDCs has been greatly underestimated by *dependistas* and the impact of foreign investment greatly overestimated. Such investment is typically a very small proportion of gross capital formation in developing countries.

The historical experience of Egypt, it should be noted, offers an ambiguous picture of these phenomena. It was not imperialism that choked its early efforts to industrialize; Muhammed 'Ali's ventures were already foundering, and the measures implemented after 1838 by the great powers were not the cause of the demise of these ventures but rather sealed their fate (Mabro and Radwan 1976, p. 18). The Anglo-Turkish Treaty of 1838 abolished state monopolies in Egypt, reduced the size of the armed forces, and reduced or abolished external tariffs. These restrictions ushered in a century in which the option of industrialization was denied Egypt and in which the country was cemented into classic monoculture and monoexport dependency.

Warren wrote before the oil crisis of 1973-74 and the general surge in global inflation. While LDCs experienced some deterioration in their terms of trade in the middle 1970s, they were able to weather the storm without massive dislocations to their economies (Holsen 1979). A crucial factor here was their ability to borrow heavily in international capital markets, themselves flooded with petrodollar earnings of various OPEC members. Egypt was but one of several LDCs that accumulated short-term commercial debts in excess of one billion dollars in those years, while other more credit-worthy LDCs such as Brazil and Mexico contracted billions of dollars more in medium-term commercial debt. The debt itself, in combination with periodic servicing crises, IMF stabilization programs, and "creditor club" consolidation loans, accentuated a kind of dependency that Warren overlooked.

In 1980, the elements of a new global payments crisis seemed to be emerging. The sharp increase in OPEC prices after 1979, coupled with rising international grain prices due to an anticipated shortfall in Soviet harvests, set the stage for a further LDC onslaught on international capital markets. This new demand, however, came at a distinctly unfavorable moment. The terms of lending have become much stiffer since the early 1970s, and private creditors more insistent on IMF-type reform packages. At the same time developed countries' level of public assistance has stagnated or even declined. Finally recession of varying magnitudes among the DCs and consequent resort to protectionism may mean that LDCs are not to be given the opportunity to export their way out of debt—a strategy that has been urged upon them by the IBRD and the IMF among others (Helleiner 1979).

Creditors, public and private, are partially able to call the tune of development strategy. As import-substituting industrialization as a growth strategy has increasingly been called into question in both the periphery and the core, the new orthodoxy urges export-led industrialization. The examples of South Korea and Taiwan are held out to the LDCs to urge them along similar paths. Yet it is not at all sure that more than a handful of LDCs could profit from such a strategy, for exports, as mentioned above, will be dependent upon growth of core economies and preferential access to their markets. Samir Amin has defined the dilemma simply (Amin 1976a, p. 289):

Let us assume a growth rate of 7 percent per annum in a peripheral economy. For a capital-output ratio of about 3 (a modest estimate), investments should represent 20 percent, approximately, of the gross domestic product. Let us assume that half these investments are financed by foreign capital rewarded at rates of 15 percent (again, a modest estimate). If imports increase at the same rate as the product, it will be possible for the balance of external payments to be kept level only if exports can grow at a rate much greater than 12 percent per annum.

Some countries may successfully follow this path, but, above all during times of recession in the DCs, only a chosen few will be able to hold their own (cf. Roger Hansen 1979, p. 138).

Still, whatever the risks involved, a process that Peter Evans (1979) has called "dependent development" is underway in several LDCs. Tables 2.1 and 2.2 give a few important statistical indicators on twenty-seven of them. Before discussing their implications, it is important to stress two factors: first, some 120 LDCs do not even qualify for inclusion in this select company, and second, the degree of variation in terms of the variables presented among this small group is extreme, far in excess of anything one could find among the members of the OECD.

Two crucial variables are size of population and size of GNP. All these states have GNPs of $3 billion or more (Brazil is the leader with $158 billion) and populations in excess of 15 million. These are countries with large markets and large capital needs. They attract MNCs because of the former, and they plunge heavily into international capital markets because of the latter. In general they have legitimate aspirations to and frequently the reality of a significant industrial base. Whether or not they have material resources the developed world covets (despite Gabon's oil and Mauritania's iron ore, neither qualify for inclusion in this group) is not as important as the fact that they have the economic and demographic weight to bargain with the core. Evans (1979, p. 297) has used the term semiperiphery to refer to such countries, mediating between the core and the rest of the LDCs and therefore "increasingly central to the overall growth of the imperialist system." Indeed, although Evans does not so argue, such countries, if faced with restricted markets in the developed countries, may seek export expansion among the rest of the peripheral states. India, Brazil, and Korea have already made major strides in that direction. Egypt would dearly love to follow suit among its own Arab neighbors.

Even within this group variations are so pronounced that they defy generalizations; yet I would argue, as Evans did for Brazil, that the Egyptian model may provide us considerable insight into the development process in the other twenty-six countries. Nearly all are food deficit countries, although India at the time of writing was in surplus and Brazil and Sudan are likely to be so before the turn of the century. By and large these countries are dependent upon international grain markets dominated by the US and Canada. There is a very strong possibility that the major grain-exporting countries will

Table 2.1
Basic Indicators of the Semi-Periphery

Country	GNP (bn. US$) 1977	Population (millions) mid-1977	GNP/ capita (US$) 1977	External Public Debt (bn. US$) 1977	Debt Service as % of GNP 1977	Net Direct Foreign Investment (bn. US$) 1977
Afghanistan	2.7	14.3	190	1.1	1.2	—
Algeria	18.9	17.0	1,110	8.2	5.3	173
Bangladesh	7.3	81.2	90	2.3	1.2	—
Brazil	157.9	116.1	1,360	19.2	1.5	1,719
Burma	4.4	31.5	140	.5	0.8	—
Colombia	17.7	24.6	720	2.6	1.6	42
Egypt	12.1	37.8	320	8.1	8.8	98
Ethiopia	3.3	30.2	110	.5	0.9	6
India	94.8	631.7	150	14.5	0.8	−8
Indonesia	40.1	133.5	300	11.4	2.9	235
Iran	75.2	34.8	2,160	6.2	1.1	802
Kenya	3.9	14.6	270	.8	1.8	54
Mexico	70.9	63.3	1,120	19.2	5.2	555
Morocco	10.1	18.3	550	3.5	2.4	54
Nigeria	33.2	79.0	420	.9	0.3	245
Pakistan	14.2	74.9	190	6.8	2.1	15
Peru	13.8	16.4	840	4.7	5.4	55
Philippines	20.0	44.5	450	3.0	1.3	213
S. Korea	29.5	36.0	820	8.5	3.7	73
Sri Lanka	2.8	14.1	200	.8	4.4	−1
Sudan	4.9	16.9	290	1.7	1.5	20
Taiwan	19.7	16.8	1,170	2.6	2.4	42
Tanzania	3.1	16.4	190	1.0	1.5	—
Thailand	18.4	43.8	420	1.1	0.7	105
Turkey	46.5	41.9	1,110	4.3	0.8	184
Vietnam	8.1	50.6	160	NA	NA	—
Zaire	3.3	25.7	130	2.7	2.4	—

SOURCES: *National Basic Intelligence Fact Book* (Washington, D.C.: GPO, 1979).
IBRD, *World Development Report 1979* (Washington, D.C., 1979).

not be able to market enough grain to meet anticipated demand in the next ten to fifteen years (Hopkins and Puchala 1978, p. 15).

To pay for these and other imports nearly all members of this group have incurred heavy external debts. Some are clearly more credit-worthy than others: countries like Brazil or Zaire with a broad range of material resources, or like Algeria and Iran with oil and gas, are able to borrow heavily despite

Table 2.2
Average Deficit in Cereal Trade
(thousands of metric tons)
(1974-1976 average)

Afghanistan	7	Indonesia	1,803	S. Korea	2,861
Algeria	2,062	Iran	1,937	Sri Lanka	1,012
Bangladesh	1,841	Kenya	−69	Sudan	105
Brazil	1,422	Mexico	2,508	Taiwan	N.A.
Burma	−346	Morocco	1,182	Tanzania	327
Colombia	283	Nigeria	576	Thailand	−3,596
Egypt	3,248	Pakistan	555	Turkey	617
Ethiopia	4	Peru	1,166	Vietnam	1,967
India	6,400	Philippines	847	Zaire	391

SOURCE: Calculated by dividing net imports of cereals (imports-exports) for the years 1974, 1975 and 1976 by three. Trade figures are from Food and Agriculture Organization, *FAO Trade Yearbook* 1976 (Rome, 1977).

their growing servicing charges, and to roll over their loans. Egypt, Peru, Turkey, and others have not been so fortunate and have experienced repeated payments crises. Many of these countries, however, have a geopolitical significance, either due to location or resource endowment or both, that makes them candidates for large bailing-out operations by core countries. India, Indonesia, Zaire, and Turkey have received such treatment, and Egypt in the past five years has achieved similar status (see Chapter Seventeen).

One may note finally a few other characteristics of these countries. Several rely upon worker remittances as a major, if not *the* major source of their foreign exchange (e.g., Turkey, Algeria, Mexico, Colombia, Pakistan, Egypt). Like earnings from visible exports these remittances are dependent upon the buoyancy of labor markets in DCs or among the oil-rich. Recession affects worker migration as negatively as it does visible exports.

Nearly all these countries, given their geopolitical significance and the scope of their development plans, are susceptible to a high level of technological dependency. All have relatively sophisticated military establishments and must rely on DC suppliers especially for advanced aircraft and electronic gear, radar, missiles, etc. Their civilian industries likewise are dependent on DC technological assistance (viz. Algeria's gas liquification plants or Egypt's Aswan High Dam power station). Only a handful, again Brazil, India, Korea, have begun to develop their own intermediate technology.

To sum up, Egypt finds itself among a select group of LDCs that has in most respects the human and material resources to build sophisticated and potentially prosperous economies. Nearly all have made important strides into manufacturing and the processing of raw materials. To further their efforts they must continue to import capital goods, advanced technology, and certain raw materials of which, for several, oil is the most important. They are good clients for commercial banks, and, because of their weight in global and regional politics, sought-after recipients of core country public aid. Their development needs and even their poverty is big business. Egypt's annual invasion of the international grain market is second only to that of Japan, but in the case of Egypt the imports serve mainly to stave off widespread malnutrition and hunger. Simultaneously, all these countries demand sophisticated armaments in large quantities which lock them into complicated financing and technical support arrangements with developed countries. Finally, they are the LDCs most likely to attract investments and projects from MNCs lured in by the size of their markets and their depressed wage levels.

This raises the question of the role of the MNCs in the evolution of external dependency. Many of the hypotheses concerning MNCs have arisen out of Latin American experience, in which analysts have seen them as the prime instrument in the perpetuation of dependency, the co-optation of local elites, and the transfer of surplus to the core economies. They create, as Phillip O'Brien (1975, p. 19) has pointed out, an international sector that displaces the focus of social antagonism from class struggle to the sectoral struggle between those who are in it and those who are without. Peter Evans, for example, builds his model of dependent development upon a process of capital accumulation engineered by an alliance of state, indigenous private, and foreign MNC investment (the so-called *tri-pe*). The maintenance of relatively low wage levels and standards of living is essential to the continuation of the process so that manufactures will be competitive in foreign markets (cf. Lewis 1978 and Emmanuel 1972). Evans refers to a kind of bureaucratic-authoritarian model as the inevitable result of this formula, for rising wages would threaten the country's comparative advantage and, in any event, the most dynamic manufacturing sector typically caters to middle-class consumer demand. Thus, as Brazil would demonstrate, the triple alliance is rooted in another alliance, that of a state bourgeoisie that masterminds the process of accumulation, multinationals that provide the technology and occasionally the equity to promote accumulation, and the military that polices the process (Evans 1978, p. 48).

For Evans and nearly all others who have carried out empirical studies of Latin American dependency, the MNC is an essential cog in the process (for example, Fitzgerald 1979, p. 37). Egypt, by contrast, offers an example of a country in which most if not all the signs of marked external dependence have been present for nearly twenty years but in the absence, until recently, of any significant involvement of MNCs. Nonetheless there has been a kind of triple alliance in Egypt of considerable importance. Two actors, the state bourgeoisie as strategists and the military as policemen, are the same. The third actor, until 1972, was the Soviet Union. Its presence changed the logic of the process of accumulation in major ways. International competitiveness was not an important goal for two reasons. First, Egypt in the period 1956-1972 was still pursuing an ISI strategy. Second, the array of turnkey manufacturing operations set up by the USSR were to be paid for partially by exports of their products to the USSR at prices negotiated (and not market-determined) between the two partners. Consequently public sector wages were allowed to rise dramatically in the 1960s, and public sector enterprises were obliged to take on workers and managerial personnel for which there was no economic justification. Ultimately these policies cost Egypt whatever edge it might have had in international markets for manufactured exports, but the net result was a kind of double-dependency: reliance upon the USSR for technical support of existing projects and the servicing of the debt; and reliance on Western capital markets to finance the growing trade deficits that emerged in the late 1960s.

Despite rising public sector wages, authoritarianism was still necessary. The numerically important private sector work force was not enjoying the same increases, and the rural population was being sweated in order to engineer a transfer of resources from agriculture to industry. These were by no means the only reasons for authoritarian rule, but we shall postpone discussion of the others for future chapters. One can conclude from the foregoing that the Egyptian experience demonstrates that MNCs need not be present as external dependency develops, and that close interaction with the socialist core can produce the same effects as interaction with the capitalist core.

Since the early 1970s Egypt has moved toward patterns of external dependency similar to the Latin American paradigm. Indeed, the kind of triple alliance analyzed by Evans may be taking shape (see Chapter Seven). I have tried to trace out in Table 2.3 the evolution of certain dependency variables through both the periods of unconventional (presence of USSR; absence of MNCs) and conventional (presence of MNCs and US) external partners.

Some of the indicators I have used are somewhat unusual, especially arms imports, imported wheat per capita, and workers' remittances (indicators 7 through 10 in the table), but let us start with those that are most familiar. Until the revolution in 1952 Egypt had been a classic example of an export-dependent country whose foreign exchange earnings rose and fell with the sale of raw cotton on international markets. The first indicator shows that this kind of dependency has been steadily anad thoroughly dissipated over the last three decades regardless of regime and political philosophy.

The second indicator is interesting for its phasing. It tells us that from 1950 to the early 1970s the GNP grew at a faster rate than the trade deficit, but that under Sadat and the open-door policy (see Chapter Seven) a steady flood

Table 2.3
Selected Indicators of Egypt's External Dependence, 1950–1980

Indicator	Monarchy			Nasserist Era			Sadat Era		
	1950	1955	1960	1965	1970	1976	1978	1980
1) Cotton Exports/Total Exports	85%	78%	71%	56%	45%	26%	19%	4%
2) Visible Trade Deficit/GNP	4.1%	4.4%	.5%	3.8%	4.7%	13%	26%	10%
3) Foreign Loans/GI	(1952) 26%	23%	11%	33%	38%	85%	108%	71%
4) External Debt: £E million	—	—	—	247	1,340	4,970	10,500	11,200
5) External Debt/GNP	—	—	—	11.8%	42%	49%	107%	85%
6) Debt Service Ratio	—	—	—	22%	25%	44.3%	65.5%	53%
7) Imported Arms: US$ million	—	336	170	810	1,070	2,690	2,000	1,500
8) Imported Wheat: kgs. per capita	24.3	30	44.5	71.6	39	88.6	103	129
9) Wheat Aid: kgs. per capita	—	—	13	27	6	24	37.6	35.7
10) Worker Remittances: £E million	—	—	8	29	84	612	1,730	2,860

SOURCES:

1) Mead 1967, Appendix V; Nashashibi 1970; unpublished IMF surveys. 2) Mead 1967, Appendix V; IBRD 1978a, vol. 6; unpub. IMF surveys. 3) Saqr 1978, 32l; IBRD 1978a, vol. 6; IBRD 1980. The figures include undisbursed credits. 4-6) Hansen and Marzouk 1965, p. 270; IBRD 1978a, vol. 6; unpub. IMF surveys. 7) Glassman 1975; US Dept. of State, Research Memoranda, various issues; USACDA 1978; NYT, various issues; Barkai 1980. 8) FAO Trade Yearbook, various issues; Von Braun 1980; Mead 1967; Issawi 1963. 9) Von Braun 1980. 10) CBE Bulletin, various issues; AI, no. 607, 9/1/80; no. 666, 10/19/ 81. Note that (4-6) refer only to nonmilitary debt. The ratio in (6) is that of servicing to value of visible exports. The entries in (7) are cumulative totals of disbursed and undisbursed military credits for the intervening time period. Wheat aid in (9) is almost exclusively from the US, except in the 1970, when it comes from other sources.

of imports drove up the trade deficit to the point that it reached 26 percent of GNP in 1978. The strength of petroleum exports after 1978 brought it back down to 10 percent in 1980. In neither period are foreign arms acquisitions included in the trade figures. Nor do deficits on visible trade say much about the balance of payments. In 1966, with the trade deficit at about 4 percent of GNP, Nasser's Egypt faced a severe foreign exchange crisis; in 1978 with the deficit at 26 percent of GNP, Egypt was awash in hard currency.

Egypt has always been heavily dependent upon foreign credits to finance investment, but once again there was a marked acceleration in this dependency under Sadat. The source of credits was mainly Western in 1955, but the Soviet Union and Eastern Europe provided the bulk thereafter (exclusive of US food aid) until 1970. From then on the West (in combination with Saudi Arabia and Kuwait) once again became Egypt's major creditor. Much the same pattern holds for Egypt's trading partners: the West was gradually displaced by the USSR and Eastern Europe which, starting from less than 10 percent of Egypt's total trade in the 1950s, accounted for over half of it (exclusive of arms) in the late 1960s. After 1972 dependence on the Eastern bloc was rapidly exchanged for dependence on the West and Japan.

Until Egypt depleted its sterling balances in the late 1950s, it had no large external debt. Financing the first Five-Year Plan (1960-1965) and the Aswan High Dam set Egypt on a course that saw its external debt nearly quintuple between 1965 and 1970, and, allowing for devaluation of the pound, did so again between 1970 and 1978. Moreover both under Nasser and Sadat the debt grew far more rapidly than GNP and stood at 107 percent of the latter in 1978. Likewise, the cost of servicing the debt grew more quickly than the value of visible exports, so that the debt service ratio soared to 65.5 percent in 1978. Again because of petroleum exports both these ratios began to improve after 1978.

Latin American analysts have seldom dealt with the question of arms supplies and costs as a major factor in maintaining links of dependency, but there are only four or five countries that can sell sophisticated war material, and two of them are the superpowers. Nearly all LDCs want some of this equipment, especially aircraft, and to obtain and maintain it dictates putting themselves in the hands of a great power patron. Until 1974, Egypt had only one such patron, the Soviet Union, which sold it over $5 billion in arms between 1955 and 1973. The US has taken over that role, agreeing in 1979 to begin shipping to Egypt $1.5 billion in arms.

Like arms supplies, there are only a handful of countries that can regularly export wheat, and all of them are Western. As indicators 8 and 9 show, keeping Egyptians alive, if not well-fed, is a matter settled in international grain markets or through bilateral trade agreements with the US. Every man, woman and child in Egypt receives on average over 100 kilograms of imported wheat per year or about 70 percent of their total consumption. Egypt's jugular vein runs through Iowa, Nebraska, and the Dakotas.

Finally, Egypt, like Turkey, Algeria, Pakistan, Upper Volta, Colombia, and Mexico, to name but a few, is a country with a large expatriate work force whose foreign earnings have become vital to keeping the foreign exchange imbalance within tolerable limits. The migrant workers are dependent upon the economic vitality, job opportunities, and official tolerance of the host countries, and because most of the migrants are unskilled, the dependence is not really mutual. With over a million workers abroad, Egypt is receiving in remittances nearly as much as the proceeds from all its visible exports.

There is no question that in most respects Egypt's external dependency intensified, sometimes dramatically, under Sadat. And that intensification was accompanied by close collaboration with the capitalist West. The important question is whether or not that collaboration caused the intensification. I argue that it did not. The intensification began as a result of poor economic performance during the Nasserist era that forced Egypt to borrow abroad to finance investment and basic consumption. Had Nasser lived longer I doubt that the external debt, wheat imports, and foreign credits would have been substantially smaller. Arms imports might have been larger and worker remittances smaller. The point is, it seems to me, that the seeds for the exuberant growth of Egypt's dependency linkages were planted in the early sixties at the height of the country's "socialist transformation." They simply came to fruition coincident with but not because of Egypt's reentry into the capitalist world.

Elite Will

Criticisms emanating from those who doubt the utility of dependency theory or from those who wish to recast it have come together on the crucial assertion that dependency may be the effect rather than the cause of the internal political configurations and class alignments in the nations of the periphery. Such assertions stand early *dependencia* arguments on their head and suggest that some societies are more or less dependency-prone. It is elites and not societies that cast themselves into the arms of the core. The Shah's Iran is a case in point. The crucial question is how political elites confront the problems of income distribution, sectoral investment, and national savings. To understand these one must in turn examine closely class alignments, the degree to which the state is rooted in a given class or stratum, and the development strategies of those who retain power as the major *causal* factors in the generation of external dependency. "What produces underdevelopment is not the 'transfer of surplus' appropriated by the metropolitan capital from the periphery to the metropole, significant though this may be. Rather, such transfer should be seen as an *effect* of structures at the periphery which militate against the productive investment of the surplus at the periphery" (Leys 1978, p. 9; emphasis added).

The questions of agricultural policy and agrarian change are a litmus test of elite will and intentions. Most LDCs are or were until recently agrarian societies. The agricultural sector is frequently viewed as both a dead weight on the economy *and* the sector that must somehow provide the savings that will fuel growth in other, more "modern" sectors. Nearly all developing countries, including radical states such as China, have experimented with various formulae for transferring resources from agriculture to industry. It is not so much whether or not, over the long run, such strategies are wise as it is the manner in which they are implemented. Michael Lipton contends that too often implementation is wasteful, undermining agriculture without promoting industrial growth. Rural populations are held in poverty and thus cannot generate sufficient demand to sustain the new industries. The latter remain costly and inefficient, unable to absorb surplus labor from the depressed countryside. The cities fill up with the unskilled and the educated unemployed who are put on the dole or plugged into artificially created jobs. The "informal" and service sectors of the cities, the bureaucracies, and overstaffed public enterprises become yet another dead weight on the economy. Yet these predominantly urban constituencies at a minimum must be fed and, for the middle classes, have some of their luxury consumption demands satisfied. National savings rates inevitably suffer and the entire economy becomes victim of what Lipton calls "urban bias." In such situations political elites are more inclined to import capital than to undertake the politically formidable tasks of forcing additional domestic savings. Lipton contends that this pattern, more than an international division of labor imposed by the core, is what is at the heart of external dependency (Lipton 1977, pp. 74-85; and Lewis 1978, pp. 43-44). It sustains the low level of wages in the LDCs that Arthur Lewis and Arghiri Emmanuel have, from their differing vantage points, singled out as the most important factor in the maintenance of unequal exchange between the core and the periphery.

For some non-oil-exporting developing countries the alternative to increased dependency is to engineer the structural change necessary to convert the "traditional," predominantly agrarian sector into an engine of savings and growth. This can be done through violent revolutionary action as in China and Vietnam, or in the wake of war as in South Korea and Taiwan. But it is testimony to the recalcitrance of rural populations and the resiliency of patterns of influence and power in the countryside that even the combination of war and revolution in Algeria produced so little change in rural areas.

Short of violent change, the policy options for structural transformation are limited and distasteful even to regimes with no vested interest in the status quo. To apply such policies requires tremendous determination and staying power and the temptation to defer the attendant decisions is difficult to resist. What one might call vividly but perhaps unfairly "the failure of elite will" is captured by Clive Bell's summation of Indian experience (Bell 1974, p. 211; cf. F. Frankel 1978, p. 548):

An elite which is no longer dependent on landed interests and likely to preserve that independence in the future can both bid for "popular" support and strike at the basis of the landlords' power by effecting a redistribution at the latter's expense. In mild reforms, the intention may be more subtle: to get rid of the "feudal" elements, while giving the emerging agrarian capitalists full rein and improving only temporarily the position of some sections of the smaller and middle peasants. Plainly, the more radical the reform, the greater the spoils to be distributed— and the larger the number of disaffected big and middling farmers. Thus in the absence of a mass agrarian movement, the reforming elite will probably settle for a less radical option, benefiting enough middle peasants to ensure a solid rural power base and relying upon the post-reform structure to maintain in peaceful acquiescence the unrewarded mass of the peasantry.

Likewise in Peru Ramón Zaldívar observed the hesitation of the military regime to pursue agrarian reform to the point that "kulak" interests would be harmed. Through the reform actually carried out ". . . the two extremes of the social pyramid have been neutralized: the upper bourgeoisie on the one hand, and the proletariat with the peasants on the other. The middle and petty bourgeoisie will provide a reserve of political support for the government and will also guarantee the sustained productivity which is necessary as an alternative political solution to a mass movement of the peasantry" (Zaldívar 1974, p. 58). The Peruvian regime, like the Nasserist before it, was in effect promoting class formation and consolidation. It was also enhancing a kind of low-level economic performance that eventually dictated, as it had in Egypt, a great surge in foreign borrowing.

Fitzgerald puts the matter somewhat differently. He sees the economies of several LDCs in dualistic terms, divided into what he calls a corporate and a noncorporate sector. The former encompasses all capital-intensive enterprise, whether in industry or agriculture, utilities, transport, and the civil service. It is only in this sector that there is reproducible capital, financial profit, and wage relations on an appreciable scale (Fitzgerald 1979, pp. 23, 91). Value added per worker in the corporate sector is five and six times that in the noncorporate.

The failure, in his view, to overcome dualism and to integrate the noncorporate into the corporate sector go hand in hand with external dependency.

Any policies that try to cope with only one of these problems will fail, for the two are inseparable. Outside the corporate sector income is inequitably distributed and savings are low. The corporate sector is unable to expand because of the concomitant constraints of domestic markets. It in turn is unable to generate the savings and investment necessary for efficient operation. Turning outward entails maintenance of depressed wage levels and, typically, resort to heavy foreign borrowing and involvement with MNCs (Fitzgerald 1979, p. 24).

With respect to Peru, Fitzgerald points out that the Velasco regime after 1968 in essence took over much of the corporate sector but was unable to appropriate the surplus it generated, which remained in private or MNC hands. Without this surplus the state could not reduce the dualism in the economy. What income distribution took place was confined to the corporate sector, but did not occur between it and the noncorporate. Deficit financing and external borrowing were undertaken as the way out, but without larger domestic markets there was no way for productivity to keep pace with debt. After a decade of military rule, Peru had met neither the challenge of structural integration nor of lessening external dependency.

We now come once again to the question of class and class-based regimes. Colin Leys, among others, insists that to understand dependency we must examine the historical formation of indigenous classes under colonial auspices and trace their evolution into the period of independence. In Kenya, Leys sees the growth of a Kikuyu landed bourgeoisie, brought into agriculture by the British in the early 1950s in order to augment colonial commodity production and to ease Great Britain's postwar dollar crisis. This class went on to capture the independent state and to apply policies that originated in the colonial era (Leys 1978 and Leys 1975). Two themes are inherent in this argument. First, the dependent state must be seen as the instrument of a dominant set of interests, increasingly manifesting all the attributes of class. Second, the drift into dependency is the result of a long process originating in the colonial experience.

Leys is not happy with the idea of an autonomous, class-free state, no matter how short-lived, although his own analysis of Kenya demonstrates that the colonial state, at any rate, was able to create *ex nihilo* a local bourgeoisie. The latter eventually captured the state and applied policies that deepened Kenya's external dependency.

Leys's emphasis on continuity with the colonial past as a determining element in the persistence of dependency is not of general validity. Egypt's experience has been one of sharp discontinuity with its colonial past, *followed by* growing external dependency. The essential features of this discontinuity are fourfold:

1) After the Second World War Egypt left the Sterling Zone with all the implications of such a move for foreign exchange balances and foreign trade.

2) Egypt established real political independence by 1957 and the final evacuation of British troops.

3) Egypt massively realigned its foreign trade after 1955 away from traditional Western markets.

4) Again, beginning in 1955, Egypt sought its arms and technology in socialist countries.

It is in fact the independent state, without class underpinnings, often in military hands, that engineers these breaks. And it is the inability of such elites to address internal problems of development that leads them back into new forms of dependency.

In very general and antiseptic terms I conceive of the challenge of economic development and of lessening dependency as hinging on the ability of the state to encourage or mobilize high rates of domestic savings and investment. Real growth sustained over relatively long periods of time presumably leads to fairly substantial self-reliance and economic sovereignty in countries of the size and complexity of those listed in Table 2.1. In turn real growth may be fueled by a combination of domestic savings and imported capital. As the Chenery-McKinnon two-gap model suggests, both may be in short supply. It is my contention that the greater the reliance upon imported capital the greater the likelihood that the structural changes outlined above are not being affected. Rigorous economic analysis (within the limits of the data) have tended to support the conclusion that domestic savings rates are negatively related to capital inflow, although the causal hypotheses vary widely (Mikesell and Zinser 1973, p. 19; Bhatt and Meerman 1978, p. 48; Griffin 1976, p. 130; for application to Egypt, cf. E. Montasser 1974). External borrowing is the most significant element of dependency and, by letting regimes avoid the hard questions of domestic resource mobilization and extraction, tends to perpetuate itself. India's communist newspaper, *The Link*, reacting to the country's "surrender" to the IMF in 1966, put the matter in polemical terms (cited in Frankel 1978, p. 300): "Devaluation of the rupee is the final admission of an abject administration that it has not got enough belief in itself to go to the people and make them work for their independence" (June 12, 1966). Frankel goes on to show that in India after 1965 domestic savings rates declined as external borrowing increased (Frankel 1978, p. 326).

In Figure 2.1 I have tried to depict the relationship of some of these variables graphically for the period 1950-1979, embracing most of Egypt's revolutionary experience to date. GNP has been plotted in constant prices as have the other variables. An ideal gross investment level of 20 percent of GNP, the

36

FIGURE 2·1. EGYPTIAN GNP AND THE RESOURCE GAP

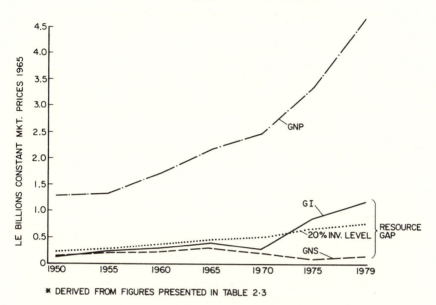

* DERIVED FROM FIGURES PRESENTED IN TABLE 2·3

kind of rate that could yield self-sustaining growth, has been calculated. Next we see the real level of gross investment which consists in national savings, external borrowing, and deficit financing. National savings are calculated as gross investment plus net exports, the latter generally being negative. The difference between investment (GI) and savings (GNS) represents the nation's resource gap which is met through external borrowing.

Egypt has rarely achieved an investment level of 20 percent of GNP, and when it has it has been at the cost of heavy capital importation and printing money. In the past decade foreign capital has not been a major constraint, although the resultant servicing of the external debt has led to periodic payments crises. The growing recourse to foreign borrowing has been accompanied by steadily declining shares of national savings in gross investment. Egypt has looked to the outside world to meet its investment needs and to cover its balance of payments deficits, and in these respects is more dependent than ever before.

What would it take to reverse this trend? Where must the shoe pinch in the process of extracting greater domestic savings? Who will pay the price of deepening the revolution or of economic autarky and self-reliance? Is there any alternative to the iron fist, to Stalinism of the left or the right, in promoting rapid capital accumulation? Nasser refused to use the iron fist, not because of signals from the countries of the core (they abounded) nor because of his

Table 2.4
Growth of GNP and Savings and Investments Levels, 1950-1979

(In £E millions constant 1965 prices)

Year	GNP	20%/GNP Investment Level	GNS	GI
1950	1,213.9	242.7	165.1	144.4
1955	1,332.5	266.5	194.5	218.5
1960	1,701.4	340.3	217.7	265.4
1965	2,321.9	464.4	315.7	392.4
1970	2,637.4	527.5	205.7	311.2
1975	3,367.0	673.4	144.7	848.4
1979	4,644.1	928.8	162.5	1,184.2

SOURCES: Figures for constant GNP taken from IBRD 1978a, 6: Table 212. Gross National Savings and Gross Investment were calculated from current price figures from the Ministry of Finance, by using their proportion to current price GNP to derive their value in constant 1965 market prices.

class predilections, if he had any. Rather his course was set by his very real unwillingness to sacrifice, as he put it, the present generation for those of the future and to unleash potentially uncontrollable elements of class conflict. In criticizing countries that drift deeper into external dependency, one must be very clear about feasible policy alternatives.

Stalinism or some variant of revolutionary authoritarianism *is* an option, but it may well be one reserved to continental powers that have the resources and domestic markets to go it alone. Even then, if chronic food deficits plague the country, it will probably have to generate sufficient foreign exchange to bid in international grain markets. Short of this, giant LDCs, such as China, India, or Brazil, have had to accept some level of technological dependency in order to assure their own growth. Recent events would suggest that China has over the years merely suppressed rather than overcome these needs. The industrial core, capitalist and socialist, has a hold over virtually every developing country whatever its political regime.

Another gambit that is currently being pursued with mixed results is what might be called South "unionism." For this to succeed national elites must be prepared to ignore whatever special advantages they may enjoy in the world economy in order to promote collective bargaining vis-à-vis the core. So far such action has been limited, despite the somewhat suspect posturing of various Third World "spokesmen" such as the late Houari Boumedienne of Algeria or Echeverría of Mexico. Ranks have constantly broken as the core offered individual states on the periphery special deals they could not refuse.

For the group of southern states with which this chapter has been particularly concerned, a very real option is to conquer the resources that they lack. The neighbors of Brazil and India are all well aware of this danger. Egypt's leaders have surely been tempted from time to time to bring the Sudan or Libya under their sway. There have been only small-scale enactments of this scenario (China in Tibet or Libya in Chad) and not sufficient to change the conquering country's geopolitical weight.

Finally there is the option, already explored above, of dependent development. It is clear that the process can be initiated with the knowing help of the core. But to the extent that continued growth will depend on access to core markets and core financing it may be that only a lucky few will be able to maintain their momentum. For the rest it will be only a question of time before steps toward decoupling will become unavoidable. For that reason moving toward regional solutions to resource and capital problems should be pursued with determination. That is much easier said than done, especially among differing political regimes as the Andean Pact, the East African Union, or various attempts at Arab unity have demonstrated.

Conclusion

What I would like to retain from all the foregoing are these points:

1) Development and dependency are compatible; the prosperity of the core is not premised on the pauperization of the periphery.

2) Dependency can be nurtured in the absence of MNCs and in interaction with socialist core states.

3) The direction of causality in the perpetuation of dependency is not from core interests to subordinate elites in the periphery. Rather it is the inability of such elites to muster the political will to undertake far-reaching redistribution of domestic assets that forces them into the arms of the core.

4) Such elites are not necessarily the creatures of the core nor need they have sprung from a dominant class in their own countries. There are autonomous elites able to use the state as an autonomous instrument to accomplish their goals. For a time Nasserist Egypt was run by such a state and such an elite.

5) Political expediency leads the elites to borrow abroad the savings they are unwilling to force from their own populations. Such borrowing entails financial orthodoxy, economic austerity, and the revivification of private sector interests that then infiltrate the state.

6) Austerity and retrenchment require political authoritarianism. Democracy and liberalism will be momentary aberrations, oscillating

with longer periods of dictatorship, more often than not under military auspices (cf. Roger Hansen 1979, p. 120).

7) Egypt is one of nearly thirty LDCs of sufficient size and geopolitical significance to set it above the rest. This "semiperiphery" is where core interests are most at stake and where economic interaction between core and periphery is most intense. If co-optation is to succeed it will have to succeed here; if it does not succeed it is among these states that decoupling will begin.

Chapter Three

DEMOGRAPHIC REALITY AND
REVOLUTIONARY INTENT

Our density is our destiny.
[Hamdan 1970, p. 366.]

A revolution, like any other form of politics, is made with people. To some degree Egypt's revolution was made because of too many people. When the monarchy was overthrown in 1952 Egypt's population was approaching 21 million. At that level and under the modes of production prevailing at the time, Egypt's limited resources were already under severe strain. Twenty-five years later the number of inhabitants had swollen to 40 million without any marked alterations in Egypt's resource base and little more in its basic modes of production.

A Statistical Sketch

Egypt's principal nonhuman resource remains its land. Only 3.5 percent of Egypt's surface is inhabited, although 15.5 percent has been designated as currently habitable. We may examine in Table 3.1 Egypt's impressive population concentration from 1947, the year of the last national census before

Table 3.1
Population Density, 1947-1976

	Inhabited Area km²	No. persons per km²	Habitable area km²	Projected No. persons per km²
1947	35,580	534	—	—
1960	35,580	730	—	—
1976	35,580	1,028.6	55,039*	664

SOURCE: Figures drawn from official census results.

* CAPMAS included in this figure areas around Fayyum, Alexandria, Ismailia, and Buhaira that are designated for new population.

41

the military takeover, to 1976, the year of the last national census. Densities on that order rival those of Bangladesh or Java, famed for their degree of crowding. The cultivated portion of Egypt's surface is even smaller, amounting to no more than 2.4 percent of the total (23,928 km²). More than a century before Nasser came to power, Egypt's Ottoman governor, Muhammed 'Ali, searched in vain for sufficient labor to farm the land available. But Egypt's population at that time was only about three million. As a result of rapid population growth throughout the first half of the twentieth century, labor became abundant and cheap. There were too many hands to farm the land. A glance at land per capita of rural population registers the declining ratio, and these figures do not reflect actual distribution.

More than half of Egypt's population is rural but somewhat less than half the work force is actively employed in agriculture. While average per capita income in the country may be about £E250 ($350 in 1978), it is twice as high in the cities as in the countryside. When this low standard of living is taken in combination with land fragmentation, high rates of illiteracy, and

Table 3.2
Cultivated and Cropped Acreage Per Capita Rural Population, 1947-1976

	Cultivated Millions of Feddans	Cultivated Per Capita Rural Population	Cropped* Millions of Feddans	Cropped Per Capita Rural Population
1947	5.7	.44	9.13	.71
1960	5.9	.36	10.2	.62
1976	5.7	.27	10.7	.52

* The statistic for cropped surface measures the extent of multiple-cropping of a given cultivated *feddan* in a given year. This is made possible by perennial irrigation. One *feddan* = 1.038 acres.

Table 3.3
Egypt's Rural and Urban Population, 1947-1976

	Total Population (Millions)	Rural (Millions)	% of Total Population	Urban (Millions)	% of Total Population
1947	19.01	12.8	67	6.3	33
1960	26.08	16.3	62.6	9.75	37.4
1976	36.6*	20.5	56.1	16.06	43.9

SOURCE: Figures drawn from official census results.
* Net of migrants.

high exposure to endemic disease, one has described a major obstacle to Egypt's prosperity and, at the same time, the mainstay of the economy.

One must allow considerable margin of error in interpreting Egyptian employment statistics (or virtually any others) because of inconsistencies in the active population covered (sometimes six years old or five years old and older), varying measures of full-time employment, and problems of categorization. Still, in addition to the fact that Egypt's socio-economic center of gravity remains situated in the countryside, two other characteristics emerge from the statistics loud and clear. The first is the low participation rate in the work force of those six and over. Since 1947 the overall participation rate has hovered around 30 percent (31 percent in 1976). That means that for every employed Egyptian there are over three dependents. Moreover, activity rates are heavily sex-biased. While female labor in rural areas on the family farm is difficult to measure, and is not always reflected in official statistics, there is little doubt that officially recognized "work" is predominantly a male prerogative.

In a similar vein, education, with all that it portends for future employment, is heavily sex-biased. This will be clear in Table 3.6. It is also heavily rural-biased, with 70 percent of all illiterates residing in the countryside in 1976. Impressive percentage gains in the spread of literacy have still left Egypt with more illiterates than ever before. Between 1960 and 1976 the illiteracy rate for those ten years old or older was reduced from 71 percent to 56 percent. But the country's 15.1 million illiterates in 1976 is a figure nearly equivalent

Table 3.4
Distribution of the Work Force by Sector, 1947-1976

(In thousands of workers)

	1947	1960	1976
Agriculture	4,085	4,406	4,878
Mining and Quarrying	13	21	33
Industry	560.6	713.1	1,367
Construction	113.3	158.8	424
Commerce	590.4	641.4	944
Transport and Communications	203.3	260.2	479
Electricity, Gas, and Water	22.6	36.8	62
Other Services	1,051.8	1,369.4	1,860
Unspecified	353.9	119.3	182
Total	6,994.6	7,726.6	10,229

SOURCE: Figures drawn from official census results.

Table 3.5
Male/Female Work Force Participation, 1947-1976

	1947*	1960	1976
Total Male Population (Mils.)	9.3	13.1	19.5
Active Male Population (Mils.)	5.2	6.5	9.88
% Males Active	55%	49%†	50%
Total Female Population	9.7	12.6	18.6
Active Female Population (Mils.)	.799	.585	1.66
% Females Active	8%	5%	9%

* Fifteen years old or older. Figures for 1960 and 1976 are for six years old and older. The decline in overall activity since 1947 can be attributed to the spread of primary education.

† CAPMAS (Al 1976) claims a 55 percent male activity rate in 1960 without giving figures. My figures for 1947 and 1960 are derived from Mead 1967, pp. 32-33.

Table 3.6
Illiteracy Levels for Those Four Years Old or Older, 1947-1976

	Male Illiterates		Female Illiterates		Total	
	No. (Millions)	% of All Males	No. (Millions)	% of All Females	No. (Millions)	% of Total Population
1947	4.4	66.1	5.9	88.2	10.3	77.2
1969	5.2	56.6	7.3	83.8	12.5	70.3
1976	5.7	43.2	9.4	71.0	15.1	56.5

SOURCE: Calculated from official census returns.

to the total population of 1937, when the men who were to rule Egypt after 1952 first entered the military academy.

There may be more effective ways for Egypt to educate its masses or organize its agricultural production, but it is also the case that a declining rate of population growth would in and of itself ease those tasks.

The development of the population for the next twenty-five years has already been determined and can only be changed slightly through family-planning efforts. Our population will double in the next twenty-five years with only a 20 percent possibility of variation. . . . Therefore for the next twenty or twenty-five years the problem in Egypt is mainly to meet the requirements of an increasing population, and if industry and technology develop quickly this will help reduce the population as happened in all advanced societies. [Hilmi 'Abd al-Rahman (advisor to PM on technology) *Egyptian Gazette*, February 9, 1975.]

44

Hilmi 'Abd al-Rahman is of course right when he argues that Egypt's population is going to grow prodigiously whatever one does to lower fertility. But he is less than scrupulous when he suggests that the 20 percent variation he so summarily dismisses is of little significance. According to various hypotheses concerning stable or declining fertility rates, Egypt would have a population between 62 and 74 million in the year 2000 and 84 or 139 million in 2030 (Waterbury 1978a, pp. 70-71). A difference of 12 million people in 2000, not to speak of 55 million in 2030, is not to be sniffed at, yet in some ways it is.

When Nasser came to power, population was seen as a problem not of numbers but of mass poverty, the inequitable distribution of land and other forms of wealth, and the mix of alienation and political apathy that seemed to flow therefrom. Thus the problem was to overcome these obstacles to progress through land reform, state-led industrialization, and political mobilization of the masses in the name of goals nominally aimed at pulling them out of their misery, ignorance, and backwardness.

By the time Egypt's first Five-Year Plan was formulated in 1959-60, it had become abundantly clear to a number of Egypt's leading economists (e.g., 'Ali al-Gritli 1962) that no matter how determined the state, its investment efforts would be wiped out as long as the population grew in excess of 2.5 percent per annum. Equity goals would likewise recede. For example, in 1976 perfect equality in land distribution would yield only a quarter *feddan* per rural inhabitant and perhaps only an eighth in the year 2000. Nasser somewhat reluctantly acknowledged the problem, and Egypt's National Charter of 1962 made explicit mention of the need to curb population growth in order to promote economic growth. In 1966 a nationwide, state-administered family-planning program was launched. While the crude birth rate did decline after 1967, it was probably more an effect of the military defeat of that year than the result of the family-planning program. In any event the rate crept upwards once again after 1973. Conventional family-planning techniques (pills, IUDs, condoms, etc.) were judged a failure and all the talk shifted to industrialization, emigration, and populating the deserts as a way out of the dilemma. Then a sudden resurgence of interest in conventional techniques manifested itself in the summer of 1978 as former prime minister Mamduh Salim made a number of surprise visits to family-planning clinics. The new concern was directly provoked by Egypt's reliance on outside sources of funding. To cite the *Financial Times* (July 31, 1978)

> Overpopulation replaced external debt as the top issue for Egyptian development when the Consultative Group (of foreign creditors) for Egypt met in Paris in June. This made it implicitly clear that continued foreign support for the economy is conditional on President Sadat's

Government taking serious steps to curb population increase. Since the international body of Egypt's creditors is the single most powerful directing force in the economy, it seems possible that Egypt may now be obliged for the first time to take serious steps in this direction.

Whatever that statement reveals about official Egyptian concern with population growth, it tells us a great deal about relevant actors in the country's policy-making process.

It has been Egypt's unhappy distinction to have experienced a decline in the crude birth rate and natural rate of reproduction in the late 1960s only to be followed by a resurgence of both in the 1970s. Some credence must be lent to the explanation that over a million men were in uniform during the period of decline and their release to civilian life since 1973 has triggered the new growth. Unfortunately the current phenomenon does not appear to be a "boomlet" but a real boom.

Several radical political economists, including mainstream *dependistas*, have tended to reduce rapid population growth to the status of a false problem, a symptom and not a cause of backwardness. There are a few observers of the Egyptian scene that share this perspective:

> We reject, specifically, the notion of demographic pressure . . . which gives a central place in the interpretation of social contradictions. . . . For us the fraction of the working population that fails to find work is

Table 3.7
Crude Birth Rates, Death Rates, and Net Reproduction Rates, 1952-1978
(Per thousand)

Year	Crude Birth Rate	Crude Death Rate	Natural Reproduction Rate
1952	45.2	17.8	27.4
1960	43.1	16.9	26.3
1966 (June War)	41.2	15.9	25.3
1972	34.4	14.5	19.9
1973 (October War)	35.7	13.1	22.6
1974	35.7	12.7	23.0
1975	36.0	12.1	23.9
1976	36.4	11.7	24.7
1977	38.4	11.9	26.5
1978	38.7	10.6	27.1

SOURCE: *Al*, no. 572 (June 15, 1979), citing official CAPMAS data.

not a biological or physical phenomenon, a given in and of itself, but a *class phenomenon* (emphasis in the original). It is one of the aspects of the system of blocked transition and of unequal international specialization. [Hussein 1971, p. 50; emphasis in original.]

It is thus argued that those who urge LDCs to devote heavy attention and resources to this problem are, in essence, defenders of the status quo, sending the elites of developing countries off on fruitless quests that distract them from dealing with the *real* problem: attacking economic backwardness and its benefactors in the developed core. It is my contention that one can perfectly well accept the validity of their suspicions of core motivation in advocating population control while rejecting the notion that rapid population growth is simply not a real problem. Few informed Egyptians, at any rate, whatever their ideological preferences, are prepared to dismiss the problem so cavalierly. One can attack backwardness at its roots *and* attempt to control fertility. Egypt has not been conspicuously successful in either endeavor. But it is essential to realize that what may have been symptom becomes with each turn of the wheel, a causal element in the perpetuation of poverty and backwardness. Distinguishing cause from effect thereby boils down to a futile semantic game.

Political Demographics

When Anwar Sadat made Husni Mubarak his vice president in 1975, he proclaimed that he was beginning to hand over power to the "October Generation," i.e., to those who had conducted the battle with Israel in October 1973. With Sadat's assassination in October 1981, effective power may well now lie in the hands of people of Mubarak's generation. He was born in 1928, graduated from the War College in 1949, and was only twenty-four when the July Revolution took place in 1952. Acceding to power at the age of fifty-three, the new president is a relatively young man.

However, Mubarak's youth renders him little more representative of the Egyptian population as a whole than Sadat was. Rapid population growth has produced an age pyramid heavily skewed toward the young. Well over twenty million Egyptians have been born since 1952 and probably about seven million since the October War of 1973. All of these dates provided symbols of legitimacy and set national goals for incumbent elites. But as wave after wave of young Egyptians move toward adulthood, these symbols rapidly become part of history, no more real or vibrant to them than are the 1919 revolution or even the Arabist movement of 1879. Fresh as Mubarak may seem to the outside world, or even to his peers, he is representative of a small and relatively aged segment of the Egyptian population.

Revolutionary Intentions

It was neither the demographic nor the economic situation that led to the overthrow of the monarchy in July 1952. One need not go in any detail into the goals that Nasser and the Revolutionary Command Council set for themselves, for that has been done more than adequately elsewhere.[1] Nor should one take fully at face value the commitments the regime undertook to fulfill at its inception. Still these commitments can and should serve as marks against which the achievements of the revolution can be measured. The six fundamental pledges of the RCC were: 1) an end to imperialism and its agents; 2) an end to feudalism; 3) an end to monopoly and the capitalist control of rule; 4) establishment of a powerful national army; 5) establishment of social justice; 6) establishment of sound democracy.

There were, then, three negative and three positive goals. Once imperialist (i.e., British) control was ended; once their allies among the feudal, cotton-growing landowners or the parasitic industrial bourgeoisie were purged from positions of political power; once the exploitation of landless peasants and sweatshop labor was ended—then Egypt could establish its full economic and political sovereignty through a credible army, the redistribution of wealth to the poor, and the practice of politics free from the bonds of economic exploitation. Until 1962 and the proclamation of the National Charter there was very little more by way of programmatic or ideological gloss than these six principles.

When Nasser died in 1970, the Egyptian army had been twice defeated at Israeli hands and ingloriously contained in the Yemen. "Zionist imperialism" had extended its grip over all the Sinai. The "feudal" landowners had been swept away through successive land reforms, but there were still millions of landless peasants and about half the agricultural surface was still farmed by tenants. A new kind of capitalism, state capitalism as some call it, had taken over the power structure of the country and instituted monopolies in the name of the people in several domains. The distribution of income remained sharply skewed, absolute poverty probably continued to involve most of Egypt's population, and disease and illiteracy were only marginally eroded. Instead of a new generation of educated, motivated Egyptians whose members would be an asset, the revolution sired a generation whose more fortunate members were poorly educated, misemployed, and unmotivated and whose less fortunate members would have a hard time discerning what distinguished their lot from that of their fathers.

It is characteristic of Egypt's leaders that while not unaware of economic problems they tended to seek their resolution in the political domain: ending

[1] *Inter alia* J. and S. Lacouture 1958; Abdel-Malek 1968; Vatikiotis 1961; Wheelock 1960; Wynn 1959; Vaucher 1959.

the British occupation, containing Israeli expansionism, liquidating the domestic allies of imperialism, and more recently ending the costly drain on the economy of war preparedness by negotiating a settlement with Israel. Moreover, beyond a vague aspiration toward industrialization and modernity, policy formulation tended to be dictated by real and perceived threats to the regime and not as part of a coherent economic strategy.

Real as opposed to false problems, like beauty, are in the eye of the beholder. To my eye the period since 1952 has often involved a search for solutions to real problems by stepping outside their parameters. There is the phenomenon of flight from responsibility of the kind—"imperialism is responsible for our backwardness, but imperialism is the weapon of the superpowers whom we cannot combat, therefore we must suffer our backwardness indefinitely." A variant of this outlook gave rise, it seems to me, to Egypt's active pursuit of Arab unity on Egyptian terms. Here the line ran or runs "imperialism is out to get us by direct threat (i.e., Suez War 1956) or through its local allies (i.e., Saudi Arabia or Jordan). We cannot lead our internal revolution as we see fit, for it is too threatening to imperialist interests. Our goals can be attained only insofar as we make the region as a whole safe for the Egyptian revolution. Therefore we must neutralize or eliminate the local agents, rally the hesitant, and shore up any friendly regimes. Egyptian leadership must be acknowledged in all collective Arab efforts." This outlook is at the heart of what Hamdan (1970, pp. 193-98) terms Egypt's enracinated impulse toward defensive imperialism. Its correlate is the assumption that Egypt cannot tend to its own affairs until the region is put in a supportive mood. A third type of "flight forward" is to treat knotty problems as insoluble and end-run them. Thus if the challenge of changing the behavior of 5 million peasants is too awesome, one may still modernize agricultural production by farming the peasantless desert and by transplanting people to a new way of life. Or if modifying fertility behavior contains unacceptable political costs among a conservative Muslim population, one can ponder the possibility of large-scale population transfers to the rich agricultural voids of Syria, Iraq, or the Sudan.

There is little evidence that Nasser and his officer colleagues gave much thought to economics before coming to power and some would say decidedly insufficient thought thereafter. None had any economic training and only two, Khalid Muhi al-Din and Yussef Sadiq, because of their Marxism, were attuned to questions of political economy. Yet an understanding of recent Egyptian history, their own political socialization, and a little intuition surely sufficed to drive home the economic lessons of the recent past.

Muhammed 'Ali, the founder of the dynasty Nasser toppled, is the only member of the *ancien régime* to receive favorable evaluation in Egypt since 1952. Although a non-Egyptian, Muhammed 'Ali wished to put Egypt on a military footing with Europe and had the wit to realize that this would require an economy with an autonomous industrial base, utilizing as much as possible Egyptian raw materials and labor to fuel it. Muhammed 'Ali's state and all its appendages were to become the major consumers in the new order. European intervention in 1839 put an end to the experiment. Protective tariffs were abolished and the army so reduced in size that it could no longer generate much demand for manufactured goods. It could not defend Egypt either. Egypt was forced to rely almost exclusively on agriculture for survival. When British cotton supplies from the southern US were interrupted during the Civil War, Egypt moved to fill part of the gap, thereby launching itself irrevocably into export-oriented monoculture.

Massive external debt and monoculture became the hallmarks of Egypt's nineteenth-century dependency. Default on external obligations and state bankruptcy in 1876 put Egypt into receivership; the country's principal European creditors established a Public Debt Commission to administer Egypt's finances and ensure rapid servicing of its obligations. Egypt's economic sovereignty had been severely circumscribed in 1839, and, for all intents and purposes, it ceased to exist after 1876. The commission's budgetary measures, an IMF stabilization plan in the nineteenth-century manner, led to widespread unhappiness, especially among Egypt's middle income groups. Their diverse interests came to be represented by Col. Ahmad al-'Arabi (like Muhammed 'Ali a legitimate national hero in the eyes of the RCC) who urged the khedive to stand up to the Debt Commission. So threatening did he, 'Arabi, become that the British decided to intervene militarily and unilaterally to rid Egypt of him. The military occupation of Egypt began in 1882 and did not end until 1954-1956. Thus the dissolution of economic sovereignty was followed quickly by the loss of political sovereignty.

Most Egyptian schoolchildren would know at least this much of the story. Most could draw the appropriate lessons: Egypt is coveted and vulnerable. Muhammed 'Ali could not be left alone to remake Egypt without great power interference. Economic diversification is threatening to powers that want to keep Egypt dependent and compliant. Nasser and his colleagues surely were able to pursue these lessons further. Essentially what had happened to Egypt was that its course toward development on the Western model had been willfully interrupted and disrupted for more than a century. Unlike Tokagawa Japan, Egypt could not make the transition to modernity and industrialization. While many doubt that Muhammed 'Ali was in fact an Ottoman shogun (viz. Ramdan 1975) official Egyptian history has been written to suggest that he was.

So the argument goes, had it not been for European intervention, Egypt might have led the Third World, along with Japan, in forging ahead toward self-sustaining growth. Instead it was brought to heel by the European "core."

For a century Egyptians have thus been acutely aware of their economic and military vulnerability. They also learned that their loss of economic sovereignty in the last century was the prelude to ensconcing the country in near-total dependence on cotton cultivation and export to fuel the economy.

After 1882 the British engineered an agricultural revolution in Egypt (Patrick O'Brien 1968, p. 180). Large public outlays in rehabilitation and expanding the water-delivery grid led to agricultural intensification through the spread of "perennial" irrigation. The ability to grow a summer crop, not dependent on the flood, was at the heart of Egypt's surge into long-staple cotton.[2] It was also at the heart of the emergence of an Egyptian landowning class closely wed to British cotton markets and British predominance in Egypt. Neither this class nor the British had any major incentive to promote the country's industrialization. The modest efforts in the 1920s and 1930s of Tala'at Harb's Misr Group notwithstanding, Egypt's economy continued even after World War II to limp on one foot: cotton.

Many, if not all of Nasser's associates had direct contact with the countryside. They saw and probably appreciated what Egypt's agricultural "machine" meant for the peasantry. The *fallah* was occupied nearly all year round in cultivation and the maintenance of water-delivery systems. His livelihood, whether as owner, tenant, or laborer, depended on cotton production and marketing. The latter was subject to all the unpredictable gyrations of international market prices. For instance, the average price per *qantar* of ginned cotton (50 kgs) fell from £E 7.8 over the period 1918-1927 to £E 3.1 over the period 1928 to 1942. The Korean War boom saw it rise from £E 7.5 over the years between 1943 and 1947 to £E 16 for the period 1948 to 1952 and then fall to £E 12 just as the new regime came to power (Issawi 1963, p. 28). Because agriculture accounted for the bulk of national employment, most of the country's exports by value, and about a third of GDP, when it stuttered so did the whole economy.

One major result of this situation was that between the end of the First World War and the revolution of 1952 per capita GNP did not improve, averaging about £E 43 (in 1954 prices) at both ends of the period and dropping down to about £E 35 by the time of the Second World War (Hansen and Marzouk 1965, p. 3). No matter how efficient this cotton-producing machine had become, its essential cog, the *fallah*, was still immersed in poverty and chained to a productive process that functioned without stop. With population growth the value of the peasant's labor was continually diminished relative to the scarce factors of land and capital.

Without any clear blueprint on how to go about it, the new regime was

[2] The construction of the first Aswan Dam in 1902, which became the key to summer water supply, contributed directly to increasing waterlogging and soil salinity in the poorly drained Delta and to stagnation in yields after nearly three decades of spectacular increases.

determined to make the economy walk on two feet and to break those economic linkages to the British metropole that perpetuated Egypt's backwardness. It should not be forgotten that in the early months and even years after the July 1952 revolution the RCC's attention was only sporadically focused on the economy. Far more pressing, in their view, was dealing with anticipated challenges from disgruntled civilian elements—primarily the Wafd Party and the Muslim Brethren—and from the British.

Still, it was clear from the outset that the new regime would seek to promote industrialization. Toward this end they needed to reach out beyond their ranks to tap the expertise of civilian elites—some of the same groups and personalities that the RCC wanted to choke off politically. The Federation of Egyptian Industries and the Misr Group both contributed members to the National Councils of Development set up after 1952. Civilian economists, academicians, and members of the free professions were brought into ministerial positions and strategic liaison roles.[3] One source of civilian expertise was the Pioneers (*rawwad*), a nominally apolitical group organized by a member of the royal family in the interwar years, dedicated to put their competence to the service of Egypt. Hilmi 'Abd al-Rahman was one of their number.

In terms of day-to-day administration and to some extent of the formulation of policy, Egypt's finances, trade, and investment programs have remained in civilian hands until the present time. In many ways the RCC and its successor officer groups knew what it wanted economically in very broad terms but never showed much enthusiasm for or attention to the mechanics of implementation. This contrasted sharply with the close attention paid foreign policy and dealing with domestic politics. The divorce at the elite level between politics and economics is by no means peculiar to Egypt. It tells us a good deal about what such regimes regard as "real" problems. Despite occasional evocation of Marxist themes, domestic and international politics are seen as the determinant elements; the economy and the organization of the means of production are subordinate. Political will sets the course of the nation; economics flows therefrom.

The goal of the RCC after 1952 was the restoration of Egyptian power after an eclipse, some would argue, that had lasted millennia. Restoration of power meant full independence and political sovereignty, an end to the British military presence, avoidance of alliances with either of the superpowers, rehabilitation of the Egyptian army and the establishment of Egypt as the foremost military force in the Arab world. That power had to be founded on a new society in which the average Egyptian could have automatic access to

[3] Fu'ad Galal, Professor of Psychology, was an important recruiter, but each officer probably had his own civilian protégés. Some of the most prominent civilians of these years were Hassan Baghdadi, 'Ali al-Gritli, 'Abd al-Galil al-'Amari, 'Abbas 'Amar, Ahmad Sharabassi, 'Abd al-Razzak Hassan, Hilmi 'Abd al-Rahman, and Sayyid Mar'ai.

a decent standard of living, education, and good health. This in turn required a diversified economy, no longer shackled to agricultural performance, an economy whose center of gravity would be a heavy industrial sector that would simultaneously act as a catalyst to further industrialization and agricultural modernization *and* protect Egypt against dependency on the manufactures of advanced economies. Nasser et al. sought to take up where Muhammed 'Ali had been obliged to leave off. With the passage of more than a century, new social welfare considerations had become important, but the impulse was the same: the restoration of Egyptian national power and broad-based prosperity. In terms of both ends and means Egypt in the last quarter century has fallen far short of its initial ambitions.

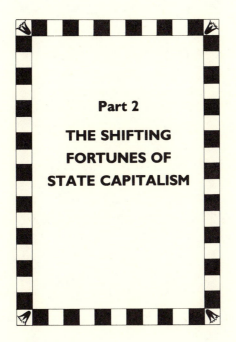

Part 2

**THE SHIFTING
FORTUNES OF
STATE CAPITALISM**

Chapter Four

THE EMERGENCE OF
EGYPT'S PUBLIC SECTOR

> It should be recognized that public enterprises are not
> necessarily easier to guide than private ones, nor are
> they more likely than their private counterpart to give
> desired results when unguided.
> [IBRD 1979a, p. 68.]

Egypt in the 1950s and the 1960s found itself among a handful of developing
countries drawn into state-guided, state-dominated economic growth. One
should not forget that among the LDCs Turkey had pioneered in this direction
in the 1930s, as had Mexico, without benefit of a Marxian socialist rationale.
India followed suit after the Second World War with the same kind of ideological underpinning. Of the "nonaligned" developing nations only Yugoslavia had an ideological commitment to the edification of a dominant public
sector. The needs to which the pioneers were responding involved the rational
and economic use of scarce resources (the private sector with its partial view
and narrow interests could not be entrusted with resource management) and
the undergirding of regime stability by preempting economic resources from
potential domestic rivals for power. Finally growth meant national strength.
Each increment of growth generated, especially in nonagricultural sectors,
was seen in a kind of zero-sum context as restoring the balance between the
recently independent and their former colonial overlords (cf. Killick 1978,
p. 41).

The RCC immediately showed its commitment to industrialization after
July 1952. However rudimentary its understanding of economics, it operated
according to a number of fundamental assumptions that were echoed in other
LDCs. First, it was clear that the state would have to assume those tasks of
infrastructure development, capital mobilization, and big-project sponsorship
of which the private sector was manifestly incapable. But private initiative
was in no way to be discouraged nor was foreign private investment to be
avoided. Second, industrialization had to be far more than cosmetic. It would
follow classic paths of import substitution for finished products, but through

backward linkages eventually move the country into heavy industrial processing and the manufacture of capital goods. Third, the agricultural sector, no matter how impoverished, was Egypt's major economic asset and would therefore have to be enlisted to pay for a good deal of the industrial effort.[1]

This set of assumptions, like nearly all others that have become associated with so-called Nasserism, was not original to the RCC. It merely rooted about in the box of Egypt's recent past to find those themes, analyses, judgments, and policies that others had previously espoused or applied. Arguments in favor of import-substituting industrialization (ISI) had long lain about, specifically for adding fertilizers and cement to Egypt's existing ventures in textiles; electrifying the old Aswan Dam (constructed in 1902) or building what in 1960 would become the Aswan High Dam to provide power for industry. What one cannot take away from the RCC is that it moved ahead, oblivious to the risks and obstacles, along paths that its predecessors had merely discussed. The originality of the new regime lay not in the policies it devised but rather in its policy "packages" and in the fact that it sought, however unsuccessfully, to implement them.

The first stimuli toward ISI came in the early twentieth century. Since the 1860s Egypt had pursued an export-oriented path anchored in unprocessed cotton. There is no question that the economy grew on this basis although benefits were poorly distributed and much of the surplus produced was siphoned off into servicing the external debt. This strategy, if one can call it that, received its first jolt in the early 1900s. Depressed world market prices for cotton and other raw produce combined with moves initiated by the British High Commissioner, Lord Cromer, in 1901 that effectively removed tariff protection from many budding Egyptian manufacturing enterprises (Hansen and Nashashibi 1975, p. 207; Mabro and Radwan 1976, p. 23; Radwan 1974, p. 245). In addition, the rapid introduction of perennial irrigation into the poorly drained Nile Delta provoked serious soil salinity and decreasing cotton yields.

In the aftermath of the First World War, Egyptians of considerable stature who were in no way hostile to the British nor ostentatiously nationalist voiced their apprehensions concerning the long-term implications of monoculture in unstable world markets, rising population, and the absence of any tariff pro-

---

[1] With this in mind, I cannot concur with Clement Moore's allegation (1980, pp. 2-3) that Nasser's approach should be placed in a Durkheimian, Weberian, US developmentalist mode that separates modernization from industrialization and in which modernization becomes tantamount to the proliferation of professionals. I believe that for the RCC industrialization and modernization were indissolubly linked, although as the former failed to develop according to expectations, there may have been a tendency to suggest that because the professional-technical strata of society had developed so spectacularly, modernization was therefore taking place. See Chapter Eleven.

tection for Egyptian industry. Isma'il Sidqi was among this group, a man of wealth and conservative political and economic views, but nonetheless something of a spokesman for Egyptian capitalists who increasingly sought investment opportunities outside the agricultural sector. One of the first Egyptians to try to provide institutional channels for the placement of this investment was of course Tala'at Harb, founder of Bank Misr and of the Misr Group of industries and trading companies. These men not only felt that import-substituting industry was necessary (for example in textiles and fertilizers) but that the government should play an active role in initiating them. With proper protection there seemed no reason why such ventures could not be made attractive to foreign investment. The 1929 Bank Misr report on ISI calling for a ten-year industrial development plan, joint public-private ventures, and a state-sponsored industrial development bank differs little in its spirit from what Nasser brought forth thirty years later. However far-reaching the implications of these ideas, the goal was not to remake Egyptian society but to stave off mass upheaval and to find nonagricultural outlets for investment. As members of the Commission on Commerce and Industry, Tala'at Harb, Isma'il Sidqi, and Amin Yahya wrote in 1918 that industrialization was the only protection against social discontent and perhaps even revolution (Tignor 1977a, p. 162; Tignor 1976, pp. 50-55; Patrick O'Brien 1966, p. 55). A year later, as nationalist hopes for postwar independence were thwarted by British obduracy, large segments of Egypt's rural population did erupt into violence, attacking all manifestations of the British presence, but, as well, the rural gentry that had so visibly benefited from British protection.

World commodity crises in 1920, 1921, and 1926 followed by the 1929 Depression ushered in the era of ISI with substantial tariff protection. In 1930 P.M. Isma'il Sidqi shepherded through increased customs duties on a broad range of imported goods, thereby giving a fillip to Egyptian industry at a time when world cotton prices had tumbled disastrously. For example, employment in industries employing ten or more workers rose from 95,000 in 1927 to 155,000 in 1937; cement production rose from 61,000 to 353,000 tons over the same period, and mechanically woven cotton cloth from 20 million to 159 million square yards between 1931 and 1939 (Issawi 1963, p. 44). The interruption of much of Egypt's foreign trade during the Second World War gave further protection and impetus to this process.[2] For their part, the British, who in the 1920s may have felt Egyptian inexperience would have prevented any major strides toward industrialization, tried in the 1930s and 1940s to

---

[2] Dr. 'Ali al-Gritli (1947, esp. pp. 574-75) perhaps typified the growing consensus, without political or nationalist coloring, that ISI was a necessity—in his view because of fixed land resources and rising population. The sectors he singles out are textiles, fertilizers, glass, paper, leather, and some local assembly. And, significantly, he called upon the state to be the catalyst to the process.

make ISI work in favor of British technology, expertise, and supplies (R. L. Tignor, personal communication, September 26, 1977).

Still Egypt's progress toward industrialization was modest and remained almost exclusively under private auspices. Large projects in which the state would have to play a major role, such as the electrification of the Aswan Dam, simply hung fire. It, for instance, was not the victim of colonial hostility to Egypt's industrialization but rather of the clan infighting over award of contract, and the difficulties of financing. Capitalization of industry was also modest. Paid-up capital in Egyptian industrial joint-stock companies rose from about £8 million in 1919 to £24 million in 1939 and £33 million in 1946— all presumably in current prices (Issawi 1963, p. 45 and Da'ud 1973, pp. 61-62). These figures probably underestimate industrial capital, for they do not reflect capitalization of small-scale enterprises. Hansen and Marzouk, for example, put paid-up capital in 1939 at £30-40 million (1965, p. 129) and Muhammed Anis (1950, p. 791) puts the figure at £70 million for 1945. Probably about 40 percent of this capital was tied up in spinning and weaving, then and today Egypt's leading industrial branch. In all, industry accounted for only 13 percent of gross national income in 1945 while agriculture accounted for 43 percent (Mead 1967, p. 45).

The RCC and ISI

It is almost always conveniently overlooked in contemporary Egypt that despite foreign economic preponderance, despite the absence of energetic state intervention, and despite the alleged shortsighted greed of private interests, the manufacturing sector grew at an annual rate of 10.5 percent between 1946 and 1951 with high rates of capital accumulation. In 1949 the state fostered the establishment of an Industrial Bank to facilitate the flow of credit to private entrepreneurs. The advent of the military regime in 1952 did not so much mark a new era as it signaled the end of the phase of "easy" import-substitution (primarily textiles and processed food) and the beginning of state-led import-substitution that would come to include intermediate and capital goods (Radwan 1974, p. 245 and Mabro and Radwan 1976, p. 88; Patrick O'Brien 1966, p. 20).

The RCC moved quickly on several fronts. In September 1952 it pushed through a land reform that had been talked about for six years but which had remained a dead letter. Later in the fall decisions were made to press ahead with the electrification of the old Aswan Dam as well as to study the feasibility of constructing a single giant dam at Aswan to assure Egypt a steady supply of water through over-year storage (Waterbury 1979, pp. 87-115). The forum in which these decisions were debated if not taken was the Permanent Council for the Development of National Production (PCDNP) grouping technocratic ministries and technical experts that rode herd on specialized subcommittees. Other projects that PCDNP advocated were the Kima fertilizer plant at Aswan to draw on the hydroelectric power generated at the old dam, and the Helwan Iron and Steel complex just south of Cairo. The PCDNP initiated several things: the regime's commitment to long-term development projects; state planning in embryo; the establishment of a file of projects that informed subsequent formal planning exercises; and, by reserving public shares in new projects, laid the groundwork for Egypt's public sector (Mabro and Radwan 1976, p. 65). In so doing, however, it seemed only to be responding to private sector appeals for greater state sponsorship and activity that had gone largely unanswered since the 1920s.

Problems that for years have been described as chronic in Egypt had not yet made themselves felt. The country emerged from the Second World War with £425 million in sterling reserves and thus foreign exchange was no particular problem. The regime did not yet feel compelled to squeeze the peasantry by purchasing their cotton cheap and exporting it dear to maximize foreign exchange earnings. Nor did it evidence much concern for an export-oriented thrust in the nonagricultural sectors; Egypt's foreign exchange position could be protected adequately by ISI. Agricultural price manipulation and the verbal commitment to export manufactures were the children of the economic crises of the 1960s and 1970s. In the 1950s Egypt had only to confront political crises, whether of the domestic or international variety.

The regime did try to stimulate new investment outside agriculture by three devices: the first in some ways may have rendered the others too impracticable. It devised the land reform of 1952, which placed a ceiling on individual landholdings of 200 *feddans* (this reform will be discussed in greater detail in Chapter Twelve). The intent of the act was at least threefold: 1) to destroy the resource base of Egypt's landed elite that had dominated politics in the 1919-1952 period; 2) to lead to some modest redistribution of rural assets; 3) to encourage rural capitalists to place their funds in industry. It was hoped that landowners affected by the reform would invest in the industrial sector the proceeds of legal land sales of acreage held over the ceiling, the bonds they received as compensation for land taken over by the state, and any other earnings they might have planned to invest in their prereform holdings. This was the first tentative step to make agriculture pay for industry.

Despite consultation with the Misr Group and the Federation of Egyptian Industries, and the inclusion of civilian experts in the cabinet and the PCDNP, the private sector did not follow the RCC's lead. It was, after all, a military regime whose open hostility to civilian political parties was far more disturbing than its enmity toward the British and the monarchy, an enmity that important segments of the civilian elite shared. Secondly, the direct assault on private property that the land reform embodied (the first civilian prime minister, 'Ali

61

Mahir, resigned over the issue) was an ominous precedent. There was no telling where these young officers might strike next, and after 1953, with political parties officially dissolved, parliament disbanded, and the constitution suspended, no way of checking them. For about four years, or until the Suez War of November 1956, there was an uneasy standoff between the regime and the private sector. It is reasonably certain that private industrial investment, running in the early 1950s at about £E 30 million a year, stagnated or fell, while that in urban real estate rose from £E 40 million in 1954 to £E 59 million in 1958. Private industrial companies paid ever larger proportions of their earnings out as dividends rather than reinvesting them. The dividend share of profits rose steadily from 59 percent in 1954 to 80 percent in 1958 (Mead 1967, p. 121).

As he was to do in other policy domains, Nasser backed away from the nationalist stances and policies put forth primarily by the Wafd, before 1952. Thus within three years Egypt dropped all claims to sovereignty over the Sudan and negotiated an agreement with Great Britain for the evacuation of its troops from the Suez Canal Zone that provided for the reoccupation of the canal in the event of an attack upon Egypt or Turkey. These otherwise extraneous examples are mentioned to indicate the room for policy maneuver enjoyed by the RCC once it had suppressed all prerevolutionary forms of political expression. In the same manner, a number of laws were issued in 1953 and 1954 that sought to encourage foreign and domestic private investment by making concessions that governments before 1952 had found

Table 4.1

Public and Private Shares in Industrial Investment, 1952-1960

(£E millions current prices)

	Public	Private	Total
1952-53	1.4	28.1	29.5
1953-54	4.6	22.6	27.2
1954-55	6.0	27.6	33.6
1955-56	7.9	41.3	49.2
1956-57	8.5	22.6	31.1
1957-58	5.1	30.5	35.6
1958-59	17.4	30.4	47.8
1959-60	49.4	—	49.4

SOURCES: Figures for public investment from Patrick O'Brien 1966, p. 328, citing NBE *Bulletin* 4 (1961): 408-9. Total figures from Mead 1967, 290; UAR Statistical Atlas, 1962. I subtracted column 1 from column 3. It does not seem plausible that there was no private investment in 1959-60. These figures therefore must be taken as indicating general trends and relative orders of magnitude.

unacceptable. Law 26 of 1954, for example, eased regulations on the repatriation of earnings and revised a 1947 law so that foreign investors could take up to a 51 percent interest in a firm as opposed to the previous 49 percent. The 1953 Mining and Quarrying Law revised that of 1948 and allowed foreign interests to undertake new petroleum concessions. Laws 430 of 1953 and 25 of 1954 extended tax holidays of seven years to new industrial ventures and of five years for existing companies that undertook capital expansion. Tax rates on undistributed profits were also reduced (Issawi 1963, p. 53). It has already been noted that the Egyptian private sector was relatively impervious to these blandishments. So too foreign investors brought in only £E 8 million between 1953 and 1961, the bulk of it concentrated in petroleum and tourism. As these domestic and foreign interests prudently assessed the real intentions of the RCC, the RCC returned the compliment and by 1958 found them wanting.

The existing entrepreneurial bourgeoisie could never quite see all the possibilities that the budding public sector held open to it. Its members perceived only the menace, and in preparing for it brought about in some measure the fulfillment of their own suspicions. It remained for a new bourgeoisie to adopt wholeheartedly a parasitical relationship with the public sector: from menace to manna. As we shall see, in the era of the open-door (*infitah*) (Chapter Seven) the new bourgeoisie can have the best of two worlds by continuing to exploit the largesse of a malfunctioning public sector while demanding that the state get out of those areas (administered pricing for example) that restrict profit margins. No two figures better symbolize the old and the new entrepreneurial bourgeoisies than Ahmad 'Abboud, the pre-1952 sugar baron, and Ahmad Osman, "the man who built the Aswan Dam." 'Abboud needed from the state only its protection of his industrial undertakings. Osman by contrast could not have prospered without the state's business (cf. Fitzgerald 1979, p. 35). New or old, it is a fact of considerable significance that Nasser was profoundly suspicious of the private sector bourgeoisie in whatever guise, not on ideological grounds but because he saw them, like the communists, as those most likely to act as agents of foreign adversaries or to use their financial resources to engineer his overthrow. Leaving aside remnants of the "pasha" class, such as Fu'ad Serrag al-Din, who were active in the Wafd, Sadat did not share Nasser's misgivings regarding the reliability of the entrepreneurial bourgeoisie.

It has been suggested that Egypt backed or fell into socialism without really knowing where it was going. There is certainly a substantial element of truth in this judgment. Yet from the very outset of the regime there was an unmasked will to propel the state directly into the management of the economy, and there was no struggle within the RCC over the principle (as opposed to the extent) of public ownership. Gamal Salim could declare early on that "We are not socialists,'' but the preoccupation with rational resource management and preempting resources for political purposes obliged the regime to reach for administrative instruments first tested in socialist economies. It was then a question of ideology catching up with practice.

One project, above all others, summarizes the various policy objectives the regime pursued in the early years. The Aswan Dam symbolized rationality in resource management, national sovereignty and strength, and the leading role of the state in finding technocratic solutions to Egypt's socio-economic problems. All are closely interlinked. No one contested the two premises that underlay the project—that Egypt needed *some sort* of over-year storage facility (i.e. capable of impounding more than one flood without silting up its storage capacity too rapidly) that could deliver an assured supply of water to Egypt's major summer and export crops of cotton and rice. The debate on this point was whether or not the High Dam was the best over-year facility (Waterbury 1979, pp. 117-53). The second premise was that only the state could mobilize the capital necessary to implement this project or any alternative to it. (Final costs for the dam, power station, and downstream facilities were about $820 million: Waterbury 1979, p. 112).

Beyond the question of *assured* water supply to make the existing agricultural sector more viable, was that of *additional* water supply to make the deserts green. The temptation to which the regime yielded was to skirt the complex and politically loaded questions of reorganizing traditional agriculture, that involved compulsory crop rotations, consolidation of fragmented holdings, producers' cooperatives, mechanization, etc., and to seek Egypt's agricultural salvation in the deserts. Beginning with the Tahrir Province experiment in desert reclamation in 1954, the regime evinced a constant preoccupation with "horizontal" expansion in Egyptian agriculture. Rather than setting their priority as the intensification of agricultural production in the valley proper (vertical expansion), the officers looked to the new lands. The threefold appeal of this assault on the desert was to characterize many of their quests for solutions to Egypt's other economic problems. Land reclamation had an element of size and sweep that captured the mood of remaking Egypt. It was susceptible to physical engineering and would depend upon advanced hydrotechnology. Second, it represented, literally, a social tabula rasa, a broad canvas upon which the regime could sketch in the agricultural communities of the future. Nothing need be destroyed in order to build the new order. Finally, it cast the state in the role of social engineer creating new group relations and new roles which the rest of society would then emulate (cf. Magdi Hassanain 1975, *passim*). The Free Officers were by no means of one mind on these issues, but those personalities that came to predominate in the 1960s believed that the new societies in the reclaimed areas would become demonstration models for the eventual reordering of Egypt's traditional peasant society. Once funding for the Aswan Dam became available from the USSR in 1958, the regime pursued horizontal expansion with single-minded purpose, leaving the traditional sector to flounder along as best it could.

Using existing water supply, the regime pushed ahead with reclamation on 77,000 *feddans* (25,000 in Tahrir Province) even before 1958. Then, in anticipation of the water that would become available as a result of the High Dam, reclamation was begun on some 600,000 *feddans* between 1960-1965, the equivalent of one-tenth of Egypt's existing cultivated acreage. Once the body of the dam was completed in the mid-1960s, the pace of reclamation slowed markedly both as a result of a general economic crisis and because of difficulties inherent in the reclamation process. When further reclamation was virtually suspended in 1972, 920,000 *feddans* were in various stages of preparation. Of total public investments between 1960 and 1970 in agricultural production, irrigation, and drainage, £E 483 million was devoted to horizontal expansion projects and only £E 192 million to vertical expansion (Muhammed 'Abd al-Ra'uf 1973, Table 8).

To sum up what we have looked at so far, the High Dam was to underwrite a holding operation in traditional agriculture by guaranteeing summer water and protection against flood, while furnishing additional water (7.5 billion m³ according to Egypt's 1959 agreement with the Sudan) to irrigate 1.2 million new *feddans* which would become the patrimony of a new agricultural order under public aegis.

There remained the all-important goal of heavy industrialization. One of the major obstacles to moving in this direction was the country's inadequate power supply, a problem with which Egypt has continued to live despite completion of the High Dam. Modest petroleum reserves precluded any major development of thermal power generation unless the country was to use up precious foreign exchange in importing oil. The electrification of the old Aswan Dam would merely respond to a small part of existing demand: indeed, the Kima fertilizer plant that was constructed at Aswan in the middle 1950s consumed nearly all the output of the old dam's power station (1.8 billion kwh). The High Dam, however, was designed with an installed capacity of 10 billion kwh per annum, enough to meet Egypt's existing demand and much of what was anticipated for the 1960s. Not only would the High Dam assure abundant hydroelectric power, but, as a public project, the price of its electricity could be subsidized in order to stimulate industrial use.

As was the case with land reclamation, the regime initiated a number of industrial projects while awaiting completion of the power station. A project that had been tabled as early as 1951 was resurrected whereby an iron and steel plant would be constructed at Helwan with a 300,000-ton annual capacity, utilizing low-grade ore from Aswan and imported coke. The German firm, Demag, both managed the project and took an equity position in it. The bulk of the capital, £E 11 million, was provided by the government. A minority share in the company was put up for private subscription in Egypt. The Kima fertilizer company followed a similar format with a public investment of £E 8 million. Thus the dam was to be vital to the success of the "hard" phase of ISI, during which the state would have to develop crucial backward linkages in the stead of the private sector. In sum, industrialization was seen and still is seen as the only long-term solution to Egypt's development needs. Unlike many LDCs, Egypt's agricultural sector was already functioning at high levels of productivity and only marginal improvements could be expected. There was also the phenomenon of diminishing returns to growing agricultural labor inputs. The High Dam could help ease the strain on the traditional sector while opening up virgin areas to which excess population could be transferred (that hope proved illusory). Further down the road the country's industrial momentum would lead to the occupational relocation of the work force out of agriculture.

In terms of national sovereignty and power the High Dam assuaged some of Egypt's most profound geopolitical apprehensions. It was a single hydraulic edifice entirely within Egypt's borders. As such it greatly reduced reasonable fears that some combination of the eight upstream states, many of which were at the time under colonial control (Sudan, Tanganyika, Kenya, the Belgian Congo), might interfere with Egypt's only source of fresh water, the Nile. In addition, the dam had the kind of massive international visibility, both physical and symbolic, that represented the regime's will to assert its sovereignty in the face of neo-imperialism. The scale of the project could not fail to capture the nation's imagination.

The Transfer of Assets

Having taken some early steps toward state-guided industrialization, Egypt's policy-makers had to come to grips with financing and investment. There were essentially five avenues open to them. We have already considered one, private sector investment, and have seen that it could not be relied upon as a major source of financing. The other four will crop up regularly throughout this book. They are: 1) once-and-for-all transfers of assets to public ownership through nationalization and sequestration; 2) fiscal revenue-gathering through income tax, sales and value-added taxes, customs duties, and forced savings; 3) foreign borrowing and deficit financing; and 4) administered pricing to engineer intersectoral transfers. Egypt has tried them all with more or less success and more or less enthusiasm. For the moment we shall be concerned only with the permanent seizure of private assets, the principle instrument of the late Fifties and early Sixties.

The first such transfer came about as a result of land reform and furthered state investment goals in at least two ways. Land redistributed to landless peasants or small-holders was organized in state cooperatives which supplied production inputs and credit and which could require that peasant beneficiaries follow certain crop rotation programs within financial terms determined by the state. Further the state retained effective ownership of the land during the period in which the beneficiaries paid for their lots by installment. As late as 1977, moreover, the state was still collecting rent on 200,000 *feddans* taken over in the reforms of 1952, 1961, and 1969 awaiting final assignment of title (*RY*, no. 2615, July 24, 1978). These revenues were never very large, but they represented a net gain inasmuch as the landowners affected by the reform were compensated in bonds with long maturation periods and low interest rates. Some 460,000 *feddans* were taken over in the 1952 reform, the market value of which was about £E 161 million. Only 40 percent of market value was calculated for compensation and even then actual payments were delayed. Legislation of 1958 stipulated that payments would take place in forty annual installments at 1.5 percent interest. By 1959 £E 42 million in compensatory bonds had been issued. Given these delays and the overall terms of compensation which Gabriel Saab (1967, p. 25) rightly qualifies as confiscatory, it is no wonder that these bonds did little to promote industrial investment. In the second reform of 1961, lowering the ceiling to 50 *feddans*, over 257,000 *feddans* were affected. Compensation was more favorable: this time the bonds could be traded on the stock exchange; they were redeemable in fifteen annual installments at 4 percent interest. By 1964 some £E 50 million in bonds had been issued. Beneficiaries of the 1952 reform were to pay the state the assessed value of the land (again 40 percent of market value) in forty annual installments at 1.5 percent interest plus 10 percent of assessed value for administrative costs. In 1964, Law 138 stipulated that all subsequent payments would be on the basis of 25 percent of the assessed value of the land in forty annual installments free of interest.

In August 1955, in a dispute over sugar pricing, the government sequestered Ahmad 'Abboud's sugar refineries, thus breaking his monopoly over that sector. But the state's first *major* leap into nonagricultural activities came as the unanticipated consequence of an international imbroglio. There is no need to go over the oft-told tale of the High Dam and the Suez War, but it may be useful to call attention to a few crucial elements that had a profound impact upon the Egyptian regime (and the Third World in general). Egypt, it will be recalled, in 1955 defied the Western embargo on arms to Arab nations in a state of war with Israel by contracting with Czechoslovakia for delivery of some $200 million in advanced Soviet weaponry and aircraft. By so doing Nasser jeopardized Western funding of the High Aswan Dam. Even when the arms deal became known, the IBRD maintained its offer to help finance construction, but its conditions were stringent and complex. Its credits were totally contingent on the US and Britain maintaining theirs, and, once the credits had been advanced, the bank insisted that Egypt 1) divert one-third of its internal revenues to the project over ten years; 2) that the bank review key aspects of Egypt's economic performance and statistical reporting on a periodic basis; 3) that contracts be awarded on a competitive basis but with none going to a communist state; 4) that Egypt would incur no new external obligation (i.e. arms acquisitions) without prior bank approval. Needless to say these conditions shocked the Egyptians, who saw in them a reincarnation of the kinds of controls imposed by the Caisse de la Dette Publique in the 1870s. Nonetheless Nasser accepted them, for he suspected that the terms were made offensive deliberately in the expectation that Egypt would refuse them. His acceptance called the Western bluff, and it was Secretary of State Dulles who in July 1956 informed Egypt's ambassador in Washington that the US was withdrawing its credit offer because it was believed that Egypt's economy was incapable of sustaining its end of the deal (Waterbury 1979, p. 107).

Nasser reacted by nationalizing the Suez Canal Company, a French company headquartered in Paris but a relative majority of whose shares had been acquired by the British eighty years earlier. Nasser's argument was that this asset, built with Egyptian sweat and money, was returning to its rightful owners, and that its annual revenues would be used to replace the Western financing for the High Dam. The company's assets were worth about £E 95 million in 1956, but for those actually held in Egypt, the government eventually agreed to pay £E 27.5 million in compensation over the period 1958-1962. Revenues from the canal did increase dramatically, from the £E 2.3 million royalty which the company paid Egypt in 1955 to direct revenues of £E 42 million in 1958, rising to £E 77 million by 1964. It is doubtful, however, that much of this income was actually engrossed in the High Dam budget.

The seizure of the canal was the pretext for a war in which Britain, France, and Israel openly sought to destroy Egypt's military potential, provoke Nasser's overthrow, and recapture the canal. Although the conspiracy failed, it is little wonder that many Egyptians felt vindicated in their conviction that their country could not undertake a far-reaching overhaul of its own society and economy without great power interference. Be that as it may, once hostilities were over, the government seized all French and British assets in Egypt.

By Laws 22, 23, and 24 of January 1957 all commercial banks, insurance companies, and commercial agencies for foreign trade were fully Egyptianized in management and capital. Nine banks, including Barclay's and Credit Lyonnais, were sold to Egyptian public sector banks. Nearly two hundred foreign-owned insurance companies were purchased by three newly created Egyptian insurance companies. Other French and British assets were placed under the control of the Economic Organization, a public holding company created in January 1957.

The real market value of the assets taken over at that time is hard to estimate. Doubtless it was grossly undervalued in the final arrangements for compensation. By an accord of 1959 Egypt agreed to pay the UK £E 25 million for its assets. It is not clear what compensation the French received beyond that awarded to the Suez Canal Company.

The Suez War was thus a major watershed. The state found itself the owner of considerable assets and from then on until 1967 there was no turning back in the systematic expansion of the public sector. The months of 1956-57 had a bittersweet quality as far as the private sector was concerned. On the one hand the elimination of foreign interests opened up new opportunities for Egyptian and Levantine capital. On the other, the state was now more than ever an economic force to be reckoned with, particularly in its control of the banking sector. It could only be disquieting that private property, even if foreign, was put into the public domain.

It was at this point that the first signs of dissent regarding the *extent* of public ownership began to appear among Nasser's associates. Most of the original members of the RCC plus several civilian advisors felt that Egypt had gone about as far as it should in expanding public ownership. They tended to advocate rationalization in the administration of existing public assets (that is, making them pay their own way), but some suggested that sooner or later the state should divest itself of many of its properties once the private sector proved capable of taking them over. This, after all, was the course that Turkey had followed with qualified success. The divestment issue was, as we shall see, put to rest by 1960 only to be resurrected with some fanfare in 1973.

By contrast, in the "second circle" of the Free Officers and among some civilian technocratic "high-risers" there was a marked determination to seize the opportunity of the 1957 expropriations to consolidate and expand the public sector. This current won out and its various apostles came to dominate economic policy-making in the 1960s. With rare exceptions (e.g., Kamal Rifa'at, Magdi Hassanain, Ahmad Fu'ad) this current was not ideologically motivated. Rather, they seemed primarily concerned by questions of efficiency in resource utilization and the need to concentrate economic power in the hands of the state in order to be able to determine sectoral investment priorities. 'Ali Sabri, Muhammed Hassanain Heikal, and 'Aziz Sidqi all shared this view.

'Aziz Sidqi was the driving force behind the expansion of the public sector. After receiving a doctorate in regional planning in the US, Sidqi returned to Egypt where he rose to some prominence in the administration of Tahrir Province. In 1956, when only in his mid-thirties, he was made minister of industry. He then carved a remarkable career for himself, establishing a close working relationship with Nasser. Only one other civilian ever enjoyed Sidqi's degree of access to or influence upon the president, and that was Hassanein Heikal. Though he suffered a period of eclipse in 1965-66, Sidqi was master of Egypt's industrialization for over a decade. He reemerged as minister of industry in October 1967 after the June War, and in 1972 President Sadat appointed him prime minister. Few ministers, military or civilian, exhibited his longevity, and fewer still his tenacity. Predictably, he had his share of rivals and adversaries, and Nasser, as he was to do with all those who disposed of relatively great power, hedged him in among countervailing personalities and institutions.

The creation of the Ministry of Industry came in July 1956, well before the expropriations of the following January. Its establishment represented an escalation in the regime's intent to replace a faltering private sector in the promotion of Egyptian industry. Within a year, Sidqi had prepared a five-year industrial development plan which was the first planning effort of any kind that the state had undertaken. It relied heavily and somewhat unrealistically upon private initiative: total investments were projected at £E 114 million of which 79 percent was to come from private sources. The Ministry of Industry, however, scarcely consulted with private interests about their role in it. The Agency for the Consolidation of Industry, set up in May 1958 with ten public officials and five representatives of the Federation of Industries, was not enough to offset the malaise. Sidqi made clear his belief that if left to their own devices private interests would not invest in industrial projects vital to the national interest. He must have convinced Nasser to give him his head. The president announced in December 1958 that the five-year industrial plan would be completed in three. "We have to work twice as fast," he warned, "once for the hundred years of backwardness that have passed, once to provide work for the 350,000 persons who are born to us each year" (Abdel-Malek 1968, p. 124). In that year Egypt negotiated its first major loan for economic purposes from the USSR: 700 million rubles (or about $126 million) payable over twelve years at 2.5 percent interest with a five-year grace period. Upon the plan's formal fulfillment in 1960, some £E 90 million had been invested over the three-year period, of which the state furnished 30 to 40 percent, while several projects begun by the PCDNP were continued or completed (Mabro and Radwan 1976, pp. 67-68).[3]

---

[3] Turkey's more telescoped experience in the 1930s makes for instructive comparisons. In 1931, at the height of the Depression, Ataturk dispatched Ismet Inonu to Moscow where he negotiated an $8 million loan and Soviet advice on the design of the first Five-Year Plan launched in 1933. Soviet advisors urged ISI projects, especially in textiles. By the end of the plan two public banks, the Eti and Sumer, were set up to act as holding companies for public sector enterprises, and to be run on cost-effective grounds. The USSR had helped launch state capitalism in Turkey in 1933 just as it would in Egypt after 1957. See Okyar 1975, pp. 32-34.

Simultaneously two other institutional innovations were initiated. In 1957 the above-mentioned Economic Organization was founded to supervise all existing public enterprises and mixed enterprises in which the public share was 25 percent or more (shares valued at some £E 17 million in 1957). To this was added the French and British assets taken over in 1957, so that by the end of 1958 the Economic Organization controlled enterprises worth £E 58 million. By 1960 the EO controlled sixty-four companies (including five banks and six insurance companies) employing 80,000, and assets worth £E 80 million (Abdel-Malek 1968, p. 111). Under heavy state pressure several firms in the Misr Group and the 'Abboud Group entered into association with the EO. Initially the EO was put under the direction of Hassan Ibrahim, a conservative member of the RCC, who, like several of his peers, looked somewhat askance at the ambitions of the upstart Sidqi.

Another hedge to Sidqi's domain was the National Planning Committee, founded in 1957 to replace the PCDNP. In 1958 it was organizationally divided into the High Council for National Planning, attached to the Presidency, and the original National Planning Committee, to act as its executive arm. With the dissolution of the PCDNP formal interaction with major private sector spokesmen came to an end. Another archconservative of the RCC, Hussain Shafa'i, was initially put at the head of the planning apparatus and let it be known that all industrial projects would have to conform to the NPC's general strategy. His successor, RCC member 'Abd al-Latif Baghadi, was of like mind. A third institutional check was embodied in the Ministry of Finance, traditionally a civilian enclave, where profligate spending was viewed with misgiving.

Sidqi was not to be so easily contained. In 1958 his Ministry was empowered to rule on the acceptability and to license the establishment of all new industrial plants, private and public, as well as any expansion, change of location or change of purpose of existing enterprises (Patrick O'Brien 1966, p. 89). To this day the Ministry of Industry has never relinquished this power. Sidqi also invaded the EO's territory in 1958 when the Ministry wrested from it control over the Industrial Bank. Hassan Ibrahim, who had not been informed of the transfer, temporarily resigned in protest only to be persuaded by Nasser to reassume his duties (*RY*; no. 2578, April 11, 1977). Even so Ibrahim was eventually removed from this position amidst rumors of corruption and mismanagement, to be replaced by the civilian economist, 'Abd al-Mun'aim al-Qaissuni.

With the benefit of hindsight two trends emerged in the period 1957-1960. The government had acquired the leverage (banks, agricultural coops, the EO) to begin to plan national investment and evidenced every intention of doing so. Secondly, and despite occasional assurances to the contrary, the private sector was to play an important but subordinate role in future development. Measures were enacted that appeared calculated to alienate private interests, thereby providing the state grounds for further inroads into private assets.

In 1958-59 it was decided that Egypt would draw up its first Five-Year Development Plan for 1960-1965. The NPC projections, again in the absence of much meaningful dialogue between public and private interests, reserved a dominant place for private investment in general strategy. Over the five-year period, private savings were to equal 55 percent of all local investment. Private interests were to be responsible for 64 percent (£E 104 million) of all industrial investment, and in the first year of the plan alone, the private sector was called upon to furnish 70 percent of all domestic investments (Mursi 1976, p. 66).

Under the most harmonious circumstances, such expectations would have been unwarranted, but in the months before the launching of the plan several measures were enacted that precluded any effective private sector cooperation. In January 1959 laws were issued that obliged joint stock companies to invest 5 percent of their net distributions to stockholders in state bonds and to limit profits distributions to 10 percent of the nominal value of company shares. The bottom fell out of the stock market and the Ministry of Finance had to fix floor prices for traded issues. This did not prevent black-market trading of stock below the floor.

A year later, in February 1960, the Misr Bank and the Central Bank (Bank Ahali) were nationalized. At the time of nationalization, the Misr Bank had £E 100 million in deposits but more important acted as a holding company for twenty-seven industrial and commercial enterprises with paid-up capital of over £E 20 million. The Misr Group owned the largest textile center in the Middle East at Mahalla al-Kubra and its various affiliates accounted for 60 percent of all textile production and 53 percent of employment in the textile sector. Although all Misr enterprises since 1952 had been closely integrated into plans for industrial expansion, nationalization was justified on the grounds of breaking up an effective monopoly that *could* use its weight to thwart public development policy. No one accused it of actually having done so.

The National Bank of Egypt had been founded in 1898 by private Jewish entrepreneurs, and while it came to exercise many of the functions of a central bank, including the issuance of currency, it remained a private sector institution. During the 1950s it obtained the power to control the volume and flow of credit in the banking sector and was instrumental in financing the marketing of the cotton crop. In the fall of 1956, after the nationalization of the Suez Canal, it refused to carry out this function. Once absorbed into the public sector, the NBE was stripped of its central banking powers—assumed thenceforth by the newly created Central Bank—but allowed to continue as a commercial bank. For a time the presidents of both the NBE, 'Abd al-Galil al-

'Amari, and of Bank Misr, Muhammed Rushdi, were kept on in their functions. As a final note on this absorption of banking institutions, the Belgian and International Bank was nationalized in early 1961 as a result of the crisis in the Belgian Congo as it moved toward independence.

Thus by the time the state launched the Five-Year Plan in 1960 it had not once retreated from its invasion of the private sector. Yet it continued to rely upon that sector to carry the major investment load and repeatedly sought to reassure private interests that the state would go no further and might even begin to divest. 'Abd al-Latif Baghdadi went on record in February 1957, just after the first wave of nationalizations and sequestrations, to state that the government's goal was only to fill in for the private sector in areas in which it was deficient. Once Qaissuni had taken over the EO he prophesied in November 1959 that government shares in its enterprises would be sold off to the public (it was sixteen years before he and the others raised the issue again). As the Nasserist regime moved toward the greatest wave of nationalizations yet contemplated, various officials tried to still the alarmists. "The objective of government intervention is to avoid losses," the under secretary of the Ministry of Economy stated in July 1960, ". . . once a project has become successful, the government will sell the share that it owns" (Abdel-Malek 1968, p. 143). Two months before the July 1961 decrees, Qaissuni declared that the state was contemplating no further nationalizations (Patrick O'Brien 1966, p. 130).

Was all this mollification only dissimulation? Were the financial technocrats of the regime kept in the dark as to what Nasser and a few others had in mind? Because with the passage of time the wisdom of the July decrees of 1961 has been universally questioned, it is now nearly impossible to obtain an accurate picture of how this momentous decision was taken. But because of its importance, some attempt must be made.

First, let us inventory briefly what the state nationalized in July 1961 and then sequestered for political reasons through 1964 (the best accounts are in Issawi 1963; Patrick O'Brien 1966; and Abdel-Malek 1968). In the welter of legislation issued that summer, the heaviest blows were struck by Laws 117, 118, and 119, putting a considerable portion of the nonagricultural sector of the economy under public ownership or control. The first law provided for the nationalization of all remaining private banks and insurance companies as well as fifty shipping companies and firms in heavy or basic industries. Their shares were simply converted into fifteen-year government bonds bearing 4 percent interest.[4] Law 118 obliged another eighty-three companies to sell 50 percent or more of their shares to public agencies. The third law,

---

[4] Nationalization bonds inspired so little confidence that even public sector banks refused them as collateral on loans (Guwaida 1976c, p. 121).

affecting 147 medium-sized companies, stipulated that the state would acquire all shares in excess of a limit of £E 10,000 in shares per shareholder (some 44,000 shareholders were affected of which 7,300 owned 62 percent of all outstanding shares). In addition to these sweeping laws that applied to foreigners and Egyptians alike, others were issued that nationalized privately owned utilities, and that brought under state monopoly all aspects of foreign trade as well as the Alexandria cotton exchange.

The market value of the shares of the companies affected by Laws 117-119 has been estimated at £E 258 million, of which the state acquired £E 124 million (Issawi 1963, p. 60). In 1963 and 1964 most of the shares that remained in private hands were transferred to the state. Moreover, nationalization was extended to other spheres after 1961, such as pharmaceuticals and large construction firms, which were brought under public ownership in 1963 and 1964. Parallel to these measures was the enactment of a new land reform law in 1961 (Law 127) which lowered the ceiling on individual land ownership to 100 *feddans* and to 300 *feddans* per family.

These actions constituted economically justified transfers. By contrast there were a number of politically inspired takeovers in the wake of the socialist decrees. To explain them, some contextual detail must be presented. In February 1958 Egypt and Syria entered into the political union that was known as the United Arab Republic (UAR). Syria had not proceeded as far as Egypt in the building of a public sector, and when the socialist decrees were promulgated, the Syrian business community was alarmed, to say the least. Indeed the decrees were applied to a handful of Syrian firms and the expectation was that they would be extended to others.

Undoubtedly the socialist decrees triggered the army-business alliance (allegedly abetted by Saudi financing) that seized power in Syria in September 1961 and led to the dissolution of the UAR. In turn Nasser was deeply alarmed. Not only had his image and power in the Arab world been badly damaged, but the kind of conspiracy that took place in Syria appeared all too possible in Egypt. It has been widely but unauthoritatively reported (*inter alia* Patrick O'Brien 1966, p. 132) that leading Egyptian businessmen approached Gen. 'Abd al-Hakim 'Amir, a man at once close to Nasser, reputedly conservative in his economic views, and chief of staff of the armed forces, in the hope that he could shackle Nasser, perhaps remove him, or at least persuade him to rescind the socialist decrees.

'Amir remained loyal to his president, or so it would seem. For his part Nasser lashed out at his real or supposed bourgeoisie adversaries. On October 22, 1961 the property of 167 ''reactionary capitalists'' was sequestered and widespread arrests took place. The measures, including the ''political isolation'' or withdrawal of all political rights, was extended to another 600 persons, among whom was Ahmad 'Abboud. In all some 7,000 persons who had been affected by the two land reforms, the nationalizations, or were accused of political deviation, were deprived of their political rights and in most cases were subjected to sequestration. None of those sequestered was to receive compensation beyond a maximum living allowance of £E 5,000 per annum and up to £E 15,000 for seized property. Although sequestration orders were subsequently dropped in several instances, the names of those initially sanctioned were given wide publicity and read like the honor roll of Egypt's prewar bourgeoisie (Abdel-Malek 1968, pp. 160-66; Mahmud Murad 1975, *passim*).

Estimates vary widely as to the value of the assets taken over by the state from 1952 on. The land reforms of 1952 and 1961 involved land worth up to £E 203 million; the market value of Suez Canal Company shares taken over in 1965 was £E 27 million; British and French companies' shares seized in 1956 were valued at £E 30 million; Bank Misr, nationalized in 1960, had deposits worth £E 100 million; the nationalizations of 1961 comprised shares worth £E 252 million and real estate worth another £E 50 million, while, finally, the sequestrations of 1961-66 involved assets worth £E 100 million. These figures are not well documented; they are derived sometimes according to the market or book value of shares and at others according to the market value of the nationalized asset, and, in the case of Bank Misr, according to the deposits it controlled. Note also that in those instances when the state did not take a majority share position in a company, the value of its shares in no way reflected the value of the asset it effectively came to control. Having pointed out these various discrepancies, it would appear that something like £E 700 million in shares and physical assets were transferred to public ownership between 1952 and 1966 (Issawi 1963, pp. 60-61 and Abdel-Malek 1968, pp. 151-55). Faruq Guwaida, probably referring to the market value of shares and all physical assets brought into the state sector, put their worth at £E 2 billion (Guwaida 1976c, p. 39).

Accompanying these transfers of private assets were acts designed to emphasize the new, self-consciously socialist phase of the revolution. Gross incomes in excess of £E 10,000 were to be taxed at a 90 percent rate. No public sector director could receive a base salary in excess of £E 5,000, and could occupy no more than one public position. Joint stock companies were to place 5 percent of all profits in government bonds and allot 10 percent to workers in cash and 15 percent to worker housing and community infrastructure. Each board of directors would have no more than seven members including a statutory two from the clerical staff and the workers. The work week was reduced to forty-two hours and the minimum wage set at twenty-five piastres (ca. sixty cents) an hour. It shall be shown below to what extent these regulations had teeth.

As Egypt moved into the second year of its Five-Year Plan and adumbrated a new, aggressive regional policy founded on Arab socialism, it had these economic levers in state hands:

1) all banking and insurance
2) all foreign trade
3) all "strategic" industries, and, in a general way, all medium and heavy industries; all major textile, sugar-refining and food-processing plants
4) most maritime transport and all air transport
5) all public utilities and urban mass transit (except taxis); some interprovincial transport, modest public housing
6) limited portion of urban retail trade
7) major department stores, hotels, cinemas, and theaters
8) all newspapers (taken over in 1960) and publishing houses (monopolistic control of importation and distribution of newsprint and other paper)
9) all reclaimed land, a large segment of land taken over through land reform, all main irrigation and drainage canals
10) agricultural credit and basic agricultural inputs—fertilizers, certified seed, pesticides
11) all major construction companies
12) large infrastructural assets such as the High Dam (and all others) and the Suez Canal; all ports and port facilities

The principal escapees, and then only in a relative sense, were private cultivators (subject to administered pricing of inputs, credit and crop purchases), small-scale retail and service firms, most wholesale traders (although attempts were made to cut into their domains in 1966) and small manufacturers generally employing less than ten persons. In the aggregate, the private sector after 1961 was not to be scoffed at, but it no longer had any autonomy and was beholden to the state for foreign exchange and controlled by the state in terms of allowable profits, prices, credit, and supplies.

Few developing countries other than those that are professedly Marxist ever cut so deeply into their private sectors as Egypt. We must now try to explain what prompted this somewhat novel and certainly profound reorganization of the Egyptian economy. It has already been noted that Egypt's planners assigned an investment role, which few could have believed realistic, to a private sector that had already been severely buffeted. Foreign analysts of unimpeachable economic orthodoxy wrote what could be seen as an invitation to the socialist decrees:

It is apparent that a major obstacle in the path of Egypt's economic development is a critical capital shortage. Unless it is resigned to a continuance of the decline of the living standards of the masses, the Government of Egypt must find the means for sharply increasing the accumulation of capital and directing it into productive channels. This is likely to require deficit financing and a program of forced savings. [Harbison and Ibrahim 1958, p. 34.]

The private sector, it was alleged, failed to meet its national obligations to invest as the plan period began.[5] The private sector was further accused of violating the restrictions placed on profits distributions. The government had therefore, in consonance with the view of Harbison and Ibrahim, to force savings.

Still, if one accepts that the game was so structured that the private sector had to fail, the question then becomes why and when did those at the top decide it was no longer worth trying to enlist private sector cooperation?

It is sure that only a few men had any role in the decision to nationalize, but with the passage of time the tendency has been to attribute the decision almost exclusively to Nasser. Those who were in control of the Ministries of Finance and Plan, for instance, claim that they were never consulted on the advisability of the measures. There were a few second-echelon "radicals" about, such as Ahmad Fu'ad and Kamal Rifa'at, who may have influenced the president. But I would surmise that the nationalizations did reflect Nasser's view of the domestic situation, and that he received strong support from 'Aziz Sidqi and perhaps Hassanein Heikal and 'Ali Sabri as well.

Nasser announced at the time of the socialist decrees that they represented the first application of true socialism, and that they had become necessary because an exploitative private sector seemed bent on milking the public sector and that if allowed to continue it would be the major beneficiary of the Five-Year Plan and not the masses. For Isma'il Sabri 'Abdullah (interview with the author, December 5, 1973) what had happened was that the petit bourgeois elite had scrapped its belief of the 1952-1959 period that growth could not be achieved with redistribution, gradually coming to the position that growth could only be achieved with redistribution.

'Aziz Sidqi, building his own public sector industrial empire, naturally wanted to add to it at private expense if need be. He is frequently touted as the man who drew up the nationalization lists. Sidqi himself, in private and

---

[5] All the investment statistics I have been able to consult for this period report gross figures with no public/private breakdown. There is a drop-off in gross investment from £E 181 million in 1958-59 to £E 171 million in 1959-60, and it is reasonable to suppose that the private share declined substantially. The following year gross investment surged to £E 225 million, presumably on the strength of public outlays (Mead 1967, p. 290, Table 3.3).

public, has denied such a role. He countered that the origin of the nationalizations remain obscure. Before the decrees, his Ministry issued an inventory of all Egyptian industries called the *Dalil as-Sina'at*. In May 1961 Nasser had a luncheon at Ma'mura in Alexandria, and he kept Sidqi after the others had gone. They went to his office where Sidqi saw on his desktop a copy of the *Dalil*. Nasser then asked how could the state plan anything if the industrial sector was under the control of "individuals." Sidqi saw that Nasser had marked various companies with a lead pencil and that was that (*RY*, no. 2536; January 17, 1977).

That the decrees were improvised is undeniable; equally so is the fact that they were not primarily motivated by economic factors. Mabro (1974, p. 128) notes without elaboration, "nationalization is ultimately a political action related to Nasser's persistent drive for hegemony." Nasser was a leader acutely conscious of potential threats to his regime and his control. Whenever possible he anticipated these threats (real or imaginary) and tried to preempt them. He manifestly endorsed the notion that the best defense, in politics at any rate, is offense. Perhaps also he had a zero-sum image of power struggles and saw each incremental diminution of the resource and power base of likely adversaries as a proportionate enhancement of his own strength. Dismantling the upper reaches of the private sector therefore contributed directly and commensurately to regime strength by placing the levers of economic control in its hands.

With this control he could better defend Egypt's stature among the Arabs through a regional policy founded on aggressive Arabism and socialism. In this manner he sought to steal the thunder of the Ba'ath Party of Syria and Iraq. Simultaneously he sought to place the process of economic change and development in Egypt beyond the reach of external interference, such interference, in his view, inevitably effectuated through domestic interests hostile to the regime.

With eighteen years' hindsight Muhammed Hassanein Heikal presented his own understanding of the sequestrations (as opposed to the nationalizations) to the author (interview, January 2, 1979). He stressed Nasser's abiding distrust of the Egyptian bourgeoisie and suggested that the rough outlines of what was to be nationalized and who was to be sequestrated had been prepared in the spring of 1961. Very few people were consulted, for Nasser was prepared to act nearly alone. In consequence Syria's break from Egypt was the pretext and not the cause of seizing the assets of those accused of political crimes. Had the Syrian crisis not occurred, another pretext would have been found. The hit list had been drawn up long in advance.

Heikal dismissed two elements of interpretation mentioned above. First, he argued that nationalizations would have weakened Nasser's position in the Arab world because most of his support in other countries came from bourgeois elements. Second, he rejected the notion that 'Amir had been approached by private sector opponents to the decrees because he had just returned from Syria in near-total disgrace. Neither of Heikal's disclaimers seem particularly convincing to me, but his main point on the conspiratorial nature of the whole maneuver, rooted in Nasser's single-mindedness and understanding of the situation, is, by contrast, compelling. In many ways Nasser confused ends and means. At heart I suspect he wanted to assure Egypt's regional preeminence and to endow it with some modicum of stature and dignity in an international arena dominated by the two superpowers. But to achieve these goals he had to make Egypt an instrument for the implementation of his goals for regime survival. Indeed, from its inception in 1952 the military regime equated its incumbency with the national interest.

Finally, the socialist decrees came at a time of relative optimism within Egypt's elite. The country had survived direct neo-imperialist aggression in 1956 and had come away with its international image greatly enhanced. It had dealt with nearly all its domestic adversaries and had made the domestic arena relatively safe for its own survival. It was benefiting from the aid of both the USA and the USSR, and it had taken the first practical step toward Arab unity in forming the UAR. It remained to link the material well-being of the mass of Egyptians to the regime through rapid economic growth and at the same time so intensify Egypt's industrial transformation as to render the country the unchallenged economic center of gravity for all the Arab world. All this seemed possible in 1960-61.

Managing the Assets

Once all these formerly private assets had been absorbed into the public sector, the regime was faced with three fundamental questions: how to organize the public enterprises, how to staff them at the managerial level, and what sorts of criteria to apply to judge their performance. Seventeen years later none of those questions had received satisfactory answers.

An initial response was the formation of three public holding companies. We have already noted the first, the Economic Organization, which grouped the French and British assets taken over in 1957. It was followed in 1960 by the Misr Organization, to administer the Misr Group assets, and finally by the embryonic Nasr Organization (twenty-four companies capitalized at £E 40 million), which was to manage state enterprises arising from the first Five-Year Plan. The formula followed at that time was to construct diversified holding companies that would compete against one another and demonstrate their efficiency on a profit-and-loss basis. As near as one can tell managerial personnel was to be retained from the former private sector firms or trained in the course of the development plan.

This formula did not survive the socialist decrees. The state capitalist philosophy that it embodied gave way to one according to which the success of an enterprise would be judged by its ability to meet strategic needs, reduce imports, provide employment, meet domestic demand at low cost, and promote regional development. Central planning would replace competition among public entities to assume rational allocation of resources and maximum production levels. The real return on investment and the overall productive efficiency of the enterprise became matters of secondary concern.

Again 'Aziz Sidqi seems to have been at the heart of the shift. On December 16, 1961, Decree No. 1899 effectively abolished the three existing General Organizations, replacing them by thirty-nine General Organizations grouping 438 companies, organized along sectoral lines. Thus the Ministry of Industry alone had eight General Organizations (foodstuffs, spinning and weaving, metallurgy, chemicals, etc.) and 168 companies. Each ministry with a sectoral domain would supervise the General Organizations within that domain (e.g., Ministry of Health supervised pharmaceuticals or Tourism supervised hotels). All companies within a General Organization would be within the same sphere of activity or production so that competition among diversified General Organizations became a dead letter. Moreover, the four major public sector banks were alloted sectoral roles that precluded competition among them. The NBE specialized in foreign trade operations, the Misr Bank in financing internal trade and agriculture, the Bank of Alexandria financing industry and handicrafts, and the Bank of Cairo financing the service sector.

While this supposedly streamlined reorganization was to be guided by a central plan, there was certainly resistance on the part of Sidqi to the idea that the Ministry of Plan should be the dominant power in that design. Sidqi staunchly asserted his ministry's right to determine the basic strategy of industrialization, and, industry being the locomotive of national growth, the course of development in general. Both Plan and Finance obviously saw the situation with a different eye.

What Sidqi created then was a series of parallel sectoral pyramids with near-monopoly control of their productive spheres. Rational planning on the one hand combined with close auditing on the other were to insure maximum production at a reasonable cost. Neither the market nor intersectoral competition were to be meaningful forces in the process. For years the debate centered on the proper mix of company autonomy, the concomitant definition of the supervisory role of the General Organization, and the relevance of the minister, if any, to sectoral performance. Sidqi had little difficulty in keeping his ministry relevant: after 1961 all industrial production targets were established at the ministerial level as were appointments to the boards of directors of both companies and General Organizations. In spirit, at least, the reorganization of late 1961 marked a step away from the unabashed state capitalism of the preceding four years.

At this point only passing reference will be made to the question of managerial staffing. To a very great extent professional managers in industry and banking were held over from the prenationalization era, if and when they proved willing to work at lower salary levels. It is also undeniable that the opening up of the public sector allowed some lateral migration of army officers from the barracks to the board of directors. The extent of this migration has probably been exaggerated, however (see Chapter Eleven).

In the course of the Five-Year Plan Egypt's slogan for industrialization became: "From the needle to the rocket," suggesting the range of industrial activity in which Egypt would become self-reliant. Sidqi worked like a man possessed, pushing ahead at breakneck speed with projects that had too often been inadequately studied, and patching up the record with some statistical fantasies. He earned the enmity of a good many of his peers in the process. But one suspects that his motives were good. He recalled once (interview with the author, December 11, 1973) that in the course of the Five-Year Plan he had gone to Nasser with a list of the ministry's accomplishments. Having perused it, Nasser said simply, "Good, but we need more." Sidqi was somewhat miffed and pointed out that the accomplishments were pretty extraordinary and that his personnel were exhausted from the effort. Nasser was unmoved: "We will die soon," he said, "but the factories will not be torn down. We must have as much as possible, do all we can. We will not live forever."[6] Both men were clearly smitten by what Warren Ilchman has called the "edifice complex."

By 1965 the public sector had been expanded to its greatest extent to date, and Egypt's economy as a whole grew at remarkable rates. Never before had such investment ratios been achieved. The public sector accounted for nearly 40 percent of total output, 45 percent of domestic savings, and 90 percent of gross domestic capital formation (Radwan 1974, p. 207). The period 1960-1965 represented the most dynamic phase of state-led ISI, but a phase that ran its course in five years. From then on further accumulation could be financed by a formula combining the following elements: 1) transfer of more private assets to public ownership and the nationalization of their profits; 2)

---

[6] Nehru had a similar relationship with P. C. Mahalanobis of the National Planning Commission. See Francine Frankel 1978, pp. 114, 122-23. There have been other Sidqi-like economic czars in the Arab world. 'Abd al-Salam Bil'aid, Algeria's minister of industry for fourteen years, was one of them. So too was Ahmad Ben Salah, Tunisia's ill-fated minister of economy whose view of development and relation to his president were similar to Sidqi's. He claims that the massive overhaul of the Tunisian economy that he initiated and that cost him his job came about at a time when Bourguiba was convinced he was dying and urged him to push on at top speed as long as he, Bourguiba, could legitimate the upheaval. See Nerfin 1974, p. 106.

generating high rates of return and reinvested profits in existing public sector enterprises; 3) increased domestic savings, forced or otherwise; and 4) external borrowing. Small and tentative steps were taken along the first path while only partial success was achieved with respect to the second. Domestic savings failed to increase as did exports and foreign exchange earnings. The result was a major economic crisis that could be met only by retrenchment and increased external borrowing.

Chapter Five

THE PUBLIC SECTOR IN CRISIS

> Egypt thus ended the sixties devoting almost as low a
> share of GDP to investments as it had in 1947. But
> public consumption had more than tripled (to almost
> 25%) while that of private consumption had shrunk by
> one-fourth (to about 65%). A largely unchanged pay-
> ments deficit persisted.
>
> [Hansen and Nashashibi 1975, p. 15.]

Egypt's gamble on state-led ISI needed time. It could not settle into any kind
of comfortable rhythm in the space of one Five-Year Plan, and, in the opinion
of cautious Egyptian experts, not even in the space of four such plans. At a
minimum what was begun in 1960 needed a decade to show results. The first
Five-Year Plan was not self-contained and would not amount to much if not
followed by a second Five-Year Plan. Although drawn up, a second Five-
Year Plan was never implemented. The main points of weakness in the whole
strategy lay in assumptions about labor productivity, sources of investment,
national savings, and export performance.

In this chapter I shall try to set forth the general lines of economic performance in the 1960s, and the nature of the crisis that called the whole
experiment into question. Several themes are common to both state-led ISI
and the subsequent "open-door policy," discussed in Chapter Seven. I have
been obliged to introduce some issues and leave them dangling—deficit financing, export-performance, balance of payments, etc.—to be taken up again
in Chapter Six. Finally, a full discussion of the travails of the private sector
will be postponed until Chapter Eight.

The Strategy

In the late 1950s, Egypt had already taken a major stride toward heavy
industrialization with the launching of the Helwan Iron and Steel Complex.
The intent of the first FYP was to ensure that consumer needs were not
neglected in the pursuit of a heavy industrial base. As the National Charter
put it in 1962, the goal was "to strike a humane balance between the re-

quirements of production and those of consumption'' (cited in E. Montasser 1974, p. 155). Expansion in consumer goods was to go beyond food processing, beverages, textiles, soaps, etc., and into a full range of consumer durables: automobiles, refrigerators, washers, radios, fans, and so forth. At the same time the textile sector was to undergo thorough overhaul and expansion.

Two further objectives of the first Plan were to promote industries with export potential (in the event, the textile sector) and to achieve an equitable regional distribution of industry in Egypt (Fouad H. Awad 1973, pp. 7-8). Progress toward these goals in the 1960s was excruciatingly slow.

Egyptian planners wanted to advance on all fronts. They wanted heavy industry without sacrificing consumer interests, import-substituting projects but not to the neglect of export-oriented projects, labor absorption and efficiency. When one adds in the Aswan High Dam project, the resulting formula is one of balanced growth for which no sector of society, save exploitative elements of the upper bourgeoisie, was to be asked to pay an exorbitant price. As in India, administered pricing, market regulation, and production targets of public enterprises were to combine to replace market forces in the orientation of savings and investment.

The sequence of industrial development that was envisaged was expansion into consumer durables with backward linkages into basic metals. In a similar vein, 'Aziz Sidqi advocated a vast expansion of the textile industry to a scale that would warrant the establishment, in the second Five-Year Plan, of Egypt's own industry for the manufacture of textile machinery.

Much if not all the logic of the strategy hinged on the ability of the economy to follow it for a decade. It would require at least five years for new industries to achieve full capacity and levels of efficiency that would warrant the further expansion that might make them competitive in foreign markets. The industrial employment drive of the early 1960s would help form new demand for ISI enterprises. The Aswan Dam was crucial to this evolution in at least two respects. Its completion in the late 1960s would yield enormous amounts of cheap hydroelectric power that would feed into new ventures in aluminum, fertilizers, and other petrochemicals. It would also provide the additional water needed for agricultural modernization and hence the creation of a large rural market for the industrial sector. As mentioned above, Egypt was caught in midstream at the end of the first Plan.

Sources of Savings and Investment

The first Plan was initially drawn up before the July Decrees of 1961. These, of course, represented not only a qualitative change in the philosophy of the Plan but in the entire outlook of the regime. I stress this point because it underscores my earlier argument that Nasser, by this time, no longer saw much compatibility between his economic goals and those of "big" capital. From 1961 on, the Plan and state capitalism were not (willingly) to service private sector needs.

Yet a glance at the underlying assumptions of the Plan as it was elaborated in 1960 yields a picture generally supportive of the arguments of Fitzgerald and Kaufman *inter alia* who see state intervention on a broad scale as an effort to restructure the process of accumulation in the long-term interests of private capital. During the first industrial plan, 1957-1960, the state proposed to undertake only 21 percent of planned investment (£E 114 million) leaving the rest to the private sector. It is likely, however, that the state in fact met about 40 percent of the investment load as several uncompleted projects were carried over to the first Five-Year Plan (Mabro and Radwan 1976, pp. 67-68).

Despite the seeming failure of the private sector to meet the responsibilities unilaterally assigned it, the state gave it another vote of confidence in the 1960-1965 Plan. It was called upon to undertake 40 percent of *all* planned investment and 70 percent of all locally financed investment (Fu'ad Mursi 1976, p. 66). But, as noted earlier, this backhanded compliment may well have been intended to place a burden on the private sector that it could not assume, hence providing a rationale for the state takeovers in July 1961. Whatever the ulterior motives of those at the top, the drafters of the plan were presumably sincere in their expectations.

> [The] massive increase in domestic savings was supposed to appear in all major sectors of the economy: *in retained corporate profits, which were presumed to double*; in the current account of the government, with a planned surplus of £E 90 million; and—perhaps most surprising—in household savings, which were expected to rise to £E 80 million, exclusive of life and social insurance installments; this would imply a marginal savings rate in households of 16%, compared to an average savings rate of this group in 1959-60 of barely 3%. [Mead 1967, p. 242; emphasis added.][1]

After 1961 most retained corporate profits were expected to accrue to the state and be available for reinvestment. By 1963 the state was responsible for 45 percent of domestic savings and 90 percent of gross domestic capital formation (Radwan 1974, p. 707). The state mobilized nearly £E 500 million ($1.4 bn) for investment in the industrial sector over the period 1960-1965.

Of total planned investment in the first Plan of £E 1.6 billion, about a third

[1] The basic economic treatments of the 1960-1965 period are Hansen and Marzouk 1965; Mead 1967; Patrick O'Brien 1966; and Abdel-Fadil 1980.

was to come through foreign borrowing. This came mainly in the following forms: Soviet loans for industrial projects in 1958, 1963, and 1964 of $496 million, another $325 million in Soviet loans for the Aswan High Dam, and nearly $300 million in US Food for Peace grain shipments. In addition, according to F. H. Awad (1973, p. 16) credits and loans worth $840 million were made available by several other countries, both socialist and capitalist. Thus more foreign assistance than anticipated was put at the disposal of Egypt, but still not enough to stave off a growing balance of payments crisis.

The third principal source of investment was to be generated by allowing the terms of trade to deteriorate between agriculture and industry. There are many facets to this policy, but we shall examine here only the major elements. The agricultural sector, whatever its weaknesses, was the center of gravity of the Egyptian economy in terms of employment, contribution to GDP, and exports. In Egypt, as in several other LDCs, planners looked to this sector, above all others, as a source of savings taxed to finance industrialization. The basic mechanism was to establish mandatory state purchase prices for essential crops well below their world market value and to sell the agricultural sector needed inputs manufactured in Egypt or imported from abroad at above world market prices (B. Hansen 1972, p. 83; Abdel-Fadil 1975, p. 120). The most important exchange was rice and cotton purchases against fertilizer and pesticide sales. The benefit to the state was threefold: it realized a net profit in foreign exchange from sales of cotton and rice abroad which could then finance the importation of raw materials, intermediate and capital goods for further industrial expansion; and it could shore up its fertilizer industry through sales to a captive market. The same degree of captivity would hold if and when Egypt moved into manufacture of agricultural machinery (tractors, mechanical threshers, pumps, etc.) and pesticides. Finally, with regard to cotton, the state could supply its own textile industry with its basic raw material input at an artificially low price, helping these companies to maximize profits and to compete abroad.

Until the international petroleum crisis of 1973-74, Egypt probably did engineer a net transfer of assets from the agricultural to the industrial sector, although the record is not crystal clear. Essam Montasser, for example (1975), estimated that in the period 1960-1971 public investment in agriculture (private investment has been negligible) totaled £E 893 million, including the water storage component of the High Dam. Against this, the agricultural sector paid £E 176 million in taxes, and the state realized net profits on the sale of rice and cotton abroad of £E 736 million. This yields a modest transfer out of agriculture of only £E 19 million, which would easily be offset by delivery of water to all cultivators free of charge and the availability of agricultural credit at subsidized interest rates.

Still, one must look closer at these figures. First it should be noted that the High Dam is frequently treated statistically as an agricultural investment although its power plant was destined for industrial use. But leaving aside the dam, one finds that of the remaining investment in agriculture £E 483 million went into land reclamation, or horizontal expansion, and only £E 193 million into improvement and intensification of cultivation in established agricultural areas. Yet it is these old lands that have generated 90 percent of all agricultural income and there is no question that they have been taxed very heavily. One may draw two conclusions from this: the major transfer in favor of industry came through foreign exchange earnings from cotton and rice that could be used to meet industrial import needs; and through the supply of low-priced inputs (principally cotton and sugar cane) to public sector enterprises. By contrast, the bulk of the transfers into agriculture went into horizontal expansion. Land reclamation, as it turned out, was and remains a net drain on public resources.

One may well ask how Egypt's planners believed domestic markets for Egyptian manufactures could grow while the state soaked the peasants. The answer seems to be that the problem would be taken care of through the employment drive on the one hand, and the benefits of the High Dam on the other. The public sector and civil service were expected to grow by 20 percent and 36 percent respectively (or the equivalent of over 400,000 new jobs) over the five-year period, thus bolstering lower middle class, predominantly urban consumer demand. The High Dam was expected to have an impact on agriculture in two ways. The old lands were to be more intensively cultivated, especially in upper Egypt, allowing the peasants to earn more by growing more. Improved irrigation and drainage in combination with the spread of cooperatives to encompass all the peasantry and to supply seed, fertilizers, pesticides, and subsidized credit were to ensure higher yields and higher earnings. The second effect of the dam was to expand Egypt's cultivated surface by 16 to 20 percent, to transfer substantial numbers of the near-landless to the reclaimed areas, and thereby to increase agricultural production further. Both assumptions were risk-laden. The employment surge might not be accompanied by commensurate production increases and the agricultural target might be too distant in time to be felt during the plan period. In both instances worst-case outcomes prevailed.

Performance

Implementation of the Plan was troubled from its inception. Throughout there were problems of jurisdiction and final authority. The newly created Ministry of Planning never became the instrument of coordination and surveillance that could have exacted compliance to Plan guidelines from other ministries. Before the Plan was underway, there was a major shake-up in its leadership.

Hilmi 'Abd al-Rahman headed up a small team of civilian technocrats, including Nazih Daif, Ahmad Murshidi, and Mahmud Shafa'i, that drew up the draft plan in 1959-60. They reconciled the growth targets of the National Planning Commission, set up in 1957, and of six mixed committees bringing public and private sector experts together to undertake sectoral planning (Patrick O'Brien 1966, pp. 104-5). Their recommendation was to double real per capita income in twenty years. They recommended modest real growth rates in GNP at the beginning of the period of 3 to 4 percent per annum, rising to 6 or 7 percent toward the middle and end.

Nasser found this target far too conservative, and announced that Egypt would double real GNP in ten years. The economy was to accelerate its growth rate to 7 percent per annum from the outset. 'Abd al-Rahman found these targets unrealistic and asked to be removed from the Ministry of Planning. His wish was met, and he was put in charge of the Institute of National Planning and then went on to be the first head of the United Nations Industrial Development Organization (UNIDO).

Critics of the Plan claim that another civilian, the perennial minister of finance, 'Abd al-Mun'aim al-Qaissuni, got the president's ear and painted a best-case picture of real growth that was opportunistic and irresponsible. It was, however, what the president wanted to hear, and so the die was cast.

It was an officer and a member of the defunct RRC, Vice President 'Abd al-Latif Baghdadi, who was in nominal charge of the Ministry of Planning. 'Abd al-Rahman worked under him and helped devise a monitoring system that would have had other ministries reporting to Plan to show their monthly progress toward attaining sectoral targets. This elicited charges that Baghdadi was trying to create a superministry, a state within the state. 'Aziz Sidqi (Industry), Sayyid Mar'ai (Agriculture), and Qaissuni (Economy) were all unhappy with the monitoring system, and it was quietly scuttled. From then on, as Patrick O'Brien notes (1966, p. 159)

> . . . the initial macro-frame worked out at the centre exercised only slight influence upon the sectoral plans drawn up by different ministries. Egypt's First Five Year Plan [was] really an amalgam of investment projects loosely coordinated into a single document. [Cf. B. Hansen 1972, p. 76.]

In his memoirs (1977, 2) Baghdadi sheds light on *his* motives: he neither mentions the first Five-Year Plan nor the fact that he was in charge of the Ministry of Planning. This is probably not intentional oversight but an accurate reflection of the importance he attached to those functions.[2]

---

[2] One may contrast this situation with that of the National Planning Commission in India. It was Nehru's habit to meet with it once or twice a month and to attend all meetings at which major policy issues were discussed. He participated directly in the drafting of the second Five-Year Plan. "From 1955 to 1964 Nehru's pivotal position permitted a handful of men to determine national economic and social policy and methods of development" (Frankel 1978, p. 114).

We come now to actual performance during the Plan period. Perhaps the first point to be made is that real growth rates were quite high: Bent Hansen (1972) and Mabro (1974) concur on an average rate of about 5.5 percent per annum. But to no small extent this growth was caused as much by inflated civil service and public sector payrolls as by production gains.

Of total investments of some £E 1.7 bn, over £E 380 million were devoted to industry and another £E 138 million to electricity, including the High Dam power station. The bulk of this investment went into intermediate goods (wood, paper, chemicals, rubber) and textiles. Throughout the 1960s industry continued to attract between 25 and 28 percent of all investment. For the period beginning in 1957 with the First Industrial Plan and ending in 1970, £E 945.3 was invested in industry (F. H. Awad 1973, p. 15). Consequently industry's share in GDP rose from 16 percent in 1956 to 24 percent in 1964 and then declined slightly to 23 percent in 1970 (Hansen and Nashashibi 1975, p. 12; cf. Mabro and Radwan 1976, p. 47).

On the whole investment targets in the first Plan were adequately met. Most observers agree that between 92 and 96 percent of planned investment was actually effected (*inter alia* Radwan 1974, p. 207; F. H. Awad, 1973, p. 117). But there were shortfalls: industrial investment fell short by 10 percent of planned investment, electricity by 22 percent, and housing by 20 percent. These shortfalls may indeed be understated in that they make no explicit allowance for inflation nor the devaluation of the pound in 1962. It is particularly interesting to note the composition of industrial investment targets and realization.

It is clear from these figures that, despite industrial expansion, product composition was more biased toward consumer goods at the end of the period than at the beginning. Moreover, as both Agwah and Mabro and Radwan

Table 5.1
Distribution of Planned and Actual Investment in the Manufacturing Sector in the First Five-Year Plan, 1960-61-1964-65

(£E millions)

	Planned Value (1)	Planned Inv. % (2)	Actual Value (3)	Actual Inv. % (4)	% change (3)-(1)
Consumer Goods	92.7	24.0	140.6	40.6	+51.7
Intermediate Goods	154.7	40.1	122.8	35.4	−20.6
Capital Goods	138.8	35.9	83.1	24.0	−40.1
Total	386.2	100.0	346.5	100.0	−10.5

SOURCE: Agwah 1978, p. 306.

demonstrate, forward linkages for intermediate goods remained weak and the share of capital goods in the final demand for industrial products increased only marginally from 2 percent in 1959 to 3 percent in 1967 (Agwah 1978, p. 308).

In many respects what we have outlined so far constitutes a commendable level of performance. But, similar to the experience of other LDCs with good growth records, the balance of payments conundrum proved a near-insurmountable obstacle. Much hinged on the predicted impact of ISI upon the import bill and the ability of the industrial sector to find foreign markets for its products.

Egypt's planners expected an absolute decline in the value of imports at the end of the Plan, from £E 229 million to £E 215 million in 1960 prices (Mabro 1974, p. 123), with a resulting positive balance on visible trade in the final year. In fact Egypt wound up importing £E 413 million in goods in 1965 and registered a negative balance on current account (including invisible exports) of £E 166 million. At the beginning of the Plan the value of imports stood at 15 percent of GDP and at the end at 20 percent (Nashashibi 1970, p. 75).

The goal of import substitution was partially served. In every industrial category, save food processing, some progress was made in meeting local demand by local manufacture, and in the instances of leather, furniture, and clothes, local industry met total demand. But, looking at the manufacture of intermediate goods, the real value of imports saved in 1962, for example, was only £E 6 million (Mabro and Radwan 1976, p. 204).

Table 5.2 speaks pretty much for itself. In current prices the value of manufactured exports nearly doubled over a six-year period, but it was one that included a major devaluation of the Egyptian pound. The ratio of the value of manufactured exports to GNP increased marginally. Not shown in the table is the fact that the share of yarn and textile in these exports increased from 53 percent at the beginning of the period to 63 percent at its end. Heavy industrial exports increased not at all (F. H. Awad 1973, p. 48). Many reasons have been adduced for this disappointing performance, and we shall consider them all below. The main reason, however, lay in a drop in labor productivity, overprotection of public sector industry, and a great surge in public consumption.

A major factor here was the employment drive launched in 1961. Over the Plan period the work force grew by nearly 22 percent, or from about 6 to 7.3 million. In absolute terms, 40 percent of the increase occurred in agriculture, 17 percent in industry, and 31 percent in the service or tertiary sector. The more rapid *rates* of growth in the latter two sectors, however, brought about a proportional shift such that their shares in the labor force rose from

Table 5.2
Percentage Value of Manufactured Exports to GNP

(In current £E million)

	Value of GNP (1)	Value of Manf. Exports (2)	% (2):(1)
1959-60	1,379	34.1	2.4
1960-61	1,461	37.0	2.5
1961-62	1,512	38.4	2.5
1962-63	1,679	42.4	2.5
1963-64	1,882	58.0	3.1
1964-65	2,192	65.4	3.0

SOURCES: GNP figures are from F. Awad 1973; p. 44. Manufactured export figures are from Awad as well, p. 48 and accord with Nashashibi's 1970, p. 79. Agwah 1978, p. 320 has a similar table but seemingly confuses total export figures with manufactured exports. One should note that the figures in column 2 reflect a 23% devaluation of the pound in May 1962.

9.8 percent to 11.4 and from 35 to 38 percent respectively while that of agriculture fell from 55 to 51 percent (Mabro 1974, p. 207).

Per capita labor productivity declined after 1962 after twenty years of steady if unspectacular growth. The key textile sector was no exception, where overstaffing reached 20 percent of the work force (Hansen and Nashashibi 1975, p. 223). Correspondingly the share of returns to labor in total value-added rose from an average of about 32 percent in the late 1950s to a high of 54 percent in 1964-65 (Mabro and Radwan 1976, pp. 179, 183). Between January 1962 and January 1964 average wages for manual workers rose by 32 percent, a larger increase than that of the preceding decade (Mabro and Radwan 1976, p. 135).

As part of the package of socialist laws in 1961, the working week was reduced from forty-eight to forty-two hours, the number of shifts in enterprises increased, and restrictions placed on overtime. All these measures aimed at increasing productive employment. In fact the weekly average of hours worked in industry fell from forty-nine in 1960 to forty-four in 1964 but then rose to fifty-three in 1965. "This rise," as Mabro and Radwan assert (1976, p. 141), "is associated with a decline in output growth, not with a reduction in employment."

The employment drive was an integral part of Egypt's "socialist transformation," marking the first efforts at planned income redistribution. It gave teeth to the inclusivist rhetoric of the period that bestowed legitimacy upon workers and peasants and granted them 50 percent representation in the par-

Table 5.3

Employment by Sector during the First Five-Year Plan Period Compared to 1959-60

(In thousands of workers)

Sector	1959-60	1960-61	1961-62	1962-63	1963-64	1964-65	Total Increases during Plan Period	% Increase over Base Year
Agriculture	3,245.0	3,600.0	3,600.0	3,632.0	3,673.0	3,751.0	506.0	15.6
Industry	601.8	625.6	679.0	725.9	789.7	825.0	223.2	37.1
Electricity	11.9	13.1	15.1	17.4	17.9	18.0	6.1	51.3
Construction	185.0	166.0	263.0	315.7	334.2	345.2	160.2	86.6
Total Commodity Sector	4,043.7	4,404.7	4,557.1	4,691.0	4,814.8	4,939.2	895.5	22.1
Transport and Communication	218.6	252.7	239.2	249.2	258.3	277.7	59.1	27.0
Trade, Finance	635.7	663.0	680.9	702.2	719.0	729.7	94.0	14.8
Housing	16.0	16.0	18.0	18.1	18.5	21.0	5.0	31.2
Public Utilities	25.2	24.3	27.1	28.7	29.5	30.3	5.1	20.2
Other Services	1,066.8	1,151.2	1,134.6	1,179.0	1,244.9	1,306.5	239.7	22.5
Total Services Sector	1,962.3	2,107.2	2,099.8	2,177.2	2,270.2	2,365.2	402.9	20.5
GRAND TOTAL	6,006.0	6,511.9	6,656.9	6,868.2	7,085.0	7,304.4	1,298.4	21.6

SOURCE: CAPMAS 1973, p. 200. Between 1960 and 1965 the work force of industries employing ten or more workers increased from 344,830 to 559,309.

liament and all elective bodies including cooperatives and worker-management boards.

Padding of civil service rolls and imposing redundant labor on parastatal companies placed a heavy burden on economic efficiency. Yet public sector managers had little incentive to protest, given their level of external protection and captive domestic markets.

The cornerstone of protection was the new system of tariffs introduced on January 1, 1962. It grouped all imports in three categories of raw materials, semi-manufactured goods, and finished goods. Tariffs in each category were determined by the possibility or actuality of local production, so that levels varied widely. The effective rates of protection (erps.) ranged upwards from 22 percent for food products, to 68 percent for fabrics, 34 percent for machinery, 61 percent for chemicals, 248 percent for clothes, 240 percent for paper, 262 percent for tires, 305 percent for automobiles, 599 percent for iron and steel, and 990 percent for leather (Mabro and Radwan 1976, pp. 111-12; Hansen and Nashashibi 1975, p. 310).

Total final consumption as a proportion of GNP failed to drop, as the planners had anticipated, and domestic savings failed to increase. It is true that private final consumption fell from 68 percent of GNP in 1960-61 to 66.7 percent in 1964-65, but public final consumption grew from 17.5 percent to 20 percent. Thus total final consumption remained at a level between 85 and 87 percent of GNP, and because about two-thirds of public consumption consists in wages and salaries, it helped finance demand for consumer goods (Agwah 1978, p. 317). Because of the stagnation of gross domestic savings, a cumulative investment gap of £E 417 million over the period 1960-1965 had to be financed by external borrowing. Had Egypt's export performance been less disappointing, the country could have maintained its international credit-worthiness and its ability to service its debt. Instead it faced its first payments crisis in 1962, followed by another in 1965 that effectively delivered the *coup de grâce* to all further planning efforts.

Retrenchment

Apologists for Egypt's economic performance, regardless of the period, have tended to attribute all deficiencies to external causes and chance events beyond the experts' control. In looking at the crisis of the mid-1960s the blame has often been put upon the failure of the cotton crop in 1961, the costs of involvement in the Yemeni civil war, the suspension of US food for peace shipments after 1965, and defense outlays "imposed" upon Egypt because of the state of war with Israel.

All these factors clearly did contribute to Egypt's problems, but they surely would have been manageable had the economy rested on solid foundations.

It is important to assess their real weight in Egypt's economic decline, for if they are seen as causes, then one can conclude that, to the extent the crisis deepened Egypt's external dependence, the process was random and not really a function of deliberate policy-making. In like situations in other countries similar random events of "bad luck" have been adduced to explain economic decline. In India at precisely the same time, there was a failure of the monsoons, costly military confrontations with China and Pakistan, and in August 1965 the suspension of US wheat shipments. At the beginning of the 1970s Peru's military bureaucrats had to deal with the failure of the anchovy catch, unfavorable movements in world copper prices, and military confrontation with Chile. In all three countries, I think it would be an error to confuse these trees with the forest of public sector performance and state intervention in the agricultural sector.

This said, let us look at the immediate causes of the 1962 balance of payments crisis. First was the 40 percent drop in the 1961 cotton harvest due to leaf worm infestation. This disaster was the pretext for the dismissal of Sayyid Mar'ai from the Ministry of Agriculture, a story to which we shall return in future chapters. The immediate impact was a drop in foreign exchange earnings from £E 121 million in 1960-61 to £E 75 million in 1961-62. Because of rapidly increasing domestic consumption, earnings from rice exports declined slightly in the early 1960s and then recovered. Still, the reluctance to curb home consumption bore a high opportunity cost in foreign exchange.

Further drains on foreign exchange reserves came as a result of payments to Great Britain for property nationalized in 1956 (£E 25 million), compensation paid to shareholders in the Suez Canal Company (£E 27.5 million), and payments to the Sudan to defray the costs of resettling Nubians who were to be displaced by the High Dam reservoir (£E 15 million).

Much ink has been spilled on the costs of Egypt's expeditionary force in the Yemen after September 1962. Most of it is ill-informed because no official accounting has ever been made public. The involvement also came too late to have any bearing on the 1962 payments crisis, although it did have an impact upon the crisis of 1965-66. Anthony Nutting (1972, p. 379) offers without reference to sources a figure of £E 500 million for the period 1962-1965. Vatikiotis advances a figure of £E 4 bn without reference to time period or source (1978, p. 162). Journalistic broadsides, such as Ibrahim Sa'ada's in *Akhbar al-Yom* (September 7, 1974), which put expenses in the Yemen at £E 1 million per day, probably were designed to show how costly were Nasser's "foreign adventures" and how destructive to Egypt's economic well-being. Far more conservative estimates of foreign exchange costs of £ 20 million per year were given the author in interviews with Nazih Daif and 'Ali al-Gritli. These seem too low, as Egypt kept 20-40,000 men and a great deal of equipment in the Yemen from 1963 to 1967. Still, no one closely associated with Egypt's external finances in those years feels that the Yemen entailed unacceptable foreign exchange costs. It is nonetheless the fact that in the crucial years of 1963-1965 *total* defense outlays rose rapidly from 8 percent to 12 percent of GNP, reaching £E 575 million in 1965 (Dessouki and Labban 1981, p. 69).

Export performance, however, was the major culprit, and even after the effects of the cotton failure were overcome, Egypt's trade imbalance continued to deteriorate, reaching £E 174 million in 1963. In order to cover these deficits Egypt had constantly eroded its total net foreign exchange reserves which stood at £E 109 million on the eve of the first industrial plan and at £E 7 million in December 1962 (Hansen and Marzouk 1965, p. 190). In May 1962 Egypt reached a standby agreement with the IMF and immediately drew credits of £E 20 million. Egypt made some commitments to curb internal demand and restrain government expenditures, but all that it followed through with was a partial devaluation of the pound from 35.2 to 43.5 piastres to the US dollar.

The size of the devaluation was not sufficient to have an appreciable impact on Egypt's exports (Egyptian cotton was competitive at the old rate) and, as the public sector had become the major importer, ways were found to meet its needs despite higher costs. In turn these higher costs were rarely passed on to the consumers, who were increasingly cushioned against them by price subsidies. Thus nothing was resolved by the stabilization program of 1962, and a more profound crisis enveloped Egypt beginning in 1964.

By that year the balance of trade deficits were paralleled by increasing resort to deficit financing, which averaged £E 60 million annually in 1959-60 prices for the period 1960-1966 (E. Montasser 1974, p. 16). This fueled Egypt's first major inflationary surge since the Korean War. It was exacerbated by the decision of the United States in 1965 to curtail wheat shipments to Egypt, which forced that country to restrict imports of grains and to dip into foreign exchange reserves to pay for what was imported. Food shortages occurred that drove food prices up at a compound annual rate of 11.5 percent and wholesale prices up at a rate of 7 percent (E. Montasser 1974, p. 146). The value of imported wheat and wheat flour in 1965-66 (£E 55 million) exceeded the value of all Egyptian exports to Western markets (£E 52 million). In meeting its import needs, Egypt fell into arrears in servicing its commercial external debt.

Overworked though the terms may be, Egypt had reached a watershed, the importance of which cannot be overstated. The new payments crisis came at a time when the all-important second Five-Year Plan, the Plan of consolidation and "deepening," was on the drawing boards. To finance the imports for this plan would necessitate assured access to large amounts of foreign exchange. Further nationalizations and transfers of assets to public ownership would be irrelevant to these needs, and those assets already in the parastatal sector were not earning their own way. The only remaining options lay in foreign assistance, especially from the superpowers. In Egypt's moment of need, neither power was forthcoming.

In March of 1964, 'Ali Sabri, a mildly leftist officer (but not a member of the old RCC) became prime minister and minister of planning. His appointment was intended to symbolize the intensification of the "transition to socialism" phase. His government hosted Nikita Khrushchev in his May 1964 visit to inaugurate the High Dam, and would have launched the second Plan. Instead, Sabri ran a caretaker operation, negotiating new debt schedules, wheedling the Soviets for a consolidation loan, requesting $500 million in food aid from Washington over a three-year period, and, in April 1965, announcing that the second Five-Year Plan would be lengthened to seven years. Having performed these chores, Sabri was dismissed in September 1965 and replaced by the mildly rightist Zakaria Muhi al-Din, member of the RCC, and allegedly well-viewed in the West. Muhi al-Din had been Egypt's first minister of interior and his appointment symbolized a wedding of technocratic efficiency and careful police control of the polity. Equally symbolic was the removal of 'Aziz Sidqi from Industry, over which he had presided since 1956, and his replacement by the far more cautious Mustapha Khalil.[3] The brief era of inclusivist socialism had come to an end and retrenchment (or what the Egyptians call *inkimash*: shrinkage) had begun.

Even before articulated policies of retrenchment were announced, there were straws in the wind. Imports in general declined, while imports of fuel, machinery, and raw materials fell off substantially. In early 1965 several factories were closed down or were barely operating because of raw materials shortages. In June of the same year a forced savings plan was put into effect by the Sabri government whereby all public employees paid one-half day's pay each month into a special account.

Muhi al-Din undertook negotiations with the IMF and Egypt's major creditors. By the summer of 1966 the outlines of a "background stabilization plan" had been worked out with the Fund. It would have included a further partial devaluation of the pound of 40 percent, reduction in investment, and some price and tax increases. Save one, these measures were being implemented anyway, but the devaluation, advocated by Muhi al-Din, was too bitter a pill for Nasser to swallow. The stabilization plan was held in abeyance, and the Muhi al-Din government was dismissed in September 1966, probably as much because of differences between the president and his prime minister

---

[3] These changes may have prompted Washington to approve, in November 1965, an additional £E 20 million in wheat sales.

over Yemen as anything else (Nutting 1972, p. 381). The new prime minister was yet another technocrat, Sidqi Sulaiman, an army engineer who had supervised construction of the High Dam.

Muhi al-Din was able to extract some additional grain deliveries from the US, but the continued Egyptian involvement in the Yemen precluded any real rapprochement. However, the attitude of the Soviet Union was somewhat surprising. Khrushchev had fallen in October 1964, and the new leadership was seemingly far more skeptical about the ability of Egypt's leaders to guide the country to true socialism. There may have been as well a feeling that the USSR had been overextended in its support of regimes of dubious revolutionary commitment. By mid-1965 some had disappeared anyway: Ben Bella, Sukarno, and Nehru were all deposed or dead. It was also a time of retrenchment for the Soviet Union. One of Khrushchev's last gestures to Egypt, coming in May 1964, had been to arrange for a $277 million consolidation loan to enable Egypt to meet payments on its debt to the USSR and to provide some financing for projects in the second Plan (Goldman 1967, p. 74). Yet when Egypt needed assistance most, the annual increment from 1965 to 1966 dwindled to $7 million (Mabro 1975, p. 310).

Kosygin, Podgorny, and Brezhnev in their advice to the Egyptians advocated retrenchment policies not dissimilar to those of the IMF (Valkenier 1970, p. 26; Guwaida 1976c, p. 22). Robert Stephens has even discerned a link between Nasser's trip to Moscow in August 1965 and the dismissal of Sabri at the end of September (Stephens 1971, p. 371). The fact that the USSR supplied Egypt 300,000 tons of wheat in 1965 may have been more an effort to counter China's gift of 250,000 tons of corn than to shore up a failing economy. Both socialist countries were jockeying for leverage at the upcoming Afro-Asian Solidarity Conference in Algiers scheduled for June 1965. More typical of the new attitude was Kosygin's trip to Cairo in May 1966. Egypt requested yet another postponement of payments on its debt to the Soviet Union, but Kosygin became bankerish and said that any such postponement would be a bad precedent for all those other LDCs that were heavily indebted to the USSR (Heikal 1978, p. 163).

The Soviet Union, prior to the June War of 1967, may have advocated fiscal responsibility and retrenchment in order to protect Egypt's socialist experiment. But after the war, when the then Deputy Prime Minister Zakaria Muhi al-Din (Nasser had become his own prime minister) proposed closing down public sector establishments operating at a loss, giving incentives to the private sector, and removing redundant labor from the public payrolls, the Soviet Union objected. Given the magnitude of Egypt's military defeat and the divisions among the elite, the Kremlin may have felt that retrenchment would lead to the liquidation of the socialist sector rather than its reform.

Thus, on the eve of the 1967 debacle, Egypt was in serious economic straits. Three monthly loan repayments to the IMF worth $13.5 million were missed, and "stretch out" loans with France, Britain, and Italy were negotiated to avoid default (Griggs 1967; Guwaida 1976c, p. 25). Palliatives were applied to ease the situation. The investment budget, in current prices, increased imperceptibly from £E 364 million in 1965 to £E 383 million in 1966 and then fell to £E 365 million in 1967. Imports dropped from £E 465 million in current prices in 1966 to £E 344 million in 1967. Economic growth came to a halt, and there were absolute declines in per capita income.

Nasser's options were limited and unpalatable. He could have given in to the counsels of economic orthodoxy urged upon him by the likes of Qaissuni and Muhi al-Din. That would have entailed faithful adherence to the IMF stabilization plan, a reordering if not partial liquidation of the public sector, and greater reliance on market pricing mechanisms in allocating scarce goods whatever the cost in individual welfare. It would also have obliged Nasser to mend his political fences with the West, and he was simply not ready for that kind of humiliation. Nor, even had the Kremlin's leaders been more sympathetic, did Nasser wish to increase Egypt's dependence on the Soviet Union. It would have meant putting the second Five-Year Plan in the hands of Gosplan experts at the same time that Egypt's armed forces were equipped almost exclusively by the Soviets. My guess is that Nasser saw both the domestic and international costs of rapprochement with the US as too high, while deepening links with the USSR would bear a heavy cost primarily in terms of diminished sovereignty.

Nasser waffled and made gestures that indicated that he was thinking of both alternatives. It is an important point to which we shall return that economic retrenchment corresponded to a period of political radicalization (see Chapter Thirteen). The regime waged political war on the religious right and upon "feudal" remnants in the countryside. Under the impetus of the ASU lobby, legislation was prepared in 1966 and 1967 to nationalize most of the contracting and construction sector, several trucking firms, and most wholesale trade.

These nationalization laws were not implemented. The president emitted signals of another order. At the end of 1966, he set up the Supreme Control Committee under Field Marshal Hakim 'Amir. On May 1, 1967 Nasser announced its purpose to be surveillance of the public sector and detection of opportunists and deviationists. Much of the rhetoric accompanying the committee's creation implied greater politicization of public sector management. But its true purpose was given away by those in charge of it. P.M. Sidqi Sulaiman and Hakim 'Amir reviewed procedures for appointing managers to public sector General Organizations and companies. Significantly 'Aziz Sidqi was not a member of this committee. It prompted the removal of thirty-eight out of forty-eight chairmen of General Organizations and engineered some

220 new managerial appointments. Nasser addressed all public sector company heads on March 18, 1967 at the opening of the Congress of Production. His message was essentially economic and can be summarized in three points (as reported in *Middle East Record* 3 [1967]:550-51).

1) Management is a science and its rules do not change under socialism or capitalism. The only difference between the two economic systems stems from the ownership of the means of production and the control of profits.
2) Wages must be linked to productivity. Socialism does not mean equal wages but equal opportunity to work.
3) The Arab Socialist Union is to involve itself in public sector operations only to the extent that it can contribute to implementation of plans and smooth relations between workers and management. In no way is the ASU to interfere in the production process itself.

This was Nasser's message to the *bourgeoisie d'état* and it was fittingly state capitalist in tone.

The June War of 1967 obviated any obligation on Nasser's part to choose Egypt's economic path. Retrenchment and austerity were the *only* options left. The one "luxury" that Egypt enjoyed was the commitment to rebuild its armed forces regardless of financial costs, contingent upon Soviet help. By contrast, a series of measures, some regressive, were adopted to dampen consumption and generate savings. Annual bonuses were abolished and representational allowances reduced. A defense tax on incomes was introduced, stamp taxes were increased, as were duties on cars, televisions, theater tickets, and beer. The price of cigarettes, tires, and cooking oil were increased, while the sugar ration was reduced (RAU 1968, pp. 82-114). But Nasser was no more willing after the war than before to accede to the prescriptions of the IMF. It was a question once again of stabilization and devaluation, and its proponents in the cabinet were Zakaria Muhi al-Din and 'Abd al-Mun'aim al-Qaissuni. Counterarguments came from leftists outside the ruling circle, principally from Isma'il Sabri 'Abdullah. They were supported by 'Aziz Sidqi who argued strongly from outside the cabinet for a return to expansionist policies. His line carried the day, and in the government formed in March 1968, he reemerged as minister of industry, while Qaissuni and Muhi al-Din were dropped (Mar'ai 1979, 2:550-51). *Inkimash* from then on was a pejorative term, but the stark fact was that Egypt did not have the resources to undertake much else.

In closing this section, I want to emphasize an obvious fact that is too easily overlooked. A head of state and his entourage cannot give single-minded attention to a given policy issue with the same facility as a scholar shuffling through his index cards. We would do well to keep in mind the plethora of policy issues and crises that engulf a leader all at once. If we take only 1965 as an example, we find Nasser coping with the following:

In the Economy: balance of payments crisis, negotiations with IMF, mobilizing resources for the second Five-Year Plan.

In the Domestic Arena: meeting an alleged plot from the Muslim Brethren, mediating rivalries between the armed forces and the Arab Socialist Union, changing ministerial teams.

In the International Arena: watching the overthrow of major allies: Nkrumah, Ben Bella, Sukarno, and the death of another, Nehru. The suspension of US wheat shipments, and King Faisal's announcement of the formation of an Islamic Alliance must have led Nasser to believe he too was a marked man. Finally there was the actual combat in the Yemeni "cockpit" from which Nasser seemed unable to extricate himself.

In all this it is little wonder that the first death throes of state-led ISI went unnoticed.

The crisis that overtook Egypt in 1965-66 was first felt in 1964 and was exacerbated, but not caused, by Egypt's military defeat in 1967. It was also not caused by MNCs pumping Egypt's foreign exchange reserves dry through remitted profits, nor by deteriorating terms of international trade, nor by the unchecked consumption of luxury imports for the middle classes, nor, finally by the international capitalist banking community. It was caused by the gross inefficiencies of a public sector called upon to do too many things: sell products at cost or at a loss, take on labor unrelated to production needs, earn foreign exchange, and satisfy local demand. It was also caused by the neglect of the traditional agricultural sector which, while taxed, was not reformed so as to become an engine of growth in its own right. In essence Egyptian agriculture, US Food for Peace and Soviet aid financed the birth of Egyptian state capitalism, but none of these sources was willing or able to help it through adolescence.

Chapter Six

THE PUBLIC SECTOR: PERFORMANCE AND REFORM

All the profits of industrial companies are fictitious. Every industrial enterprise in Egypt runs at a loss. Take for example the Egyptian Spinning and Weaving Co. It buys Giza 68 cotton at £E 16.75 while the world price is £E 31.65. After that they pull out their accounts and say we're making profits.
[M.P. Mustapha Kamal Murad, A, December 4, 1975.][1]

We must not overlook that the principal objective [was] an increase in national income in general and not an increase in value-added in one sector at the expense of another. An increase in profits of industrial companies as a result of failing to pay interest to banks does not lead to an increase in national income. Nor do wage increases that eat into profits earned by the General Organizations without an increase in production.

[Gritli 1974, p. 170.]

Profits and Losses

It would be hard to find among the several commentaries on the Egyptian public sector any accolades regarding efficiency in management and production (see esp. Guwaida 1976c; Gritli 1977, pp. 175-218; Hansen and Nashashibi 1975, pp. 255-308). There are two exceptions that in many ways prove the rule. The operation and management of the Suez Canal, between 1956 when it passed into Egyptian hands and 1967 when it was closed as a result of war, was exemplary. Volume of shipping increased as did state revenues, the waterway was adequately maintained, and the safety record was

[1] Murad is an amalgam of several currents in the Egypt of Nasser and Sadat: a former army officer who took over a public sector cotton-exporting company, as well as the leader of the Liberal opposition in Sadat's first parliament and a persistent critic of the public sector.

excellent. The second exception was the construction of the High Dam and its power station. Some mythology has inevitably crept into this mammoth undertaking, and the careers of some of the protagonists, especially Ahmad Osman and Sidqi Sulaiman, were enhanced by their reputed genius. The role of Soviet equipment and engineers has surely never received the credit it deserves. Yet neither of these ventures, once the dam was completed, involved management of large work forces involved in complex production and marketing operations. In enterprises where such factors did come into play the record is somber.

The record was not even visible until the early 1970s and then only in bits and snatches. The Nasserist regime was secretive about all its activities. Public industrial performance in particular, and public sector performance in general, were regarded as state secrets and as sensitive as military information. While there was oversight through the Central Auditing Agency, which eventually was put under the charge of Sidqi Sulaiman, there was no public accounting. This situation began to change gradually after March 1968 when the new finance minister, 'Abd al-'Aziz Higazi, was given something of a mandate to see what was really going on in the public sector.[2] Still, it was not until 1973, well after the death of Nasser and after 'Aziz Sidqi's removal from the prime ministership, that a parliamentary committee was allowed to make a full investigation of some public sector companies.

The Plan and Budget Committee of the Maglis al-Sha'ab (the People's Assembly or Parliament), chaired by Ahmad Abu Isma'il who became minister of finance in 1975, issued two lengthy reports in May 1973 concerning sixteen public sector companies (Maglis al-Sha'ab 1973).[3] All had experienced repeated losses in their operations.

Let us take one case study, the Egyptian Shipbuilding Company, which, given the state of our knowledge, appears not untypical. The project had first been discussed in 1955 in the NPC, but it was not until 1962 that a contract for equipment was signed with the USSR. It received its first contract for a ship in 1969, and, in 1973, delivered the 12,000-ton *Alexandria* to the Egyptian Navigation Company. At the time of the parliamentary investigation that was the only ship it had built. Against that meager record the company in

---

[2] According to Higazi (interview with Yussef Idriss, *A*, October 25, 1974) Nasser met with him in March 1968 and told him: "By God [Wallahi], I want to know where we are . . . some people say we're on the brink of disaster . . . others have a different view. I want to know exactly what the state of our economy is." "Those," said Higazi, "were my only instructions when being entrusted with the Ministry of Finance."

[3] Companies covered were Tourhotel Co.; Edfina Co.; Egyptian Bottling Co.; Food & Dairy Co.; Rural Construction Co.; Egyptian Printing & Publishing Co.; Egyptian Land Reclamation Co.; Greko Co. for Engineering and Refrigeration; Egyptian Navigation Co.; Egyptian Shipbuilding Co.; Canal Storage and Loading Co.; Land Transport Co.; Nasr Coke and Basic Chemicals Co.; Chemical Dyes Co.; Nasr Pressed Board Co.; Ahram Cooperative Stores Co.

1972 employed 5,107 workers, up from 4,465 in 1971. According to Soviet experts the yards were designed to employ no more than 3,000, and construction of the *Alexandria* still took about twice as long as it would have in the Soviet Union.

Three public sector operations have been the perennial butts of journalistic criticism (it has always been permitted the Egyptian press to decry bureaucratic bungling if names are not mentioned): Cairo International Airport, Egyptair, and Alexandria Port. The airport was always an exemplar of confusion as some twenty-three different administrative jurisdictions, employing 26,000 people, haggled over the movement of passengers and goods (*A*, July 10, 1973). Alexandria Port is accurately depicted as perpetually buried in unmoved goods while ships lie in the harbor receiving millions of pounds in hard currency fines against delays in scheduled unloadings. Egyptair, the national airline, has been a particularly savory bone to gnaw. As of 1976 it had accumulated losses of £E 80 million (Gritli 1977, p. 52). Its profile was as follows (*A*, January 14, 1977):

Fixed capital	£E	2,207,000
Wages (1975)		7,116,609
Debts		34,815,013
Debt service (1976)		4,500,000
Overdrafts		14,292,298
No. of passengers		1,459,000
No. of employees		9,003

Egyptair has been plagued, like much of the public sector, by overemployment, mismanagement, and corruption.

The Helwan Iron and Steel Complex is certainly the best-known of Egypt's public sector industrial projects. Prior to its inception, the country's small private sector steel industry relied on scrap metal to produce some 200,000 tons of steel each year. As scrap became scarce, the industry urged exploitation of Egypt's iron ore deposits in the Aswan region (29 percent to 44 percent iron content) to facilitate the next phase. In 1954 the PCDNP approved a project to be located at Helwan near Cairo utilizing imported coke. With public financing, the Misr Group entered into a contract with the Demag Corporation of West Germany to produce 300,000 tons of ingots annually at 12 to 36 percent below the price of competitive imports.

The industry proved highly inefficient due to faulty installation (Demag was accused of selling Egypt substandard furnaces and installing them poorly), the low quality of the ore, the rising cost of imported coke after the devaluation of 1962, and the fact that the oxygen conversion process employed was obsolete by the time the plant started production. By 1963-64 it was producing only 144,000 tons and had an effective rate of protection of 599 percent

(Hansen and Nashashibi 1975, pp. 289-97; and Isma'il 1973). 'Aziz Sidqi's solution was to increase the scale of operations in order to achieve output of 1.5 million tons. In 1965 the USSR was awarded a contract to carry out the expansion. Like the Nag Hammadi aluminum smelter, the Helwan project was suspended until 1967 when the USSR again agreed to carry out the expansion at the 1965 price of $156 million (*RY*, no. 2536, January 17, 1977). The expansion has not gone well either, although better quality ore from the western desert is now used. The last of three blast furnaces had not been installed as of 1978 due to the complexity of a gas conversion process that was to fuel it. Production at Helwan has never exceeded 800,000 tons (*FT* survey, July 31, 1978). The steel complex was saddled with an enormous debt. In 1976, when it was still capitalized at only £E 19 million, its long-term obligations had reached £E 235 million (Gritli 1977, p. 210). It had been obliged to absorb out of its own budget the development of the new iron ore deposits at Wahhat and the costs of building a railroad to transport the ore. But the consistent losses registered by the company predate the opening up of the new deposits and are rooted in chronic underutilization of capacity, very high rates of coke and ore consumption per ton of finished steel, and the high share of labor costs relative to the value of output (Hansen and Nashashibi 1975, p. 295). The component parts of the complex have not functioned smoothly. The coking plant was started in 1964 but only reached full capacity in 1974 at 310,000 tons. An ammonium nitrate plant, designed to produce annually 120,000 tons at 33.5 percent nitrogen, never operated at capacity because the amount and quality of coking gas it needed from the coking plant were always insufficient (Maglis al-Sha'ab 1973, Pt. II). The iron and steel industry, which was to be the vanguard of the public sector, has instead brought up the rear.

The heart of Egypt's public sector and industry has remained the textile industry. With some 300,000 workers it employs over half the public sector workforce, accounted in 1978 for 46 percent of the value of public sector industrial production, and in the same year contributed 30 percent of *all* exports exclusive of petroleum. Yet since the middle 1960s it has not been a very dynamic sector. Whereas at the end of the Five-Year Plan the textile sector, however heavily protected, was meeting over 96 percent of local demand, that no longer is the case. The Federation of Industries (1977 *Yearbook*) gave these production figures:

	1952	1972	1976
tons of yarn	55,700	179,000	193,065
millions of meters of cloth	40	708	874

Expansion has slowed in the 1970s while urban lower and middle class demand for cheap, subsidized cloth has surged ahead. Since 1975, when the Ministry of Commerce decreed that textiles, subject to duty, could be imported through the "own exchange" system, whereby an importer with the necessary foreign exchange at his disposal could import without seeking a license. The country was flooded with cheap Korean and Chinese imports with the upshot that Egypt in 1977 imported over £E 55 million in textiles while the textile sector was burdened with £E 41 million in inventories it could not move. According to one estimate (*AI*, no. 557, November 1, 1978) the amount of imported cloth in 1977 was equivalent to 20 percent of domestic production. Since the early 1960s domestic spinners have bought cotton at a price well below that of the world market. By 1975 the local price was one-third the international price (IBRD 1978a, 3:92). Despite this subsidy, production costs have remained high, and part of the reason may lie in the 20 percent labor redundancy in this sector that Hansen and Nashashibi discerned in 1970 (1975, p. 223).

'Aziz Sidqi wanted Egypt to move into new lines of consumer goods production, particularly consumer durables: refrigerators, washing machines, radios and televisions, air conditioners, stoves and heaters. All are now available in Egypt but at very high cost. The company that has justifiably drawn the most critical attention is Nasr Automotive, which started up as a truck assembly in combination with Deutz, and then, in 1962, went into automobile assembly with Fiat. In 1969 Egypt began to import its Fiat knock-down assembly kits from Poland through barter arrangements in order to conserve foreign exchange. The original goal for this industry was to produce 20,000 automobiles, 4,000 trucks, and 4,000 buses with 90 percent of components manufactured locally by the late 1960s. Over a decade later, this goal had not been remotely approached, as the following figures show:

	1963-64	1970-71	1976
automobiles	5,406	4,241	9,799
buses	1,155	407	307

'Ali al-Gritli (1977, p. 215) uncharitably noted that Nasr Automotive employed 10,000 workers to produce 10,000 vehicles a year while a similar Fiat plant in Spain turned out 100,000 with the same number of hands.[4] Throughout the period the Nasr Automotive Company suffered from foreign exchange shortages and seldom operated at more than 70 percent capacity. In 1977 locally manufactured components did not exceed 30 percent of the total (*A*, April 28, 1975; also Hansen and Nashashibi 1975, pp. 290-300).

If the industrialization strategy laid down in 1960 had worked properly, the center of gravity of industrial production would have shifted from consumer to intermediate and capital goods industries. The first step in this direction was the establishment at Aswan of the Kima Fertilizer Company.

---

[4] In 1977 plans were announced to manufacture a so-called "Popular" Nasr 133 to retail at £E 1,950, when average annual per capita income was ca. £E 120.

For some years, under the direction of Taha Zaki, this plant was touted as one of Egypt's industrial success stories. It took its power from the power station at the old Aswan Dam but at a highly subsidized rate that many feel explains the company's profits (*AI*, no. 530, September 15, 1977). But even with this advantage the company experienced a sharp decline in production in the late 1960s when it could not extract from the Ministry of Finance the foreign exchange necessary to replace used equipment. Egypt has remained a net importer of fertilizer although the new Talkha plant, utilizing natural gas, may help meet local demand for nitrogenous fertilizers. But this, like similar ventures in cement, petrochemicals, synthetic fabrics, and sponge iron, has come in the "open-door" era to be discussed in the next chapter.

The final project to be discussed here is the Nag Hammadi Aluminum Complex. 'Aziz Sidqi had advocated this project prior to his eclipse in 1965. When he returned to the Ministry of Industry in 1968 he revived it. The Soviet Union agreed to finance the plant on its usual soft terms (see Chapter Sixteen) and to buy up to 40,000 tons of plates and molds annually at world market prices. The plant was located downstream from the High Dam, which supplies its power. In an initial stage, with production at 100,000 tons annually, the plant required about a quarter of the total energy generated at the High Dam. This could rise to half if production is increased to 170,000 tons. Like Kima, Nag Hammadi is receiving its energy input at a highly favorable rate—but its bauxite is imported from Australia and unloaded at the Red Sea port of Safaga. Because of the high subsidization of its energy supply, the aluminum complex has been quite profitable and has been able to compete successfully for export markets (*FT*, July 23, 1980).

The production figures in Table 6.1 clearly reveal the overall stagnation of Egyptian industry beginning in the late 1960s, particularly in the strategic sectors of chemicals, metallurgy, and engineering products. These trends were not reversed until the late 1970s.

It is difficult to obtain consistent statistics on the value of public sector assets. This is so in part because they were deliberately undervalued at the time of nationalization. The parliamentary investigatory committee in 1973 put the total worth of public sector companies at about £E 1.7 billion, and in the same year the minister of industry, Salim Muhammedain used a figure for fixed public sector industrial investment of £E 1.4 billion (*A*, February 12, 1973). Both these figures clearly exclude such assets as the Suez Canal or the High Dam power station, which are not considered companies. A third source (Handoussa 1980) examined 107 of 160 industrial companies in the public sector and found that their "employed capital"—equity, reserves, and long-term loans—totaled £E 2.6 billion. It is interesting to contrast this figure with that of Anis (1950, p. 791) of £E 70 million in industrially employed capital in 1945.

Table 6.1
Output of Selected Industrial Products
(In thousands of metric tons unless otherwise stated)

	1952	1969-70	1974	1977	1979
SPINNING AND WEAVING					
Cotton yarn	56	163	179	210	216
Cotton textiles	40	110	120	97.5	100
FOODSTUFFS					
Tomato sauce	.4	1.2	.18	2.4	3.9
Beer (million liters)	10	23	29	38	34
Cottonseed oil	100	139	149	169	177
Oilseed cakes	410	565	536	716	442
Cigarettes	11	17	23	31	37
Cooking butter	12	64	99	133	160
CHEMICALS					
Soap	63	136	183	217	245
Paper	20	119	130	153	169
Superphosphates	106	354	464	505	483
Ammonium nitrate					
fertilizer (15.5%)	111	—	639	1,247	1,689
Tires (thousands)	—	711	814	920	933
ENGINEERING PRODUCTS					
Cars (units)	—	2,800	8,169	13,990	15,670
Trucks (units)	—	1,117	1,082	1,684	2,304
Tractors (units)	—	1,071	1,260	2,761	2,783
Refrigerators (thousands)	—	68	55	91	207
Washers (thousands)	—	16	31	126	273
ELECTRICAL PRODUCTS					
Televisions (thousands)	—	64	71	150	249
METALLURGIC PRODUCTS					
Reinforced iron	50	135	262	347	302
Steel sections	—	126	78	143	151
Steel sheets	—	43	39	34	50
Cast iron products	17	48	210	70	119
BUILDING MATERIALS					
Portland cement	951*	3,760	3,264	3,232	2,987
Pipes and beams	18	38	39	41	32
Plate glass	4	15	16	21	27

SOURCE: CAPMAS, *Statistical Yearbook (1952-1977)*, July 1978, pp. 74-88, and "Industrial Egypt," *AI*, no. 612, October 6, 1980, pp. 38-42.

* Production in 1952 was of "ordinary" cement, not Portland.

The only source at my disposal that summarizes profits and losses for all public sector enterprises was a published synthesis (Banna 1979)[5] of a long report of 372 companies carried out by the Central Auditing Agency. In current prices it estimated the total capital employed of these companies at £E 22.5 billion in 1977.

These figures include everything in public ownership, and as al-Banna points out, the modestly improving trend in profits is accounted for in 1977 by the rapidly growing earnings of the petroleum sector and Suez Canal (£E 461 million of total profits of £E 814 million). Handoussa, by contrast, found that the number of *industrial* companies registering losses in the same period was increasing. In general however the net rate of return on capital employed, despite the great surge in current price profits, has changed little: in 1973 the parliamentary committee put it at 2.4 percent and by 1977 it had risen to 3.2 percent.

Although it is a point to which I shall return, it is the case that whatever its imperfections the public sector has brought the Nasserist and post-Nasserist regimes substantial economic and political dividends. It is above all an instrument of political and economic control, and no Egyptian leaders, however hostile they might be to the ideology of public ownership, will lightly will it away. It employs about 10 percent of the total work force; more particularly the elite of the industrial proletariat. Its wage bill in 1974 was over 20 percent of the national total. At the same time it is a source of savings to which the government has direct and uncontested access. Table 6.3 shows how the financial surplus of all profit-making public sector companies was actually distributed in 1976. From the point of view of the state, the public sector was the source of £E 475 million in savings (the entire financial surplus minus the discretionary reserves and about £E 20 million in private shareholder

Table 6.2
Gross Profits and Losses of Public Sector Companies, 1975-1977

(£E millions)

Year	Gross Profits (1)		Gross Losses (2)		Net Profit (3)	Capital Employed (4)	(3)/(4) %
	no. of cos.	value	no. of cos.	value			
1975	301	397	54	73	324	15,547	2.1
1976	323	589	44	80	509	19,005	2.7
1977	325	814	40	84	730	22,507	3.2

SOURCE: Banna 1979, p. 31.

[5] See also 'Ali al-Gritli 1977, p. 216.

Table 6.3
Allocation of Financial Surplus of
All Profit-Making Public Sector Companies, 1976

(£E millions)

	Amount	%
FINANCIAL SURPLUS	582.3	100
Company profit tax	120.7	21
Mandatory allocations	169.8	29
(Bank Nasser	10.2)	
(Statutory reserve	21.2)	
(Gov't. bond reserve	21.2)	
(Asset inflation reserve	21.2)	
(Admin. supervision	27.5)	
(Workers' profit, share, cash	27.4)	
(Workers' profit, local services	13.7)	
(Workers' profit, gen. services	27.4)	
DISCRETIONARY SURPLUS	291.8	
Discretionary reserves	86.7	15
Income tax on dividends	83.2	14
Net dividends to public and private* shareholders	121.9	21

SOURCE: Unpublished statistics, Ministry of Finance.

*There are some thirty public sector companies that have private shareholders, including Rakta Paper Co., Kima Chemical Co., and Helwan Iron and Steel. Of total dividends paid, only about £E 20 million went to private shareholders.

dividends). By 1978 the transfer of earnings to the state reached £E 708 million and has likely gone much higher since because of the skyrocketing profits of the petroleum sector (*AI*, no. 574, July 15, 1979). Because of the size of this fiscal bite, companies have every incentive to minimize declared profits and to maximize retained earnings.

The public sector has thus been a serviceable milch cow for the regime, but presumably with better management it could have been far more productive.[6] Its malaise stems from several causes, some of which have been alluded to but which I shall outline here. The units that suffer chronic losses are victims of unfavorable administered pricing, foreign exchange shortages, and idle capacity. All three factors may be interlinked or work separately—it simply depends on the enterprise.

Heba Handoussa produces evidence that industrial companies that show repeated losses are those that must sell their produce at artificially low prices

[6] For two general critiques see Guwaida 1976c and Salmi 1969. For general and rather uncritical treatment see Badawi 1973. Ayubi (1977 and 1980) provides thorough accounts.

Table 6.4
Public Sector Employment and Wages by Type of Activity, 1974

Sector	No. Employed	Net Wages
Agriculture and Irrigation	18,041	8,673,000
Industry, Petroleum Mineral Wealth	69,452	222,235,600
Electricity	2,413	1,540,000
Transport, Communications	64,523	1,540,000
Supply, Internal Trade	76,581	26,558,000
Finance, Security, Foreign Trade	54,117	29,959,660
Housing, Construction	41,973	35,026,000
Health Services	19,780	7,940,000
Culture, Information	1,282	703,000
Tourism	7,693	3,198,000
Insurance	7,290	3,946,000
Total	913,145	£E 366,680,460

SOURCE: Figures presented by First Deputy Prime Minister 'Abd al-'Aziz Higazi, published in *The Egyptian Gazette*, August 30, 1974. Figures do not include the civil service.

imposed by the state and absorb the loss on their own accounts. Fertilizers are a notable example. The problem has been greatly exacerbated in the 1970s as production costs, due in part to exchange rate adjustments, have soared. Erratic shifts in exchange rates first were felt with the devaluation of 1962 (see Hansen and Nashashibi 1975, pp. 95-101), and in the mid-1970s the state monopoly in foreign trade, in effect since 1961, was partially ended. It maintained that monopoly for nineteen imported commodities to be bought at the official exchange rate of thirty-nine piastres to the dollar.[7] All other imports, including raw materials and intermediate goods, were to be imported at the "incentive rate" of the pound (designed to attract hard currency earnings of Egyptians abroad) of sixty piastres to the dollar. In 1977 Yussef Shahin, the minister of industry, testified before parliament that the shift to the new rate would increase the import bill of public sector companies by £E 242 million (*A*, April 13, 1977). On January 1, 1979 Egypt moved to a unified exchange rate, at the incentive price, for all foreign trade.

Whatever the exchange rate, foreign exchange needs have not been met by the producing units themselves, with the exception of the petroleum sector and Suez Canal. Some industries that could be competitive abroad, such as

[7] The commodities were wheat, flour, maize, beans, sesame, bulk tea, sugar, edible oils, animal fats, tobacco, cotton, yarn, jute, coal, petroleum, fertilizers, insecticides, military production means, and armaments.

fertilizers and cement, are prohibited from exporting in order to satisfy local demand. Despite the natural tendency of many companies to stockpile excessive amounts of vital raw materials, the need to replace worn equipment, as in the case of Kima Fertilizers, cannot be met in the same way. Its production fell from 437,000 tons in 1967-68 to 152,000 tons in 1973. Some public sector firms in the 1970s, such as Nasr Automotive, gave priority to Egyptian customers who could pay in foreign exchange requirements. The anomalous situation that resulted was that in 1974 Egypt contracted with Iran to import 200 Mercedes buses at twice the cost of Egyptian buses, while Nasr Automotive's assembly of buses had fallen from 1,500 units in 1965 to 360 in 1974. The company did not have the foreign exchange to import assembly kits.

The problem of idle capacity is rooted in the retrenchment policies introduced in 1965. The value of lost production in 1967-68 was put at £E 153 million rising to £E 271 million in 1973, £E 285 million in 1976 and £E 300 million in 1979—all in current prices and including the private sector. For the public industrial sector alone the situation in 1972-73 is depicted in Table 6.5. The Ministry of Industry estimated in 1974 that an additional £E 42 million in foreign exchange would yield £E 230 million in new industrial production.

Table 6.5
Fixed Capital, Production, Workers, and Idle Capacity
in the Public Industrial Sector

	Fixed Capital thru 1972 £E mil.	Value of Production, 1973 £E Mil.	No. of Workers, 1972	Value of Lost Production, 1973 £E Mil.
Spinning and Weaving	540	406	267,701	14.2
Food	351	426	76,345	82.2
Chemicals	393	111	56,358	29.2
Engineering	263	110	142,853	35.2
Building Materials	116	57	25,147	2.2
Metallurgy	387	103	27,826	26.0
Total	2,050	1,213	396,230	189.0

SOURCES: This table has been compiled from several sources. Fixed capital figures were provided by Mohammed 'Abd al-Fattah Ibrahim, undersecretary of state for industry in *The Egyptian Gazette*, July 18, 1973. Column 2 contains official Ministry of Industry figures published in July 18, 1973. The number of workers was provided in Dr. Mungi's study (1975) and idle capacity in Ministry of Industry "Unutilized Productive Capacities," unpublished 1974. The same source estimates idle capacity in the private sector at £E 43 million.

Not all the problems of idle capacity and high per unit costs can be attributed to foreign exchange bottlenecks. In a survey carried out by the Institute of National Planning in 1972 (Mungi 1975), it was found that 61 percent of all public sector companies operated only one shift a day, 8 percent two shifts, 23 percent three shifts, and 8.4 percent (including Kima Fertilizer) four shifts. Even when operating, public sector plant is underutilized. Idle capacity has gone hand in hand with the stockpiling of raw materials and the holding of large inventories of unmarketed or unmarketable produce. The value of such goods was £E 78 million in 1966 and £E 100 million in 1977 with textiles taking the lion's share in both instances.

The employment drive of the early 1960s proceeded with a life of its own despite repeated public endorsement after 1968 of limiting job openings to real production needs and wage levels to production levels. Nonetheless it probably remained the case that total public sector employment was 20 to 30 percent above the requirements of production. Over the period 1971-1976 the public sector work force grew at a rate of 5 percent per year, and did not begin to taper off until 1977 when the rate decelerated to 3.6 percent (Handoussa 1980). By Deputy Prime Minister Higazi's reckoning, the public sector wage bill increased 20 percent between 1973 and 1974 alone.

The Seven Lean Years: 1967-1974

There is no telling whether or not Egypt could have undertaken the necessary streamlining in its public sector after 1965 to render it an effective instrument in socialist transformation. As was noted in the previous chapter, Nasser vacillated on a number of painful policy choices and then lost altogether the possibility to choose after Egypt's crushing defeat in June 1967. From then on, and until the time of writing, there has been no seven- or five-year plan, although such documents are perpetually on the drawing boards, but rather a series of poorly integrated one-year public investment programs. As Egypt's foreign exchange crisis deepened after 1967, the crux of the planning effort resided in the management of the foreign exchange budget. But even the series of unimplemented plans have a thoroughly retrospective, corrective cast to them rather than containing strategies for the future.

For seven years economic retrenchment (*inkimash*) was complemented by political and military steadfastness (*sumud*), which meant asking the Egyptian people to support the enormous military expenditures needed to avoid capitulation to Israel. Everything else in the realm of social and economic policy was held in suspended animation; the apparatus of the public sector, the programs of the welfare state, as well as the country's infrastructure, were barely maintained, and in per capita terms, if not in absolute terms, production levels and the quantity and quality of services began to deteriorate.

This state of affairs is partially reflected in investment data. In Table 6.6, I have presented figures for the period from the end of the first Five-Year Plan through 1975, a full year into a new era of expansionist investment. The message is fairly dramatic. As a proportion of national income, gross fixed investment fell off markedly from its peak of the middle Sixties only to make a spectacular recovery in the mid-Seventies. But the remarkable aspect of this is that domestic funding as a proportion of national income continued its precipitous decline throughout the period. What growth took place in national income went into private and public consumption, not investment, while the impressive investment levels of the latter part of the period were attained only by massive borrowing abroad and deficit financing. The political costs of extracting greater savings from the Egyptian masses appeared higher than those of printing money and increased external dependence. The regime's will to save was invariably eclipsed by its will to survive.

Under Nasser there was redistribution of income in favor of the rural and urban lower middle classes while the upper bourgeoisie paid for the redistribution and the middle classes found their consumerist proclivities thwarted. In the early 1970s, under Sadat, everyone was allowed to consume. While levels of production remained low, the *laisser aller* of the new Egypt could be paid for only by foreign credits and deficit financing. Some indication of the volume and rate of growth of both phenomena is provided in Table 6.7.

Table 6.6
Growth in GNP and Sources of Investment, 1965-66-1975
(£E Million at current market prices)

Year	GNP (1)	Domestic Investment (2)	% (2)/(1)	Gross Fixed Investment (3)	% (3)/(1)	Resource Gap Met by Deficit Financing and External Credits (4)	% (4)/(3)
1965-66	2,455.5	309.6	12.6	446.2	18.2	136.6	30.6
1966-67	2,500.3	328.9	13.1	385.6	15.4	56.7	14.6
1967-68	2,584.8	221.9	8.5	342.2	13.2	120.3	35.1
1968-69	2,793.4	215.8	7.7	318.2	11.4	102.4	32.1
1969-70	3,006.6	255.7	8.5	416.1	13.8	160.4	38.5
1970-71	3,180.4	219.6	6.9	432.0	13.6	212.4	49.1
1971-72	3,380.1	291.9	8.6	420.4	12.4	128.5	30.5
1973	3,625.5	278.7	7.7	502.0	13.8	223.3	44.4
1974	4,085.0	197.3	4.8	730.0	17.8	532.7	72.9
1975	4,713.0	207.4	4.4	1,466.0	31.1	1,258.6	85.8

SOURCES: GNP figures from IBRD 1978, 6: Table 2.2. Columns 2,3, and 4 are from unpublished data issued by the Ministry of Planning, September 1975.

Table 6.7
Total Deficit, Net Deficit, and Net External Borrowing

Year	Total Deficit	Net Deficit	Net External Borrowing £E million current prices
1962-63	194	70	28
1963-64	300	150	83
1964-65	208	72	81
1965-66	253	116	67
1966-67	95	75	57
1967-68	106	50	24
1968-69	54	48	−13
1969-70	47	80	−15
1970-71	5	79	—
1971-72	101	77	18
1973	310	183	51
1974	560	380	119
1975	1,388	731	210
1976	1,265	437	488
1977	1,532	374	464
1978	2,149	332	705
1979	3,195	1,197	690
1980	3,119 (est.)	976 (est.)	350 (est.)

SOURCE: 1962-63-1974: IBRD 1978, 6:54. 1974-1979: annual Egyptian budget outlines and IMF statistics.

To cover the total deficit the state primarily borrows against social security and insurance funds, and, since 1978, utilizes the proceeds of sales of development bonds.

Nineteen seventy-six was a crucial year in enracinating Egypt in the inflationary game of printing money. In that year the investment budget of the annual Plan was divided into two *tranches* of £E 798 million and £E 574.4. When the Plan was drawn up, domestic and foreign funding were in hand to cover the first *tranche*, but the second would depend upon a massive infusion of Arab credits. It was announced publicly that these were likely to be forthcoming. At the same time Egypt was negotiating a standby agreement and stabilization plan with the IMF. This would have entailed a substantial reduction in the current account deficit essentially through the elimination of several consumer goods subsidies. The net deficit, which stood at over £E

700 million in 1975, would have been reduced to about £E 150 million. Instead, what transpired was that funding for the second *tranche* did not materialize, but public sector companies had gone ahead and borrowed from Egyptian public sector banks on the assumption that it would. Their uncovered borrowing reached nearly £E 400 million in 1976, and they continued to borrow beyond authorized limits to the tune of £E 389 million in 1977. Meanwhile, for political reasons that we shall examine in Chapter Ten, the price subsidies were maintained.[8]

The upshot was that, despite some governmental belt-tightening, the total deficit was not reduced. Moreover, the hitherto exceptional resort to uncovered issuance of treasury bills and banknotes became the norm, expanding the money supply and fueling inflation. Three years later, in presenting the 1980 budget, Minister of Finance 'Ali Lutfi stated (*Al* Supplement, January 1, 1980): "The primary cause of the currency expansion and, by derivation, the increase in inflationary pressures inside the country, is increased governmental borrowing from the banking system and accumulated governmental indebtedness, which reached 75.3 percent of all net credit at the end of September 1979." Dr. Lutfi was right on both counts: liquidity increased by 22 percent in 1972-73, 29 percent in 1973-74, 20 percent in 1974-75, 26 percent in 1976, and 32 percent in 1977 (Gritli 1977, p. 134 and NBE 1978). By the middle 1970s it was widely believed that inflation was running at 25 to 30 percent per annum, although the administered pricing system makes such estimates hazardous.[9] In these same years the outstanding government *domestic* debt grew from £E 3.4 billion in 1975 to £E 5.9 billion in 1979.

It has been necessary, mainly because of data availability, to carry my argument beyond 1974, the last of the seven lean years. I have done this because the seeds of what I see as public sector profligacy took root between 1967 and 1974 but blossomed most spectacularly thereafter. There are many other facets involved here, and I want to take some of them up now. Not only was the public sector heavily indebted to the banking system but to other branches of the same sector. As none of Egypt's putative "economic czars" ('Abd al-'Aziz Higazi, Ahmad Abu Isma'il, 'Abd al-Mun'aim al-Qaissuni) was ever given a mandate on such practices, neither public sector debtors nor creditors had any incentive to clear their books. The two most striking examples were the Egyptian customs administration and the Egyptian railways. By 1975 the cumulative public sector debt to the railways, representing unpaid bills for the movement of passengers (especially military personnel) and goods was £E 93 million, while in the same year the cumulative backlog of unpaid

[8] On this period see Tingay 1976; Ghaith 1977; Sabbagh 1978.

[9] Choucri and Eckaus (1979, p. 785) see these same phenomena in a more positive light. The greater amount of money in circulation in combination with certain assumptions about money velocities, would, despite increased inflation rates, yield some real growth, especially through private sector investment.

customs duties was £E 176 million (*A*, July 27, 1975; and Gritli 1977, p. 75).

The seven lean years were lean only in terms of foreign exchange, savings, and investment but not, as has been already noted, in terms of consumption. This was reflected in the growing deficit in the balance of payments on visible trade. The initial efforts of retrenchment to restrain imports gave way in the early 1970s to a significant expansion in all kinds of imports. The overall shares of consumer, intermediate (raw materials), and capital goods in total imports scarcely changed from what they had been in the mid-1960s, except that the shares of food in consumer goods rose perceptibly. These points will be discussed in greater detail in Chapter Nine.

The Draft Plan for 1976 indicates the extent of control of the Minister of Planning over the deficit (ARE: Ministry of Planning 1975, p. 8): "When there occurs in the next few years—God willing (*insha' llah*)—the rectification of the current deficit in the balance of payments, GNP will be sufficient to cover popular and governmental consumption as well as participating increasingly in financing development." After eight years of retrenchment none of the original problems had been resolved. Public sector enterprises had not improved their export performance, agriculture fell further and further behind in meeting basic food needs, and there seemed no politically acceptable way to curb public and private consumption. Added to this was the growing defense burden that meant that by 1970 Egypt was spending over £E 1 bn per annum

Table 6.8

Egypt's Balance of Payments on Visible Trade, 1966-1975

(£E millions current prices)

Year	Exports	Imports	Balance
1966	259.5	410.9	− 151.4
1967	258.7	413.2	− 154.5
1968	258.7	369.3	− 110.6
1969	319.7	418.4	− 98.7
1970	355.4	517.8	− 162.4
1971	369.7	540.8	− 171.1
1972	353.7	559.2	− 205.5
1973	396.3	662.3	− 266.0
1974	653.9	1,357.5	− 703.6
1975	612.5	1,691.1	− 1,078.6

SOURCE: All figures from various IBRD reports. A 1974 IMF report calculated a *quantity* index for exports, 1965 = 100. The results were 1969 = 99.8, 1970 = 100.7, 1971 = 105.9, 1972 = 105, 1973 = 102.

to maintain its armed forces. In 1971 these outlays represented 20 percent of GDP, although half came in the form of Arab aid and was funneled through the Emergency Fund. In all this Sadat was trying to be all things to all people; the only losers in the process were the peasants and private sector workers whose incomes did not keep pace with the rise in prices.

Tinkering with the Public Sector and the Plan

When in doubt, reshuffle. From its inception the public sector underwent periodic reorganizations which came across as quixotic attempts to patch over more profound structural problems in protection, monopoly position, over-staffing, and inadequate management. We have already noted the shift in 1961 from a limited form of competitive state capitalism based on three holding companies to one of sectoral monopolies under the supervision of relevant ministries. These monopolies in 1972 consisted in twenty-nine General Organizations that supervised companies operating in their sphere of production. For example, the 106 companies under the umbrella of the Ministry of Industry were supervised by seven General Organizations: Metallurgy, Spinning and Weaving, Petroleum, Chemicals, Building Materials, Food Processing, and Engineering/Electrical. Alongside the General Organizations were twenty Authorities. While the General Organizations were nominally involved in direct production and trade, the Authorities were engaged in the provision of services of one kind or another. The absence of a tangible product and the welfare implication of the services involved lent emphasis to nonfinancial criteria in judging their performance: typical examples are the Cairo Transport Authority, High Dam Electrical Authority, and the Egyptian Railroad Authority (cf. Ayubi 1980, pp. 218-25).

The General Organizations and Authorities were supported by five specialized public sector banks, themselves in a monopoly position. In September 1963 six small commercial banks were merged with the five major banks nationalized between 1957 and 1961. Then, in July 1969, each bank was assigned a specific task:

Ahali Bank:	Agriculture, agrarian reform, Suez Canal, railroads, and communications.
Misr Bank:	Textiles, general insurance.
Alexandria Bank:	Industrial General Organizations with the exception of textiles; also General Petroleum Organization.
Cairo Bank:	External trade, housing, tourism and information.
Pt. Said Bank:	Health, supply, pharmaceuticals, internal trade.

As Muhammed Rushdi, president of the Board of Directors of Misr Bank before and after nationalization, put it, this arrangement had two principal advantages: 1) each bank was responsible for mobilizing the foreign exchange necessary to implement the projects assigned its sector by the Plan; 2) supervision of Plan implementation. All banks, in turn, came under the supervision of the Central Bank (Rushdi 1972, 2:237-39).

As laid down in Law 30 of 1963, each General Organization had the right of oversight of personnel lists, proposed budgets, financial accounts, production, marketing and export, and financial and investment programs of the companies in its sphere. The relevant minister served as president of the Board of Directors of the General Organizations, but there is some evidence that ministerial control must have been found wanting during the first Five-Year Plan. In 1966, with retrenchment underway, Law 32 increased direct ministerial control of the General Organizations while encouraging greater autonomy at the company level. After Nasser's demise, in 1971, Law 60 was issued to clarify procedures that were now a decade old. This law stressed that the primary role of the General Organizations was preview of company production and investment plans and evaluation of implementation, but that there was to be no interference in day-to-day management and operations (in general see Gabr 1975).

In 1975 a major shake-up occurred. Law 111 of that year abolished the General Organizations altogether. Their abolition is intimately linked to the economic liberalization measures adopted in 1974, so that a complete discussion must be postponed until the next chapter. Still, a great deal of the impetus for this change reflected growing unhappiness with public sector performance and was not dependent upon the regime's will to stimulate the private sector or attract foreign investment.

Law 111 was issued in the spirit of honoring fairly strict benefit/cost criteria in running public sector enterprises. The best way to achieve this, it was felt, was to maximize the autonomy of each company so that the weaknesses and strengths of its management, production line, and marketing would be readily apparent. It was, in theory, to usher in an era of sink or swim. In practice, however, everyone understood that certain companies would continue to benefit from subsidized inputs (cotton, electricity) while others would be penalized by subsidized sales of output (fertilizers, soap, matches, etc.). Yet others, like Helwan Iron and Steel, because of their presumed strategic importance, would not have to submit to close scrutiny.

At the time of its issuance, Law 111 led to the abolition of thirty-five General Organizations comprising over 300 companies. It did not apply to the General Authorities, and as the directors of General Organizations felt administrative sinecures slipping from their grasp, some asked that they be reclassified as Authorities. Otherwise the rather elaborate bureaucracies that the General Organizations had spawned were to be dispersed among the other ministries. In Industry alone Law 111 did away with six General Organizations

(Petroleum became an Authority) with 117 companies. Some 1,110 employees of the industrial General Organizations were to be reassigned.

Replacing the General Organizations were twenty-three Supreme Sectoral Councils. Each has a full-time president, not infrequently the former chairman of the General Organization, a small secretarial and research staff, and several part-time members including parliamentarians, company heads, university professors, and representatives of consumer interests. There was no provision for worker representatiion although there had been in the General Organizations.

As most public sector politicos had suspected, the Sectoral Councils turned out to be window dressing. They did not meet regularly, they had no power, and their part-time members did not take them seriously ('Issam Rifa'at 1976, pp. 14-16). What Law 111 brought about was the dissolution of power at an intermediate level, and its reconcentration at the ministerial level. If lessening of red tape was a prime objective of the abolition of the General Organizations, it is hard to imagine how this could be served when the minister of industry was now directly responsible for supervising 117 companies (Waterbury 1978a, pp. 295-99). The Cotton General Organization, for example, had 245 full-time employees. They were replaced by 45 part-time appointees and 7 full-time staff members.

Even long-standing critics of the General Organizations, such as Mustapha Kamal Murad, who referred to them as states within the state (*AY*, April 20, 1974), were dismayed at their abolition. He and others would have liked to see a return to the holding company format that prevailed between 1957 and 1961, but whatever the arrangement some supervisory and coordinating mechanism at a level intermediate between the company and the minister was deemed necessary. Likewise 'Ali al-Gritli noted the positive functions undertaken by the General Organizations. They were able to anticipate foreign exchange and financing crises for individual companies under their umbrella. For example, in 1970 the General Organization for Chemical Industries was able to help a number of companies over liquidity problems by arranging long-term loans at 3 percent interest from the surplus earnings of Kima Chemical Company. General Organizations could also help ease raw material and spare parts shortages by shifting stocks among their companies. Similarly, nothing has been done to overcome the sometimes anomalous assignation of companies: before Law 111 one found that sugar refineries fell under the General Organizations for Food Industries, while sugar cane production came under the Ministry of Agriculture. Since Law 111 the jurisdictional splits in supposedly integrated industries have been transferred to the ministerial level.

The reorganization of 1975 was designed to encourage company heads to take effective charge of their operations without undue interference from above. Law 111 became effective on January 1, 1976. A little over a year later, in March 1977, the minister of industry, 'Issa Shahin, issued a decree firing twenty-one board chairmen and 95 members of the boards of directors of seventy-three industrial companies. The victims included some very powerful public sector figures such as Taha Zaki, chairman of Kima Fertilizers. The reasons for the firings were obscure and could only lead one to believe that the minister was consolidating his grip and settling scores on behalf of himself and others. It was obviously too early to have judged the success or failure of company heads acting under Law 111.[10]

Since 1977 steps have been taken to enlarge the financial autonomy of public sector companies. Parliament voted out a bill in 1979, effective in 1980, that placed the budgets of the public sector companies outside the state budget, although the net surplus or deficit of these entities will continue to be financed by the state. The investment budget alone for public sector companies in 1980 was projected at over £E 2 billion (*AI* Supplement, January 1, 1980, p. 33). At the same time, the thrust of policy is to force public sector units to deal with the new banking system, on an orthodox financial basis, for their funding needs. The principal instrument of this will be the National Investment Bank, first chartered in 1978. At least in intent, it would become a giant holding company, arrogating to itself all the financial and management rights of the defunct General Organizations (*A*, July 24, 1978).

The new bank, whose operations had not yet begun in 1980, was put under the aegis of the Ministry of Planning. It was the creation of 'Abd al-Razzaq 'Abd al-Magid, minister for the economy as of May 1980. It marked an astounding assertion of the Ministry as the prime shaper and controller of public sector growth strategy. This is a role that had always been denied it by the Ministries of Finance and Economy. The fact that Hamid Sayyih, minister of economy, and 'Ali Lutfi, minister of finance, left the government signalled 'Abd al-Magid's apotheosis. Sadat began to refer to him as Egypt's Erhard.

If chartered, the NIB will serve several purposes. First, it will control all lending to the public sector in accord with the Plan. While its charter does not refer to exclusive rights in this domain, the NIB has such other powers of preinvestment review, implementation oversight, financial disclosure, and priority in recuperating its own credits that it would have an effective veto over any outside loans. It is responsible for mobilizing local resources, contracting foreign loans, and issuing bonds toward implementation of the Plan and is likewise responsible for servicing these obligations.

Secondly, the NIB will absorb the Insurance and Deposits Investment Fund

---

[10] See full listing of changes in *A*, March 13, 1977; protests by victims, *AY*, March 26, 1977; 'Issa Shahin's explanation, *A*, March 13, 1977; Taha Zaki's letter, *AY*, April 9, 1977. According to Shahin, Law 111 modified but did not displace Law 60 of 1971, section 52 of which empowers the minister to appoint and dismiss board chairmen in consultation with the members of the board. In 1980 Taha Zaki had his revenge, returning to prominence as minister of industry.

that had grouped social security, pensions, and postal savings payments. Thirdly, the NIB, in the words of Dr. 'Abd al-Magid, will deal with public sector companies "according to appropriate economic criteria to assure a continuous financial return on capital" (*A*, July 24, 1978). Finally, beginning with the Five-Year Plan 1980-1984, the NIB will take over most of the functions of the Ministry of Planning, which will be concerned in the future only with long- and medium-term investment planning (*AI*, no. 596, June 16, 1980). With projected capitalization of £E 3.2 billion, the NIB will have considerable leverage. Complementing the NIB, there are plans for an Import-Export Bank to act as a holding company for public sector trading companies. The latter will have their activities restricted to trade in "strategic" goods designated by the Ministries of Supply, Military Production, and Petroleum.

While it is too early to advance firm judgments, and cognizant of the fact that nothing is irreversible in Egypt, the general tendency is clear. Planning will no longer be comprehensive but confined to the public sector. Public sector units will have to justify themselves to a bank that in turn will justify itself in terms of its ability to recover costs on its operations. Presumably the NIB will have the power to hasten the death, promote the merger, or engineer the selling off of failing units.

A final word with respect to planning is in order. Egypt has not had a multiyear plan since 1965. It replaced the second Five-Year Plan with a Seven-Year Plan of readjustment. It was scrapped because of the June War. By 1970 there was talk of a Ten-Year Plan, but external finance was not remotely in hand, and the October War sent everyone back to the drawing boards anyway. Next there came talk of another Five-Year Plan to be launched in 1976, but the balance of payments crisis, the inability to implement an IMF stabilization plan, cost of living riots in January 1977, and Sadat's trip to Jerusalem in November led to a further postponement. Each year led to further delays, although USAID helped translate the multivolume 1976 plan into English, and various versions of it were served up at annual meetings in Paris of Egypt's Consultative Group comprising Western and Arab creditors.

At last count, a new Plan was to go into effect during 1980 involving £E 20 billion in investments over five years. By sector investment was allocated as follows:

Agriculture	£E 3.6 bn	18%
Housing and Infrastructure	4.5	22.5
Transportation and Communication	4.2	20.8
Power	1.8	
Industry	2.5	12.5
Export Sectors (incl. oil)	1.8	9.2
Social Services	1.6	8.0

Industry's share has ostensibly diminished but that is somewhat misleading. If one adds in power, those two sectors account for 22 percent of all investment, and it does appear that the now separate investment budgets of public sector companies have not been included in these figures.

Conclusion

In the late 1950s Egypt initiated an experiment in state capitalism in which publicly owned holding companies were to compete among themselves for local and foreign markets. The allocation of scarce resources would go to the most efficient. While not excluded, foreign capital was not expected to play much of a role in the economy. By contrast a subordinate domestic private sector was to undertake a major investment load. All this changed after 1961. Local private capital was no longer regarded as of significance and foreign private capital was viewed with suspicion. Competition among public sector companies was superseded by comprehensive planning and the allocation of scarce resources according to this plan. Profits and losses meant little in measuring the success of companies and management, and bargaining for resources became a more highly rewarded managerial skill than efficiency in meeting production norms. Moreover there was no incentive anywhere in the system that would have encouraged an honest appraisal of performance—in the name of protecting socialism's good name and Egypt's international stature, all failures had to be swept under the rug. In this era, the managers of the public sector could use their control of the means of production to consolidate that control, build empires, and otherwise enhance their power. They could not legally enhance their earnings. That could come about only through corruption: deals with private sector contractors, manipulation of black markets, payoffs from foreign suppliers, and so forth.

The model of sectoral monopolies and comprehensive planning began to disintegrate after 1966 and was abandoned for all intents and purposes in 1974-75. The ideals of the new era are close to those of the period 1957-1960. State managers are supposed to run efficient operations and make money, not for themselves but for the treasury, and now for the NIB. However, the possibilities for personal aggrandizement have been expanded enormously as the local private sector has been resuscitated and the doors thrown wide open for foreign capital. Since 1974 Egypt has officially entered the era of an opening to the outside world, and the course it is now following may produce economic configurations similar to those of Latin America.

Chapter Seven

THE OPEN DOOR
TO THE TRIPLE ALLIANCE

> ... whatever the state of resources that we can mo-
> bilize locally, we are still in the most urgent need of
> external resources. The circumstances of the world
> today render it possible that we obtain these re-
> sources in a manner that strengthens our economy
> and hastens growth. On this basis we have called for
> an economic opening (*infitah*), and it is a call founded
> upon the calculation of our economic needs on the
> one hand, and available external funding on the other.
> [Anwar al-Sadat, *The October Paper*,
> April 1974 (*Al* [1974a] Supplement).]

> I think that Egypt has come to realize that socialism
> and extreme Arab nationalism ... have not helped the
> lot of the 37 million people they have in Egypt. And if
> President Sadat wants to help them, he has got to look
> to private enterprise and assistance. ...
> [David Rockefeller, *NYT*, February 8, 1974.]

The formal adoption of the "economic open-door policy" (*infitah*) was not
forced upon Egypt by domestic capitalist lobbies nor by Western creditors.
Both sources of advice, to the limited extent that they had access to the Sadat
regime after 1970, tended to confirm the course upon which the country had
already set itself. That course was chosen in light of internal economic and
external political factors. While I shall stress the economic considerations in
this chapter, it is important to understand the broader context in which *infitah*
became state policy.

As with most other major shifts in Egyptian policy (the socialist decrees
of 1961, the expulsion of the Soviet military mission in 1972, etc.) the people
consulted and the range of considerations that led Sadat to the open door are
subjects for speculation and just plain hearsay. I am unable to assign weights
to those people and issues that I know were involved in the elaboration of

the policy; I can only inventory them. However, I am fairly convinced that Sadat's primary consideration was with the international arena. Secondly, the policies he was contemplating represented a major shift in Egypt's relations with conservative Arab regimes, the United States, and the Soviet Union. Yet this shift came at a time when Egypt had no diplomatic relations with the US[1] and when adopting a truculent posture toward both Washington and Israel was the order of the day. It was therefore very hard for Sadat to reveal his hand even to his closest associates. Consequently he was systematically misread by the political elite as they sought to package the few thematic hints that he let drop. For his part the president picked and chose among the diverse counsel available to him from his first prime minister, Mahmoud Fawzi; his minister of finance, 'Abd al-'Aziz Higazi; Hassanein Heikal, editor of *al-Ahram*; and Sayyid Mar'ai, the minister of agriculture.

Mahmud Fawzi, long-time minister of foreign affairs under Nasser, a civilian and a career diplomat, probably was a seminal figure in helping Sadat define the issues (for example see Mar'ai 1979: 3:635). Like Heikal he wanted to see bridges to the West reopened without sacrificing Soviet support. He also recognized that rapprochement with Saudi Arabia could lead to the mobilization of Arab ''surplus'' oil earnings in favor of Egyptian development. The president and Fawzi were sufficiently of like mind in 1971 to instruct 'Abdullah Marziban, minister of economy and foreign trade, to begin work on a coherent framework for the economic side of the open door. Marzipan in turn involved Sharif Lutfi in the process, who subsequently became the principal architect of the Foreign and Arab Investment Code of 1974 (Guwaida 1976c, p. 105).

For Fawzi and Sadat it was the advent of Soviet-US détente in 1972 that gave impetus to a policy of political and diplomatic *ouverture*, yet, as mentioned, it was a door that had to be opened stealthily. Détente foreclosed some opportunities for Egypt while opening up others. It implied that countries like Egypt that had been able to exploit superpower rivalries to their material advantage would no longer be able to do so. With specific regard to Egypt it looked as though the USSR, in order to avoid confrontation with the US, would not help Egypt liberate the Sinai from Israeli occupation. The opportunity it bore was in the form of precedent: the Soviet Union and China, like Yugoslavia before them, could do business with the West without selling their souls. It would be unreasonable to deny Egypt the same opportunity.

The various threads of this line of reasoning were first pulled together in a political document issued by a joint committee from the ASU and the

---

[1] Egypt broke relations with the US in June 1967 after which Washington was represented by an interests section of the Spanish embassy.

parliament in August 1973 and known as the Dialogue Paper (*warqat al-hiwar*). The relevant passages are:

> The policy of global détente between the superpowers has led the US to be more daring in its military, political, and economic support of Israel, and more open in its enmity toward the Arabs in its denial of the legitimate rights of the Palestinian people and the UN Charter. Its disregard for world public opinion is aimed at blocking all paths to a just political settlement.
>
> The policy of détente has weakened the UN in that many agreements and settlements have been reached outside its confines. In conformity with this trend, the USA has begun to endeavor to remove the Middle Eastern case from the UN framework in an effort to monopolize this arena for itself and to strengthen its grip on the Arab world.
>
> The Middle East problem has become part of the strategy of the two superpowers. In light of this situation the Soviet Union, in accordance with the policy of global détente and [its] shared interests, is committed to prior review with the US in several instances, for example in easing restrictions on the emigration of Soviet Jews.
>
> *Our reliance upon external forces, no matter how determined we are to nurture our relations with them, has become in the context of global détente, less effective and of reduced scope.* [ASU 1973; emphasis added.]

But the drafters of the Dialogue Paper misjudged the logic of the directions Sadat had cautiously selected. The Paper went on to declare: "We must cherish and protect the friendship of our friends, especially that of the Soviet Union, by placing these friendships in their true and frank context." Further, the Paper urged greater reliance upon Arab resources, both military and economic; the strengthening of the eastern front with Israel; diversification of sources of arms; more effective utilization of Third World arenas, such as the Non-Aligned which was to meet in Algiers in September 1973; and an economic open-door policy to attract Arab capital and Western technology. The tone of the Paper suggested a period of revitalization of the Egyptian economy and military, of steadfastness (*sumud*) in the conflict with Israel, and continued estrangement from, if not confrontation with, the United States.

Gamal al-'Utaifi, deputy speaker of the People's Assembly and frequent contributor to *al-Ahram* and the now-defunct *al-Tali'a* on matters of national and foreign policy, produced several articles in the summer of 1973 which developed the basic points of the Dialogue Paper. His tone, however, was somewhat different. He notes ('Utaifi 1973c, pp. 38-50) that in the official US-Soviet Declaration of May 29, 1972, following Nixon's visit to Moscow, both sides pledged not to maneuver for advantage at the other's expense. At the same time, al-'Utaifi pointed out, after Brezhnev's return visit, it became apparent that the two powers had not reached any detailed understanding on how to settle the Middle East conflict, other than in endorsing UN Resolution 242 and calling for a "peaceful" solution.

But al-'Utaifi was relatively sanguine about Egypt's ability to maneuver in this arena. While acknowledging that the military equilibrium between the two superpowers would render disruptions of regional security anywhere in the world extremely difficult, he nonetheless saw factors at work in the opposite direction. He alluded to the strengthening of the Afro-Asian bloc, the Non-Aligned (prematurely citing the success of Allende's Chile), and "the strengthening of moral force in the world." All these factors strengthen the hand of the developing nations in their dealings with the great powers. Moreover, the emerging world energy crisis, alluded to in Nixon's address to Congress on May 3, 1973, gave the Arabs special leverage in their dealings with the industrialized West. In essence, al-'Utaifi suggested that Egypt could continue as in the past to use both superpowers to its advantage.

In other articles al-'Utaifi took up the implications of *infitah*. For example, in "Are Foreign Investments Compatible with Socialism?" (*A*, August 16, 1973), he justified Egypt's new course by likening it to the experiences of other socialist countries, beginning with Lenin's New Economic Policy and continuing through the investment codes of Yugoslavia in 1966 and Rumania in 1972. If these countries could benefit from foreign investment, why not Egypt? The Egyptian left had an answer: that Egypt was dealing with foreign capital from a position of weakness, and that its leaders might lack the will to protect the socialist sector. Abu Saif Yussef criticized 'Utaifi and the Dialogue Paper for making erroneous comparisons with the NEP. There is a great difference, he noted, between changing "socialist" legislation to grant ownership rights to foreign capital and the Soviet Union's practice of public sector units contracting with foreign capital to carry out projects in strict conformity with the Plan (Abu Saif Yussef 1973, pp. 51-71). The caviling came too late to deflect a policy process already in train. The principal economic expert associated with *infitah* was 'Abd al-'Aziz Higazi, promoted from minister of finance to deputy prime minister for the economy in March 1973. The term *infitah* was first given official blessing in Higazi's presentation of the government's economic program to parliament, April 21, 1973, and was subsequently amplified through interviews with relevant officials and the exegesis of various pundits. In an interview with Faruq Guwaida, Higazi envisioned the future wedding of Arab capital and Western technology, and he justifiably later took credit for the first and only *major* project of this nature, the Suez-Mediterranean Pipeline (Sumed). At the same time, there was in his mind no special policy to be adopted toward the US, no special role to be reserved for the West in the context of *infitah*. All he was prepared to advocate was greater equilibrium in Egypt's trade between socialist and capitalist countries (*A*, July 19, 1973):

> We cannot deny the role played by the agreement countries in Egypt's economic growth, especially that of the Eastern Bloc countries which advanced us long-term credit at a time when the West refused to advance us anything. No Egyptian can deny the results achieved as a result of technical and economic cooperation with the Eastern Bloc, led by the USSR. There are the giant projects such as the High Dam and the Iron and Steel Complex, etc., which are undoubtedly the foundation of the Egyptian economy. However, our foreign trade in the next phase must be redistributed. 50 percent of our imports are from agreement countries while they take 70 percent of our exports. This has created a disequilibrium in our foreign trade balance with other countries. This in turn requires a broader *infitah* to the world so that we can put our foreign trade on a footing that achieves the greatest economies possible.

In sum, détente dictated new policies, but Egyptian policy-makers in 1973 saw these in terms of continued cooperation with the USSR, increased solidarity with the Arabs with a view toward confrontation with Israel and toward external finance, a search for arms and markets in the European West, and continued alienation from the US. Sadat, we now know, had other scenarios in mind. The conclusion he drew from détente was that 1) the post-1967 Arab-Israeli situation had been "frozen" in favor of Israel, and the USSR would do nothing to unfreeze it; 2) that the US "held all the cards" in the dispute, and that only American action could break the stalemate. But American action needed a catalyst, hence the October War. Moreover, Sadat could not really accept the notion of *sumud* as the economic situation worsened. There could be little expectation of foreign investment, Arab or otherwise, as long as war lay on the horizon. In one of those masterstrokes of which he was occasionally capable, Sadat went to war in October 1973 in order to cooperate with the US and to make his country safe for *infitah*. A year after the hostilities, he conceded the link between Egypt's economic situation and the war, while admitting that the pay-off had been meagre.

> So that I can give you an idea of what the opening is all about, I must go back to the fourth of Ramadan of last year [October 1, 1973], six days before the battle. I invited to this same house in which we are now seated the members of the National Security Council consisting of the vice-president, the presidential assistants, the prime minister and deputy prime ministers, the minister of defense, the director of military intelligence, the national security advisor, and the minister of supply . . . and I laid before them the situation and asked them to advance their own

127

opinions. . . . We debated for a long time. There were some who advocated fighting, and others who said we were not ready. . . . At the end I said that I wanted to tell them one thing only, that as of that day we had reached the "zero stage" economically (*marhalat al-sifr*) in every sense of the term. What this meant in concrete terms was that I could not have paid a penny toward our debt installments falling due on January 1 [1974]; nor could I have brought a grain of wheat in 1974. There wouldn't have been bread for the people, that's the least one can say. . . . But as soon as the battle of October 6 was over, our Arab brethren came to our aid with $500 million . . . and this sum would never have come had we not taken effective action as regards the battle. But despite these dollars, we are now in the same situation we were in a year ago, perhaps worse. [Sadat, *al-Usbu' al-'Arabi*, October 9, 1974.]

Thereafter it was necesary to provide foreign and Arab investors the positive, legal incentives that would lure them to Egypt.

Economic Objectives and the Legal Framework

A fair amount has been written about the legal framework of foreign investment in Egypt,[2] and there is no need to go over it in any great detail here. Until 1971 foreign investment was regulated by a series of laws issued between 1952 and 1954. In important respects these laws represented a backing away from more restrictive regulations formulated by nationalist governments in the waning years of the monarchy. For instance, Law 120, issued on July 29, 1952, just a week after the RCC took power, waived the stipulation of a 1947 law that foreign investors could own no more than 49 percent of a private Egyptian company's equity. The major legislative landmark, however, was Law 156 of 1953, applicable to foreign investment, granting tax holidays for foreign investors and the right to repatriate up to 10 percent of gross earnings each year. This latter clause was modified in 1954 to allow repatriation of all earnings. Again in 1953, Law 66 did away with the requirement that companies engaged in mineral exploration be of Egyptian nationality. The Companies Law (26) of 1954, applying to all joint stock companies regardless of nationality, consolidated these disparate pieces of legislation.

This sort of wooing of foreign capital is compatible with the view that assigns the RCC the role of representative and arbiter of the interests of an

[2] Salacuse and Parnall 1978, pp. 759-77; Salacuse 1975, pp. 647-60 and 1980, pp. 315-33; Ahmad al-Shalaqani 1975 unpub.; *AI*, no. 593, May 1, 1980; Stephen and Hayek, eds. 1974; Egypt-US Business Council 1976. Although the Egyptian Investment Authority has printed English versions of the basic investment legislation, I have relied upon the Arabic originals and English translation of Law 43 published as a supplement to *AI*, September 1, 1974; and Law 32 of 1977, Arabic version only, published as a supplement to *AI*, February 1, 1978.

industrial bourgeoisie unable to master the process of accumulation requisite for its own advancement (see Chapter One). The measures were inspired by the PCDNP upon which there was substantial private sector representation and whose mandate (Law 213, 1952) charged it to "benefit from Egyptian and foreign capital in economic development projects without preference to one or the other" (*AI*, no. 593, May 1, 1980, p. 14). Whatever the intent of the regime, the legislation failed to attract much foreign investment, and, in any event, after the nationalization of the Suez Canal, Nasser did not care. In fact, he probably never did care, and merely tolerated the efforts of the PCDNP as he was preoccupied with establishing his regime politically, and wresting power from General Naguib.

From 1956 to 1971 little effort was made to attract foreign capital. 'Aziz Sidqi insisted to me that he would have welcomed foreign private investment had it come on terms acceptable to Egypt or had it been competitive with Soviet assistance. There were no ideological blinders in use, he said, and went on to point out the successful conclusion of exploration agreements in the 1960s with a few Western oil companies, notably Mobil. The product-sharing formula favored by Egypt skirted the question of equity ownership. Oil companies contracted with the public sector Egyptian Petroleum Company to carry out exploration at their own expense and risk in a defined area. If no oil were found, the foreign company absorbed the loss. If oil were discovered, the foreign company received crude sufficient to cover its initial exploration expenses, after which the production of the wells was split between the Egyptian Petroleum Company and the foreign partner. In the 1960s, the split was generally 60/40, although since 1973 it has become 80/20.

Product-sharing in the petroleum sector, hotel management contracts in tourism (Hilton), licensed pharmaceutical production within the public sector (Swisspharma, Ciba, Pfizer, etc.), and provision of Fiat assembly kits for Nasr Automotive constituted the major manifestations of multinational involvement in Egypt's socialist economy of the 1960s.

Whatever Sidqi's disclaimers, the 1962 Charter could hardly be considered welcoming. As a general principle it stipulated: "All heavy and intermediate industries and most mining operations must be within the framework of public ownership; and if private ownership is permissible within this sector, it must be under the guidance of the public sector, the property of the people . . ." While untied foreign aid and credits are cited as the most desirable form of external resources, there is "acceptance of foreign investment in those instances where there is no alternative and in those domains requiring advanced scientific expertise . . ." (as cited in Waterbury 1978a, pp. 214-15).

The first legislative step toward the open-door policy came with Law 65 of 1971 for foreign investment. The new code provided for a five-year corporate tax grace period, the establishment of free zones, and stated that joint ventures between foreign investors and public sector units would be considered autonomous. A foreign investment authority was established under the direction of 'Abdullah Marziban. In its own right this clarion call was too uncertain to attract much notice, but coming as it did during a year that Sadat warned would be "decisive" in Egypt's struggle with Israel, Law 65 was stillborn.

Between 1971 and June 1974, when it was superseded by Law 43, 250 projects with a total value of £E 171 million were submitted for approval within the terms of Law 65. Of these some fifty projects were approved with a value on paper of £E 13 million. By 1974 not a single project had actually started up. Nonetheless Egypt adopted other measures to signal its intent. In 1971 the Egyptian International Bank for Trade and Development was chartered and put under the chairmanship of 'Abd al-Mun'aim al-Qaissuni. The bank hoped to attract Arab petrodollars for investment in Egypt. In October of the same year Egypt signed the IBRD international accord for the settlement and arbitration of foreign investment disputes, a token of the country's earnest in adhering to Western norms in the handling of foreign capital.

A general consensus developed within the first Sadat government that the industrial sector needed technological overhauling, and foreign exchange shortages had to be addressed. For Higazi the objective was to wed Western technology and management to Arab capital and Egyptian resources. The test case was the Suez-Mediterranean Pipeline (Sumed), a project under consideration since 1968. With the Israelis on the east bank of the canal and the waterway closed to shipping, Egyptians proposed to recoup some of their transit trade by building a 210-mile oil pipeline from the Red Sea to a point on the Mediterranean just west of Alexandria. Its initial capacity was to be 80 million tons per annum rising eventually to 120 million tons.

'Aziz Sidqi and his protégé in the Ministry of Petroleum, 'Ali Wali, took the lead in seeking funding from a consortium of European banks. This was not forthcoming on terms acceptable to Egypt, and the project appeared to founder. 'Abd al-'Aziz Higazi revived it by lobbying with the Arab states of the Peninsula for support. Eventually, in December 1973, he engineered the SUMED Pipeline Company, capitalized at $400 million, with the Egyptian Petroleum Company taking up $120 million in local currency and $80 million through a Chase Manhattan Bank loan. Saudi Arabia put up $60 million, Kuwait $60 million, Abu Dhabi $60 million, and Qatar $20 million in hard currency. The construction contract was initially awarded the Bechtel Corporation of San Francisco, but it lost its bid to Italian parastatals (Montubi-SAP, SNAM-Progretti, Saipen) in 1974 as the dollar revalued in world markets. Still, the sought-after triangular deal had been achieved and on no small scale. Ironically it was the first and, at the time of writing, last such deal of any scale—and it came under neither Law 65 of 1971 nor Law 43 of 1974.

The October War of 1973 created a more congenial atmosphere, so the Egyptians hoped, for luring in foreign capital. It also prompted the issuance in March 1974 of the president's *October Paper* in which he let it be known that a new era, the Sadat era, had been born and that he had come out from under the shadow of Nasser. The *October Paper* stated the need for resolute steps toward *infitah*. The Paper was submitted in its entirety to national referendum and overwhelmingly approved. Sadat could then claim a popular mandate to pursue *infitah*. With the passage by Parliament of Law 43 for Arab and Foreign Investment in Egypt in June 1974, the legal underpinning for the open-door policy was in place.

I shall single out here only the most important provisions of Law 43. Potentially the most important clause in the law is that any project approved within its terms is automatically considered part of the private sector even if the Egyptian partner is a public sector firm with a majority share of the equity. It will become evident further on what this portends for the public sector. At a minimum it means that all private investment projects are not subject to the labor laws, stipulations of worker representation on management boards, profit-sharing formulae, and salary ceilings applied to the public sector.

Law 43 sets priorities for investment. These include projects that will be self-sufficient in foreign exchange and that will promote Egyptian exports; projects that bring in advanced technology and management techniques; projects that substitute for imports, and projects that enhance Egypt's strategic position. At the same time Law 43 represents a major easing of certain preexisting priorities. No sector of the economy is ruled off limits, as had been the case after 1962. Foreign investors can take majority interests in firms in basic metals, minerals, chemicals, and textiles that had been reserved for the public sector. Most important Law 43 put an end to the public sector monopoly of banking. Within a few years of its issuance there was talk of allowing foreign investors to move into the domain of public utilities and transportation services. Finally, and public protestations notwithstanding, there would be no real effort made to see that Law 43 projects conformed to the Plan. Indeed, there was no Plan.

The law created an Investment Authority, within the Ministry of Economy, that was to screen all investment applications and then obtain the approval of all other relevant governmental agencies for those projects initially selected. The Board of Directors of the Authority, grouping representatives of several ministries, would meet regularly to grant final approval to proposed investments, passing them on for the president's signature.

Approved projects fall either into the in-country category or the free-zone category. These latter were aimed at creating extraterritorial enclaves on the South Korean model geared to export. The zones, set up in Cairo, Alexandria, Port Said, and elsewhere, are not subject to Egyptian taxes, but pay an annual

1 percent levy on the value of all goods moving through them. Capital transfers can be made without restriction between the free zones and all foreign countries. Free-zone enterprises may sell to the Egyptian market subject to normal customs duties. Conversely, free-zone and in-country projects purchase raw materials at world market rather than the subsidized prices prevailing in Egypt.

In-country projects are entitled, on a discretionary basis, to tax exemptions of five to eight years after starting operations and to the duty-free import of equipment and raw materials needed for production. Initially it was stipulated that companies could freely repatriate earnings only within the limits of their own foreign exchange holdings: hence a premium was placed on projects self-sufficient in foreign exchange.

Before moving on to consideration of the application of Law 43, two other facets need mention. First, Arab investment is considered different from all other sources of funding and is granted special privileges, such as the right to acquire urban real estate and housing. This distinction reflected the ongoing determination of Egypt's policy-makers to attract Arab petrodollars. Second, Law 43 provided for the establishment of private commercial banks. Those dealing in Egyptian currency were required to have 51 percent Egyptian ownership, although it was not clear if this 51 percent was to be taken up by public sector banks or could be partially subscribed by private Egyptians.

For reasons that will be spelled out in greater detail below, Law 43 did not elicit the response among foreign investors its authors had anticipated. By the end of 1976 sixty-six projects had begun operations under Law 43. They were capitalized at £E 36 million and had 3,450 employees (*FT*, August 1, 1977).

In February of 1977 a workshop was held to consider revisions of Law 43, bringing together over one hundred businessmen, lawyers, and government officials. The recommendations emanating from the workshop led to the issuance of Law 32 in June of the same year, which introduced important modifications to Law 43. Of these, the three most important addressed obstacles that had held foreign investors at bay for three years. Law 43 had required that foreign currency invested in a project be transferred through an Egyptian bank at the official exchange rate. It then went on to say that repatriated earnings and proceeds from the liquidation of a project would be valued "at the exchange rate prevailing at the time of transfer." The specter this raised was that, as seemed all too likely, the pound might be devalued between the time of initial investment and the time of repatriation of earnings. Law 32 laid it down that all capital transfers would take place at "the highest rate prevailing," that is the so-called incentive rate that is periodically adjusted by the Central Bank.

Most investors have wanted to take advantage of Egypt's large domestic market and were put off by the unofficial requirement that their projects be self-sufficient in foreign exchange. Law 32 did away with this constraint by interpreting claims of import substitution as liberally as possible and waiving the stipulation that such projects be in "basic" industries. Finally, as some of Egypt's foreign exchange constraints eased, Law 32 made it possible for foreign investors to purchase foreign exchange with local currency, to sell products locally for foreign exchange, and to purchase hard currency in the "parallel money market" that had first been set up to help the Egyptian private sector meet its foreign exchange needs.

Egyptian Objectives

At the beginning of this chapter I indicated the broad concerns that prompted Sadat to endorse the open-door policy. These concerns changed with time and the new configurations in the Arab world itself (inter alia al-Tali'a, 1974: 10:14-59. The October War led to a great outpouring of Arab bilateral aid for Egypt, and some private investment. Rapprochement with the United States opened the prospect of US private investment in Egypt, and the preoccupation of oil-dependent EEC nations with their balance of payments after 1973 rendered the triangular formula all the more attractive.

Thus an initial objective of easing Egypt's balance of payments problems through foreign investment gradually receded. More emphasis was placed on revitalizing the public sector through competition with foreign projects or through joint ventures with them; on developing new export capacity; on establishing Cairo as a major regional money market, especially as Beirut burned; and on resuscitating the private sector.

The export factor became particularly important in the mid-1970s. As Egypt emerged from the hiatus of the seven lean years, 1967-1974, the ISI strategy was in shambles. Further, several LDCs had demonstrated the merits of export-led growth, South Korea and Taiwan foremost among them. This growth path was forcefully backed by the IMF and the IBRD. Egypt's planners also adopted this line. In general they felt there was no alternative. Essam Montasser, in charge of long-range planning in the Ministry of Planning, offered some sobering estimates in 1976 (E. Montasser 1976). He calculated that if per capita income were to quadruple by the year 2000, total exports would have to grow from £E 560 million in 1975 to £E 12 billion at the end of the century. *Industrial* exports would have to increase twenty-nine times over from £E 206 million in 1975 to £E 6 billion in the year 2000. Montasser's projections were for the most part incorporated in the Draft Five-Year Plan of 1976, and came at a time of intense negotiations with the IMF.

The challenge that Egypt had never been able to meet was to open markets for its manufactures in Europe and the Arab world where its exports would not be bartered, as was the case with the USSR and Eastern Europe, but would earn foreign exchange. It was hoped that *infitah* would attract MNCs whose technology and renown would guarantee foreign markets for brand names marked "Made in Egypt." The new imperative was reflected in the exhortation of an Egyptian parliamentarian during the debates on Law 43 who cried "Like Japan, we must export or die!" With less bombast it was taken up by Gamal Nazir, later to be head of the Investment Authority, when he outlined the similarities between the Egyptian and Japanese worker (discipline, loyalty, hard work) and Egyptian and Japanese productive units. With outside assistance and reduced government interference Egypt, he believed, could replicate Japanese successes (Nazir 1975).

Much, of course, hinged on maintaining and consolidating peace in the region, and Sadat may have thought that that would be more easily achieved than in fact was the case. Sadat had made himself valuable to the West after 1973 by demonstrating his willingness to deal with the Israelis and by his good will toward major regional oil exporters, Iran and Saudi Arabia, that had always been targets of Nasser's wrath. Sadat, as always and not unreasonably, assumed that in return for the geopolitical advantages he offered the West, he could expect financial support, including the encouragement of foreign private investment. In other words, Egypt was a good investment in its own right with substantial nonfinancial dividends for its benefactors. When Richard Nixon visited Cairo in June 1974 the official joint communiqué talked of $2 billion in investment projects under serious consideration.

Nonetheless, by 1977 peace was not at hand, and most of the Sinai remained occupied. In November Sadat went to Jerusalem and a little over a year later signed the Camp David accords. For one pundit, at least, he thereby changed the complexion of the open-door policy. The talk of close economic cooperation between Egypt and Israel was seen as a ploy to prompt Israel to mobilize Jewish capital for Egypt "not so much to refloat the Egyptian economy as to guaranty the security of the Jewish state. . . . The Egyptian economy must be organically linked to that of Israel to such an extent that never again will there be any question of war" (Sid Ahmed 1978). Whether or not this was Sadat's vision is moot, as the Israeli-Egyptian negotiations foundered for reasons having little to do with their economies.

Internal Debate

It should come as no surprise that the open-door policy was greeted with misgivings and hostility in several quarters, but especially among those associated with the public sector and, in general, those on the left. Sadat, after all, was careful not to make an open assault on socialism per se, but only upon the distortions that had crept into its application in Egypt. Nor could he be seen as refurbishing the tarnished image of international capitalism that had justifiably been saddled with the blame for retarding Egypt's development throughout the first half of the century. Conversely, the Egyptian left could not openly accuse the president of selling out the socialist experiment or of willingly falling captive to neo-imperialist interests. Sadat insisted that the revolution could not be undone and that it could deal with foreign capital from a position of strength, and the left insisted it was not against foreign investment per se so long as it neither threatened the public sector nor did violence to priorities laid down by the Plan.

The artillery of the left was puny. It consisted mainly in a handful of Marxist or Nasserist parliamentarians,[3] staunchly assisted by the unaffiliated Dr. Mahmud al-Qadi, an M.P. since 1957, familiarly known as "Doctor No." On specific issues they were joined by Gamal al-'Utaifi, a gifted legal mind and deputy speaker of parliament. Outside the legislature the critics of the open-door could snipe at Law 43 in the pages of *al-Tali'a, Ruz al-Yussef*, and *al-Katib*. In many ways those that were the most vocal in their opposition were the least puissant, while those in a position to undermine the open-door, the public sector managerial corps, chose extrapolitical, bureaucratic channels to defend their sinecures.[4] The labor unions, so thoroughly coopted under Nasser, for the most part remained quiescent. The only warning labor issued came in a declaration of the General Confederation of Public Sector Labor, drawn up at a meeting in February 1974 (*al-Tali'a*, 5/74:113-14). The Confederation warned that any return to a situation in which labor was ground between imperialism and local capital would be refused. Further, if public sector profits were in any way allowed to accrue to private individuals, that would contravene all the basic documents of the revolution and the rights of the workers.

The debates of Law 43 in June 1974 took place in two stages. Gamal al-'Utaifi presided over a special, enlarged parliamentary committee including members from the Committees on Legislation, Economy, Budget and Plan, and Labor. The argument for Law 43 was presented to this committee by Sharif Lutfi. It reported out the draft law to the full parliament where the subsequent debate was led by 'Abd al-'Aziz Higazi (ARE: Maglis al-Sha'ab 1974).

Much of the debate revolved around the implications of the open-door policy for the ownership of vital assets. In committee Ahmad Taha stated his

[3] On the left were Ahmad Taha, a Marxist labor leader from Cairo's Shubra district, Khalid Muhi al-Din, an original member of the RCC, and Abu Saif Yussef of *al-Talia*. From the Nasserists and center left were Kamal Ahmad, Mumtaz Nassar, Qubari 'Abdullah, Hassan 'Arfa, Mahmud Zainhum, and 'Abd al-Salam al-Zayyat.

[4] Some representative critiques are Mutwali 1973c; 'Abd al-Mughani Sa'id 1974; Hussain 1975; Mursi 1976.

fears that areas reserved to the public sector by the 1962 Charter would be invaded. Al-'Utaifi summed up the spirit of the Law as follows:

> The text of the Charter states that the majority [of basic industries] must be within the framework of public ownership for the people. This does not preclude a project, in mining for example, in which private capital is invested along with public. *So long as the majority of projects remain under public ownership there is no contradiction with the principles of the Charter* [emphasis added].

Although I think al-'Utaifi was sincere in his interpretation, what we see here is the first breach in the dikes against the penetration of foreign capital into strategic sectors. 'Abd al-'Aziz Higazi hinted at the elasticity of the principles underlying Law 43:

> When we speak of the framework of public ownership we mean that the majority or the bulk of it is under the control of Egyptians. . . . I believe that the principle of public ownership is fully protected . . . as long as 51 percent is in trustworthy, nonexploitative hands.

In response to a question from Mahmud al-Qadi, whether or not a foreign investor could set up an electric power company or tram line in Cairo, Higazi replied in the affirmative. At one point in the debate Sharif Lutfi appealed to critics to trust the Council of Ministers to protect vital public sector interests, citing specifically the textile sector. As we shall see below with respect to the al-'Amiria project, within four years of passage of Law 43 no sector was sacrosanct.

The question of foreign banks proved to be the lightning rod of the debates. If public sector banks lost their monopoly of public and private deposits to private sector banks linked to the giants of the Western financial world, Egypt could revert to a situation where major credit policies and investment decisions were made in the bank board rooms of New York, London, or Zurich. There were basically three positions on this issue: 1) there should be no joint-venture banks authorized to handle local currency deposits; 2) joint-venture banks accepting local currency deposits must have 51 percent ownership by public sector banks (Gamal al-'Utaifi); 3) joint-venture banks accepting local currency deposits should have 51 percent *Egyptian* ownership regardless of the public/private mix (Sharif Lutfi).

Ahmad Taha put the matter bluntly. If there were 49 percent foreign ownership, 49 percent public and 2 percent private Egyptian "it would be possible for the 2 percent Egyptian private subscribers to combine with the foreign subscribers to dominate the Egyptian economy." Defenders of Sharif Lutfi's position queried whether or not Taha and others doubted the patriotic motives of the private sector. To which the critics protested their faith in the private sector but wondered what might happen if the private sector subscribers ''inadvertently'' failed to show up for a board meeting—unfortunate decisions might be made. In the event, Law 43 simply stated that joint-venture banks operating in the local currency must have Egyptian ownership of not less than 51 percent. Western bankers read this to mean that *eventually* the Egyptian private sector could take an equity position in such banks, and that the public sector could find itself in a minority position.

One other disputed point is worth some elaboration here: the potential role of foreign investors in agriculture. Here some voices on the left advocated positions that can only be qualified as petty bourgeois while the government happily found itself defending public ownership. Most of the debate focused on the several hundred thousand *feddans* reclaimed from the desert after 1954. Little of this acreage was producing, and the state was paying large sums of money into the reclaimed areas for maintenance and improvement. An easy way out, so it seemed, would be to *lease* this land (there was never any question of ownership) to foreign agribusinesses that could use it to produce export crops or to supply their own processing operations elsewhere. Their capital resources, advanced technology, and market knowledge would make profitable for them what was a dead loss for Egypt.

Dr. No, as usual, was opposed. He argued that Law 100 of 1964, that limited private reclamation efforts to twenty *feddans* per family, should be repealed so that the Egyptian private sector could try to make a profit in the desert. Sharif Lutfi countered by referring to a project under consideration with an American firm. It would start with 33,000 *feddans* and expand within a decade to 270,000. It would involve cultivation of several commercial crops combined with animal breeding and raising. The total investment, Lutfi said, would be £E 270 million.[5] How could small-scale private cultivators contemplate anything of this size?

But the left would not give up on this point. Abu Saif Yussef, in the full parliamentary debate, contended that giant leasing operations would be in violation of the Charter in which it was stated that the two goals of agrarian reform were broadening the base of ownership and distributing reclaimed land to the landless. ''Thus,'' he concluded, ''the formation of companies operating on thousands of *feddans* will violate the rights of poor peasants to the land of their country.'' It might be noted that there is no record of Yussef having protested the creation of the 10,000 *feddan* Soviet mechanized farm in the late Sixties, an undertaking that was supposed to serve as a model for the rest of the reclaimed areas.

This time it was 'Abd al-'Aziz Higazi who replied, asking Abu Saif Yussef

[5] The project had been put together by FMC and several important Egyptians had a stake in it. Yet it eventually was dropped as it became clear that FMC saw it mainly as a means to sell agricultural equipment to Egypt.

if he would favor breaking up the citrus orchards of South Tahrir district into holdings of three to five *feddans*. Is it not more reasonable, he queried, to keep this land within the framework of public ownership in order to promote the twin goals of industrial food-processing and exports?

These rear-guard actions were insufficient to impede progress toward enactment. Still, the industrial public sector indicated that it would not be easily moved. In a document put together before the debates, but released after them, the Ministry of Industry and the General Organization for Industrialization (GOFI) looked ahead to 1982. Their plans made no mention whatsoever of possible joint ventures, foreign investment, or even Egyptian private sector investment in industry.[6]

Selling Off the Public Sector

Law 43 was passed with very few amendments. Once it came into effect, the right gained heart, and in a general onslaught on the Nasserist legacy began an offensive against the public sector and socialism. A former civilian minister of trade and industry, Saba Habashi, set the tone (*A*, April 28, 1974). The declared object of the July decrees, he wrote, was to dissolve the differences among classes. In fact all that they dissolved were national savings.

A favorite target of the right, by name or innuendo, was 'Aziz Sidqi. A former Wafdist newspaper editor, Ahmad Abul Fath, exiled under Nasser, returned to Egypt in the mid-seventies. He called for the abolition of all laws impeding the Egyptian private sector and the trial of all those who had committed crimes at the expense of the people (*A*, April 17, 1975). After parliamentary elections in November 1976, 'Alawi Hafiz, newly elected from a district in Cairo, accused Sidqi by name of mismanagement, falsification of records, corruption, rigging of elections, and of having been bought by Fiat (*A*, December 30, 1976). Sidqi replied (*RY*, no. 2536, January 17, 1977), demanding that he be put on trial to see if these allegations had any substance to them.

These were but pyrotechnics on the surface of more far-reaching moves against the public sector. As early as 1973 various Egyptians began to call for the liquidation of failing public sector enterprises. Foremost among them was Fu'ad Sultan, who had worked with the IMF in North Yemen and who went on to head the Egyptian-Iranian Investment Bank set up in 1974. He also advocated revision of labor laws so that public sector companies could rid themselves of unwanted labor (*AI*, no. 429, July 1, 1973; and no. 432,

[6] ARE: Ministry of Industry and GOFI 1974. The program of National Action was Sadat's first major policy pronouncement, delivered July 23, 1971 to the ASU. In fairness to the Ministry of Industry this speech made no reference whatsoever to foreign investment or the open-door policy.

August 15, 1973). The call was picked up by M.P.s Mustapha Kamal Murad and Abu Isma'il, head of the Budget and Plan Committee. The latter, on the strength of his investigation of public sector losses, recommended that 49 percent of all equity in public sector firms be put up for private subscription.

Predictably this recommendation raised a general hue and cry. When Presidential Decree 262 of 1975 was issued, authorizing such share subscriptions, all the worst fears of the defenders of the public sector appeared confirmed. 'Abd al-Salam al-Zayyat, who had defended Sadat in his moment of need in May 1971 (see Chapter Fourteen), attacked the decree as unconstitutional, as did Lutfi al-Kholi in *al-Tali'a* (June 1975). The apprehensions of the left were accentuated with the passage of Law 111 on July 28, 1975, after only one day of debate in parliament, abolishing the General Organizations. This seemed a device to cast loose all public sector companies to determine which were intrinsically solvent. The weak would be sold off or liquidated; the strong would be put up for general share subscriptions. Moreover, it was widely noted that under Law 111 companies were given much greater latitude in handling their labor force. They could sack unneeded labor after paying a severance fee equivalent to 60 percent of the last six months' wages, and they would not be obliged to take on personnel assigned to them by the Ministry of Labor and Human Resources (Mursi 1976, p. 174). These measures, in combination with the provision of Law 43 that all joint ventures between public sector companies and foreign investors would be legally within the private sector, convinced many observers that the public sector would be dissolved.

It had appeared to me in 1975-76 (Waterbury 1978a, pp. 275-301) that this conviction was ill-founded. As mentioned in the previous chapter, the public sector was extremely important as a source of savings and as an instrument of labor control. In addition it was an important source of business for Egypt's private sector, a factor to be explored in the next chapter. Consequently it was relatively easy to inventory powerful constituencies that had no stake in the liquidation of the public sector (public sector labor and management, Ministries of Finance and Plan, important segments of the private sector) and difficult to locate its enemies. My guess was that it would be allowed to go its uncertain, inefficient, and overprotected way as long as it fulfilled its control functions. A dynamic enclave economy, founded on foreign investment, would be allowed to grow up beside it, but integration between the two would be minimal.

This scenario has not been invalidated, but in the late 1970s one could discern a new dynamic. The erosion of the public sector may ultimately be far more profound than I would have suspected. The reasons are at least threefold. First, the pressure of foreign investors, bankers, and counselors from the IBRD and IMF has been persistent and unattuned to the political ramifications of "streamlining" the public sector. Second, some elements of public sector management itself have found that they can prosper from joint ventures and have become active promoters of such arrangements. Their zeal is reciprocated by foreign investors who have found that there is access to decision-makers, reliability, and a scale of operations characteristic of the public sector that the Egyptian private sector cannot match. Finally, the embryo of a new entrepreneurial class in Egypt is taking shape, and it looks to the foreign investment sector more than the public sector for its source of business, contracts, and commissions.

That said, let us look at the record of the public sector in the open-door era since the promulgation of Decree 262 and Law 111 of 1975. The process of generating capital expansion of public sector enterprises through share offerings has proved very difficult. Gamal al-'Utaifi identified the dilemma early on: why should successful companies bother to bring private capital into their operations; why would the private sector want to invest in losing ventures? Despite the Presidential Decree there was a very real fear that a public subscription might fizzle due to lack of private sector interest. So careful preparation was requisite if the authorities were not to be embarrassed.

One set of parastatals looked like natural candidates for partial or total privatization: the hotels, department stores, and other consumer service enterprises that had fallen under public ownership since 1961. However, nothing to date has been done about them. Beginning in 1976 the Ministry of Industry came up with a list of sixteen industrial companies, that, during the proposed (but never implemented) Five-Year Plan (1976-1980), would expand their capital by selling shares worth £E 50 million.[7] It was not until 1978 that such capital expansion was actually budgeted, although the list of companies had been changed and reduced (*AI*, no. 558, November 15, 1978). But it was just a question of time before the process was put in train.[8] It was a function to no small degree of the reorganization and rebirth of the Egyptian stock exchange, moribund since 1961, and itself a highly complex operation. Pending that, not much could be done, although some companies under Law 43 were selling shares for foreign exchange.

In a private study prepared by Ford Foundation experts for the Ministry of Economy, a set of specific proposals was made on how best to engineer the share offerings. The crux of the recommendations was that private Egyptian

[7] The list included nine textile plants, two food-processing companies, the Rakta Paper Co., National Cement Co., Egyptian Chemical Co., Nasr Transformer Co., General Ceramics Co.

[8] It had been proposed since 1976 that workers in public sector companies be given options to buy stock issues. If they did not exercise their options, the remaining shares, after six months, would be open for public subscription. Nabil Sabbagh of *al-Ahram al-Iqtisadi* repeatedly attacked this proposal, saying that *existing* private sector shareholders in parastatals should have first option on all new share offerings.

investors primarily valued net dividend income after taxes. For new issues to be attractive they should have a dividend yield of 8 to 10 percent. In turn such yields could be attained by several companies, *if* their mandatory allocations due the state (see Table 6.4) were reduced by 60 percent and made available for distribution to private shareholders. The ceiling on the value of shares held by any one shareholder, in effect since 1961, should be repealed. The report identified ten companies that were financially sound enough to offer the desired yield.[9] The implications of this proposal are clear: the state must be willing to surrender its control over a significant portion of public sector savings in order to promote the partial privatization of public assets.

Once Taha Zaki had returned to the Ministry of Industry, he prepared his own project for the expansion of public sector capital through "citizen participation" (*AI*, no. 612, October 6, 1980). It would, if enacted, abolish clauses in Law 60 of 1971 and Law 111 of 1975 forbidding the public sector to diminish its share in any state enterprise, although not below 51 percent. All new ventures resulting from public share subscriptions would henceforth be considered part of the private sector. As such they would not be subject to compulsory hiring of graduates, salary ceilings for management, compulsory profits distribution, and the requirement to represent labor on management boards. The most unusual proposal, however, was to fix the rate of return on private investment at 1 percent above the interest rate prevailing on commercial bank deposits. As Nabil Sabbagh pointed out, this would make shares more like bond holdings and totally at variance with conventional capitalist participation, the return on which varies with profits and losses (*AI*, no. 614, October 20, 1980). Zaki's proposal can be fairly seen as a counter to 'Abd al-Magid's project for the NIB.

No one was very happy with the draft law: the private sector felt it did not go far enough in separating management from ownership (the state would remain majority owner) and in giving full discretion to management to fire redundant labor. The General Confederation of Labor was hostile to the project because it undermined labor's acquired rights to profits and representation (*AI*, no. 615, October 27, 1980; and *AI*, no. 618, November 7, 1980). Despite these various objections, it is likely that privatization of larger segments of the public sector will be pursued through capital expansion. It may be that the new National Investment Bank will be a prime instrument in financing such expansion.

To date, however, joint ventures with foreign investors are leading to the greatest shift of assets from the public to the private sector. Because all parastatals, except for the petroleum companies, are starved for foreign ex-

[9] Paints and Chemicals Co., Egyptian Electric Cables, Misr/Shabin al-Kum, Nasr Bottling, National Plastic, Delta Industrial (IDEAL), Bisco Misr, Alexandria Confectionary, Alexandria Oil and Soap, Egyptian Starch and Glucose.

change, they have tended to offer their existing plant and real estate as equity in joint ventures. The new joint ventures formed in the private sector overshadow their public sector partners in capital concentration and level of technology. They tend also to siphon off the best public sector managers and workers because there are no legal constraints on salaries.

Joint ventures in manufacturing have been difficult to negotiate, so that the process here described is only in its inception. Yet it is legitimate to speculate how it will develop. One example is the Nasr Tire Company, a small producer of a limited range of overpriced tires for the Egyptian market. Michelin and Goodyear have competed with each other to establish a joint venture with Nasr Tire which would have a large export component and access to the local market. Eventually the local market was split between them, but while the Nasr Tire Company survived de jure it was swallowed up de facto. Similarly, Nasr Automotive is negotiating with Fiat for expansion of private automobile manufacture, Calabrese for trucks, Ford for truck engines, and Caterpillar for tractors. IDEAL Company, which manufactured 125,000 refrigerators in 1978, contemplated a joint venture with Thompson Company of France to turn out 500,000 refrigerators annually.

By the end of 1978 the Investment Authority had approved 134 projects with public sector participation. The value of public sector investment in projects underway or planned was £E 440 million of a total of £E 1.66 billion. Two years later, at the end of 1980, of total approved investments of £E 3.1 billion, the public sector share was 30 percent or £E 920 million. This investment has mainly taken the form of fixed assets (Handoussa 1980; AI, no. 635, March 16, 1981).

The most striking development in recent years is that aid-granting bodies such as the IBRD are actively promoting this process. The World Bank approved a $50 million loan to Egypt to modernize its paper and pulp industry, if Rakta Paper Company and the National Paper Company enter into joint ventures under Law 43 with foreign companies that will handle the rehabilitation program. The IBRD felt this necessary so that the new companies could benefit from tax and customs exemptions, avoidance of mandatory surplus allocations, and public sector labor legislation (Sabbagh 1979; and MEED, May 30, 1980). Equally remarkable is that the Investment Authority, in August 1979, agreed to transfer a public sector company, the Abu Qir Fertilizer and Chemical Company (founded in 1976) to the private sector upon a request from the annual meeting of its shareholders. They had voted for this change in order to assure a decent return on the investment of its founders, to escape state-determined fertilizer prices, and to avoid mandatory surplus allocations (AI, no. 576, August 15, 1979). In sum, the legal arrangements and some precedents necessary for the liquidation of the public sector are in place, and there is increasing evidence that they will be used.

Table 7.1

Public Sector Investment in Open-Door Projects

(Cumulative approved investment 1974-1979)

Sector	No. of Projects	Public sector investment £E millions	Share of public sector in total investment
Investment cos.	17	65	35%
Banks	16	49	36
Tourism	17	42	11.5
Housing	6	83	38.4
Transportation/communications	2	2	8.7
Health and hospitals	2	11	31.5
Agriculture, animal husbandry	11	51	48.5
Contracting	11	4	15.6
Educational training, services	2	1	.6
Spinning and weaving	2	41	38.9
Food processing	8	8	30.8
Chemicals	7	8	9.8
Wood industries	2	2	16.8
Engineering	14	29	33.6
Building materials	7	43	50.0
Metallurgy	3	2	6.6
Pharmaceutical	2	1	12.8
Mining	3	2	46.5
Petroleum	2	1	22.1
Total	134	445	

SOURCE: *AI*, no. 571, June 1, 1979.

There is little clear evidence of the effects of the open-door policy upon organized labor. By the end of 1978 there were only 13,553 workers employed in some 191 functioning projects. Their average wage was £E 836 per annum, which is a little less than twice the average public sector industrial wage (Muhammed Ali Rifa'at 1980). The potential employment of Egyptians in in-country projects that had been approved up to mid-1979 was 139,000, or about 2.2 percent of the total nonagricultural work force. In her survey of 107 public industrial companies, Heba Handoussa (1980) found that their work force actually declined by 2.6 percent in 1978. She advances no explanation of this phenomenon, and one wonders if it could be accounted for by reclassification of public sector partners to joint ventures in the private sector.

For some years labor was relatively quiescent in the face of *infitah*. Workers involved in potential joint ventures occasionally used their unions to try to block them. Such was the case with the proposed Wilkinson Sword Blade venture that actually was approved. It led to the liquidation of Egypt's existing razor blade factory, so the workers claimed, and the flooding of the Egyptian market with imported blades (*RY*, no. 2739, December 8, 1980). Similarly, workers in the General Battery Company protested a proposed joint venture with the Chloride Battery Company of England, which involved their company and left a 67 percent interest to the foreign partner (*AI*, no. 617, November 10, 1980). The general drift toward privatization, both through Law 43 and the proposed subscription of public sector shares by local private capital, has called into question the "revolutionary gains" of the 1960s. The erosion of these gains has spread to the public sector itself. For example, the *Conseil d'Etat* issued a legal writ (*fatwa* 882 of 1976) stating that worker represent-atives or management as stipulated in the constitution need not be elected and could be appointed. Appointment is now the practice in public sector banks and probably will be extended to other sectors (*AI*, no. 595, June 9, 1980).

The Evolution of the Open-Door Policy

> We have been clearly aware at times that the Egyp-
> tians have great difficulty dealing with our concepts of
> return on equity and are lacking in sufficient business
> experience to recognize a fair deal when one might
> by struck.
> [Egypt-US Business Council 1976, p. 61.]

There was no stampede on the part of foreign investors to take advantage of Law 43, and, as we have seen, Law 32 of 1977 was drafted to meet some of their reservations. Others, however, could not be dealt with by legislation. The very complicated and time-consuming authorization procedure, the in-creasing willingness of well-placed Egyptians to accept payoffs for greasing the rails, the inadequacy of the staff of the Investment Authority and frequent changes in its leadership,[10] and the surliness of vested public sector interests frustrated investors and the proponents of *infitah* alike.

Sometimes the only way to get action was to complain to the president,

---

[10] Between 1974 and 1980 the head of the Authority changed frequently. Sharif Lutfi left it to become a financial advisor to the government of Oman. Tahar Amin, former head of GOFI, left the Authority to head up the Saudi-financed Arab Investment Co. Zaki Shafa'i left it to become minister of economy. 'Abd al-Razzaq 'Abd al-Magid left it to become minister of planning. Gamal Nazir was moved out to become minister of tourism and civil aviation.

and his own exasperation soon became evident. On April 15, 1975, he dismissed Higazi as prime minister, and denounced bureaucratic foot-dragging in applying open-door policies. Higazi was replaced with the minister of interior, Mamduh Salim, who, it was believed, would deal with the situation as only a professional policeman could.[11]

Mamduh Salim (A, April 24, 1975) made it clear early on that nothing would stand in the way of foreign investment:

> Every condition is a restriction, and every restriction is incomprehensible. The thing is to let the investor direct himself to his natural place according to his own freedom of action and the dictates of the needs of the Egyptian market. . . . Anything that leads to an increase in production and self-sufficiency—or prosperity—we must accept and not refuse. We must welcome all Arab and foreign capital that finds its way to investment in Egypt.

The advent of the Salim government coincided with the laborious but successful negotiations of the second Egypt-Israeli disengagement agreement in September 1975. That event, in the view of the Minister of Economy Zaki Shafa'i, was determinant in setting the proper regional atmosphere for *infitah* (A, May 14, 1976).

Still, very little happened. By the end of 1976 the value of approved projects totaled £E 735 million, and the share of US investors in them was only £E 24 million (AI, no. 519, April 1, 1977). There was also a wide gap between approval of a project, which commits the investor to nothing, and the actual disbursement of funds. Many investors were merely trying the water, and the cost of a feasibility study and prospectus could be written off. By the end of 1977, of 482 approved projects, 110 had their authorization withdrawn because there was no followup on the part of the investor (Ibrahim 'Amr, AI, no. 544, April 15, 1978).

Equally disturbing to the Egyptians was the fact that both approved and functioning projects tended to cluster in three areas that had little to do with direct production: investment companies, banks, and tourism. At the end of 1977, 32 percent of all investment in projects underway or under implementation was taken up by these three categories (*MEED*, April 1978, p. 121). What Egypt wanted was a big, visible joint venture in manufacturing with a well-known MNC. When 'Abd al-Razzaq 'Abd al-Magid was head of the Investment Authority, he took draconian measures to accelerate Egypt's quest. On March 27, 1977, a day now notorious in the annals of the open-door

---

[11] Higazi had been consistently thwarted in his tenure as prime minister by three "superministers" who refused to report to him and dealt only with the president. They were Isma'il Fahmi, minister of foreign affairs; Ahmad Osman, minister of housing and reconstruction; and Mamduh Salim, minister of interior. The first two were active in promoting open-door deals.

policy, the Investment Authority approved 102 projects in five hours, including joint ventures with Union Carbide, Ford, Goodyear, Michelin, and Xerox (Mahmud Maraghi, *RY*, no. 2629, October 30, 1978).

With this kind of official encouragement and the issuance of Law 32 in June of the same year, the investment climate improved markedly. Table 7.2 shows in detail the distribution and value of approved projects as of September 1979. In-country projects alone were capitalized at £E 2.1 billion with projected investment outlays of £E 3.9 billion. Within fifteen months new approvals had raised these totals to £E 3.1 billion and £E 5.7 billion respectively. In general, service and finance projects accounted for about half of the projected capitalization with a third going to banks and investment companies. Two-thirds of this capital was to be raised locally. At the end of 1980 there were 352 open-door projects actually underway. Table 7.3 clearly shows the continued bias toward investment in nonproductive sectors.

It should be noted that none of these figures include petroleum product-sharing accords. These do not come under Law 43 nor do they involve foreign equity ownership, but they do involve sums of money that have grown prodigiously. Between 1973, when the Ministry of Petroleum was founded, and 1980, seventy-nine agreements were concluded with $1.42 billion committed to exploration and $144 million in signature bonuses (*FT*, July 23, 1980). These investments, taken together with the equivalent of $15 billion in projected capital and investment costs for approved open-door projects, leave little doubt that *infitah* could substantially change the face of the Egyptian economy.

The scope of what is afoot has come to alarm even some of the staunchest proponents of *infitah*. There is a feeling that there is so much money around, and so many projects approved, that development strategy has been cast to the winds and a scramble among well-placed Egyptians to get in on the action has begun (cf. *AI*, no. 601, July 21, 1980).

I want to examine in the remainder of this chapter some specific problems and projects that have drawn widespread public comment and aroused public fears. The most sensitive issue, although in some ways the least visible, has been that of foreign banks.

Some supporters of *infitah* had envisioned Cairo as superseding Beirut as the Arab world's regional money market and financial clearinghouse. What they tended to overlook was the fact that foreign banks in Beirut were only minimally interested in business and investment in Lebanon, while Egypt, no matter how impoverished, offered a vast market for investment and merchant banking. It became clear after 1974 that no major international bank would pass up the opportunity to do business in Egypt. The pioneers were Chase, Citibank, Bank of America, American Express, and Barclays, but literally dozens followed in their wake. By 1981, sixty-two banks had been

Table 7.2
Approved In-Country Projects by Sector, Cumulative to September 30, 1979
(£E millions)

	No.	Capital			Investment Outlays			Labor		
		Local	Foreign	Total	Local	Foreign	Total	Foreign	Local	Total
Banks and investment companies	139	235,363	344,649	580,012	235,363	373,304	608,617	163	2,643	2,806
Tourism	100	192,974	204,864	397,838	258,869	448,007	706,876	315	13,442	13,757
Housing	42	59,100	100,267	159,367	82,471	145,293	227,764	—	701	701
Transportation, health, other services	49	22,218	176,664	198,882	25,954	248,592	274,546	944	6,710	7,654
Agriculture	36	59,561	52,240	111,801	118,817	146,118	264,935	74	8,774	8,848
Contracting	61	16,502	32,583	49,085	22,327	60,970	83,297	236	13,163	13,399
Textiles	38	66,530	49,014	115,544	182,750	427,878	610,628	145	45,929	46,074
Other industries	263	230,036	265,678	495,714	402,851	723,608	1,126,459	474	46,208	46,682
Total	728	882,284	1,225,959	2,108,243	1,329,402	2,573,770	3,903,172	2,351	137,570	139,921

SOURCE: AI, no. 583, December 1, 1979, p. 14. Figures do not include private and public free-zone projects. At the end of 1980 there were 331 approved free-zone projects, capitalized at £E 420 million with projected investment costs of £E 1.3 billion (AI, no. 635, March 16, 1981).

Table 7.3
Distribution of Capital by Sector and Source in Law 43
Projects Underway as of December 31, 1980

	Gross Capital (£E 1000)	Egyptian %	Arab %	US %	Other %
Services and finance	634,412	68	19	2	11
Agriculture and construction	92,426	72	12	.4	15.6
Industry	175,497	56	25	6	13
Total	902,335	65	19	3	13

SOURCE: *AI*, no. 635, March 16, 1981.

authorized and forty had begun operating in Egypt. Thirteen had entered into joint ventures with public sector banks and were therefore authorized to handle local currency accounts. The remainder were "off-shore" banks, permitted to deal only in foreign exchange but able to make loans or to invest locally. The banks were joined by 129 investment companies, authorized as of December 1980, and of which 47 had gotten underway (*AI*, no. 636, March 23, 1981). For all intents and purposes the open-door policy in its first four or five years amounted to nothing more than a scramble among foreign banks and investment firms for a foothold in Egypt.

It was to be expected that public sector bank managers would feel threatened by the invasion, although many of them had been active in private banking prior to 1960. 'Ali al-Gritli, who had worked with Credit Foncier prior to the revolution and then in the 1970s for the Arab-African Bank, strongly doubted the need to involve giant Western banks in Egypt's development. He argued that joint Egyptian ventures with Arab banks would be able to borrow abroad without difficulty (Gritli 1977, p. 275).

As private sector banking under Law 43 got underway, the real bone of contention became the privileges extended to the new banks that were denied public sector banks. The latter were constrained by statutorily low salaries and fixed, noncompetitive interest rates. 'Abd al-Mun'aim al-Qaissuni, who had helped implement the nationalization of the banks fifteen years earlier, evoked the past he had helped bury in a speech in 1976 (*AI*, no. 494, March 15, 1976): "When, I wonder, shall we see the illustrious Bank Misr, and our other Egyptian banks, active once again, seeking Egyptian capital participation in executing projects for which they will have priority over all other investors?"

A first step in this direction was the ending in 1975 of the specialization of public sector banks. Thenceforth they became full service banks. They were granted some greater flexibility in adjusting interest rates and competing for foreign exchange held by Egyptians, but, for the most part, they remained the conduits for public sector savings and financing.

Off-shore and joint-venture banks have gradually acquired greater room for maneuver. Law 97 of 1976 granted these banks the right to have foreign exchange accounts held by Egyptians, and such accounts could be freely transferred abroad. This law gave the private sector banks direct access to the savings of Egyptian migrant workers, and residents abroad. On April 1, 1978 the condition that all joint-venture banks place 20 percent of their reserves in noninterest-bearing deposits in the Central Bank was waived (*FT*, July 31, 1978).

In 1977 and 1978 the Central Bank published reports on the banking sector that tended to demonstrate that Law 43 ventures had done very little by way of local investment. Instead, they had attracted foreign exchange deposits held by Egyptians and then transferred these holdings to accounts in parent banks abroad. 'Abd al-Mun'aim Rushdi, chairman of the Ahali Bank, stated flatly that the foreign banks were not doing their job (*RY*, no. 2597, March 20, 1978). A report of the Central Auditing Agency showed that these banks had invested £E 560 million in local projects. This sum represented about 42 percent of their total deposits, with most of the rest being held with correspondent banks abroad (*AI*, no. 628, January 26, 1981).

After five years of the application of Law 43, public sector banks, in terms of the volume of deposits and investments, still held center stage: they held 81 percent of £E 5.9 billion in deposits and 83 percent of all credits. Included in these figures are the ''specialized'' public banks: the Agricultural Credit Bank, Development Industrial Bank, and the Mortgage Bank, in addition to the four full service public sector banks.

It can therefore be said that foreign banks have not come to dominate the direction of investment in Egypt as some had feared. However, they have gotten a strong hold on foreign exchange accounts; £E 816 million of total holdings of £E 2.05 billion. This is to be compared with their local currency deposits of £E 284 million of a total of £E 3.9 billion (*A*, June 14, 1980). The explanation lies in interest rate variance where the gap between the public and foreign private sector is generally on the order of 7 to 10 percent. For example, at one point in 1980 foreign exchange accounts in Law 43 banks were earning 19 percent, when the legal ceiling on public sector bank accounts was 9 percent. Moreover, foreign exchange depositers in the private banks could borrow local currency against these accounts at only 7 percent interest from public sector banks. Consequently the major negative effect of Law 43 banks has been to deprive the public sector banks of a good deal of foreign exchange savings of Egyptians abroad, and to place this money abroad rather than invest it locally. But public sector banks, with £E 1.2 billion in foreign exchange deposits, drawn mainly from remittances, have also tended to place these holdings abroad (Bawwab 1980).

In the summer of 1981, as high interest rates in the US drove up the value of the dollar in international markets, the Egyptian treasury found itself unable to defend the pound. The gap between the official and the black-market rates widened alarmingly, and 'Abd al-Magid was forced to devalue from sixty-nine to eighty piastres to the US dollar. This move was followed by an inflationary surge commensurate with the rise in the import bill. The weakening of the pound drove 'Abd al-Magid to curb the freedom with which Law 43 banks could transfer their holdings abroad to take advantage of high interest rates. Similarly, he sought to force worker remittances through the official banking system to prevent private merchants from buying these earnings at premium and then holding them abroad. But if Cairo truly aspires to become the Middle East's banking center, it may have to forego a good deal of control over foreign currency movements.

Some open-door ventures have evoked what might best be called "the rape of Egypt" reaction. This reaction is rooted in fact, and there are many well-placed Egyptians all too willing to enter into contracts with foreign investors with attention only to rapid profits, licit or otherwise. Before outlining two particularly notorious examples, I want to indicate some of the ways in which "exploitative" behavior has been called to public attention.

One type of complaint has arisen out of tariff policies that, after 1974, have been skewed in favor of Egyptian importers (a new and dynamic breed to be discussed in the next chapter) and foreign investors. Imported luxury foods, cigarettes, and ready-made clothing have driven local private producers out of business and left public sector producers with growing inventories. Decree 1058 of 1975 allowed unrestricted importation of textiles and apparel, subject to duty. Asian textiles flooded the Egyptian market, and at the end of 1978 public sector companies were holding unsold inventories of £E 129 million (Khamis al-Bakri, *AI*, no. 543, April 1, 1978; *AI*, no. 573, July 1, 1979). Law 32 of 1977 allowed for the importation with 50 percent reduction in duties of free-zone products, the components of which are 40 percent or more Egyptian-supplied. Frequently duty-free import privileges for foreign investors are abused: tourist projects are allowed to bring in equipment duty-free and this has led to heavy traffic in imported refrigerators, air conditioners, furniture, and kitchen equipment sold in the local market.

A second order of alleged abuse has come in the conditions demanded by foreign partners in joint ventures. Predictably the latter have sought monopoly sales rights in the local market. For example, Ford requested such rights with respect to a proposed truck assembly (*AI*, no. 583, December 1, 1979), and

Michelin and Goodyear have been allowed to split the Egyptian market, each one to monopolize sales of a particular kind of tire. A foreign investor may try to underwrite sales from the parent company. This is the gambit played by the French Thompson Company in its joint venture with IDEAL Company of Egypt. The French side insisted on importing compressors from France for 500,000 locally manufactured refrigerators while the Egyptians want to make the compressors locally. Over and above that issue was the French partner's insistence on placing five out of nine members on the board of directors and its valuation of the assets of the Egyptian partner. 'Abd al-Razzaq 'Abd al-Magid, deputy prime minister for economic affairs in 1980, denounced the deal (*MEED*, July 4, 1980, p. 3): "[It] was a sell-out. They valued the whole factory at £E 1.2 million while the land alone was worth £E 12 million."

The two *causes célèbres* of *infitah* have been the Pyramids land deal and the al-'Amiria synthetic fiber complex. The first, in the nature of its objectives, is representative of the run of projects under Law 43 in its first five years. The second, in its scale and production goals, could be a harbinger of what Egypt will see in a second phase.

In September 1975 a joint venture was approved between the newly formed Egyptian Company for the Development of Tourism and the Southern Pacific Properties Company (SPP), registered in Hong Kong. Part of the deal consisted in leasing to the joint-venture company 10,000 acres of desert land at concessional rates for ninety-nine years. SPP proposed to develop this land into a giant tourist complex, on the order of Disneyland, along with a residential development project destined for Egyptian purchasers.

Because the acreage involved is still presumably loaded with undiscovered Pharaonic artifacts and tombs, archaeologists who had been excavating the area were alarmed at the destruction and loss that would take place as a result of the project. One archaeologist, Dr. Ni'amit Fu'ad, single-handedly publicized the dangers in the Egyptian press and eventually brought about the cancellation of the deal (Fu'ad 1978).

Her protestations triggered a parliamentary investigation of the project, a special report of the Lawyers Guild, and a newspaper crusade. The Lawyers Guild, never known as a hotbed of radical protest, declared the project a "national disaster," and asserted Egypt's economic and political sovereignty in the face of foreign multinationals, "the most recent form of neo-imperialism" (*RY*, no. 2608, June 5, 1978).

The various investigations uncovered details of the project that indicate the kinds of actors and motives that may often combine in promoting an investment. The Egyptian partner was a public company created by the Ministry of Tourism, an active promoter of joint ventures of dubious utility such as Kentucky Fried Chicken and Wimpy's. The Ministry was one of the better known conduits for licit and illicit open-door deals.[12] The foreign partner, SPP, was scarcely a giant. It had been founded by a Canadian businessman, Peter Munk, who had left Canada because of his shady business practices. Once in Hong Kong he attracted some powerful investors: Adnan Khoshoggi's Tri-Ad Corporation, held 29 percent of SPP's shares while Saudi Princes Nawaf ibn'Abd al-'Aziz and Fawaz held 25 percent (Roger Matthews, *FT*, May 30-31, 1978). The Saudis in turn had considerable influence in Egypt.

Munk's approach was unoriginal but profitable. SPP put up equity capital worth $500,000, while Egypt's equity consisted in 10,000 acres. By 1977 SPP had sold, without improvements, lots covering 500 acres, and received $1.7 million and £E 1.2 million in payment from Egyptian purchasers. Many purchasers were members of the Egyptian elite, looking for second residences and a good investment. So, for an investment of half a million dollars, Munk got about $4 million back, and there were still thousands of acres left. Eventually the project was supposed to yield villas and hotels for tourists, an eighteen-hole golf course, an artificial lake, and a residential city for Egyptians. The whole package would have been worth $500 million and it is evident that key people were promised a material stake in its successful outcome.

Dr. Fu'ad's counterattack compared Peter Munk to a new de Lesseps and the ninety-nine-year lease to that of the Suez Canal Company. The historical analogy was telling, and informed public opinion was aroused. When, in the spring of 1978, the parliamentary investigatory committee found the project in violation of parts of Law 43, aesthetically disastrous, and potentially destructive of Egypt's historical heritage, President Sadat annulled its authorization.

In most respects the al-'Amiria textile and synthetic fiber complex is a far more formidable undertaking than the Pyramids venture. The project was energetically promoted by Misr Bank and its President Ahmad Fu'ad. The foreign partners in the project were to be Chemtex of the USA and the Misr-Iran Textile Company (MIRTEX).

The statistical shape of the project is as follows:

location:	on undeveloped land near Alexandria
production:	115,000 tons yarn
	400 million meters fabric
	100 million meters knitwear
	53,000 tons polyester
work force:	37,000
total value:	$1.3 billion

[12] When Gamal Nazir took over the ministry in the spring of 1980 he promptly sacked some seventy of its most senior staff.

The project was one of those rushed through on March 27, 1977 in the mass authorization engineered by the head of the Investment Authority, 'Abd al-Magid. A little over a year later he and Ahmad Fu'ad were the project's main defenders, but they were nearly alone.

For the first time public sector interests openly expressed their opposition to a joint venture, and the attack was launched on several fronts. The major adversary was the General Organization for Industrialization (GOFI), watch-dog of the Ministry of Industry, whose case was put by Ibrahim Shirkiss, its deputy chairman (*AI*, no. 558, November 15, 1978).[13] His arguments were supported by a diverse set of allies, including the Federation of Egyptian Industries (private sector), the IBRD, and yet another parliamentary committee of inquest.

The basic charge was that the Bank Misr's feasibility study substantially overestimated Egyptian domestic demand for textiles and made totally un-realistic assumptions about the project's exports. Consequently it posed a grave threat to existing public sector firms on several counts. It would compete directly for a market it overestimated;[14] it would impede for that reason the planned expansion of public sector production; it had no clear idea of where it would export its production, which would probably be dumped on the domestic market but would in any event compete with public sector exports; the project would inevitably raid the public textile companies for its managers and 37,000 workers. GOFI's case was given considerable credibility when the IBRD suspended its offer of credits to finance the expansion of the National Spinning Company because of the approval of the al-'Amiria complex.

The matter did not stop there. Bank Misr was accused of playing fast and loose with its cost calculations. It calculated the value of imported equipment at the official, overvalued exchange rate while it valued local cotton purchases up to 1.5 million *qantars* per annum at the subsidized price enjoyed by public sector firms; Law 43 forbade the extension of such privileges to foreign investors. Thus the real costs of the project were seriously underestimated, a fact that made its proposed debt to equity ratio of 6 to 1 all the more alarming. Bank Misr set capitalization at £E 70 million with the remaining £E 460 million to be raised on international capital markets. Indeed, when the scandal broke in 1979, the bank had already contracted for loans worth

[13] Besides Shirkiss's case, see "The Battle of 'Amiria in the Parliament," *AI*, no. 564, February 2, 1979; M.P. Dr. Shamil Abaza, "After the Pyramids scandal the 'Amiria scandal," *AI*, no. 561, January 1, 1979; "The IBRD refuses financing because of 'Amiria" *RY*, no. 2621, September 11, 1978; "These are the ones who grabbed 'Amiria commissions" *RY*, no. 2636, December 18, 1978.

[14] In 1977 public sector production amounted to 670 million meters and private sector to 405 million. Planned expansion of existing capacity would easily meet projected domestic demand in 1982 of ca. 1.3 million meters. Al-'Amiria's production of 400 million meters would simply flood the market.

$248 million. Finally the bank assumed that the state would finance the very considerable infrastructural investments in roads, railroads, utilities, schools, and medical facilities that would be required by the complex.

With the smell of such large amounts of money wafting about, it was inevitable that charges of profiteering would be leveled at people involved. Egyptian middlemen acting as agents for textile equipment suppliers in Switzerland and Germany were said to have received commissions ranging from hundreds of thousands to over one million pounds. Similarly Chemtex contracted with Bank Misr to supply equipment worth $58 million; the same equipment had been offered a year earlier to a public sector firm (Egyptian Synthetic Silk Company) for $38 million. *Ruz al-Yussef*, which ran the story (no. 2636, December 18, 1978) all but accused bank officials of having split the difference with the American partner.

Unlike the Pyramids project, the hue and cry about al-'Amiria did not bring about its downfall. As its shortcomings became known, the Supreme Investment Committee suspended its authorization on August 16, 1978. This was followed by an investigation carried out by a special parliamentary committee that published its report in February 1979. It was somewhat Delphic in its pronouncements, acknowledging the validity of many of the charges leveled against the project but coming down in favor of it nonetheless. The report suggested that the feasibility study be revised, that Bank Misr look more closely at the problem of financing, that public sector textile companies be brought into the venture, and that they in turn pay greater attention to overhauling and improving their own production. Eventually it appeared that only the polyester production unit would be retained from the original project (*FT*, July 23, 1980 and *AI*, no. 620, December 1, 1980).

Conclusion

Neither the Pyramids nor the al-'Amiria projects have been presented here to suggest that they are typical of what is or might be the course of foreign investment in Egypt. Rather they demonstrate the flux and confusion inherent in *infitah*. All attempts to define and insist upon priorities in foreign investment have been pretty much abandoned, although the Egyptian authorities do bargain hard over the terms of proposed investments. Still, a premium is placed on the numbers of projects, their aggregate capitalization, and their gross worth. These aggregates are advertised as evidence of Western confidence in the Egyptian economy.

The lack of strategy toward private investment merely reflects the lack of comprehensive planning for all sectors. The constant elaboration of plans since 1966 has gone hand in hand with their constant revision, postponement and nonimplementation. It may be that with the creation of the National

Investment Bank, there will be some attempt to devise a medium-term plan for the public sector, but I suspect the foreign, joint-venture, and private sectors will be left to go their own way. There is also the danger that an institution so closely identified with one man, as the NIB is with 'Abd al-Razzaq 'Abd al-Magid, will rise or fall with his fortunes, or become the prize in intraelite power struggles. Indeed, the devaluation of summer 1981 dulled his luster, and it was widely believed that he would not long survive the advent of President Mubarak.

Another aspect of flux is the diversity of interests that are at stake in *infitah*. Moreover, these interests are by no means fixed and tend to shift erratically. For example, public sector management has not acted as a lobby in its own defense. Rather individual managers have sought to make their own deals with foreign investors or have left the public sector entirely. Others have dug into their sinecures and prayed that enough lip service be paid to socialism to protect them. A project the size of al-'Amiria—and there have not been any others to equal it—is so laden with promise and threat that alliances do take shape. We saw that the public sector textile companies, the Ministry of Industry, and the Egyptian private textile sector were of one mind in trying to torpedo the project. Yet it was a public sector bank that masterminded the deal, and it became clear that too many Egyptians had a stake in it to allow it to go under. In such circumstances, to exercise real oversight of incoming investments puts the overseer at considerable risk. It is significant that former prime minister Sidqi Sulaiman, who for years headed the Central Auditing Agency, resigned without explanation after the Pyramids and al-'Amiria "scandals."

On the other side of the equation, foreign investors have been tentative in their approach to Egypt. Outside the banking sector, their presence has yet to be felt. If, however, all approved projects are actually implemented, within five years the Law 43 sector could dwarf the public sector in terms of productivity and sophisticated technology. There are major obstacles to such a development. Many joint ventures are premised on access to the domestic market and to Arab markets, especially among the oil-rich. With Egypt's semi-ostracism in the Arab world after the 1979 Camp David accords, access to these markets cannot be assured, and the lure of the Egyptian market may not be sufficient to hold investor's interest. Nonetheless, Egyptian plans, such as they are, anticipate a major influx of foreign private capital, rising by 1983 to £E 465 million or 9 percent of total planned investment (*FT*, July 30, 1979).

In the meantime prospective investors want to minimize their risks by riding the wave of Arab and Western *public* financing that has poured into Egypt since 1974. I shall have a good deal more to say about this in the final section of the book, but I want to stress here that in a manner unequalled in Latin

America, foreign private investment has become a matter of US and Western foreign policy. The US and other Western countries actively encouraged private investment in order to consolidate Egypt's return to the Western camp and to underwrite Sadat's peace effort. There is little doubt that the IBRD has been a tacit ally in this process, as were the conservative oil-rich states prior to the Camp David accords. It has already been noted that the IBRD has made loans to public sector companies contingent on their entering joint ventures under Law 43, and USAID has supplied the foreign exchange component of at least one Law 43 project, the Egyptian Cement Company. In essence foreign investors have sought to limit their equity commitments by taking advantage of abundant public and private financing, or by assigning equity value to their technology and know-how.

There is little point in speculating on the likely scale of foreign investment in Egypt over the next decade. Much will depend on Egypt's relations with its Arab neighbors and upon its balance of payments position. Manufacturers of sophisticated consumer durables, intermediate goods (cement, petrochemicals, etc.) and luxury goods will need Arab markets to justify their scale. Companies selling primarily to the Egyptian market (e.g., soft drinks) will be able to repatriate earnings only so long as Egypt does not relapse into the foreign exchange crises that typified the early 1970s.

While awaiting more dramatic surges in foreign investment, Egyptian policy-makers have realized that one facet of *infitah* requires fairly immediate attention. *Infitah* must rid itself of its speculative, consumerist image, born of the own-exchange system (discussed in the next chapter) and liberalized controls over foreign currency transactions. Soon after Sadat's death, President Mubarak denounced middlemen who exploited the people and called for a productive *infitah*. "There are already enough projects such as soft drinks or luxury goods. What we need are productive projects that will benefit the great bulk of the people. Ready-made clothes, low-cost refrigerators, and all that can be produced to go into the home of the man in the street, I would welcome" (*A*, October 23, 1981). Many people interpreted this as an indirect criticism of Sadat's winking at the fast-and-loose conduct of his associates. It is of course a long way from words to effective action, but the social malaise arising from the consumerist *infitah* has now been officially recognized.

Looking toward the more distant future, it is fairly certain that the Egyptian regime would like to move toward a triple alliance formula of local private, public, and foreign investors that has been fairly successful in Brazil. Only the most efficient public sector enterprises would be allowed to survive. The rest would be broken up or prodded into joint ventures that would transfer them to the private sector. 'Abd al-Magid in 1980 was categoric on this subject (*MEED*, July 4, 1980, p. 3):

Unless the public sector improves itself and its technology through joint ventures with foreign companies it will have no hope of survival. . . . We cannot afford to provide the new technology and the new investment needed for the public sector from the government budget. So each public sector company will have to find a partner to get things done more efficiently.

I suspect that 'Abd al-Magid would not spare either Helwan Iron and Steel or the Nag Hammadi Aluminum Complex from this injunction, and with the NIB will be the instrument by which this philosophy can be imposed. If it survives, the NIB will become the financial heart of a new form of state capitalism in close alliance with multinational corporations and the Egyptian private sector.

Chapter Eight

THE PRIVATE SECTOR: OUT OF THE SHADOWS

The relationship is complicated by the fact that ever since the formation of nation states in Latin America the securing of profit within their oligopolized economies has depended upon privileges and concessions obtained by access to government, so that a "proprietary" rather than an "entrepreneurial" business ethos obtains based on control over a limited market and exclusive licenses instead of mass sales and price competition. This has reduced the ideological antagonism between "public" and "private" sectors observed in developed economies.

[Fitzgerald 1979, p. 35.]

Above all, the implication was that African traders learned to make their profits through monopoly, in some cases adding no value whatever to the goods they handled, or even reducing their value. In the most successful—that is to say, the most thoroughly protected—cases, they could best be regarded as being an extension of the parastatal system, receiving a commission on turnover instead of a salary, a new and politically powerful section of the "auxiliary bougeoisie" to be provided with a share of the national surplus.

[Leys 1975, p. 156.]

Over time the *infitah* wrought profound changes in the symbols of legitimacy that were forged after 1952. Egypt's foreign enemies had been the Western powers, especially as they acted through NATO or through regional ''puppets'' like Saudi Arabia. From 1974 on these actors were portrayed as the providers of advanced technology and capital, interested mainly if not solely in a fair return on their investment. Internally three institutions were implicitly discredited: the armed forces insofar as they assumed any nonmilitary roles; the Arab Socialist Union; and the public sector. I shall deal with the first two in subsequent chapters, but the discrediting of the last produced its dialectic opposite, the rehabilitation of Egypt's private sector.

I have already stressed what I think was Nasser's genuine antipathy for the private sector, save its weakest elements which could not constitute a real political threat to him. These he was prepared to tolerate, but no more. This appreciation of Nasser is contrary to the belief that he was all along the captive of private interests, and that his acts against some of them served merely to resolve certain conflicts within their ranks. To the extent that one adheres to this interpretation, the *infitah* can be seen as the necessary reassertion of private interests in the wake of changes imposed upon them by a bureaucratic-authoritarian regime.

One who argues forcefully along these lines is Fu'ad al-Mursi (1976, cf. Iren Cihat 1975). In his view important elements of the private sector were allowed to prosper under Nasser. However, they were denied profitable outlets for speculative reinvestment and simply accumulated savings. To find such outlets, they brought concerted pressure to bear, and over time, forced the regime to relax "socialist" controls and to open up to the outside world. The two elements of Mursi's hypothesis are irrefutable, but he does not demonstrate any causal relationship between them. His approach, be it noted, feeds into a more general proposition that in many LDCs the public sector serves as the training ground of a new generation of private sector managers at the taxpayers' expense (Ajami 1982). This too seems accurate enough, but it is produced, at least in Egypt, not by design but as a function of the "soft" approach to making the public sector work.

President Sadat moved toward *infitah* with two considerations in mind. First, he wanted to lessen Egypt's dependence upon the Soviet Union, and he saw the surplus oil earnings of some Arab states as the way out. Second, he wanted greater US intervention in the Arab-Israeli stalemate in a manner favorable to the Arabs. He rightly concluded that progress toward both goals would require creating a more hospitable environment for private activity, and a move away from the socialist practices that alienated conservative Arabs and the US Congress alike.

While Sadat manifestly felt uncomfortable with Nasser's socialist experiment, he did not begin to dismantle it under pressure from private Egyptian interests but in light of the logic of Egypt's place in the global arena. Nonetheless, once the process was underway, it stimulated the efflorescence of private interests that may now be on the brink of capturing the experiment and perhaps even the regime.

The Public / Private Balance of Interests

At the beginning of the revolution the private sector contributed over 85 percent of GDP. Twenty years later, after the expulsion or nationalization of most foreign interests and a decade of socialist transformation, its share had declined to 56 percent. That was probably the nadir of the private sector, for in subsequent years the open-door policy stimulated an impressive, albeit uneven, renaissance.[1]

The resiliency of the private sector in the face of official animosity lies in its nominal domination of agriculture. Because nearly all producing acreage in Egypt is in private hands, its contribution to GDP is attributed to the private sector. This is misleading in two respects. Agriculture's contribution is made up of the production of about four million members of the rural work force, the bulk of whom own a *feddan* or less or are landless. Their aggregate economic weight is large but their political weight is practically nonexistent. Second, the indirect controls exercised by the state through cooperatives, agricultural credit banks, compulsory crop deliveries, and administered prices vitiates the reality of private property of much of its substance.

We should also take note of private sector contributions in trade and services. As in agriculture, these categories cover hundreds of thousands of self-employed, tradesmen, peddlers, venders, and the like. Only a small percentage of them, such as butchers, grocers, barbers, food retailers, etc. are able to

Table 8.1

Output from Public and Private Sectors in 1953 and 1973

(£E million, current prices)

	1953			1973		
	Public	Private	Total	Public	Private	Total
Agriculture	—	272.8	272.8	22.3	1,040.1	1,062.4
Industry and electrical	1.4	74.3	75.7	459.5	220.3	679.8
Transportation and communications	16.6	55.0	71.6	132.2	26.4	158.6
Financial services	—	20.8	20.8	49.1	—	49.1
Trade	—	129.4	129.4	105.0	157.3	262.3
Housing	—	57.7	57.7	14.6	109.4	124.0
Construction	—	20.3	20.3	98.1	9.4	107.5
Services	110.0	106.3	216.3	529.0	244.2	773.2
Total	128.0	736.6	864.6	1,409.8	1,807.1	3,216.9

SOURCES: 1953 figures from Patrick O'Brien 1966, p. 154. 1973 figures from *Economic Bulletin*, 15 (1975): 141 and adjusted to conform to O'Brien's entries. I have seen no more recent figures giving total sectoral breakdown by public and private sources.

[1] General sources on the private sector are Mabro and Radwan 1976, pp. 115-29; Hansen and Nashashibi 1975, pp. 203-55; Waterbury 1978a, pp. 275-300; Roy 1978; IBRD, IDF Division, December 1977; Salih 1975; FEI 1976.

rise well beyond subsistence or to employ labor. In 1977, with 1.6 million members, they made up 18 percent of the work force. In most respects these people are as much like potatoes in a sack as Marx's French peasants.

It is only within the construction and industrial categories that one could reasonably expect to find a capitalist lobby that would urge the kind of policies that became identified with *infitah*; and even then there is little evidence that such a lobby existed by the late 1960s and early 1970s *except* among a limited number of Egyptians interested in the import trade. There is evidence that the upper stratum of landowners lobbied for a relaxation of state controls over agricultural prices, crop deliveries, and export trade, but their objectives went no further than that.

Between 1956 and 1961 the expatriate and Egyptian industrial *haute bourgeoisie* was decapitated. Nonetheless, over the period 1961 to 1967, the private sector maintained its share of total industrial production and it increased it thereafter. The number of establishments employing ten to forty-nine workers actually expanded by 32 percent over the same period despite restricted access to credit, foreign exchange, and raw materials. Moreover, after 1958 the Ministry of Industry was empowered to license all new industrial

Table 8.2
Employment (1977)
Distribution between Public and Private Sectors

(In thousands)

Sector	Public	Private	Total
Agriculture	120.0	3,983.5	4,103.5
Industry and mining	747.0	479.6	1,226.6
Petroleum and its products	18.7	—	18.7
Electricity	53.9	—	53.9
Construction	337.0	120.0	457.0
Total Commodity Sector	1,276.6	4,583.1	5,859.7
Transportation and communications	322.0	122.3	444.3
Trade and finance	141.9	908.7	1,050.6
Total Distribution Sector	463.9	1,031.0	1,494.9
Housing	11.4	133.7	145.1
Utilities	54.0	—	54.0
Social development services	1,320.5	844.9	2,165.4
Total Services Sector	1,385.9	978.6	2,364.5
GRAND TOTAL	3,126.4	6,592.7	9,719.1

SOURCE: IBRD, 1978b.

ventures and to authorize all expansion, reduction, or modification in the type and level of production of all industrial enterprises. Throughout the 1960s the Ministry was notably unsympathetic to private endeavor.[2]

Thus with the advent of the open door and more general economic liberalization the private sector accounted for nearly a quarter of total industrial production for sectors under the supervision of the Ministry of Industry (see notes to Table 8.3), its share rising to over 30 percent by the late 1970s. It is important to keep in mind, however, that because certain industries (especially cement and paper) were removed from the Ministry's supervision in 1976, the figures for 1975 and 1978 are not strictly comparable. Nonetheless the private sector has advanced in textiles and chemicals and held steady in food processing. It continues its total domination of woodworking and tanning and leather products, the last accounting for its substantially larger share of total production in 1978.

The figures in Table 8.3 understate the real private sector contribution to industry because they refer only to activities under the Ministry's purview. According to the estimates of the Ministry of Planning the private sector contribution to total industrial production was 37 percent in 1973. They arrive at this estimate by attributing £E 600 million of £E 923 million in food processing to the private sector. They include under this rubric meat preparation and packaging, skins and stomachs, butter, clarified butter (*semna*), cheese, salt fish, *baladi* bread, and nonwheat flours (millet, barley, fenugreek), cracked beans, and lentils. Much of this production is only tenuously industrial, and I would guess that a good deal of it is artisanal or familial. But because the Ministry's are the most detailed estimates I have seen, I present them here in Table 8.4.

Its aggregate productive weight should not lead us to believe that the private sector as a whole is greater than the sum of its parts. These are indeed small and myriad. In the middle 1970s, 93 percent of the total 116,000 private sector firms were artisanal or semi-artisanal, employing fewer than five workers. Half of them employed no workers at all (Mabro and Radwan 1976, p. 119). Some 113,000 businesses operating in 1974 employed 501,000 owners or workers, equal to 80 percent of the entire private sector industrial labor force. The remaining 20 percent were scattered through 3,000 firms employing ten or more workers. Only ten of these firms could be classified as "large-

[2] The Industrial Supervision Department of the Ministry, first set up in 1956, took over licensing in 1958 as well as distribution of state-monopolized raw materials, and foreign exchange and the application of quality controls. The General Organization for Industrialization assumed these tasks in 1973 for all enterprises capitalized at £E 8,000 or more or employing twenty-five or more workers. Projects capitalized at £E 5,000 or less are under the tutelage of the Supreme Committee for the Supervision of Handicrafts and Artisanry. All licensed private industries must be members of the Egyptian Federation of Industries. Membership in 1977 totalled 3,000 firms.

Table 8.3

Contributions of Public and Private Sectors to Gross Industrial Production, 1972-1978*

(£E millions current prices)

	1972				1975				1978†			
	public	private	total	priv./tot.	public	private	total	priv./tot.	public	private	total	priv./tot.
Spinning and weaving	395.9	129.5	525.4	24.6%	503.9	186.3	690.2	26.9%	798.3	299.2	1,097.5	27.2%
Foodstuffs	410.0	108.5	518.5	21.0	548.4	149.6	698.0	21.4	755.9	202.2	958.1	21.1
Chemicals	102.3	32.8	135.1	24.2	207.1	60.3	267.4	22.5	235.0	78.5	313.5	25.0
Engineering	118.6	26.6	145.2	18.3	327.9	57.6	385.5	14.9	569.1	84.7	653.8	12.9
Metallurgy	98.5	6.6	105.1	6.2								
Building materials	49.3	9.2	58.5	15.7	83.8	16.6	100.4	16.5	33.6	26.7	60.3	44.2
Mining	7.1	—	7.1	—								
Woodworking	—	36.0	36.0	100.0	—	39.8	39.8	100.0	—	99.9	99.9	100.0
Leather	—	39.0	39.0	100.0	—	86.6	86.6	100.0	—	248.9	248.9	100.0
Total	1,181.7	388.2	1,569.9	24.8	1,671.1	596.8	2,267.9	26.4	2,391.9	1,040.3	3,432.2	30.3

SOURCES: 1972 figures from *FT*, August 1, 1977, citing Ministry of Industry. 1975 and 1978 from unpublished IMF sources also citing Ministry of Industry.

* Covers only industries under the supervision of the Ministry of Industry. Does not cover national defense production, cotton ginning, flour milling, bakery production, tea packing, printing, pharmaceutical production, iron ore mining, or the production of village industries.

† In the beginning of 1976 the wine and spirits industry was placed under the supervision of the Ministry of Agriculture, the paper industry under the supervision of the Ministry of Information, and the cement industry under the supervision of the Ministry of Housing. Therefore, data on the output of the footstuffs, chemicals, and building materials sectors (in which these industries had been included) after 1976 are not comparable with the earlier figures.

Table 8.4

Public and Private Shares in All Branches of Industrial Production, 1973

(£E millions current prices)

	Public	Private	Total	% Private/Total
Ginning, pressing	206.2	—	206.2	—
Food processing	323.0	600.0	923.0	65.0
Beverages	25.3	3.5	28.8	12.1
Tobacco	190.0	13.0	203.0	6.4
Spinning and weaving	377.0	78.7	455.7	17.2
Clothes and shoes	17.9	101.8	119.7	85.0
Wood, wood products	3.4	36.5	39.9	91.4
Paper and paper products	31.0	.8	31.8	2.5
Printing and publishing	15.2	18.5	33.7	54.8
Leather and leather products	5.5	24.0	29.5	81.3
Rubber and rubber products	14.6	1.3	15.9	8.1
Chemicals	116.3	24.3	140.6	17.2
Coal products	10.2	—	10.2	—
Building materials	54.5	11.1	65.6	16.9
Basic metallic products	105.9	11.9	117.8	10.1
Other metallic products	31.9	21.2	53.1	39.9
Non-electric machines	16.4	3.0	19.4	15.4
Electric machines	43.6	6.0	49.6	12.1
Means of transport	55.6	10.6	66.2	16.0
Miscellaneous	3.8	11.6	15.4	74.3
Total	1,647.3	977.8	2,625.1	37.2

SOURCES: Ministry of Planning figures as cited in Salah 1975. Ministry of Industry figures put total private production in the same year at £E 436 million with the discrepancy accounted for almost entirely by their estimate of private sector food processing at £E 115 million.

scale'' with 500 or more employees.[3] Private sector industrial employment in the same year represented 54 percent of all industrial employment, and 13 percent of the nonagricultural work force. These figures tell us a great deal about the *rapport de force* between private and public sector workers and the strategy of the regime in maintaining discipline within the proletariat. Private sector workers outnumber public but are seldom unionized and in general receive substantially lower wages. While public sector workers are well or-

[3] There is little detailed data regarding levels of capitalization, but 74 percent of the artisanal establishments have fixed assets of less than £E 100 and 97 percent less than £E 1,000 (IBRD, IDF, December 1977, p. 13).

ganized, they are also an economic elite, caught between the job-hunger of the urban poor and the authoritarianism of the regime. *Both* segments of the industrial labor force were outnumbered by Egyptians in uniform (ca. one million in 1972).

Both before and after the July Decrees, the private sector, outside of agriculture, financed its investments largely out of retained profits, although the creation of the Industrial Bank in 1949 did provide an alternate source of financing.

The bulk of private sector investment has always gone into housing with much smaller shares for industry and transportation. Private agriculture has traditionally relied upon the state for investment in basic infrastructure, undertaking itself only the acquisition of farm machinery. Before the revolution total private fixed investment reached £E 122 million in 1950 and tailed off thereafter. Some recovery was registered after 1954 and the promulgation of Law 26 regulating joint stock companies and Law 430 granting five-year tax holidays to all new industrial ventures. Up to the eve of the 1956-57 nationalizations and the first industrial plan, the picture looked like this (Table 8.5). Despite Law 430 very little new private investment found its way to industry (F. H. Awad 1973, p. 49). In 1954 and 1955 private sector investment in industry was only £E 17 million while £E 83 million went into urban housing (Da'ud 1973, p. 69).

Two decades elapsed before any marked resurgence of private investment became manifest. Throughout the 1960s and up to 1976, its share of total investments hovered around 10 percent and began to pick up modestly thereafter. Housing, as usual, has led the way, but industrial investment has grown impressively. Since 1961 the private sector's share in total industrial investment has never exceeded 4 percent. Just prior to the launching of *infitah*, in 1971-72 it stood at only £E 6 million. By 1975 that figure had grown in current prices to £E 31 million, and in 1978 to £E 95 million or 14 percent of total planned industrial investment. However, in the same year the private sector was to undertake £E 140 million in housing investment. In Table 8.6 we have a complete picture of public and private sectoral investment for 1977.

Table 8.5
Public and Private Gross Fixed Investment, 1950-1956

(£E millions)

Investment	1950	1951	1952	1953	1954	1955	1956
Private fixed	122	115	87	70	72	94	72
Public fixed	19	26	28	35	44	57	49
Gross fixed	141	141	115	105	116	151	121

SOURCE: Hansen and Marzouk 1965, p. 321.

Table 8.6

Actual Fixed Investments according to Economic Sectors in Public and Private Enterprises in 1977

(£E millions)

Sector	Public £E	% of Public Investment	% of Total Investment	Private £E	% of Private Investment	% of Total Investment	Total £E	% of Total Investment
Agriculture	122.2	8.6	7.4	16.3	7.5	1.1	138.5	8.5
Industry and mining	449.4	31.9	27.5	63.0	29.1	3.8	512.4	31.3
Petroleum	58.2	4.1	3.5	—	—	—	58.2	3.5
Electricity	99.3	7.0	6.1	—	—	—	99.3	6.1
Contracting	33.9	2.4	2.1	8.2	3.8	.5	42.1	2.6
Total Commodity Sector	763.0	53.7	46.6	87.5	40.4	5.4	850.5	52.0
Transport, communications, and storage	417.6	29.4	25.5	23.0	10.7	1.4	440.6	26.9
Trade and finance	26.9	1.9	1.6	2.0	0.9	.2	28.9	1.8
Total Distribution Sector	444.5	31.3	27.1	25.0	116.0	1.6	469.5	28.7
Housing	59.5	4.2	3.6	102.5	47.3	6.3	162.0	9.9
Utilities	60.6	4.3	3.7	—	—	—	60.6	3.7
Other services	92.2	6.5	5.6	1.5	0.7	.1	93.7	5.7
Total Services Sector	212.3	15.0	12.9	104.0	48.0	6.4	316.3	19.3
GRAND TOTAL	1,419.8	100.0	86.6	216.5	100.0	13.4	1,636.3	100.0

SOURCE: Adapted from IBRD 1977.

The industrial bourgeoisie, centered on the Misr, Abboud, and Delta groups, was, like the landed aristocracy, dismantled. A heteroclite almost faceless private sector was left to make its own way in a system that stacked the deck in favor of public enterprise. After 1974, however, the private sector was given new legitimacy and positive legal and financial incentives. These in turn have created a suitable terrain for a new private sector bourgeoisie.

Encouraging the Private Sector

In the space of two years, between 1966 and 1968, the Nasserist regime grudgingly began to reverse its position on the desirability of private sector activity. It would have been hard for anyone in the private sector to detect the shift, but by 1968 it was real. Moreover, some of the measures adopted at that time derived from the same logic that produced *infitah* six years later. What was most apparent in the year prior to the June War was the public display of radical intent and socialist "deepening"—even as Sidqi Sulaiman's government undertook to apply policies of economic retrenchment and fiscal orthodoxy.

In a speech at Damanhur, in June 1966, Nasser announced that all wholesale trade would be nationalized and transferred to public ownership over a three-year period. Initial measures were to be applied to trade in building materials, chemical and mechanical products, office equipment, food products, and cigarettes. Eventually all semi-wholesale trade was to be taken over, and all retail trade to be split 75/25 between the private and public sectors. Former wholesalers and semi-wholesalers were to become retailers, and, except in villages, they would be obliged to specialize in a single line of products. In addition, the regime drew up legislation to take over private sector trucking (RAU 1968, 130:92; Mutwali 1972; *RY*, no. 2496, April 12, 1976).[4]

Largely as a result of the June War, these measures were never applied. In the case of the truckers they proved unworkable, and one may conjecture that they would have failed in wholesale and retail trade as well. To nationalize or manage the activities of several hundred thousand tradesmen was well beyond the capacity of the Egyptian (or perhaps any other) state. Yet, along with the possibility of lowering the landholding ceiling again, which Nasser in fact did in 1969, this proposed incursion into petty capitalism was the only avenue of socialist deepening left to the regime. On paper at least, the "free" professions were already under public economic control. Journalists all worked for nationalized publications, university professors were on the Ministry of Education's payroll, and lawyers were tethered to business handed out by the

---

[4] According to *RY*, no. 2496, April 12, 1976, "The Adventures of the Merchants," there were 219 wholesalers eligible for nationalization, doing £E 600 million of business in 1966. In 1973 the public sector truck fleet stood at 2,191 and the private sector's at 36,659.

state. Only doctors, through private practices, were in a position to become rich. All were subject to absolute ceilings on total earned income or to public sector salary ceilings.

The regime's failure, whatever its causes, to apply the measures adopted in 1966 marked the beginning of its retreat from socialism. At the same time other measures were adopted that suggested a new strategy. Again in 1966, legislation was prepared to make Port Said a free zone and to attract foreign investment to it. The partial destruction of the city and the evacuation of its population after 1967 left this policy a dead letter until 1973.

The reason that it was adopted in the first place was to take some positive steps to redress the country's foreign exchange imbalance. In the same spirit, but with much more far-reaching consequences, incentives were introduced to encourage private sector exports to the Soviet Union and Eastern Europe. These exports were to figure directly in annual bilateral trade agreements between Egypt and the socialist countries. The latter were already taking as much public sector export as they wanted, and it was hoped that private sector exports could at once help adjust the trade imbalance and act as partial debt servicing to the Eastern bloc (see Chapter Sixteen).

It was crucial to the success of this policy that the private sector have access to the credit, foreign exchange, and raw materials needed to increase its production. For the first time since 1961, the state lent the private sector a helping hand. The bellwether of the new policy lay in the lending practices of the Industrial Bank. In 1966-67 the private sector received only 18 percent of all its £E 4.5 million in loans. In the following year the private sector's share rose to 34 percent and in 1969-70 to 71 percent or £E 5.8 million (F. H. Awad 1973, Table 13; CBE 1969, 3:173).

Little more was done before 1973 to reanimate the private sector. Lack of foreign exchange had always been a major obstacle to its operations, severely limiting its ability to import raw materials and intermediate goods. State monopolies controlled the distribution and pricing of imported and many domestic raw materials (wood, paper, chemicals, dyes, cotton, synthetic fibers and so forth), resulting in chronic shortages, inequitable distribution, and black markets. One cabinetmaker lamented in 1974 (*A*, November 18, 1974): "Two years ago a high-quality bedroom suite cost £E 180, with an honorable profit; today a similar suite of lower quality costs £E 350, with an honorable loss."

In September 1973, the state established a parallel foreign exchange market to bring partial remedy to the situation. To feed this market, the state offered to buy foreign exchange at a premium, or "incentive rate" well above the official rate (e.g., in 1973 sixty piastres to the US dollar rather than the official thirty-nine piastres). In turn private sector firms could apply to buy foreign exchange from the parallel market at slightly higher than the buying rate. If their applications were approved, they were required to pay half the amount they wished to convert and then wait months until their turn came up to draw funds. Throughout, the public sector was able to purchase its foreign exchange at the official overvalued rate.

The foreign exchange resources for the parallel market came essentially from three sources: tourist revenues, savings of Egyptians abroad, and proceeds of nontraditional exports (e.g., anything but cotton, yarn, rice, onions, petroleum, and a few other products). There is no doubt that the market's creators hoped that the incentive rate would be sufficiently attractive to make workers' savings the principal source of foreign exchange. As Table 8.7 shows, that has not been the case. For reasons to be set forth in the next section, other exchange markets, legal and illegal, offered higher rates and drew off most worker remittances. Nonetheless the parallel market provided an important source of import finance. In 1977 the private sector resorted to it to import £E 237 million in various commodities.

The extension of a wide range of privileges and incentives to foreign investors under Law 43 prompted reciprocal measures for the Egyptian private sector. For example, Law 86 of 1974 extended to local currency investors some of the same tax incentives provided in Law 43, although it was not published until June 1976. Egyptian businessmen were also allowed to act as commercial representatives of foreign firms, a privilege hitherto reserved to companies in which the state had at least a 25 percent interest. Moreover Law 118 of 1975 broke the monopoly of the state in import-export. Except for strategic commodities, such as imported wheat, petroleum, and coal, or exported cotton, rice, or cement, the private sector was authorized to engage directly in foreign trade. With the passage of time the state has gradually ceded its remaining monopolies in this sphere. The same law abolished the complicated and sluggish system of "bidding committees" that had formerly

Table 8.7
Evolution of the Parallel Market, 1973-1977

(£E millions current prices)

	1973		1975		1977	
	Amount	%	Amount	%	Amount	%
Tourism	37.2	26.1	72.0	30.0	239.2	38.6
Nontraditional exports	24.4	17.2	45.3	19.1	135.2	21.8
Workers' savings	72.6	51.1	105.7	44.6	193.5	31.2
Other	7.8	5.5	13.7	5.8	52.2	8.4
Total	142.0	100.0	236.7	100.0	620.1	100.0

SOURCE: CBE, *Annual Report: 1977*, Table 23

processed all import applications from private sector firms. It also allowed virtually unlimited imports of goods by Egyptians working abroad that could plausibly be considered for personal use (Roy 1978, pp. 25-26; Salacuse 1980, pp. 315-33).

Parallel to these measures was the introduction in June 1974 of the controversial "own-exchange" import system. Although it will receive separate treatment further on, let it be noted that after June 1974 private sector importers were not required to acquire or convert foreign exchange through public sector banks. In short there would be no questions asked as to how the importer got his foreign exchange, and he was entitled to use it to import whatever he saw fit so long as he paid the stipulated duties.

Other decrees and laws have trickled down in the last five years, opening the way to increased private sector activity. In 1975 the private sector was allowed to import building materials duty-free and all new housing projects were exempted from taxes for five years (*A*, May 18, 1975). The following year Egyptian private and foreign investors were authorized to undertake mineral exploration. In 1978 it was decided that contracting and construction companies would qualify for operation under the foreign investment code, and that foreign and private Egyptian contractors could bid on all public sector contracts. Up to that time private sector contractors could not bid on any project valued at more than £E 7 million.

The most important legislation affecting the private sector was contained in Law 32 of 1977 that revised the Arab and Foreign Investment code (Law 43) of 1974. It extended to private sector investments several of the privileges granted foreign investments, although guarantees against nationalization were conspicuously not among them. These included exemptions from prevailing labor legislation, the right to dispose freely of foreign exchange earned by the project, free importation without license of goods necessary to the production process, the right to export directly without permit, exemption from corporate profits tax for eight years, exemption from taxes on all foreign currency loans, etc. (Arab and Foreign Investment Code, *AI*, Supplement, February 1, 1978, pp. 9-15). Whether or not private sector projects qualified under Law 32 was left to the judgment of the General Authority for Arab and Foreign Investment.

By the time Law 32 was issued both USAID and the IBRD had taken concrete steps to promote private sector activity. The World Bank played a major role in the creation of the Development Industrial Bank in 1975. The IBRD has lent $130 million and USAID $32 million to the DIB. The DIB is designed to meet the credit needs of small-scale private industry, and by 1979 had committed £E 150 million to 3,000 of them (*MEED*, April 18, 1980). For its part USAID has established the Special Fund for Private Projects worth $30 million. It will make loans to four public sector banks and five joint venture banks, which they will then lend out to private sector projects (see Chapter Sixteen).

The Public / Private Symbiosis

Munfatihun

Over the decade between 1969 and 1979 the private sector responded impressively to the stimuli of the state. It is still difficult to discern *what* private sector or sectors seized the opportunity. Surely its roots are shallow, having little to do with the pre-1961 bourgeoisie. Just as surely important cohorts active in it are upwardly mobile petty tradesmen, wholesalers, small-scale contractors, black-market speculators, *contrabandiers*, and the like; or public sector figures who know well how to manipulate administrative licensing, regulations, and personal contacts to feather their private nests.

It was the traditional sectors of private manufacturing and artisanry that began to export heavily to the USSR and Eastern Europe after 1966. In four years, between 1970 and 1974, their exports to socialist countries—known as "agreement" countries because of annual bilateral trade agreements between them and Egypt—more than tripled, from £E 14 million to £E 50 million. Over the same period their share of total industrial exports to these markets increased from 19 to 31 percent and their share in industrial exports to all markets from 14 to 24 percent (Salih, 1975).

The pattern of private sector exports reveals a peculiar kind of dependence. The bulk of them consisted in leather products, textiles, knitwear, soaps, detergents, furniture, and bazaar goods. The socialist countries annually negotiated values for these exports that had little to do with world market prices and even less with quality. On that score the Egyptian public and private sectors were treated alike. The result was that the private sector, and parts of the public sector, became habituated to a market that took all they could produce regardless of quality.

The balloon burst in 1975 and 1976. In the former year, as relations between Egypt and the USSR soured after the second Sinai disengagement agreement, trade between the two countries was sharply curtailed. Voices on the Egyptian right attributed the reduction solely to Soviet plotting to kill off the private sector. Tuhami Ibrahim (*A*, May 7, 1977) accused the Soviet Union of having encouraged the establishment of hundreds of private sector firms, whose sole function was to produce for export to the "agreement" countries, only to drive them into bankruptcy by restricting imports (cf. 'Issam Rifa'at 1975). There may be some truth in the accusation, but it is equally true that Egypt was balking at servicing its massive military and civilian debt to the USSR.

Although the causes may have been political and diplomatic, the net result for the Egyptian private sector was not much different from that of North African industries in the late 1970s that had been called into being by preferential accords with the EEC only to have import restrictions unilaterally imposed by EEC countries to protect their own depressed industries.

In mid-1976 the Federation of Industries reported that some 300 private sector plants were on the verge of shutting down. Textiles and knitwear were particularly hard hit. Their dilemma was compounded by Ministry of Trade Decree 1058 of 1975 (referred to in the previous chapter) that allowed the duty-free import of textiles and clothes. The Egyptian market was flooded with mainland Chinese and South Korean textiles while the 1,000 private textile firms, with their 50,000 workers, felt the pinch (*AI*, no. 583, April 1, 1978; and OPNUR 1977, p. 27). In August 1977 Sadat deepened the crisis by suspending *all* bilateral trade with the agreement countries, which amounted to a default on Egypt's debt to them.

Perhaps this politically produced crisis has been a blessing in disguise, forcing the private sector to look for markets in so-called "free" or hard-currency areas. The going will be no easier for the private than the public sector as they both try to penetrate the growing protectionism in OECD markets.

As traditional, small-scale industry marks time, it may be that a new entrepreneurial class is taking shape. Despite the private sector export crisis, GOFI was approving record numbers of investment projects at high levels of capitalization and in production areas where the private sector had feared to enter. In 1975 GOFI approved 525 new private sector projects, and in 1977 the number of approvals rose to 693. While textiles and food processing continued to play a prominent role, it is the surge in large projects in chemicals, engineering, and metallurgy that indicates the new forces at work. The kind of production and level of capitalization envisaged suggest a group of entrepreneurs ready and able to enter into joint ventures with foreign capital and to constitute the missing leg in *tri-pe* arrangements. It is significant in this respect that steps are underway to establish three new business associations (the Bankers' Club, the Investors' Association, and the Businessmen's Association) independent of the Chambers of Commerce and the Federation of Industries, long under the thumb of the state.[5]

If these new entrepreneurial groups represent the future of *infitah*, the *munfatihun*, those known pejoratively as the "openers," represent its present. They have been the architects of a speculative, commercial open-door rather

[5] The three groups have so far chosen to avoid founding unions or federations which would require laborious parliamentary debate and a presidential decree. Instead they have registered with the Ministry of Social Affairs as societies with "charitable or social purposes" (*AI*, no. 595, June 9, 1980).

Table 8.8
Private Sector Exports
(£E millions current prices)

Industry	1973		1974		1975		1976	
	Amount	Share %	Amount	Share %	Amount	Share %	Amount	Share %
Leather	11,023	36.5	21,661	39.9	17,263	29.3	11,007	24.8
Textiles	6,608	21.8	12,577	23.1	12,254	20.8	8,598	19.4
Chemicals	5,650	18.7	10,909	20.5	19,888	33.8	13,937	31.5
Woodworking	3,812	12.6	5,449	10.0	5,683	9.6	4,947	11.2
Khan al-Khalili*	2,436	8.0	2,797	5.1	3,272	5.5	3,115	7.0
Food	442	1.4	119	0.2	30	—	1,306	3.0
Engineering and metalurgical products	140	0.4	467	0.8	381	0.7	1,240	2.8
Building	91	0.3	332	0.6	177	0.3	144	0.3
Total	30,202	100.0	54,311	100.0	58,947	100.0	44,294	100.0

SOURCE: Ministry of Industry and Mineral Resources, cited in IBRD 1977, p. 23.
*Khan al-Khalili refers to the bazaar and artisans section of old Cairo and is used to designate all artisanal production.

Table 8.9

GOFI-Approved Private Sector Industrial Projects by Level of Capitalization, 1977

(In £E thousands current prices)

Sector	Total no. of proj.	Under £E 25,000			£E 25-100,000			Over £E 100,000		
		No. proj.	Capital	Average cap. per proj.	No. proj.	Capital	Average cap. per proj.	No. proj.	Capital	Average cap. per proj.
Food	175	31	599	19.3	35	1,756	50.1	109	21,029	192.9
Textiles	250	82	632	7.7	75	1,799	25.0	96	23,923	249.1
Chemicals	118	14	173	12.3	35	1,182	33.7	63	21,693	344.3
Engineering	100	12	118	9.8	32	1,184	37.0	56	14,000	250.0
Electrical	9	9	155	17.2	—	—	—	—	—	—
Metallurgy	13	1	5	5.0	7	203	29.0	5	821	164.2
Leather	24	3	32	10.6	5	134	26.8	16	4,214	263.3
Mining	4	1	20	20.0	1	55	55.0	2	486	243.0
Total	693	153	1,734	11.3	187	6,313	33.7	347	86,166	248.3

SOURCE: Adapted from IBRD 1977.

than a production-oriented liberalization. Their activities have been basically of two kinds: importing and acting as middlemen between foreign firms and the government. Many are, were, or have direct links to, public sector officials and the political elite. They trade in influence, inside knowledge, and fixing deals. They profit from feeding seemingly insatiable middle and lower middle class demand for imported consumer goods. So successful have they been in shaping policy to favor their interests that they have become the major Egyptian beneficiaries of *infitah*. Moreover the latitude they have been given through liberalized import regulations has struck directly at the interests of the traditional private sector manufacturing groups. It is not mere hyperbole to see in the two groups a near-classic clash of interests between the national bourgeoisie and the compradors. Sadat openly favored the latter, but Mubarak may build a constituency among the former.

The *munfatihun* were sired in the period of state-monopolized foreign trade and unmet consumer demand. The "suitcase merchants" (*tuggar al-shunnat*) stepped into the breach to elevate smuggling to a major industry. Often to be successful required the collusion of public authorities, which was just as often forthcoming. Suitcase merchants, frequently migrant workers, were given foreign exchange and a commission to bring in consumer items in their suitcases. Knitwear, radios, automobile spare parts, perfumes, etc. were the staples of this trade. The goods were generally acquired in Beirut, Saudi Arabia, or Libya, and the merchant bought the foreign exchange illegally from foreigners resident in Egypt or Egyptians resident abroad. Libya was particularly lucrative, in that travel to and from Egypt was generally effected by overland taxis that could be loaded with goods. It was common for new Libyan Peugeot taxis to be driven to Alexandria or Cairo, stripped of all moving parts and tires, and rebuilt with old parts and sent back to Libya to be refitted with new parts for a new sortie.

In the years prior to 1973 it is estimated that illegal imports of this kind were running at £E 100 million per year (A, September 15, 1977). Many found their way to a cluster of tawdry boutiques along Cairo's notorious Shawarbi Street, where they fetched astronomical prices. Occasional raids by the customs police on Shawarbi, once prompted by the fatal beating of a prominent elderly Egyptian who protested the cravat he had just bought was not really a Cardin, were more for show than correction. In curious obeisance to Egyptian demand for foreign goods (*min barra*), local manufacturers successfully imitated European brand products. Egyptians paid hefty prices for falsely labeled goods that they would otherwise have scorned.

The suitcase merchants have been eclipsed by a new breed of importer, but they are still active and ingenious. 'Adil Hamuda (*RY*, no. 2592, February 2, 1978) observed that entire planeloads of Egyptians descend on London during January white sales, clean out the department stores, and cart the booty back to Egypt. He entitled his article, "The Arabs buy in the summer; the Egyptians buy in the winter." Of more than suitcase size were Israeli automobiles buried in the Sinai desert by Bedouin and unearthed once the Israeli occupying forces had withdrawn making the territory Egyptian.

Concomitant with the creation of the parallel market in 1973 were measures permitting Egyptians to import private automobiles without permits and, for migrant workers, to bring in large amounts of consumer goods for personal use. The rapid growth in the earnings of these workers prompted the creation of the parallel market, but in June 1974, the "own-exchange" system was introduced, which sapped the parallel market of its effectiveness.

The own-exchange system was designed to expedite the import of raw materials and other production inputs for the private sector. This, after all, was the purpose of the parallel market, and the new system was an implicit recognition of the failure of the parallel market to pull in workers' remittances and to process rapidly foreign exchange requests from the private sector. As mentioned above, the own-exchange system allowed the importer to acquire foreign exchange however he could, without any obligation to convert it through an Egyptian bank. Importers, whether middlemen or final users, could buy foreign exchange from workers abroad at a premium above the purchase price of the parallel market. They were competing for a burgeoning source: in the middle Seventies total workers' savings rose to about $250 million a year, then to $700 million in 1976, $1.7 billion in 1978, and $2.8 billion in 1980. Over half the earnings are remitted through the parallel market or the own-exchange system. In 1980 that represented the equivalent of $1.5 billion, mainly because the importers' price for the dollar was 86 piastres while the parallel market price was 70 piastres (*A*, June 4, 1976; *Egypt Newsletter* 1980b; *AI*, no. 648, June 15, 1981). After the devaluation of summer 1981 the respective rates were 80 and about 106 piastres to the dollar.

The own-exchange system came under fire early. In December 1975 the parliament's Budget and Plan Committee recommended its abolition because it was undermining the parallel market and leading to an explosion of luxury imports. *The Economic Ahram* (*al-Ahram al-Iqtisadi*), cited so frequently in these pages, launched a campaign against what it called "provocative" goods. *AI*'s editor, Lutfi 'Abd al-'Azim, a man who had called for *infitah* before it became official policy, denounced its perversion in favor of the new profiteers. In one issue, 'Abd al-'Azim ran a signed article comparing Zakaria Tawfiq 'Abd al-Fattah, the minister of commerce and the own-exchange system's most fervent backer, to Marie Antoinette facing the Parisian rabble (*AI*, no. 531, October 1, 1977).[6]

---

[6] 'Abd al-'Azim was reprimanded by the editor-in-chief of *al-Ahram*, Yussef al-Siba'i, and eventually removed from editorship of *AI*. It was after Siba'i's assassination in Cyprus by Palestinian terrorists that 'Abd al-'Azim was reinstated.

'Abd al-Fattah, a man who had once been in charge of sequestered properties under Nasser, argued all along that own-exchange imports would put an end to suitcase merchants, give a boost to private sector production, and eventually drive down consumer prices. He took as success the spectacular volume of approved imports under the system: £E 265 million in 1975 and £E 334 million in 1976 (*A*, January 4, 1976; and *AI*, no. 534, October 15, 1977). After six years of own-exchange imports, it does not appear that any of its three advantages are real. Suitcase merchants still thrive, easier access to imports for the private sector has been offset by floods of cheap and competitive finished imports, and middle class demand has proved so resilient that prices have continued to climb.

In the face of charges that all own-exchange has done is to promote luxury imports, 'Abd al-Fattah insisted that the bulk of the imports consisted in capital and intermediate goods. Official statistics, however, are highly ambiguous and do not appear to include two kinds of exemptions under the own-exchange law. First, no import permit is required for individual shipments valued at less than £E 5,000 and there is no limit to the number of such shipments any importer may bring in in a given year. It is estimated that in 1980 alone imports of this kind were worth £E 477 million (*AI*, no. 666, October 19, 1981). Second, no permit is required for imports valued at less than £E 10,000 of industrial producers goods. It is not clear how or if imports of this kind are recorded. The categorization of imports is not always helpful with production and consumer goods lumped together in entries such as "electrical products," "vehicles," "metallic products," etc. Table 8.10, however, attempts to regroup Ministry of Commerce figures so that they show

Table 8.10
Own-Exchange Imports 1975-1979
(£E millions current prices)

	1975	1976	1977	1978	1979
Fuels	—	—	.1	.3	.18
Raw materials	—	—	—	—	2.2
Intermediate goods	—	38.9	68.5	188.3	389.8
Capital goods	—	69.1	99.2	214.2	331.4
Consumer goods	—	68.4	97.3	184.6	250.2
(Durables)	—	(12.8)	(33.1)	(55.7)	(109.9)
(Non-durables)	—	(55.6)	(64.2)	(128.9)	(147.9)
Total	107.7	176.4	265.1	587.4	973.8

SOURCES: From IMF data for 1975-1978; and *Egypt Newsletter*, June 9-22, 1980 for 1979. Goods brought in under special provisions, mainly for personal use, are not included.

clearly the distribution of own-exchange imports between consumption and production spheres.

While there has been rapid growth in the importation of capital and intermediate goods, the level of consumer imports, *not* including goods for personal use or brought in under the £E 5,000 ceiling, has reached impressive heights. These consumer goods are what is on display in the streets and shop windows of Cairo and other cities and constitute the "provocative" goods that the *Economic Ahram* and other publications have criticized. Whatever their composition, it is striking that own-exchange imports represented only 3.5 percent of the total import bill in 1975 but over 21 percent in 1979.

The own-exchange system has fueled a more general surge in consumer imports. In the name of "food security," all food products may be imported duty-free, and these products include pâté de foie gras or Danish cheese as well as cooking oil or wheat flour. In 1975 it was estimated that £E 300 million in food products (exclusive of basic grains and tobacco) were imported duty-free (Ghaith 1978a). Consumer durables have also flooded in: 48,000 automobiles, 340,000 televisions, 175,000 radios, 238,000 sewing machines, 24,000 tape recorders, and 13,000 refrigerators were brought in in 1978. These were all dutiable goods, but official statistics do not record goods that are brought in under "temporary admission." They also do not reflect the Topsy-like growth of nondutiable goods from the Port Said free zone. In less than three years after 1976 £E 395 million in duty-free imports entered the country from Port Said while another £E 312 million were imported subject to duty (*AI*, no. 571, June 1, 1979). When all these factors are taken into account, one finds that whereas imported consumer goods represented about 10 percent of total imports in the late Sixties, their share grew to 28 percent in the period 1970-1973, and then to 34 percent between 1974 and 1977 (*AI*, no. 589, March 1, 1980).

Presumably the halcyon days of the *munfatihun* will not go on indefinitely. Their speculation and profiteering have been sufficiently ostentatious to call down the wrath, real or feigned, of the regime. Law 119 of 1977 sought to fix profit margins at 30 percent for imported consumer goods sold in the Egyptian market. The Ministry of Commerce was charged with applying the law, but the importers protested so vigorously that the law was referred to the Economic Committee of the parliament for review and has apparently remained a dead letter ever since. Sayyid al-Misri, deputy minister of commerce and a determined backer of Law 119, was transferred from his post (Mahmud Maraghi, *RY*, no. 2601, April 17, 1978; *Tigarat al-'Arab*, March 1978).

The state's other line of attack on the *munfatihun* was to try by various means to tap their hard currency sources. In August 1979 the Ministry of Economy issued Decree 600, requiring that duties charged on own-exchange imports be deposited, prior to importation, in one of the four public sector banks. Many observers felt that this measure would not lead to any reduction in consumer prices but rather an increase in them as well as a rise in the free market price for foreign exchange. They were proven right on both counts.

Less than a year later, when 'Abd al-Razzaq 'Abd al-Magid took over as deputy prime minister for economy, the decree was abolished. Its place was taken by an equally controversial piece of legislation that required importers to deposit Egyptian pounds in public sector banks equivalent to 25 percent of the value of imported foodstuffs, 40 percent of the value of imported intermediate goods, and 100 percent of the value of finished and luxury goods. In return the banks would issue letters of credit for the value of the imports with the balance due upon delivery. 'Abd al-Magid saw this as a useful hybrid of the own-exchange system and the "open licensing" system urged by the IMF. After June 15, 1980 private sector banks came to a "gentlemen's agreement" with 'Abd al-Magid to deposit 15 percent of their foreign exchange holdings with the Central Bank and thus earned the right to issue letters of credit to importers on the same basis as public sector banks (*MEED*, July 4, 1980; *FT* "Egypt Survey," July 23, 1980).

The new regulations drove a wedge into the ranks of the *munfatihun*. Only those with substantial liquidity could afford to tie up funds in letters of credit for the six or more months it would require for imported goods to arrive in Egypt. Small-scale importers would be hard-pressed to compete. What they anticipated was that the most powerful importers would build effective monopolies of certain imported goods and drive their prices up on domestic markets.[7] This would be especially true for goods requiring 100 percent advanced payment. Second, these same merchants would be able to act as bankers for the small-scale importers, advancing them the funds necessary to take out letters of credit. In short, the new regulations consolidate the power advantage of the elite of *munfatihun* (Hassan 'Amr 1980).

The import boom and *infitah* in general have attracted so many participants that it is nearly impossible to characterize them in any way. One must treat with some skepticism Faruq Guwaida's claim (1976a) that there were, in 1976, some 50,000 private import-export and consulting offices operating in Egypt. Still, even allowing for an enormous margin of overstatement, the figure is impressive. Far more plausible is Guwaida's estimate that twenty-two ex-ministers and two ex-prime ministers were active as importers or consultants to foreign businesses. 'Aziz Sidqi, 'Abd al-'Aziz Higazi, the ex-prime ministers, former Minister of Agriculture Mustapha Gabali, former

---

[7] Perhaps as a countervailing measure the government reduced customs duties across the board. The maximum duty became 150 percent, where it had been 300 percent. Duties were slashed on consumer durables, small cylinder automobiles, and furniture (*MEED*, May 16, 1980, p. 24).

Director of the Institute of National Planning Isma'il Sabri 'Abdullah, former Minister of Social Affairs 'Aisha Ratib, former directors of the Investment Authority Tahar Amin and Zaki Shafa'i, former First Secretary of the ASU Rifa'at Mahgub, former Foreign Minister Isma'il Fahmi were willing or unwilling converts to *infitah*.

Several former public sector figures have shown up in the new, private Egyptian banking sector. I do not want to imply that those persons, or any of those mentioned above, are somehow by definition unscrupulous profiteers or parasitical middlemen. But neither have they gone into manufacturing or other directly productive lines of activity. Former Free Officer Ahmad Tu'aima, heading a small textile firm, is an exception. The rest in essence market their inside knowledge of the system and their ability to provide access to it.

At the interstices of all branches of private activity are the new, private Egyptian bankers, gradually building their capacity to finance local industry or imports. Some are purely Egyptian banks, others are joint ventures. All are well-connected. The largest is the Suez Canal Bank with shareholders that include the Suez Canal Authority and Osman Ahmad Osman's Arab Contractors Company. Former Finance Minister Ahmad Abu Isma'il is at the head of the Cairo Far East Bank, and another former minister of finance, Hassan 'Abbas Zaki, heads the Société Arabe Internationale de Banque. Higazi, Tahar Amin, and former Finance Minister 'Ali Lutfi were instrumental in founding the Merchants Bank. President Sadat himself was one of the founders of the National Bank for Development (£E 50 million in capital), which is affiliated to his political party and not to be confused with 'Abd al-Magid's superbank, the NIB.

Many of the *munfatihun* are first-generation entrepreneurs. Others have their roots in the era before the Socialist Decrees of 1961. Still others launched their careers by learning how to beat the system of socialist controls erected in the 1960s. Some examples may help give the flavor of the group.

1) Basyuni Guma' was tried and convicted in 1967 for illegal manipulation of import permits. After 1974 he was back in business, legally, and richer than ever (cf. Rifa'at Sa'id 1972, pp. 61-71).

2) Rushdi Subih, a rich businessman from Minia, living in England since 1961, has promoted various British interests in Egypt since 1974, including Leyland Motors. His close contacts with the most highly placed Egyptians are well-known.

3) Mahmud Isma'il, "the new De Lesseps," passed himself off as an engineer. He was forced to flee the country in 1964, and made his fortune in Kuwait. After 1973 he established the first private sector shipping and navigation company since 1961. Public sector shipping handles only about 14 percent of Egypt's foreign trade. Isma'il was

able to extract from the Egyptian parliament an act that gave his company priority on all shipping not undertaken by the state (Mahmud Maraghi, *RY*, no. 2477, February 1, 1975).

4) Mansur Hassan, a wealthy young importer of cosmetics among other things, rose after 1976 to become a confidant of President Sadat, a top leader of the Egypt Party, and, in May 1980, minister of information. He, as much as Osman Ahmad Osman, represented the kind of business interests with which Sadat felt most comfortable. Hassan's father had his property sequestered after 1961.

Muqawalun

Muqawalun are contractors, and in Egypt they have been the masters of the public/private symbiosis. As the public sector was built in the early 1960s, it delegated a good part of its voluminous business to private sector interests. For the latter, public enterprise was anything but threatening; it was rather a steady source of livelihood. Public sector managers tolerated or promoted links that many have described as parasitical for many reasons: lack of experience or competence, convenience, and kickbacks.

Convenience has determined the symbiosis between public and private sector textile producers. Since 1961 the state has tried to assure an ample supply of cheap "popular" fabrics to Egypt's masses at subsidized prices. Public sector companies were responsible for producing this cloth, the consumption of which had risen to about 400 million meters in 1975. It was not a profitable undertaking for public sector firms, so they tended to contract with smaller private producers to supply the cloth. Through such contracts, private sector firms not only won a steady customer but also supplies of cotton at subsidized prices. Public companies were able to concentrate on producing fancier fabrics for domestic consumption or for export.

By the late 1970s the private sector was supplying well over 100 million meters of popular cloth annually. In addition, its total cloth production rose from 220 million meters in 1974 to 405 million meters in 1977, while that of the public sector grew from 530 million to 670 million meters (*A*, June 12, 1974; and *AI*, no. 557, November 1, 1978). Many bogus private sector firms have been registered so that their owners can have allotments of subsidized cotton, which they then sell on the black market to legitimate manufacturers. A café in the Mouski district of Cairo serves as the unofficial *bourse* for transactions in this cotton market.

Private sector construction companies have made off with the most lucrative contracts. In the first Five-Year Plan, 40 percent of all public investments went into construction projects. This proportion represented about £E 700 million, and as much as 80 percent of that may have been farmed out to private sector firms (Ghun'aim 1965, p. 471; Habashi 1973, pp. 27-31; Mutwali 1972, p. 51; cf. Benachenou 1973, p. 339 on similar phenomena in Algeria).

The new "fat cats" of the construction sector attracted enough opprobrium that Nasser contemplated nationalizing 80 percent of their interests in 1966. That intention was never carried out. After 1973 and the rehabilitation of the Canal Zone cities, public investments in construction swelled to new heights: £E 391 million in 1974 to £E 654 million in 1975. In 1980 the level declined slightly to £E 509 million. During those years the government drew up plans for new satellite cities in the desert, port construction, and continued rebuilding of the Canal Zone cities.

Contracting and subcontracting in construction provided limitless possibilities in kickbacks, and the siphoning off of building materials into the black market. As in the textile sector, public companies abetted private sector production of goods they would then purchase. For instance, public sector imports of scrap metal helped fuel the unauthorized private production of £E 10 to 20 million in construction steel each year. However, the figure who has come to personify the construction sector symbiosis is Ahmad Osman, president of the Arab Contractors Company, with 50,000 employees and annual business worth about £E 200 million in and outside Egypt.

Osman has, in recent years, been bluntly critical of socialism and state enterprise, yet one wonders how he could have prospered without it. As a young civil engineer in Ismailia, Osman launched his career by contracting with the British military authorities in the Canal Zone. Later, when construction of the High Dam began, he won a major contract for supervising the construction of the earth-fill segment of the dam. His success earned him fame, official favor, and fortune. His domestic operations were nationalized, but he was allowed by Nasser to run his foreign operations as a private company and to maintain foreign exchange accounts abroad. From these he was able to do favors for the Nasserist elite when they traveled abroad. He also built certain of them private villas, exacting only a token price for his work.

As the head of a nationalized company, Osman was in theory like any other public sector manager. In 1974, when Sadat appointed him as minister of housing and reconstruction, the question of conflict of interest that had been muted for a decade rose to the surface. He reigned supreme over the entire reconstruction budget, including hundreds of millions of dollars flowing in from Saudi Arabia, Kuwait, Qatar, and Abu Dhabi. A special law, 62 of 1974, gave him the right to ignore general procurement and import regulations for all materials and equipment that were required for reconstruction. He was responsible for importing a large amount of Spanish construction steel at what many members of parliament thought were suspiciously high prices. A special committee in 1976 drew up a list of twenty-six accusations that ranged from nepotism and conflict of interest, to bribery and receiving foreign kickbacks. He dismissed the charge of conflict of interest by saying that either as minister or as head of Arab Contractors he was a simple salaried public servant who stood to gain nothing by channeling Ministry business to his company. He admitted that not many other public sector managers had a company helicopter to ferry them between the Ministry and company headquarters (*A*, February 2 and April 19, 1976). Prior to Sadat's assassination, Osman lost his Ministry but continued on as the *éminence grise* of his company and as principal presidential advisor on "food security." This allowed him to promote agro-industrial ventures like the Pepsi Cola citrus project near Ismailia. The president sought Osman's advice in all spheres, and their friendship was cemented by the marriage of one of Sadat's daughters to Osman's son. It is highly unlikely that Osman will enjoy the same favor under Mubarak.

There is not room in Egypt for too many Osmans. The scale of his operations are not typical of the private construction sector as a whole. They do, however, highlight the more general process of accumulation that took place in this sector in the 1960s under public auspices. The experience and liquid assets gained at that time have enabled the entrepreneurs of this sector to profit from the investment opportunities opened up by *infitah* while continuing to do heavy, and now unrestricted, business with the state.

Bayyumiyun

The housing market has always been the preferred area of private investment and speculation. It was the one area during the 1960s that offered something more than a token return. The public sector has tried to meet some small portion of the huge demand for low-cost housing, seldom more than 10 percent of the approximately 120,000 units that would be needed annually to give adequate shelter to the urban masses (Waterbury 1982). The private sector has been allowed to provide middle- and upper-income housing, and their construction of such units has frequently outstripped that of the public sector. A disparate group of entrepreneurs has, occasionally, literally made a killing in meeting urban middle-class demand.

On December 24, 1974, an eleven-story apartment building in the middle-class district of Doqqi in Cairo collapsed. The building was put up by a contractor, Hassan Bayyumi, and sold to Muhammed al-Qasabi for £E 60,000. Al-Qasabi, his two daughters, and an unidentified guest were buried in the rubble. They were the only occupants of the building at the time it collapsed. It turned out that Bayyumi had been authorized by city engineers to build a six-story structure. He had exceeded his authorization by five stories.

Table 8.11
Housing Production in Egypt, 1960-1975

	Public Sector		Private Sector		Total	
	No. of Units	Cost (£E thousands)	No. of Units	Cost (£E thousands)	No. of Units	Cost (£E thousands)
1960-61	2,296	2,556	11,564	10,684	13,860	13,240
1965-66	20,509	18,380	13,000	17,400	33,509	35,780
1970-71	5,250	5,484	22,520	19,050	27,770	24,534
1975	17,700	22,400	24,000	45,600	41,700	68,000

SOURCE: USAID, Ministry of Housing and Reconstruction, Ministry of Planning, *Immediate Action Proposals for Housing in Egypt: Statistical Appendix* (June 1971), p. 51.

What Bayyumi had done was typical of private sector building entrepreneurs. Until 1977 when the private sector was allowed to import building materials duty-free, the public sector had a monopoly of the distribution of cement, steel bars, wooden door and window frames, and some kinds of window glass. To obtain these materials private sector builders had their blueprints approved by city architects, and on the basis of their specifications, appropriate quantities of building materials were allotted to them.

These materials were always in short supply as the public sector had prior rights to them. Months would elapse after approval for building and delivery of materials which would often arrive out of phase—cement but no steel bars or vice versa. A booming black market in building materials developed. Once a builder's plans were approved he would buy what he needed on the black market at prices well over the subsidized state levels.[8] When his state allotments were finally delivered he would simply sell them on the black market.

In the meantime, with approved plans, he could borrow from the Real Estate Bank up to 80 percent of estimated construction costs. Real costs would be higher, of course, because of black market purchases, and the gap could be made up by advance sales of apartments or accepting advance rent or down payments before ground had even been broken at the building site. Indeed, Hassan Bayyumi had gathered £E 35,000 in advance rents or key money (*khalu al-rigl*) before selling the building outright.

Bayyumi had elected one of the two most prevalent modes of fraud. He violated his building permit to coax a large building out of limited construction materials. After it collapsed it was found that no steel reinforcing had been

[8] For example, in 1975 the official price for a ton of cement was £E 13 but £E 40 on the black market. In 1976 the value of imported cement was calculated at the incentive rather than the official rate. The state price for a ton became £E 14.5, the import price £E 35, and the black market price £E 60 (Housing Committee, *AI*, no. 522, May 12, 1977).

used at all. If Bayyumi had had any, he probably sold it on the black market. His other option would have been to apply for a larger building, put up something considerably smaller, and sell all excess materials on the black market.

Either way real costs would exceed by substantial margins official estimates based on subsidized building material prices. To earn a good return on his investment, the builder would then have to violate the elaborate rent control laws enacted by the regime after 1952. The first attempts at rent control in Egypt came during the Second World War when, under martial law, orders were issued forbidding the expulsion of tenants and fixing rents at the level prevailing on April 1, 1941. Subsequently rents were lowered by 15 percent in 1952 on all apartments built between 1944 and 1952 and then lowered again by 20 percent in 1958 on all apartments built between 1952 and 1958. There was a further sweeping decrease of 20 percent at the time of the Socialist Decrees in July 1961. The most important legislation, however, was issued in Law 46 of 1962. It effectively removed rents from all supply-and-demand influence and made them a function of administered profit margins. Rents on new buildings could not exceed annually 5 percent of the value of the site and 8 percent of the value of the building. Because the urban real estate market was depressed precisely because of state regulation, and because the state subsidized the cost of building materials, profits remained low and stable.

As inflation became a major factor in Egypt's economy toward the end of the 1960-65 Plan, and as private sector entrepreneurs and contractors sought investment outlets, rent controls were increasingly violated. There was (and is) a large pent-up middle class demand for urban housing. State officials, professionals, private sector investors all turned to real estate as the safest investment in a period of rising inflation and growing state control of all sectors of the economy. It was inevitable that this demand would create black-market conditions. For instance, key money became a requisite for access to rent-controlled flats; a second gambit was to require several years advance rent. By 1974 average (illegal) key money was £E 1,000 per unit. Commercial leases, such as shoe shops in central Cairo, were worth £E 100,000 to 200,000 in advance rent.

Furnished flats had always been exempted from rent controls, and it became a sound investment for builders, building owners, or apartment renters to furnish and sublet rent-controlled units to foreigners or Arabs at high prices. I myself sublet an apartment in Cairo for £E 500 per month that cost the lessor £E 18 per month. More and more, however, the favored course was to sell apartments in order to avoid rent controls. Units or buildings could be sold well in advance of construction, particularly as Arabs invaded the urban housing market. It was not unusual for the same building to be sold several times over.

All of these practices were well known, but the Bayyumi incident provoked a flurry of public protest and official indignation regarding them.[9] The leftist editor of *al-Tali'a*, Lufti al-Kholi, borrowed Bayyumi's name to characterize a whole group of speculators, exploiters, and profiteers who trafficked in basic needs. He dubbed them all *"Bayyumiyun"* (Kholi 1975b), and he had in mind more than private housing entrepreneurs.

Speculation in scarce goods other than housing has become a studied art among the tens of thousands of small-scale entrepreneurs, retailers and wholesalers of the private sector. These figures are not well known, coming out of places like Wikalat al-Balah where they recycle scrap metal, or from the Rod al-Farrag vegetable market where they deal in wholesale fruits and vegetables. Their profits often were diverted into urban housing and perhaps now importation. These men are more likely to wear a *gallabia* than a business suit; they are unlikely to have had a university education or to speak more than a few words of a foreign language. If they vacation it will be at down-at-the-heels Ras al-Barr rather than in Europe. To my knowledge only one of their number, Sayyid Galal, has achieved national prominence as a member of parliament since 1957 (Springborg 1975, pp. 89-90). He made his fortune in fresh produce trade, but has branched out since. He was one of the founders of the National Bank for Development.

The fresh produce wholesalers of Rod al-Farrag market in Cairo have always attracted a good deal of comment. When Nasser thought seriously of nationalizing wholesale trade, an official report claimed that 219 wholesalers at that market each year sold produce worth £E 130 million and made gross profits of £E 25 million (*A*, October 19, 1967). That would average out to over £E 100,000 per wholesaler per year, ten times the maximum gross income allowable after 1961. The wholesale market is monitored by the Ministry of Supply (traditionally shot through with corruption: see Chapter Fourteen), and legal profit margins are not to exceed 8 percent. The 250 wholesalers operating there in the mid-1970s flouted the regulations, paid fines set so low that they could be easily absorbed, and increased profits by loading on handling charges and other commissions. It is widely believed that the most successful wholesalers gross £E 1,000 to 1,500 per day (Muhammed Yassin 1973, p. 35; *RY*, no. 2613, July 10, 1978).

Similar accounts are related about meat wholesalers and retailers whose kingpins are in the beef-fattening business, buying up animals cheap from the peasants and selling the slaughtered animal dear to the butchers. In 1975 a special parliamentary committee sustained the opinion of the Ministry of Supply that meat should be retailed at no more than ninety-four piastres per

[9] Bayyumi's property and other assets were put under a temporary freeze by the socialist prosecutor. His property had already been sequestered in 1962. It is not known to me if Bayyumi was ever tried.

kilogram. Meat retailers countered that anything less than £E 1.25 per kilo-gram would be impossible. Both parliamentarians and the Ministry of Supply caved in (A, November 18, 1975).

One could go on in this vein through other wholesale-retail sectors, such as paper, school notebooks, cloth, medicine, etc. Nonetheless a particularly sensitive commodity has been shoes. Most local tanning and virtually all shoe manufacture is in the hands of the private sector. A small number of tanners have controlled the trade in skins. Only about 45 percent of Egypt's needs for hides are met locally, the rest being imported, along with many of the chemicals used in tanning. The result has been that a lively black market in skins and chemicals grew up with phony tanning firms obtaining allotments of imported goods from the state. The inevitable result was that the cost increases were passed on to the consumer. The Ministry of Industry in 1973 set the price of a pair of men's leather shoes at £E 2.45, but retailers sold them with impunity at £E 7. Two cartoons by Salah Jahin of al-Ahram captured the public image of these merchants. One depicts a little schoolboy asking for a notebook from a towering, fat-cat shopowner who says: "Go next door to the shoemaker; he bought all my notebooks to make shoes." The second cartoon shows a young lady in a police station, her dress ripped, evidently reporting an incident of rape to the duty sergeant. In tears she wails, "He took my most precious possession." In the balloon over the head of the bemused sergeant is a pair of shoes.

Conclusion

The Egyptian revolution emasculated the large foreign and small indigenous industrial and commercial bourgeoisie. It left unharmed a sprawling sector of petty manufacturers and tradesmen that it referred to as the national, nonexploitative capitalists. For the most part they were self-employed and capitalized so minimally that exploitation was hardly an option for them. Hemmed in by foreign exchange shortages, complicated distribution of vital production inputs by public monopolies, and administered price ceilings, this highly fragmented private sector managed to hold its own in total industrial output and to continue its domination of wholesale and retail trade.

The advent of infitah produced policies that encouraged private sector activity and that tended to restore that sector's public legitimacy. Gradually investment incentives similar to those granted foreigners were extended to the private sector. In addition it was provided greater flexibility in obtaining foreign exchange and in engaging in direct import and export. Yet policies adopted out of political considerations undermined the renaissance of an export-oriented industrial group that had arisen after 1968. Sadat's decision to suspend all bilateral trade arrangements with the USSR and Eastern Europe deprived this group of its only reliable export markets at a time when lowered customs duties permitted a flood of competitive goods from abroad.

There was some evidence in the late 1970s that a new industrial group is taking shape, moving into more sophisticated product lines (chemicals, metallurgy, fine textiles) and using much higher levels of capital. These entrepreneurs seem to have the know-how and sophistication to enter into joint ventures with foreign investors, but it is too early to tell how much economic weight they will take on. It is toward them that the state is looking to provide £E 4 billion of total investments of £E 24 billion during the 1980-1984 Five-Year Plan.

The main beneficiaries of the more liberal economic era inaugurated by Sadat have been the importers and consultants to foreign interests. Riding the wave of middle-class consumer demand, and tapping the foreign exchange savings of migrant workers, the importers have made great fortunes in importing consumer durables, fancy clothes and foods, and other luxury items. Some of what they import is directly competitive with private sector industries, but the importers have several voices in court and their kind of *infitah* has prevailed. One would assume that the moment will come when middle-class demand, especially for consumer durables, will be sated but that moment is not yet upon us.

To no small extent, however, both the new industrialists and the *munfatihun* are dependent upon the earnings of migrant workers who earn Egypt as much foreign exchange as petroleum exports. The state is thus able to meet the foreign exchange needs for imports of the industrialists and to afford to tolerate the own-exchange system of imports preferred by the *munfatihun*. Should anything occur to impede worker migration, the private sector renaissance would be imperiled.

Alongside these interests are some older, more traditional private sector actors, untutored, unglamorous, and rapacious. Housing is their preferred field of activity, but wholesaling in various vital goods has proven to be equally rewarding. Whatever segment of the private sector one looks at, its interpenetration with the public sector is striking. For some, such as the contracting and construction groups, their livelihood is dependent upon the enormous volume of business dealt out by the state. They have grown with the public sector. Others, like the builders or tanners, have thrived through manipulation of "socialist" measures to regulate economic activity. Mastering black markets to cater to middle-class demand has been their forte. Only the new industrialists, financed to some extent by new private Egyptian banks, appear to be in a position to take their distance from the state. Unless, however, they become self-sufficient in foreign exchange, they will have to pay the public piper or go in league with foreign investors and creditors.

Chapter Nine

REPRISE: ACCUMULATION
AND DEEPENING

Egyptian industry is essentially a producer of consumer
goods. Its largest components can be viewed as the
last stage of an integrated agricultural system.
[Mabro and O'Brien 1970, p. 419.]

Developing countries that, like Egypt, adopted state-led ISI as their basic
economic strategy, have been quite explicit about what they hoped to achieve.
The very fact that public political authorities took the initiative, as opposed
to the private sector itself, already says a great deal about their motives which
had to do primarily with national economic sovereignty and strength. Poor
agricultural societies, it was rightly judged, would have little weight and even
less room for maneuver in the international arena.

It was expected that industry would replace agriculture as the motor of the
economy, absorb its excess labor, and, as it sold the agricultural sector the
inputs needed for its own modernization, lead to agriculture's absolute decline
as the dominant source of livelihood in the society.

It was accepted that initially industrialization would cater to existing consumer demand. But that would only be temporary. The real objective was
the establishment of heavy, ''strategic'' industries that were the hallmark of
the power of the West and of the Soviet Union. These would produce the
inputs (fertilizers, tractors, pumps, etc.) necessary for agricultural modernization. They would also produce the intermediate products necessary for a
new generation of manufactures: steel plates, aluminum ingots, tubeless pipes,
copper cable, cement, synthetic fibers, plastics, glass, paper, and so forth.
These would feed into basic consumer goods and consumer durables, and,
eventually, as scales of economy were achieved, into exports. As labor shifted
from subsistence-income agriculture to urban-based, high-salaried industrial
employ, a market would be created sufficient to sustain these economies of
scale.

With urbanization, rising incomes, and literacy, the birth rate would fall,
and excess population growth would take care of itself. A revitalized agri-

cultural sector could then feed a stable population. The average Egyptian would have his own dwelling, a modest range of appliances, perhaps even a car. He or she would, as often as not, work for the state which in turn would own the basic means of nonagricultural production and control what it did not own. While accepting modest consumerism on the part of the citizenry, the state would be able to tax the population's growing prosperity to generate the investment for further growth. The process would become essentially self-sustaining. This, I think, was the socialism envisaged by Nasser, and he may have thought that it would be within Egypt's grasp at the end of a decade of planned growth.

All of these profound structural changes in the economy, had they been effected, would have amounted to the "deepening" process mentioned in Chapter One with respect to Latin America. What I propose to do here is to break down this process into five components and present some summary statistics of the changes brought about in each one. The components are:

1) the structure of industrial output and employment
2) the structure of Egyptian imports and exports
3) the growth of basic food imports
4) the importance of foreign private capital
5) the evolution of national savings and investment.

The Structure of Industrial Output and Employment

The relative weight of industry in Egyptian gross domestic product has unquestionably grown substantially since the beginning of the revolution. During the period corresponding to concerted state-led efforts at ISI, 1956-1965, the industrial share grew from 16 to 24 percent of GDP (Hansen and Nashashibi 1975, p. 12). In 1975 the industrial contribution, *including petroleum, mining, and electricity*, was 22 percent. On the strength of Egypt's petroleum boom, that share had increased to 27 percent by 1979, but when one excludes petroleum it is reduced to 14 percent (unpublished IMF data).

It is true that, as expected and desired, agriculture's share fell from 33 percent to 24 percent, but industry, exclusive of petroleum, did not pick up the slack. Rather it was the service, trade, and finance sectors that grew to contribute 30 percent of GDP by 1979 with the Suez Canal, housing, transportation, and storage also making impressive gains.

In short, between 1956 and 1965 Egypt underwent a process of industrial "broadening," but did it also include deepening? If we look at the gross value of production and value added by industrial subsector, the answer is a very qualified yes. Table 9.1 requires several warnings. It includes only those public and private sector projects under the supervision of the Ministry of

Table 9.1

Gross Value of Industrial Production by Major Subsector 1952-1978

(£E millions current prices)

	1952		1965-66		1970-71		1975		1978	
	Amount	% of Total	Amount	% of Total	Amount	% of Total	Amount	% of Total	Amount	% of Total
Spining and weaving	84	31.3	358	36.3	470	33	690	30.4	1,098	32.0
Foodstuffs	122	45.5	285	29.0	481	33.8	698	30.8	958	28.0
Wood and leather	—		—		—		126	5.5	349	10.2
Chemicals	20	7.4	140	14.2	180	12.6	267	11.8	314	9.1
Engineering and metallurgy	30	11.1	160	16.2	200	14.0	385	17.0	654	19.1
Building materials and nonmetallic products	8	3.0	31	3.1	93	6.5	93	4.1	—	
Mining products	4	1.4	11	1.1	—		7	.3	—	
Total	268	100.0	985	100.0	1,424	100.0	2,266	100.0	3,433	100.0

SOURCES: Data for 1952-1975 from Gritli (citing CBE and FEI) 1977, p. 315. Figures for 1978 from Ministry of Industry as cited in unpublished IMF reports.

Industry. *Not included* are defense industries, publishing and printing, cotton ginning, electricity, petroleum extraction, and, after 1975, public sector building materials, which were put under the supervision of the Ministry of Housing and Reconstruction. I cannot explain why there was no entry until 1975 for private sector manufacture of wood and leather products.

With these gaps in mind we may take note of the unchanging share of consumer goods in total production across the entire period. Were we to have added in small-scale cotton ginning and food processing as defined by the Ministry of Planning in the previous chapter, total industrial production would be even more heavily weighted in favor of consumer goods. The only deepening one can discern came in engineering and metallurgy where its share rose from 11 to 19 percent of the total. Chemicals peaked in 1965-66, and their share declined thereafter. It is useful in this context to refer back to Table 6.1 which shows the evolution of industrial production in quantitative rather than monetary terms. Consumer durables, cars, and television sets have registered the most impressive growth while metallurgical and construction products have lagged behind. In brief, the quarter century covered by Table 9.1 shows little deepening despite the determined efforts of the 1960s.

This picture could change under, but not necessarily as a result of *infitah*. Intermediate goods industries will probably increase rapidly as aluminum, cement, fertilizer, and other petrochemical projects come on-stream. At the same time, however, textiles have attracted most foreign industrial investment under Law 43, with the al-'Amiria project leading the way, and consumer durables and automobiles are also likely to grow substantially.

When one considers value added in manufacturing a considerably different situation is encountered. A slow but steady transformation in favor of inter-

Table 9.2
Percentage Distribution of Gross Value Added
in Manufacturing by Main Group, 1950-1975

Group	1950	1952	1960	1970-71	1975
Consumer industries	72.8	69.8	68.4	63	40.7
Intermediate goods industries	23.8	25.2	27.1	29.6	44.0
Capital goods industries	2.2	3.8	3.5	6.3	8.7
Other	1.2	1.2	1.0	1.2	6.4
Total	100.0	100.0	100.0	100.0	100.0

SOURCES: Entries for 1950-1970-71 from Mohie Eldine 1978, p. 188. The 1975 entry was calculated from data in IBRD 1978a, 6:114. Not included in these percentages are mining, quarrying, and petroleum extraction although petroleum products are included in intermediate goods. Cf. Radwan 1974, p. 211; and Mabro and Radwan 1976, p. 101. Both cover the period 1952-1966-67 in detail.

mediate goods is observed up to 1970-71 and then a marked surge occurs that boosts their share to 44 percent of total value added.[1] These figures reflect the heavy public outlays in the intermediate sector throughout the period. Between 1957 and 1965 46 percent of all public industrial investment was devoted to chemicals, rubber, paper, petroleum, and basic metals (Mabro and Radwan 1976, pp. 113-14). Yet there was a long lag time before these investments were reflected in the new distribution of value added in the mid-1970s. As a result of retrenchment after 1965 a number of projects were suspended and many others operated below capacity because of raw material shortages. It was not until these problems were partially overcome after 1973, that the deepening begun in the first Five-Year Plan became apparent.

If one were to exclude private production from the calculations, the diminishing weight of consumer industries in value added would be all the more noticeable because private efforts are still concentrated in that branch. The private sector contribution to total industrial value added, exclusive of the artisanal sector, may be on the order of 25 percent (IBRD, IDF 1977, p. 24).

The share of industry in total investment outlays has varied widely, but with two exceptions has not exceeded levels achieved prior to the revolution. Industry accounted for 28, 39, 31, and 35 percent of all investment between 1948 and 1952. It was only during the first Industrial Plan, 1957-1960, that these prerevolutionary investment levels were equalled or exceeded. Between 1960 and 1975, with the inclusion of outlays on the High Dam power station and power grid, industry's share was in a range between 25 and 38 percent, but in the late 1970s, as priorities shifted toward housing, infrastructure, and power generation, its share fell precipitously. In that vein it should be noted that the figures in Table 9.3 do not reflect the outlays on the High Dam power station and national electrical grid.

There is no reason to expect that industrial deepening would lead to any major increase in the size of the industrial work force, because the deepening process is inherently capital intensive. On the other hand, one would expect the "broadening" process of the early 1950s to have produced such an increase. That has not been the case. The modest increase in industrial employment reflected in Table 9.4 occurred as much before 1960—especially between 1937 and 1947—as after.[2] For most of the period the service sector

[1] Intermediate goods include building materials, metallic products, chemicals, rubber, petroleum products, basic metals, paper, glass, leather, and wood. K. M. Barbour 1972, pp. 59-68 lists all principal industrial plants founded between 1952 and 1964.

[2] Egypt is not really a newly industrialized country. However inefficient, Muhammed 'Ali's industrial ventures had given rise by the 1830s to a very large industrial work force that may have involved well over 30 percent of the active population (from Barbour 1972, p. 39):

Table 9.3
The Share of Industry in Public Investment Outlays 1952-1980
(In £E millions current prices)

	Total Investment	Industrial Investment	Industrial Investment as % of Total
1952	118.6	29.5	25
1957-58	165.4	35.6	21
1960-61	225.6	67.8	30
1966-67	358.8	98.4	27
1970-71	355.5	125.7	35
1975	1,228.0	394.1	32
1980 (proj.)	3,100.0	546.1	17.6

SOURCES: 1952-1975 from IBRD 1978, 6: 117. 1980 from Gov't. Budget Proposal published as a supplement to *Al*, January 1, 1980. Industry includes manufacturing, mining, and petroleum but not electricity.

has been the major sponge of underutilized agricultural labor, consistently representing about a quarter of the work force. Even with the out-migration of half a million Egyptians in the mid- and late 1970s, persons who could not be readily absorbed into the industrial sector, the service sector grew from 23 to 24 percent of total employment, with 2.5 million workers in 1979. There were another 1.2 million in trade and finance for a total of 3.7 million workers against industry's 1.3 million.

Moreover, since the end of the first Five-Year Plan, private industrial employment has grown much more rapidly than public. In the middle 1960s the private share of total industrial employment was about 46 percent, but rose to 55 percent by the mid-1970s (IBRD, IDF 1977, p. 24). Although it is quite possible that there will be renewed employment drives, it appears that the rate of increase of industrial employment has slowed in the late 1970s. It was 3.2 percent per annum over the period 1975-1979 as opposed to 4

Textiles	174,000
Foodstuffs	11,000
Military stores	15,000
Processing raw materials	20,000
Construction	40,000
Total	260,000

Although the figures are not comparable (nor is there any reason to attribute much accuracy to those of the 1830s), industrial employ in 1927, a century later, stood at 215,000 ('Ali al-Gritli 1962).

194

Table 9.4
Share of Industry in Total Employment, 1937-1980

	Total Employment (thousands) (1)	Industrial Employment (thousands) (2)	(2)/(1) %
1937	5,783	377	6.5
1947	6,590	589	8.9
1960	7,833	771	9.8
1965-66	7,607	842	11.1
1970-71	8,506	1,053	12.3
1975	9,433	1,175	12.5
1980	10,694	1,347	12.6

SOURCES: 1937-1960 figures from Mead 1967, p. 33; and 1965-1980 unpublished IMF data and Al, no. 666, October 19, 1981. The data for the latter period are not consistent with the former, probably excluding female agriculture labor. Also compulsory universal education may have led to an absolute decline in the total work force. In industry some artisanal establishments seem to be excluded after 1960. See Mabro 1974, pp. 205-8.

percent for the period 1966-1975. Consequently, it is not unreasonable to expect that for some time to come industrial employment will hover around 15 percent of the total work force.

It is hard to unearth recent statistics presenting the distribution of the industrial work force by major branch of activity. Mabro and Radwan (1976, p. 103) provide detailed data for the period 1952-1967 for public and private firms of ten or more employees. As was the case with the distribution of value added, we find that in terms of employment, textiles and food processing more than hold their own with 62 percent of the total at the beginning of the period and 67 percent fifteen years later. Considerable deepening, however, is manifest in the rapidly growing share of chemicals, metals, and metal products in overall employment: 8.5 percent at the beginning of the period and 31 percent at its end. Had private sector employment been included in the 1978 figures, it is likely that the share of these basic industries would have been reduced and that of food, textiles, leather, and wood increased still further.

The Structure of Imports and Exports

The changing pattern of imports represented in Table 9.6 confirms that ISI had its desired effect. When "food," primarily grain, is separated out from

Table 9.5
Industrial Employment by Major Branch of Activity, 1972-1978

	1952		1960		1966-67		1978*	
	No.	%	No.	%	No.	%	No.	%
Food	47,606	18.3	47,625	14.8	76,484	13.2	89,088	15.7
Textiles	115,357	44.3	164,163	51.1	246,505	42.7	289,624	51.2
Chemicals	11,052	4.2	16,906	5.3	46,058	8.0	56,331	10.0
Metals and metal products	11,092	4.3	16,125	5.3	47,894	8.3	120,569	21.3
Mining	—	—	—	—	—	—	9,945	1.6
Building materials	13,946	5.4	12,511	3.9	31,992	5.5	—	—
Other	60,999	3.5	63,753	19.6	128,870	22.3		
Total	260,052	100.0	321,083	100.0	577,803	100.0	565,557	100.0

SOURCES: Mabro and Radwan 1976, p. 103 for the period 1952-1966-67, covering public and private establishments of ten or more employees.
* 1978 entry from Ministry of Industry for public sector only. Building materials in 1978 were no longer under Ministry supervision.

Table 9.6
Structure of Egyptian Imports, 1947-1976

	Food	Consumer Goods	Intermediate Goods	Capital Goods	Other	Total %
1947-1952 avg.	21.4%	34.3%	25.5%	18.1%	.7%	100.0
1953-1959 avg.	17.9	28.7	30.4	22.7	.3	100.0
1960-1965 avg.	30.0	16.0	31.3	22.7	—	100.0
1968-1970 avg.	26.4	9.7	36.0	27.9	—	100.0
1971-1973 avg.	25.7	7.0	46.5	20.7	—	100.0
1973-1976 avg.	32.3	7.5	41.0	19.2	—	100.0

SOURCES: 1947-1965 from Mabro and O'Brien 1970; 1965 and 1968 from Hansen and Nashashibi 1975; 1971-1976 from IBRD 1978, vol. 6.

consumer goods, we find a steady decline in the latter from 34 percent at the beginning of the period to about 10 percent at the end. As indicated in the previous chapter however, consumer goods imports are accelerating, and the figures in Table 9.6 do not include own-exchange imports. Capital goods imports remained fairly steady, while intermediate goods, including raw materials, came to dominate imports and to favor production in import-substituting industries. Preliminary figures for the period 1977 to 1979 reveal a major proportional increase in capital goods imports, as, on the one hand, the importation of petroleum products has declined, and, on the other, imports of "machines and appliances" have increased from £E 158 million in 1975 to £E 540 million in 1979 (*AI*, no. 666, October 19, 1981). One may guess that this upsurge corresponds to the expansion in housing and construction since 1975. During this same period, own-exchange imports came to represent between a quarter and a third of total imports, and the consumer goods component of own-exchange imports on the order of one-sixth of all imports. Even excluding own-exchange imports, the gross value of imports has grown vertiginously since the revolution. In current prices the import bill grew from £E 213 million in 1952 to £E 6.9 billion in 1980. As 'Amr Mohie Eldine has noted (1978, p. 193), the deficit in the balance of external payments grew from 1 percent of GDP in the early 1950s to 6 percent at the end of the first Five-Year Plan to 37 percent in 1975. Import substitution has thus had little to do with export promotion and nothing to do with import reduction.

Unlike the value of imports, which grew thirty-two times over between 1952 and 1978, exports grew in the same period and in current prices from £E 135.8 million to £E 2.9 billion, or about twenty-one times. The composition of exports, however, changed markedly with the share of primary exports, mostly raw cotton, pared down from 88 percent in 1953 to 32 percent in 1978. That was certainly the direction intended by Egypt's planners, but this displacement was only partially the result of industrial deepening. It is clear from Table 9.7 that by the end of the period, the most spectacular gainers were fuels and semi-finished products. With respect to the first, crude petroleum exports account for most of the gain. The loss of the Sinai fields after 1967 produced a temporary downturn, but the world price boom after 1973 coupled with recovery of the Sinai fields made petroleum Egypt's leading export. Not shown in the table are the exponential gains registered in the wake of the Iranian crisis at which point Egypt took full advantage of the

Table 9.7
Structure of Egyptian Exports, 1953-1978

	Fuels	Primary Prod.	Semi-Finished Prod.	Finished Prod.
1953	.7%	88.6%	1.4%	9.3%
1959	2.7	83.9	9.0	4.4
1965	6.6	71.4	18.0	4.0
1970	4.6	63.1	13.9	18.3
1975	4.2	49.5	16.2	30.0
1978	20.6	32.2	21.7	25.4

SOURCES: 1953 computed from Mead 1967, Table V-A5; 1959 and 1965 from Nashashibi 1970, p. 79; 1970-1978 IMF statistics, various years.

international spot market.[3] In 1979 with export earnings of £E 1.2 billion, petroleum accounted for 66 percent of the value of all visible exports.

As far as semi-finished exports are concerned, the basic component has always been cotton yarn and waste. Other less important exports of this variety are dried onions, edible oils, perfume essences, etc.

The substantial growth in the export of finished products may seem to say more about deepening than is in fact the case. In 1976, woven cotton, other textiles, refined sugar, footwear, alcoholic beverages, furniture, and books accounted for 65 percent of all finished exports. By contrast, the value of exported fertilizers, automobile tires, rubber pipes, asbestos products, steel sheets and fittings, copper products, household utensils, other metal products, refrigerators, automobiles, and buses was a mere £E 4.2 million or 2.1 percent of the total (FEI, *Yearbook* 1977, pp. 106-7). The export failure of the public sector in the mid-1960s that put in jeopardy the entire ISI strategy is still manifest in these figures a decade later. Only public sector textiles and private sector finished goods showed much growth.

Egypt's external payments crisis would have led to receivership had it not been for the country's invisible exports. These consist primarily in foreign exchange receipts from tourism, workers abroad, and Suez Canal tolls. Their levels were modest throughout the 1960s, but by 1975 their value was the equivalent of one-third of Egypt's visible exports. Four years later their value was equivalent to *all* Egypt's visible exports. The fact that most worker remittances to Egypt come in the form of own-exchange imports or consumer durables for personal use, and were therefore not available to the Treasury, should not detract from this phenomenon. Without this explosion in invisible

Table 9.8
Growth of Major Invisible Exports, 1960-1980
(£E millions current)

Invisible Export	1960	1965	1970	1975	1979	1980
Suez Canal	50.1	86.2	—	33.2	363.0	400.0
Workers' Remittances	—	—	—	143.2	1,449.8	1,888.3
Tourism	—	19.2	25.6	129.8	384.6	500.0
Total	50.1	105.4	25.6	306.2	2,197.4	2,788.3

SOURCES: Computed from published data of IBRD, IMF, CBE, and *Al*, no. 648, June 15, 1981.

NOTE: More recent estimates of remittances yield much higher figures for 1979 and 1980, i.e., £E 2,221.6 and £E 2,861.9. The figures in Table 9.8 are surely an underestimate, but may also reflect use of a lower exchange rate and noninclusion of goods accompanying returning workers (*Al*, no. 666, October 19, 1981).

[3] Egypt is not a member of OPEC and is not bound by its pricing agreements.

exports coupled with the petroleum export windfall, the Egyptian economy, whether guided by Nasserist socialism or Sadatist liberalism, would have been moribund, or put in the trust of the highest international bidder.

Food Imports

Far from approaching self-sufficiency in basic food production Egypt imports more than ever of those commodities that have always been in short supply, and has become a net importer of a number of commodities it has traditionally exported. Over the past two decades Egypt lost self-sufficiency in sugar, sesame seed, corn, and the staple of most of the population, broad beans (*ful*). Its exports of rice have shrunk drastically as domestic consumption has risen, but most striking of all has been the country's total rout in meeting its needs for wheat and wheat flour. These together with Egypt's other food imports have made it one of the major actors, year in, year out, in international grain markets.

Average wheat production for the period 1945-1949 was 1,127,000 tons per year. Already, however, domestic consumption had begun to outstrip supply, and modest amounts of wheat were imported. In 1950, for instance, these amounted to about 500,000 tons. At the end of the first Five-Year Plan, domestic production stood at 1,272,000 tons, while imports, exclusive of flour, reached 1,230,000 tons. It is true that much of the imported wheat came under the US PL 480 program, but even when that supply was no longer available, after 1965, total consumption, carried along by population growth and rapid urbanization, did not decline. By 1973 the situation had become near catastrophic, and one of the reasons adduced by Sadat for going to war in October of that year was to call forth Arab aid that would allow Egypt to pay for its next round of grain imports (*A*, October 9, 1974). In 1974 Egypt produced 1,884,000 tons of wheat, and imported 2,251,000 tons more. Added to this was 258,000 tons of wheat flour. As PL 480 deliveries started up after a ten-years' halt in 1975, the foreign exchange constraint eased somewhat, and imports went on unabated. Production in 1978 reached 1,933,000 tons, but imports of wheat (3,560,000 tons) and flour (837,000) totaled 4,397,000 tons. In the space of thirty years domestic wheat production had increased by 71 percent, the population by 102 percent, and imports of wheat alone by 612 percent. The value of wheat and flour imports had grown to nearly half a billion dollars annually by the late 1970s and food imports in general to over $1 billion when own-exchange imports are included.

Egypt's new kind of dependency, worker migration, resulted in earnings that just about offset its old form of dependency, basic food grains imports. There is no reason to expect any diminution in grain imports and many reasons to assume that they will grow at a rate perhaps double that of the population.[4] By contrast, there is nothing inevitable about continued, no less increasing, worker migration, given Egypt's inimical relations with other Arab states and their desire to phase out *all* imported labor in the long run.

Foreign Private Capital

The urge to deepen, as it were, springs from considerations of national economic sovereignty. For many Third World leaders, Nasser among them, such sovereignty is incompatible with the presence of an important foreign private sector in the economy, linked to the money markets and MNCs of the industrialized core.

It is certainly the case that the dominant role of foreign capital in Egypt from the late nineteenth century up to the Second World War has been blamed as the cause of Egypt's backwardness and dependence. Even as the era of *infitah* dawned, Egyptian scholars continued to decry the historical influence of foreign capital in Egypt (Mutwali 1973c, 150:89):

> . . . the penetration of foreign capital impacted upon the Egyptian economy in a manner without parallel, depriving the country of a natural stage in its economic growth. This capital undertook an international operation to abort the growth of the Egyptian middle class and to deny Egypt and Egyptian national capital any capability to compete.

But while this is the prevalent view all along the Egyptian political spectrum, it is not entirely accurate.

The place of foreign capital in Egypt on the eve of the First World War was overwhelming: of a total of £E 100 million in fixed capital formation in industrial, commercial, and financial enterprises in 1914, 92 million was foreign-controlled (Crouchley 1936, p. 73). As a result of the world depression and the cessation of certain privileges for resident foreigners in 1936, the picture began to change rapidly. According to some estimates, of all companies founded between 1933 and 1948, Egyptians owned 79 percent of the capital (valued at £E 21 million). Thus as the monarchy approached its demise, of the £E 128 million in fixed capital in all enterprises, Egyptians owned 39 percent and foreigners 61 percent. The Egyptian share may in fact have been even greater, as several firms (Sugar Company, Khedival Mail Line, Delta

---

[4] Possibilities for increased production are limited. Wheat is grown in the winter and competes for acreage with clover and other fodder crops. To increase wheat acreage would require reductions in fodder (animal traction is still the heart of the agricultural process), and disruptions in the cotton rotations. Production increases will have to come vertically through improved yields. Egyptian experts estimate the total grain deficit at 6.3 million tons in 1985, 8 million in 1990 and 11.2 million in 2000 (*AI*, no. 616, November 3, 1980).

Light Railways) founded before 1933 were subsequently "Egyptianized."[5] The weight of Egyptians in management was similar: in 1951 32 percent of all industrial and commercial company directors were Egyptian, while 38 percent were European, 18 percent Jewish, and 11 percent Syro-Lebanese. Nonetheless, although it had perhaps been retarded in its growth, there is little doubt that an Egyptian capitalist class was taking shape when the monarchy was overthrown in 1952.

As I have already noted, very little new foreign investment entered Egypt after 1952, in all about £E 8 million between 1954 and 1961, concentrated in petroleum and pharmaceuticals (T. Labib 1974, p. 8). For obvious reasons, after 1961 and until 1973-74 foreign private investment was negligible. At the same time, beginning in 1956 the private assets of Europeans (British, French, and Belgian) were nationalized, followed by the piecemeal liquidation of Syro-Lebanese, Jewish, Greek, and Armenian interests. By 1965 the slate was wiped clean. Foreign private capital no longer played any role in the Egyptian economy. The only exception concerned oil exploration that by 1967 involved contracts worth about £E 30 million, but inasmuch as no equity was involved in the product-sharing contracts, this does not really count. In this sense, to the extent that deepening entails indigenization of foreign-owned assets and capital, the Nasserist regime was eminently successful.

That state of affairs was willingly undone by Sadat, but it is still too early to forecast where *infitah* may take Egypt. At the end of 1978 the foreign capital component of all approved Law 43 investment projects reached £E 1.2 billion, an impressive figure but one that probably involves very little equity capital. Actual foreign investments in the same year were £E 189 million or 8 percent of Egypt's total investment outlays. It was hoped that by 1984 annual infusions of foreign private capital would be running at £E 450 million or over 10 percent of planned investments (*FT*, July 30, 1979). What will be of greater significance than size is their location in the economy. It is only logical to expect that they will be concentrated in the leading industrial and financial sectors where, through joint ventures, they will determine far larger investment outlays and where they will be in a position to orient basic sectoral choices.

National Savings and Investment

There is no need to retrace here the argument made in Chapter Two. Readers need only refer to Table 2.3 and Figure 2.1 to refresh their memories. The point is that in the best of all possible worlds, deepening and self-reliance

[5] These figures were drawn from 'Abdullah Fihri Abaza Bey, "The Position of Foreign Capital in our National Economy," *Magalla Ghurfat al-Tigara al-Qahira* 16 (July-Aug. 1951):642-48. They correspond closely to those of 'Aziz Da'ud 1973, pp. 61-62. I am grateful to Robert Tignor who provided Abaza's estimates from his personal files.

are inseparable phenomena. Self-reliance in turn presupposes a high and sustained rate of domestic savings and investment. If such a rate is not attained, development plans must be shelved or the required capital borrowed from abroad.

Egypt was not able to achieve a high and sustained rate of national savings. The best that it could achieve was a savings rate in 1965 of 13.5 percent of GNP. Thereafter it declined, reaching an all-time low in 1975 of 4.3 percent. In the same year Egypt's resource gap, i.e. the difference between domestic savings and gross investment, reached 21 percent of GNP and was filled by external borrowing.[6]

Although there has been some improvement in the situation since 1975, the rate of increase in national savings is projected to lag behind the rate of increase in external borrowing. This fact is apparent in Table 9.9. Although the guesswork involved makes the calculation almost useless, if one were to suppose that Egypt's GNP rose to £E 16 billion in 1984, projected foreign-funded investment would still be 16 percent of that figure.

Conclusion

Deepening of a quality and kind sought by the Egyptian regime since 1957 and the first industrial plan has not taken place. Its greatest success has been

Table 9.9
Sources of GOE Total Revenues 1981-82

	Revenue £E billions	%
External sources	1,634.0	13.3
Taxes	5,479.7	44.7
(Direct	2,484.0	20.3)
(Indirect	2,995.7	24.4)
Returns on public assets	2,409.8	20.0
Social security, etc.	1,317.8	10.7
Autofinance of public companies	629.0	5.0
Proceeds of bonds, etc.	789.4	6.4
Total revenues	12,259.7	100.0

SOURCE: Figures released by Deputy Minister of Finance Muhammed 'Abduh, Al, no. 651, July 6, 1981.

[6] Voluntary private savings as a proportion of total private savings (which include social security and bank financing of the private sector), reached 25 percent in the late 1970s. This, however, was due largely to the increasing share of worker remittances in savings (IBRD 1980, p. 22).

in the elimination of foreign capital as a significant factor in the determination of development strategy and sectoral priorities. The implications of the open-door policy are that, if all goes well, foreign capital will once again take on considerable weight in the economy but not so much, so it is officially argued, that basic decisions will be warped in its favor.

The major failures have been in the generation of national savings and in agricultural modernization. On the one hand, financing the deepening process has increasingly come to rely on external sources, which rob it of much of its raison d'être. On the other, agriculture has not yet become a significant market, except for fertilizers, for the new industrial sector, nor has it achieved levels of production sufficient to meet most of Egypt's demand for food. Food and capital have been imported in increasingly large doses.

There has been considerable horizontal and some vertical industrial expansion. The industrial sector now accounts for 25 percent of GNP while agriculture's share has fallen to 24 percent. But much of industry's growth is the result of increased earnings from petroleum exports, and if they are excluded, the rest of industry accounts for only 14 percent of GNP. Vertical expansion is evident in the increased share in total manufacturing of chemicals, metallurgy, and metal products, but textiles and foodstuffs, so-called traditional industries, have consistently contributed 60 percent or more of the total value of industrial production. A similar pattern emerges in terms of employment, with 65 percent of public sector workers concentrated in textiles and food processing.

It may be that the structure of Egyptian imports and exports will signal the shape of the future. Consumer goods imports, exclusive of food, have lost their top ranking to intermediate goods that feed into the industrial production process. So, too, primary exports have ceded their place to the export of semi-finished and finished goods, although these include only a very small amount of heavy industrial products.

There has been a new surge of growth in the Egyptian economy since 1975, the first since the early 1960s. It is founded on a radically different strategy, dependent on foreign capital and technology and the reintroduction of market mechanisms to determine the pattern of resource and capital allocation. It may be that more industrial deepening will take place under these new policies than under those of state-led ISI and economic planning.

That said, it would be wrong to suppose that the new growth has resulted mainly from *infitah*. Rather the new growth is rooted in four phenomena none of which was "planned" in any meaningful sense, none of which is intimately bound to *infitah*, and three of which would have been perfectly welcome to Nasser's socialist experiment. They are: worker migration, tourist receipts, Suez Canal receipts, and petroleum export earnings. Together they have provided a foreign exchange cushion that has allowed Egypt to afford its new capitalist experiment but that might just as well have enabled Egypt to pay for its socialist experiment (cf. Iraq and especially Algeria). Nasser would have and did balk at the notion of substantial worker migration, for he believed that anyone with the skills to find work abroad would be sorely needed at home. The real question was and is whether or not worker remittances are to be more highly valued than their skills. The answer for the time being is yes, and Nasser, like the Algerians, might well have come to see that as well.

As for petroleum, canal tolls, and tourism, the first product-sharing agreements in the early 1960s, the nationalization of the canal, and the construction of Egypt's basic touristic infrastructure were all measures undertaken by Nasser's regime. He was unable to reap their benefits. His major error lay in foreign policy, leading him to the 1967 defeat. His economic policies, while far from brilliant, were never really given their day in court. One wonders what his regime would have done with $2.5 billion in annual petroleum revenues.

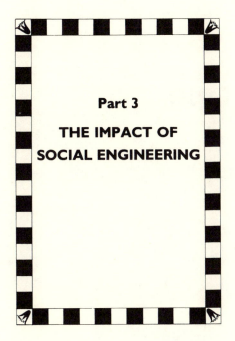

Part 3

THE IMPACT OF
SOCIAL ENGINEERING

Chapter Ten

EQUITY AND INEQUITY
WITHOUT PAIN

> . . . Reforms have often followed upon rash decisions
> from the top based on intuition rather than on cool
> and careful expert advice. Too often they have just
> been expedient palliatives and piecemeal measures
> chosen along the line of least popular dissatisfaction.
> [Bent Hansen 1972, pp. 72-73.]

Capital accumulation and investment have been the central themes of the preceding six chapters, but intimately linked to, and often working at counterpurposes with regime strategies for growth have been policies for social equity and income redistribution. There is no question that Nasserist policies led to far-reaching socio-economic leveling. In the span of two decades Egypt moved from a society in which the inequitable distribution of wealth was of the highly-skewed Latin American variety to one which by nonsocialist LDC standards was among the more egalitarian. Part of the cost of redistribution and greater equity, however, was inefficiency in public sector production and the stimulation of consumption at the expense of production. In Egypt, growth and equity were wedded only during the early 1960s.

Income Distribution

Income maldistribution and absolute poverty were public issues in prerevolutionary Egypt (Tignor 1982). In 1952 Muhammed Sa'id Bey, director-general of Customs, wrote in *al-Musawwar* (February 8, 1952, as cited in S. Yassin 1977, p. 21) an article entitled "Half Egypt's population lives like animals." The concern of this titled gentleman was not unusual. It was above all the question of rural poverty and the concentration of land ownership that preoccupied a number of Egyptian politicians, some of whom, like Ibrahim Shukri and Sayyid Mar'ai, remained active after 1952. They had good cause. By 1950 44 percent of all rural families were landless while .4 percent (2,042 families) owned 35 percent of the cultivated area. The top 1 percent of landowners (4,182 families) controlled 72 percent of Egypt's agricultural land, yielding a Gini coefficient of inequality of .61 (Abdel-Fadil 1975, pp. 4-12). Few other countries of the world could rival this concentration of rural resources.[1]

Rural overpopulation and land hunger fed a steady exodus to the cities. Mobilization of able-bodied men during the Second World War accelerated the process, and Cairo's population grew at 4.8 percent per annum between 1937 and 1947. Probably half of the 800,000 new Cairenes of those years were of rural origins, and many of the recruits among them stayed in the city after demobilization. A large *lumpen*-proletariat was crammed into Cairo's decaying medieval quarters, many of whose members were precariously anchored in the informal sector. Elements of this *lumpen*-proletariat set fire to Cairo in January 1952 and set in motion the collapse of the monarchy. After that fire urban poverty became as much an issue as rural.

Estimates of real income distribution have generally been unsatisfactory in Egypt, although periodic household budget surveys since 1960 have provided us a clearer image. For the period preceding 1960 available estimates are highly impressionistic albeit dramatic. Fathi 'Abd al-Fattah (1975a, pp. 118-19) advances the following table:

Table 10.1
National and Agricultural Per Capita Income, 1952-1964

	Nat'l. Per Capita Income		Agric. Per Capita Income	
	£E current prices	£E 1939 prices	£E current prices	£E 1939 prices
1952	37.1	11.7	19.3	6.1
1955	40.1	14.2	22.2	7.8
1957	44.6	15.2	23.7	8.2
1959	46.3	15.3	25	8.3
1962	52.5	17.2	22	7.2*
1964	57.9	19.4	28.7	9.6

SOURCE: Fathi 'Abd al-Fattah 1975a, p. 119.
* This figure reflects the failure of the cotton crop in the fall of 1961.

In constant 1939 prices, rural per capita incomes were exceedingly low: $20 per annum in 1959 for example. It must be remembered that peasants consume a good deal of what they produce, and the value of autoconsumption is not included in the figures above. Still, the overall poverty is undeniable. 'Abd al-Fattah goes further, however. He contends that in 1958, the 73 percent of the rural population without land earned £E 3.5 ($8.40) per capita per annum, while those owning twenty or more *feddans* earned £E 773 ($1,855) per capita

[1] See Chapter Twelve for a fuller treatment of rural stratification.

per annum. That yields a ratio of 220:1. It is well to keep this in mind, for when we look at gaps in average *expenditures* per capita, we shall see that the degree of skewedness is not as pronounced.

A survey carried out by a group of French social scientists in the late 1950s produced an equally grim profile of urban poverty (I.E.D.E.S. 1961, pp. 183-210; and Riad 1964, pp. 60-64). They calculated the total gainfully employed urban work force at 1.9 million with an average *per worker* income of £E 198 per annum. However, *per capita* urban incomes worked out to only £E 40, and this is an economic milieu that was and is almost entirely monetized.

As in the countryside, official statistics do not reflect the inactivity of women who, unless employed, are not considered part of the work force, nor of children of school age who are not in school and not employed. Thus while unemployment in Cairo in 1970 was officially put at 58,000 against 1.5 million employed, a more accurate figure would probably be over one million un-employed in Cairo alone (Wissa Wassef 1973a, pp. 37-39). Of the urban employed in 1960 (1.9 million) over a fifth were household servants earning £E 50 per capita and accounting for only 5 percent of the urban incomes, while the uppermost 2 percent of the urban employed accounted for 22 percent of urban incomes.

It is safe to say that postwar Egypt resembled faithfully Hollis Chenery's general characterization of income concentration in LDCs (Hollis Chenery et al. 1974, p. 40):

> The combined share of the top 40 percent of the population amounts to about three-quarters of the total GNP. Thus the rate of growth of GNP measures essentially the income growth of the upper 40 percent and is not much affected by what happens to the income of the remaining 60 percent of the population.

Nasser, like Nehru in India, believed, long before Chenery wrote about it, that this kind of concentration could be eroded, that wealth could be redis-tributed to the poorest and that rapid economic growth would be not only compatible with redistribution but its sine qua non. It was left to his economic advisors to work out policies of redistribution—land reform, the employment drive, commodity subsidies, free education through the university—while simultaneously taxing the redistributed wealth through compulsory crop de-liveries, forced savings, regressive sales taxes, and the like. As already noted, there was one brief moment, roughly 1961-1965, when the policies worked, but after that there was a period of no growth and no redistribution (1966-1973), followed by the current phase of rapid growth and worsening distri-butional equity.

Let us look first at a statistic that is frequently passed off as meaningless but which over time can indicate general trends. The statistic is per capita

GNP. There are, to my knowledge, no long constant-price series for this statistic in Egypt, but some facts are well-established. Hansen, al-Gritli, and others have shown that in real terms per capita income declined substantially from the mid-1920s to the end of the Second World War (from £E 37 to £E 28 in 1954 prices: Gritli 1962, p. 197) and by 1957 had still not made up the lost ground (£E 32). Over the course of the revolution per capita income gains have been modest.

Table 10.2
National Per Capita Income, 1952-1979 in Constant 1952-53 Prices

Year	Nat'l. Income (£E millions)	% Annual Increase	Per Capita Income (£E)	% Annual Increase
1952-53	806	—	37.1	—
1955-56	881	2.3	37.7	.4
1959-60	1,091	4.6	42.6	2.6
1964-65	1,480	5.9	50.7	3.2
1969-70	1,746	3.0	53.2	.8*
1976	2,137	3.2	58.3	1.3
1979	2,742	7.1	66.8	3.6

SOURCE: 1952-1970 figures from CAPMAS 1973, p. 243. The entries for 1976 and 1979 were derived from the figures used in Table 2.3 and include only the population resident in Egypt.
*Dr. Ahmad al-Murshidi contended that there was an absolute decline in per capita income between 1965 and 1970. See al-Tali'a, July 1974, p. 24.

Taken only as indicating trends and general orders of magnitude those estimates are quite plausible and adhere closely to the performance of nearly all Egypt's economic indicators: a gathering of momentum in the late 1950s, a strong growth peaking in 1965, marked decline until the early 1970s, and then a new rise in growth.

The various studies now available that estimate the size distribution of income on the basis of the household budget surveys of 1960, 1965, and 1975 (e.g., Osman al-Kholie 1973, pp. 33-56; Lance Taylor in IBRD 1978a, 1:82-96; Issawy 1982, pp. 88-131) present a picture of unexcessive and fairly unchanging inequality (see Table 10.3).

These statistics, as Lance Taylor commented (IBRD 1978a, 1:82), are slightly more egalitarian than most LDCs. But what is perhaps more significant is that despite the great effort at socialist transformation in the 1960s, so little redistribution took place. Unsurprisingly the income gap between rural and urban areas widened in favor of the latter throughout the period (Osman al-Kholie 1973, p. 365) and average incomes were and are about twice as high in the cities as in the countryside.[2] Two caveats regarding the difficulties of

[2] In 1975-76 roughly £E 198 per capita in the cities to £E 99 in rural areas: Waterbury 1982;

Table 10.3
Relative Shares in Rural (R) and Urban (U) Household
Expenditures with Gini Coefficients, 1958-1975

| Relative Shares | 1958-59 | | 1964-65 | | 1974-75 | |
of Income	R	U	R	U	R	U
Lowest 40%	17.6	16.4	19	16.5	18.8	18.3
Lowest 60%	34.2	30.9	35.2	31.2	35.5	34.4
Middle 30%	37.7	38.7	37.2	38.0	37.8	38.0
Top 10%	28.0	30.4	27.4	30.8	26.7	27.6
Gini coefficient	.37	.40	.35	.40	.35*	.37

SOURCE: Issawy 1982.
* Radwan 1977, p. 43, using the same sources, comes up with rural Gini coefficients for the same years of .37, .35, and .39. Cf. Mohaya Zaytoun 1982.

these extrapolations are in order. First, household expenditures are a poor surrogate for real income. In particular what they can tell us about the real wealth of the better-off is limited. Second, in the urban areas in particular, they overweight the "regularly employed," the salaried, and the middle-class strata. The lowest and uppermost deciles of the population tend to get lost in studies based on these data.

Because the urban informal sector is inadequately reflected in expenditure surveys, the income gap between urban and rural areas may be even less than that stated above. However that may be, two analysts have separately calculated that in the mid-1970s about 11 million Egyptians, rural and urban, lived below the poverty line. Samir Radwan (1977, p. 42) set that line at £E 270 per household, per annum for *rural* families in 1975. He found that 44 percent of all rural families and 28 percent of the rural population fell below that line. The same figures in 1964-65 were 27 percent and 17 percent, so that one finds here the same decline registered with respect to other indicators. Sa'ad Ibrahim (1982) argues that the poverty line for urban households in the same year is about £E 350 per annum. Ibrahim estimates that 35 percent of all urban households fall below that floor. A study by Mona Serageldin in general shows a highly skewed pattern of income distribution in the cities. Using her figures and Ibrahim's threshold, we find that 48 percent of the urban population is living in absolute poverty (in USAID 1976, p. 89). Using the population breakdown of 1976, Radwan's and Ibrahim's estimated shares yield the total of 11 million Egyptians living in absolute poverty.

All of the available data on income distribution take us no further than 1975. Yet as we know the open-door policies initiated in 1974 have had far-reaching effects upon the economy and probably upon the distribution of

cf. Amr Mohie Eldine in Eckaus et al. 1978, pp. 94-98 for income estimates computed from sectoral returns to factors.

wealth. The logic of *infitah* is to encourage middle- and upper-class investment and speculation while allowing inflation (20-30 percent per annum since 1975) to hold down the real wages of the lower-middle class and poor. The better-off are supposed to become richer and to save and invest; otherwise, *infitah* will not be a vehicle for growth. Likewise as wage increases lag behind the rate of growth in national income, wealth will be redistributed upwards.

Even by 1975 that trend could be measured. Issawy (1982) demonstrated that the share of wages in GDP increased from 45 percent in the late 1950s to 50 percent in the early 1970s only to fall back to 44 percent in 1975. The Economic Analysis Unit in the Ministry of Economy put the share of wages in GDP at 43 percent in 1975, 40 percent in 1978 and 36 percent in 1979. Property income has of course followed the exact inverse of this trend. More-over, the new redistribution upwards is predominantly an urban phenomenon, for the share of wages in agricultural income has been *increasing* since the early 1970s (Mohie Eldine 1982).[3] This is as one would expect, for private sector revival, real estate speculation, the import traders, foreign investors, and the like are concentrated in the cities.

There is an offsetting factor mitigating the effects of growing inequality. Available data do not measure the impact of migrant workers' earnings upon income distribution. Although remitted earnings were running at over $1.5 billion by the late 1970s, it may be nearly impossible to measure their impact upon families with any accuracy. This is because most remittances enter the country through unrecorded foreign exchange sales under the own-exchange system or as consumer durables. Still the impact can only be enormous. In the aggregate remittances are the equivalent of one-third the total domestic wage bill and bear directly upon at least half a million households and over two million people. While it may not be the most destitute who migrate, the majority are poor. What would be extremely important to know is the share in remittances of the 10 percent of the migrants who are highly skilled and middle class (Birks and Sinclair 1978), but that information is not available. If they accounted for 30 percent of all remittances, it would mean that, in 1980, about $1.4 billion would be the share of the remaining 90 percent, or something like $2,800 per capita. This is to be compared to the average per capita income in 1979 and in 1979 prices of $358. Using more recent estimates yields roughly similar results. The Development Planning and Technological Research Center (DPTRC) of Cairo University put the active Egyptian work force abroad in 1981 at 1 million (1.7 million with dependents). Taking the revised estimate of £E 2.8 billion in worker remittances in 1980, we come up with 900,000 workers earning £E 1.96 billion, or £E 2,177 per capita,

---

[3] Although increasing since the early 1970s, they had fallen from their peak in 1966 of 33 percent to 26 percent in 1976.

(i.e., about $3,110 per capita at 70 piastres to the dollar) (DPTRC estimate given by 'Amr Mohie Eldine in an interview with the author, October 19, 1981). The figures do not include income spent in the workers' countries of employment. Choucri and Eckaus (1979, pp. 789-90) are probably right that in a general sense the failure of national accounting statistics to record adequately migrant workers' savings and remittances has led to a major underestimate of Egypt's real GNP.

Indirect Redistribution: Subsidies and Services

The welfare state that the Egyptian regime gradually constructed after 1960 has had a major impact upon the redistribution of valued goods in Egyptian society. The provision of free or highly subsidized services and commodities has, in theory and to a considerable extent in fact, afforded the poorest 60 percent of the population benefits they might otherwise not have been able to afford.

In January 1979 the Minister of Planning 'Abd al-Razzaq 'Abd al-Magid claimed that while average per capita income was £E 250, or over £E 1,000 per family, the state paid out an additional £E 150 per *family* in subsidies and £E 275 per *family* in services. In short, through indirect means the state was increasing each Egyptian family's effective income by 35 percent on average (*AY*, January 6, 1979). Average indirect income figures are not much more useful than the per capita GNP statistic, but there can be little doubt that the poor are the major beneficiaries of these programs.

Price subsidies have taken on a life of their own in the Egyptian economy and now require financial resources equivalent to over 50 percent of all central governmental expenditures. From their modest beginnings in the Second World War, they have centered on reducing prices of basic food commodities— wheat, flour, edible oils—primarily for the urban poor. Food subsidies have grown prodigiously over the years and never account for less than half of the total subsidy bill. In 1979, if subsidized foodstuffs had been distributed equitably, each Egyptian would have received £E 22 of such commodities. Actual milling and distribution of the flour is clearly aimed at the urban poor, however, and is almost unabashedly designed to disarm potentially volatile and strategically situated disadvantaged populations. Sadat's pledges never to raise the price of Egyptian flat loaves, set in 1945 at 5 millemes, had little meaning for peasants who mill and bake their own, nor for the well-to-do whose diets no longer rely on low-quality starches.

Egypt grows relatively little of its own wheat and has had to resort to the international market and bilateral aid to meet demand as distinct from needs. In eighteen years, from 1960 to 1978, the per capita share of imported wheat and flour rose from 45 to 103 kilograms (see Table 2.3). Because imports

Table 10.4
Subsidies as a Proportion of Total Public Current Expenditures, 1960-1980
(£E mil. current)

	Current Expenditure (1)	Subsidies (2)	(2)/(1)
1960-61	340.5	9.0	2.6
1964-65	611.6	45.0	7.3
1968-69	561.9	8.0	1.4
1970-71	661.4	51.0	7.7
1974	839.7	355.5	42.3
1976	1,289.6	433.5	33.6
1978	1,664.0	710.0	42.6
1980	2,182.0	1,279.0	58.6

SOURCES: Entries for 1960-1971 are from IBRD 1978a, 6:57; the remaining figures have been drawn from unpublished IMF data and published Egyptian budgets for 1979 and 1980. *Actual* subsidies in 1980 were £E 1.8 billion.

constitute over 70 percent of consumption, the costs of subsidies fluctuate with the import price of wheat. The US-Soviet wheat deal of 1972 drove the price up dramatically, while increased supply and renewed PL 480 shipments to Egypt have subsequently reduced it. Still, because the amounts imported increase inexorably while local production lags behind, the overall trend is for the bread subsidy to grow steadily: wheat and flour subsidies stood at £E 80 million in 1970 and £E 586 million in 1979 (*AI*, no. 588, February 15, 1980).

Other commodities have taken on greater weight in the subsidy program as demand has outstripped local production, causing a sharp rise in imports. By 1976 these commodities accounted for more than half of the food subsidy bill.

In two stages, July 1978 and January 1979, the import price of subsidized goods was reevaluated at the incentive rather than the official rate of exchange. This had the effect of driving the import bill upward by about 70 percent, and, as the government was reluctant to pass much of the increase on to the consumer, to increase the subsidy budget by at least that much as well.

Subsidies have become a kind of Kafkaesque nightmare for Egyptian economists. Their initial welfare objectives were and are well-intentioned, and they have been partially successful. On the other hand their unchecked growth, and the profligate use of foreign exchange to maintain them, have been dictated by political expediency. The economic price has been distortions in the al-

214

Table 10.5
Evolution of Government Subsidies to Some Food Commodities, 1969-1976
(£E millions current)

Commodity	1969-70	1970-71	1971-72	1973	1974	1975	1976
Wheat	4.9	21	20	69.5	191.7	265.8	182.8
Wheat flour	—	—	—	8.2	27.6	31.1	33.0
Maize	.2	.9	.6	—	16.5	43.7	30.3
Beans	—	—	—	—	.4	4.7	4.5
Lentils	—	.1	—	.5	2.1	4.9	11.5
Oil	6.5	10.5	19.5	16.8	44.7	69.7	65.0
Fats	—	—	—	2.9	12.7	24.2	27.0
Frozen meat	—	—	—	—	.007	.2	—
Fresh meat	—	—	—	—	.04	.3	.3
Sugar	—	—	—	—	16.2	17.2	15.3
Other	.01	.6	2.6	3.3	13.1	21.9	23.7
Total	11.6	33.1	42.7	101.2	325	483.7	393.4

SOURCE: 'Issam Rifa'at 1978c, p. 9.

location of material resources and entrepreneurship, which can only be judged as harmful. In laborious negotiations with the Egyptians, the IMF has urged, as part of a broader stabilization program, the gradual phasing-out of the subsidies. Yet in complying with other aspects of IMF recommendations, such as the adjustment of exchange rates in 1978 and 1979, Egypt has actually increased the size of the subsidy bill. No policy-maker since the riots of January 1977 (of which more later) has recommended higher prices for basic commodities nor curtailing consumption. Characteristically, in taking over the role of "economic czar" from Hamid Sayyih in May 1980, 'Abd al-Razzaq 'Abd al-Magid redrafted the budget with a 22 percent increase in the subsidy bill, up to £E 1.5 billion. He increased allocations in nearly every category, doubling the popular cloth subsidy and quintupling industrial subsidies (*MEED*, June 13, 1980, p. 22).[4]

In terms of their distorting effects, subsidies should not be viewed separately from administered prices in general. They have led predictably to reenforcing patterns that cannot be easily undone. Wheat subsidies have caused a major shift in diets away from Egypt's traditional corn flour and toward reliance upon a commodity Egypt does not and cannot produce in sufficient quantities. Moreover, the artificially low price of wheat and bread has made them at-

[4] In an interview in 1975 'Abd al-Magid told the author that he believed foreign investors should favor subsidies because they allowed the state to hold down the wage level, a factor that should be attractive to investors.

Table 10.6
The Evolution of Total Direct Subsidies, 1977-1980
(£E millions current)

	1977	1978	1979	1980§
Gen. Org. for consumer goods				
(foodstuffs, tobacco, tea)	313.4	432.7	884.6	944.0
Housing coop. credit*	.3	.8	2.9	6.7
Agric. credit†	5.7	9.9	17.4	22.4
Bottled gas	10.2	15.1	32.5	70.0
"Popular" cloth	16.3	46.0	46.0	55.1
Crop price adj.*	13.0	32.8	66.1	85.8
Cotton pest control	—	30.0	30.6	46.0
Cotton purchase increase‡	—	—	30.0	—
Cairo Transport Authority	9.7	13.5	22.2	13.8
Alexandria Transport Authority	1.8	4.0	6.2	5.5
School notebooks	2.5	2.0	2.0	2.0
Newsprint	3.5	8.0	5.0	—
Medicine, powdered milk	—	—	6.0	6.0
Middle East News Agency	—	1.3	1.3	1.3
Egyptian Navigation Co.	—	4.0	5.0	—
Industrial subsidies	—	79.4	19.0	10.0
Miscellaneous	4.5	.3	—	1.0
Total	380.9	679.8	1,176.8	1,269.6

SOURCE: From annual budgets as presented to parliament.

* Represents subsidized interest rates on loans.

† Consisting mainly in fertilizer subsidies.

‡ Presumably increase in subsidy to textile industry resulting from increase in cotton purchase price. Note also that cement and other building material subsidies are not included in these figures.

§ Planned. Actual subsidies reached £E 1.8 billion in 1980 and £E 2.3 billion in 1981.

tractive substitutes for various freely marketed animal and poultry feeds. Cairo's cart owners have been known to feed bread and beans to their donkeys because they are cheaper than dry fodder or clover.

Subsidized goods that are in short supply, such as tea, sugar, unbroken rice, cooking oil, etc., typically find their way into black markets where higher-income customers buy them up. Beginning in the 1960s the Ministry of Supply began running fair-price shops, loosely referred to as coops, in the urban areas to market basic commodities. Ration cards were required for only tea, sugar, and oil in these shops, while other subsidized goods could be bought in monthly allotments according to family size. Rich and poor have equal access to the goods. What happened was that private retailers would dispatch "buyers" with false ration cards or family books to stand in the endless lines at the coops to buy up butter, oil, tea, chickens, frozen meat, or whatever else was available. These goods would then be resold in middle and upper-middle class neighborhoods at a handsome profit. Frequently managers of coop stores simply sold off their deliveries of coveted goods to private buyers before they even entered the shop.

So far no serious attempt to introduce a rationing system based on real need has been made.[5] Nor has there been much zeal in monitoring abuse in distribution. The coops are still run like private enterprises, and the city bakeries that handle much of the subsidized flour are not held to weight and quality specifications in the bread they sell to retailers.

In 1980, according to figures from the Ministry of Supply (reported in Von Braun 1980, Table 20), there were 30,530 fair-price shops nationwide. In terms of numbers, rural areas were better served than the cities. In Cairo, there were 688 ration-card carriers for each shop while most rural provinces had ratios of 200 or less. Most subsidized consumer goods are sold through licensed private retailers and here again rural dwellers appear to fare as well on a per capita basis as urbanites (H. Alderman et. al. *Egypt's Food Subsidy System*, IFPRI, 1982).

A visitor to Egypt will see no starving people, and few people in rags. The efforts made since 1952 to provide housing, clothing, and food for all Egyptians have borne fruit. However, a World Bank basic-needs survey of Egypt picked out certain areas in which improved welfare has been superficial or deficient. In clothing there has been an unmistakeable improvement. Per capita consumption of shoes doubled between 1970 and 1977, and that of cotton textiles increased by 21 percent. Per capita consumption of wheat, domestic and imported, grew from 120 kilograms per annum to 130 over the same period, while sugar grew from 16 to 21 kilograms per annum. In contrast per capita consumption of beans, relatively rich in protein, declined, as did that of meat. The same report found that over 20 percent of all preschool children suffered from chronic malnutrition (IBRD 1979c). In sum, the record of consumer subsidies in Egypt is not unlike that of the employment drive: they have partially reached their target but poverty has been no more eliminated than unemployment, and both policies have saddled the state with costs it can ill-afford but is seemingly incapable of reducing.

Indirect subsidies do not show up in official statistics, yet they may represent in value as much as the direct subsidy bill. For instance, public sector industries, especially Kima Fertilizers and Nag' Hammadi Aluminum, purchase

---

[5] 'Abd al-Magid on television tore up his rationing card to show its inappropriateness for someone of his income. In other countries, because of various forms of "leakage," subsidies are believed to benefit the 60 percent of the population least needing them (Bhatt and Meerman 1978, p. 51).

their electricity at a highly subsidized rate. On an entirely different scale is the provision gratis of irrigation water and drainage to Egypt's cultivators. The cost of construction and maintenance of this vast infrastructure has simply been absorbed by the state.

Far and away the most significant indirect subsidy attaches to petroleum and gas products. Because Egypt produces a good deal of these itself and is a net exporter, petroleum subsidies as such are seldom reported. As world petroleum prices soared after 1973, the indirect subsidy has grown commensurately: in 1976 it stood at £E 206 million, in 1977 at £E 310 million, and in 1980 at £E 867 million (*A*, January 27, 1977 and *AI*, no. 645, May 25, 1981). In 1980 three-quarters of the total indirect subsidies were accounted for by oil for thermal generators, diesel fuel, and kerosene. The subsidy of bottled gas, used for cooking and heating, stood at £E 73 million and that for high octane gasoline at £E 18 million.

The *infitah* era marks a sharp break with the socialism of the 1960s, at which time consumer subsidies first gained some importance. Yet for all the talk about increased efficiency, benefit-cost criteria, belt-tightening and so forth, Sadat actually increased the flow of resources into welfare programs that sustain high levels of consumption. Likewise, the 1970s witnessed some resurgence of spending on social services and education, areas that had been relatively neglected during the industrialization drive and absolutely neglected in the wake of the June War.

The principal efforts in this latter domain have come in health and education. Both are directly related to income distribution; both have great symbolic value in politics. The state has made it its obligation to raise the general health standard of the population. The image of malnourished peasants, ridden with bilharzia and trachoma, toiling in the cotton fields for the benefit of the mills of Lancaster and Manchester was a staple of nationalist propaganda. With independence, the emphasis shifted from poor health as a facet of colonial exploitation to that of health as the key to increased productivity and, presumably, higher incomes. Similarly, the state's commitment to mass education sought to overcome the elitism of the colonial system and to provide all Egyptians an opportunity for upward mobility through literacy and specialized training.

The results of these efforts have been very uneven. As Table 10.7 shows, per capita outlays on services increased substantially during the 1950s, peaked in 1965, fell off after 1967, and regained momentum in the 1970s. If one takes inflation into account, however, there has probably been no real increase in per capita expenditures since 1965. The evolution of investment outlays has followed the same pattern except that there is a marked growth in the share of services in the middle 1970s. The figure of 19.3 percent is highly misleading. The great bulk of the investment went into housing, and most of

Table 10.7
Recurrent Per Capita Outlays on Services, 1951-1976

	1951-52	1964-65	1967-68	1976
Population (millions)	21.2	29.0	31.3	38.2
Education £E per cap.	.12	1.15	.76	6.3
Health £E per cap.	.48	1.5	1.2	2.1
Housing and utilities £E per cap.	.28	3.4	2.0	1.1
Soc. Serv. £E per cap.	.27	.69	.67	.75
Total £E per cap.	1.2	6.8	4.6	9.8
% Total invest. devoted to services	5.6%	6.1%	2.4%	19.3%

SOURCE: From CAPMAS 1973, Table 2.1.3; and IBRD 1978a, 6:57.

this consisted in reconstruction of the Canal Zone cities. If housing investment is removed, then the share of services in total investment drops to only 3.3 percent. Projected investments for the period 1980-1984 would raise the share of services, exclusive of housing, to 8 percent of the total.

Much of the growth in recurrent and investment outlays in the middle 1960s consisted in the development of basic health and educational infrastructure, especially rural health units and schools. By 1978, for example, all rural inhabitants were served by over 2,500 health units and centers (nearly one for every two villages), and 24 hospitals. While there appears to have been only marginal improvement in the eradication of endemic disease, overall health standards have improved to the point that the crude death rate has dropped from fifteen to eleven per thousand in a decade. Likewise all citizens have access to primary schools (the total number doubled to 10,000 between 1952 and 1976), and the proportion of the population over ten that is literate has grown. This notwithstanding, the already meager resources devoted to services have been swamped by population growth. Moreover, once the physical infrastructure was in place, most of these resources have gone into salaries for the personnel that operates it. For example, in 1969-70 the budget of the Ministry of Education was £E 104 million. Of that £E 87.2 million went to salaries, £E 1.3 million to building maintenance, and £E 15.6 million to administration, printing, and sports.

Without question the pledge to provide primary education to all Egyptians between six and twelve years old, to eradicate adult illiteracy, and to abolish fees for all levels of instruction, has elicited an enthusiastic social response and endorsement unequaled by *any* of the regime's other major goals. This commitment was and is one to enlightenment, upward mobility, respectability, and, to no small extent, old-age security for parents who were denied similar opportunities. With the exception of the abolition of fees, the pledge has not been fulfilled. It was, then, with no degree of exaggeration that a special National Council observed that in the 1950s "the people received their right as citizens to education in the same manner as their right to water and air" (ARE: Presidency, Specialized Councils 1974, p. 12). The Council's 1974 investigation, however, documented the extent to which this right had been denied a large segment of the Egyptian population. It was a familiar tale and ended with a familiar appeal: a crash program to enroll all eligible children between six and twelve years old in primary school within five years and to extend basic literacy training to Egypt's adults.

The distance to be covered is daunting. In 1976 there were 15.6 million illiterate Egyptians, ten years old or older (CAPMAS 1976a). As noted in Chapter Three, while the proportion of the population that is illiterate is dwindling, the absolute numbers of illiterates are increasing.[6] It has been left to the public primary education system to overcome this embedded ignorance.

Over a twenty-five year period, 1951-1976, primary school enrollments more than quadrupled, from 1 to 4.2 million. At the beginning of that period less than half the children of school age were in school. Since then progress has been rapid, but how rapid is a matter of some conjecture. The World Bank estimated the total eligible population between six and twelve years at 7.4 million, and, using the Ministry of Education enrollment figure of 4.2 million, concluded that only 56 percent of those eligible were in school (IBRD 1979c, p. 11). It is hard to know how the total eligibility figure was obtained, for it appears much too high. In 1974 the total eligibility figure was put at 5.8 million (Yussef Khalil Yussef 1974, p. 6), and increasing that base by the annual average growth rate of 2.3 percent yields a total of 6.2 million in 1976-77. As Table 10.8 reveals, about 67 percent of all eligible children were

Table 10.8
Male/Female Primary School Enrollment, 1976

Sex	Population aged 6-12 (millions) (1)	Number of children enrolled (millions) (2)	(1)/(2)
Boys	3.17	2.54	80.1
Girls	3.05	1.61	52.7
Total	6.22	4.15	66.7

SOURCE: From ARE: Ministry of Education, *Development and Flow of General Education, 1950-1977,* Cairo, 1977. Total eligibility figure derived from Yussef Khalil Yussef 1974, p. 6.

[6] The Specialized National Council estimated that in 1974 the government and public sector employed 130,000 illiterates, and the armed forces had another 100,000 in its ranks.

in school. If that is a close estimate, it represents a marked decline from the 74.6 percent enrolled in 1965-66. One need hardly be surprised. The table also shows the marked sex bias of primary education, rural families in particular attaching little value to female education. However, the decline in enrollments has been less severe for females than for males. The situation is even more somber than the table indicates. The Specialized National Council reported that about 25 percent of all primary schoolgoers drop out, only one in three move on to the preparatory or intermediate level, and that over 60 percent of all primary schoolchildren eventually revert to functional illiteracy (ARE: Presidency Specialized Councils 1974, p. 95).

When one reviews the evolution of enrollment figures for all levels of education, an unacknowledged triage can be observed. The ideal of universal primary education will doubtless be extolled, but the commitment necessary to attain it may no longer be there. The rate of growth of the eligible population has been more rapid than that of new enrollments. Further, there are 155,000 teachers to handle over six million students at all levels below university. Student-teacher ratios are deteriorating, but the Ministry of Education regularly approves the annual delegation of over 30,000 teachers to Arab and African countries.

Intermediate education is expanding rapidly while secondary and university education have grown since 1969-70 at over 20 percent per annum. By contrast public technical institutes that were to have bolstered the ranks of literate, skilled labor (electricians, mechanics, typists, etc.) have languished. Secondary and university education are intimately joined, forming the track to high-prestige employment. Those who have already followed this path are an important political constituency, and they want their children to have the same opportunity. The enrollment figures in Table 10.9 are solid evidence that their desire is being met.

The secondary school or university diploma has been justifiably seen as a free ticket to high-status employment, above all in the public sector. The nationalizations of 1961 and the expansion of the state thereafter created a large demand for highly trained cadres, which was more than met by the educational system. Sa'ad Ibrahim, on the basis of a limited survey, has postulated that the *rate* of upward social mobility for the educated is slowing perceptibly in the 1970s. By comparing the educational status of a sample of Egyptians to that of their fathers, it was found that of forty-eight respondents with college educations only thirteen had college-educated fathers. The ratio of 4:1 held also for respondents with secondary education. However, Ibrahim found that the offspring of the respondents were no more likely than their fathers to have a college education and only twice as likely to have a secondary education (Sa'ad Ibrahim 1982). A similar conclusion is reached by Clement Moore in his study of Egyptian engineers (Moore 1980, pp. 126-30). He

Table 10.9
Evolution of Enrollment All Levels of Education, 1952-1977

	1952-53	1965-66	1969-70	1976-77	% Growth 1969-1977
Primary	1,540,202	3,417,753	3,618,663	4,151,956	15
Intermediate	348,574*	574,420	793,891	1,435,529	81
Secondary	181,789	208,991	293,144	796,411	161
Tech					
Institute	5,285*	34,702	35,300	31,541	−10.6
University	51,681	140,143	161,517	453,696	180

SOURCES: From CAPMAS 1973, p. 220; Mead 1967, p. 300; CAPMAS 1970, pp. 148-69 and *Statistical Yearbook*, July 1978, pp. 155-81.
* Figures are for 1953-54.

Table 10.10
Growth of the Social Security Program, 1964-1980

Year	Participants (millions)	Pensioners (thousands)	Pensions (£E mill. current)
1964	1.7	102	8.2
1970	2.9	153	43.0
1975	4.0	270	142.0
1980	10.5 (proj.)	430 (proj.)	320.0 (proj.)

SOURCE: *TME*, March 1976, p. 81; and *AI*, no. 613, October 13, 1980.

measured a great expansion in the training and placement of engineers in the 1960s. He then projected output of engineers over a fifteen-year period against the likely creation of posts and came up with 50,000 engineers vying for 10,000 public sector openings in 1990. Only emigration or private sector employment could save them from a dramatic loss in status.

There remains one program to consider that could have considerable impact on social welfare and individual incomes, and that is employees' pensions. To date social security payments have been used by the state as a means of forced savings, but as the number of pensioners grows so will the size of payments to them. The growth in their numbers can be seen in Table 10.10. One should note that in 1975 less than half the work force participated in the program, and the participants consisted overwhelmingly of public sector employees and civil servants along with some regularly employed private sector workers. The figures projected for 1980 are probably unrealistic, for they imply coverage of most of the "active" population. For those who benefit from it, it may ease anxieties about old age and reduce the impulse to produce progeny as a form of old-age insurance. On the other hand the prime beneficiaries for the foreseeable future will come from the urban working elite and middle classes to the exclusion of peasants and those in the urban informal sector who are most in need of some sort of protection (Garrison 1978, p. 290).

In sum, the ambitious welfare programs, including the employment drive of the 1960s, could have been sustained only if the economy itself had expanded rapidly. But as stagnation set in in the late 1960s and early 1970s, without any corresponding slowdown in population growth, the goals of extending basic services to all Egyptians had to be quietly abandoned. The abandonment is, in effect, the abandonment of the socio-economic inclusion of the "socialist" phase, coupled with the official tolerance of policies of benign neglect of basic welfare programs, and the acceptance of growing inequity in the distribution of income and in the quality of social services. High rates of inflation on the one hand, with the explicit policy of stimulating middle-class savings and entrepreneurship on the other, have produced a situation in which large segments of the population are losing ground to the better-off in relative and absolute terms. Further, the state has shown itself willing to revert to a moderately elitist educational system that caters to the offspring of the already educated while it arouses the aspirations, without augmenting the skills, of the poor. The socio-professional advancement of whole strata of Egyptian society under state auspices has come to an end. Egypt's leaders are not blind to the longer-range implications of this growing inequality. Their steadfast support of the consumer-goods subsidies represents an attempt to buy acquiescence to this situation from the poorer strata of the cities.[7] They will not concede that the costs to the economy in terms of deficit-financing and inflation may make these programs self-defeating.

It is Husni Mubarak's fate to face this situation directly. He and his peers in age, in their early twenties at the time of the revolution, are the oldest among those Egyptians who reached adulthood between 1952 and 1965 and experienced the greatest degree of upward mobility in the Nasserist era. They moved up rapidly in the expanding ranks of the armed forces, civil service, and public sector. Mubarak, who became commander of the air force in 1972, is a perfect example. But now, given the youth of this generation (thirty-five to fifty-five years old), the upper strata of the state apparatus and armed forces are clogged, and those who reached adulthood after 1965 cannot hope to achieve similar heights. Inevitably, frustration has become acute. It has been

---

[7] It would be a bit like serving free coffee and doughnuts to the drivers in the stalled lane of Hirschman's "tunnel-effect" analogy.

in part voiced through extremist Muslim politics (see Chapter Fifteen) and in part defused through the exit of workers abroad.

Taxes

In advanced industrial societies, personal income tax-returns can provide a fairly accurate profile of the size distribution of income. In Egypt, by contrast, the bulk of the population is exempt from income tax, and many of those who are subject to it evade it. The progressive income tax has neither been an important source of revenue for the government, nor an instrument for redistributing wealth.

It was not until 1937 that taxes on business profits and in 1939 that taxes on personal income were introduced in Egypt. Prior to those dates most direct government revenues came from customs duties, production levies, and taxes on agricultural land and urban real estate. Despite the application of a progressive income tax since 1939, revenues from it have never been very significant, although in recent years the business profits tax has grown impressively (see Table 10.11).

Indirect taxes, even net of customs duties, have always brought in revenues far in excess of income tax: in 1979, for example, the stamp tax generated £E 155 million in revenues while all taxes on personal income generated only £E 47 million. The stamp tax, like most indirect taxes, falls equally on rich

Table 10.11
Development of Tax Structure, 1952-1979

(£E million current)

Tax	1952-53	1959-60	1965-66	1970-71	1975	1979
Business Profits	12.1	17.5	71.9	115.3	189.3	572.0
Personal Income	9.3	10.8	18.4	28.2	31.1	47.3
salaries, wages	3.4	5.2	14.5	24.0	26.9	NA
gen. income	5.7	5.2	3.3	3.0	1.9	NA
free professions	.2	.3	.7	1.2	2.3	NA
Real Estate and Inherit.	17.7	15.0	23.6	31.6	17.2	17.5
agric. land	13.7	13.6	8.6	13.1	9.6	NA
Stamp Tax	5.1	8.2	15.5	36.1	52.2	154.7
Commodity Taxes	87.7	103.9	226.1	367.4	623.8	1,602.3
customs	75.8	80.7	172.0	196.3	399.9	822.7
Other	16.7	57.9	1.1	6.3	52.5	94.5
Total	148.6	213.3	356.6	584.9	966.1	2,488.3

SOURCE: From Edel 1982; and 1980 Budget as published in supplement to Al, January 1, 1980.

and poor. It is the fee exacted to push any official paper through the administrative labyrinth. The same nonprogressive character inheres in all commodity and sales taxes—the rich pay more only if they buy more.

The yield of profits and income tax is heavily dependent upon the public sector and the public payroll. Public sector companies and organizations, above all in recent years the petroleum sector, account for the bulk of profits and other business taxes. Concomitantly, all those on public payrolls are taxed at the source and thus make up the bulk of contributors to Egypt's IRS. The rest of the population is either exempt from tax or randomly ensnared by revenue officers. Foreign residents and businesses may be more scrupulous than most in honest disclosure of income and tax payment for they are highly visible and subject to expulsion. On the other hand, doctors, lawyers, and other professionals who collect unrecepted cash fees are very difficult to monitor. The same holds true for wholesalers, retailers, small businesses, contractors, and real estate speculators. Their records are imperfect, falsified, or nonexistent; they may legitimately plead illiteracy, or they may easily buy off tax inspectors (*ma'mur al-dara'ib*) who are few in number and poorly paid. The press is often full of unsubstantiated stories of gross evasion by the ''new fat cats'' such as an illiterate scrap metal merchant in Cairo's Wikalat al-Balah who owed £E 1.2 million in back taxes (*RY*, no. 2659, May 28, 1979) in a country where gross income over £E 10,000 per annum is taxed at a rate of 95 percent. Agricultural incomes, with a few exceptions (see Chapter Twelve), are not taxed at all.

Regime stalwarts and parliamentarians periodically inveigh against tax evasion, threatening draconian measures to deal with it. Legislation has followed slowly with little attention as to how it is to be implemented. Still, the threat and sometimes the reality of strong measures have been over the last two decades a bellwether of official concern about distributional issues.

In April 1978, for the first time since 1949, the tax burden on large incomes was reduced. In the intervening thirty years the burden was steadily increased until it became nearly confiscatory in 1965. For example, in 1949 incomes over £E 100,000 were taxed at a rate of 50 percent, but in 1950 that was changed to 70 percent on incomes over £E 50,000, and then, in 1952 to 80 percent of such incomes. Just prior to the socialist decrees of 1961, the rate was raised once again to 80 percent on incomes over £E 30,000. Then Law 115 of July 1961 imposed a rate of 90 percent on all incomes over £E 10,000, and Law 52 of 1965 raised that to 95 percent (Issawi 1963, p. 56; and Edel 1982).

Was the fact that general income tax revenues, exclusive of those on wages and salaries, declined from £E 5.2 million in 1960 to £E 3 million in 1970 evidence that few Egyptians earned more than £E 10,000 per year or was it evidence of gross evasion? As the decline continued to £E 1.9 million in 1975 at the height of *infitah*, Sadat's regime reasonably concluded that evasion was the culprit, and the solution to the problem was to reduce the tax burden on large incomes.

In the early 1970s the growth of the black market, the resurgence of private speculative activity, and the booming urban real estate market made it impossible to turn a blind eye to untaxed incomes (Azbawi 1973, pp. 101-9). In 1972 a special committee of the parliament found that there were £E 170 million in unpaid taxes owed the Ministry of Finance (*A*, December 10, 1972), and in 1974 all those with taxable incomes were required to take out tax I.D. cards that would then serve as evidence that they were not in arrears. Despite this, tax arrears remained around £E 150 million in 1975, and one source estimated that of 790,000 eligible payers (presumably outside the civil service) only 243,000 filed returns (*AY*, August 16, 1975). Of the 84,000 Egyptians suspected of earning more than £E 10,000 only 32,000 filed returns (*RY*, no. 2444, April 14, 1975; 'Abd al-'Azim, *AI*, no. 472, April 15, 1975; and 'Adil Hussain, *al-Tali'a*, 11).

The system had become a public joke, and a complete overhaul of the tax structure was promised. It was five years in coming. As legislation was prepared, modified, and dropped the regime attempted to contain the situation. In February 1976 Sadat called for taxes on all revenues and profits. He had in mind the urban real estate speculators who were making sizeable fortunes through the construction and sale of apartment buildings. Only the legal rent and officially assessed value of the property were subject to tax, each at a rate of 7 percent. These rates, as Mahmud Maraghi rightly pointed out, were an incentive to further speculative investment in real estate inasmuch as business profits were taxed at a rate of 40 percent (*RY*, no. 2596, March 13, 1978). Legislation was issued to deal with this situation, but it was not applied with any enthusiasm.[8]

A year later Sadat faced the crisis of doing away with some subsidies of consumer goods. While he and his economic advisor, 'Abd al-Mun'aim al-Qaissuni, expected some trouble, they thought they could head it off by announcing new measures to tax large incomes. The riots that took place in January 1977 showed that this was a futile gesture, but they in turn prompted the issuance of Law 2 of 1977, calling on all Egyptians to make a declaration of personal wealth. At the same time the parliament began debates on a unified tax system that produced a law only in June 1978.

The new law lightened the tax burden for all Egyptians. First, all bachelors with incomes of £E 600 or less and all married wage-earners with incomes of £E 660 or less were exempted from income tax. This was to placate the

---

[8] My landlady nonetheless seized upon this occasion to raise my rent by £E 200 per month in anticipation of a bigger tax bite.

great mass of the Egyptian population faced with soaring inflation and the visual affirmation in the urban areas of the big spenders of the *infitah* era (see text of law in *AI*, no. 547, June 1, 1978). At the other end of the income spectrum, the following tax rates were to be applied:

Income	Tax Rate
£E 10,000-15,000	35%
15,000-20,000	40
20,000-30,000	45
30,000-40,000	50
40,000-50,000	55
50,000-60,000	60
60,000-70,000	65
70,000-100,000	70
100,000 +	80

The regime concluded that: 1) the confiscatory nature of the previous system had merely provoked widespread evasion, and that a more lenient rate structure would *increase* receipts, and 2) penalizing the accumulation of large fortunes would be contrary and harmful to the spirit of *infitah*. In short, one can become rich legally in Egypt once again.

The new tax law was riddled with exemptions, so many in fact that Sadat sent it back to parliament three times to close loopholes. Bureaucratic interests, for example, were able to see to it, even in the final draft, that representational allowances up to £E 2,000 would be exempt from all tax (*AI*, no. 561, January 1, 1979). The 1978 law underwent further revisions and was reissued in the fall of 1981. The net effect of the law cannot yet be gauged, but one suspects that it will, so far as personal income tax is concerned, reduce total receipts still further because of the exemptions at the lower end of the income scale. It is moot whether or not the well-off will feel any more inclined than in the past to comply with the law. As is common when a new law is issued, or a public scandal breaks that cries out for official action, the new tax law elicited a campaign to uncover delinquent taxpayers (Wren 1979). Such campaigns are generally short-lived, and this one, significantly, concentrated on lower middle-class districts where the negligent could not bribe their way out.

While the income tax will probably remain an indifferent tool in the process of income redistribution, business and profits tax is already generating almost as much revenue as customs duties. The breakdown of public and private sources of profits tax was not available to me, but the size of new private actors under the umbrella of *infitah* should make monitoring and collection much easier. Because Law 43 firms are granted tax holidays of up to eight years, it will be some time before the potential of this source can be measured.

The Political Dole

Authoritarian regimes, no less than democratic polities, buy incumbency through strategically timed giveaways. In Egypt the tactic followed has always been to give publicly and take away indirectly. The giveaway is a one-shot affair, while the indirect take is permanent. The object is to take in more than is doled out, but that cannot always be achieved.

In agriculture, compulsory crop deliveries at prices set by the state were the counterpoint to the land distributed as a result of the reforms of 1952, 1961, and 1969, land for which the peasant beneficiary was required to pay anyway. In industry periodic wage increases and profit-sharing formulae were offset by forced-savings deductions for social security, defense and *jihad* taxes, and the like that often amounted to 30 percent of a worker's take-home pay.

Nonetheless, under Nasser squeaking wheels received little grease. It is true that protests generated by economic conditions were rare until inflation became a serious problem after 1965. But then there was the national crisis following the June War that was invoked to impose across-the-board austerity. Political challenges, such as that of the Muslim Brotherhood in 1954 and in 1965, were met with generally repressive political measures without complementary giveaways.

It is significant in this respect that when Nasser died the legal minimum monthly wage stood at £E 7.5. It had been raised only once before, in February 1962, so that it stood at about 10 percent above the minimum established at the beginning of the revolution. In other words, over an eighteen-year period the minimum monthly wage declined relative to the rate of inflation. In the spring of 1968, however, Nasser behaved in a manner that was to be a hallmark of his successor. The student-worker riots of February 1968, coming in protest of the lenient sentences meted out to high-ranking officers responsible for the defeat in the June War, shook Nasser's grip on power. He responded by moves on several fronts: retrial of the officers, the March 30 Declaration, and, in his annual May Day speech, pay increases for public sector workers.[9] He clearly wanted to buy off the workers and in so doing split them off from the students. He may have then launched the War of Attrition against Israeli positions in the Canal Zone to thwart any further challenges.

Sadat was thoroughly at home with the giveaway. Because his incumbency was so closely associated with rapid inflation, he had little choice. He raised the minimum wage four times, beginning in 1972 when it rose to £E 9 per month and lastly on May Day 1981 when it reached £E 25. To shore up his rural constituency, in 1973 he exempted all owners of three *feddans* or less

[9] His finance minister, Nazih Daif, left the cabinet over the increase because it played havoc with his policy of linking wages to production increases.

from all agricultural taxes. A year later, to give some substance to the general expectation that the October War would result in widespread prosperity, he raised the minimum wage to £E 12 (again on May Day), raised the tax exemption floor from annual incomes of £E 250 to £E 360 thereby affecting 1.8 million people, and raised the minimum pension payment from £E 3.6 to £E 6 per month. He followed this at the beginning of Ramadan and on the first anniversary of the October War with a one-month's salary bonus up to a maximum of £E 30 and ended the practice of docking salaries one-day's pay per month.

On May Day 1975 the president announced cost-of-living bonuses of about 10 percent of total annual wages for 2.6 million public sector employees and civil servants. As was the usual practice, the president urged the private sector to follow suit. A year later, as inflation really began to take hold, he increased the cost-of-living allowance by 40 percent for all those earning £E 50 per month or less.

These highly publicized giveaways, along with the continued expansion of subsidy programs, exacerbated problems of deficit financing without arresting the downward slide of Egyptians on fixed incomes. Violent protests became commonplace. In 1972, Canal Zone refugees and private sector workers rioted in Shubra al-Khaima over working and living conditions. Mahalla al-Kubra in 1975 and 1976 was the scene of bloody demonstrations by private sector textile workers demanding that their employers apply legislation on bonuses and minimum wages. On New Year's Day 1976, downtown Cairo was taken over by angry public sector workers unable to get to Helwan because the electrified train line was not functioning.

Despite these straws in the wind, Sadat and Qaissuni decided that they must take some measures to comply with the IMF's insistence that the public deficit be reduced. Qaissuni chose to approach the problem by lifting subsidies on a carefully selected list of ''luxury'' goods: butagas, beer, fine flour, unbroken rice, granulated sugar, French bread, macaroni, and so forth. He estimated that the resulting price increases would cost the average middle-income Egyptian family no more than £E 1.25 per year. Still, in anticipation of grumbling it was promised that pensions would be raised 10 percent, and that the public sector wage bill would be increased by £E 200 million.

The regime was taken by surprise by what occurred. Rioting broke out on January 20 up and down the Nile Valley, but especially in Cairo and Alexandria. Police precincts were besieged, the homes of officials ransacked, shops and nightclubs looted and burned. The police lost control of the situation, and army units, for the first time since 1952, had to be brought in to restore order. In Cairo alone seventy-seven people were officially listed as killed.

The government's response highlighted its confusion. First of all it immediately rescinded the price increases but solemnly pledged to go ahead with the salary increases. Simultaneously it was declared that communist agitators and other destructive elements had fomented the riots. Several hundred people were promptly arrested, but all but a handful were subsequently acquitted in the courts. Few Egyptians thought that the riots were anything other than a despairing protest against the new liberalism. For some, such as the conservative and pro-*infitah* editor of *al-Ahram al-Iqtisadi*, Lutfi 'Abd al-'Azim, the riots were the first salvo in an avoidable class war (*AI*, no. 515, February 1, 1977):

> Sadly, the majority of the Egyptian people have come to feel that they are unwelcome in the new consumer society. They live under a regime of "economic apartheid," a kind of economic discrimination that deprives the majority of the essentials of life while bestowing fantastic benefits and advantages upon a tiny segment of society. Whether this segment is that of the parasites and the individuals of the new class in Egypt, or from the Arab tourists who come to Egypt with an incredible buying power, they destroy Egyptian society and break its continuity.

It has become a given of Egyptian politics that the bread subsidy cannot be touched except at the peril of the regime. Bread has become the staff of life and the staff of regime survival. If Egypt's leaders consulted the recent past, however, they might question this premise. Up until 1966 per capita grain consumption in Egypt rose steadily to 115 kilograms per year. Because of the US suspension of PL 480 sales and the balance of payments crisis, per capita consumption fell precipitously to 72 kilograms per capita in 1969-70. That is a drop of 33 percent, and it must have been borne disproportionately by the very poor. This being the case it is instructive to note that there were no political disturbances related to curtailed grain supply. Perhaps the overriding crisis associated with the June War muffled economic protest, but the impression one has is that the Egyptians simply somehow made do.

The situation since the 1977 riots has changed little. Ever greater resources are pumped into the subsidy system to cushion the masses against inflation and to give them at least a taste of middle-class consumerism. Selective wage increases are aimed at defusing popular protest. One can only speculate as to the impact of these policies on economic performance and income distribution. Some trends, however, have become discernible. The beneficiaries of *infitah* are becoming very rich by the standards of any country. Less well-off segments of the society have also improved their position as a result of economic liberalization. Worker migrants have been able to import and trade in middle-class consumer goods and to use their earnings to buy land, urban real estate, or small businesses. Skilled craftsmen and workers—masons, plumbers, mechanics, electricians—are in heavy demand. Certain kinds of clerical staff, bilingual secretaries or accountants, now earn large salaries in

Law 43 enterprises. Peasants close to major urban centers may be able to take advantage of booming markets for fresh produce. In short, the benefits of *infitah* in its broadest sense have not been confined merely to the upper bourgeoisie. At the same time, other segments of society have seen their relative position deteriorate, although the means to measure their decline with any accuracy are not in place. The urban informal sector, the employees of small, artisanal enterprises, subsistence farmers and tenants, and two million or so public employees earning less than £E 50 per month cannot have kept up with inflation. Egypt's leaders know this and have kept them quiet through subsidies and the dole. The bill for this is steep, but Sadat hoped that the West would find it in its interest to help him pay it until something better turned up. As long as this hope was fulfilled he was able to continue to follow the line of least popular dissatisfaction.

Chapter Eleven

STATE AND CLASS

The socialist bourgeois want all the advantages of modern social conditions without the struggles and dangers necessarily resulting from them. They desire the existing state of society minus its revolutionary and disintegrating elements. The bourgeoisie naturally conceives the world in which it is supreme to be the best; and bourgeois socialism develops this comfortable conception into various more or less complete systems. In requiring the proletariat to carry out such a system, and thereby to march right into the social New Jerusalem, it is only really requiring that the proletariat should remain within the bounds of existing society, but should cast away all its hateful ideas concerning the bourgeoisie.

[*The Communist Manifesto,*
reproduced in Mendel, ed. 1979, p. 39.]

The existence of a capitalist bourgeoisie in Egypt is a twentieth-century phenomenon. Its indigenous wing took shape in the 1920s and achieved its maximum power after the Second World War. But its economic and political power was never great, paling beside that of foreign interests and hemmed in by a state and regime it could never fully penetrate, no less control. A brief flirtation with the Nasserist state after 1952 seemed to hold some promise, but what hopes existed were dashed by 1962. It can be said, therefore, that at no time in the modern history of Egypt has a capitalist class captured the state. Rather it has been the quasi-autonomous state and its manipulators—the Muhammed 'Ali dynasty, the British, or the military—that have broken up, reassembled, or created out of whole cloth existing and new class interests. Class formation and state policy are intimately bound, with the traditional path to economic status lying through access to political power. In Egypt and elsewhere in the Middle East, in contrast to the experience of the capitalist West, no group has obtained an enduring grip on political power or on economic resources.

There has been a very deep-rooted tradition of state autonomy in Egypt. It is the product of several factors. Egypt's rulers have typically been non-Egyptians. It is not nationalist hyperbole to state that Nasser was the first native son at the head of the state since the (pre-Ptolemaic) pharoahs. The foreign dynasts themselves were sustained to varying degrees by foreign powers, the last two being the Ottoman and British Empires. Whatever classes may have dominated those entities, and surely in the Ottoman Empire no class did, Egypt's class structure, such as it was, had no consistent links to the forces that controlled its state.

As Egypt entered the twentieth century the only class that might have asserted a claim to control the state in its own interests would have consisted of the middle and large landowners, the major producers of cotton for export. In some measure the Arabist movement represented an attempt, by no means unanimously supported, of this class to wrest control of the state from the Ottoman dynasts. The British intervened and thereby underwrote state autonomy for another seventy years. Muhammed 'Ali's dynasty was left in formal control of the state apparatus with the British in a position, at a minimum, to veto any state action they found unpalatable. The largely unregulated economy was in the hands of European bankers, insurance companies, and utility concerns with a Levanto-Jewish bourgeoisie that handled internal commerce and some foreign trade. Tala'at Harb and his allies could scarcely make a dent in this exogenous capitalist monolith, and Egypt's landowners had little desire to do so. There was no question, except perhaps briefly under Isma'il Sidqi in the early 1930s, of the Egyptian bourgeoisie capturing the state.

But we should not forget that it was a very limited state. No Keynes or FDR burst upon the Egyptian scene in the 1930s to deal with the economic crisis. Add to this the fact that the Egyptian military, since 1839, had been no more than an elaborate police force, and one sees that there was not all that much to capture. There are two exceptions to that assertion however. The British presence promoted and confirmed an expanded role for the state in financial regulation and in irrigation. The first arose out of the Caisse de la Dette Publique and the need for the state to impound substantial revenues to pay off foreign creditors. The second was but the continuation of policies initiated by Muhammed 'Ali to extend summer cultivation of cotton. So state expansion came down to water and taxes. It was really only under Nasser that the industrializing Egyptian welfare state set policy for and extended its regulatory and proprietary grip to vast areas of the economy. With the demise of the Muhammad 'Ali dynasty, the withdrawal of the British, the liquidation of Syro-Lebanese and Jewish interests, and the decapitation of the landed aristocracy, the weakened, not to say spavined, Egyptian bourgeoisie could finally contemplate a state truly worth seizing. But that state had, by the middle 1960s, its own vested interests, and its own class, many of whose members were the scions of bourgeois families done in only a few years before. State autonomy was now underwritten by the growing presence of a large managerial class whose interests lay in its control—not ownership—of the means of production. At present I want first to examine the expansion of the state in terms of personnel and its role as employer of last resort for the educated. Second, I shall explore the implications of its invasion of all sectors of the economy for the formation of a "state bourgeosie," and, third, I shall outline the links its upper echelons have nurtured with private interests existing along its fringes. The questions of rural stratification and class interests are important to this account but will be left for the following chapter.

Higher Education

No one within or without Egypt doubts that both the system of higher education and the public administration are plunged deep in crisis and that the causes of their respective plights spring from the same set of political considerations. Higher education has been a guarantee of a steady income if not of prosperity, and financing the expansion of the university system has responded to the aspirations of the upwardly mobile while providing those who have already arrived with the means to protect their advantage. But the awarding of degrees of varying prestige would count for little if employment opportunities did not keep pace with the supply of educated job-aspirants. It did not and does not require a university education to plant cotton, run a grocery store or restaurant, or repair a car. Once the state bottled up the modern private sector while curtailing out-migration, its alternatives were to absorb the educated or create an intellectual proletariat. It understandably chose, or perhaps more accurately had forced upon it, the first course.

The obligation of the Egyptian civil service and public sector to offer employment to all graduates of universities, higher and technical institutes was codified in Decree 185 of 1964. The principle, however, had a long history. Lord Cromer, as Mahmud Faksh pointed out (1977, p. 232), "made the school certificate not only a requirement for a job in the civil service but also a guarantee for one." What has happened since is a steady inflation in degrees so that the equivalent of a B.A. or B.S. is now necessary to activate the state's legal obligation.

The ills of the educational system have been visited upon the civil service. With rare exceptions there has been no attempt to structure secondary school and university curricula to the real needs of the bureaucracy, nor, indeed, have these needs ever been defined. The right to education, mentioned in the previous chapter, was transformed from a nationalist demand to a legislated reality. The first step came in 1925 when elementary school education was made both free and compulsory, but implementation of this law proceeded slowly. Primary schools, which, unlike elementary schools, led on to secondary schools, were made free by the Wafd Party in 1936, and in 1950, in what Malcolm Kerr refers to as a "demagogic bid" (Kerr 1965, p. 176), the Wafd made secondary schools tuition-free and open to anyone passing the primary school final exams. The Wafdist stalwart, Fu'ad Serrag al-Din, claimed in 1977 (Serrag al-Din 1977, pp. 58-59) that had the 1950 Wafd government survived, it would have made all higher education free as well.

The Free Officers could hardly roll back this tide, for it involved every adult Egyptian's aspirations regardless of social class. What they did in 1953 was to unify elementary and primary education into one six-year sequence, followed by a two-year preparatory stage (i'adadi) which would be the cutoff point for entry into four years of secondary school. Secondary school remained free, although minimal scores had to be achieved in preparatory school examinations to qualify for admission. Finally, at the end of the secondary school period, students sat for General Secondary Exams, the results of which would determine their entry into universities. Table 10.9 in the previous chapter shows aggregate growth figures for all stages of education. I add here only the fact that in 1971-72, for instance, 328,000 primary students out of a total primary school population of 3.8 million moved on to the preparatory level. Of the approximately 800,000 students enrolled at this level, 203,000 qualified for admission to secondary school, while 94,000 out of a total secondary school enrollment of 300,000 qualified for university or higher institute admissions.

The crucial gap lay between secondary school and university. There has been enormous pressure from all sectors of Egyptian society to render that gap as narrow as possible, and while educational planners and the already well-educated urge that these pressures be resisted, this is an issue over which Nasser and Sadat both avoided confrontation. In a revealing episode in 1957, Minister of Education Kamal al-Din Hussain, member of the defunct RCC, sought some modest controls of admissions to university. He presented his proposals to the parliament (known as the Council of the Nation—*Maglis al-umma*—at that time) and found himself confronted with vociferous and near-unanimous opposition. This tame body that had never taken on the military elite before ordered Hussain, as Abdel-Malek put it (1968, p. 121), "to open the doors of the university to every secondary school graduate who requested admission." Abdel-Malek also suggests that the ire of the MPs resulted partially from Hussain's plan to purge the students' movements in the universities, but if that were the case it would have been the first and last time that political heavy-handedness ever moved civilian politicos to public protest.

Whatever the nature of the confrontation, Hussain felt obliged to resign, and was reinstated by Nasser at the same time he dissolved the Maglis.

Having lost its case in parliament, the government in 1963 finally codified the principle of open admissions to university of all successful secondary school graduates. In 1964, as already noted, it took on the obligation to hire all those who graduated from university. So the rush was on, and while the logic of the policy sprang from the employment drive of the early 1960s, its major impact began to be felt during the period of stagnation and retrenchment (*inkimash*). The state has never been able to put down the burden it shouldered in 1964, and, like the maintenance of consumer subsidies, its obligations in this domain have become politically sacrosanct.

Let us look more closely at the consequences of this policy for the quality and organization of higher education. One result has been that higher technical institutes and other ''lower'' forms of post-secondary school education have lobbied to obtain university equivalency for their degrees. Such lobbying has been resisted by the universities and graduates of professional faculties (Moore 1980, pp. 58-59), but the resistance smacks of elitism and was criticized during the 1960s, although less so now. Still, the result has been that several technical institutes were absorbed into the universities after 1975.

A second consequence has been the obsessive concern with exams. The first hurdle is the General Secondary Exam (GSE) that gives rise each year to a national trauma producing in equal measure parental and student breakdowns and journalistic satire. In the desperate struggle for comparative educational advantage, competition to do well in these exams has spawned a parallel system of secondary education: the tutorial.

On the demand side of this equation are tens of thousands of well-to-do and not-so-well-to-do families willing to pay for private tutoring of their children so that at a minimum they pass the GSE and perhaps even achieve a high score. On the supply side are tens of thousands of poorly paid secondary school teachers trapped between inflation and an increasingly low-status profession. It is frequently alleged that tutorials given by these teachers have become obligatory if parents want to avoid retributive grading of their children's work. ''Fees'' vary substantially, but it would not have been unusual in the mid-1970s for a determined family to spend upwards of £E 100 per year in tutorial expenses.[1] Thus, at the secondary level, and as we shall see in the universities as well, a nominally free service has given rise to its own fee-based black market in which the better-off can compete at unfair advantage against the poor. But given the range of starting civil service salaries, even the not-so-well-off may see tutorial fees as a good investment. In 1980 all

---

[1] In 1980 average secondary school rates for tutorials were £E 8 per hour in mathematics and £E 6 per hour in languages.

graduates of universities and Higher Technical Institutes started off at £E 33 per month, while those with intermediate school degrees started at £E 23-25 and, of course, without guarantee of placement.

The same phenomenon has taken root in the universities, and is reinforced by the extraordinary crowding that has arisen out of easy admissions policies. To grasp this problem, something must be said about the process by which students gain entry to various branches or faculties of the university. According to their prestige, schools and faculties set minimal admissions standards according to the student's GSE scores. The most sought-after faculties, medicine and engineering, set the highest qualifying standards, while teacher-training institutes set the lowest. This procedure obviously places a premium on high GSE scores and is the underpinning of secondary school tutorials.

The revolutionary regime after 1952 invested a good deal in rehabilitation and expansion of the four major universities[2] and was able to orient the flow of students into the pure and applied sciences. During the 1960s when large infrastructural projects were being undertaken, the demand for engineers led to a real explosion in this field. For the entire period 1910-1951, Egypt's engineering faculties turned out 4,822 engineers, while between 1952 and 1967 18,678 were graduated. By 1972 there were 40,000 engineers registered with the officially recognized Engineers' Syndicate.

Medicine, which had always been highly regarded, maintained its appeal, but perhaps because of the stiff language requirements and the efforts of the state to regulate the profession, medical faculties did not expand at the same rate as engineering faculties: between 1910 and 1951, 15,000 MDs were graduated, while between 1952 and 1967 11,400 were graduated (*AI*, no. 299, February 1, 1968). With the liberalization of emigration in the early 1970s, combined with the saturation of the engineering profession, there has been renewed growth in medical school enrollments (see Table 11.1).

The applied sciences were given a great boost by the military regime, as were agriculture and veterinary medicine. The distribution of the student body was pried away from the previous concentration on law, commerce, and the humanities toward training in areas that were most necessary for modernizing Egypt. Nonetheless, as Table 11.1 shows, the great majority of university students is still in nonapplied fields, especially law and commerce. Moreover, these fields have become the receptacles for those whose scores precluded entry to more prestigious faculties and have had to absorb more than the others the influx of secondary school graduates. It is the cohorts of graduates in the nonapplied fields, probably unhappy with their lot, that, for want of employment alternatives, flood the government offices and the schools of the

[2] Cairo University, 'Ain Shams, Alexandria, Al-Azhar.

Table 11.1

**Distribution of Students in Institutions of Higher Education
by Specialization, 1968-69 to 1976-77**

Faculty/ Specialization	1968-69	% of Total	1976-77	% of Total
SCIENCE				
Engineering	20,464		37,134	
Agriculture	11,796		37,924	
Medicine	17,956			
Dentistry	2,000		49,628	
Pharmacy	4,268			
Veterinary	3,013		5,347	
Sciences	7,862		18,661	
Subtotal	67,359	38.6%	148,695	32.6%
ARTS				
Literature (*Adab*)	12,098		47,496	
Law	12,495		41,226	
Commerce	20,729		103,876	
Normal Schools	7,891		34,778	
Girls' College	2,492		5,738	
Girls' Religious and Linguistic College	—		25,001	
Nonscientific Institutes	—		12,326	
Subtotal	55,705	32.0%	270,441	59.6%
Al-Azhar	18,748	10.7%	—*	
Nursing	442	.2%	1,001	.2%
Higher Technical Institutes	32,159	18.5%	33,499	7.4%
GRAND TOTAL	173,971	100.0%	453,696	100.0%

SOURCE: From CAPMAS *Yearbooks* for 1970 and 1978.

*Figures for al-Azhar are not listed separately for 1976-77, but are included in the totals for the arts and science faculties.

Ministry of Education. *Infitah* and emigration have given the best among them new employment opportunities, but the civil service is left with the rest.

The ability of the prestige faculties to resist the onslaught, at least in relative terms, of the secondary school students, has reinforced the premium placed on high scores. Nonetheless, as discriminating as they may be, these same faculties have been physically swamped by new entrants. Very little physical expansion or refurbishment of existing classrooms or laboratories has gone on since the late 1950s. Cairo University, which was designed for 35,000 students, now handles about 90,000. Its engineering faculty was designed for 700 students but in 1977 had 9,000; its medical faculty should accommodate 300 but deals with 1,700. It is possible for an Egyptian medical student to complete his medical studies without ever having seen a cadaver (*RY*, no.

2567, August 22, 1977). Again at Cairo University teacher-student ratios range between 1/70 and 1/666. For the period 1967-1974 average annual per student budgetary outlays were only £E 15. In 1974 per student outlays in medicine and engineering totaled £E 159, but net of wages the figure dropped to £E 8 (*A*, July 31, 1974).

It is in the prestige faculties that private tutoring reigns supreme, and it has been alleged that even deans have lined their pockets with tutorial fees that may ensure success in crucial examinations. In medicine and engineering semester tutorial fees in individual courses ran between £E 250 and £E 1,000 in the middle 1970s.[3] Once again a nominally nonelitist system has recreated an elitism that favors the offspring of the well-to-do.

The regime has responded to the overall situation in ways that make some political but very little educational sense. It has, as already noted, debased university diplomas by absorbing the Higher Institutes into the university system. More importantly it has created several regional universities in the name of decentralization without giving them the physical plant and teaching personnel that could lend them credibility. The following list gives some indication of the scale of this phenomenon.

University	Enrollment 1976/1977
Cairo	88,217
'Ain Shams	84,413
Alexandria	71,902
Assiut	28,028
Al-Azhar	43,063
Tanta	19,680
Mansura	29,459
Zagazig	25,377
Suez Canal	7,184
Helwan	35,211
Minia	10,277
Menufia	10,885
Total	453,696

Assiut University, while in a sense regional, has a fairly long history, but the seven last entries in the list are recent creations. With 138,000 students they accommodate 30 percent of the total university population, but in many respects they exist more on paper than in reality. However that may be, they award degrees, including medical degrees from Mansura and Tanta. The trend

---

[3] It was reported in *AI* (no. 613, October 13, 1980) that tax inspectors were after a medical school professor who had grossed £E 250,000 in one year in tutorials.

is to allow the creation of other such campuses, and there already exist nonautonomous units in agriculture and veterinary medicine at Kafr al-Shaikh and Shabin al-Kum. The head of the Physicians' Syndicate, Hamdi al-Sayyid, lamented the deterioration in standards which had given rise to eight medical faculties with 30,000 students. Assiut University, he noted, had founded a new medical faculty at Suhag in 1977, and the Syndicate decided not to recognize its degree (*RY*, no. 2629, October 30, 1978).

Often teaching staff commute from Cairo or Alexandria to the regional campus, exacerbating an already overextended workload. It is estimated that the main universities lack about 25 percent the staff they need, while the regional universities are short 50 percent of their needs. One professor at 'Ain Shams, for example, gave seventeen lectures per week in addition to four others at regional campuses (*A*, January 18, 1976). At the same time the salaries of the teaching personnel are held low. A full professor earns about £E 120 per month, but is allowed to supplement his or her income by selling books and lecture notes to the students. I personally knew a full professor of economics who earned extra income by grading exams at roughly ten cents an exam. The safety valve for alienation that has inevitably arisen out of the scramble to survive is migration abroad. There are over 30,000 primary and secondary schoolteachers abroad, and the unwritten rules at the university level entitle all teachers to a "turn" in an Arab country where they may earn fifteen times their Egyptian salary. The best of these teachers stay away longer, thus adding to both the depletion of the ranks of teachers as well as lowering the quality of what little instruction is offered. That reference is used advisedly for, barring strikes, the effective academic year does not exceed twenty weeks.

There is a general sense that matters cannot continue in this fashion, but so far the regime has carefully tread the line of least popular dissatisfaction. For over a decade there have been official pledges to limit university admissions that have gone unfulfilled.

The first such pledge came in 1968 when it was decided to restrict new university admissions to 35,000 per year and to channel 60 percent of these into engineering and sciences and another 10 percent into teacher training (Mabro 1974, p. 157). Neither goal was even remotely attained. A decade later it was decided to put the lid on at 65,000 new admissions, and in 1979 the government announced that 60,000 would be the outer limit given the limited capacity of the universities (*RY*, no. 2669, August 6, 1979). Within weeks of that announcement, the High Universities Committee approved 80,000 admissions for the academic year 1979-80 (*RY*, no. 2678, October 8, 1979).

Higher education has become mired in one of those systemic crises that Egyptian policy-makers typically regard as insoluble. There is a tendency to let the crisis worsen because, it is felt, whatever its dimensions it is no longer susceptible to reform. The standard tactic is then to seek a solution outside the afflicted institutions. Thus it was that just prior to the era of *infitah*, talk circulated about establishing a private university (*AI*, no. 431, August 1, 1973). It was merely an idea, officials alleged, fully recognizing that such an institution would totally shatter all remaining pretenses to egalitarian higher education. The rationale advanced was that thousands of Egyptians went abroad for university education, using foreign exchange that might just as well be spent at home. Conversely thousands of Arabs earned university degrees in Egypt, paying out little more than their own living expenses. A private university, charging tuition, could offer the quality education that would attract the offspring of the rich and oblige visitors to pay a fair price for their degrees. Implicit in this was the fact that a private institution would have the latitude to recruit Egypt's best teachers and scholars to its classrooms. It was not without some justification that proponents of this idea defended it by pointing out that it would rationalize the existing state of affairs in which people with sufficient financial means were illicitly buying advantages for their children. Whatever the rationale, the proposal has so far been too politically and symbolically loaded to permit implementation.[4]

It will be very difficult to modify the cluster of incentives within the educational system that has prevailed since 1964. Families have operated on the assumption that the successful fulfillment of secondary school requirements will lead their children to steady jobs and reliable if modest incomes. The realities of economic survival in Egypt render meaningless all considerations of job satisfaction and personal fulfillment. Any major change in the system now would inevitably catch hundreds of thousands of families in midstream and could provoke political resentment similar in its intensity to that following the suspension of some consumer subsidies in January 1977. In the meantime government offices, companies, and factories literally fill up with unneeded clerks and paper-pushers. They may not have even a desk of their own, nor do they enjoy much social status, but they do have an income.

The Employer of Last Resort

"In January 1969, the public bureaucracy was actually employing over 153,300 (University) graduates, or some 60 percent of the three-quarters of a million graduates that the country had produced"
[Ayubi 1980, p. 355]

It is not surprising that the inability or lack of will of the regime to deal with the universities has been translated into an inability or an unwillingness to make the civil service and to some extent the parastatals more than parking

---

[4] It was decided in 1980 that university students who failed twice, necessitating repetition of an academic year, would be required to pay their own fees.

lots for the educated, or for any other segment of the population seeking pacification. As a result the bureaucracy is far more a dead weight upon the economy than an instrument for growth. But, as we noted with respect to the public sector, its ability to employ enhances its ability to control.

About one-third of the Egyptian work force is on the public payroll, i.e., 3.2 out of 10 million persons. This figure does not include the armed forces, which are commonly estimated at 350,000, but which swelled, according to Chief of Staff Sa'ad al-Din Shazli (1980, p. 48) to just over one million in 1973. Nor does it cover the 150,000 teachers employed by the Ministry of Education.

Let us retrace the evolution of this "bureaucratic inflation" (Atribi 1972; Rashid 1970). As is often the case, only highly aggregate figures are available and they do not always accord with one another. At present we shall examine only the civil service exclusive of the public sector. In 1947 the civil service totaled about 165,000 employees, net of the armed forces, police, judiciary, and teaching corps (Mead 1967, p. 134). By 1952 various estimates put the civil service at a minimum of 200,000 (Rashid 1970, p. 8) and to a maximum of 381,000 (Berger 1957, p. 82; Ayubi 1977). With the advent of the first Five-Year Plan more detailed breakdowns became available. In overall terms the civil service grew by 7.5 percent per annum during the period represented in Table 11.2, a rate well in excess of the 2.2 percent annual growth rate of the national work force. The most rapid rates of growth, however, were recorded by superior and specialized personnel, each of which expanded at more than 9 percent per annum. As a whole, the civil service had reached 2.1 million in 1980. In less than thirty years it had sextupled.

Table 11.2
The Growth of the Egyptian Civil Service, 1962-1971

Civil Service Level	1962-63	1964-65	1966-67	1971-72
Superior	967	1,184	1,544	1,905
Specialized	71,661	89,596	103,587	137,814
Technical	126,090	140,251	161,030	208,044
Administrative	13,671	16,772	19,862	25,281
Clerical	63,451	75,976	76,011	85,928
Skilled and unskilled employees	494,472	567,308	675,713	831,566
Other	—	—	63,507	—
Total	707,312	891,068	1,035,747	1,290,538

SOURCES: From Atribi 1972, p. 74; and Ghun'aim 1968; Harik 1972, p. 293 gives a figure of 1,255,000 for 1968-69 which includes 400,000 in state organizations. The figures in this table do not include state organization employees.

Predictably the expansion in personnel was accompanied by a proliferation of agencies and ministries. The latter doubled from fifteen to thirty between 1952 and 1970; microcosms of the central administration were created in twenty-five governorates, with the *diwan* of Cairo alone employing 5,000 bureaucrats. In addition, as noted earlier, the growth of the public sector entailed the founding of forty-six General Organizations and Authorities, to oversee some 370 public companies.

The grand total of all those employed as labor and civil servants by the state reached about 3.2 million in 1980. The breakdown for that year is provided in Table 11.3. Between 1966 and 1980, *after* the employment drive of the early 1960s, the civil service alone doubled in size. Public sector employment grew rapidly as well, although not at the same rate as the civil service. On this point the few statistics we have are somewhat confusing. In Table 11.3 personnel in the Economic Authorities (e.g., Suez Canal, High Dam, petroleum) are included in the civil service rather than in the public sector. Other sources apparently include them in the public sector. Thus 'Abd al-Salam Badawi (1973, p. 162) estimated public sector employment at 965,000 in 1969-70, and 'Abd al-Fattah Mungi (1975) put it at 970,755 in 1972. Thus between 1970 and 1980 public sector employment may have grown at an average annual rate of 4 percent (i.e., from 966,000 to 1,360,000 when the Economic Authorities are included).

Let us look more closely at the managerial and bureaucratic component of the public sector. In 1975 this personnel was made up of the following categories (Muhammed Hassan 1975, 65):

Table 11.3
Distribution of State Employees, 1980

Sector	General Cadre	Special Cadre	Total	%
Central Gov't. Admin.	274,856	291,345	566,201	17.6
Local Gov't. Admin.	1,067,178	959	1,068,132	33.2
Service Authorities	188,158	32,869	221,027	6.9
Economic Authorities	264,791	15,481	280,272	8.7
Total Civil Service	1,794,983	340,654	2,135,637	66.4
Public Sector Cos.	1,080,886	—	1,080,886	33.6
GRAND TOTAL	2,875,869	340,654	3,216,523	100.0

SOURCE: Employment survey, Central Agency for Organization and Administration as of 1/1/80; not including local government personnel which was estimated from budget requests for 1979. Reprinted from 'Afifi 1980. By 1981, the gross figures had risen to 2,150 in the civil service and 1,476 in the public sector, for a total of 3,626,000 state employees (*Al*, no. 666, Oct. 19, 1981).

Directors	1,860
Specialists	6,272
Technical/Supervisors	11,605
Clerical	15,500
Skilled	60,663
Semi-skilled	44,572
Unskilled	53,061
Total	193,533

In 1972 CAPMAS (1974) carried out a survey of 34,000 top-level public sector bureaucrats. It produced some fairly surprising results. Of some 25,000 bureaucrats recorded, it turned out that over 15,000 had been in service for fifteen to thirty years. That is, they had been recruited before the nationalizations of 1961 and were probably holdovers from the time when many public sector units were in private hands. This is borne out by the finding that nearly half of all those sampled were fifty years old or older. It is clear that the old guard had managed to keep its grip on the public sector at the upper levels. The expansion in employment, not surprisingly, took place in the lower echelons of the bureaucracy. It is not without interest to note that as part of the same survey the respondents were asked to rank professions of "greatest importance in contemporary Egyptian society." They were given a choice of twenty, and the top five were:

1) University professor
2) Doctor
3) Governor
4) Army officer
5) Engineer

The least important was judged to be "public sector employee."

Civil service wages, like employment itself, grew at a rate well in excess of the national wage bill: for the period 1962 to 1971, the rate was 13.6 percent per annum in the civil service as opposed to 8 percent per annum nationally. The civil service share in total wages rose from 28 percent to 38 percent over the same period. In the eight years after 1971, the civil service wage bill grew by about 25 percent per annum, but because of the high rates of inflation in those years, that extraordinary growth produced a slight decrease in the civil service share of total wages. In Table 11.4 I have also entered the growth of the public sector wage bill, largely paid out to workers in parastatal companies. It too has shown phenomenal growth, nearly doubling between 1975 and 1979. What one may draw from this data is that the state employs about a third of the total work force and pays out nearly two-thirds of the total national wage bill.

Table 11.4
Share of Civil Service in Total Wages, 1962-1979
(£E millions current)

	1962-63	1966-67	1971-72	1975	1977	1979
Total Wages	707	1,002	1,180	2,181	2,784	3,600
Civil Service	200	336	446	754	946	1,258
Public Sector	—	241	328	482	620	896
Civil Service/Total	28%	33.5%	38%	35%	34%	35%
Civil Service and Public Sec./Total	—	57.5%	65.5%	56.6%	56%	60%

SOURCE: Total wages have been drawn from various IBRD and IMF publications. The first three columns are from Atribi 1972, pp. 74-75; and 'Abd al-Salam Badawi 1973, p. 162. Figures for 1975, 1977, 1979 are drawn from A, January 30, 1977 and draft budgets for 1978 and 1979, published as supplements to AI, January 1, 1978 and January 1, 1979.

Salary differentials within the civil service are substantial. In the middle 1970s, when the minimum wage was £E 12 per month or £E 144 per annum, the top administrative salary for a company head or deputy minister was £E 2,100 per annum, for a ratio of 1:15. If one adds to this representational allowances ranging between £E 1,500 and £E 2,000 per annum, the ratio becomes 1:25. These allowances, which are untaxed, have been tantamount to second salaries. Between 1962 and 1967 they grew in aggregate from £E 72 million to £E 183 million, or by 154 percent. At that level they constituted 21 percent of the entire civil service wage bill (Ghun'aim 1968, p. 89). At that time, prior to reductions in representational allowances introduced after 1967, the ratio of highest to lowest salaries and allowances was 40:1. This ratio was achieved at the height of Egypt's socialist transformation and is to be compared to a similar ratio in Great Britain of 5:1 (Galal Amin 1973).

Survival for the two-and-a-half million middle- and low-ranking bureaucrats has come to depend on holding down two jobs, sometimes both on the public payroll. This sort of scrambling is crippling to morale and to the level of performance. A survey carried out by the Ministry of Human Resources and Training, in conjunction with the General Confederation of Labor Unions, found that the average workday in the ministries and public sector varied between one-and-a-half and three hours (AI, no. 609, September 15, 1980). One may presume that for many, the rest of their official working hours were not spent idly. Along with the moonlighting, petty corruption in such circumstances is unavoidable, and civil servants carry out functions the importance and financial implications of which are totally incommensurate with their salaries. Warehouse supervisors, tax assessors, infirmary attendants, those that process applications, etc., may earn in 1980 as little as $40 per month at a time when cigarettes are $.80 a pack and a kilo of meat $3.50. Sayyid Mar'ai recounts (1979, 2:536) that in 1968 the linchpin of the Agriculture Ministry's rural programs, the 4,000 inspectors (*mushrifin*) earned £E 8 per month. These officials are but a small segment of the ranks

> . . . of not-so-bright young men in their soiled collars and cheap suits [who] eke out a shabby and insecure but desperately respectable existence on ten pounds a month as minor clerks, bookkeepers, schoolteachers, and journalists. They are assured from time to time in the press and in the president's speeches that as educated men they are the "vanguard" of the nation's progress, but they are impotent to fashion even their own progress, and they can only listen anxiously to the officially propagated theme of equal and widening opportunities under the new socialist economic development plan which ambitiously pledges to double the national income in ten years. [M. Kerr, 1965:187.]

With the unofficial passing of Egyptian socialism new anxieties have been sown throughout the civil service. The need to reform the administration and put an end to the state's obligation as employer of last resort has been openly recognized. The word of the day is the right man or woman in the right place. An official report on the problem (cited in *RY*, no. 2672, August 22, 1979) noted that in 1975 for example, the Ministry of Human Resources requested from the Ministry of Agriculture the number of graduates it would need in the following year. The answer was 261 with university degrees and 495 with secondary agricultural diplomas. This was the civil service demand at a time when supply consisted in 8,000 graduates of agriculture faculties and higher institutes, and 11,000 bearers of agricultural secondary school diplomas.

The press frequently talks of the 20 to 25 percent redundancy throughout the public work force (e.g., *A*, September 18, 1975), and Egypt's foreign creditors and friends have urged for years that civil service rosters and payrolls be trimmed in the name of efficiency. No direct measures in this sense have so far been taken, although it is claimed that public sector companies need not hire anyone they do not really need. Whatever the cause, it is the case that there is an enormous backlog of educated Egyptians awaiting public jobs, as many as 250,000 at the beginning of 1981. Often the wait is three years or more. For instance, in June 1980, 88,000 new appointments were made: 20,000 from the 1977 and 1978 graduates of universities and higher institutes, and 68,000 who had graduated from preparatory and secondary school in 1976 (*A*, June 14, 1980). It may be the unofficial policy to allow graduates to languish among the ranks of the unemployed for long periods of time in the hope that they will be forced to find work in the private sector, in *infitah* joint ventures, or outside the country altogether (see remarks of Ahmad Osman, *AI*, no. 626, January 22, 1981).

The State Bourgeoisie and Its Allies

The Egyptian state has become a social entity in itself, a layering of strata and interests held together by the source of their income and promotion. It in turn has called forth and nourished private interests that live parasitically on state business. But does this social entity constitute a class or even an alliance of interests? Scholars such as Manfred Halpern (1963) and Richard Sklar (1979), from their differing vantage points in time and place, share the conviction that high-ranking state personnel and their counterparts in a subordinate private sector do constitute a class. Moreover they share the conviction that a Marxian definition of class is inadequate, and that, at least in Sklar's view, control over, as opposed to ownership of, the means of production *and* the means of "consumption and compulsion" is the real hallmark of dominant classes in LDCs.

In a corps as vast as the Egyptian civil service it is essential to go beyond the delimitation of strata and say something about self-awareness and common goals. For example, in his original formulation Halpern included in his new middle class all those drawing salaries as well as the "would-be salariat" (Halpern 1963, p. 54). "Leadership in all areas of Middle Eastern life is increasingly being seized by a class of men inspired by non-traditional knowledge, and it is being clustered around a core of salaried civilian and military politicians, organizers, administrators and experts. . . . The thrust toward revolutionary action on the part of the new middle class is overwhelming" (Halpern 1963, pp. 52 and 75). In a more recent defense of his original thesis Halpern jettisons the salaried aspect of the new middle class as unessential to its definition. He redefines it as a "transiently modern" class devoted to the transformation of society, leading one to wonder if the term "middle" has any relevance to his conceptualization (Halpern 1977). Be that as it may, neither the original nor the revised formulation do justice to the subject. These enormous groups to which Halpern attributes common motives, drives, attitudes, and fears are too fragmented and differentiated to be treated as a class or even as an integrated set of subclasses.

In the first chapter I defined class as any group within society sharing the same relationship to the means of production and the same level of material well-being, privileges, and power. Some classes or class fractions are dominant because of their control and/or ownership of the means of production and distribution, as well as their control over the means of coercion. Others are in varying degrees subordinate. It borders on the obvious to say that dominant class fractions, whatever their intramural rivalries, will be the most aware of the common interests that bind them, and to the extent that these include *control* over the means of production, it is legitimate to speak of class consciousness. By contrast, subordinate class fractions need not share any such awareness. In fact, their perception of class may be limited to their aspirations to join the dominant groups. If upward mobility is a real and widely available possibility as it was in the 1960s in Egypt, then no underclass mentality need develop.

On the other hand, if avenues of promotion are sealed off at the same time that inflation erodes real income, subordinate strata in the civil service and the public sector will become very different kinds of class actors. It is not at all clear that the lower and middle echelons of the Egyptian bureaucracy ever had any collective or individual will to modernize and transform society in the Halperian sense, but to the extent that they are or were so motivated, it is unlikely that their will could survive the alienating pressures of closed careers and status loss. As indicated earlier, their recourse takes the form of individual survival tactics—corruption, moonlighting, migration. Collective demands and collective action may come later if individual strategies of ''exit'' fail to keep them afloat. So far collective action through union bargaining and strikes has been surprisingly absent in the civil service and even in the public sector work force.

There are at least four administrative strata within the personnel of the civil service and the public sector with fairly distinct interests and career perspectives.[5] There is a managerial elite of a few thousand, made up of ministers, deputy ministers, division heads, presidents and members of the boards of directors of companies and agencies, and provincial governors. Members of this group may legally earn about £E 4,000 per year or about $5,700, which is high relative to the rest of the bureaucracy but increasingly low relative to their formal status, accustomed life styles, and self-image. It was always power more than income that set them apart, but more and more often they have had to convert power into illicit or quasi-legal incomes.

It is important to keep in mind that contrary to impressionistic observations, the weight of the military in this stratum was never very great and is currently declining. Dekmejian, Sami Qassem, but especially Nazih Ayubi have shown that at the height of military influence in the Egyptian economy and polity, officers were not prominent in the administrative and public sector elites. In 1967, of 18,000 top-level civil servants, exclusive of the Ministry of Interior, the military accounted for only 370 positions or 2 percent of the total. They were marginally better represented in the public sector, occupying 8 percent of all board chairmanships and 3 percent of all upper-level management positions. However, their sinecures, to the extent they had any, were in Interior and Foreign Affairs (Ayubi 1980, pp. 347-53).

Below this topmost stratum are some 170,000 high-ranking civil servants

---

[5] For a somewhat different system of categorization of all these strata see Abdel-Fadil (1981, pp. 95-109).

and managers (ARE Ministry of Planning 1977, 1:31) out of a total national pool of about 350,000 in 1976. Average earnings for this stratum are £E 900 to 1,500 per annum, clearly insufficient for senior officials with university degrees and technical competence. This stratum, however, feeds directly into the elite, but only a minority (one in thirty?) will be selected. And, given the declining real income of the elite, promotion may have lost some of its appeal. In any event, it is within the ranks of the elite and this second civil service stratum that the state bourgeoisie is situated.[6]

Within this second stratum one can discern a subgroup of technocrats traditionally made up of engineers (civilian or military), but now supplemented by management experts, computer programmers, financial analysts, and the like who have the greatest likelihood of promotion within the civil service, but especially the public sector, as well as lateral movement into the private sector. Richard Sklar has described members of this stratum as a "managerial bourgeoisie," a term reflecting "the coexistence of a newly developing and private enterprise sector with a preponderant yet protective public sector. . . . Inasmuch as this term clearly refers to the private business elite as well as the managers of public enterprise and high government officials, it may be preferred to either 'bureaucratic' or 'state' bourgeoisie" (Sklar 1979, p. 546). I would add that in the Egyptian case its members are probably ideologically indifferent to the question of public or private ownership of the production and consumption means they supervise.

Descending one step further down takes us directly into the subordinate cohorts where differentiation comes mainly in the form of rather finer income gradations. There were in 1975 about 2.7 million employees spread between the civil service and the public sector. This mass fell in an income range of £E 144-£E 540 per annum. However wide in absolute terms this range may be, it is both narrow and low in cost-of-living terms. Saad Ibrahim (1982) estimates that the minimum urban income in 1976 required to keep a family from sliding into poverty is £E 350. From Table 11.5 it would appear that the bulk of the bureaucracy, or some 2.4 million employees, hovers on the brink of poverty if it has not fallen into the pit already. A walking tour through Sayyida Zainab or Shubra in Cairo would provide ample visual evidence of the precarious material conditions of these subordinate groups.

Few of these nearly three million employees can hope to ascend very far within the bureaucratic hierarchy. The rest must content themselves with riding the seniority system of slow but automatic promotions. At the end of a full career they may have doubled their incomes, and for the illiterate or semi-

---

[6] In 1974 an MP, Mahmud Nafa', urged that all civil servants earning more than £E 1,200 per annum accept a 25 percent reduction in salary to be reallocated to the lowest grade civil servants. *Al-Ahram* (December 12, 1974), reporting the suggestion, noted "great commotion (*dajja*) in the ranks of MPs." The suggestion, of course, was not adopted.

Table 11.5
Stratification of the *Lumpen*-Salariat, May 1975

Civil Service Level	No. of Employees	Monthly Salary (£E)	Yearly Salary (£E)
10	840,000	12	144
9	400,000	13.5	162
8	650,000	15	180
7	350,000	25	300
6	210,000	27.5	330
5	120,000	35	420
4	65,000	45	540

SOURCE: From A, May 2, 1975.

literate among them without secondary or university degrees even that kind of advancement may be too much to expect. For the most part this "*lumpen* salariat*" (to abuse *lumpen*, yet one more time) engages in individual, frequently desperate survival tactics of which the second job is the cornerstone. The day-to-day scramble, quite often in the physical sense given the state of Cairo's public transport system, to meet their basic needs and maintain a modicum of dignity, undermines any tendency toward class or group awareness. It is rather a question of each man and woman for him or herself, a contest in which the negligence and corruption of each civil servant is paid for by all in their capacity as citizens who cannot avoid recourse to the administration.

Al-Tali'a published a long interview with "Ibrahim 'Iraq," entitled "Preoccupations of a Young Civil Servant" (October 1976:21-42). His account conforms in most respects to the general impression one has of civil servants in the lower echelons. 'Iraq was thirty-one at the time of the interview. His father was a *fallah* who took up factory work first at Mahalla al-Kubra then at Shubra al-Khaima. 'Iraq had seven siblings but was still able to receive a university education, earning a B.A. in commerce in 1967. He then spent two-and-a-half years in the military in Libya. He was able to save £E 200 and with that to marry. The couple's only child died within twelve hours of birth because of "medical neglect." He worked as an accountant at £E 32 per month or £E 29 net of taxes. His wife worked as a nurse at £E 28 per month. With net monthly income of £E 58 the couple paid out £E 12.50 in rent, £E 16 in commutation, £E 4 for electricity, and £E 7.50 for cigarettes. The remaining £E 18 had to cover food, medicine, entertainment, and installments on their appliances: a TV, water heater, and refrigerator. In short, they were a two-income family, creating through appliances the illusion of middle-class existence, but too poor to afford children or even a decent diet. Their combined annual income of £E 699, however, placed them well above the household poverty line of £E 350.

The question of the attitudes of these substrata toward change and transformation of society, modernity and tradition is simply irrelevant to their basic concerns. My own feeling is, and in the absence of survey data it is only that, the fact of being urban, literate, and salaried will tell us very little about collective attitudes and aspirations.

The question is only marginally easier with respect to dominant elements of the state bourgeoisie. 'Adil Ghun'aim in his original article on the "new bureaucratic class" rightly insists on the social and ideological heterogeneity of its members (1968, p. 92). It is probably safe to say that most members of this class are simply careerist, but to the extent that their careers depend on implementing programs and projects that bring about structural change in the economy and society, they can also be seen as committed modernizers. But for a rare few, who would include figures such as 'Aziz Sidqi, Sidqi Sulaiman, or even Ahmad Osman, I suspect that their urge to modernize did not go beyond protecting their careers.

It has always been difficult in all systems, including revolutionary and/or Marxist states, to indoctrinate and mobilize bureaucrats. Even in socialist, party-dominated states, the apparatchiki tend over time to reduce the party to yet another bureaucratic agency. In Egypt, where many of the top-ranking figures had begun their careers before 1952 or had been drawn from the officer corps, little attempt was made to imbue the bureaucracy with socialist ideals. Some, surely very few, came to their careers with socialist or leftist predilections. Others, more numerous, identify with the religious right, especially the Muslim Brethren (see Chapters Fourteen and Fifteen).

These wings notwithstanding, the more centrist, managerial outlook is probably dominant. To underline what I believe is a prevalent set of values, I shall cite verbatim judgments made by members of the administrative elite in interviews I conducted. All, I should note, are in the spirit of Nasser's remarks of March 18, 1967 to public sector company heads. In these he emphasized that there is no difference between socialist and capitalist management, only a difference in the ownership of the means of production and the control of profits. A guiding principle in both systems is that wages must be linked to productivity.

Engineer Samir Hilmi, a member of the Free Officers group, minister of industry in 1964-65, and in 1974, deputy director of the Central Auditing Agency, put the matter in similar terms [interview, June 5, 1974]: "The whole distinction in this day and age between public and private ownership pales beside the question of professional management." He went on to invoke the desirability of competitive public sector holding companies as had existed in Egypt between 1957-1961. Mustapha Murad, another Free Officer, MP, and head of the Cotton General Organization also looked back on that period as the halcyon days of Egyptian state capitalism: efficient, competitive, and profit-oriented.

The nemesis of these and other stalwarts of the public sector was 'Aziz Sidqi. Yet how different was he? The heart of his disagreements with his peers consisted in his conviction that planning must take the place of profit-oriented competition. Industrialization in the socialist framework, he told me,

> has two objectives: efficiency and justice. It must generate jobs and goods for local consumption. We cannot afford to have our reinvestible surplus drained off through low wages, foreign markets, and repatriated profits. The state must generate the investment burden and control its sources. The socialist solution is the only way to generate capital. . . .
> We have always been pragmatists of the national interest, not idealogues. [December 11, 1973.]

Taha Zaki, the civilian director of Kima Fertilizers, and in 1980 minister of industry, put the question more bluntly (February 7, 1974): "All these debates between capitalism and communism can be reduced to one thing—who gets the money. I don't care about the debates. The question is to get some money first, otherwise the debates are about nothing."

'Adil Ghun'aim (1968, pp. 92-93) delineated four basic perspectives among his "new bureaucratic class," to which I think we can fairly attach some names of personages who have appeared in these pages. The first is an elitist perspective grounded in a faith in science and technology, suspicious of political mobilization, democracy, and capitalism in equal measure. 'Aziz Sidqi typifies this outlook. The second believes in a close alliance between state capitalism and private capital, but is also suspicious of political mobilization and democracy. Sidqi Sulaiman, 'Abd al-Mun'aim al-Qaissuni, and Samir Hilmi represent this perspective. The third flows from the civilian old guard, seeking foreign capital to play a major role in nonsocialist development. 'Abd al-Galil al-'Amari, Hassan 'Abbas Zaki, 'Abd al-Razzaq 'Abd al-Magid of the *munfatihun* mentioned earlier adhere to this view. Finally there is the democratic-socialist perspective advocating intensification of socialist transformation and mass mobilization. Isma'il Sabri 'Abdullah, Fu'ad Mursi, Ya-hya Gamal, and a few others embody this trend. The first perspective prevailed in the 1960s when Ghun'aim wrote. It is by no means absent in the 1970s but has been rivaled if not eclipsed by the second and third. The fourth has always been a marginal phenomenon.

It would be a major error to suppose that the members of the state and managerial bourgeoisie spend much time thinking about their philosophies of social transformation. Rather it is understandably their careers that most concern them. Some of the information furnished by the previously cited CAPMAS survey of public sector management (1974) sheds light on the varying prospects open to different segments of this class. First, it was the case that of 34,000 managers surveyed, 31 percent had begun their careers in the private sector before the 1961 nationalizations. One may logically assume that this older group, kept on because of their experience, would feel threatened by younger recruits with strong technical backgrounds and untainted by a past in the private sector.[7]

Second, we find that 37 percent of the managers had neither university nor secondary school diplomas (N = 12,633). The data did not present the overlap of this subgroup with the first but I would suspect that it is substantial. In any event people with such low educational qualifications must cling defensively to their jobs in the face of waves of younger, presumably better-educated competitors.

Nearly 60 percent of the managers (N = 19,744) had secondary or university degrees, while 1.5 percent (397) had advanced degrees, including 57 Ph.D.'s. It is within this group that the technocratic-managerial elements are concentrated. In 1967 Nazih Ayubi found that 24 percent of all top-level public sector posts, and 50 percent of all public sector board chairmen, were engineers. Commenting on this Akeel and Moore (1977, p. 281) noted on the basis of their own survey that the engineering profession was increasingly "colonized" by the urban middle and upper middle classes. They also showed that engineers of this background were more prevalent in the public sector, where salaries are generally higher than in the civil service. The best prediction of rapid promotion, however, were graduating grades from university and not class origins.

Until the era of *infitah* the state bourgeoisie was a pampered elite relative to the rest of Egyptian society. But even in 1972, 22,000 of the 34,000 public sector managers surveyed claimed that their salaries were not commensurate with the cost of living and most (74 percent) felt that their jobs did not match their skills. Believing themselves underpaid and misemployed, these bureaucrats and their counterparts in the civil service have engaged in games of manipulating perquisites, personal enrichment, and other forms of what the French call "les délices du pouvoir."

One of these forms was high-level moonlighting. In 1975 it was determined that the majority of Egypt's 750 highest-ranking bureaucrats held more than one public job. At that time it was decided to make this practice illegal,

[7] How many private sector managers have stayed on successfully in the public sector is not known to me. At the summit one encounters people like Ahmad Osman or Muhammed Rushdi of Bank Misr. Occasionally the press reveals holdovers at lower levels, i.e., Muhammed Rida al-Damyati, director of the Tanta Oil and Soap Co., the son of the owner of the plant, which was nationalized in 1963.

although membership on the board of directors of a public sector company was not considered a second job. Some of those immediately affected were Mustapha Abu Zaid Fahmi, minister of justice *and* "socialist prosecutor," and Salah Gharib, minister of labor *and* president of the General Confederation of Labor Unions.

Beyond this, there was the more general trend of proliferating high-level administrative positions and budgeting salaries for positions unoccupied. In 1980, for instance, there were 2,531 bureaucrats with the rank of deputy minister or director general (*AI*, no. 624, December 29, 1980). More piquant was the phenomenon of "fictitious ministers" (Shafiq Ali, *RY*, no. 2560, July 4, 1977). It was claimed in 1975 that there were 500 to 700 posts of ministerial rank whose nominal occupants had no real function. One ministry alone, it was alleged, had twenty employees with the rank of deputy minister who never went to work (*AY*, November 16, 1974). Deputy P.M. Higazi had to testify before parliament on this issue and stated that the public budget carried no more than eighty-four persons at ministerial rank (*A*, January 26, 1975).

There are many ways in which the high-ranking bureaucrat can legally make his material life more pleasant (cf. Maraghi 1975). They had in the mid-Seventies something like £E 15 million annually in representational allowances to play with in addition to which they frequently awarded their companies and themselves production bonuses. Subsidized housing, private clubs, low-cost vacations, and government cars were also available to them. At the time of the revolution, the government owned 500 cars; by 1964 the number had increased to 12,000, then to 18,000 in 1975. Most were reserved for use by high-ranking officials. The reported sighting of a minister's wife using an official vehicle and driver to do the shopping or take the children to school is standard journalist fare ('Issam Rifa'at 1978a).

Bureaucrats are not legally permitted to engage in private business, but it is significant that in 1974 the Conseil d'Etat ruled that owning taxis is not a commercial activity and hence open to civil servants. Many bureaucrats must have heaved a sigh of relief, for taxi ownership had been a favored device for supplementing salaries. Another avenue was investment in urban housing and real estate which also fell outside the strictures on commercial activities.

Outright corruption, however, was from the very outset rife throughout the civil service and public sector. I will have a good deal more to say about the general phenomenon in Chapter Fourteen, but for the moment I want to concentrate on high-level corruption.[8] Kickbacks, embezzlement, "marketed" services, black market operations, and the like were common features

---

[8] The Egyptian slang expression for corruption is *kusa* or squash, because, it is said, it spreads thickly and horizontally like the squash vine. In the 1970s Egyptians said that squash had become ivy (*al-kusa yib'a liblab*) spreading thickly and *vertically*.

of public life in "socialist" Egypt. One of the more notorious figures of these years was a former officer hired as a broker by the public-sector Wadi Company, which exported citrus fruit to the USSR. Between 1964 and 1974, when he came under investigation, the officer received £E 1.2 million in "commissions" (Guwaida 1976a). In a detailed account of other cases, Muhammed 'Abd al-Salam, the state prosecutor in the 1960s, summed up his experience thus (1975, p. 64):

> It is said that this kind of deviationism occurs in all countries and in all times. But I do not believe that it ever reached at any time in our country, or in other civilized countries, this degree of pervasiveness; a pervasiveness that reduced the exception to the rule, and the rule to an exception. Corruption became the rule and honesty the exception.

Fathi 'Abd al-Fattah (1975b, p. 257), a Marxist imprisoned in the early 1960s, recounted his conversations with the ebullient millionaire, Basyuni Guma', also in prison for capitalist crimes.

> [Guma'] was certain that he would one day get out and that once again he would turn dust to gold. "How," I asked him, "could you do that?" "Native wit," he replied. "But nearly everything is nationalized," I said. Guma' smiled and countered: "God in His infinite wisdom has left us high-ranking bureaucrats."

Basyuni's prophesy came true, and by 1976 he was running full throttle under the umbrella of *infitah*.

With the advent of the open-door policy, high-level corruption has taken on new dimensions. Indeed, it is instructive to remember that the corruption scandals that literally shook the monarchy in the 1940s and tarnished the image of Nahhas Pasha and the Wafd involved sums of no more than £E 5,000 or £E 10,000. Today Egypt's public officials have joined the big leagues, and certain observers of the current scene look back on the bad old days with a certain nostalgia (Zakaria 1975a).

One of the most highly publicized scandals did much to discredit *infitah*, for it involved a triangular deal of precisely the wrong kind. The deal consisted in the purchase by Egyptair of four Boeing 707/200s. Kidder-Peabody's Beirut representative, Roger Tamraz, arranged the financing and reserved 5 percent of the value of the contract as his firm's commission. He began to put the deal together in 1973, perhaps in conjunction with Kamal Adham, an advisor to King Faisal of Saudi Arabia, an agent for Boeing, and a man known to have close links to the CIA (*Wall Street Journal*, March 1, 1977).

The deal was a long time gestating, and some of the officials involved fell from favor, so that details of it leaked to the press in 1976. Two loans of $53 million and $7 million were negotiated in October 1972 and October

1973 to purchase the four aircraft at a price per aircraft $500,000 more than that prevailing elsewhere. After a three-year grace period, loans would be repaid in ten equal installments in the currency of the creditor's choice. Interest on the loan would have amounted at the end of ten years to 108 percent of the principal, i.e., approximately $68 million. Presumably Kidder-Peabody would have picked up a $6 million commission.

It was stipulated that if Egypt missed any installments on the loan, the aircraft could be seized anywhere in the world and sold by the creditors. These terms were reviewed by Bank Ahali, which recommended that the deal be refused and suggested that more favorable financing could be found. But a ministerial committee overruled this recommendation, approved the loan, and designated the Central Bank as guarantor. The then-governor of the CB, Nazmi 'Abd al-Hamid, later testified that he, too, opposed the loan but was likewise overruled (A, January 7, 1977). The persons subsequently accused of accepting bribes and kickbacks in this affair were the director of Egyptair and former Deputy P.M. 'Abdullah Marziban, who was simultaneously implicated in a foreign exchange smuggling scandal. I have seen no evidence that any official was subsequently convicted on these charges, although Muhammed Hilmi Shams, technical advisor to the Ministry of Civil Aviation, later wrote a check for $200,000 to the socialist prosecutor representing his cut in the deal.

In 1976 US investigations of Westinghouse Electric Corporation's operations abroad led to the disclosure of a bribe of $322,000 having been paid to Egypt's minister of electricity, Ahmad Sultan, a civilian technocrat (details in J. Hoagland, WP, October 26, 1976). The quid pro quo consisted in contracts for the purchase of $30 million in Westinghouse equipment for Egyptian power stations. Sultan was dropped from the cabinet. So too was Ashraf Marwan, Nasser's son-in-law, advisor to Sadat on Arab affairs, and director of the Arab Military Organization which was to start a weapons industry in Egypt. For years rumors had circulated on Marwan's five-percenting of the flow into Egypt of funds and projects originating in the Arab peninsula. His visibility had become too great, as had that of Ahmad Osman in his capacity as minister of housing and reconstruction, and they both left the cabinet.

In short, corruption became a major political issue under Sadat. So much so that in April 1975 he dismissed the Higazi government with oblique hints that if Higazi had not indulged in personal aggrandizement himself he had at least been too accommodating with others in his cabinet. The president called for the strict application of Egypt's "Where-did-you-get-it" law.

High-level corruption has nearly always paid in Egypt. Important figures are rarely prosecuted, never mind convicted. In 1958 an Administrative Surveillance Agency with 120 investigators was set up to monitor bureaucratic corruption. Muhammed 'Abd al-Salam, the former public prosecutor, referred to this agency as the "graveyard" of accusations of high-level wrongdoing. Fahmi Huwaida, a pundit for *al-Ahram* (June 3, 1975), decried this lack of pursuit. The only corruption case he could recall came in 1969, involving three public sector officials who could not agree on how to divide up $180,000 in illegal commissions. They were simply dismissed after paying back the money. Two later resurfaced with the rank of deputy minister. As another columnist, Muhammed 'Abd al-Tawwab, put it (*A*, April 22, 1975), "We convert embezzled funds—if discovered—into long-term loans that the employee can pay back in easy installments."

Petty bureaucrats have frequently been tried. The first case after Sadat's call for firmness was a civil servant at £E 32 per month who had bought a car at £E 1,150 and rented an apartment at £E 20 per month. He was acquitted. But the high-ranking continue to escape unscathed and are spared public exposure. A master's thesis by Shadia 'Ali Qinawi found that 454 high-ranking bureaucrats had sentences pending against them that had never been imposed (*RY*, no. 2609, June 12, 1978).

This kind of widespread cover-up that disproportionately benefits the administrative elite can be taken as an important indicator of shared interests and class solidarity. The major levers of the economy are at their disposal, and they are used for several purposes: to transform society, to build careers in the professional sense, and to line their pockets. The state bourgeoisie controls important means of production and knows it. However, unlike its capitalist counterparts in the developed countries, this bourgeoisie is also aware of the fragility of the regimes with which it collaborates as they face development challenges and international pressures. Handing on power to their offspring or even keeping it for themselves for very long may appear to them as the height of hubris. Hence a premium is placed on personal aggrandizement as a hedge against that unavoidable moment when they are stripped of power.

It remains for us to examine the links between the state bourgeoisie and its allies in the private sector. In combination they have come to form a class that has earned the opprobrium of the left and to some extent of the right. Its members have been individually decried as "parasites" (*inter alia*, Ghazzali 1973, pp. 22-26), and collectively as the "new millionaires" (Lutfi al-Kholi *al-Tali'a*, April 1974), or the "new aristocracy" (Saaty 1977, pp. 196-204).

In the popular or at least journalistic mind, this class, while encompassing more than public officials, is nonetheless built around them and the business they individually or institutionally dispense. What Egyptians are aware of is its highly visible, ostentatious levels of consumption and living style, and its less visible corruption.

This class became the object of widespread attention with the advent of *infitah*, although it had already taken root in the 1960s. Lutfi al-Kholi, who denounced the *bayyumiyun* in the building sector (see Chapter Eight) referred to them as "the legitimate offspring of the 1967 defeat." Galal Amin in 1973 noted the presumed gap in consumption and life styles between Western middle classes and their Egyptian counterparts and concluded, "A strong desire of a small minority to catch up with Western ways of life was thus translated into a desire of the whole population, the majority of whom are either completely unaware of the existence of such a 'gap' or, because of their much simpler needs, would find its existence completely irrelevant" (1973, p. 31). Nazih Ayubi (1977, p. 75) echoed the same theme, attributing to the alliance of the administrative class with private sector interests fundamental distortions in development strategies. Otherwise, he queries, why would Egypt produce consumer durables at the expense of cheap cloth and shoes,[9] concentrate on higher education when two-thirds of the population is illiterate, guarantee jobs for university graduates while ignoring the unskilled.

Egypt's last, fleeting attempt to constrain the consumption of the managerial and parasitic bourgeois came under 'Aziz Sidqi's government in 1972. The austerity measures imposed at that time had particular effect on imports—the number of private automobiles imported for instance dropped off from 10,000 to 4,000—but the October War and the rush to liberalize foreign trade opened the doors wide to a middle-class consumption binge. It manifests itself at several levels, from the flood of imported "provocative goods" that all can see but only the well-off can afford, to the parties of the rich. To arrive in Egypt's new bourgeoisie, one must at the very least fête the nuptials of one's children in the Sheraton or Hilton Hotels. The guest list should run into the hundreds and the price into the thousands of pounds. So gaudy had these nightly displays become that legislation was proposed to place a flat-rate tax on whatever was paid out to hold them. In the same vein, the marriage of one of Sadat's daughters to the son of Ahmad Osman was celebrated in a

---

[9] *Al-Tali'a* 8 (June 1972):121-35; "The Situation of the National Bourgeoisie," published the following, contrasting consumption figures during the first Five-Year Plan.

Consumer Durable Increase		Basic Goods Increase	
refrigerators	215%	wheat	29%
washers	390	corn	40
heaters	1,543	broad beans	35
butane gas	117	cloth	26
radios	152	shoes	60

Many consumer durables are so costly, e.g., TVs and automobiles, that only the wealthiest Egyptians could afford them. Such persons could import their consumer needs as well. For example, the number of imported automobiles rose from 1,811 in 1966 to 10,196 in 1971.

well-attended but modestly catered ceremony arranged by the president. Osman was not satisfied and held a more private, lavishly catered affair that, like all he does, raised eyebrows and tempers.

Somewhere between imported beer at two dollars a can and catered meals flown in from Paris is the determined quest for the latest accoutrements of middle-class existence. When it was announced that Egypt would assemble its own color TVs, £E 8 million was paid out in one day by private Egyptians as down payments on sets unseen and as yet unassembled.

The existence of "the new class" became an important political issue in 1974 and 1975. Lutfi al-Kholi (*al-Tali'a*, April 1974) claimed that undisclosed sources in the Ministry of Finance were convinced that there were 187 millionaires in Egypt. In January 1973, the Price Planning Agency released for limited circulation Memo 181, prepared by Ahmad Murshidi, that indicated that there were 2,376 families with annual incomes of over £E 30,000 per year. *Ruz al-Yussef* published Murshidi's figures October 28, 1974. Deputy Prime Minister Higazi first denied the existence of these families, dismissing the figures as "prattle" (*Sawt al-Gama'*, January 13, 1975), then, pulling back a bit, said that the PPA study was not very reliable (*RY*, no. 2432, January 21, 1975). Murshidi later reported that government officials asked him "what foreign powers are behind your work?" (cited in Galal Amin 1978, p. 144).

The issue was now out in the open. First there was debate as to whether a class of "fat cats" had come into being. Sa'id Sinbal, columnist for the rightist *Akhbar al-Yom*, wrote indignantly ("Talk, talk, talk," *AY*, January 17, 1976): "Who are these parasites, these brokers, these commission grabbers? Who are the fat cats? Name them or shut up." But a year later he denounced a new breed of exploiters in an article entitled "Infitah and the New Class" (*AY*, February 5, 1977).

After 1976 the existence of this class was no longer in doubt. The question then became to what extent was the concentration of wealth in its hands tolerable. Members of it began to advocate the abolition of confiscatory taxes on gross incomes that had proved "counterproductive." The Shaikh of Al-Azhar, 'Abd al-Halim Mahmud, argued that Islam placed no obstacles in the path of those fortunate enough to become wealthy. Even 'Abd al-'Aziz Higazi, defending his policies before Egyptian students and the parliament, resorted to Islam. To the students, he said, "I personally believe in an important Islamic principal: the necessity of differentiation among people. For people are not all equal in wealth, knowledge and health" (*Sawt al-Gama'*, January 1, 1975). For the parliamentarians he invoked a phrase in the Quran: "We have placed some of you above others in rank" (cited in *al-Tali'a*, March 1975, p. 23).

By the middle 1970s the managerial bourgeoisie, with its administrative core, private sector allies, and foreign benefactors, had consolidated itself and, because of its partial control over the state, conferred legitimacy upon itself. It was out in the open, courted by foreign businessmen, praised for its perseverance under Nasserist socialism, and promised a vanguard role in the development of Egypt's mixed economy. Whether it would accept that or any other role of social and economic transformation with any degree of commitment is moot.

Conclusion

The Nasserist regime regarded the civil service and public sector as instruments of change and preemption. To change Egyptian society, to promote mass literacy, to shift the country to an industrial footing, and to achieve the rates of growth required to bring about broad-based prosperity, were dependent on the growth of a powerful, interventionist state apparatus. Preemption consisted in cornering markets in human and material resources and transferring them to public control, thereby denying their use to potentially hostile groups in the private sector. The will to transform was never a class phenomenon but was confined to a few among the top leadership. As the capacity of the state itself to transform waned in the late 1960s, its importance in preempting and controlling strategic resources waxed. The private sector could only vie for crumbs from its table, while its payroll and personnel list were the regime's major hedge against political unrest. When Nasser died the economy was stagnant, the bureaucracy expanding, and vested public sector interests cashing in their control over resources and the flow of communications.

Any Egyptian with a higher education could aspire to find his niche in this elite, and during the 1960s its expansion was so rapid, especially among its technocratic elements, that hope and reality were not far apart. It was this burgeoning group of managerial technocrats that led Manfred Halpern to observe that Egypt and other Middle Eastern countries were undergoing a managerial revolution before their industrial revolutions had gotten underway. Clement Moore seized upon the same phenomenon to argue that Egypt's leaders had confused the proliferation of technical and managerial cadres with modernization itself (Moore 1980, pp. 3-4).

The one-third of the work force in public employ breaks down essentially into two classes: the first and dominant class is what we have referred to as the state bourgeoisie. With its private sector counterparts it resembles Sklar's managerial bourgeoisie, controlling although seldom owning the means of production and distribution. It may number about 200-300,000, but any such estimate must be very tentative. The top-level elite of the state bourgeoisie, perhaps 2,500 individuals in public economic activities, is recruited from this pool. What is most interesting now (1980) is the changing weights of its components. The military technocrats that took over important civilian functions in the public sector are fading from the scene. General Gamal 'Askar, head of CAMPAS until his death in 1980, and Col. Samir Hilmi, head of the Central Auditing Agency until he was killed along with Sadat in October 1981, outlasted most of their peers.

The weight of public sector managers is itself changing. *Infitah* has led to a noticeable migration of skilled managers to more lucrative posts in the private sector. In the 1960s, managers and technocrats had exit options of only one kind: work with international agencies. Several, having fallen out with Nasserist policies, exercised this option: Hilmi 'Abd al-Rahman (UNIDO), Nazih Daif (IMF), Fu'ad Sultan (IMF), 'Abd al-Galil al-'Amari (IBRD), 'Abd al-Razzaq 'Abd al-Magid (IBRD), Hassan 'Abbas Zaki (Abu Dhabi Fund), Hilmi Murad (UNESCO), etc. Now private consultancies or direct managerial positions in foreign enterprises have led to new forms of migration in which public-private lines of demarcation are increasingly blurred. Public sector companies, especially banks and insurance companies, invest in and place representatives on the boards of directors of joint ventures under Law 43, and, of course, public sector companies are parties to the joint ventures themselves. The recent movements of Taha Zaki may indicate the new career paths. After being fired from his position as head of Kima Fertilizers, he became an advisor to Ahmad Osman, himself advisor to the president for Food Security. Zaki visited the US where he had contacts with Robert Strauss. This led to their joint promotion of a project run by Pepsi Cola to develop 20,000 acres of citrus near Ismailia. In May 1980 Zaki returned to the cabinet as minister of industry.

The possibility that has opened up since 1974 is that the weight of economic activity will shift to private Egyptian and foreign interests, sustained by a migration of the state bourgeoisie out of the state. The result would be the gradual rebuilding of a private entrepreneurial class where the control and ownership of the means of production are increasingly coincident.

This leaves us with the three-million strong administrative underclass whose only alternative to blocked careers and salaries undermined by inflation is migration out of the country. From the outside this mass, and its private sector counterparts, appear economically homogeneous. My own first impressions of Egypt in 1971 were of a classless society whose members tenaciously sought to assert class differences. Only the elite had succeeded in that quest. In 1972 a jointly produced Soviet-Egyptian film (*Hikayat al-Nil*) about the Aswan Dam portrayed a bourgeois Egyptian girl who falls in love with a worker at the dam site. But the filmmakers knew they could not allow this to happen, and it turned out that the worker was really a well-educated journalist posing as a worker to get an authentic story. In this way class lines were respected.

At the lower deciles class is not predominantly a function of income. A tenant farmer and smallholder may live identically, but there is no question which is superior in class terms. A college graduate may earn nine times as much a year as a peasant cultivator: £E 360 versus £E 40. In the US that kind of ratio would apply to a $10,000 per year schoolteacher as opposed to a $90,000 per year executive. But in Egypt the £E 360 will not provide the graduate with a car, a house, a vacation trip, or even decent furniture. His status is rooted in his education and the nature of his job, not his superior earning power. In 1975 the starting civil service salary for those holding primary school diplomas was £E 13.50 and those with secondary diplomas £E 15. The difference between the two diplomas was only £E 1.50 ($2.15) per month in salary, but much more in social ranking.

This economic leverage for the strata of the underclass is finely gradated and cannot be expressed in the ostentatious accumulation of material goods. Although such accumulation is important, differentiation is expressed more in terms of social prestige, the demand for deference, the right to exploit or protect others. Each narrow income differential is developed to its fullest and the status attached to it stolidly defended and overlaid with the intangibles of education, nature of employment, marriage, style, and dress. This system for years allowed the constituent elements of the salariat to maintain a sense of dignity, self-respect and hope for modest advancement. The rampant inflation of the 1970s and the growth of migration on a major scale has upset the old values and expectations. The civil service continues to grow, but it is now, in every sense, the employer of last resort.

Chapter Twelve

LAND TENURE AND RURAL CLASS

[The Revolution] wanted to liberate the *fallah* by abolishing large landownership, but when it announced that the *fallah* in its political lexicon is he who owns twenty *feddans* or less, it handed over the political, economic, social, and cultural leadership of the Egyptian countryside, not to the *fallahin*, but to the state bureaucracy and to the class of small big landowners or big small landowners.

[Louis Awad, A, October 11, 1974.]

Students of contemporary Egyptian society, whatever their ideologies, are nearly at one in attributing great political weight to the agrarian bourgeoisie. This class has been variously named rural middle class, second stratum, kulaks, middle-range landowners, rural capitalist class, and so on. Some have attributed to it the paternity of Egypt's ruling elite since 1952, and others have depicted it as the single most dominant political force in the country. It is my contention that while an observable rural bourgeoisie does exist, it sired neither the regime of Nasser nor Sadat. It can best be seen as a class fraction subordinate to the state bourgeoisie and its predominantly urban private sector allies.

Land Reform and Land Tenure

The class that we are to examine can or should no longer be called middle. The successive land ceilings imposed in 1952, 1961, and 1969 have rendered it the topmost stratum in the countryside. Its members, in the Egyptian context, are the big landowners, but it is understandable that certain writers refer to them as "middle" when the largest legal landholding in Egypt is fifty acres. The relative position of this class, although not its existence, is owed to the policies of the Nasserist regime. The destruction of the large landowners through land reform left the "kulaks," by default, at the top of the rural heap. For some observers this outcome could not have been inadvertent and therefore proves that the Free Officers were intentionally servicing the interests of a class from which they had sprung and to which they owed ultimate allegiance (for example, Mursi 1975c, p. 113).

In this section I want only to present the basic quantitative evidence concerning the evolution of this class, leaving for subsequent sections the assessment of its political weight. The initial operation is by no means simple. Despite Egypt's millennia-old tradition of keeping detailed cadastral records, contemporary registration categories are subject to widely varying interpretations. There has been no agricultural census in Egypt since 1961. Since then there have been two land reform measures and, presumably, a great deal of unlegislated change in tenure patterns. The principal means at our disposal to capture the existence of rural strata and classes is landowning statistics. Yet there is systematic confusion in Egyptian data between landowning (*mulkia*) and landholding (*hiyaza*). The latter term refers to operational units as registered with the agricultural cooperatives. One suspects that holdings are frequently erroneously reported as ownership units. I cannot resolve these ambiguities, but they become very important in interpreting tenure data since 1961.

Agrarian reform was a political issue of great saliency even before the 1952 revolution. The full implications of a labor-surplus society with relatively fixed cultivable land resources had made themselves felt after World War II. Land hunger drove up cash rents to the extent that about 60 percent of all Egypt's land was let out each year at rates that equaled 75 percent of net income, and in the late 1940s sporadic rural violence was one of the results (G. Saab 1967, p. 11).

In the face of mounting rural tension, a small number of parliamentarians introduced various proposals for land reform. Naturally enough they focused on the tiny band of large landowners, some 2,000 strong, who constituted no more than .1 percent of all landowners but owned among them 20 percent of all cultivated acreage. The major issue revolved around the question of imposing ceilings on landownership. For example, Ibrahim Shukri, elected to parliament in 1949, proposed a ceiling of fifty *feddans*. He was joined in the senate by Muhammed Khattab, who argued that the ceiling should apply only to future acquisitions, not existing holdings. Another M.P., Mirit Ghali, advocated a ceiling of 100 *feddans*, warning that anything lower would "restrict the initiative of the rural middle class, those rural notables, who, in our opinion, have the vital task of infusing life into rural society" (Baer 1962, p. 212). More conservative voices, such as that of 'Ali Shamsi, president of the National Bank of Egypt, were raised to reject property ceilings in favor of distribution of state lands and introduction of a progressive tax on agricultural incomes.

No measures were adopted before the *coup d'état* of July 1952, but in light of these debates it is difficult to believe, as 'Abd al-'Aziz Ramadan has contended, that the RCC had given little or no thought to agrarian reform. Instead, apparently on the strength of Khalid Muhi al-Din's recollections, he attributes the concern of the military leadership to an article by Dr. Rashid al-Barawi appearing in *al-Zaman* (August 4, 1952). Barawi stressed the desirability of undermining the political strength of the large landowners as well as that of promoting social harmony in the countryside by reinforcing the stratum of smallholders. Again according to Ramadan, the civilian, Ahmad Fu'ad, a member of the Marxist movement Haditu[1] and a liaison person with the Free Officers, and Ahmad Hamrush, a Marxist officer, read the article and brought it to the attention of the RCC (Ramadan 1976, pp. 14-18 and 320).

Hamrush himself partially confirms this account but stresses the extent to which the principle of agrarian reform was in the air. On the one hand he chronicled the growing violent resistance to rack-renting during the summer of 1951, and the urging of the Americans, through the M.P. Ahmad Hussain who later became ambassador to the US, that some reform measures be undertaken. On this point Hamrush concludes: "When the armed forces moved on the evening of July 23, the abolition of feudalism was one among the goals they sought to attain, but they had not prepared a project or an integrated plan . . ." (Hamrush 1974, 1:255).

He confirmed that he, along with Rashid al-Barawi and Ahmad Fu'ad, brought such a plan to the attention of Gamal Salim of the RCC. He in turn was charged with forming a committee to devise means of implementation, with the legal help of 'Abd al-Razzaq Sanhuri. P.M. 'Ali Mahir balked at the draft law, preferring the introduction of a progressive income tax, but once he was removed from the prime ministership, and Gen. Muhammed Naguib installed in his place, the Agrarian Reform Law was immediately issued.

It fell to the civilian and former M.P. Sayyid Mar'ai to implement the reform, although he had had no part in drafting it (Mar'ai 1979, 1:241). The Agrarian Reform Law of September 9, 1952 limited individually owned landholdings to 200 *feddans* with the right to transfer another 100 *feddans* to wives and children. In that way an effective, legal farm unit could be as much as 300 *feddans*. The right to transfer 100 *feddans* to family members as well as that to dispose of land above the ceiling through legal sales were clauses insisted upon by the civilian 'Abd al-Galil al-'Amari who became minister of finance in Naguib's cabinet (Hamrush 1974, 1:27). The right to sell excess lands in fact prompted a wave of panic sales of some 150,000 *feddans*, and

[1] Acronym of al-Haraka al-Dimuqratiya lil-Taharrur al-Watani or Democratic Movement for National Liberation.

within a year, Law 300 of October 1953 was issued suspending this privilege (G. Saab 1967, p. 20; Fathi 'Abd al-Fattah 1975a, p. 21).

The ceiling on landownership was further reduced in 1961-62 to 100 *feddans* per nuclear family with the right to all those affected to dispose of the excess by 1970 (Law 127 of 1961 and the National Charter of 1962). These acts were followed in 1962, 1963, and 1964 by individual sequestrations for political reasons, and in 1966 by seizures prompted by the Committee on the Liquidation of Feudalism (see below) of properties held illegally above the 1961-62 ceiling. Finally, in September 1969 the ownership ceiling for individuals was lowered to 50 *feddans* and that of a nuclear family kept at 100 *feddans*.

The distributional impact of these reforms is reasonably clear and is presented chronologically in the following listing (drawn from 'Abd al-Hamid 1973, p. 115; Fathi 'Abd al-Fattah, 1975a, p. 23; Radwan 1977, p. 16).

Law 178 (1952)	450,305 *feddans*
Law 152 (1957), taking over public *waqf* land	110,451
Law 127 (1961)	214,132
Law 44 (1962), taking over private *waqf* land	38,336
Law 15 (1963), prohibition of ownership of agricultural land by foreigners	61,910
Law 150 (1964), transferring sequestered property to public ownership	45,516
Coop purchases of land	25,807
Land turned over to agrarian reform by organizations and agencies	25,979
Law 50 (1969)	30,000?
Total	1,002,436
Land returned as a result of legal appeals	72,137
Net takeover	930,299
Distributed as of 1967	754,487 to 318,000 families

Two comments are in order at this point. First, the Committee for the Liquidation of Feudalism found that landowners had held 90,000 *feddans* in excess of the 1961 ceiling and that their total holdings, temporarily put under sequestration, were about 200,000 *feddans*. 'Abd al-Fattah (1975a, p. 30) claims that nearly all this acreage was returned to its owners in 1967 and 1968. Law 50 of 1969, it is commonly believed, involved no more than 30,000 *feddans*, and it is also widely believed that very little land was actually taken over. In any event no official statistics regarding the application of this law have ever been released. What we are left with, then, is a series of reforms that involved at most about 16 percent of Egypt's cultivated land, leading to the actual redistribution of 13 percent of that land to about 10 percent of Egypt's rural families. The state, even as late as 1978, retained control of at least 200,000 *feddans*, which it leased, although it is a matter of debate whether or not this is a function of the poor quality of the land ('Abd al-Fattah, 1975a, p. 30) or that they were under litigation (Ibrahim Shukri in *RY*, no. 2615, July 24, 1978).

Obviously agrarian reform in and of itself did not lead to any major redistribution of land, and the object of the 1952 reform was above all political. Given Egypt's limited land resources, Gabriel Saab, who is scarcely a radical, predicted that the landownership ceiling would eventually be lowered to 5 *feddans* (Saab 1967, p. 188). But even perfect equality would have been a self-defeating goal anyway. Had every rural family received an equal share of Egypt's cultivated land in 1965, its plot would have amounted to only 1.8 *feddans*. Then and now a holding of that size is regarded as subsubsistence. With continued population growth even these dwarf holdings would have been further reduced through inheritance. Moreover, Egypt's cultivated surface has actually been diminishing due to the expansion of cities and villages and the construction of roads, schools, factories, etc. In 1980 the cultivated surface was probably no more than 5.5 million *feddans* as opposed to about 6 million at the beginning of the revolution.

Some of the major elements of the impact of land ceilings in political and socio-economic terms can be discerned in Table 12.1. Throughout the period covered, large landholdings tended to diminish as a proportion of the total cultivated surface. On the eve of the first agrarian reform .4 percent of all owners controlled 33 percent of the cultivated area, but as mentioned earlier, a mere 2,000 still owned 20 percent of this land. As a result of the reforms of 1952 and 1961 the share of those owning fifty *feddans* or more dropped to 15 percent of the cultivated area, although by registering land in the names of brothers and other associates operational holdings could still be maintained in the hundreds of *feddans*.

The poorest stratum of the landowners, those owning five or less *feddans*, saw their relative position in both numbers of owners and proportion of cultivated surface owned increase throughout the period. When the 1952 reform was issued, they constituted 94 percent of all owners and controlled 35 percent of the cultivated surface. After the first two reforms they still made up 94 percent of all owners but now owned 52 percent of cultivated acreage. They were the prime beneficiaries of the 700,000 *feddans* distributed as a result of the land ceilings.

In all this I want to emphasize the stability of the two middle strata but particularly those owning eleven to fifty *feddans*. This stratum was the former rural middle class but is today the rural upper class. The smallholders in the five-to-ten-*feddan* range have shown extraordinary stability over time, num-

Table 12.1
Evolution of Major Strata of Landowners, 1896-1961

	0-5 feddans	6-10 feddans	11-50 feddans	Over 51 feddans
1896				
Owners	1,005,000	77,663	57,866	12,475
% All Owners	87.2	6.7	5.1	1.0
Surface	1,264,084	544,264	1,123,822	2,366,602
% Cult. Surface	24.5	9.5	20.8	45.3
1914				
Owners	1,414,920	76,044	46,160	12,480
% All Owners	90.7	4.9	3.5	8
Surface	1,425,060	529,620	1,098,380	2,396,940
% Cult. Surface	26.1	9.7	20.3	43.9
1936				
Owners	2,242,000	85,000	61,000	12,000
% All Owners	93.4	3.5	2.6	.5
Surface	1,837,000	561,000	1,185,000	2,254,000
% Cult. Surface	31.5	9.6	20.3	38.6
1952*				
Owners	2,642,000	79,000	69,000	11,000
% All Owners	94.3	2.8	2.5	.4
Surface	2,122,000	526,000	1,291,000	1,983,000
% Cult. Surface	35.4	8.7	21.6	33.1
1961†				
Owners	2,919,000	80,000	91,000	11,000
% All Owners	94.1	2.6	2.9	.3
Surface	3,172,000	526,000	1,456,000	930,000
% Cult. Surface	52.1	8.6	24.0	15.3

SOURCES: 1896-1939 from Rushdi 1972, Pt. I, p. 180 and Pt. II, p. 119; 1952 from Gabriel Saab 1967, p. 183; 1961: Abdel-Fadil 1975, p. 16.

* Prereform.

† After reforms of both 1952 and 1961.

bering between 76,000 and 85,000 and owning between 6.7 percent and 9.7 percent of the cultivated surface. The new upper class has been nearly as stable. Between 1896 and 1952, the numbers of its members, despite a drop prior to 1914, varied between 57,000 and 69,000. The acreage they owned varied between 1.1 and 1.2 million *feddans*. As a result of the land reforms this stratum increased in numbers and acreage controlled so that with 3 percent of all landowners it owned 24 percent of the cultivated surface. Its new assets were acquired mainly through purchase of excess land sold off in 1952-53 by landowners affected by the land ceiling. If we take this stratum in combination with the remnants of the old upper rural class, we have a group of roughly 102,000 landowners controlling 40 percent of Egypt's cultivated acreage. Moreover, the position of the stratum in the eleven-to-fifty-*feddan* range has been remarkably stable over a seventy-year period and has been relatively strengthened through the reforms of the 1950s and 1960s.

We seem therefore to have before us impressive statistical evidence as of 1961 of the property assets of a clearly defined class that had, by inference, transferred its property from generation to generation. This evidence notwithstanding, more recent statistics emanating from the Ministry of Agriculture give a different, albeit ambiguous picture. To understand this we must return to the distinction between agricultural properties and agricultural holdings. An agricultural holding is the cumulative size of all plots *operated* in the same district (*markaz*) by the same person, whether tenant or owner or both (Harik 1979, p. 38; and Abdel-Fadil 1975, p. 14n). On that basis, the agricultural census of 1961 revealed the following pattern:

Table 12.2

Comparison of the Distribution of Ownership (*Mulkiyat*) and Landholdings (*Hiyazat*) in Egypt, 1961

Size Class	1. No. of ownerships (thousands)	2. Area of ownerships (thousands)	3. No. of holdings	4. Area of holdings (thousands fed.)	4/2
< 5	2,919	3,172	1,381	2,354	74%
5 < 10	80	526	170	1,101	209
10 < 20	65	638	57	743	117
20 < 50	26	818	24	689	84
50 < 100	6	430	6	430	100
< 100	5	500	4	906	181
Total	3,101	6,084	1,642	6,223	

SOURCE: From Abdel-Fadil 1975; p. 16. The author speculates that the area of holdings exceeds that of ownership because government properties are recorded only in the former.

Egypt's tenurial system involves a combination of pure tenancy, pure ownership, and mixed tenancy and ownership. Table 12.2, for example, tells us that smallholders tend to lease out over a quarter of their land, while those in the five-to-ten-*feddan* range double their operational holdings by leasing in. So too the largest landowners leased in 406,000 *feddans* in addition to the 500,000 they owned. For the strata between 10 and 100 *feddans*, there is little overall difference between holdings and ownerships, although the better-off of what we have described as the new upper class (twenty to fifty *feddans*) lease out, while the less privileged of this stratum (ten to twenty *feddans*) lease in. It is, of course, impossible on the strength of these data to know to which strata the lessors-out are renting. This said, it is the fact in 1961 that those owning ten *feddans* or more had title to 40 percent of the cultivated surface while those operating ten *feddans* or more had control of 45 percent of that area.

Ilya Harik, using the results of a 1975 Ministry of Agriculture survey of holdings registered with cooperatives, has called this picture into question in a major way. His figures and the somewhat different ones of Mohaya Zaytoun are presented in Table 12.3. Harik justifiably concludes from his figures that:

> . . . the holders of 10 *feddans* or more are fewer now, 2% of total farm operators instead of 5.5 in 1961. The area of land they controlled declined sharply from 44.5% to 18% of the total area. In absolute figures they lost 1,676,600 *feddans*. . . . It is clear from these findings that in the second stage of land reform, it was the rural middle class who started to lose ground to the landless and small farmers [1979, pp. 42 and 43].

Harik concludes that middle-range landowners have sold a great deal of land to smallholders or the landless, and have allowed their retained holdings to fragment through inheritance (Harik 1979, pp. 42-43). Mohaya Zaytoun reaches somewhat similar conclusions, although her data, drawn from the same source as Harik's, is significantly different. She too stresses the important growth in small holdings, rising since 1961 from 67 percent to 83 percent of all holdings and from 22 percent to 48 percent of all cultivated acreage. The decline in cultivated area of those controlling ten or more *feddans* is partially explained by Zaytoun as the result of sales by those owning fifty *feddans* or more. In general she suspects that the redistribution of holdings has come at the expense of the richest (fifty-plus *feddans*) and the poorest

Table 12.3
Distribution of Holdings (*Hiyazat*) in 1975 and 1977-78
according to Harik and Zaytoun

	Holdings				Area Cultivated			
	Harik 1975 no. (thousands)	%	Zaytoun 1977-78 no. (thousands)	%	Harik 1975 no. (thousands)	%	Zaytoun 1977-78 no. (thousands)	%
0 < 3	2,284	80.0	2,359	83	2,762	46	2,446	45
3 < 5	355	12.4	293	10	1,185	20	1,013	19
5 < 10	148	5.2	126	4.4	944	16	773	14
< 10	65	2.3	69	2.4	1,091	18	1,220	22
	2,852	100.0	2,847	100.0	5,982	100	5,452	100

SOURCES: From Zaytoun 1982; and Harik 1979; p. 39.

(ten to twenty *feddans*) strata of the new rural upper class. She mentions fragmentation through inheritance and adds to this the possibility that middle-range landowners registered holdings in different names in order to take advantage of the tax exemption on holdings of three *feddans* or less introduced in 1973. She summarizes her findings thus:

> . . . all groups of landholders, with the exception of the group of small landholders, show a continuous decrease in their relative number over the whole period 1961-1977/78. This reflects a transformation in Egyptian agriculture towards smaller holdings and larger numbers of poor peasants, with fewer and fewer peasants holding a relatively large area of land . . .

This speculative foray into unpublished statistics of the Ministry of Agriculture may become obsolete if and when the projected agricultural census, the first since 1961, is tabulated and analyzed. In the meantime the trends indicated by Harik and Zaytoun are too important to hold in abeyance. In essence Harik is suggesting that a class that had stolidly maintained its relative strength in the rural pecking order for over seven decades had committed hara-kiri. They had, Harik argues, succumbed to Muslim inheritance laws, to which they had been impervious in the past, and found the financial conditions of capitalist agriculture in Nasser's Egypt so discouraging that they sold off land.

I cannot believe this. By all accounts capitalist agriculture for the upper stratum has become extremely lucrative in the last fifteen years, because of, rather than despite, state intervention in the agricultural sector. There are more incentives now than ever before for the new upper class to consolidate its position rather than disinvest. I shall explore this question further in the next section. I am also skeptical that tax evasion could tell much of the story. Assuming average ownership of nineteen *feddans* for the stratum under scrutiny, the tax savings through subdivision would be about £E 57 per annum. This is not negligible but, as we shall see, probably represents no more than 1 percent of the net income of a prosperous farmer.

Other than the possibility of statistical error, not unlikely given the discrepancy in data between 1975 and 1977-78[2], the observed dissolution of this class, can be explained in other ways.[3] Zaytoun may well be right that the

---

[2] Evident not only in the large variations in shares among strata but in the cultivated area itself: 5,982,000 *feddans* for Harik and 5,452,000 for Zaytoun. Zaytoun's is the more plausible.

[3] Statistical ambiguities of several sorts are rife. I cite here a problem that arose with the application in 1973 of the tax exemption on properties of three *feddans* or less. Inheritors of small fragmented plots frequently never bother to reregister the property in their name, leaving it in that of the deceased—this may involve 40 percent of the properties of three *feddans* or less. About half of all holders (*ha'izin*) have no official papers in their name, either having inherited

upper stratum of those owning fifty-plus *feddans* is the source of most of the redistribution.[4] According to Abdel-Fadil's 1961 figures, this would mean the transfer of properties of at least 450,000 *feddans* and perhaps 650,000 *feddans* in holdings. In any event the ten-to-fifty-*feddan* stratum could have been uninvolved in the redistribution. It may also be the case that wealthier peasants are leasing out a substantial portion of their lands. Finally there may be a good deal of double-counting because the same landholder may have plots in more than one district or even lying astride district lines. Harik contends that errors from this source are no more than 4 percent of the owners and acres involved, but officials in the Ministry of Agriculture believe that the percentage may be far higher.[5] In short, in the absence of a solid economic rationale or reliable statistics I am not prepared to write off the new upper rural class.

The Second Stratum

Sequestration merely takes power away from those who own fifty acres and gives it to those with over twenty-five acres. This will not change village life very much.

[A village doctor as cited in Mayfield 1971, p. 64.]

Noting the apparent continuity of this class over time is a far cry from proving that status within it has been inherited. Leonard Binder, however, has set out to prove just that, and his effort must be cited for its ingenuity and rigor.

It would be both tedious and nearly impossible in a limited space to trace out all the steps in Binder's elaborate argument. Suffice it to say that he has identified a group that he refers to as the "second stratum" and has attempted to measure its influence on and relations with the regimes of Nasser and Sadat.

---

the land or bought it through "customary" (*'urfia*) contracts (*AI*, no. 445, March 1, 1974). Some years ago Charles Issawi reported similar difficulties ". . . it should be remembered that the figures indicate not the number of owners but the number of land tax returns; thus an individual who owns land in different localities will be registered several times over and, conversely, several people owning one plot of land (acquired, for instance, by inheritance) will be registered in a single return" [Issawi 1954, pp. 124-25].

[4] In an earlier study, Harik gives partial support to this thesis. The Kura family in a Delta village that Harik studies began selling off land after 1961 in anticipation of a lowering of the ceiling and invested in livestock (Harik 1974, p. 203).

[5] I cite here one example which may or may not be representative. Sayyid Mar'ai (*AY*, November 13, 1976) listed his holdings as follows: in his name seventeen *feddans*, nineteen *qayrat*; in his wife's name, twenty-two *feddans*, nine *qayrat*; for each adult son, twenty-five *feddans* (adult sons no longer are legally part of the nuclear family) for a total of 114 *feddans*. Of the nuclear family's land, sixteen *qayrat* were in Markaz Banha; fourteen *feddans* in Markaz Ashmun; three *feddans* in Giza, and twenty-two *feddans* in 'Azizia, Sharqia Province.

I will not have much to say about his methodology of measurement, except that his estimate of the size of the second stratum at 700,000 to one million is a mystery. Binder comes up with this figure, he says (1978, p. 156), by multiplying the number of landowners in the twenty-to-fifty-*feddan* range by an average family size of five. Figures cited in Table 12.2 and elsewhere show the number of owners in that range to be no more than 25,000, which would yield a second stratum of about 125,000.

Be that as it may, the more interesting question is the weight of this stratum in Egyptian politics. Binder is not always consistent in his assessments although I concur with many of his summary statements (pp. 28-29). The thrust of these is that this stratum is "second" in the sense that it is the underpinning of the "first" stratum which is similar to the managerial bourgeoisie depicted in the previous chapter. "The second stratum does not rule but is the stratum without which the rulers cannot rule. The role of the second stratum is expressed neither in collective action nor consciously—certainly not 'class consciously' " (p. 26). He goes on to assert, "The predominant social characteristic of the Egyptian elite is its derivation from the rural bourgeoisie, rural notability, or well-to-do peasants" (p. 28). Binder in these remarks claims too little and too much. Too little in that I believe the second stratum has demonstrated the capacity for collective action (see below), and too much in that I believe the regime could rule without this stratum and that the elite is by no means drawn predominantly from its ranks.

Still, I think Binder's emphasis upon the subordinate and passive nature of the second stratum is well-placed. At times, however, he seems to contradict this proposition. The very title of his book is drawn from Marx in the "The Critique of Hegel's Philosophy of Law" in which he wrote ". . . a section of civil society emancipates itself and *attains universal domination*. . . . No class in society can play this part unless it can arouse, in itself and in the masses, a moment of enthusiasm in which it associates and mingles with society at large . . . *and is recognized as the general representative of this society*" (as cited by Binder 1978, p. 19; emphasis added). By implication the Egyptian second stratum in some measure fits this description, but that implication is certainly in error. The second stratum has never been dominant or recognized as the representative of society. Only the managerial bourgeoisie has, since 1952, been dominant, but it too has never been recognized or legitimized. Nonetheless in at least one instance Binder attributes considerable political leverage to one segment of his rural middle class, a term used interchangeably with second stratum, when he asserts that "the same socio-political element [of the RMC] has *structured* regime-level change processes both before and after the revolution" (p. 143; emphasis added). He goes on to say "In its concern to establish its legitimacy and to provide a functional equivalent of a political organization, the revolutionary regime did not attempt merely to exploit the traditional influence of the village notables. The Nasserist regime attempted, rather, to transfer the spirit of village Egypt to the seat of power in Cairo'' (p. 376).

I have cited Leonard Binder extensively because some aspects of his argument are at direct variance with my own hypotheses. Were the post-1952 regimes in fact so enmeshed in rural class interests that they could not rule without them? Was the Egyptian state at the service of these interests no matter how passively they may have been expressed?

To answer these questions I want to begin with some consideration of the social background of the Free Officers and to elaborate upon the very important and useful analytic category that Binder has called the "mixed family set." As noted earlier, several observers have depicted the Free Officers as the offspring of the kulaks or of poorer landed strata. Even Binder, stretching the evidence, refers to Nasser as "a son of the soil" (p. 303). What information we have reveals a much more heterogeneous set of social and economic origins.

By examining the members of local committees in Egypt's National Union, the country's only legal political organization in 1959, Binder was able to identify over 2,000 "family sets" out of 27,000 individuals; that is, people bearing the same family name indicating local prestige and influence. Over half of these sets were "mixed," in which members were engaged in both agrarian and nonagrarian professions. Binder hypothesizes that the RMC has fostered nonagricultural callings among its children who become urban and professional but who maintain important social, cultural, and economic links with the rural remnants of their families (p. 28).

A good example of what Binder has in mind has come from an unexpected source (al-Mayo, October 26, 1981). Among those arrested in connection with Sadat's assassination were two brothers, Tariq and 'Abbad al-Zumr, from the village of al-Nahaya near Cairo. One brother, 'Abbad, was a colonel in military intelligence. As it turned out, they came from an illustrious family that had dominated the village for generations. An ancestor, Admiral Tahar al-Zumr, had died in the Arabist cause a century earlier, and General Ahmad al-Zumr was killed in the October War. The family's property had been sequestered in 1966, but after 1971 various members reentered active political life. In 1981 Ahmad Hassan al-Zumr was village 'umda, and Aziz al-Zumr, after two terms as an MP, was appointed by Sadat to the Consultative Council (Maglis al-Shura).

Both Eliezer Be'eri and Ahmad Hamrush have demonstrated the relevance of the mixed family set in explaining the social backgrounds of the Free Officers. But they have shown as well that a significant proportion of them had little or no rural roots or interests. Hamrush sums up his reading of the situation thus (Hamrush 1974, 1:214):

The Free Officers were from the middle class varying between sons of petty or high-ranking bureaucrats or some rich peasants with small properties. . . . The sons of petty bureaucrats whose shoulders bore the heavy burdens of life and drove them deep into debt to pay the fees of their sons in the War College, which in general reached £E 80 per year at a time when the monthly salary of a university graduate did not exceed £E 12.

Hamrush in interviews with members of the Free Officers conspiracy came up with the following information on agrarian links (See Table 12.4; Hamrush 1977, vol. 4 *passim*). The first column lists those whom we may consider true sons of the soil although that should not preclude offspring of absentee landowners. Of those listed only Tawfiq 'Abdu Isma'il claimed himself to own much land (106 *feddans*) and to depend on it for his livelihood. Two of those listed are or have been in positions to aid rural interests: Fathallah Rifa'at has been for many years head of the Central Agricultural Credit Bank, and Zakaria Tawfiq 'Abd al-Fattah was for a time in charge of sequestered properties, and then minister of commerce at the beginning of *infitah*. Khalid Muhi al-Din and his cousin Zakaria, both members of the RCC, come from well-to-do farming families near Mansura. Both still own land, but Zakaria is, to my knowledge, the only former RCC member to be engaged predominately in commercial farming. Khalid, like Ahmad Hamrush himself, is a Marxist and whatever his property, not ideologically well-disposed toward the RMC. We should include in this group Hakim 'Amir, the son of a middle landowner and *'umdah* from Minia, and Anwar Sadat. I believe that Kamal al-Din Hussain, in the ''unclear'' column, also came from a landowning family near Banha. None of the Free Officers were from large landowning families, and nearly all have pursued careers that have kept them divorced from the rural world. 'Abd al-Magid Nu'man, for instance, lists his current occupation as sports editor for *Akhbar al-Yom*. Although not a member of the RCC, Husni Mubarak's background faithfully mirrors that of most older officers. His father was a court functionary in Shabin al-Kom (Menufia) and resided in the nearby village of Masilha, where Husni was born. The family lived there until 1952, when the father was transferred to Cairo, but Husni had already become an urbanite upon entering the War College four years earlier.

It is the second column that shows the reality of mixed family sets. The fathers of these respondents were already ensconced in nonagricultural pursuits such as trade, banking, engineering, law, civil service, officers corps, etc. Landowning was a sideline, and the sons have seemingly continued to move away from agriculture. Finally, in the third column, we encounter officers for whom the break with the rural world is at least a generation old if it ever

Table 12.4

The Rural Links of the Free Officers

N = 49

Sons of Landowners	Sons of Professionals Owning Some Land	Sons of Professionals/ Businessmen w/o Land	Unclear
Ahmad Lutfi Wakid	Ahmad Anwar	Ibrahim Baghdadi	Hassan Ibrahim (RCC)
Tawfiq 'Abdu Isma'il	Ahmad Hamrush	Ibrahim al-Tahawi	Hassan 'Abd al-Magid
Husni al-Damanhuri	Ahmad Qadari	Ahmad Fu'ad	Zakaria Imam
Husni 'Abd al-Magid	Ahmad Kamil	Amal al-Marsafi	Sa'id Halim
Khalid Muhi al-Din (RCC)	Amin Huwaidi	Tharwat 'Ukasha	'Abd al-Hamid Sabur
'Abd al-Halim al-'Asr	Salah Nasr	Hussein 'Arfa	'Abd al-Muhsin Murtagi
'Abd al-Latif Baghdadi (RCC)	'Abd al-Ra'uf Nafi'a	Shawqi Hussain	Fu'ad Habashi
'Abd al-Magid Nu'man	Magdi Hassanain	'Abd al-Mun'aim al-Naggar	Kamal al-Din Hussain (RCC)
Fathallah Rifa'at	Muhsin 'Abd al-Khaliq	'Abd al-Mun'aim Amin	Muhammed Riad
Fu'ad Hillal	Muhammed Wagih	Fu'ad al-Mahdawi	Sidqi Sulaiman
Muhammed Ahmad Bultagi	Muhammed Naguib (RCC)	Kamal Rifa'at	
Zakaria Tawfiq 'Abd al-Fattah	Munir Muwafi	Mahmud al-Gizawi	
		Muhammed Abu Nar	
		Yussef Sadiq (RCC)	

SOURCES: Hamrush 1977, vol. 4, *passim*. Be'eri (1970, p. 320), it is interesting to note, in analyzing the relatives of eighty-seven officers killed in the war with Israel in 1948, found that of 345 relatives, 30% were officials, 20% officers, 15% academics, but only 7% were village notables.

existed at all. Hrair Dekmejian undertook a similar exercise, examining the backgrounds of 131 top leaders in the 1960s, and came to the tentative conclusion that "the real socio-political significance of the military's rural middle class connection remains somewhat obscure" (Dekmejian 1971, p. 212).

Finally, Nazih Ayubi (1980, p. 362) compared the findings of Morroe Berger in 1953-54 with those of M. S. Qassem in 1966-67 concerning the social background of members of the bureaucratic elite in those years. Over those thirteen years the proportion of elite members whose fathers were predominantly involved in agriculture declined from 39 to 10 percent. The bulk of the elite, 31 percent in 1966-67, had fathers who were civil servants, 15 percent businessmen, 16 percent white collar, and 13 percent independent professionals. Seventy-six percent of the elite was born in cities, and 98 percent resided in cities for most of their lives.

On the strength of this evidence I think it is unwarranted to argue that the Egyptian elite is predominantly derived from the rural bourgeoisie and less so to attribute to those with rural interests or backgrounds a cultural or moral set of values that would lead them to defend the interests of the rural middle class. It is the case in general that members of the Egyptian elite own land and farm it as absentees. This stems as much as anything from atavism and nostalgia as from a desire for income. The holdings are generally small, visited on weekends or holidays, farmed by tenants, and treated as a hobby. While it is probably true that few elite members would advocate the collectivization of Egyptian agriculture, the simple fact of land ownership tells us little about elite attitudes toward rural propertied strata.

In fact the record of the Nasserist era is ambiguous on this score. Official attitudes toward the RMC ranged from hostile to tolerant, but they were never supportive. Binder is closest to the mark when he portrays the RMC as a convenient but by no means indispensable ally of the regime, an instrument of political and social control in the countryside that was manipulable and subservient. Its economic interests were never directly serviced in any major way, but it was allowed to become the local overseer for much that the state undertook in rural areas. With the exception of the period 1966-1968, the regime turned a blind eye to its manipulation of official pricing arrangements, its violation of rent and wage laws and of landholding ceilings. It was allowed to control, directly or indirectly, much of the political infrastructure that Nasser introduced into the countryside. This was the extent of the collaboration between the regime and the RMC.

Let us look more closely at the question of influence. Ilya Harik has given us a fine case study of one village that confirms many of Binder's macro-suppositions. In the large village of "Shubra" in Buhaira governorate, Harik focuses on the varying fortunes of three families: the Samads, traditionally powerful but gravely weakened by the land reforms; the Kuras epitomizing the RMC, and 'Ali al-Shawi, a poor peasant who rose to some prominence locally through the efforts of the ASU in the middle Sixties to bring *fallahin* into active political life. It is the Kuras who will concern us.

The Kuras, witnessing the eclipse of the Samads after 1952, made their move to assert their primacy in the village in the late Fifties. In 1959 Muhammed Kura was elected as a M.P. from Buhaira to the National Assembly, and his brother Sayyid became mayor of Shubra. This is precisely the kind of family set that is crucial to Binder's argument. Moreover it is a mixed family set. Muhammed Kura was an executive in a government-owned cotton firm in Tanta, and Sayyid had taken a law degree at Alexandria University. Both inherited land but in amounts not affected by the 1952 ceiling. Sayyid elected to be a farmer rather than a lawyer, while for Muhammed "farm work provided him with after-hours and weekend pleasure . . ." (Harik 1974, p. 72).

The Kuras were challenged by peasants in the local agrarian reform cooperative, led by 'Ali al-Shawi, the son of a tenant farmer. In the first elections to ASU local committees (the so-called Committee of Twenty) in 1963, the Kuras edged out al-Shawi and his allies with eight seats to seven with the rest scattered among independents. This is symbolic of the precarious position of the RMC in those years, and when 'Ali Sabri took over the ASU in 1965 a campaign was launched to dislodge the kulaks from local power. The spearhead of this campaign was to be the newly created Socialist Youth Organization in alliance with smallholders and tenants. A new unit, largely appointed, called the Leadership Group, replaced the Committee of Twenty and was composed in such a way as to restrict the influence of the Kuras and their allies. Sayyid Kura was removed from the office of mayor in 1965.[6]

While I am anticipating a fuller discussion of the ASU and of this period in Chapter Thirteen, those moves directly affecting the second stratum have their place here. The middle Sixties, as we know, witnessed a shift of power within the regime toward those advocating intensification of socialist transformation and greater political mobilization of the "masses." On both counts they were frustrated by the RMC, seeing it as maintaining capitalist and exploitative relations of production in the countryside and as incorporating into its own power networks, and thereby paralyzing, local cells and committees of the ASU. Rather than as an instrument of control and rule, Sabri and his allies saw the RMC as an impediment and an enemy. In November 1965 some 2,500 members of the ASU were dismissed as "reactionary, deviationist, and negative," and in 1966 the Committees of Twenty were

[6] Much of the reorganization of the ASU was engineered by Buhaira's governor, Wagih Abaza (column 2, Table 12.4), scion of a prominent albeit sprawling family of the former large landowning class. He was an ally of 'Ali Sabri, himself of quasi-"aristocratic" background.

dissolved all over the country and Leadership Groups put in their place with appointed members reflecting Sabri's desiderata. "Temporarily," Sabri said in October 1966, "until we have a peasantry sufficiently enlightened to take up a leading role, we will have to depend on the cultured elite of the villages, such as the physician, the agricultural supervisor (*mushrif*), the school headmaster, and the veterinarian" (Mayfield 1971, pp. 133-34).

Important elements of the Nasserist regime, however superficial their socialism may have been, were not loath to ferret out the RMC, isolate it, and try to destroy it. This was no more dramatically revealed than in the constitution of the Committee for the Liquidation of Feudalism. A great deal of ink has been spilled regarding this committee, for it was linked to what later became known as the nefarious "centers of power" that Sadat undertook to root out (see Chapter Fourteen). At this point we will only consider it as a token of the regime's resolve to confront rural interests that many had regarded as essential to its survival.

The committee was formed as the result of the murder of an ASU activist, Salah Hussain, in the village of Kamshish in 1966. It was alleged that the major landowning family of the village, the Fiqqis, had had Hussain murdered because he was about to expose their violations of the landholding ceilings. Indeed, as early as October 1961, when Sayyid Mar'ai was in disgrace, the new minister of agrarian reform, 'Abd al-Muhsin Abu al-Nur (a Free Officer close to both 'Amir and Sabri), received complaints from Salah Hussain about the evildoings of the Fiqqis. On the strength of these complaints their lands were sequestered, but somehow, by 1966 they were still farming large units.

With Hussain's killing there were in place all the symbolic elements of a Manichaean confrontation between good and evil, the downtrodden led by an intellectual militant against the Simon Legrees of rural Egypt (cf. *inter alia* Hussein 1971, p. 234).[7] The regime may have wanted to demonstrate its revolutionary fervor at a moment when its ratings were sinking: balance of payments crisis, inflation, Muslim Brotherhood conspiracy, and a great mass outpouring for the funeral of the old, officially discredited leader of the Wafd, Mustapha Nahhas. Be that as it may, Sabri and Nasser decided to appoint a committee in May 1966 to investigate all cases of the violation of agrarian reform laws and to destroy feudal remnants in the countryside. Something of a witch hunt led by local ASU committees ensued.

The Committee to Liquidate Feudalism was presided over by Hakim 'Amir and had forty members. Some felt that the choice of 'Amir was an attempt to embarass him as a landowner himself and to erode his power base in the armed forces by investigating his own military clients, who, it was supposed,

[7] The tale is far more complicated obviously, involving, as in "Shubra," an upwardly mobile RMC family, the Muqallids, of which Salah Hussain was a member, versus the declining Fiqqis— see Binder 1978, pp. 341-46; and Chapter Fourteen.

had substantial illegal rural properties. It turned out, according to Sayyid Mar'ai who subsequently reviewed the minutes of the committee's meetings, that 'Amir did play a moderating role, as well as his *chef de cabinet* Shams Badran and also Kamal Rifa'at, one of the more politically radical of all the Free Officers. The extremists were 'Ali Sabri, Salah Nasr (head of intelligence), Hamdi 'Abid (minister of local government), 'Abd al-Muhsin Abu al-Nur, Sha'rawi Guma' (minister of interior), and Sami Sharaf (special advisor to the president). One point of confrontation came over Sabri's proposal to lower the land ceiling to twenty-five *feddans*. 'Amir objected, saying, "We must not go beyond the Charter [of 1962] and thereby shake the confidence of the people in the regime forever" (Mar'ai 1979, 2:502-4).

As a result of the investigations, measures were taken against several hundred feudalists and nearly 60,000 *feddans* were seized. So arbitrary were the procedures involved, however, that by March 1967 acts of seizure had been rescinded in at least sixty cases. After the June War of 1967, when Mar'ai was brought back to the cabinet, Nasser announced that there had been widespread abuse in the seizure of land and ordered restitution where justified. With 'Amir's suicide/death in the summer of 1967, the Committee to Liquidate Feudalism was disbanded. By the time of Nasser's death in September 1970, all but 3,117 *feddans* had been returned, and Sadat returned these shortly thereafter.

Let us return to the Kura brothers in Shubra. During the period 1966-1968 they had lain low in order to avoid investigation by the 'Amir Committee regarding some local scandal involving the activities of the Socialist Youth Organization and the Leadership Group. They received a new lease on political life in 1968 when elections were held within the ASU and to the National Assembly. These came in the wake of the June War, worker-student riots in February 1968, and Nasser's March 30 Declaration, admitting the failure of the ASU and promising real democracy. In some ways political barriers to the RMC were actually heightened prior to these elections. *'Umdahs* or village mayors were not allowed to stand for election to any ASU office, and not more than one person from a single extended family (parents, children, grandchildren, aunts, uncles, nephews, nieces) could be elected to an ASU "basic unit" (Harik 1974, p. 223).

In "Shubra," Muhammed Kura came out of hibernation, acting as a healer and unifier and espousing a strong socialist line. His rivals from the Youth Organization and agrarian reform peasants in the ASU had lost their momentum as a result of Nasser's March 30 Declaration implicitly criticizing the manner in which they and others throughout Egypt had obtained local influence. The upshot was that Shubra's newly elected Committee of Ten in July 1968 saw Muhammed Kura and three allies in control while 'Ali al-Shawi and an ally had only two seats.

1968 was a turning point in the fortunes of the RMC, but we must be very careful in interpreting it. Muhammed Kura may have sniffed a new era coming and was successful in exploiting the opportunity offered by a regime that had in most respects been a failure. Yet Muhammed Kura was probably in the minority. Binder has looked closely at the 1968 elections to measure continuity with persons active in the National Union in 1959. He concentrated in 1968 on delegates elected to the provincial and national congresses of the ASU. There were 1,006 of these, and 236 or 24 percent bore names that Binder was able to trace to the 1959 National Union register. He takes this as evidence of considerble continuity in the political influence of the RMC (Binder 1978, pp. 362-63). I take it as evidence of the opposite: i.e., that in ten years the regime had brought about the elimination, voluntary or otherwise, of over 70 percent of those politically active and influential in the countryside.

That elimination was temporary, not definitive. It would seem that many members of the second stratum, like Kura, lay low during the Sixties. Kura's distinction lay in his willingness to resurface before many of his peers. The Nasserist regime was in desperate quest of allies among its citizenry, and the question of the fate of the RMC had simply become embroiled in a game with fairly high stakes. Nasser had always used the ASU to counterbalance the "power center" of the armed forces where Hakim 'Amir reigned supreme. With the military debacle of June 1967 and 'Amir's death, one of the two poles in that confrontation was missing, leaving Sabri and the ASU in a menacing position. Nasser had to whittle that power center down to size and "democratic elections from top to bottom" within the ASU was how he set about it. Elements of the RMC may have been the unwitting and *unintended* beneficiaries. But once again, I think it is fair to say that measures benefiting certain class interests were not taken as a result of class pressures or lobbying or in light of common social origins and values.

Once the door was opened a crack to the RMC, it got its foot in it. The door was opened as part of a return to economic orthodoxy part and parcel of the phase of retrenchment and liberalization begun in 1967/68. It may seem paradoxical to argue that the imposition of a lower landholding ceiling exemplifies the new mood, but that is what I shall do.

Law 50 of 1969, limiting individual landownership to 50 *feddans* and that of a family to 100, came as the result of a resolution of the National Congress of the Arab Socialist Union. My reading of this act, based mainly on interviews, is that it was intended to be largely cosmetic. The amount of acreage involved was small, for what was at stake was a redefinition of individual ownership from 100 *feddans* maximum to 50, while permissible family ownership remained at 100 *feddans*. As we have already noted, the fact that the Ministry of Agriculture and Agrarian Reform has never published statistics regarding this reform is indicative of its marginal impact. Nor did Sayyid

Mar'ai, the person entrusted with implementation of this law, provide any estimates of the acreage affected. Instead he paid dutiful homage to Egypt's socialism (introduction to text of Law 50, supplement to *AI*, January 9, 1969: "The deliberations of the National Congress were characterized by a clear tendency toward the realization of socialism founded on justice; and aimed at socialist transformation based on sound, comprehensive planning, with the understanding that this socialist transformation represents the principal state in the battle against imperialism and the forces of tyranny."[8] Probably the regime wanted to demonstrate its revolutionary bona fide without threatening in any fundamental way allies that it needed in a time of troubles. Nasser, it is said, told the ASU National Congress with respect to the fifty *feddan* ceiling that there would be no further reductions. The process of redistribution of agricultural land had thereby come to an end.

The Second Stratum in Sadat's Egypt

And then the president [Sadat] and engineer [Ahmad] Osman laid out the plans for the various stages of the project, and he [the president] showed his pride and happiness. And I found him listening attentively to each detail of the engineering designs. Then the president said to me, "I want to do for the people of my village—those who are my people, my relatives, my townsmen—the best possible thing, the closest thing possible to the nature of the English countryside . . ."
[Engineer Mustapha Hassan, director of Arab Contractors Company in Tanta, reporting on the overhaul of Mit Abu al-Kom where Sadat was born (A, December 28, 1978).]

There is no question that since 1970 an active lobby in defense of the interests of the rural middle class has taken shape. In order to define these interests I propose to concentrate on two areas: tenancy and rents on the one hand, and returns to crops on the other.

The other major facet of agrarian reform in Egypt has consisted in laws regulating rents and the terms of tenancy. Prior to the revolution, land hunger had driven up rents astronomically with the result that between 1939 and

---

[8] It is doubtful that the phrase "socialist transformation" ever crossed Mar'ai's lips after 1973 and the advent of the open-door policy. In December of 1969 Nasser ordered that the southern sector of Tahrir Province be sold off to private cultivators inasmuch as the project had been pilfered by state employees, "from the *ghafir* [watchman] to the manager" (Ayubi 1980, p. 284).

1950 the proportion of tenanted land to cultivated surface rose from 17 percent to 60 percent (Radwan 1977, p. 7). The 1952 agrarian reform set maximum cash rents at seven times the basic land tax. The tax itself is a function of the assessed value of the land, and inasmuch as until 1976 no reassessment took place, rents remained fixed as the value of agricultural produce rose. For instance, average legal rents in 1975 were £E 25 per *feddan*, roughly what they had been in 1952. The rent freeze produced two phenomena: 1) a return by *rentiers* to direct cultivation because of higher returns, 2) illegally high rents with unwritten contracts due to continued land hunger.

Abdel-Fadil has rightly emphasized the difficulties in measuring tenancy in Egypt because "pure" tenancy is relatively rare. More common is mixed tenancy with small and medium-sized holders leasing out part of their land (Abdel-Fadil, 1975: 17). It is probably the case that nearly all owners of dwarf holdings lease out all their land ('Abd al-Fattah, 1975:45). In 1961 there were 593,930 owners of one feddan or less controlling 322,202 feddans. But, again according to Abdel-Fadil 1,214,000 feddans were let out in pure tenancy,[9] an equal amount in mixed tenancy, and about 600,000 feddans in seasonal tenancy. Thus, between 1950 and 1961 the tenanted area had fallen from 60% to 51% of the cultivated area (Abdel-Fadil 1975, p. 22). Fifteen years later, as is shown in Table 12.5, the tenanted area had been reduced

Table 12.5
Distribution of Rented Agricultural Land, 1975

	Cash Rent Land Area	Average Rents per *Feddan*
Delta	1,015,410	£E 23,5
Middle Egypt	500,509	£E 22.1
Upper Egypt	438,006	NA
Total	1,953,925	

	Sharecropping Land Area		Rented Land as Percentage of All Cultivated Land Area
Delta	310,755	Delta	38.2%
Middle Egypt	103,964	Middle Egypt	51.2
Upper Egypt	29,545	Upper Egypt	46.1
Total	444,264	Total	42.4
GRAND TOTAL RENTED 2,398,189			

SOURCE: ARE, Ministry of Agriculture, Statistical Division, unpublished figures. Cited in Waterbury 1978b, p. 14.

[9] It may be that the remaining 900,000 *feddans* are let out by urbanites with title to or shares in title to small holdings, and by a proportion of those in the one-to-two-*feddan* range.

further to 42 percent, but these figures presumably do not include seasonal tenancy. Despite the political opprobrium habitually attached to tenancy and absenteeism, both continued to flourish after twenty years of agrarian reform.

Security of tenure was the second principal facet of laws affecting tenancy. From 1952 on the regime tried to enforce legislation that gave tenants minimum three-year rent contracts, a period of time corresponding to the basic crop rotation. Special acts were passed throughout the 1950s as leases expired to grant automatic renewals. Moreover tenants were granted in 1956 a three-year period in which to retire cumulative unpaid rents. These had become substantial because many tenants believed that the 1952 law was but the first step toward the expropriation and redistribution of all agricultural land.

In 1960 the RMC briefly flexed its muscles. The government introduced yet another bill to the parliament to extend all tenants' contracts another three years, but the Agricultural Committee rejected the measure "under pressure from medium-size landowning groups" (G. Saab 1967, p. 145). A few years later, however, as the "socialist transformation" intensified, the government was able to implement Law 52 of 1966 that stipulated that all tenancy contracts would be considered permanent unless the tenant voluntarily failed to meet his obligations.

The way around these regulations was through unwritten contracts. Initially, as Gabriel Saab points out (1967, pp. 145-46), it was absentee owners of small plots who exacted illegally high rents, occasionally reaching in 1959 £E 50 per *feddan* when average legal rents were £E 21. Large landowners were more circumspect for they feared exposure and possible sequestration of their lands.

Within a decade abuse of tenancy laws became more widespread. On the basis of a survey of three villages near Beni Suef, carried out in 1971, 'Abd al-Basit 'Abd al-Ma'ati was prepared to argue that the fundamental class cleavage within the Egyptian countryside lay along the line dividing tenants from owners, however small the properties of the latter. In those three villages he found that 70 to 90 percent of the villagers were landless, and that most landowners owned less than five *feddans*. Of 141 landowners surveyed, 92 cultivated all their land, 45 cultivated part and leased part, while only 4, of which 3 were large landowners, leased out all their land. 'Abd al-Ma'ati also identified a group of middlemen who simply leased in land from larger landowners and then sublet it at higher rents to the landless. Such men had been a standard feature of the countryside before the revolution (Ramadan 1975, p. 36), and are common still today (Sa'dni 1975a; and Mahmud 'Abd al-Ra'uf 1974, pp. 32-38).

By examining the records of special Disputes Committees in the villages that were designed to handle disputed contracts, 'Abd al-Ma'ati found that the most frequent complaint was the imposition of unwritten contracts by the landlords, and the second most frequent complaint the nonpayment of rents by the tenants. Except for the middle 1960s, the committees tended to find in favor of the landlords. The author contended that tenants and owners had well-formed negative attitudes toward each other that represented class consciousness.[10] Harik's earlier study of ''Shubra,'' be it noted (1974, p. 171), concluded that landlords were not regarded as exploiters (although merchants were) and only 8 percent of 135 villagers sampled thought that socialism had anything to do with abolishing class differences and exploitation.

Once the short-lived fervor of the 'Ali Sabri period at the head of the ASU had died down and the final cosmetic land ceiling legislated in 1969, the second stratum grew more assertive. For example, 136,000 *feddans* in *waqf* land were sold off in 1971 by the ministry of *waqf*, presumably to the RMC (Mursi 1975c, p. 117). Its major objective, however, was to regain some leverage over tenants. While the phenomenon was by no means uniform, tenants were receiving increasingly higher returns for many crops (especially vegetables, *bersim*, rice, *ful*, etc.) while paying fixed cash rents and enjoying protection from eviction. Many landowners wanted to take advantage of the new market incentives (and as we shall see, many did), and the means to do so was through eviction of tenants and resort to hired labor and mechanization.

The RMC achieved a major victory toward this end in 1975. On June 23 of that year, after only six hours of debate,[11] the People's Assembly passed a law submitted to it by the agricultural committee that provided for the following measures:

1) Reassessing the value of land, which would have the effect of raising taxes, but more importantly of raising rents which would now be calculated on the basis of ten times rather than seven times the basic land tax. It seems to be the case that rents have in fact at least doubled.

2) With the consent of both parties rent contracts could be converted to sharecropping.

---

[10] Sayyid Mar'ai recounts that when his family was investigated by the Committee to Liquidate Feudalism, tenants on their land defended the Mar'ais. ''They all insisted upon the links that bound us together, and they all said that they did not deal with the Mar'ai family on the basis of tenants and landlords, but rather on the basis that the Mar'ai family was their fathers, and brothers and sons, and that they always considered us their refuge from distress and their source of aid in times of need'' (Mar'ai 1979, 2:508).

[11] In what little debate took place, rural interests followed an astute line of defense. They insisted that productivity in agriculture had gone up steadily since 1952 and that rents should follow. In fact productivity since the mid-1960s had stagnated, but leftists in parliament, in order to protect the socialist experiment, were loath to admit this and would not challenge the landowners' claims (Guma' Qassim, *al-Tali'a*, August 1975, p. 100).

3) Failure to meet any clause of the contract, including specification of the crops to be cultivated, could result in eviction and three-year contracts would not be binding.

4) The Dispute Committees were disbanded and all landlord-tenant disputes were henceforth to be handled by the regular court system. Here the backlog of cases of all sorts was enormous, sometimes the courts were distant from villages, and in any case an illiterate tenant would find himself at a distinct disadvantage in them (Dib 1975, pp. 78-83; and *A*, June 14, 1975).

Parallel to this victory was a ruling by the Conseil d'Etat permitting a family to lease in up to 100 *feddans* of agricultural land.

In a manner parallel to the nonagricultural private sector, the RMC was able to profit from the intervention of the state in the rural economy. Its ability hinged on its direct and indirect influence over the operations of the agricultural cooperatives and agricultural credit banks. The cooperative movement received a great boost through the reform of 1952.[12] Receipt of redistributed land bore with it the stipulation that the new owner would join an agrarian reform cooperative that would provide him with credit in the form of seed, fertilizers and pesticides, and purchase from him, at centrally determined prices, the crops he produced in conformity with rotations prescribed by the Ministry of Agriculture.

After 1961 the cooperative system was extended rapidly to the entire cultivated area, and virtually all Egypt's tenants and owners became members. Table 12.6 shows the timing of this expansion.

Table 12.6
The Expansion of the Cooperative System, 1952-1972

	1952	1962	1965	1970	1972
No. of Cooperatives	1,727	4,624	4,839	5,049	5,008
No. of members (thousands)	499	1,777	2,369	2,830	3,118
Capital (£E thousands)	661	2,178	2,653	7,415	7,915

SOURCE: Radwan 1977, p. 53. There are nearly as many coops as there are villages, but there are only 750 agricultural credit banks for all of Egypt, each bank serving a cluster of villages and coops.

While it represented a major stride in the state's effort to assert control over private farming, the burden of the new controls fell more upon the shoulders of smallholders and tenants than upon those of the RMC, thus widening the

---

[12] In Egypt's mixed economic system, there are, officially, three sectors: the public, the private, and the cooperative. While the latter includes fair price shops and artisans' coops, the center of gravity lies with agricultural cooperatives.

gap between them. For instance, when the agrarian reform coops were set up, each new peasant proprietor was given his land (generally two *feddans*) in three separate plots. In any one season he could cultivate three different crops, thereby protecting himself against unfavorable conditions or pricing arrangements affecting one. He could for instance grow wheat, clover, and beans in the winter; corn, cotton, and melons in the summer. He would have food for family consumption (corn, beans, wheat), fodder for animals and poultry (clover, corn, wheat, chaff) and crops for market (cotton, melons, clover, wheat). His plots of land would be laid out in such a way as to be contiguous with other plots under the same crops, thereby facilitating mechanical land preparation and the use of herbicides and pesticides.

The post-1961 expansion could not provide so rational a system. Smallholders, dwarf-holders, and tenants frequently found that all their land had to be under one crop, and when that was cotton, as it frequently was, the best they could hope for would be to precede it with as many clover cuttings as possible. Still the smallholder would be dependent on the terms of trade (price of inputs versus purchase price of crop) set by the state. These turned against the *fellahin* throughout the 1960s and until 1975. In that year, as rural wages soared, production costs for one *feddan* of cotton averaged £E 165 while the purchase price for the average output of one *feddan* stood at £E 125 (Sa'dni 1975b). Cuddihy (1980, p. 117) estimated the producer transfers to the state on major crops (rice, wheat, cotton, sugar, maize, meat), net of input subsidies, at £E 1.2 billion in 1974-75.

The only way around this "taxation" for smallholders was to violate prescribed rotations by late plantings of clover which could be freely marketed, by planting cucumbers between the cotton rows (cucumbers earned £E 300 per *feddan* in 1975) or by selling fertilizer allocations on the black market and accepting the resulting production loss in what became known as the "government's crops." Because of skyrocketing meat and poultry prices in the cities, fodder of any kind became one of the most valuable cash crops. Peasants resisted planting Mexipak wheat varieties because of their short stalks. The higher yields in grain, the price of which was set by the state, could not begin to match the value of the dried stalks of taller, lower-yielding varieties that were sold as fodder. Violations of rotations became rampant: 43,000 in 1973, 180,000 in 1974, and 269,000 in 1975. After 1975 the state began to move away from compulsory marketing and administered pricing, retaining its grip only on cotton, more than doubling its purchase price, and setting floor prices for other basic crops.

Larger landowners had more latitude to deal with the new system. First they took full advantage of the agricultural credit system. Between 1962 and 1967 short-term credit was interest-free, and medium term, for which substantial collateral was necessary, had subsidized rates. Most borrowers, whatever the size of their holdings (tenants could not borrow) were delinquent in paying their debts, but by 1967 owners of twenty-five *feddans* or more owed £E 60 million of £E 80 million in cumulative arrears. 'Abd al-Ma'ati found this pattern systematically reflected in the three villages he surveyed. In one, 525 coop members owed the agricultural credit bank £E 25,000 of which £E 16,000 was owed by forty owners of ten to fifty *feddans* ('Abd al-Ma'ati 1977, pp. 125-29). Medium and long-term loans, used to finance land improvement and acquisition of machinery, while a small proportion of total agricultural credit, was monopolized by the RMC.

In recent years, as shown in Table 12.7 (and in Radwan 1977, p. 63), there has been a marked tendency for short-term production loans to go predominately to smallholders. On the other hand, over the decade 1969 to 1978 public loans for livestock and machinery purchases rose from 2 percent of total agricultural credit to 25 percent (i.e., £E 1.5 million of £E 75 million in 1969-70 to £E 26 million of 132 million in 1978: Ahmad Hassan 1982). The result has been that the average debt per borrower and per *feddan* of the stratum owning more than ten *feddans* is much higher than for smallholders. Cheap, subsidized credit has not been monopolized by the well-to-do, but it has served to underwrite their existing economic advantage.

In many instances, so it is alleged, the RMC has controlled all local institutions, including the coop board, the credit bank, and the warehouse. This could be done directly[13] or indirectly through the placement of clients. It is significant in this respect that Law 51 of 1969 introduced the stipulation that all coop board members must be able to read and write and that they could own up to ten *feddans*, where previously there had been no literacy requirement and the ownership ceiling had been five *feddans* (*al-Tali'a*, October 1972, pp. 56-62). With this local leverage the RMC could manipulate existing controls to its advantage, setting up private credit schemes, renting out machinery, controlling the black market in inputs, and coopting poorly paid government functionaries (*inter alia*, see the case studies of Girgis 1974, pp. 251-320).

With much greater acreage at their disposal, members of the RMC were able to pursue more lucrative cultivation strategies, mixing freely marketed, high-return crops with government crops. Estimates vary widely as to the incomes they have been able to generate through crop production, and I can do no more than explore some of the more plausible hypotheses. In what follows I have made two assumptions: 1) that in the mid-1970s there were still very roughly 70,000 owners in the range of ten to fifty *feddans*, controlling about 1.2 million *feddans*; and 2) that as in 1961, the owners in the twenty-

[13] In the village of Abishna in Daqhilia governorate in 1966 the Sawaylim family held the positions of *'umdah*, assistant *'umdah*, secretary of the ASU Committee of Twenty, chairman of the Village Council, and director of the Coop Board (Mayfield 1971, p. 163).

Table 12.7

Agricultural Credits Provided by Banks of Development and Agricultural Credit to Individuals according to Holding Categories, 1978

Size Class	Borrowers		Credits provided		Area served feddans		Average share per borrower	Average share per feddan
	No. (thousands)	%	(£E millions)	%	(thousands)	%	(£E)	(£E)
<5 feddans	2,651.4	93.2	71.07	56.25	3,459.0	64.7	26.80	20.54
5<10 feddans	125.6	4.4	19.44	15.38	772.5	14.5	154.73	25.16
<10 feddans	69.3	2.4	35.84	28.37	1,114.6	20.8	517.54	32.16
Total	2,846.3	100.0	126.35	100.00	5,346.1	100.0	44.39	23.63

SOURCE: Collected and computed from the Bank of Development and Agricultural Credit, unpublished data. Reproduced from Ahmad Hassan 1982.

NOTES: The share of each holding's category in the total amount of agricultural loans provided to individuals, and hence the average loan per *feddan* and per borrower (holder) in each category was worked out on the following bases:

1) The average share per *feddan*, of the loans of field crops is equal in the three categories, since the conditions of providing them apply to all cultivators in the same degree.

2) The total amount of orchards and vegetable loans was allocated to the various categories in the same proportion as the allocation of areas of orchards and vegetables to them. The basis for this allocation was the fourth agricultural census of 1961. We have assumed that it represents their distribution in 1978, though we believe that change in these proportions occurred in favor of large and middle categories of cultivators.

3) The total amount of loans for livestock provided to individuals was divided equally among the areas across the three categories of holding after dropping the holders of less than three *feddans*; though we believe that the category of large holders in particular, would secure bigger shares than estimated on this basis.

4) Loans to purchase agricultural machinery were allocated to large owners only, since only they are able to provide the property—guarantee required, ten *feddans* at least—for these loans.

to-fifty-*feddan* range leased out acreage while those in the ten-to-twenty range leased in equivalent amounts for no net change.

All strata, as Mohaya Zaytoun has shown, have moved away from field crops (wheat, rice, cotton, sugar cane, corn) and into cash and freely marketed crops (broad beans, lentils, peanuts, sesame, soya, vegetables, fruits, potatoes). According to the results of a 1979 survey that one must treat with caution, landholders of ten or more *feddans* had 58 percent of their acreage under cash crops. Those holding between three and ten feddans about 50 percent, and holders of less than three feddans, 37 percent (Zaytoun 1982). As we shall see, returns to cash crops are frequently three to four times as high as those of field crops.

One of the most striking changes in Egyptian agriculture in the last two decades has been the expansion into vegetable and fruit production, itself a function of burgeoning urban and, to some extent for citrus, export markets. By Zaytoun's calculations, all cultivators have participated in this shift, especially with respect to vegetables in which smallholders can compete with large landowners. Fruit is another matter, for orchards require considerable capital investment and long lead-time before any returns are earned. Only melons and berries can be grown with the capital resources normally at the disposal of smallholders. Thus we find that the RMC, with about 22 percent of the cropped surface at its disposal, controls 30 percent of the vegetable acreage and 56 percent of the fruit acreage. But Zaytoun's figures also indicate a more intriguing phenomenon: cultivators in the three-to-ten-*feddan* range control 40 percent of vegetable acreage and 23 percent of fruit. In other words, 17 percent of landholders in the three-plus *feddan* category are responsible for 70 percent of all vegetable acreage and 80 percent of all fruit acreage. As appears to be the case with agricultural credit, those who have gained most in recent years from shifts to freely marketed crops are not so much the members of the RMC as we have defined it, but the group of 400,000 smallholders just below them (see Table 12.3).

Table 12.8
Fruit and Vegetable Acreage as a Proportion
of Total Cropped Acreage
(In thousands of *Feddans*)

	1961	1978
1. Vegetables	386	950
2. Fruits	141	330
3. Total Cropped Acreage	10,634	11,112
$\frac{1+2}{3}$	4.9%	11.5%

SOURCE: CAPMAS *Statistical Yearbooks*, 1962-1979.

In geographic terms, much of the action is concentrated in what a USAID report (1976a, p. 59) labeled as the Cairo Vegetable Zone. This consists in nearly 500,000 *feddans* of Egypt's best soils (classes I and II) in the southern Delta. In the mid-1970s it was already three-quarters equipped with tile field drains for improved yields. It also grew a great deal of full-term clover for use as animal feed in meat production for urban areas. One would like to know a great deal more about landownership and use in this zone, and the degree to which urban-based absentees draw revenues from it.

What might the gross income of a RMC family look like in the late 1970s? Using the estimated shares of the RMC in field crops, vegetables, fruits, and livestock, we come up with this picture:

Table 12.9
Share of the RMC in the Value of Gross Agricultural Income, ca. 1977

	Gross Value of Crop or Product (£E millions)	Share of RMC (%)	Gross Income of RMC (£E millions)
Field Crops	1,384	20	276.8
Vegetables	378	30	113.4
Fruit	133	56	74.5
Livestock	731	20	146.2
Total	2,626	23.3	610.9

SOURCE: Reconstructed from Zaytoun 1982.

If we assume that about 70,000 families are involved in the RMC, then per family gross income would work out to £E 8,727 per annum or perhaps £E 1,750 per capita; about eight times the national average. These are impressive incomes, and in the aggregate result in 2.3 percent of the landholders controlling 23 percent of agricultural income. Following the same calculating procedure for smallholders below three *feddans*, we come up with an average per family income of £E 472 and a per capita average of £E 78.7.[14] The ratio between the richest and poorest individuals is 22:1.

My impression is that in terms of income, the RMC has held its own over the past fifteen years, but has not notably improved its position. Relative to the other strata, the real gainers are those tenants and owners in the three-to-ten-*feddan* strata. Still, the generation of real fortunes out of agriculture is too well-known to be pure myth, and it is certain that some substratum of the RMC is doing vastly better than the rest. Let us take a hypothetical example

[14] Poor rural families are on average larger than the better-off: 6.4 members versus 5.2 (see Harik 1979, p. 103).

of a rich capitalist farmer, using widely accepted gross return figures for specific crops.

Cultivated area	50 *feddans*	
cropped area	80 *feddans*	
orchards	20 *feddans* × £E 300 per *feddan* =	£E 6,000
vegetables	20 *feddans* × £E 500 per *feddan* =	10,000
clover	10 *feddans* × £E 250 per *feddan* =	2,500
watermelon	10 *feddans* × £E 200 per *feddan* =	2,000
potatoes	20 *feddans* × £E 700 per *feddan* =	14,000
livestock sales		500
machinery rentals		1,000
	Total income	£E 36,000

If that farmer is able to double the cultivated surface through a family ownership of 100 *feddans*, he could double family income. Groups of brothers can bring the operational units well above the 100-*feddan* ceiling (for example: N. Hopkins 1980, p. 5). Until 1978 all their income would have been untaxed; their land tax might have been £E 150-300.

These owners are what have become known as "fat fallahin" (*RY*, no. 2503, May 31, 1976). They are well represented in parliament and have some allies in the elite. They have begun to diversify their interests. They and the RMC in general own most of the 20,500 privately owned tractors, and most of the 27,000 mechanical pump sets in the country. Coops, by contrast, own only 4,190 tractors, a large proportion of which are out of service at any one time. According to the Era 2000 report on mechanization (1979, pp. 111-21), 40 percent of cropped acreage is plowed by tractors each year and 70 percent of all farmers use custom-hire tractors for some plowing regardless of the size of their holdings. Nicholas Hopkins found in one village in Upper Egypt that ownership of tractors, mechanical threshers, and diesel pumps is dominated by a handful of wealthy villagers (N. Hopkins 1980). Zaytoun's 1979 survey produced similar results. To qualify for public credit for tractor purchase one must own at least 10 *feddans*, and such loans increased from £E 1.1 million in 1970 to £E 4.9 million in 1978.

A second line of diversification has been into poultry, and beef-fattening and finishing. The official figures from CAPMAS show that between 1967 and 1980 the average price of a kilo of meat increased at a rate of 36 percent per year, poultry at 33 percent per year, and eggs at 46 percent (*AI*, no. 608, September 8, 1980). A common practice is for wealthy farmers and urbanites to own shares in animals with smallholders or to pay fees to smallholders to raise animals for them. Harik (1979), N. Hopkins (1980), and Dewidar (1977) are agreed that a large proportion of Egypt's cattle and buffalo population is held in such partnerships. In addition, owners of five or more head of cattle are those solely entitled to insurance for their animals and to 150 kilograms of dry fodder per month at subsidized prices. Subsidized credit for the purchase of livestock going primarily to large landowners increased from £E 440,000 in 1970 to £E 21.5 million in 1978 (Ahmad Hassan 1982). Some owners are able to fatten and market up to 5,000 head per year, which, in 1976, earned them £E 200-250,000 in gross income (*RY*, no. 2503, May 31, 1976). Concomitantly, the state is encouraging large-scale poultry and egg production, in the name of food security, through easy credit, tax exemptions, and customs exemptions on imported chicks and equipment.

The returns on citrus, guava, mangoes, bananas, and other orchard crops, as well as on apiaries and flowers, have been very high, and have lured in owners with the requisite capital to start up. From the late 1950s on, taxes on the incomes from such crops were abolished in order to encourage production. In 1972, however, 'Aziz Sidqi proposed as part of his austerity budget that an £E 20 tax per *feddan* of orchards be levied. The members of the parliament's Agricultural Committee voted down the proposal, 98 to 2 (*A*, June 14, 1975). But as profits became ever larger and more visible, a new effort was made in 1977 to implement a tax on the profits from apiaries, orchards, truck farms, flowers, poultry, livestock, and the renting of agricultural machinery (*RY*, no. 2573, October 3, 1977), with the support of the Ministry of Finance. It was fiercely and successfully resisted by the Agriculture and Irrigation Committee, chaired by Ahmad Yunis, a man who was achieving unsought notoriety of another sort. Members of the Agricultural Committee made their stand in the name of Egypt's food security and protecting smallholders. In 1978, however, probably as a result of Sadat's need to demonstrate real concern for equity and distribution, parliament approved a tax on profits from orchards, poultry, livestock, and some other products on holdings of three *feddans* or more, but the revised version of the law, issued in 1981, dropped all reference to such a tax.

In general the tax burden on the agricultural population has been falling. Hamid Draz estimates that the average land tax fell from 4.4 percent of the average income of one *feddan* in 1952 to 2.3 percent in 1964 (Draz 1976), well before the abolition of all taxes on holdings under three *feddans*. After 1973 the Egyptian government received only £E 9 million in taxes from a sector whose contribution to GDP in 1974 was valued at £E 1.2 billion. Nonetheless Ahmad Yunis and his colleagues in parliament argued that all owners of five *feddans* or less be exempt from taxes and that the clause stipulating that owners of three *feddans* or less who earned more than £E 150 from nonagricultural sources would not qualify for the exemption, be waived (see *al-Tali'a*, October 1973, pp. 134-46). A few years later Yunis led the charge for the total abolition of the land tax. He made the not implausible claim at that time that £E 63 million in land tax arrears had actually been collected and simply pocketed by the tax inspectors (*Egyptian Gazette*, May 5, 1976).

Yunis unintentionally provoked the reorganization of the cooperative system to his personal, albeit temporary, detriment but to the benefit of the RMC. He was president of the National Federation of Agricultural Cooperatives, under the tutelage of the Ministry of Agriculture and Agrarian Reform, and responsible for overseeing the activities of the coops and their officers. He was and is a capitalist farmer, practicing what he called "heavy agriculture." He has never tried to hide his antipathy for socialism and state interference in agriculture. At a 1973 meeting of peasants in Qaliubia Province (*A*, November 23, 1973) he declared:

I have been in the People's Assembly, and along with many colleagues we tried to stand firm in the face of tyranny and the issuance of a new cooperative law. . . . Then came the March 30 Declaration, and it appeared that our effort had failed . . . because the centers of power controlled everything in Egypt. We opposed the issuance of a new cooperative law out of concern for the peasants, until Sayyid Mar'ai, beloved of the peasants, returned as minister of agriculture and issued a new law that we could accept.

He went on record in 1976 as opposing compulsory cotton deliveries and purchases, and recommended the reopening of the Alexandria cotton futures market. At the same time he backed a new cooperative law in parliament that would have merged the 700 agrarian reform coops with the rest, ended the tutelage of the Ministry of Agriculture, and put the whole system under the control of the Federation.

The then-minister of agriculture and irrigation, 'Abd al-'Azim Abu al-'Atta, perhaps in reaction to an unwarranted invasion of his ministerial turf, simply dissolved the Federation by decree in July 1976, leaving the entire cooperative movement in limbo. Yunis was charged with corruption and abuse of office. Specifically he was accused of padded expense accounts and unjustified foreign travel at Federation expense, taking cuts on contracts for migrant workers, manipulating bonuses to pay off clients, and running the Federation as a closed shop with elections by acclamation.

In the course of the investigation of Yunis it was revealed that he received the following salaries and honoraria (in addition to his income as a farmer):

Potato Growers Coop:	£E 1,600
Nat'l Fed. of Agricultural Coops:	3,130
Gen. Authority for Coops, Ministry of Agriculture:	700
Fruit and Vegetable Marketing Coop:	190
Arab Federation of Agricultural Coops:	ca. 1,200

Dar al-Ta'awan Printing House: 450
President, Parliamentary Agricultural Committee: 1,960
Total 9,230

In addition to Yunis there were fifteen other M.P.s on the Federation board, including Nasif Tahun who subsequently became minister of supply, Hafiz Badawi, once deputy speaker of parliament, and Mahdi Shuman, head of the Peasants Secretariate in the ASU. Another twenty M.P.s had been recipients of "bonuses" from the Federation (*AY*, July 24, 1976; *RY*, no. 2513, August 9, 1976). Despite all these allies among the M.P.s, the People's Assembly voted to suspend Yunis' legal immunity. His proposed bill for the autonomy of the Federation was withdrawn, and in October President Sadat issued a decree confirming the dissolution of the Federation, abolishing the General Authority for Agricultural Cooperatives, and replacing it with a deputy minister of agriculture to supervise the coops.

Yunis was unrepentent, and as parliamentary elections approached in 1976, he left the president's party and ran successfully as an independent. Once returned to parliament, his immunity was restored and the charges against him were never pursued.

Whether pretense or cause, Yunis' comportment had led to the emasculation of the cooperative system as it had existed since 1962. The most significant change was that cultivators would now deal directly with the 750 village agricultural credit banks rather than through the more than 4,000 elected coop boards. Indeed the cultivator no longer had to be a member of a cooperative to qualify for credit, and, concomitantly, the coops lost an important source of revenue that had come through a 5 percent commission charged on the handling of loans.

In the future the coop was to serve mainly as a local council to "promote agricultural production" in various unspecified ways, to identify local investment projects, and to market some crops. The real power had shifted to the village banks, themselves supervised by the National Agricultural Credit Bank. Its director, Fathallah Rifa'at, told me in October 1977 that the banks would be run on a strictly businesslike basis, with close attention paid to the credit-worthiness of the borrower, and with seizure of land used as collateral in the event of default on repayments. In addition to short-term production credit, the banks would encourage local savings through time deposits at 6½ percent interest, and would make loans to local investment projects at 10 percent interest. He noted to me that banks in Sharqia governorate had already loaned £E 1 million for cattle-raising and in Giza £E 500,000 for poultry projects. The banks could also take an equity position in local investments (and had done so with an Italian firm in a Law 43 project). Rifa'at summed

295

up by saying: "We are returning to our true mission as a commercial bank for the servicing of the agricultural sector."

Along with the restructuring of rural credit has come an effort to pump more funds into local development at the governorate and district levels. The Organization for Rehabilitation and Development of Rural Egyptian Villages (ORDEV) has provided capital for rural agribusiness and has received support from some international aid agencies such as USAID. What one may expect from all these developments is the reenforcement of the relative strengths of the RMC, as its members receive the financial support to specialize in or diversify their agricultural pursuits. They will probably continue to dominate production of those cash crops, poultry, and livestock ventures with the highest returns, monopolize ownership and custom-hiring of agricultural machinery, and perhaps reestablish private credit systems for those judged bad risks by the village banks. With the quasi-scuttling of the cooperative system, there will be no public institutional means to challenge their dominance or to offer the rural poor an alternative to their services.

If the RMC is the winner in this process, it is somewhat more difficult to discern the losers. There is little dispute that both landlessness and rural poverty have increased in Egypt in the last decade. Estimates vary but it is probably the case that landless families as a proportion of total rural families declined between 1952 and 1965 from 30 percent to 28 percent, and then rose to 33 percent in the early 1970s (Abdel-Fadil 1975, p. 44; cf. Radwan 1977, p. 22). This may represent as many as 1.2 million families, an unknown portion of which are pure tenants, or employed outside of agriculture, or agricultural laborers, or migrants. Be that as it may, both Harik (1979, p. 93) and Radwan (1977, p. 42) following different methods of computation, argue that between 44 and 39 percent of all rural households live below a poverty line (£E 50 or less per capita annual expenditures) and 28 to 44 percent of all individuals. For Harik this amounts to over 9 million people.

Against this bleak picture, one should note the marked real increase in rural wage rates since 1973, well in excess of the rural rate of inflation. This phenomenon is due to several factors. First, labor demand is highly seasonal and "full employment" is achieved only during May-June and November. For the rest of the year supply is well in excess of demand. The seasonal shortages are the result of a growing proportion of school-age children actually in school and not available for field work; the trend toward small, family-operated holdings that restrict the supply of seasonal labor; conscription into the armed forces, and migration. Era 2000 (1979, XXIV.21/22), referring to unpublished estimates made by an MIT study, puts annual rural migration at 200,000, 135,000 of whom go abroad, while the rest go to Egyptian cities. This migration is the major safety valve for a situation that is otherwise deteriorating. Rising wages are a function of increasing family labor absorp-

tion on dwarf-holdings at the subsistence level, with inheritance and fragmentation continually pushing the marginal operators into the ranks of the
tenants. For those who can neither rent nor find full-time employment, migration is the only solution.

Policy Issues of Today and Tomorrow

For the RMC the central policy issue has always been the degree of state
intervention in agriculture, and the extent of socialization or collectivization
of cultivation. The RMC has welcomed state intervention when it has been
supportive of private initiative (cheap credit and inputs), but hostile when it
has been regulatory (prescribed crop rotations, administered purchase prices).
The cooperative system has been neutralized, and the administered pricing
system significantly eroded. There remain, however, two policy issues that
go to the heart of property arrangements and class interests: land reclamation
and mechanization.

Once the Nasserist regime made the decision to go ahead with the Aswan
High Dam, the means for transforming Egyptian agriculture appeared to be
in hand. What Nasser and his associates sought was to build a new society
in the desert that would then serve as a model for the conversion of the old
lands to modern collective agriculture. Tahrir Province was the first attempt
in this direction, and Magdi Hassanain has laid out his vision of it in great
detail (1975). There would be no owners; men and women would share all
labor; most operations would be mechanized; and every village would be
fully equipped with schools, clinics, and recreational facilities. The farmers
would wear standard, practical uniforms to the fields.

Tahrir Province was mismanaged and failed, and in 1965 Nasser publicly
criticized it as an example of muddled planning and confused thinking (*al-
Tali'a*, April 1965). Nonetheless the regime continued to attach great hopes
to reclaimed lands. Indeed, once funding for the High Dam was in hand, the
regime could think of little else in the agricultural sphere. Sayyid Mar'ai
recalls receiving a directive from Nasser in 1958 calling upon him as minister
of agriculture to double the area under reclamation in one year. (Mar'ai 1979,
2:436). Three years later Mar'ai argued that even with the High Dam waters,
40,000 *feddans* per year would be the maximum rate of expansion in reclaimed
areas. When Mar'ai was removed in 1961, 'Ali Sabri, Muhsin Abu al-Nur,
and others insisted that 200,000 *feddans* per year should be the target, and
in fact with Abu al-Nur at the head of the Ministry of Agriculture something
like that rate was approached.

Until the June War the model the regime wished to follow was clear. It
had been taken as given that about two million reclaimed *feddans* could be
added to Egypt's cultivated area. This new land would be organized into

large, mechanized, state-managed farms producing for both domestic and foreign markets. Cropping patterns and land use would be centrally determined. The question of ownership, however, nagged the regime throughout the 1960s. The National Charter was categoric in its commitment to expand and consolidate private ownership of land and referred to the High Dam as the symbol of this policy. Nonetheless Sabri, Abu al-Nur, and others warned against hasty distribution of reclaimed areas, citing the long lead-time needed to bring the acreage up to marginal levels of productivity and the risks involved in reducing the scale of operations. Hassanain Heikal backed these views in an editorial in *al-Ahram* (January 8, 1965) and then debated Sayyid Mar'ai, champion of the yeoman private proprietor, in the pages of the same newspaper in March (for Heikal's position, see 1965, pp. 185-202).[15]

During the first Five-Year Plan reclamation was begun on over 600,000 *feddans*. Mustapha Gabali, who was active in the reclamation effort in those years, summed it up to me in these words:

> Mushin Abu al-Nur, in his military way, took on reclamation like a military campaign, announcing new *feddans* like a body count; each year more and more casualties. In the first Five-Year Plan there was no agricultural strategy, just the dam and land reclamation.

The military in fact stood squarely behind the campaign. Abu al-Nur's former boss, Hakim 'Amir, supported him after 1961. "In order to service his extensive network of clients in the armed forces, Field Marshal 'Abd al-Hakim 'Amir required numerous civil service and public sector patronage jobs, and the area of land reclamation provided a real bonanza" (Springborg 1979). Sami Sharaf, 'Ali Sabri, and Kamal Hinnawi were also part of this constituency. With Sidqi Sulaiman heading the High Dam project, the military had control over all aspects of agricultural policy as well as large investment budgets.

In May of 1964, on the occasion of the completion of the coffer dam at Aswan, the USSR and Egypt signed an accord by which the Soviets would supervise reclamation of 300,000 *feddans* in Western Nubaria. As part of the accord the USSR gave Egypt a 10,000-*feddan* fully mechanized farm ('Izz al-Din Kamil 1976). The Soviets and probably many Egyptians hoped that this farm would be the model for the future. Simultaneously it was hoped that the new comprehensive cooperative system would begin to bring about the mechanization of agriculture in the old lands and the introduction of rational cropping practices on consolidated land holdings. Once again Egypt's military leaders, or at least one important group of them, espoused policies that could only be inimical to the long-run interests of the RMC. The reason

---

[15] Law 100 of 1964 limited privately owned reclamation sites to twenty *feddans*.

is simple enough: the power of these men did not lie in the land, even for those like 'Amir who owned land. Rather it lay in the state, and by backing increased state intervention in the economy, they were enhancing their own power and careers.

By 1969-70 reclamation had begun on over 900,000 *feddans*, but beginning is a long way from reaching marginal levels of productivity. No soil survey of the designated reclamation areas had been carried out before 1964, and it turned out that most of the soils were poor. Without enormous investments, they could not be expected to sustain intensive cultivation. Moreover the irrigation grids that were installed were not suited to the lighter soils of these areas, and no drainage systems were provided. Reclamation costs soared, but by 1970 only about one-third of the area under treatment was producing anything at all. Few people could actually live on these lands, and the bulk of these were salaried agricultural laborers (Waterbury 1978a, pp. 85-113 and 279-81).

On July 23, 1969 Nasser publicly acknowledged the failure of the land reclamation programs. He recommended that the new lands be oriented toward production for export, and that substantial parts of them be leased out or sold to individuals or placed at the disposal of state companies that would seek a solid financial return. (F. 'Abd al-Fattah 1975a, p. 98). These were recommendations put into practice by Sadat after 1971. 'Ali Sabri was in Moscow at the time they were made and allegedly criticized them to his Soviet hosts. When he returned to Egypt charges of smuggling were hastily brought against him, and he was dismissed from his post in the ASU (Springborg 1979; Nutting 1972, p. 447).

The Soviet mechanized farm was officially opened with great fanfare in 1970, but what then happened reflected the new mood. "The day after the opening, orders were issued by the Reclamation Authority to stop all work on uncompleted buildings, and the contractors were transferred to other zones. . . . The opening was the end of the road, not the beginning of work and production" ('Izz al-Din Kamil 1976, p. 92). Two years later, in March 1972, the then-minister of agriculture, Mustapha Gabali, announced a moratorium on the opening of all new reclamation sites, and ceased all state activities in South Tahrir, Wadi Natrun, and the New Valley, regarded as total losses because of salinity.

Land reclamation has been in limbo ever since. Because of population pressure and growing food imports, the state is more committed than ever to reclamation, hoping to add 2.8 million new *feddans* between 1980 and the turn of the century. At the same time the state is aware of its ineptitude in the past and wants to avoid the financial outlays that would be required to rehabilitate old reclamation sites (e.g., installation of appropriate irrigation grids and drainage systems) and to begin work on new ones. The way out, so far only in theory, has been to seek foreign agribusiness investors under Law 43 to take over the lands on long-term leases and run them as they see fit. Foreign investors, however, have been in no rush to seize this opportunity.

In the meantime the state has set up companies to manage existing sites. It is also encouraging graduates of agricultural faculties and institutes to take up farming in the reclaimed areas by granting them title to holdings on easy terms. Some land has been auctioned off to private interests, and Sadat's National Democratic Party recommended that other lands be sold off in plots in excess of fifty *feddans* if need be. It has also urged that no landowning ceiling be placed on private individuals who undertake reclamation (*AI*, no. 553, September 1, 1978; and *RY*, no. 2599, April 3, 1978). Nearly anything can be justified in terms of "food security," and increased production. With Ahmad Osman as special advisor to the president on food security, one can assume that the privatization and internationalization of the reclaimed lands would have proceeded apace. Sadat was not reluctant to phrase the policy issue in ideological terms (speech in Ismailia, early 1977):

> I say that people who practice collective agriculture will lose from it, and I want to know the meaning of socialism when it doesn't provide food and prosperity. . . . As I've said before, we built an idol called socialism and worshipped it. We have reclaimed land that is supposed to produce enough so that we don't have to import. But this land has lain idle because of those socialists [*butu' al-ishtirakia*—i.e. Sabri et al.]. Whenever we said to them we'll start companies to manage these lands, they said no . . .

Whether or not Law 43 joint ventures take over horizontal expansion from the Egyptian state, there remain pressing policy questions concerning the vertical expansion of the old lands. In the past decade or so the debate on these questions has been less explicitly ideological than that in respect to land reclamation. Nonetheless the implications are equally momentous for the rural bourgeoisie.

The advocates of sweeping change are by no means leftists but rather efficiency-minded technocrats. They have all grappled with a three-sided dilemma involving land fragmentation, animal traction, and mechanization. Mustapha Gabali's views are typical in this respect. He sees the Gordian knot of agricultural backwardness to lie in reliance upon animal traction and the allocation of three million *feddans* every winter to fodder crops. To cut the knot will require the substitution of machines for animals. This would allow food grains to be grown in place of fodder, and it would raise productivity. Ideally, for mechanization to have its maximum impact would require the strengthening of the cooperative system, and extending the model of the old agrarian reform cooperatives with their compulsory land-use schemes to the entire countryside. Scattered land parcels would be consolidated and brought into blocs of, say, 1,500 *feddans*, all under the same crop. This would facilitate all mechanical land preparation, tillage, planting, irrigating, and harvesting operations. Animal husbandry for milk, cheese, and meat would be taken over by the coops and carried out in local feed-lots (see M. Gabali, *A*, May 5, 1974).

Were Gabali's recommendations to be implemented they would represent a far-reaching assertion of state control over private agriculture with all basic production and allocation decisions taken out of the hands of the farmers. It also would strip the RMC of its control over the custom-hire of agricultural machines and their corner on animal-raising for market. Yet Gabali's views are widely shared. Ibrahim Shukri, stalwart of the old Socialist Party, former Minister of Agriculture, and head of the "loyal opposition" in parliament, lamented the effects of land fragmentation on irrigation. Most branch canals, he noted, service 1,000 *feddans*, but these *feddans* are usually a patchwork of different crops with different water requirements. He urged that each 1,000-*feddan* irrigation bloc be put under the same crop to maximize the efficient use of water. The then-minister of irrigation, 'Abd al-'Azim Abu al-'Atta, concurred in this judgment and stressed the waste of irrigation water that results from fragmentation (*RY*, July 24, 1978). The authors of the draft 1978-1982 plan sought the middle of the road in their recommendations (ARE, Ministry of Planning 1977, 4:83-84). They propose:

1) Land Consolidation in the form of shared or joint cultivation by which individuals and their implements come together for agricultural purposes and carry out agricultural operations jointly.
2) The sharing of costs and returns while safeguarding individual ownership. *For the family unit is the effective foundation of consolidated lands and the cohesive family order prevailing in rural areas is a positive and efficient support for this orientation.* [emphasis added]

Since 1952 there have been laws on the books to prevent subdivision through inheritance of plots of less than five *feddans*. Clearly, however, these laws have never been applied. The 1961 agricultural census revealed that the 1,642,160 holdings (*hiyazat*) were subdivided into 4,394,540 parcels. For holdings of two *feddans* or less (716,480 *feddans*) the number of parcels was 1,527,660 or an average of .47 *feddans* per parcel (Mayfield 1974, Table XI). There is no reason to believe that the situation has improved since 1961.

The extent of fragmentation and the scattering of plots under single ownership are major obstacles to mechanization in the Egyptian countryside. USAID and other Western aid-granting bodies would like to promote mechanization as well as the sale of Western machinery and technology. The Era 2000 study is an impressive brief for moving ahead with mechanization within the existing system. This would mean facilitating the sale of tractors, threshers, and pump sets to the RMC, which could then hire them out to the rest of the rural population. Although at one point they cite a survey that shows the resentment of smallholders who must lease machinery from the "fat fallahin" (ERA 2000 1979, VIII.15), they nonetheless conclude that this sense of exploitation is little more than standard peasant bellyaching (ERA 2000 1979, XXIV.35). While the study makes a good case for higher productivity through mechanization without major labor displacement, it nowhere tries to deal with the fragmentation issue. Tiny scattered plots are not susceptible to efficient tractor or pump set use, and that may be why 60 percent of Egypt's cultivated surface is still farmed with human and animal traction. Unless the state follows Gabali's interventionist path by regrouping fragmented holdings in prescribed blocs of uniform cultivation, further mechanization of Egyptian agriculture will amount to the rural rich hiring out their machines to the not-so-rich. Dwarf-holders, owners of scattered plots, and small-scale tenants will not share directly in whatever production benefits accrue (cf. Alan Richards 1982).

Conclusion

It is surprising that in a country in which agricultural statistics have been kept for seven millennia that we could be so adrift in understanding the changes in rural tenure of the last quarter century. A new agricultural census should go a long way toward explaining what has transpired since 1961. While awaiting those results, certain generalizations can be ventured, although not proven.

The first point to be made is that the military elite that took power after 1952 in part traced its roots to the RMC, but only in part. More important is the fact that those origins have had little observable impact on the kinds of policies adopted by the military elite, or its civilian allies, toward the agricultural sector.

If anything the Nasserist regime demonstrated considerable hostility toward the RMC, above all between 1961 and 1967, at the same time that it was clipping the wings of the Egyptian private sector in general. It mitigated its policies after 1967, not because the RMC had been able to assert its influence over a regime nominally sprung from its ranks, but rather because the desperate balance of payments situation and the June War had forced upon Nasser and his advisors a wrenching realignment of all domestic policies. The seeds were planted at that time that germinated into *infitah*; they fostered as well an atmosphere in which the RMC could, like the Kuras in "Shubra," come out of hiding. However beleaguered and however frail, the RMC, like the urban private sector, were reeds upon which Nasser could lean in a time of troubles.

We will never know if Nasser would have cast aside this stratagem at some future point when he felt sufficiently confident to resuscitate the socialist experiment.

A second point is that while the RMC could not claim paternity of the post-1952 regime, it has hardly been passive or unaware of its collective interests. It was on the defensive during most of the 1960s, although it was able to take disproportionate advantage of the subsidized credit system set up by the state after 1961. In the years after 1969, however, it began to lobby effectively for policies in its favor. It apparently reexerted control over the cooperative movement at both the local and national level; it was heavily represented in parliament, and it had the tacit support of leaders like President Sadat, Ahmad Osman, and Sayyid Mar'ai. It was not able to stave off the imposition of a tax on certain kinds of agricultural income, but it was able to have rents revised upwards, tenant's obligations tightened, and the disputes committees dissolved.

In addition it has come to occupy a dominant position in the ownership and leasing of agricultural machinery and has diversified its activities into the most lucrative crops as well as livestock and poultry. Pending legislation regarding land reclamation will give it incentives to set up commercial ventures in the new lands.

There is considerable money to be made in capitalist agriculture, and for this reason alone it is hard to accept Harik's suggestion that the RMC has frittered away its leverage after having maintained it for decades. It may be and probably is that only a small segment of the RMC is drawing maximum benefit from these conditions, but all the elements—cheap credit, adequate landholdings, liquid capital, the ability to sell to commercial markets—are in place for anyone owning more than five *feddans* to prosper. Indeed, the most dynamic stratum in the countryside is probably that lying between five and ten *feddans*.

Thus between Binder's occasional assertion that the RMC, in a moment of enthusiasm, embodied the Egyptian revolution, and Harik's that once it came under political fire it divested itself nearly out of existence, there lies a third way. There is a RMC, and it gives evidence of being conscious of its class interests. But it never embodied the Egyptian revolution and only on occasion did it serve as a referent or source of values for the Nasserist elite. More often it was merely tolerated and not infrequently harassed.

It has not (yet) tried to project itself upon the national scene. It has not attempted to prescribe or shape any kind of national strategy for development in which its rural interests would be maximally served. India's RMC has been far more assertive in this respect than Egypt's. Instead, Egypt's capitalist farmers have, since the death of Nasser, launched a limited offensive to promote their specifically rural goals. Sadat serviced this clientele because it

303

appeared useful to him in containing a potentially hostile and uncontrollable urban milieu, because its members shared his antipathy for the socialist experiment of the 1960s and its authors, and because the private initiative and productivity of the RMC corresponded nicely to the rural growth strategies urged upon Egypt by the international donor community.

There are nonetheless problems in Egyptian agriculture that can at best be swept under the rug, but not hidden from view eternally. While food deficits grow, so too does land fragmentation, the proliferation of dwarf-holdings, and the absolute growth in rural poverty and landlessness. Productivity and equity may be very much at odds in the present situation, with the trade-offs masked only by the flow of migrants to the cities and abroad. To make the benefits of agricultural modernization—principally in the form of mechanization and land reclamation—available to all would require policies that the RMC does not welcome. It is more likely that, for the foreseeable future, policies will favor the consolidation of RMC interests, regardless of the costs in rural equity.

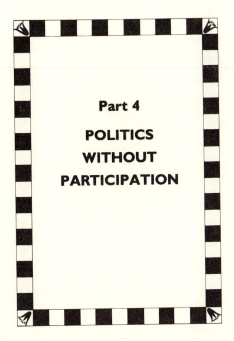

Part 4

POLITICS
WITHOUT
PARTICIPATION

Chapter Thirteen

THE ARAB SOCIALIST UNION: CORPORATISM AND CONTAINMENT

What Nasser does not like is the politics of politics. It clashes with the image of organization and is alien to a society that admits only the goodness and rationality of man. . . . [He] knows in functional terms why he needs a political party—he needs it to legitimate what is going on in the country by providing a more permanent vanguard than now exists in the persons of Nasser and his associates. But he cannot accept a political party in real behavioral terms.
[Heaphy 1966, p. 191.]

The weight given the economy and state apparatus in this book does not accurately reflect the priorities of the Egyptian elite itself. It was absorbed almost entirely in the hurly-burly of domestic and international politics, leaving to a handful of civilian and occasionally military technocrats the management of the economy. Both Nasser and Sadat and their respective entourages were immersed in a daily struggle to deal with real and perceived threats to their own survival. Nasser's style was to cope with conspiracy through counterconspiracy while Sadat preferred to lure his adversaries into the open, expose, and then isolate them. But for both, political life took on the cast of short-term maneuvering and manipulation, resting on no particular strategy and somewhat divorced from the currents of social and economic change the regime had released.

One is struck in reading the several sets of memoirs that members of the RCC began to publish in the 1970s, or the views of insiders like Ahmad Hamrush, by the adolescent egos and sheer pettiness of the men who laid claim to Egypt's revolution. To take Baghdadi, Kamal al-Din Hussain, Hassan Ibrahim, etc. at their word, we see RCC or cabinet meetings perpetually paralyzed by the theatrical exits of officers wounded by some obscure affront to their wisdom or integrity; interminable all-night mediation efforts to bring them back into the fold, the success of which might then provoke the walkout of the original offender once the offendee had been soothed. I cannot resist mentioning Magdi Hassanain, the literal strongman of the Free Officers, who, upon being slighted by Gamal Salim, shoved Salim's shoe into his mouth.

I have already noted that the military delegated the authority to manage the economy to civilians. The Ministries of Finance, Commerce, Supply, Planning, Agriculture, and Industry generally lay in civilian hands. So too the Ministries of Education, Health, and Justice. But even the civilian stalwarts of these domains, no doubt out of necessity, became tactical maneuverers with short-time horizons, rather than the far-sighted managers the regime may have wanted. As the years passed civilians like 'Aziz Sidqi, 'Abd al-Mun'aim Qaissuni, Sayyid Mar'ai, and Kamal Ramzi Stino came to resemble their masters in style and the setting of priorities. What they lacked, of course, were constituencies in the military, which made them at once less threatening and more vulnerable.

The above notwithstanding, there was, from 1953 on, a palpable need to give some sort of formal structuring to political life in Egypt, and this need ran like a thread through all the daily skirmishes, squabbles, and occasional crises that beset both Nasser and Sadat. From the outset there were two components to meeting this need. The first consisted simply in the filling of the vacuum brought about by the abolition of all political parties in 1953. The regime had to put something in their place, and whatever that was, it had to be their creature. Second, the need for structuring was dictated by the need to control and preempt. In this respect, at least, Nasser and a few others had a fairly clear vision of the social and economic tensions that lay just beneath the surface of legal political life. These tensions, rooted in Egypt's poverty and maldistribution of wealth, had to be contained until economic development could reduce them. Nasser, be it noted, never belittled the potential for class conflict in Egypt.

To the above one may add a need that was more than anything rhetorical: ideological mobilization of the masses for the tasks of development and in support of the regime. Vatikiotis is right in criticizing Western scholars for taking this rhetoric at face value (Bienen 1978, p. 55 makes similar criticisms of the analysis of African parties).

> For a long while foreign students of Egypt considered the Nasser regime a revolutionary "mobilizing" type of polity. This suited their peculiarly Western typology of regimes which tended to exaggerate differences between regimes by paying too much attention to the ideological tone of their leaders' pronouncements, but hardly any attention to their structural bases. [Vatikiotis 1978, p. 197]

Over time, the "party" in Egypt was judged successful if it occupied the political field and acted as a counterweight to the armed forces. Little more was asked of it.

Corporatist Politics

The growing literature on corporatism in developing countries helps clarify some of the dynamics at work in Egypt's approach to political organization. The term itself is frequently and accurately associated with fascism. It grows out of an image of the state as an organic unit with functioning, coordinated members directed harmoniously by a brain that is lodged in the leadership of the regime. The organic model emphasizes the fundamental harmony and compatibility of all the working parts (the *corps*), and their dependence upon the impulses from the brain.[1] It is the antithesis of a conflict model of politics except insofar as the classic theory of twentieth-century fascism emphasized the desirability of war with and coercive dominance over other states.

The designated enemies of fascism and derivatively of corporatism are class conflict and competitive liberal democracy. I hasten to add that in most developing countries where corporate forms are manifest, the tenor of the ideologies associated with them bear little resemblance to the totalitarian, racist programs of fascism and Nazism, nor do they share the will to dominate others. Nonetheless, as the case of Egypt will demonstrate, they stress, on the one hand, the inappropriateness and wastefulness of pluralist politics in poor, illiterate societies, and, on the other, the destructiveness of socialist systems that welcome class conflict.

Philippe Schmitter has given us a fine synthesis of the essential characteristics of twentieth-century corporatism (Schmitter 1974, pp. 93-94). As a program, it divides adult society into compulsory, noncompetitive, functionally differentiated categories or corps. These are recognized and licensed by the state and granted monopolistic rights in representing those that fall in the category. Because the corps are defined by function, they cut vertically across strata defined by income and wealth. Moreover because they are monopolistic and exclusive, the building of horizontal links between corps becomes structurally difficult if not illegal.

The corporatist model need not be honored in its totality for one to attribute corporatist tendencies to a given polity. Indeed, Schmitter calls our attention to the increasing resort to corporatist formulae in labor-management relations in advanced, industrial, liberal democratic societies. Nor, it should be emphasized, need the term itself or explicit reference to its ideological origin be evoked for one to discerrn these same tendencies. Nasser, for example, never employed the word corporatism and I have never encountered any rendering of it in Arabic. Nonetheless, Egypt's political formula adopted in 1961-62 was unequivocally corporatist in its intent.

The resort to corporatism lies in elite response to social crisis. Schmitter

---

[1] I have frequently heard Arabs compare society to the fingers of one's hand; parts of different size and strength working together smoothly to execute the mind's will.

has proposed that this involves for the most part the need to impose "social peace" (a phrase in the mainstream of Egyptian political jargon) following the collapse of pluralist politics in the face of mounting demands on scarce resources. ". . . The bourgeoisie is too weak, internally divided, externally dependent and/or short of resources to respond effectively and legitimately to these demands within the framework of the liberal democratic state" (Schmitter 1974, p. 108). This is the same sort of analysis that others have used to explain the phenomenon of state autonomy (see Chapter One), and Alfred Stepan, for one, sees corporatism as part and parcel of the broader process of restructuring relations between various sectors of society and the state (Stepan 1978, p. 47).

He refers in particular to the transition into and out of ISI as requiring different forms of corporatism. The "easy" phase of ISI is likely to be characterized by "inclusionary corporatism" in which all the corps are accommodated in the expanding welfare-state system. The Cárdenas period in Mexico is cited as an example of this phase. Under the military in Peru, the same phase lasted from 1969-1974 and saw the gradual incorporation of urban squatters and sugar plantation workers into SINAMOS, the only officially recognized body for political representation. As the economy enters into the "hard" phase of ISI, or of export-led growth, both generally accompanied by economic retrenchment, the state may be obliged to introduce "exclusionary" corporatism. This phase is characterized by the "demobilization" of some of the corps, especially urban labor, so that their earnings can be lagged behind the rate of inflation and some of their welfare benefits eroded. Elements of the military in league with technocrats and management within the MNC sector impose, rather than buy, social peace. Peru after 1974, Brazil in the late 1960s and early 1970s, and Turkey in 1980 would all be examples of this evolution.

The application of this sequence to Egypt, as we shall see, raises many difficulties, but they may be more apparent than real. Egypt has experienced a crisis in its development strategy. ISI has been called into question, retrenchment instituted between 1966 and 1970, and by 1973, an export-led strategy endorsed if not put into effect. Except for the period 1966-1970, a period of war and the occupation of Egyptian soil, no economically exclusivist policies have been imposed on the corps of Egyptian society. Economic inclusivism has been the order of the day at least since 1961 and Egypt's ability to tap external resources has allowed its leaders to avoid the hard social choices that streamlining the economy would entail. In Chapter Fifteen we shall see how Sadat sought to preserve the corporatist formula, summed up in the slogan "the alliance of working forces," while adding a modicum of electoral party politics on top.

Some students of corporatism have suggested that variations in its prevalence may have cultural roots. Analysts of Latin American politics have on occasion yielded to the temptation of attributing the strength of corporatism there to the cultural traditions of the Hispano-Catholic world (Stepan 1978; Wiarda 1974). Stepan, as noted in Chapter One, finds the historical origins of the purposeful, organic state in the concepts of Roman Law and the commentaries on secular power of the Catholic Church. With regard to corporatism he cites "the administrative law tradition of 'chartered' associational groups" and "patrimonial leadership patterns—both institutional characteristics that are congruent with modern corporatist patterns (Stepan 1978, p. 53).

On the strength of Clement Moore's analysis of Egypt as a "nonincorporated" society (Moore 1974), Stepan concludes that these political cultural traditions do not exist in the Arab world. I do not believe that cultural underpinnings should be given too much attention as causal elements in the emergence of modern corporatism. Rather I tend to look at this phenomenon as, in Stepan's own terms, "crisis response," and the twentieth-century crises to which corporatism provides a partial response do not have historical antecedents. This said, I think it bears noting that there are strong cultural patterns in the Middle East and in Islam that can provide a gloss for current practice. There is the traditional notion of the purposeful state emerging from the governance of the Muslim *umma*, there is the historical experience of the Ottoman *millet* system of self-administered, centrally recognized and authorized religious communities, and there is the continuing prevalence of what several observers have called patrimonial or neo-patrimonial rule (Akhavi 1975; Bill and Leiden 1979; Springborg 1979). In addition, craft, labor, and merchant guilds and associations were firmly rooted in Islamic society.

Yet it is in light of what they see as the lack of historical and cultural underpinnings that both Moore and Springborg explain the unincorporated nature of contemporary Egypt. What they have in mind is that Egypt is divided into corps on paper, but that these corps have no institutional *armature* or autonomous life. In large measure Moore and Springborg are right in their assessment of the reality of corporate organization in Egypt, but wrong in their explanation of it. Stepan puzzled over a similar situation in Peru— "Once organized by the state, these 'corporate groups' have been notable for their ineffectiveness in demanding corporate pay-offs and for their secular passivity even in the face of their own poor results."

The explanation lies, it seems to me, in the ambivalence toward political mobilization of *any* kind on the part of the leadership of Egypt, of Peru and of several other developing nations. They want the control that corporatism seems to embody without the risk that the corps take on any life of their own. Cardoso (1979, pp. 36-37) captured this ambivalence nicely. He posited that corporatism under the bureaucratic-authoritarian state differs fundamentally from German or Italian fascism because there is no mobilized party and hence no use of its extremist members to impose ideological conformity and to police the rank and file. The BA state does not seek to

> promote a doctrine of organic harmony among social groups, or to establish corporative links among them that could form a base for *political* domination. Rather, the links between civil society and the bureaucratic-authoritarian regime are achieved through the co-optation of individuals and private interests into the system. Under these circumstances, stable pressure groups are unlikely to materialize, and a truly corporatist network of links between society and the state is unlikely to emerge [p. 37; emphasis in the original].

What Moore and Springborg describe as the reality of Egyptian politics conforms to this generalization. In this and the next chapter I shall flesh out the evolution of Egypt's corporate experiment and its interaction with the more fluid, unstructured maneuvering of elite clusters, interests groups, and "power centers."

The National Alliance of Working Forces

The slide toward corporatism in Egypt was, like that toward state capitalism, gradual and unplanned. A full-blown corporatist formula was not adumbrated until 1962 and then only after two experiments in preemptive political organization had failed.

These experiments took the form of two political fronts known as the Liberation Rally (1953-1958) and the National Union (1958-1961). The first was an unabashed improvisation on the part of the regime to replace the political parties it had outlawed. Its most notable success was in the partial co-optation of the labor movement. The support of the Cairo Transport Workers Union, for instance, was instrumental in enabling Nasser to prevail in his long confrontation with General Mohammed Naguib in 1954 and to seize all the levers of political control in Egypt. Other than that the Liberation Rally, with its slogan of "Unity, Liberty and Work," did little more than stage "popular" demonstrations in favor of the regime. During its existence Egypt elaborated and adopted a new constitution, and in 1956 the RCC was dissolved and Nasser was elected president.

The 1956 constitution provided for the replacement of the Liberation Rally by the National Union, in which all adult Egyptians were to be members. The Executive Committee of the National Union, consisting of three members of the now-dissolved RCC, screened some 2,500 candidates and approved 1,188 for the first election to parliament since the overthrow of the monarchy. It was this parliament, elected in July 1957, that challenged Kamal al-Din Hussain with respect to university admissions (Chapter Eleven). The union

312

with Syria that gave rise to the United Arab Republic in February 1958 also led to the dissolution of parliament and eventually to the appointment, in July 1960, of a new legislature of 600 members: 400 from Egypt and 200 from Syria. The 1956 constitution was suspended and a new provisional constitution drawn up. The final step in this chronology came with the breakup of the UAR in September 1961 leading, inevitably, to the dissolution of parliament, the abrogation of the 1958 constitution, and the overhaul of the National Union.

This period has been more than adequately studied by Lacouture, Vaucher, Abdelmalek, and Binder among others. I want merely to emphasize a few well-known points. The intent behind the National Union was far more serious than had been the case with the Liberation Rally. Once firmly established in power after 1956, with domestic and foreign adversaries either neutralized or at bay, Nasser sought to move beyond preemption to the structuring of political life in support of the regime. Article 192 of the 1957 Constitution stipulated that: "The citizens form a National Union in order to achieve the goals of the revolution and to coordinate their efforts toward the construction of a healthy nation from the political, social, and economic points of view." The creation of the NU was simultaneous with the emergence of a strong state sector in the economy and with comprehensive planning. This phase of the revolution was reflected in the National Union's slogan of "socialism, cooperativism, and democracy."

The regime had no clear political model in mind, but snippets of the approaches of Peron, Salazar, Tito, and Ataturk were loosely blended together to produce the NU.[2] The NU, it was emphatically proclaimed, was not a party, for parties implied partisanship, conflict, and divisions with the body politic. Rather it was an assemblage, a front, and a union to serve national purposes. Representation as a goal was an afterthought. Unlike its successor, the ASU, the NU did not move toward the organization of the citizenry along functional or occupational lines, but instead imposed a comprehensive pyramidal structure based on villages, quarters, district centers, provincial capitals, and, at the top, a National Congress and executive committee. These regional strata, especially in the countryside, tended to fall under the control of established local elites.

Because of the formation and dissolution of the UAR with the attendant reorganizations of Egypt's political institutions, the National Union never was given a chance to establish itself. Syria's withdrawal from the UAR after a rightist military coup aroused Nasser's fears of reaction within Egypt and pushed him further along the radical path he had chosen with the nationali-

---

[2] Nasser's legal advisor, Muhammed Fahmi Sayyid, a man of no little influence, was dispatched to both Portugal and Yugoslavia to report on their experiences.

zations of July 1961. Nasser feared that the NU, rather than serving as a bastion against the right (and to a lesser extent against the left) in Egypt, might instead serve as a platform for their interests and machinations against the regime. It was an easy and logical step to discard the experiment and start over again. In the fall of 1961 Nasser did just that. In most respects the efforts at political organization in the first eight years of the regime's incumbency were counterproductive in the sense that they set precedents for the ineffectiveness and irrelevance of the "popular organizations" in the policy process. As Tariq al-Bishri noted (1975, p. 35) neither the Liberation Rally nor the National Union debated or had any discernible influence over the regime's most significant decisions: nationalization of the Suez Canal, unity with Syria, and the Socialist Decrees.

Throughout late 1961 and the first half of 1962 meetings and congresses were convened and texts and programs debated that culminated in the creation of the Arab Socialist Union. The debates were not window dressing, and Nasser had to pull a reluctant and mistrustful society along his leftward course. He sought many things from the ASU, and because not all of them were compatible, it led to a kind of paralysis in both the organization itself and in Nasser's conduct. Seriatim, these goals were:

1) to combine universal adult membership with a vanguard elite;
2) to contain and "melt" class differences;
3) to mobilize the dispossessed in order to isolate "reactionary" enemies of the revolution;
4) to act as a counterweight to the armed forces;
5) to carry Egypt's socialist experiment to other Arab countries, especially at the expense of the Ba'ath Party.

Let us look more closely at each of these. The Liberation Rally and National Union failed in part because universal, compulsory membership meant that no citizen could take any particular pride or derive kudos from identification with the organizations. The ASU, while maintaining the principle of universality, instituted different grades of membership, eventually moving toward the formation of a "vanguard." Moreover, membership was made voluntary. Prospective members had to apply to the ASU and pay annual dues. At the time of parliamentary elections in 1964, for example, there were over four million active members in the ASU but over six million eligible voters. Still, as Gamal al-'Utaifi noted (1969, pp. 12-13) the voluntary nature of membership was something of a fiction. One had to be a member of the ASU to be eligible for appointment or election to any cooperative board, local, regional, or national assembly, or board of any union or professional association. In some instances the right to exercise a profession (viz. journalists) was dependent upon ASU membership, and in others membership in a union automatically entailed "attributed" (*muntasib*) as opposed to "active" (*'amil*) membership in the ASU. Thus while peasants or people in the urban informal sector could pass up the opportunity of membership without grave consequence, the most politically aware and active elements in Egyptian society could ill-afford to be onlookers.

Nasser's offensive against the bourgeoisie in 1961, coming after his jailing of most of Egypt's active communists in 1959, was indicative of his awareness of the class differences upon which the forces of the left and right could feed. This led him to adopt a corporatist formula that had two basic aspects. First was the assertion that the ASU represented the "national alliance of working forces" consisting of workers, peasants, intellectuals, national capitalists, and soldiers. Second, these broad functional categories were to be organized by residence and by places of work. Thousands of basic units were to be established in factories and offices as well as in villages and urban quarters. All people in those places of work, regardless of level of income or the nature of their work, would participate in the basic unit. While the five parts of the alliance were far more a rhetorical device than an organizational reality, they served to focus attention on social categories that cut vertically across strata of income and privilege. A hotel-owner and a streetcorner soup retailer were equally national capitalists; the owner of a half *feddan*, a landless tenant, a ten-*feddan* "kulak" were all peasants; an unemployed high school graduate and the dean of the Medical School were all intellectuals, and so forth. By collaborating within their working force and under the guidance of the Supreme Executive of the ASU the members of the alliance would produce the melting away of class differences (*tadhwib al-fawariq bain al-tabaqat*).

Some people were excluded from the alliance, and two working forces benefited from a positive action philosophy. A third, the military, never became an active force in the ASU. Those excluded were persons affected by the land reform laws, nationalization of shareholdings in 1960-61, and sequestration thereafter, as well as capitalist exploiters and "enemies of the revolution." Such individuals were excluded from all political activities, and in the meetings of the Preparatory Committee of December 1961, at least one participant urged that political isolation be extended to all the male collaterals of the principal accused. Guilt by association, however, was not retained except for members of the royal family ('Utaifi 1969, pp. 18-24).

By contrast, the new National Charter of July 1962 stipulated that 50 percent at least of all elected seats at whatever level of political, union, or cooperative activity be reserved for workers and peasants. This step represented the regime's determination to mobilize constituencies that had always been on the margins of political life and that could be expected to support the regime as it combated reaction and undertook the country's socialist transformation. But even this determination was halfhearted and vitiated by qualifications that played into the hands of established groups. For example, worker-management boards in public sector companies generally had nine members, only four of whom were elected. A company could honor the 50 percent rule with only two workers out of nine members on its board. Similar ratios held for agricultural cooperative boards. The fact that an M.P. received, by the 1970s, £E 100 per month tax-free meant that some hitherto deprived peasants upon election to parliament joined the ranks of the "fat fellahin."

At the same time that plans were being elaborated for the launching of the ASU, Nasser went through a confrontation with his close friend Field Marshal 'Abd al-Hakim 'Amir. He had been seconded to Syria as Nasser's "viceroy," or as some Syrians saw it, *gauleiter*, and when the union broke up, 'Amir was seen by many to have been responsible for that outcome. There was a move by Nasser and several members of the old RCC to isolate 'Amir by kicking him upstairs. The vehicle chosen was a Presidential Council, which would be empowered to review all military promotions from battalion commander upwards. Along with this Nasser appointed five vice-presidents, including 'Amir, and laid it down that any officer exercising civilian functions would have to resign his commission and leave the military. Nasser then tried to remove 'Amir from the position of commander-in-chief of the armed forces. Unlike Harry Truman's showdown with MacArthur, Nasser did not win. In May 1962, after having acquiesced to the proposed changes, 'Amir retracted. In particular he rejected the proposed Presidential Council and refused to give up his position of commander-in-chief. He left Cairo in a huff, and when it became clear to Nasser and his allies that 'Amir's officer clients in the armed forces would remain loyal to him, emissaries were sent to bring him back. The Presidential Council never saw the light of day; 'Amir retained his command, and from then on until his death in the summer of 1967, he made the armed forces his creature. Faced with this power center, Nasser had to build up the ASU as a civilian counter to the military.

The final mission that Nasser envisaged for the ASU was providing the organizational means for exporting Egypt's revolution. The dissolution of the UAR forced Nasser to reappraise his entire approach to the Arab world. He was convinced that Saudi Arabia, probably encouraged by the US, had engineered the rightist coup in Syria. From that point on Nasser insisted that Arab unity without shared socialist values and programs would be an illusion. The reactionary pro-Western regimes of the Arab world would have to be converted, and Nasser wanted to make sure that conversion redounded to Egypt's credit rather than to that of the Ba'athist radicals of Syria and Iraq. The Ba'athist goal was to establish regional commands of their party in all Arab countries, and Nasser wanted to counter them or beat them to the punch. While Nasserist groups did emerge in Lebanon, Jordan, Syria, and Iraq the ASU never itself took root in any other country.

It remains for us to examine the ASU from the point of view of its formal ideology and from that of its organization. Nasser and those who were at any point in time in his favor had a relatively free hand with the organization of the ASU, but the definition of ideological principles never ended. It may well have been the lack of consensus, or the imposition of a false consensus embodied in the National Charter, that led Nasser to state that the Charter would have to be revised within ten years. The culmination of that decade fell conveniently at a moment when Sadat was consolidating his own grip on the state and political apparatus.

Nearly all the skirmishing from 1961 on focused on the proper definition of socialism. Once the term itself had been made part of the regime's credo by Nasser, no one challenged the desirability of some sort of socialism. The debate over its proper components, however, became a kind of shadow play in which "right" and "left" sought to capture the revolution. A number of scholars have analyzed this debate (Binder 1966; Kerr 1962; L. Awad 1976), but none better than El Kosheri Mahfouz (1972). She and others have shown that Nasser went through two distinct phases: the "Chartist" phase up to 1964, during which he demonstrated his accustomed ambivalence in his commitment to socialism, and the "post-Chartist" in which his whole approach was markedly radicalized.

But for a few associates, like Kamal Rifa'at, Murad Ghalib, and Ahmad Fu'ad, Nasser was out ahead of his troops. Nonetheless in 1961 and 1962 he was not willing to impose his own interpretation of socialism, if indeed his ideas had yet crystallized. The Preparatory Committee, which was appointed in the fall of 1961 in order to draw up an agenda and programmatic terms of reference for what was to become the National Charter and the ASU, was packed with members of the governmental and public sector elite. Of its 265 members there were 7 vice-presidents or members of the RCC; 50 ministers, state secretaries, and undersecretaries; 24 provincial governors; 34 professors; 34 members of the dissolved parliament; 9 writers and journalists; 25 coop peasants; 28 union workers; 12 lawyers; 8 doctors; 6 agronomists; 5 engineers; 6 teachers; 2 pharmacists; 5 students, and 10 women. Cutting across these functional categories were 52 Free Officers. There was only one Muslim Brother, and there were no Marxists nor remnants of the *ancien régime*. The committee was thus a fairly accurate cross-section of Egypt's power structure (Kosheri Mahfouz 1972: 90; and Binder 1966, p. 239).

Nasser participated in the deliberations of the Preparatory Committee and was at pains to counter the proponents of "liberalism" led by Khalid Muhammed Khalid who protested the notion of political isolation. He did not contest those, like Muhammed Ghazali, who advocated Islamic socialism and the derivation of Egypt's socialism from principles laid down in the Quran and the Shari'a. At one point Nasser rebuked Gabr Gad 'Abd al-Rahman for his assertion that socialism required socialists and proposed the contrary—socialism without socialists (Kosheri Mahfouz 1972, p. 174). Many would say that that is exactly what Egypt got over the next six years.

The locus of the debate then shifted to the National Congress of Popular Forces in May 1962. Here the contending parties aligned themselves under banners whose colors could scarcely be distinguished to the untutored eye: "Arab Socialism" versus "the Arab Application of Socialism." Under the former were all those concerned with the drift toward secular socialism, the increasingly close relations with the Soviet Union, and the assaults on private property. They masked their unhappiness with the prevailing trends under the slogan Arab Socialism. They meant by this that Egypt's socialism must be derived from the Arab-Muslim heritage and faith. More specifically, while distributive justice is the goal, it should be pursued with full respect for the individual and legally obtained private property. It must reject any atheistic doctrines and great power entanglements as well as the dictatorship of all society by any particular stratum. Underlying this maneuvering were the far more strident protests of religious leaders like Sayyid Qutb who subsequently wrote (in *Ma'alim fi al-Tariq* 1964) of the "new *Jahilia*," or period of ignorance[3] and of the arrogation by man of God's sovereignty (Najjar 1968, p. 189).

At the time of these first debates, the proponents of the Arab application of socialism were very few and had to fight a rearguard action. While Nasser leaned toward them, he made no effort to tilt the balance of the debate in their favor. Moreover, the most able spokesmen of the scientific socialist position were nearly all in jail or exile. In confrontation over foreign policy in 1959, Nasser had dismantled Egypt's Marxist organizations and imprisoned their leaders. They were not to be released until 1964. This meant that second-rank officers, principally Kamal Rifa'at, along with some fellow travelers of considerably less ideological conviction like 'Ali Sabri, had to carry the cudgels of the more radical position.

The National Charter of July 1962 was a careful amalgam of both major positions, although its secularism is unmistakable. The Arab-Islamic sources of socialism are not mentioned, but then again neither is "scientific socialism." But the discomfiture of many members of the Congress of Popular Forces was sufficient that they lobbied for and were granted the election of a "Committee of 100," which issued a *Report on the Charter* that emphasized their interpretation of Arab socialism. It did not depart radically in tone or in substance from the Charter itself, but it did have a long section on "Religion and Society." It asserted that there is a distinct Arab socialism characterized by an unshakable belief in God and adherence to religious values. Under this

---

[3] The *jahilia* is the period of ignorance preceding the coming of the Prophet Muhammed.

socialism there will be no sacrifice of the present generation for its successor, and there will be a constant striving for the peaceful resolution of all social conflicts. This report was never widely circulated, until, significantly, it was reissued in 1973 when Sadat began to dismantle the ASU.

All of Nasser's moves at this time revealed his reluctance to push ahead too hard. He continued his practice of putting political organizations with nominally radical missions under the supervision of the most conservative of his associates. Thus the Liberation Rally was headed by Anwar Sadat and the National Union by Sadat and Kamal al-Din Hussain. The first secretary general of the ASU was Hussain Shafa'i. All three men were well-known for their religiosity and past links with the Muslim Brethren. Indeed Shafa'i, the last politically active member of the RCC, was relieved of his vice-presidency in 1975 partly because he had taken to delivering religious harangues each Friday in various of Cairo's mosques.

In January 1963 a Tripartite Commission was set up within the ASU to elaborate the new organization's ideology and program. Its three members were Hussain Shafa'i, 'Abd al-Qadir Hatim, and Kamal Rifa'at. They accurately reflected the basic tendencies within the ASU at that time with the clear predominance of the Arab socialist path. The organization at that point was to be neither ideologically radical nor programmatically adventurous.

Nasser's own pronouncements underscored his hesitations. In March-April 1963, almost two years after the collapse of the UAR, tripartite negotiations were begun in Cairo with a view toward unity among now-Ba'athist Syria and Iraq, and Egypt. In the course of those deliberations, Nasser argued for the inclusion in the charter of union of the following definition of the "enemies of the people" ('Issa 1974, pp. 20-21): "All who have worked or are working to impose the domination of a single class upon society." A non-Egyptian countered by proposing the addition of the word "exploiting" before "class," to which Nasser replied: "That could include the Communists, because their principle is the domination of society by the proletariat, that is, the dictatorship of the proletariat. It seems to me that this clause is aimed essentially at them."

But other forces were at work at the same time that began to propel Nasser toward a more radical stance and the ASU toward a more radical role. In no small measure the explanation must lie in Nasser's fear that the ASU, whatever its organizational innovations, would become yet another paper monolith, paralyzed at the summit and coopted into local power networks at the base. Nasser began to pursue the idea of establishing a vanguard organization within the ASU to lead it and to circumvent the bureaucracy (see interview with Eric Rouleau, *Le Monde*, June 5, 1963). Secondly, he was under considerable pressure from the USSR and various leftist friends of Egypt (Ahmad Ben Bella among others) to release Egypt's Marxists from detention. Some who were considered the least integrated into the formal Marxist parties and the least obeissant to Moscow had already been released in 1961: 'Abderrazaq Hassan, Muhammed Khafif, and Lutfi al-Kholi.

The Marxists that remained in detention for the most part welcomed the National Charter of 1962 although its various sections were hotly debated as to their socialist or revolutionary content. The possibility was broached of formally dissolving their own organizations and joining the ASU individually upon their release. The latter came about largely as a result of Nikita Khrushchev's impending visit to Egypt in May 1964 to inaugurate the completion of the first stage of the Aswan High Dam. By that time the first signs of the foreign exchange squeeze arising out of the first Five-Year Plan had become apparent, and the need for additional massive credits to move ahead with a second plan could not be ignored. Lobbying for this kind of support could not be easily reconciled with Egypt's continued repression of Marxists. Consequently they were released. A Soviet loan for $277 million was agreed upon at the end of May. Other indicators of the shift leftwards were 'Ali Sabri's appointment as prime minister and minister of planning in March 1964, and the increasingly hostile confrontation with the Johnson Administration over the Yemen, and then, in November 1964, over the Congo.

It was not until January 1965[4] that the last of the Marxist holdouts, the Egyptian Communist Party (of which Fu'ad Mursi and Isma'il Sabri 'Abdullah were prominent leaders) decided to autodestruct and adhere to the ASU. Several Marxists, in so doing, cited the Cuban experience where communists merged with the 26 of July movement and shifted it toward socialism. But Egypt's Marxists miscalculated. Hassanein Heikal (A, January 29, 1965) announced the ECP dissolution as an "unconditional capitulation" stemming from the fact that Egypt's communists realized that there was no place for them in Egypt or elsewhere in the Arab world.

Heikal's crowing notwithstanding, the stage was set for a distinct step to the left. Nasser had more than once threatened to give up the presidency and devote his time to organizing the ASU. This option was dropped when he was reelected president for another six years in March 1965. Nonetheless he took the first steps toward the organization of the Vanguard Organization with its stress upon scientific socialism. With the Marxists at his disposal, he had the professional cadres and ideologues to undertake the venture.

It is difficult to ascertain when exactly Nasser began to toy with the idea of the ASU vanguard, but there is considerable evidence, as Harik has argued (1973, p. 97), that it was on the drawing boards by mid-1964, and that Sami Sharaf, director of the president's cabinet, and Sha'rawi Guma', were in charge. Both were long-time functionaries in military and civilian intelligence. Nasser's moves at this time deeply worried conservative, first-rank members

---

[4] In the same month the leftist monthly, *al-Tali'a* (Vanguard) was started under the editorship of Lutfi al-Kholi.

of the old RCC, especially 'Abd al-Latif Baghdadi and Kamal al-Din Hussain. They protested the drift toward "communism" and criticized Nasser's proposal in the Presidential Council that all private wheat and rice mills and cotton ginneries be nationalized. On March 4, 1964, at the funeral of Muhammed Fahmi Sayyid, Nasser's legal advisor, Hussain and Baghdadi clashed with Nasser over his policies. Hussain noted that the Charter had a Marxist and an Islamic face and urged that the *Report on the Charter* of the Committee of 100 be made an integral part of the Charter, to keep the country from falling under communism.

Nasser countered by pointing out that the number of mosques in Egypt had doubled since 1952. He went on to say that he felt that the people should own the means of production, not just exercise authority (*saitara*) over them as stipulated in the Charter. The size of operations was irrelevant. A private entrepreneur owning three trucks and hiring three drivers while he sat in his office, was, in Nasser's eyes, an exploiter and should be nationalized. For Baghdadi this was a startlingly new departure in Nasser's thinking, and both he and Hussain dropped out of political life shortly thereafter (Baghdadi 1977, 2:229-30; and Gawhar 1975, p. 75).

In a series of meetings with the ASU General Secretariat between November 11, 1964 and May 15, 1965, Nasser laid out his new train of thought. He felt that the real problem of the ASU was its lack of a "political apparatus" (*al-gihaz al-siyassi*), one that would take years to build: (quotes from Rifa'at Sa'id 1975, pp. 39-75; cf. Binder 1978, pp. 336-40).

Sometimes I think we should create two socialist parties, each competing in general elections. But we know this idea is mistaken for we would simply divide socialist forces that have never really been united. In fact there are two parties now—the reactionary party and the socialist party. . . . After we do away with all traces of reaction and exploitation, then we may consider two socialist parties. . . .

The workers and the peasants are the real interests but are they socialist? My opinion is that socialism is made to work by a minority that leads. Everywhere we find that any appeal/propaganda (*d'awa*) is made by a minority that is able to struggle and lead. . . .

What is needed is not the definition of the ASU but rather the formation of a socialist party in each governorate. . . . And I say "party" to be absolutely clear. Thus the ASU brings together all the people while at the same time there are well-organized socialists: and I believe our next steps must move in that direction so that we do not waste our efforts.

As Gamal al-'Utaifi and others have often pointed out, the experience upon which Nasser was drawing was that of Yugoslavia's Socialist Alliance with its Communist League core. Nasser's leftward course, however, was not designed to put real power in the hands of Marxists. That notwithstanding, it is not warranted to see the main purpose of the vanguard as preventing the left from gaining political influence (Binder 1978, p. 337). The left was never so numerically strong or well-organized to elicit such a large-scale response. All in all, Nasser wanted the ASU to do everything: preempt all other political forces, contain the entire citizenry, and, through the vanguard, turn it into a mobilizational instrument with a cutting edge.

It is very important for the general argument in this book to underscore that Nasser's leftward course was more than tactical or opportunistic. He had come with evident conviction to a stance well to the left of many of his erstwhile associates (Baghdadi, Hussain, Ibrahim, 'Amir), and he was able to neutralize them and find enough people to support him so as to set the state apparatus as a whole on a new course. Note also that this course had been well-set *before* the downfall of Ben Bella (June 1965) and Sukarno (September 1965), and before his confrontation with the Muslim Brethren (August 1965). He was under no particular pressure, psychological or situational, to move as he did. As significantly, he maintained his militant political stance even as he knuckled under to the pressures from the IMF to retrench economically. It was as if politics and economics had gone their separate ways. If at this time Nasser pursued any tactical or opportunistic policies they were surely on the economic and not the political front. Economic orthodoxy was an expedient, not socialist intensification.

The dichotomy was nicely summed up in Sabri's replacement as prime minister by Zakaria Muhi al-Din, a nonideological organization man selected to reassure Egypt's creditors, and Sabri's transfer to the ASU as secretary general. For the first time since the revolution, Egypt's official political organization had at its head someone reputedly leftist. Sabri took his new tasks very seriously.

He moved on several fronts at once. The major objective was to isolate local elites that had been elected to the "basic units" that made up the base of the ASU pyramid. These were allowed to lapse into inactivity in December 1965. Sabri then moved to form, *by appointment*, "leadership groups" in all villages, city wards, factories and other places of work. Members were selected through consultations with provincial governors and the national secretariat. The leadership groups were supposed to group committed activists frequently drawn from the ranks of younger civil servants, teachers, extension agents, etc. Intermingling with them were civil servants seconded from their ministries, with full pay and the right to return, to staff the local secretariats (Harik 1973, pp. 80-105).

Sabri also breathed life into the Socialist Youth Organization and the Higher Institute of Socialist Studies, directed by the Marxist economist Ibrahim Sa'ad al-Din. The Youth Organization was to provide a framework for politically active Egyptians between the ages of sixteen and thirty-three (it eventually had over 200,000 members) and was probably seen by Sabri as yet another instrument to bypass and isolate vested interests. For its part the Institute of Socialist Studies was designed to train professional party cadres in organization and ideology. In sum, the Sabri initiatives, had they been carried forward, would have made the ASU a formidable organization with full-time career apparatchiki, militant auxiliary organizations, and handpicked activists at all levels to lend a sense of direction and purpose to an otherwise amorphous assemblage.[5]

But Sabri's ultimate goals were far more ambitious. He subsequently summarized them in an interview with Lutfi al-Kholi (*A*, April 26, 1967, cited in Kosheri Mahfouz 1972, p. 177):

1) to place the direction of the public sector and the administration under the ASU in order to evict the "reigning bureaucracy";
2) to place the labor unions and professional syndicates under ASU control, and promote revolutionary elements within them;
3) to form a Central Committee that will be the brain of the ASU and will supervise the government.

In this vein Sabri advanced the notion of functional corporatism to an astonishing degree.

Carrying out its activities on the basis of a sectoral division, such as industry, agriculture, transport, etc., this would imply the transformation of the General Secretariat which would renounce its present form based on the division into social categories: peasants, workers, national bourgeoisie, etc. The present form was dictated by the need to create an organizational framework; but in the future there will only be branches of activity. Thus, for example, the agricultural sector will group the agricultural engineer, the peasant, the agricultural laborer and the landowner, etc. Likewise, the industrial sector will include the engineer, the manager, and the worker . . .

Nasser may not have been displeased to see Sabri take such firm command, because he wanted some ideological ferment as well as the construction of a credible counterforce to the military. However, Sabri's ambitions could only be seen as overweening by many others. For now he proposed to move beyond the destruction of old elites and vested interests (exemplified in the Committee to Liquidate Feudalism discussed in Chapter Twelve) and to take on the state

[5] In December 1964, the Tripartite Commission on ideology in the ASU was converted into the Secretariat for Ideology and Propaganda under the exclusive control of the leftist Kamal Rifa'at. Through its sponsored publications it sought to inculcate socialist ideas in a far broader audience.

bourgeoisie in the public sector and the civil service. Undoubtedly technocrats like 'Aziz Sidqi took umbrage at Sabri's plan of attack. In Egypt and elsewhere when party leaders announce, as did Sabri, that "the direction of production is a preeminently political task," public sector czars race to the battlements.[6] Several years after Sabri's pronouncements it was found in a 1974 survey of public sector management that 19,000 of 27,000 respondents agreed that the interference of ASU committees in administrative and production activities caused many errors (CAPMAS 1974).

While we have little direct evidence of the maneuverings between the end of 1965 and June 1967, it appears that Nasser and perhaps Sabri himself tried to contain the new socialist élan almost as soon as it developed some thrust. It may be that too many toes had been stepped on. The revelation in the summer of 1965 of an alleged plot to overthrow the regime by the Muslim Brethren led to mass arrests and internments. In September 1966 the venerable leader of the plot, Sayyid Qutb, was executed, provoking widespread protest throughout the Arab world. The Committee for the Liquidation of Feudalism had been used rather indiscriminately at the local level to settle old scores. The new leadership groups and activists in the Youth Organization were not always warmly received at the local level. Finally the projected harnessing of public management, the civil service, the unions and professional syndicates to the ASU was viewed with alarm.

Nasser and Sabri continued to make radical pronouncements. In August 1966, Nasser addressed students at Alexandria University in these terms (cited in Najjar 1968, p. 188).

> Socialism in general means the eradication of man's exploitation by man. But the socialist application varies from one country to another. There are people who like to call it Arab socialism on the basis that this is a socialism with a particular trademark. It is my opinion that it is an Arab application of socialism and not an Arab socialism. I believe that there is only one type of socialism and that there are basic socialist principles.

At the same time 'Ali Sabri was elaborating his own strongly leftist ideas in a series of articles in *al-Gumhuria*. Yet in the midst of all this, widespread arrests of leftists took place in October 1966 and the expulsion of Marxists in the Institute of Socialist Studies and in the Socialist Youth Organization was pursued ('Issa 1974, p. 28). The defeat of June 1967 put an effective end to the radicalization process. Having accumulated too many adversaries too quickly, "it had to be abandoned, not as a result of failure but of success" (Harik 1973, p. 97).

---

[6] A similar kind of confrontation took place in Algeria in 1967 between minister of industry, Abdesslam Belaid, and radical leaders of the FLN. Belaid won.

The Constituent Parts of the National Alliance

The constitution of the "corps" that were to make up the Alliance of Working Forces reflects the same incompatible goals that led to the quasi-paralysis of the ASU itself. The goals were preemption, containment, and mobilization. Only the first two were mutually reenforcing.

The first observation to be made is that none of the corps had ever exhibited any corporate life before 1961. Their existence and identity were granted from above and seldom escaped their fictional origins. The regime simply and minimally wanted to make sure that no other clandestine or rival groups within Egypt would capture or mobilize some part of them. Nor did the regime want to see any autonomous, spontaneous development of identity in their ranks. With respect to peasants and workers in particular, the grandiloquence of the regime's commitment to 50 percent representation of workers and peasants in all elected bodies contrasts sharply with the fact that neither peasants nor workers had made any noticeable claims to such representation. In fact the last manifestation of any collective worker movement came in the first weeks after the RCC seized power in 1952 when troops fired on striking workers at Kafr al-Dawar. There had been no major sign of peasant involvement in Egypt's political life since 1952.

Breathing corporate life into these somewhat inchoate groups (the peasants more so than the workers) was an effort to tap alternative sources of power for the regime and to outflank middle-class interests. But the approach was managerial, halfhearted and easily deflected. The peasantry, for example, found representation through three channels: coop boards, village councils, and the Union of Permanent Agricultural Laborers. The first two frequently were dominated directly or indirectly by the same village power figures, except for the few years during which Sabri shook things up. From these local councils various "peasants" found their way to governorate assemblies or to the parliament in Cairo where their official allowances inevitably transformed the true sons of the soil among them into easily manipulated votes. As for the Union, the best it could hope to do was to assure its members the legal minimum wage and protect them sporadically against arbitrary hiring and firing.

Throughout the 1960s elaborate debates on the correct definition of a peasant, worker, or national capitalist took place. They tended to reflect the ebb and flow of radical versus centrist tendencies in the polity. Typical of the ASU as a whole was that no single authoritative definition of the constituent forces was available before June 1968. The 1962 Charter itself makes no such definitions but suggests that they would be elaborated during the preparation of the country's new constitution. It was understood during the meetings of the National Congress in May and June 1962 that the *Report on the Charter* would contain authoritative definitions, but while the Charter itself was unanimously approved, the accompanying *Report* was never publically circulated.

However, virtually by default, the definitions offered by the *Report* became the de facto standards. A peasant accordingly was someone who, along with his nuclear family, owned or rented no more than twenty-five *feddans*, was not a public employee, had not been affected by any land reform acts, who resided at his place of work, and for whom cultivation was the major source of livelihood. Still, when it came time to organize elections to coop boards, specific modifications were introduced. A 1963 ministerial decree stipulated that four-fifths of all elected coop members must own five *feddans* or less (F. 'Abd al-Fattah 1975a, p. 60). At that point one can see the signs of increasing radicalization. The next major modifications came in 1968, prior to general ASU elections, and in 1969 with the issuance of a new coop law. The new definition of a peasant became anyone who, with his nuclear family, owns or rents no more than ten *feddans*, who resides in the countryside, and for whom agriculture is their sole source of livelihood ('Utaifi 1969, p. 32). While this was a more restrictive definition than that of the *Report on the Charter*, it was less restrictive than the 1963 decree in determining membership on coop boards. Moreover, the new coop law required all board members to be literate. The new definition and representation formula revealed the ebbing of the radical tide after 1967.[7]

The same sort of process occurred with respect to the definition of a worker. The *Report on the Charter* declared a worker to be anyone who worked for a wage, and was a member of a labor union. This definition was considerably tightened in 1968. First, it was noted that the labor law brought within unions all those, whether salaried or working for a wage, that participated in a specific line of production or activity, and might put production engineers and janitors in one union basket. With this in mind Nasser narrowed the definition in 1968 to exclude all graduates of universities, higher institutes, or the military colleges as well as anyone who was a member of a professional union. The only exceptions would be for those who began their careers as workers and then acquired advanced degrees while retaining membership in their original labor union. Finally the 1968 redefinition excluded self-employed craftsmen.

Because public sector industry was at the heart of the regime's entire

---

[7] In 1971 'Abd al-Ma'ati (1977, pp. 128-29) found that in the three villages in Beni Suef that he surveyed, power in the coop boards and ASU committees was concentrated in the hands of the wealthier peasants. In one village, for instance, the average ownership of the members of the ASU Committee of Ten was twelve *feddans* while the average for the village was .4. In all villages size of holding varied positively with literacy. Sixty-six percent of the sampled villagers were illiterate. 'Abd al-Ma'ati contends that the fundamental cleavage in these villages is between the class of owners and the class of tenants. Both are contained, however, within the "corps" of peasants.

development strategy, it is no surprise that what Ayubi calls the "bureaucratization" of labor was most pronounced in the industrial sector (Ayubi 1980, p. 452). In 1964 twenty-eight labor unions were chartered, corresponding roughly to the same sectors as those headed by the General Organizations. All the unions, with some 1.5 million members by the mid-1960s, were grouped within the General Confederation of Trade Unions which in turn was closely supervised by the Ministry of Labor. There was little room for maneuver left to organized labor, squeezed as it was by the ministry and the ASU.

The above definitions relegated to the residual category of the "intellectuals" all others who were not cultivators, unionized labor, petty entrepreneurs, or members of the armed forces. On the one hand nonagricultural labor was contained through unions that had institutional reality only among public sector workers. Private sector labor was confined to small enterprises in which unionization was mainly a fiction. But even as far as public sector unions were concerned, the regime was able to parachute in loyal leadership or co-opt the incumbents. The limitations of that strategy were revealed in the worker-student riots of 1968 (see below), but the tenor of regime-union relations in the 1960s is best summed up in the injunction of the ASU General Secretary of Labor in 1965 that after twelve years of "workers' gains" (*makasib*), all demands should be frozen for two years (R. Sa'id 1975, p. 75).

While members of the armed forces were designated as one of the five corps no steps were ever taken to bring them within the fold of the ASU. In all likelihood Hakim 'Amir would have resisted any attempts to do so. The national bourgeoisie, those nonexploitative private entrepreneurs who had not been targets of acts of nationalization, sequestration, or other measures of political exclusion, were also represented among the corps in name only. Between the public industry bias of the Ministry of Industry, the mandatory pricing policies of the Ministry of Supply, and the political suspicions of Nasser, Sabri, and a few others, the national bourgeoisie asked little more than to be left alone. The more successful among them, such as the subcontractors in the construction sector, had other means than the ASU to make themselves felt.

That left the civil servants, managers, and professions. There was little logic to their being lumped together under the corps of intellectuals other than the fact that all were presumably educated to some degree. The major point of control over this corps came through the professional syndicates that were licensed to represent their interests. Thus through the co-optation or selection of the leaders of the syndicates for lawyers, engineers, doctors, journalists, accountants, etc. the regime was able to contain these groups whose potential political influence and technical expertise was considerable. Indeed several of them had a rather long tradition of professional organization in marked contrast to the workers and peasants (D. Reid 1974; Springborg 1978).[8] It is instructive to note that a partial background analysis of 100 of 700 Muslim Brethren charged with conspiracy in 1965, 60 percent were professionals, schoolteachers, low-level bureaucrats and science students (Davis 1982). These were in some ways the major beneficiaries of the revolution, and yet they exhibited total alienation from it. The ASU goal of containment was in this instance not attained.

Virtually without representation were the faceless ranks of clerks, typists, stenographers, students, unemployed women, and Egyptians in uniform that made up the bulk of the adult population. Announced membership figures for the ASU generally ran between four and five million. Again as many must have been totally uninvolved bystanders except when obliged by law to vote. Egypt's demobilizing corporatist system accepted the risk of leaving without any corporate representation those who otherwise have little potential for autonomous organization.

The Containment of the ASU

In the next chapter I shall look more closely at the internal politics of the ASU and its attempts at various times to strengthen its grip over its constituent parts. At present I want only to emphasize its denouement. Leaving aside the two years in which Sabri attempted to stimulate some dynamism in the organization, it cannot be said that the ASU represented much of an improvement over the National Union from the regime's point of view. It was used for too many purposes, but even those negative ones of containment and preemption began to break down under the pressure of the religious right which refused to be contained, and the students and workers who denied its right to speak in their name. Nasser throughout could not set his own course with assuredness. At one moment he elevated the attainment of the ASU's political cause to the status of his own personal mission and threatened to abandon the presidency to make it work. At other moments he treated the ASU like any

[8] To gain some idea of the numbers involved, I have recorded below the figures for various professions provided in the 1976 census:

Engineers	132,478
Doctors, dentists,	
veterinarians	83,245
Lawyers	29,054
Teachers	264,129
Accountants	71,063
'Ulema	25,164
Journalists	4,173

cf. Ayubi's figures on syndicate membership in 1967 (1980, p. 400).

other ministerial sinecure: when he and the conservative Baghdadi were at loggerheads in the early Sixties, Nasser tried to fob him off with the ASU; some years later, in June 1967, when Nasser sought to shunt the disgraced but unrepentent Hakim 'Amir into a vice presidency which 'Amir refused, the president said "If you don't want to be vice president, how about taking over the ASU?" ("Who Killed the Marshal?" *al-Hawadis*, no. 982, September 5, 1975.)

The June War probably had a far greater impact on the course of Egyptian politics than upon the course of its economy, which had already been set before the war. Once, however, the armed forces had been humiliated and Hakim 'Amir interred, there was no longer any pressing need to have a civilian counterweight to the military. To the contrary, with Sabri at its helm, the ASU by 1968 was the only significant political force in the Egyptian arena and by that token a legitimate cause for Nasser's suspicion. He had ample call to dampen its fires.

Yet Nasser's overriding concern was to hold his political system together as he supervised the rebuilding of the armed forces. A crucial issue in this vein was the question of the sentences to be meted out to the senior officers put on trial for their bungling of the June War. It was recognized, although never restated beyond his resignation speech of June 9, that Nasser had to share part of the blame for the debacle. 'Amir had gone on to pay the ultimate price, either through suicide or liquidation, for his inglorious role. Could Draconian sentences be imposed on senior officers who had been poorly led by their top commanders, especially as the rest of the officers corps that was to be the backbone of the new Egyptian armed forces looked on?

In February 1968 the High Military Court issued fairly lenient sentences for most of the officers on trial. The gentle treatment of air force officers, whose materiel had been destroyed on the ground, particularly incensed the general public. On February 21 worker riots protesting the verdicts broke out in the military factories at Helwan. They quickly spread to other cities and factories, and eventually brought thousands of university students into the streets. Violent clashes with the police occurred and at least two civilians were killed and over 600 workers and students arrested.

There are many interpretations of what triggered the initial response in the Helwan Aircraft Factory. Mahmud Giyyar, Nasser's aide-de-camp and faithful shadow for years, later recounted (*RY*, no. 2476, November 24, 1975) his version. He claimed Nasser's own *chef de cabinet*, Sami Sharaf and the minister of interior, Sha'arawi Guma', instigated the riots in an effort to discredit Nasser. There might be some grain of truth in this allegation, although it was made long after the fact and when both Guma' and Sharaf were in jail on other political charges. The prosecutor general of those years, Muhammed 'Abd al-Salam (1975, pp. 123-24) recalled that when Nasser demanded an explanation of the causes of the riots from Guma', he was told that they were expressions of loyalty to the government and to Nasser. So incensed at this lie was 'Assam Hassuna, the minister of justice, that he denounced Guma' for his false flattery and deceit. Another piece of evidence of the complicity of Guma' and Sharaf was that the head of the ASU Youth Organization, Ahmad Kamil, himself an intelligence officer and client of Sharaf, allowed a telegram from the YO to be sent to Nasser protesting the verdicts.

But if elements in Nasser's entourage closer to the leftist position of Sabri had a hand in the riots, hoping thereby to isolate Nasser in his post-June War weakness, the movement they touched off got well beyond their control. As the riots spread, the chants became directed at all aspects of the regime: the police, intelligence, the army, and the ASU. Hassanein Heikal, Nasser's brother al-Lithi, and many others were favorite targets.

Nasser was faced with the most severe internal challenge he had ever confronted. Following the riots he went to Helwan to address the workers. He promised that the air force officers would be resentenced and justice rendered.[9] While Nasser recognized the legitimacy of some of the demands and deplored the opportunistic maneuvering of some "power centers" (see Chapter Fourteen) in his own elite, he made clear where he thought the real threat lay (*Le Monde*, March 5, 1968).

> . . . counterrevolutionary elements exploited the demonstrations in order
> to shout slogans calling for the suppression of the ASU, the dissolution
> of the parliament, the liquidation of the Youth Organization, the estab-
> lishment of democracy and of freedom of speech. The suppression of
> the ASU means the liquidation of the Alliance of Working Forces . . .
> it also means the reestablishment of several parties and the installation
> of the dictatorship of one class over another. . . . We can grant no liberty
> to the enemies of the revolution.

Despite this warning Nasser subsequently went on to promise much greater democracy. This promise came in the March 30 Declaration which became one of the "basic documents" of the 1952 revolution. The heart of his message was that the ASU had been a "top-down" organization and hence ineffective in representing the people's will. He promised free elections within the ASU from the base to the summit with each organizational layer electing the next level above it up to the Central Committee, which would elect the hitherto appointed Supreme Executive Committee.

The March 30 Declaration was put to referendum on May 2 and over-

[9] They were Air Force Commander Sidqi Mahmud, Air Defense Commander Isma'il Labib, Chief-of-Staff of the Air Force Gamal 'Afifi, and Eastern Front Air Commander 'Abd al-Salam al-Daghidi.

whelmingly approved. Elections to ASU basic units were conducted at the end of June and the National Congress of the ASU convened on July 23. It has been commonly claimed by outsiders that these elections were for the most part unrigged (Binder 1978, p. 352; Harik 1974, p. 223), but several participants dispute such claims. Figures as disparate as Mahmud Giyyar and Ahmad Baha al-Din (*A*, August 30, 1974) concur that considerable rigging took place, especially at higher levels. Baha al-Din saw an effort to purge the ASU of its last remaining dynamic youthful cadres and independent voices (including himself). Giyyar notes that Nasser wanted 'Abd al-Latif Baghdadi to supervise the elections so as to rid the ASU of "the bureaucrats" (i.e., Guma', Sharaf, 'Abd al-Magid Farid, Labib Shuqair, and their clients) but that Baghdadi declined. Dr. Mahmud Fawzi, the aging, civilian dean of Egypt's diplomats, was left to supervise the elections. He was too scrupulous and too weak to engage in infighting with Sabri and his allies of convenience. According to Giyyar, they were able to control the elections and prevent the infusion of new blood. In all this what seems clear is that the ASU was not rejuvenated; it was not given a new, democratic face. Nasser probably wanted only to neutralize it, and Sabri wanted minimally to keep his hold on its organizational levers.

That Nasser's moves were unconvincing became apparent in November 1968 when new demonstrations broke out following a totally unimpeded Israeli helicopter raid on Nag' Hammadi in the heart of Upper Egypt. Demonstrations occurred up and down the Nile Valley by November 20 and were particularly violent in Mansura. There were calls for arming the people while 'Ali Sabri became the butt of satirical slogans (Hussein 1971, pp. 307-8).

Nasser's response was twofold. In the winter of 1969 he launched the so-called "war of attrition" against the Israeli forces ensconced on the east bank of the Suez Canal. This war must be seen *in part* as a ploy to deflect popular scrutiny from the domestic scene and to appeal to national unity. Simultaneously Nasser began to move in on 'Ali Sabri. As a former air force officer Sabri had been entrusted with many of the negotiations with Moscow for advanced weaponry. Sami Sharaf, who in this instance was anything but Sabri's ally, learned through his own intelligence source that Sabri had deplored Nasser's timidity in pursuing socialist policies to his friends in the Kremlin. Nasser suspected that Sabri might be trying to work a deal with the Kremlin to replace him, especially in that Soviet doctors knew all too well the frail state of Nasser's health. In July 1969 Nasser had Sabri apprehended at Cairo airport upon his return from Moscow and charged with smuggling. He was then dropped as first secretary of the ASU (Nutting 1972, pp. 447-48).

From then on and until Nasser's death in September 1970, the ASU was moribund. Sabri remained a member of the Supreme Executive and had other allies there, especially 'Abd al-Muhsin Abu al-Nur. Some efforts were made to organize a popular militia under ASU auspices. On the other hand the leftist cadres were gone, the Youth Organization in suspended animation, and the basic units had replaced the leadership groups at the local level. Through the War of Attrition Nasser had effectively stolen center stage from the students and workers and from the ASU.

After 1967 Egypt had neither an economic plan nor a political organization with any sense of mission. Perhaps Nasser felt that he was merely in tactical retreat, biding his time until he could deal politically or militarily with Israel before returning to five-year plans and socialist transformation. Then again he may have been as tired and dispirited as he looked, increasingly crippled by diabetes and the weight of defeat. Egypt's experiments in socialist economics had lasted no more than five years and in socialist vanguard politics no more than two. Nasser never had another opportunity to demonstrate his commitment to the experiments he had begun.

For two years Nasser laid aside his fears and hesitations and tried to make of the ASU an instrument that could promote his increasingly radical goals. He seemed genuinely to want to reach out to new, underprivileged constituencies to sustain the socialist transformation. At the same time he knew that if the ASU became such an instrument it could be turned against him. Thus between 1965 and 1967 the ASU began to break loose from the policies of demobilization and clientelism masked by superficial corporatism that Cardoso finds typical of bureaucratic-authoritarian states. After the 1967 war, however, the brief initiative was abandoned, and the pattern described by Cardoso reasserted itself. The corps that had never shown any evidence of collective action before 1961 remained fictions represented mainly in ASU organizational charts. Substantive interests expressed themselves in the ASU through the maneuverings and clashes of power cliques, coteries of cronies, clients, and professional syndicates. Otherwise there were the streets and backrooms where the unincorporated or the unincorporable could hatch their plots or voice their grievances.

Chapter Fourteen

INSTRUMENTS AND
PROCESSES OF CONTROL

> It was, therefore, necessary to liquidate the centers of
> power regardless of any other considerations. This was
> no easy task in view of the positions which these cen-
> ters occupied and within the framework of the delicate
> circumstances through which the homeland lived.
> [Gamal 'Abd al-Nasser,
> The March 30 (1968) Declaration.]

If Nasser was able to lay aside his preoccupations with control and preemption only occasionally, his aides, advisors, and clients were seldom able to think beyond questions of short-term personal and regime survival. Nasser's peers from amongst the RCC began to drop away from him in the late 1950s, and increasingly in the 1960s he came to rely upon second-level Free Officers, drawn primarily from military intelligence. The major exception to this trend was Hakim 'Amir who clung to his fiefdom in the armed forces and held sway over the biggest of what became known as the "power centers." It is widely assumed that Nasser would have liked to clip 'Amir's wings, if not get rid of him altogether, although Louis Awad suggests that in fact Nasser could trust 'Amir as the perfect "second man," one who would never aspire to be first (L. Awad 1976, p. 166).

The dominant actors of the 1960s were, then, men whose careers had been made in internal and external security and who operated more or less comfortably in that nether world. Their view of "politics" had been shaped by maneuvering in high-stake, inner-sanctum games where control of information and access to the president were the keys to success. Some tried to create public images by espousing radical causes with more or less sincerity, but it can be safely said that none ever developed a popular following.

The ASU Vanguard

It was to these men that, for the most part, Nasser entrusted the organization of the ASU Vanguard Party. That fact alone says much about Nasser's hesitancy to undertake a real mobilizational effort. That they were assisted ideologically by civilian Marxists is perhaps not as significant as the fact that the latter had just been released from six years in concentration camps where they had been incarcerated by some of the men they were now supposed to serve.

The principal organizers were 'Ali Sabri, Sha'arawi Guma', and Sami Sharaf. They were not the most comfortable of bedfellows. They set about recruiting or placing their own clients throughout the Vanguard and the ASU and developed parallel intelligence networks so as not to be out-maneuvered or to lose access to Nasser. We have already noted in the previous chapter how Sharaf sought in 1969 to do in Sabri; yet two years later they were both conspiring to do in Sadat.

They were not alone in this kind of activity. Membership in the Vanguard was nominally kept secret, which meant that only a few officials knew its full extent. It had its own in-house journal, *The Socialist Vanguard* (*al-Tali' a al-Ishtiraki*) circulated to members by I.D. numbers. However, it was known that all governors and nearly all ministers were automatically made members of it, in addition to which there were perhaps thirty Marxist ideologues. One of the few civilians that Nasser had regularly used in political and ministerial positions, Dr. Nur al-Din Tarraf,[1] remarked to me that advance word on the Vanguard was that it would group only the purest socialists and the purest Nasserites. Tarraf was not asked to join and consequently knew pretty much where he stood. The others, including people like 'Aziz Sidqi, Sayyid Mar'ai, and presumably Anwar Sadat, indulged in the placement of cronies and clients in the same manner as their more powerful colleagues.

Nowhere is the apoliticism of this maneuvering better captured than in the transcript of the investigation of Ahmad Kamil in 1971 when, as director of General Intelligence, he was placed under arrest for conspiring against Sadat (see Matar 1972a, 1:97-155). Kamil graduated from the War College in 1946 and by 1958 had reached the rank of colonel. In 1964 he was transferred from the General Staff to work in the office of the president. He was immediately delegated to work in the ASU where for three months he did nothing. He then worked directly for Sami Sharaf, and after six months he was told he was to work in the Vanguard. Having by his own admission never read anything about socialism, he was nonetheless put in the secretariat of the Vanguard headed by Sha'arawi Guma',[2] as well as on the ASU committee

---

[1] For example, he and Ahmad Sharabassy were the only two civilian members of the Presidential Council that Nasser formed after the breakup of the UAR in order to neutralize Hakim 'Amir.

[2] In 1971 the Vanguard secretariat had as its members Sha'arawi Guma', Ahmad Kamil, Sa'ad Zayid, Hilmi Sa'id, Muhammed Fa'iq, Sami Sharaf, Ahmad Shuhaib, Yussef Ghazuli, Muhammed 'Aruq, and Mahmud al-'Alim.

of Masr Al-Gadida in Cairo which was headed by Sami Sharaf. In October 1965 he was appointed governor of Assiut, and then, after the June War, 'Abd al-Mushin Abu al-Nur made him deputy secretary of the ASU. Abu al-Nur had been one of his teachers in the War College. Abu al-Nur then made him secretary of the Youth Organization with the rank of minister. After Nasser dissolved the ASU Secretariat in the wake of the 1968 riots, Kamil returned to work with Sami Sharaf, eventually becoming governor of al-Minia then of Alexandria. Finally, after the death of Nasser, Sadat placed him at the head of General Intelligence.

Throughout his interrogation Kamil revealed no political sentiment other than a fine sense of patrons ascending and descending. His wagon was hitched firmly from 1964 on to Sami Sharaf's star, and he did no more, so he claims, than follow his patron's orders. Even as governor he reported privately to Sharaf. Organizing Socialist Youth or tapping phones on Sharaf's orders were routine activities that in Kamil's laconic rendering apparently had no qualitative difference between them.

Kamil referred often to "Sami's [Sharaf] group" in the Vanguard. Who were they?

Sami Sharaf—Nasser's *chef de cabinet*; Free Officer, Intelligence.

Ahmad Shuhaib—Free Officer, M.P., president of Board of Directors, Cotton Company

Mustapha Fahmi Sulaiman—president of Board of Directors, Sidnawi Department Stores.

Fathallah Rifa'at—Free Officer, deputy president Agricultural Credit Bank (currently president of the same bank)

Khalid Fawzi—secretary of the Presidency

Mustapha Kamal Murad—Free Officer, M.P., president of the Cotton Exporters' Association (currently leader of the liberal opposition in parliament)

Gamal Nazim—deputy minister of youth

There is not an identifiable militant in the lot; instead they represent the quintessence of the managerial state bourgeoisie with military backgrounds. Two, Murad and Rifa'at, have gone on to be staunch advocates of *infitah* and orthodox banking practices.

While Kamil no doubt sought to diminish his role in the Vanguard, his summary criticism is probably on the mark:

> Unfortunately I have to confirm the fact that the Vanguard never practiced freedom of opinion but rather worked with directives that came from the top, and that was its major fault. And I personally as one of its members said and wrote more than once, especially

335

when I was governor of Assiut and responsible for the Vanguard there, that this organization could never be of any use to the public interest as long as it worked that way. . . . There should have been leadership that listened to opinion from below and worked to implement it. And I said to Sami and Sha'arawi more than once what I thought, but no one listened to my words.

QUESTION: And what brought the Vanguard to this state of affairs?

ANSWER: It seems to me that it was Sha'arawi Guma'. He had been secretary of the vanguard since its beginning in 1964. He used to work in General Intelligence and he used the same methods in the Vanguard; such that his concern was to make it a source of information, no more, no less. And the whole thing boiled down after some years to members that had no role other than passing on information and receiving directives. [Matar 1972a, p. 145.]

Power Centers: Army and Police

After Sadat consolidated his grip on power in 1971, the Vanguard was denounced as a "power center," despite the fact that many of Sadat's supporters had been members of it. But what really lay at the heart of the opprobrious label of power center were the ultimate instruments of coercive control: the armed forces, the police, and intelligence.

It is not really surprising that Nasser would be, from the outset, suspicious of his own military. He was able to seize power using his alliances within it, and there was no logical reason why others still in uniform could not do the same. It may well be, as Jean Lacouture has argued (1971, 106-7), that Nasser in the beginning had no intention of expanding the armed forces and only did so reluctantly as a response to Israeli militarization and the setting up of the Baghdad Pact. There is little doubt, however, that he came to rely on Hakim 'Amir to be his eyes and ears in the armed forces and to assure that they would not turn against him. 'Amir performed that task faithfully but demanded in turn a free hand in building his own clientele within the military (see Stephens 1971, pp. 360-61).

In effect this meant that up to 1967 'Amir was able to put his fingers in many pies. He successfully kept control of the promotion process within the officers corps and was able, in addition, to place his people in upper-level management in the growing public sector as well as the diplomatic corps and the ranks of provincial governors. His *chef de cabinet*, Shams Badran, who became minister of war in 1966, was the principal artisan in this patronage process. Not all those military men who moved into civilian careers were beholden to 'Amir, but it is unlikely that many were his enemies.

Although the armed forces and the ASU can be seen as balancing and potentially antagonistic institutions, 'Amir and Sabri were allies in at least one domain—arms acquisitions through Soviet auspices. In that light 'Amir was willing to accept some radical policy packages, such as the great efforts at state-led land reclamation in the early 1960s, that conformed to Soviet preconceptions. It was, after all, his principal aid in Syria, 'Abd al-Muhsin Abu al-Nur, who became responsible for that effort.

From their positions of power the senior officers were able to trade on their influence, pocket kickbacks on everything from citrus exports to arms purchases, and to acquire property and income through appropriations or management of sequestered properties. There were no checks and balances against any of these abuses; it would hardly do in a time of war to drag Egypt's top-ranking military into the tribunals; nor would 'Amir have permitted it.

Predictably the tentacular spread of the military into the civilian sphere sapped it of its fighting capacity even as it accumulated tremendous stocks of advanced weaponry. The Yemeni imbroglio was graphic evidence of its growing problems in its nominal area of competence. The most scathing account of the military's disorganization comes from General Salah al-Hadidi (1974) who was chief of military intelligence at the time of the June War.[3] He recounts in detail the institutionalization of the principle of "loyalty before competence" that 'Amir and Badran nurtured. So industrious was Badran in placing cronies throughout the state apparatus that as war loomed in June 1967 military diplomats, managers, and administrators had to be hastily put back in uniform and in command of operational units. This, combined with the fact that tens of thousands of troops were still in the Yemen, that the military budget had been reduced in 1967, and that Nasser on the eve of the fighting decided to accept the first blow, meant that a debacle was unavoidable. Writing over a decade later, General Saad al-Din Shazly (1980, p. 41) recalled the shame of that moment:

> In their confusion and distress, the Egyptian people vented their feelings on the ordinary soldier. Anyone in uniform was ridiculed in the streets. Morale fell to near-suicidal levels.

On June 10, 1967, 'Amir and Badran resigned from their positions, but a group of ten or fifteen officers loyal to them petitioned Nasser to reinstate them both. These officers were immediately cashiered and over the ensuing weeks 600 to 850 officers were "retired." As 'Amir watched the dismantling of his clientele, he began to conspire with Badran and perhaps Salah Nasr, the director of General Intelligence, to save themselves. 'Amir began to propagate views that he had successfully muffled for years. He advocated

---

[3] Nasser made him head of the military tribunal that tried the air force officers in 1968.

greater democracy, freedom of the press, reform of the ASU, the formation of an opposition party, amnesty for political prisoners, release of arrested officers, halting the intensification of socialism, and moving away from the USSR. Sadat was to espouse the same themes four years later. To Nasser all this maneuvering may have indicated that 'Amir was no longer going to play number two and might be preparing a direct seizure of power. 'Amir was placed under house arrest in early September, and on the 15th, in circumstances that have never been satisfactorily clarified, his suicide was announced.

Intertwined, but certainly not coterminous with the military power center, were the various police and intelligence networks. The three main fiefdoms were run by Sami Sharaf, Salah Nasr, and Sha'arawi Guma'. After Sadat had pulled off his "corrective revolution" in May 1971 (to be discussed below) these fiefdoms were dismantled, or at least put under new management, while their abuses—torture, arbitrary arrest, phone-tapping, etc.—were roundly denounced. As these power centers became targets of official opprobrium, it became legitimate for those who had been their victims to publish their own, frequently vivid accounts. By the mid 1970s there was an impressive body of literature on what had been one of the murkiest and most unseemly sides of the Nasserist experiment. Part of the game of post-1971 revelations was in fact to discredit Nasser himself.

There have been police states more repressive and brutal than Egypt's of the 1960s, but it is significant that both the left and right eventually concurred that it was a question of a police state. The "right" led the charge, and because it was clear that their ultimate target was Nasser, the "left" was reluctant to join in the onslaught. For instance, Mustapha Amin, rehabilitated under Sadat as editor of *al-Akhbar*, recounted his tales of torture as an accused agent of the CIA at the hands of Salah Nasr's henchman, Hamza Basyuni. Equally sensationalist were the revelations of the well-known journalist, Galal al-Hamamsi, who went so far as to accuse Nasser of having pocketed a $15 million gift from ex-King Saud ibn 'Abd al-'Aziz. These sorts of revelations could be dismissed by the left as the concoctions of known reactionaries. It was more difficult to deal with the accusations of Egypt's dean of letters, Tawfiq al-Hakim, or of the respected, "progressive" professor of philosophy, Fu'ad Zakaria, who, in the pages of *Ruz al-Yussef*, chided the left for having been systematically manipulated by Nasser. Various leftists then reluctantly began to recount their own experiences at the hands of Nasser's police. The most important statement was that of Fathi 'Abd al-Fattah (1975b; see also Adel Montasser 1960-61), author of the two-volume study on the Egyptian village, who spent years in the Wahat concentration camp in the western desert. Louis Awad, who underwent similar treatment, put his appreciation of a figure he otherwise defends in blunt terms (1976, p. 67):[4] ". . . 'Abd al-Nasser in my view will enter history essentially for two of his most important achievements: the liquidation of communism [coming] after the liquidation of democracy in Egypt and to a certain extent in the Arab world."

One of Nasser's early supporters was Ahmad Abul Fath, the editor of the Wafdist newspaper, *al-Misri*. Abul Fath tried to resist the increasing control of the press and growing police repression but was eventually driven into exile. Writing in the early 1960s (1962, pp. 51-52), he noted the immediate recourse of the RCC to police surveillance: "During the first weeks Nasser was preoccupied by the creation of a vast network of intelligence agents. He confided the organization of this network, its control and its direction to Lt. Col. Zakaria Muhi al-Din of the RCC." It was undoubtedly Muhi al-Din that built the police apparatus and nurtured the careers of the men who came to dominate police repression in the 1960s.

It was the political sequestrations of the fall of 1961, following the July Decrees, that gave free rein to the police. Nasser felt that he was, after the breakup of the UAR, fighting for his survival. His underlings in the intelligence networks vied for the privilege of unearthing his enemies. The somewhat comical Mustapha Amin was only the most prominent of those jailed. But the initial wave of repression consisted of drawing up the "hit lists" of those subversives whose property was to be sequestered. Over the period 1961-1966 some 4,000 families were affected by sequestration measures.[5] Total assets seized during those years may have been worth £E 100 million and included 122,000 *feddans*, 7,000 urban properties, about 1,000 business "establishments" and over £E 30 million in stocks and bonds (see Gritli 1977, p. 76; Ghun'aim 1965, pp. 472-73; *A*, June 8, 1974 and July 6, 1974; *AI* 1974b Supplement). Compensation was offered in state bonds bearing 4 percent interest over fifteen years and up to a maximum of only £E 15,000 per sequestree.

[4] Some of the most important writings on police abuse are as follows: Mustapha Amin 1974 and 1975; Hamamsi 1975; Kamal Khalid, *In the tribunal of tyranny* (1975); 'Adil Sulaiman, *Martyrs and victims in the shadow of tyranny* (1977); 'Abdullah Imam, *The slaughter of the judiciary* (1976); Nassar 1974; Tawfiq al-Hakim, *The return of awareness* (1974); Muhammed 'Awda, *Awareness lost* (1975); Mahmud Murad, *Hakim . . . and his returning awareness* (1975); Fu'ad Zakaria "Is Nasser above criticism?" *RY*, no. 2444 (April 14, 1975); "Nasser bent the left to himself, not vice versa," *RY*, no. 2446 (April 28, 1975); Hassanain Karum, *Nasser slandered* (1975); Fathi 'Abd al-Fattah 1975b; Nasr 1975; 'Abd al-Salam 1975; Louis Awad 1976. All the above are in Arabic published either in Cairo or Beirut.

Film and theater picked up the same themes, especially the two films *Karnak* and *The Dawn Visitor*, and 'Ali Salim's popular satire, *The Phantoms of New Egypt* (translated by John Waterbury, *AUFS Report*, NE Africa Series, vol. 18, 1973). In general see Vatikiotis 1978.

[5] Decree 138 of October 18, 1961, based on the Emergency Law 163 of 1958, provided the first legal justification for the sequestrations. Takeovers after 1964 were based on the Emergency Law 119 of 1964.

Abuses were rife in both the takeovers themselves as well as in the subsequent disposition of properties. The system of police intelligence spoils perhaps reached its peak under the Committee for the Liquidation of Feudalism which included many of those later to be branded as heading "power centers"—'Ali Sabri, 'Abd al-Muhsin Abu al-Nur, Salah Nasr, Sami Sharaf, Shams Badran, etc. (see *inter alia* Sayyid Mar'ai, 1979, 2:502-504). This committee was used to settle scores among rival clienteles and it is clear that the victims included the innocent and the poor (L. Awad 1976, p. 25).

The Kamshish incident (see Chapter Twelve) that provided partial justification for the committee's activities is, in the eyes of many, a classic example of police abuse. There are several versions of how the whole incident was trumped up, perhaps even staged, and that it almost certainly revolved about an unsavory tale of cuckolds and philanderers, including the president's brother. But whatever else it was, it became the pretext for a wholesale settling of accounts.[6]

As noted in Chapter Twelve, many of the land seizures were fairly quickly suspended and several arbitrary arrests terminated in prompt release without trial. The principal accused were not brought to trial until two years later and most were acquitted. Some were held in military prisons without charges, tortured, and then released only after Sadat consolidated his power in May 1971. Mustapha Amin once explained in private, "the basic rule in those days was that if you were found guilty, you went to prison; and if you were found innocent, you went to a concentration camp."

There is no doubt that political arrests were widespread in the 1960s. The

---

[6] Here is the standard revisionist account of Kamshish. Salah Hussain, the "martyr," was married to Shahanda Muqallid from Kamshish. Hussain was not from Kamshish but was a member of its ASU Committee of Twenty. Shahanda's brother was a pilot and a close friend of Nasser's brother, also a pilot, Hussain 'Abd al-Nasser. The *aspect louche* of all this is that Shahanda was reputedly of loose morals, tired of her husband, and had him killed (April 30, 1966), hoping to marry a member of the Fiqqi family, the "feudalists" in the saga. She was rebuffed and then blamed her husband's death on the Fiqqis. Hussain 'Abd al-Nasser wanted to avenge the death of his friend.

Hakim 'Amir was finally dragged into the affair on May 3, turning it into the national cause it became. Three men were arrested, accused of having acted on the orders of Salah al-Fiqqi. Internal Intelligence (Mubahith al-'Amm) got into the act, carrying out widespread arrests and beating over 100 people from Kamshish in public. The accused were imprisoned for a year before any charges were brought. Twenty-two were then put on trial in the military tribunal presided over by the notorious General Fu'ad al-Dagawi. After the March 30 (1968) Declaration, the tribunal was reorganized and on May 21 a new investigation was ordered. On July 8, seventeen acquittals were handed down, although all were held in custody until Sadat released them in May 1971!

In 1976 the Fiqqi family went to court to reopen the case and sought £E 350,000 in damages. For partial corroboration of this version, see 'Abd al-Salam 1975, p. 145.

minister of interior, Sha'arawi Guma', admitted to the following (*A*, December 12, 1967):

	Imprisoned	Released	Still detained
Muslim Brethren (1965)	2,000	1,000	1,000
Communists	24-30	24-30	0
Feudalists (1966)	196	102	94
High Officials	43	40	3
Wafdists	23	23	0
Arrests during June War	119	119	0
Jews arrested during June War	257	23	234
Narcotics dealers	1,816	1,496	325
High-risk criminals	1,885	1,447	438

In addition Guma' noted that some 1,406 Egyptians who had been placed in "political isolation" in 1961-1962 had their political rights restored to them in November 1967.

It was nearly a decade later that the Ministry of Interior released a rather different set of figures (*A*, May 5, 1976):

Period	No. of Political Arrests
7/22/52-1/13/54 (trials of politicians)	679
1/14/54-3/25/54 (showdown with Naguib)	1,421
10/26/54-7/18/56 (essentially Ikhwan)	3,000
11/1/56-1/1/57 (Suez War)	411
11/2/57-3/21/64 (Communists and sequestrations)	1,288
3/22/64-5/15/71 (feudalists, Ikhwan)	7,700

In both the 1950s and 1960s the Ikhwan, or Muslim Brethren, were the principal targets of political arrest. In August 1965, the authorities believed they had solid evidence that elements within the Brethren, inspired by Sayyid Qutb, were in contact with King Faisal of Saudi Arabia with a view to bringing down Nasser's regime. He ordered a crackdown that was by all accounts spectacular. He himself admitted in December 1968 that 18,000 Ikhwanis had been arrested (Stephens 1971, p. 136), but *Akhbar al-Yom* (March 29, 1975) later claimed that 27,000 had been swept up in a single twenty-four-hour period. The bulk were held in military camps, and only about 100 were ever brought to trial. It was not until 1975 that President Sadat had the remaining Ikhwanis released and permitted the organization to undertake legal activities (see the articles of Hassan al-Ashmawi, "The Story of the Ikhwan and the Revolution," *RY*, October-November 1977).

Inevitably torture and police sadism became commonplace. Salah Nasr was frequently touted as the czar of this nether world, although when he replied to Mustapha Amin's accusations (1975) he denied that he was aware of Hamza Basyuni's depravity. He also noted that he had little to do with Sabri's and Sharaf's power centers who, he charged, plotted his downfall in August 1967 so that they could gain control of General Intelligence. He was at that time implicated in 'Amir's alleged plot and sentenced to forty years in jail.

People lost their lives in Nasser's jails, most at the notorious detention camp at Abu Za'abal. Well-known Communists and leftists—Shuhdi 'Atiyya, Rushdi Khalil, Muhammed Uthman, 'Ali al-Dib, and 'Abd al-Fatah Muftah—all lost their lives through physical torture. The family of 'Atiyya, who died on July 15, 1960, was finally awarded £E 12,000 in damages by the South Cairo Court in 1974. A year later 'Ali Grisha, a lawyer who had been tortured in 1965 but not killed, received a settlement of £E 37,000.

Nasser's second-echelon officer-allies, whom he had used to end-run his own peers from the RCC, had clearly gotten out of hand, and by 1966 he had begun trying to rein them in. When the drafting committee for a permanent constitution convened in the summer of 1966, Nasser stressed the need to "codify" (*taqnin*) the revolution in order to foil the power centers. After the June War Hassanein Heikal, Nasser's undesignated spokesman, stressed in his editorials due process, intellectual freedom, the right to criticism and so forth. At the same time Nasser acknowledged the abuses carried out by the Committee to Liquidate Feudalism and began to return sequestered property to former owners. Just as had been the case with the first hints at some liberalization of the economy in the same period, so too did Nasser adumbrate in the political realm themes that Sadat was later to seize upon and develop more fully.

Syndicates

By the mid-1960s Nasser had brought the private sector bourgeoisie and landowners to heel through nationalizations, land reform, sequestrations, and political "isolation." Yet he could still anticipate the indirect opposition of the state bourgeoisie, technocrats, and professionals. In the ASU all these groups constituted a particularly and deliberately ill-defined corps—"intellectuals"—that blurred the functional specificity of their component parts and denied them a platform for the expression of their diverse interests. As the years went by after the founding of the ASU, this corps was no longer referred to as intellectual but rather, more appropriately, as "groups" (*fi'at*). As became clear in the 1970s (see Chapter Fifteen), many resented their nonstatus and nonrecognition while workers and peasants enjoyed guaranteed and, in their eyes, unwarranted representation. Some professionals were able to don what Ayubi calls dual class identity, invading thereby the ranks of "workers" and "peasants." In one ASU general conference it was revealed that among these toilers were an ex-minister, five members of company boards, a general, twenty-five civil service directors, a university chancellor, twenty-nine high-level bureaucrats, 117 pharmacists, accountants, and clerks, two journalists, and a radio producer (Ayubi 1980, p. 447).

For most other professionals the last refuge became their syndicates, and for doctors, lawyers, and engineers these bodies had fairly deep historical roots (see D. Reid 1974; Springborg 1978; Moore 1975 and 1980). As potential sources of resistance to or sabotage of the process of socialist transformation, the syndicates inevitably became targets of the regime. There was never any question of simply abolishing them, for their main function of setting standards and regulating entry to their professions was perfectly legitimate. So the game became to co-opt or manipulate their leadership and to effect changes in their rules.

Probably the most important issue that arose in this connection was the subjugation of the judiciary and the law profession, because what was at stake was the principle of the separation of powers. Nasser was never reticent in dismissing such notions. In the tripartite unity talks of 1963, he stated:

I'm against the principle of the separation of powers, and I consider the carrying out of this separation an enormous illusion. Why? Because in reality there is no such thing as the separation of powers; because whoever has the majority in parliament takes over the executive and legislative powers. Thus the political leadership that has the majority also has two things: executive power and legislative power, and, consequently, judicial power. For, no matter what they say about its independence, the judicial power is subordinate to the legislative power. That talk [kallam] that emerged in France in the days of Montesquieu on such separation was all theory and was never implemented [cited in 'Issa 1974, p. 20].

It is indicative of the kinds of pressures that came to bear in the mid-1960s that even Gamal al-'Utaifi felt compelled to lend his own legal expertise in support of the subordination of the judiciary. In a pamphlet entitled *Socialist Justice* (*AI* Supplement, March 1, 1966), 'Utaifi pays obeissance to the independence of the judiciary but then goes on to disparage the notion of "bourgeois justice." The state, he wrote, is the emanation of popular will, itself indivisible. 'Utaifi agreed, with what one hopes was tongue-in-cheek, that if this were not the case, then how could the RCC have abolished the 1923 constitution, the monarchy, and political parties by executive order? 'Utaifi then declared that the task of law in the present (i.e., 1966 radicali-

343

zation) phase is to work toward the crushing of the resistance of classes hostile to the revolution (p. 86).

Many of 'Utaifi's colleagues in the legal profession did not share his views on the use of the courts as subordinate political instruments. Indeed, their well-known recalcitrance on this score probably led to the routine referral of political cases to military tribunals. A particularly galling instance was the question of the trial of those arrested in connection with the Kamshish affair. By the spring of 1968 it had not yet been decided how the accused would be tried. Dr. Hilmi Murad, a lawyer, but at the time minister of education, urged that civilian courts handle the cases, referring for support to the principles laid down in the March 30 Declaration. Murad believed he had won Nasser over to this view, but ultimately it was Muhammed Abu Nussair, the minister of justice and one of 'Ali Sabri's clients, who led the move for referral to Dagawi's military tribunal.

It was Nussair as well who acted as Sabri's agent in the subordination of the judiciary to the ASU. On March 28, 1968, after the February student-worker riots and two days before the March 30 Declaration, the General Association of Magistrates voted against collective membership in the ASU which, they believed, would compromise their independence. Abu Nussair eventually called for a purge of all magistrates who had voted in favor of this motion, and in August 1969 all magistrates were temporarily suspended while 112 were eventually dismissed from the bench. Some, like former Minister of Justice 'Abd al-Fattah Hassan, were held for over a year without charges (see *AY*, October 19, 1974; Nassar, 1975; 'Abdullah Imam 1976; 'Abd al-Fattah Hassan 1974). It was not until May 1973 that Sadat reinstated all of them in their professions.

Less repressive but no less effective measures had been applied to the Lawyers' Syndicate. In a general move to flood professional syndicates with members beholden to the regime, the lawyers were obliged to admit all graduates of faculties of law working in the legal departments of public sector companies. Their numbers were sufficient to assure the victory of ASU candidates for syndicate president (*naqib*) (Moore 1980, p. 58).

The medical and engineering professions fared somewhat better. The former resisted inclusion of paramedical personnel, such as nurses and orderlies, in their syndicate, while the engineers granted only provisional, nonvoting membership to graduates of higher technical institutes. Even so leadership positions could be manipulated in favor of the regime. This was particularly important with respect to the engineers for several reasons. The thrust of Egypt's economic growth strategy brought engineers to the forefront of policy implementation if not policy formulation. Many projects, like the High Dam, were so laden with political significance that the docility of potential technocratic critics had to be assured. Finally, engineers had risen to prominence in managerial positions throughout the public sector and the civil service, and their loyalty to regime goals thus became essential (Moore 1980, pp. 167-68; and Ayubi 1980, pp. 356-58).

Throughout the Nasserist period it may have been the possibility of arbitrary and often petty vengeance as much as anything that kept the professional elites in line. In 1966 Nasser strongly criticized the management of Qasr al-'Aini Hospital, contrasting it with the management of the Suez Canal. Dr. Rashwan Fahmi, *naqib* of the Doctors Syndicate, rebutted the charges, claiming that if Qasr al-'Aini had the canal's resources it would be a model of medical care and if the canal had Qasr al-'Aini's resources, navigation would come to a halt. After these remarks, Fahmi's property was sequestered and he was fired from Cairo University and dropped from the ASU (*RY*, no. 2436, February 17, 1975).

Nasser had no more respect for the independence of the educational establishment than for that of the judiciary. All currents of opposition in Egypt quite naturally found their most explicit formulation in institutions of higher learning. Nasser learned this lesson early on. In his struggle with Naguib in March 1954, he found much of the university establishment aligned with Naguib and with the demand that the armed forces return to the barracks and civilian rule be restored. From then on the universities were stripped of all autonomy. Elective deanships were terminated and appointment became the rule. Student organizations, after the purge of the Ikhwan in 1954, were strictly controlled and muzzled. The widespread arrests of leftists and communists in 1959 furthered the process, and some intellectuals like Louis Awad were never permitted to resume their teaching careers (see Fu'ad Zakaria 1974 and 1975b). By the 1960s the universities had been fairly systematically subordinated.

The schoolteachers' syndicate fared no better than other professional associations. The regime saw to it that primary schoolteachers controlled the syndicate through the sheer weight of numbers (Moore 1980, p. 58). The syndicate itself had been created in 1955 to contain the teaching profession. By the early 1970s its membership had grown to 300,000, but the leadership installed in the 1950s still prevailed. Moreover, these leaders had substantial resources at their disposal. Each member paid £E 3 in annual dues, one-quarter of their annual bonus, and 2 percent of their exam grading earnings. In addition the syndicate owned and rented out the Burg Hotel and received some revenues from the stamp tax. Adib Dimitri estimated total revenues to the syndicate in 1975 at £E 2 million but pointed out that the syndicate had reported *total* revenues of only £E 6 million for the fifteen-year period 1955-1970 (*RY*, no. 2532, December 20, 1976).

In 1959 the Egyptian press was brought under direct state control. The device by which this was done was to transfer ownership of all newspapers and periodicals to the National Union and to place newspaper content and editorial orientation under the purview of the political leadership. This formula was maintained with the creation of the Arab Socialist Union and, throughout, was undergirded by heavy censorship prior to publication. All journalists were automatically members of the ASU and suspension of their membership in that organization entailed suspension of their right to exercise their profession.

Through these measures of containment, liberally supplemented by arbitrary dismissals without appeal of anyone on the public payroll, the Nasserist regime was able to keep the professional intelligentsia constantly on the defensive.[7] Thus the only corporate actors that could conceivably have challenged Nasser came from the principal instruments of control: the armed forces, the police and intelligence groups, and the ASU.

Cronies

At least two students of Egyptian politics have singled out small clusters of cronies (*shillas*) as being the de facto operative units of Egyptian political life—"for authoritarian rule blotted out all other forms of political memory or identification" (Moore 1980, p. 56; cf. Springborg 1975). These groups of equals, joined by common educational, professional, or familial backgrounds, are not to be confused with patron-client groups which are rooted in relations among unequals. The *shilla*, by contrast, can be seen as an instrument for the defense of its member's interests and the promotion of their collective fortunes when one of them has risen to prominence. These groups tend to be fragile—cronies prefer to share good fortune but often abandon old friends who have fallen on hard times or into political disgrace.

Like clientelist politics, the concerns of *shilla* members are focused on maneuvering and short-term advantage. By its very nature the *shilla* vitiates ideological and programmatic politics and maximizes the wielding of group influence for personal gain. It is for this reason that *shillaliyya* has such a negative connotation in Egyptian politics. The view of a former public sector company head is not atypical (Khalil 1977:123):[8] "The *shilla* is a legal gang exploiting the gaps in the existing legal system to its own interest."

---

[7] The *'ulema* could have been a cohesive force of opposition on the order of the *mullahs* and *mujtahids* of Iran, but it was precisely cohesion that they lacked. Hemmed in by the essentially lay critics of the Muslim Brethren and the successful efforts of the regime to co-opt and manipulate the most visible leaders associated with al-Azhar University and the Ministry of Religious Endowments, the *'ulema* have never constituted a corporate force.

[8] Khalil added these remarks contrasing cronies with friends: "the *shilla* is the inverse of a group of friends and is held together essentially by ties of mutual benefit. . . . Can one deny that there are relations of mutual benefit among friends? Of course not. They exist but are on our personal account, while for the *shilla* they are on the accounts of others. Who are these others? Tens of millions of citizens" (Khalil 1977, pp. 121-22). Springborg (1980) has refined

It is undeniable that *shillas* occupy an important place in Egyptian elite politics (see for instance reference to Sharaf's *shilla* at the beginning of this chapter) but to attribute to them a dominant role because corporate and interest groups are weak and not institutionalized is excessive. They may be seen as one among several instruments for personal protection and advancement, and some of the others are based on impersonal processes of merit and objective qualifications (cf. Ayubi 1980, pp. 468-69). The point to be made here is that the phenomenon of *shillas* flowed naturally from the indecisiveness of Nasser in structuring the Arab Socialist Union and its "popular" organizations. The existence of the *shillas* in turn facilitated political control, at the expense of mobilization, because of their resort to the nonideological tactics of expedience and short-term gain.

Bureaucratic Corruption

It is tempting to see in Egypt's long bureaucratic tradition the ingredients of far-reaching administrative penetration and control, or what has been called oriental despotism. Under Nasser the country's already large public administration was greatly expanded and, with the growth of the public sector, took on new social and economic functions. Seemingly one then had the meeting of the historically conditioned docile Egyptian with the bureaucratic behemoth obeying the directives of the new pharaoh. However, nothing could be farther from reality. The great administrative pyramid is indeed there with a presence in every village, quarter, and factory in the country, but it has, more often than not, been appropriated by local interests, manipulated to personal advantage by its own personnel, and put to the service of those who can buy its favors and benefits. Seldom has it been the executor of the regime's will. Both Nasser and Sadat periodically heralded sweeping administrative reform measures, but their favorite tactic was simply to create new administrative structures to deal with problems mishandled by the old.

The first element leading to an explanation of this situation is the question of administrative salaries. It is said that in Odessa a bureaucrat may be the target of the particularly terrible curse: "Let him live on his salary" (Smith 1976, p. 110). Evidence from Egypt would suggest that for most bureaucrats that is an impossibility. Salary levels throughout the administration have been judged inadequate, and most civil servants have been driven to moonlighting and petty corruption. Let us recall that in 1975 over 1.2 million civil servants earned £E 14 per month or less (ca. $25 at the time). Their financial vulnerability has opened the way to the marketing of a wide range of adminis-

his concepts to distinguish between *shillas* of friends and political *shillas* that look exclusively to maneuvering in the political arena. He also introduces a new unit that he calls "family nests," created through strategic marriages, that serve political purposes.

trative services. Malak Girgis (1974) has nicely captured the ethos of the Egyptian administration. His case study of the trading in favors and services at the village level among local elites, the veterinarian, and the public clinic orderly reveals how the base of the administrative pyramid is appropriated and run for the benefit of the wealthy and the publicly employed.

Top-level public servants and managers have been prone to the same excesses. In 1975 some 750 high-level bureaucrats held down at least two jobs, frequently both in the public sector, and membership on a board of directors was not considered a second employ.

With growing state control over coveted resources, it was inevitable that illegal traffic in these goods would take on substantial proportions. Administered prices and short supplies led to thriving black markets which in turn led to the pilfering of state supplies.[9] Currency and import controls nurtured embezzlement and smuggling, and the volume of public business led to kickbacks and inflated commissions. While all of these phenomena grew in volume under Sadat, they were already present under Nasser. In the 1950s a series of scandals became public, beginning with Magdi Hassanain's alleged abuses in connection with Tahrir Province, to the machinations of Hassan Ibrahim at the head of the Economic Organization after 1957 or Rashid Barawi at the head of the Industrial Bank (Riad 1964, p. 88).

Muhammed 'Abd al-Salam (1975) has chronicled the major corruption cases of the 1960s and the inability of the judicial system to deal with them. The Ministry of Supply was particularly active, but he cites also the criminal mismanagement of the Nasr Glass and Crystal Company, Esko Silk and Cotton Company, the Tractor Engineering Company, and the Coldair Refrigeration Company.

Members of the political elite, including 'Ali Sabri and Hakim 'Amir, were implicated in all these cases, and for that reason legal follow-up was very difficult. There is abundant legislation on the books to handle such cases (Ibrahim Sabri 1978), including a "Where did you get it" law passed in 1958. But most of this legislation has remained a dead letter. Most often guilty officials are merely transferred to other posts, and, if they are able to pay back what they have illegally acquired, charges are dropped. Even if the employee goes to jail, the price may be worth it. Mahmud Abu Wafia, President Sadat's brother-in-law, once pointed out in parliament that a civil servant earning £E 50 per month could embezzle £E 30,000, suffer a maximum of seven years in jail, and wind up with more money than he could earn in a lifetime at his job.

Corruption minimally diverts administrators and other public officials from

---

[9] It is a standing joke, but rooted in observable practice, that public sector companies typically experience a rash of fires each year during "inventory season." Stolen or illegally sold goods are then said to have gone up in smoke.

their designated tasks, and channels scarce resources away from the populations for which they are allocated. But beyond this, high-level corruption can be viewed as an instrument of political control. In that sense corruption may be actively encouraged by a given regime (Waterbury 1976c, pp. 426-45). For leaders like Nasser and Sadat, whose popular mandates to rule were always of dubious validity and whose trust in their peers was always minimal, corruption could be used to wed potential rivals to the regime. The elite would be allowed to play its crass material games, records would be kept of their activities, and were they ever to become politically threatening, legal action could be taken against them.[10] 'Ali Sabri's temporary eclipse in 1969 was just such an instance of political control, but it works best when it is held in reserve as was the case under Sadat.

In many ways, then, Nasser's approach to the bureaucracy and public sector was similar to his approach to the ASU. Rather than engines of growth and transformation, he tolerated their conversion into porous networks of influence-trading, cronyism, moonlighting, and petty and large-scale corruption. Only newly created bureaucracies (such as the High Dam Authority or the Suez Canal Authority) briefly escaped this process of decay. But if the administration and public sector were not put to the service of socialist transformation, they did hold a vast salariat in occupational and material thrall. In that respect they were preeminent instruments of political control.

The Corrective Revolution

The brief flirtation with institutionalized and radical politics under the auspices of 'Ali Sabri and the ASU did not live beyond the June War. Although it took a decade before it was pronounced dead, the ASU was already in its death throes in 1967. Egypt's leaders, discredited, dispirited, and stripped of most ideological pretense, could only fall back on their control of institutional power. Sadat could truthfully claim that he stood naked in the post-1967 jungle of elite politics. He had no institutional base of power and no organized clientele. It was probably for that reason that those who did have such power—Sami Sharaf, 'Ali Sabri, Sha'arawi Guma', etc.—accepted him as president when Nasser died.[11] He must have seemed an easily manipulable figure, one the real power-wielders could tolerate until one of them gained supremacy.

[10] Generally the head of state is careful to dissociate himself from these illicit activities or, if involved, to cover his tracks. Galal Hamamsi (1975, pp. 170-74) and Ahmad Osman (1981) are the only Egyptians to have accused Nasser of personal corruption, albeit posthumously. Both men had their accusations disowned by Sadat.

[11] At a later date, when the ASU Vanguard came under intense criticism, a letter from former Vanguard members in Bahaira Province to Ruz al-Yussef (no. 2416, September 30, 1974) revealed that all Vanguard members received a central directive dated October 6, 1970 to support Sadat for the presidency.

Early on Sadat showed himself to be singularly uncompliant. In February 1971 he went before parliament to announce a proposal for an Israeli pullback in Sinai and the reopening of the Suez Canal without discussing his proposal with his foreign minister, Mahmud Riad. Riad promptly resigned. Sadat then moved ahead with plans for union with Libya, Sudan, and Syria. The project for what was to be the Federation of Arab Republics had been adumbrated with Nasser's blessing in September 1969. Sadat accelerated the pace of the process in early 1971 without reference to the Supreme Executive Committee of the ASU. He made concessions to the other partners that would have allowed decisions to be taken by majority rule and would have overrepresented the other states in supranational legislative bodies. Whether Sabri and his colleagues on the ASU Executive Committee were truly outraged or merely in search of a pretext, they decided to pick this issue to isolate and disgrace Sadat.[12]

Sadat's adversaries may have anticipated an easy victory and hence moved slowly, always leaving the initiative to Sadat. General Muhammed Fawzi, the minister of defense, told the senior officers corps on April 18 that he was opposed to the unity project. Then on April 21 the matter was referred to the Supreme Executive Committee of the ASU where Sadat did not have a majority.[13] Faced with a defeat in this committee, Sadat insisted on taking the matter to the Central Committee. Reluctantly Sabri acceded to this demand as Sadat threatened to bring it before the ASU National Congress or even put it to national referendum if need be.

On April 25 Sadat and Sabri in a rare open debate presented the issues to the Central Committee. A handful of Sadat's allies (Ahmad Darwish, Sayyid Mar'ai, Hassanein Heikal, Muhammed Dakruri) supported a motion to choke off Sabri's address. But the majority of the Central Committee (150 members) insisted that he be allowed to continue, not so much because they supported him but because this was virtually the first time they had ever been made privy to the altercations of the elite (Matar 1972a, p. 30). Ultimately, on April 29, this committee approved the unity plan but changed it so that all decisions at the federal level would require unanimity.

It was at this point that Sabri and his allies began to move against Sadat. Meetings were held in various branches of the Vanguard in which the president's "illegal" initiatives were denounced. With Sha'arawi Guma' in charge of Interior and the Republican Guard and General Fawzi, a reluctant conspirator, at the head of the armed forces, Sabri must have felt fairly confident. But Sadat seized the initiative. On May 1 he verbally attacked the nefarious

[12] The best accounts are Fu'ad Matar 1972a, vol. 1, and Binder 1978, pp. 382-96.

[13] Of the committee members, Sadat could count on Hussain Shafa'i and Mahmud Fawzi. His other ally, Kamal Ramzi Stino, was on a trip. Sabri had himself, Abu al-Nur, and Labib Shuqair. Sha'arawi Guma' was present *ex officio* but not able to vote.

"power centers" that were maneuvering against him, and on May 2 he dismissed Sabri from his position as vice president and from the ASU. In the meantime, through General Muhammed Sadiq, he engineered the isolation of General Fawzi within the senior officers corps. The crisis came to a head on May 13 when Guma' resigned as minister of the interior to be followed by the collective resignation of Fawzi, Sami Sharaf, Muhammed Fa'iq, Sa'ad Zayyid, and Hilmi Sa'id from the cabinet, along with Labib Shuqair, Dia al-Din Da'ud, and 'Abd al-Muhsin Abu al-Nur from the ASU. The resignations were broadcast by Egyptian radio with the presumed approval of Hassanein Heikal, the minister of information.[14] Perhaps the conspirators had deluded themselves into thinking that they personally and the ASU as a whole had popular roots, that having gone public some segments of the masses (students, workers, the Vanguard?) would go into the streets to shout their names, and that with control of the police, Interior, and the armed forces they could restore order and their own power.

Sadat wasted no time. He put Muhammed Sadiq at the head of the armed forces, brought in Mamduh Salim, the governor of Alexandria, as minister of interior, and ordered the Republican Guard to arrest all those who had resigned. Ninety government and ASU officials were taken into custody at this time. All this took place on May 15, which henceforth became the hallowed date of the beginning of the Corrective Revolution. Simultaneously 'Abd al-Salam al-Zayyat was put in charge of a temporary secretariat of the ASU, and also replaced Heikal at the Ministry of Information. Hafiz Badawi was made the new speaker of parliament, replacing Labib Shuqair.

In one fell swoop Sadat had cleared the arena of his major rivals, who were subsequently put on trial.[15] Most were convicted, and all had been released by 1981. Immediately after the confrontation, Sadat ostentatiously began the dismantling of the power centers, proclaiming an end to police harassment, wiretapping (he personally set fire to more than 22,000 taped phone calls), mail surveillance, and the like. He announced plans for an overhaul of the ASU and, at the meeting of the ASU National Congress of July 23-26, 1971, he presented the delegates with a Program for National Action. In many ways this document marked Sadat's first attempt to establish his own style and to take his distance from his predecessor. For example, the

---

[14] Heikal played an ambiguous role in this confrontation. The fact that he broadcast the collective resignations could indicate his complicity with Sabri et al. But it was told to me that around May 10 Heikal had purposely misled Sabri by telling him that legality was on his side and that there was nothing Sadat could do to thwart him, thereby lulling him into a false sense of security.

[15] The USSR, crucial to the rebuilding of the Egyptian armed forces, was naturally alarmed at this purge, and to allay their apprehensions Sadat entered into a Friendship Treaty with the Soviet Union at the end of May.

program proposed changing the country's name from the United Arab Republic to the Arab Republic of Egypt, thereby implying a move away from the Arabism promoted by Nasser since 1958. Sadat called for the renewal of the ASU from top to bottom, noting that the ASU had to come to be "hated" by the Egyptian people. The Vanguard was singled out as a major instrument in the abuse of power by Sadat's fallen rivals.

Within months of the May 1971 confrontation Sadat moved to release many political prisoners, reinstate civil servants who had been dismissed from their jobs, and to return property that had been sequestered for political reasons. All these measures gained him widespread support among the civilian middle class that had come to chafe under Nasser's police surveillance. Implicitly these moves called into question the quality of Nasser's leadership and planted the seeds for the process of de-Nasserization that Sadat allowed to develop.

At the end of 1971 Sadat put together what can be considered his first handpicked cabinet. The aging Mahmud Fawzi, Egypt's perennial foreign minister, left the prime ministership to 'Aziz Sidqi who had remained loyal to Sadat during the crisis. Others who had stood by him were equally rewarded: Sayyid Mar'ai was put at the head of the ASU, 'Abd al-Salam al-Zayyat was made deputy prime minister, Mamduh Salim was kept at Interior, and Muhammed Sadiq at Defense. In addition, perhaps to reassure the USSR, two Marxists, Isma'il Sabri 'Abdullah and Fu'ad Mursi, were brought in as minister of state for planning and minister of supply. In many ways the acid test for admission to Sadat's inner councils was loyalty during May 1971, but even among these stalwarts the attrition rate proved to be very high.[16]

For our purposes here the most significant move was to turn over the care of the ASU to Sayyid Mar'ai. His mandate to reorganize that body in fact entailed a concerted effort to strip it of all real power. In the first three months of 1972, Mar'ai presided over a wide-ranging debate on the deficiencies and the future of the ASU. The transcripts of those debates were published in *al-Tali'a* (1972a) and make fascinating reading. There was scarcely anyone who

---

[16] I list here those who supported Sadat and have gone into eclipse. Ashraf Marwan, married to Nasser's daughter, gave Sadat tapes that incriminated Sabri. He became Sadat's advisor on Arab affairs until 1978 and then was dropped. Muhammed Sadiq was arrested in late 1972. Mamduh Salim went on to be prime minister but then was given an honorific post of advisor after 1978. Hassanein Heikal was fired from the editorship of *al-Ahram* in 1974. 'Aziz Sidqi has had no public role since 1978. Hafiz Badawi, who became speaker of parliament, was dropped in favor of Sayyid Mar'ai. Dakruri, Darwish, 'Abd al-Akhir, and Mahmud were all put on the Discipline Committee of the ASU; two went on to governorships and two to cabinet positions. All had disappeared by the late 1970s. 'Abd al-Salam al-Zayyat survived as an M.P., but was briefly arrested in 1980 and again in 1981. Hussain Shafa'i of the RCC was made a vice-president and then replaced by Husni Mubarak in 1975. Those who fared best were Mahmud Fawzi, who retired with honor, and Sayyid Mar'ai, who remained an influential but somewhat marginal figure in the early 1980s.

spoke in defense of the ASU's past. All agreed with Mar'ai's assessment that it had become bureaucratized, had limited democratic procedures, and had become the tool of the regime rather than of the people. One participant said it was nothing more than a Ministry of Political Affairs.

Beyond this, various proposals were made that hinted at developments that would take some years to come to fruition. Some on the left, such as Khalid Muhi al-Din and Lutfi al-Kholi, called for the separation of powers and the setting up of "platforms" (*manabir*) within the ASU to encourage diversity within the ASU. Mar'ai endorsed this idea emphatically. Two illustrious men of letters, Hussain Fawzi and Nagib Mahfuz, called outright for a return to a multiparty system.

As the debates proceeded, Mar'ai decided to republish and distribute the 1962 *Report on the Charter* that for a decade had been suppressed. Consonant with this move was the warning of Muhammad Mahmud (*al-Tali'a* 1972a, no. 6, p. 25):

> Our political organization should be founded on our religious convictions, our intellectual heritage, and the reality of our society. It should be translated into an intellectual guide distinguishing our Egyptian socialism sprung from the humanitarianism of our religion. It is up to the Action Committee [appointed by Mar'ai for the purpose of the debate] to codify this and to clarify it so as to protect it from an intellectual slide that could cast it in the lap of the adventurous spiteful left.

Within a year of his triumph over Sabri, the general lines of Sadat's new look were becoming clear. The first investment code to attract foreign capital had been issued in the fall of 1971. Scientific socialism was discredited, while themes of political liberalism combined with religious values and "Egyptianness" were stressed. The expulsion on July 23, 1972, the twentieth anniversary of the revolution, of the 15,000 Soviet military advisors in Egypt, announced the beginning of the country's return to the West.

Chapter Fifteen

CONTROLLED LIBERALIZATION UNDER SADAT

> . . . for most political elites participation is, at best, an instrumental rather than a primary value.
> [Huntington and Nelson 1976, p. 29.]

> There will never come the time that one can convince the Egyptian people of the health of party life when the three parties are headed by our military colleagues. This is a situation without parallel in the world; as if the country had no politicians and no civilians.
> [Serrag al-Din 1977, p. 27.]

The marketplace reigns supreme neither in the Egyptian economy nor in the political arena. Sadat and his entourage carefully moved toward mixed systems in both domains and left themselves avenues of retreat toward increased economic statism and political authoritarianism. Real change took place in the economy and the polity in the 1970s, change that cannot be dismissed lightly but that is not irrevocable.

From *Manabir* to Parties

Anwar Sadat made it clear early in his incumbency that what he liked in the Nasserist political formula was the alliance of working forces and that what he disliked was the Arab Socialist Union. Initially he talked of reforming and reorganizing the ASU, but one suspects that he really had its abolition in mind. Unlike Nasser, Sadat felt comfortable with the idea and the reality of some political diversity, and eventually even with controlled multipartyism. He had the self-confidence to act as broker and referee of the competing interests to be unshackled. He sacrificed *some* of the control that so obsessed Nasser in order to see more clearly the forces that warranted control. In most respects Sadat was much more a risk-taker than his predecessor.

Put another way, Sadat continued the corporatist formula and through the introduction of corporate "honor codes" reinforced it, while allowing for open politics in the interstices of the corporate edifice. These open politics, however, were restricted to the religious right; links between these segments and mass constituencies were carefully monitored and constrained. At the end

Sadat imposed such severe restrictions on all forms of political activity that he seemed to have reverted to the Nasserist style he nominally abhorred.

The dismantling of the ASU was pursued in a cautious manner after 1971. The struggle with Israel was still Egypt's primary policy concern and the acid test of its leadership. Sadat could not afford to tamper with Nasserist formulae of control in the face of external threat, nor did he yet have the stature to introduce innovations in his own name. That would have to await the October War of 1973, which was the turning point in Sadat's fortunes. Prior to that he was confronted with widespread student movements in the winters of 1972 and 1973 during which he and his associates were accused of abandoning the Arab cause and the socialist revolution. Sayyid Mar'ai in fact stated that the student riots of February 1972 prompted the convening of the meetings to assess the past and future of the ASU. In so doing Mar'ai displaced the blame for the unrest from the new regime itself onto the "unresponsive" and "unpopular" political apparatus of the Nasserist years.

After the October War Sadat issued a personal statement known as the October Paper that became, along with the Charter, the March 30 Declaration, and the permanent constitution one of the "fundamental documents" of the revolution. Even in this paper Sadat was cautious in his criticism of the past (October Paper, *A*, April 19, 1974):

> Perhaps the greatest achievement of the revolution lay in its peaceful social and political transformations. Whatever the errors that occurred in application, they pale in significance when we realize that the revolution through these measures saved the country from violent class conflict. . . . Moreover, I am not exaggerating when I say that the revolution saved the country from a civil war.

A year later, in July 1975, elections were held to 6,324 basic units in the ASU as well as to the 1,500 seats in the National Congress. Membership at that time was claimed to be 4.8 million, and 97,000 offered themselves as candidates for office within the ASU. Thus, even at this late date the form if not the spirit of the Nasserist formula was being maintained. Yet within a year independent "platforms" (*manabir*) were allowed to contest parliamentary elections in the fall of 1976, and shortly thereafter independent parties were authorized. By 1978 the ASU was defunct. The shift in mood was astonishing. In a talk with Egyptian journalists in June 1977 (*A*, June 27, 1977) Sadat noted:

> It was clear to me in 1970 that what we called the socialist experiment and which we carried out in the 1960s was a 100 percent failure . . . it was a summit operation carried out in the name of the peasants and

workers, but it served only the summit and never resulted in a social revolution . . .

. . . There is no doubt that anyone who writes the history of this period will say that the Sixties were nothing but years of defeat and pain . . .

The far-reaching reassessment of the ASU undertaken by Mar'ai in 1972 can be seen more as an effort to discredit the old edifice than to put anything new in its place. Nonetheless the effort would have logically led to a major reorganization had it not been for Sadat's preoccupations with Israel and the Soviet presence in Egypt. In March 1973 Sadat became his own prime minister and moved Mar'ai out of the ASU, replacing him with a relatively unknown law professor, Hafiz Ghanim. In August of that year a joint committee of the ASU and the People's Assembly issued a report known as the Dialogue Paper, that was to be the basis for discussion between committee members and leaders of the various "corps" of the nation. That discussion never materialized as the clock wound down toward the Egyptian assault on the Bar Lev line.

The whole issue was revived with the issuance of the October Paper in April 1974. Having established his image as a national leader in his own right and not simply Nasser's heir, Sadat could turn to institutional change. The October Paper called for the overhaul of the ASU. In August of 1974 a new document, the Paper on the Evolution of the ASU, was circulated for the purpose of a national debate.[1]

The text demonstrated plainly that Sadat was not interested in sweeping changes. The president stated that the three principal errors committed in the name of the ASU in the past were: 1) its nominally optional membership had been seen by most citizens as compulsory; 2) the power centers had imposed their own notions of single-party organization upon the alliance of working forces; and 3) the ASU was so intimately linked to the executive that it could in no way censure government policy and thus rightly appeared to most Egyptians to be the mouthpiece of the authorities.

Sadat made no specific recommendations in his paper, but he did offer some suggestions as to how the ASU could be made a more effective political organization. It might be advisable to separate the presidency from the ASU. Further, it might be possible to allow for several poles of thought to develop within the ASU, and these in turn might be reflected in the press. Membership should probably become meaningfully optional so that only the motivated would join. Sadat suggested that the whole issue of collective membership needed close examination. Leadership at all levels of the ASU pyramid should be directly elected by their peers and the number of appointments greatly reduced. With these few suggestions, the president turned the whole matter

[1] The treatment of this debate is based on Waterbury 1978a, pp. 252-55.

over to a "Listening Committee" (*Lagnat-il-Istima'*) under Mahmud Abu Wafia, a member of parliament and the president's brother-in-law.

The Listening Committee hearings, conducted during the last three weeks in September 1974, were fascinating both for the substantive issues debated and for the skillful stage-managing that underlay them. Ahmad Baha al-Din, at that time managing editor of *al-Ahram*, set the tone for the opening of the hearings. He noted that Egypt's long and not inglorious experience under a parliamentary, multiparty system had rendered the nation undeniable services. While the process might work itself out over a long period, Baha al-Din implied that a return to such a regime should be open for consideration. The first meetings of the Listening Committee were devoted to the same themes.

The committee, mostly in the person of Abu Wafia, had defined its task as simply recording the diverse views of the members of various functional groups that were invited to appear before it. The first groups consisted of intellectuals, writers, and the press. Such disparate figures as Mustapha Amin and Fikri Abaza on the right traded ideas with Salah 'Issa and Yussef Idriss on the left. Curiously all were fairly unanimous in their disillusionment with the ASU and, significantly, in their hope that Egypt would once again enjoy a multiparty system. Salah 'Issa declared "I am one of those who believe that the ASU has failed and cannot be saved no matter what we try." At the same time he rejected the notion of an organized two-party system as an arbitrary infringement on the freedom of the people. He urged instead that either parties be allowed to form freely or that the ASU be kept as it is despite its faults. 'Issa may have been articulating a generally held Marxist sentiment that the 1965 dissolution of their party and their integration into the ASU on an individual basis had done considerable damage to their image. A multiparty system could give them the opportunity to reorganize legally, even though it would give the same right to conservative forces such as the Amin brothers.

After the press and urban intellectuals, the Listening Committee heard representatives of various professional unions and associations, such as the engineers and the doctors. They took up where the others had left off and some went so far as to call for the dissolution of the ASU (Mustapha Barad'ai, head of the Lawyers Union), open presidential elections, the formation of a legal opposition, and scrupulously free elections to parliament. All the middle classes' pent-up liberalism, like all their pent-up consumerism, seemed to be released at once. But even as the educated urban middle classes of Cairo and Alexandria dominated the debate, countertrends began to manifest themselves. Hafiz Badawi, at that time speaker of the People's Assembly, organized a special meeting of the Listening Committee in Suhag Province. There the rural masses affirmed their support of the ASU, although with some modifications, their conviction that the head of the ASU and the president of the Republic must be one in the same person, and their feeling that any more talk of abolishing the guaranteed 50 percent or more representation of peasants and workers in all elected positions in the country would be deeply resented. This warning was directed at several urban intellectuals who had contested the utility of the 50 percent representation clause in effect since 1962.

The counterthrust developed more momentum after September 15. Successive meetings of peasant groups insisted on the safeguarding of the alliance of working forces, seeing in the appeals for a multiparty system a lightly veiled pretense for counterrevolutionary forces to eat away at the "benefits of the revolution": peasant-worker representation, land reform, growth of the public sector, worker-management councils, profit-sharing, free education, and the like. Up to this point, the staging of the hearings was such that a number of radical departures from the prevailing political formula had been amply aired and thus given some legitimacy. They were out in the open, and without endorsing any of them, Sadat could hold them in reserve and if need be reintroduce them later. At the same time, the masses were brought forth to remind the intellectuals of their isolation and to insist upon the need for continuity with the past. The shift was reflected in the editorials of Baha al-Din. After initially praising Egypt's multiparty past, he came out, on September 24, strongly in favor of maintaining the alliance of working forces and developing a "multiplicity of *minbars*" (platforms) within that framework.

Next came the labor unions, and their representatives thundered away on all themes advanced by the peasants, adding some biting attacks on the whole purpose of the debate. They vociferously rejected a multiparty system and accused named forces, in particular the Amin brothers, of wanting to abolish not only guaranteed worker representation but the very principles of the July 23 Revolution. One anonymous voice from the floor demanded to know the significance of the president's brother-in-law directing these hearings, while at various other times unidentified voices attacked their own union leaders as puppets of the regime who had been only too willing in the past to neglect the true interests of the working masses. At this stage it was abundantly clear that the intellectual Marxists, speaking in the name of the proletariat and calling for multipartyism, were overruled by the workers themselves who remained loyal to the ASU. Moreover, the union leadership was reminded of the weakness of its own legitimacy and the fact that they had traditionally been handpicked by the executive branch of government. In short, the liberals on the left and right were held in check, but those who did the checking could not express themselves except through the regime's own men.

The final episode in the hearings came with the university professors, students, and feminist organizations. The professors reflected a variety of positions, but the women and the students were nearly unanimous in their denunciation of all attempts to tamper with the benefits of the revolution. Granted, the students were consulted within the context of 'Ain Shams University's annual colloquium on Nasserist thought, and there was thus surely a strong element of self-selection among committed Nasserists, but no other student bodies tried to refute them afterward. The students were warned by Kamal Abu al-Magd, minister of information, that they must distinguish between revolutionary Nasserism and Sufistic Nasserism. He implied by the latter term that Nasserism was becoming a sort of mystic cult for some student groups. The warning was ignored as the students voted a series of resolutions that called for strengthening the ASU, strengthening the public sector, affirming the inviolability of the principle of 50 percent worker-peasant representation, and accelerating the pace of socialist transformation. With respect to foreign affairs, they recommended closer relations with "progressive" regimes, stronger support for the Palestinians, and affirmation of the principle of nonrecognition of Israel. All this was laced with constant attacks upon Mustapha and 'Ali Amin, symbols of the right-wing press (*Akhbar al-Yom*).

After the hearings were terminated, the committee disbanded pending submission of a report to President Sadat, who remained inscrutably silent about the future for a number of months. He obviously had more pressing matters, in the form of Kissinger's shuttle diplomacy, with which to contend. The major findings of the Listening Committee were published in December 1974, but were as tentative as the original paper on the evolution of the ASU. Moreover, the report did not make any new suggestions, repeating the recommendations that optional membership be affirmed, several forums for debate opened up, and free elections be allowed at all levels. It did state, somewhat surprisingly, that only a minority of those who authored the report advocated separation of the presidency of the Republic from the presidency of the ASU. In April 1975, Sadat removed Hafiz Ghanim as first secretary of the Central Committee (he was appointed minister for higher education), replacing him with Dr. Rifa'at Mahgub, another law professor who had been in charge of ideology in the ASU. Mahgub set about preparing for top-to-bottom elections in the ASU, to be held in July 1975.

While temporarily safeguarding the integrity of the ASU and the alliance, Sadat reminded each one of its constituent parts of their vulnerability by allowing them to be subjected to a great amount of well-founded criticism. But the critics themselves were contained and given only minimal satisfaction.

Sectarian Conflict

In retrospect it appears that Sadat must have anticipated most of his political opposition from the left in the form of Nasserists, Marxists, and assorted radical students. He may have overestimated their potential, but given the disturbances of 1972 and 1973 that is understandable. To contain that threat, Sadat began to unleash the forces of religion, ranging from Muslim Brethren to supporters of Libya's Mu'ammar Qaddafi. The forces at play, which the president soon dubbed the "adventurous left" and the "reactionary right," cut across the alliance of working forces and threatened Egypt's national unity.

Like most of Sadat's political balancing acts, manipulation of religious groups and themes proved extremely difficult. Nasser, as we have seen, was compelled to repress the Ikhwan in both 1954 and 1965. Egypt's Copts, however, representing some 10 percent of the population, were relatively quiescent.[2] They absorbed the blow of the abolition of religious courts in 1955. The unified legal codes that were applied to all Egyptians thereafter reflected the *shari'a* more than any other legal source. Coptic leaders may have chosen to lie low in the face of Egypt's military and uniformly Muslim leaders and accept the token cabinet-level appointments that Nasser doled out (Kamal Ramzi Stino in the Ministry of Supply was a perennial favorite). In 1965 it was alleged that a Coptic separatist movement had been uncovered, aided by Israel and the USA, but that was the only major incident of Coptic unrest in the Nasser years.

Sadat was not so fortunate. Muslim and Coptic militancy were both on the rise at the advent of his incumbency, the first stimulated by his own policies of containing the left, and the second in reaction to this trend. Moreover, the election in November 1971 of a new and younger patriarch of the Coptic Church, Pope Shanuda, signaled an end to Christian quiescence. During 1972, especially in the summer, clashes between Muslims and Copts occurred in many areas of Egypt. There were many pretexts for them, involving alleged Christian proselytization and the operation of "illegal" Christian churches. They prompted the passage of a "National Unity Law" (text in Badawi 1980, pp. 127-29) in September 1972. This law made punishable any efforts "that expose national unity to danger by resort to violence, threats, or any other illegal means to thwart the official policies of the state or to affect its political and constitutional institutions . . ."

Despite this legislation serious clashes broke out in Khanqa, near Cairo, in November 1972, and a parliamentary commission was formed to investigate their causes. The commission was evenhanded in its conclusions, which in a way was a victory for the Copts. In particular administrative obstacles to the construction of churches were partially removed, thereby satisfying one of the principal Coptic demands.[3]

This conciliatory gesture, coupled with the nonspecific but threatening

[2] The 1976 census gave a figure of 2,264,250 Copts for all of Egypt or about 6 percent of the total population. Church officials are sure the real figure is more like five million.

[3] For background on contemporary Coptic-Muslim relations, see Wakin 1963; Hanna 1980; Badawi 1980; J. P. Peroncel-Hugoz, "Coptes d'Egypte," *Le Monde*, November 25 and 26, 1977. The Parliamentary Commission was chaired by Gamal al-'Utaifi and included three Copts: Rushdi Said, Albert Barsum Salama, and Muhib Stino. Its report was published in *al-Akhbar*, November 29, 1972.

clauses of the National Unity Law, may have been sufficient to defuse further Coptic agitation for awhile. Muslim activism, however, was on the rise. The ostensibly close ties to Libya up to September 1973 obliged Sadat to tolerate a fair degree of Qaddafite Islamic propaganda among students and parliamentarians. The shift to Saudi patronage after the October War merely opened the way to Muslim influence of a more conservative kind. One result was that some Egyptian legislators began to lobby energetically for making the *shari'a* the sole source of law in the country. This mood culminated in the deliberation by parliament of a draft law that would have made apostasy punishable by death. The Copts were particularly threatened by this because it was not uncommon for Copts to convert to Islam in order to marry Muslim women and to revert to Christianity upon death or divorce of the spouse. Pope Shanuda called for five days of fasting in September 1977 to protest the general drift toward Islamic exclusivism, and Prime Minister Mamduh Salim had the law withdrawn.

The powerful currents of Islamic revivalism emanating from Iran put most leaders of Muslim countries on the defensive vis-à-vis Muslim fundamentalists in their own countries. Sadat was no exception. The growing prominence of Muslim groups was menacing to the Christian community, and Coptic émigrés embarassed Sadat during a trip to Washington in early May 1980 by denouncing Muslim fanaticism. In his annual May 15 (Corrective Revolution anniversary) speech, Sadat lashed out at the Coptic leadership for creating "a state within the state." He asserted that there could be "no politics in religion and no religion in politics" but then submitted to referendum a constitutional amendment that would make the *shari'a* the *sole*, rather than the *principal* source of legislation. The clause was approved by 98.8 percent of the voters, which, if we are to believe the figure, means that most Copts voted for it as well. In any event, while Coptic leaders had been publicly chastised, Muslim leaders had been given a thinly veiled warning.

Modulating the revival of Islamic political activism became a major challenge to Sadat's political skills. In 1975 he authorized the Muslim Brotherhood to undertake legal activities once again, and their two publications, *al-Da'wa* and *al-'Itisam*, soon captured a broad audience. It is likely that the Saudis had urged this legitimation of the Ikhwan. Further, the Saudis had good access to al-Azhar University through its *shaikh*, Dr. 'Abd al-Halim Mahmud who, among other things, became a firm opponent of liberalized personal status law and an equally firm enemy of anything smacking of Marxism or socialism. In an exchange of articles with 'Abd al-Rahman al-Sharqawi, the editor of *Ruz al-Yussef*, Dr. Mahmud argued that there was nothing un-Islamic about disparities in wealth in Muslim society and tarred as crypto-Communists all those who advocated state intervention to promote egalitarian redistribution. Qoranic prescriptions regarding the tithe and alms are, he contended, sufficient to ensure social justice (see for instance *RY*, no. 2463, August 25, 1975).

Parallel to the Ikhwan and al-Azhar there emerged in the middle 1970s radical Muslim groups that rejected the entire political system and indeed the society itself. The best-known of these was the Repentance and Holy Flight group (Takfir wal-Higra) that had been implicated under another name in an attempted coup d'état involving cadets at the military academy in April 1974. In July 1977 members of the group kidnapped the minister of religious endowments (Awqaf) and demanded the release of all those arrested in connection with the 1974 incident. Their demands were not met, and they assassinated the minister, Muhammed al-Dahabi. The leader of the group, Ahmad Shukri Mustapha, was arrested with several others and eventually executed.

Political activism by Muslim groups is particularly hard to contain because the symbols and themes they employ enjoy such widespread legitimacy. Imagine the plight of judge and prosecution when a dozen or so accused interrupt court proceedings to prostrate themselves toward Mecca. Because of the mood in the Arab world, the sources of Egypt's regional support, and the president's own religious beliefs, bold repression of such activities was avoided until the summer of 1981. Instead Sadat tried to combat the Muslim militants with religion. After the death of 'Abd al-Halim Mahmud in 1978, the president regained some control over al-Azhar and could then use this prestigious institution to condemn the radicals. It is entirely possible that the president thought of applying the Apostasy Law against groups like Takfir wal-Higra, which the Azhari establishment could with some plausibility accuse of having stepped outside the faith.

His efforts lacked credibility. Increasingly Muslim groups, in print and in private, seized upon the various humiliations inflicted upon Egypt by Menachem Begin's one-sided interpretation of the Camp David peace process. Coupled with this were the protests against creeping Westernism, loose morals especially among women, and high-level corruption. These themes had been the stock in trade of Shi'ite opposition to the shah, and they found a ready audience in Egypt.

The most active and potentially dangerous elements among the fundamentalists were secondary school and university students organized in the "Islamic Associations" (al-Gama'at al-Islamiyya). Although representing a minority among students they gained control of student organizations in virtually all Egyptian universities. These Associations served as umbrellas for Muslim activists of widely differing philosophies. What joined them was enmity toward the regime and the desire to bring it down.[4]

---

[4] Some of the best treatments of this question are: Davis 1982; Saad Ibrahim, "Anatomy of Egypt's Militant Islamic Groups," MESA Conference, October 1980; Nazih Ayubi, "The Political Revival of Islam: The Case of Egypt," MESA Conference, Washington, D.C., October 1980.

There were clear hints throughout the spring of 1981 that Sadat would adopt measures to bring all Islamic Associations under close police and administrative surveillance. Of great concern in this respect were the 27,000 ''popular'' mosques that were spontaneously initiated and in which the ulema and imams could preach on themes of their own choosing no matter how hostile to state policies. The media frequently cited the need to bring these mosques under control.

The building confrontation was hastened by the bloody Coptic-Muslim clashes of June 17, 1981 in the Cairo suburb of al-Zawia al-Hamra. The causes were unclear but apparently involved Muslim protests at the construction of a church on an empty lot that the Muslims felt had been promised them for a mosque. The clashes officially left ten dead and sixty wounded. Jean-Pierre Peroncel-Hugoz claimed (*Le Monde*, October 8, 1981) that "Coptic infants were thrown from windows or burned alive with their parents."

Once order was restored, it was only a question of time before Sadat moved against the Muslim groups. He believed that not only had they provoked the clashes but, on the basis of information supplied by the minister of interior, Nabawi Isma'il, were conspiring to overthrow the regime. At the time, the latter allegations were not deemed credible by most observers. After Sadat's assassination, and the revelation of the penetration of the armed forces and police by the extremists, it looked rather that Sadat had underestimated his adversaries.

After a visit to Washington in early August and a meeting with Begin later in the month, Sadat proceeded on September 5 to arrest 1,536 Egyptians. All but a hundred or so (whom we will discuss below) were labeled as religious extremists, both Muslim and Coptic. There was some speculation that Sadat was responding to proddings from Begin to disarm the most vocal critics of Camp David. Be that as it may, ten Muslim associations and three Christian were dissolved. Seven publications were suspended including those of the Ikhwan. The overwhelming majority of those arrested were Muslims. Among them were 'Umar Tlamsani, the head of the Ikhwan, and Shaikh 'Abd al-Hamid Kishk whose writings on Islam circulated throughout the Arab world. Sadat simultaneously removed Pope Shanuda from the patriarchate and suspended five Coptic bishops. There had never been any love lost between Sadat and Shanuda, but the assault on the Coptic Church can best be seen as a gesture toward evenhandedness and an attempt to disarm Muslim opinion at home and abroad.

After the arrests *al-Mayo* (September 7, 1981), the official newspaper of Sadat's National Democratic Party, published biographical information on twenty-seven leaders of the Islamic Associations (referred to by their followers as Amirs, prince or commander). None were over thirty, all were employed, mostly in the public sector, and they included schoolteachers and doctors.

Only one was from Cairo. The general commander (Amir 'Am) was Hilmi Sa'ir 'Abd al-'Aziz al-Gazzar, born in the Delta town of Sirs al-Layyan in 1955. As a student he was head of the al-Gama'at al-Islamia at Cairo University. At the time of his arrest he was a practicing physician in a general hospital.

On September 12 Sadat, as had become his custom, put his acts up for plebescitary approval through referendum and received 99.4 percent of the votes in support of the arrests. With this expression of the general will, he warned those still at large that he knew there were 7,000 extremists at liberty and that unless they mended their ways they too would be arrested. Instead, on October 6, while he presided over the annual military parade in celebration of the October War, Sadat was gunned down by at least four Muslim extremists, with the backing of an unidentified number of coconspirators. Within hours of Sadat's death, bloody clashes occurred at Assiut, and on a lesser scale at Mansura.

In the massive arrests that followed the assassination (2,500 fundamentalists according to minister of interior, Nabawi Isma'il) the same type of militant activist showed up frequently. They were in their twenties, fairly well-educated and often from provincial towns and cities. First Lieutenant Khalid Islambuli, a member of Takfir wal Higra, identified as the leader of the assassination squad, is fairly typical. His brother had been among those arrested on September 5; yet Khalid was chosen by his superiors to lead a unit in the military parade. As mentioned in Chapter Twelve, he was aided by Tariq and 'Abbud Zumr, young members of an old family of rural gentry.

How deeply the fundamentalists have penetrated Egyptian society and, more importantly, the armed forces and police, is moot. There was probably some tendency on the part of embarrassed senior officers to cover up the extent of such penetration. But whatever Egyptians may have thought about Sadat, the bulk, I would surmise, approved neither of the objectives nor of the methods of the extremists. The "bearded ones" as they became known were seen as thoroughly un-Egyptian and thoroughly un-Islamic. More secular politicians who thought they could form tactical alliances with Muslim groups on certain issues (Camp David, reliance on the US, etc.) were quickly and perhaps definitively disabused of that notion.

Manabir

In the midst of Sadat's ultimately fatal skirmishes with Muslim activists, he finally moved to abolish the ASU and to introduce Egypt to a multiparty system. One facet of this evolution was the new legitimacy bestowed upon the parliament[5] of which Sadat for many years had been the speaker. The first parliamentary elections under Sadat were held in November 1971, and the new MPs emphasized the fact that they were directly and "popularly" elected to their seats while noting that ASU representatives at all levels were often indirectly elected or appointed. The parliament therefore became the symbol of the return to a more democratic and liberal style. With skilled management of parliamentarians like Sayyid Mar'ai and Gamal al-'Utaifi, Sadat was able to orchestrate debates on fairly sensitive issues. In Chapter Six it was noted that for the first time, in 1973, the accounts of selected public sector companies were made available to the Budget and Plan Committee of parliament. In the same year, P.M. 'Aziz Sidqi's proposed program for government action was roundly criticized (although approved) by 'Utaifi and others. Important national projects, such as the construction of an oil pipeline from Suez City to a point west of Alexandria (SUMED as it became known) were subjected to close scrutiny. In 1976 the Central Auditing Agency was made directly responsible to the parliament. In sum, the national legislature was given some limited autonomy lending credence to Sadat's intention of making Egypt "a state of institutions."

After issuing the October Paper and staging the debates on the future of the ASU, Sadat moved toward liberalization with some confidence. What we find in the years between 1975 and 1977 is a curious replication of the situation prevailing in the period 1965-1967. In that period Nasser found himself pursuing divergent objectives of socialist intensification and economic retrenchment. In the later period, Sadat was under heavy external pressure to introduce policies of economic austerity just as he moved to ease constraints on open political activity. In both instances political goals had to be subordinated to economic imperatives, although Sadat tried to honor some of his commitments to liberalization. His retreat, however, did not come until after the riots of January 1977.

The ASU elections of July 1975 did not signify the renewal of the organization but rather its death knell. Even at the time of the elections, leftist commentators associated with the ASU questioned the increasing "rightist" pressure for the creation of autonomous parties (al-Tali'a 1975c).

The issue hinged on the creation of platforms (manabir) within the ASU to express diverse opinions within the alliance of working forces. The first meeting of the ASU National Congress after the July elections gave the green light to the formation of platforms. Some forty ASU members leapt into the arena, sponsoring manabir of all shapes and hues including one called the Akhnaton Platform. The Executive Committee of the ASU, led by Rifa'at

---

[5] I use this term to refer to the two names used in Egypt. From 1957-1971 the legislature was known as the Maglis al-Umma (Council of the Nation) and from 1971 to the present as the Maglis al-Sha'ab, or People's Council.

Mahgub, by December 1975 narrowed the field to four (programs in *al-Tali'a* 10 [December 1975]):

"Right": Socialist Liberals led by Mustapha Kamal Murad
"Left": Progressive Nationalists; Khalid Muhi al-Din
"Nasserists": Kamal Ahmad Muhammed
"Center": Socialist Democrats; Mahmud Abu Wafia

The center was for all intents and purposes Sadat's platform. The right stressed the need for renewed private sector activity and promotion of *infitah*. The separation of Nasserists from the left signified a suspicion on the part of the former of the subordination of Egyptian Marxists to Moscow and their presumed belief in the inevitability of class warfare. While both currents have occasionally come together since 1975, the mix has always been uneasy. What they share is a concern for social and economic equity, protecting the public sector, suspicion of the USA, and hostility to the private sector bourgeoisie.

Early in 1976 Sayyid Mar'ai was entrusted with the task of convening a committee made up of 168 parliamentarians, ASU members, and "opinion leaders" to define the nature of political life in the new era. After a month of meetings and hearings, it produced a Report on the Future of Political Action which recommended limiting the political arena to three tendencies that they called organisms (*tanzims*). These were endorsed by Sadat himself on March 14, 1976, and were authorized to contest the parliamentary elections scheduled for October 1976. The only significant change in the new alignment was that the Marxist left and the Nasserists were grouped within a single *tanzim*.

Elections and the Formation of Parties

As Egypt prepared for its first openly contested elections in nearly twenty-five years, the center organization, now known as the Tanzim of Arab Socialist Egypt, was clearly although unofficially the president's party. His prime minister, Mamduh Salim, headed it, and most of the cabinet ran for seats under its banner. The media were at its disposal, and the civil service and public sector work force were assumed to be a captive electorate.

The "Egypt Party," as the president's coalition became known, won an overwhelming majority in parliament, taking 280 of 352 seats. The left won only two seats (Khalid Muhi al-Din was one of the winners) and the right only twelve. The biggest surprise was the election of forty-eight Independents who ran individually and were unaffiliated with any of the three tendencies.[6]

[6] The Independents included several prominent figures of very diverse backgrounds: Kamal al-Din Hussain, former member of the RCC; Kamal Hilmi Murad, former member of the Socialist Party who resigned from Nasser's cabinet in 1968; Ahmad Yunis, fired as head of the Agricultural

Finally, President Sadat appointed ten MPs, including eight Copts and two women. Ironically one of those appointed was Mustapha Khalil whom Sadat had placed at the head of the ASU, replacing Rifa'at Mahgub. The other major surprise was that of 9.5 million eligible voters only 3.8 million actually voted (*al-Tali'a* 12 [December 1976] and 13 [January 1977]).

Sadat, having destroyed the centers of power, now established the power of the center. With a comfortable and manipulable majority in parliament, he quickly took two decisive steps in Egypt's political reorganization. On January 2, 1977, official permission was extended to found political parties, and on January 10, First Secretary Mustapha Khalil announced the abolition of all organizations under the aegis of the ASU except for the Women's Organization. All that remained of the superstructure was a Central Committee in suspended animation. This marked the official demise of the ASU and it was carried out without convening any of its governing bodies. That, as much as any other action, demonstrated that there were no institutional guts to the ASU, no vested interests that would resist dissolution. What had been created by the top was abolished by the top.

The fall of 1976 and the first two weeks of January 1977 were the heyday of Sadat's liberal experiment. The press was remarkably free in its coverage; the television, now in the hands of the new minister of information, Gamal al-'Utaifi, televised lively and significant debates among top policy-makers, and the new parliamentarians took their role seriously. In fact on November 14, 1976, at the Sidna Hussain mosque in Cairo, the Independent MPs met and declared themselves the real opposition in the parliament, dismissing Kamal Murad and his Liberals as puppets.

The moment was short-lived, and economics overtook the political process. In the winter of 1976, the government of Mamduh Salim had begun negotiating a standby agreement with the IMF (see Chapter Seventeen) that would have entailed the implementation of a stabilization program. At the heart of that program would have been measures to reduce government spending and the subsidies of basic consumer goods. The minister of economy, Zaki Shafa'i, was in favor of moving ahead with the program as Egypt was in desperate need of foreign exchange to cover the short-term debt. Ahmad Abu Isma'il, the minister of finance and a man who was to run for parliament, counseled Sadat to postpone the implementation of the stabilization program until after the elections. This Sadat decided to do. In the new government formed after the elections 'Abd al-Mun'aim al-Qaissuni was made deputy prime minister for the economy and was given the green light to go ahead with Egypt's pledges to the IMF. On January 18, 1977, Qaissuni went before parliament

---

Coops Federation for corruption; Dr. No, Mahmud al-Qadi; Ahmad Taha, perennial communist M.P. from Shubra; the thirty-five year old leader of the Nasserists, Kamal Ahmad; and the former Wafdist minister 'Abd al-Fattah Hassan.

to announce a reduction in subsidies of a limited range of consumer goods (see Chapter Ten), and the next day massive rioting broke out up and down the Nile Valley.

Faced with visible fissures in the surface of Egyptian society, Sadat had to begin a cautious and uneven retreat from his liberalization programs. Even before the riots, the regime had laid down fairly restrictive conditions for the formation of political parties. These were finally incorporated in the Parties Law of May 1977 and included the following stipulations:

1) The party's principles must be clearly distinguished from those of the three existing parties.
2) Principles must be in accord with those of the Charter, the permanent constitution, and the October Paper.
3) No party may be founded on a class, sectarian, or geographic basis, nor upon sex or race.
4) Party members cannot come from the judiciary, officers' corps, military recruits, or police.
5) The party can have no foreign sources of funds.
6) It requires at least twenty MPs to found a party.
7) Authorization of new parties will be determined by a special committee consisting of the first secretary of the ASU, the ministers of justice and interior, the president of the Conseil d'Etat and two former heads of the judiciary appointed by the president. The special committee can dissolve any party if its leaders are convicted of crimes involving threats to "the social peace" or to national unity, the rejection of "the necessity of the socialist solution," or the alliance of working forces.

Despite these restrictions, members and sympathizers of the old Wafd Party held a boisterous meeting on May 23, 1977 and on June 1 announced their intention of reestablishing the party. Out of a quarter-century of obscurity and calumny came Fu'ad Serrag al-Din, the unofficial leader of the right wing of the party before 1952, a pasha from the old ruling elite, but for all that imbued with all the legitimacy and nostalgia that the party's name, and those of Zaghlul and Nahhas, could evoke. To a youthful audience the septuagenarian Serrag al-Din made a vigorous defense of the old Wafd, and belittled the July 1952 movement as a coup (*inqilab*) and not a revolution. That term, he said, could be used in the twentieth century only to describe the great uprising of 1919 when Zaghlul was sent into exile. He stressed all the traditional antimilitarist themes of his party (Serrag al-Din 1977).

Sadat and Mamduh Salim were deeply disturbed by this specter from the past. As the New Wafd began to line up potential members among MPs, the president and his prime minister denounced Serrag al-Din and his allies as "feudalists" and "cadavers." Nonetheless the Wafd picked up the required support among the independent MPs, eventually coming up with twenty-six members, including Hilmi Murad. On February 4, 1978 the party was given formal authorization to undertake political activities. It immediately cast itself in the role of the true opposition, criticizing in particular the corruption and speculation accompanying *infitah*. Some observers felt that the New Wafd would appeal to local manufacturers and entrepreneurs hit hard by foreign competition and the privileges granted foreign investors under Law 43. Sadat's trip to Jerusalem in the fall of 1977 and his overtures toward Israel also drew Wafdist criticism. In all this the party tried to escape its right-wing image. For instance, Professor Muhammed Anis, a well-known leftist historian from 'Ain Shams University and a former editor of the leftist review *al-Katib*, joined the new party as an official ideologue.

The party put Sadat's commitment to democracy to the test and it was found wanting. The regime began to harass the Wafd in various ways. In late March, for example, the centrist majority in parliament voted to expel the Wafdist MP, Shaikh 'Ashur Muhammed Nasr, for having "insulted" President Sadat in public session. In May Sadat attacked parliamentary critics as unconstructive and as people who pervert parliamentary life. A national referendum on political isolation was hastily arranged for May 21, 1978 that had the effect of denying political rights to all those tried and convicted for corruption in 1953: i.e. Fu'ad Serrag al-Din. The referendum yielded the desired results, and on June 1 parliament, with only ten dissenting votes, approved the implementing legislation. The following day the Wafd, in protest, dissolved itself, and a few weeks later, 'Abdal-Fattah Hassan of the Wafd was expelled from parliament. Those months revealed the weapons upon which Sadat came to rely: a tame majority in parliament and multipoint national referendums.

The economic and international challenges facing Sadat at this time were formidable. He was seeking an accord with Israel that was sure to meet with an as-yet-unknown level of internal and regional hostility. Second, his government was trying to reach an accord with the IMF for a three-year "extended facility" that would unavoidably require a reduction in subsidies and government spending. To move on both fronts while permitting significant political freedom internally looked like squaring the circle.

On the one hand, Sadat was not happy with his own majority, which patently lacked credibility. Likewise, with the Wafd out of the way, it was important that something more substantial than Kamal Murad's Liberals take over the opposition.

At the end of July 1978 Sadat announced his intention of founding a new "national democratic" party and to hold another round of parliamentary elections within a year. The president had first begun to talk of a new "ideology,'' that he referred to as ''democratic socialism,'' in May 1977. Sayyid Mar'ai, as usual, formed yet another committee to elaborate the president's ideas (*A*, May 24, 1977), but it was the rector of Cairo University, Sufi Abu Talib, who did most of the packaging (J. P. Peroncel-Hugoz, *Le Monde*, October 31, 1978).

Interim arrangements were undertaken in August 1978 to launch the new party, and at the beginning of September, the National Democratic Party published its program (*AI*, no. 553, September 1, 1978). There was little new in it, and for the most part sewed together slogans that Sadat had made familiar over the years. For the record the basic goals were:

1) the building of a modern state founded in science and faith;
2) the affirmation of spiritual values;
3) the reconciliation of individual and collective interests;
4) the affirmation of national unity and social peace;
5) striving for Arab unity;
6) the *shari'a* is the *principal* source of law.

Perhaps of greater significance was that the rare references to socialism were always accompanied by the adjective ''democratic.'' The public sector was discussed only in terms of increasing its productivity and freeing it of bureaucratic red tape. The private sector was to be liberated so long as it honored national economic objectives and safeguarded social peace. With respect to agriculture, the program stipulated that reclaimed lands were to be sold to proprietors, agricultural institute graduates, and the landless. In an earlier summary of the party's objectives, the president had probably come closer to the heart of the matter than the official program: the two main goals, he said, were enough food for every Egyptian and a house for every family (London *Times*, August 16, 1978).

Simultaneous with the birth of the NDP, the president encouraged Ibrahim Shukri, a Socialist Party MP before 1952 and in 1978 the minister of agriculture, to launch a new opposition party that became known as the Socialist Labor Party. Then in October 1978, Sadat removed Mamduh Salim from the prime ministership, and replaced him with Mustapha Khalil.[7] He also made himself chairman and appointed five principal secretaries in the NDP, most

---

[7] General Gamassi, the respected minister of defense, was also dropped from the October 1978 cabinet. It may have been that he was unhappy with Sadat's peace initiative. Or it may have been that Sadat wanted to prove to Begin that he was in full control of Egypt in that he could fire a popular senior officer as well as the man, Mamduh Salim, who had run the Ministry of Interior. Yet another interpretation is that Sadat had anticipated trouble in reaching peace with Israel and in implementing the IMF stabilization plan. He asked Gamassi to head a quasi-military government and Gamassi refused, thereby provoking Sadat's displeasure—or, again, that Gamassi agreed, but Sadat got cold feet when the coup occurred in Afghanistan.

prominent of whom were Mansur Hassan, a wealthy importer, and Makram Fikri 'Ubaid, a Copt and the son of Makram 'Ubaid who, until 1946, had been one of the principal leaders of the old Wafd. Sayyid Mar'ai, who had not wholly approved of Sadat's peace gambit, stepped down as speaker of parliament and was replaced by Sufi Abu Talib.

With the constitution of the Khalil government, Salah Hafiz (*RY*, no. 2629, October 30, 1978) pinpointed the importance of the moment. The question, he asserted, is "who owns Egypt?" and Mustapha Khalil's government, he noted, will be the first Egyptian government to face this question. Colonel 'Arabi failed to find the answer, Sa'ad Zaghlul fled from it, and Nasser left it unresolved. The distribution of wealth among Egyptians and between them and foreigners is the heart of the matter. Nasser was able to suppress the issue in the name of hostilities with Israel. But now, Hafiz pointed out: "the peace that is about to be realized in this part of the world, whatever its terms, will automatically lead to the reopening of the dossier that has been closed since the days of 'Arabi."

It was only a matter of months before Sadat signed the Camp David accords (March 1979) with Israel and the US and was then unambiguously faced with the question Hafiz outlined. Egypt was ostracized by the rest of the Arab world, and while peace in principle was popular among most Egyptians, their support was above all contingent upon improving economic conditions and second of all upon an "honorable" solution for the Palestinians. Sadat knew that quick progress was not likely on either front and set his defenses accordingly.

The first steps were yet two more referendums and new elections to parliament. The first referendum in April gave 99 percent approval to the Camp David accords. The second, multipoint referendum was held on May 21, 1979 and was overwhelmingly approved. Some of the points covered were: 1) freedom to found parties; 2) protection of national unity and social peace; 3) the constitution is the sole document upon which the state rests; 4) adherence to the principle of 50 percent representation for peasants and workers; 5) an end to partisan corruption and feudalism; 6) establishment of a Consultative Council representing all categories (*fi'at*) of the people; and 7) legalization of the press as the fourth power of the state (*A*, May 30, 1979).

Sadat's NDP then went on to a crushing victory in the elections held in early June. The party took 330 of 392 seats. Ibrahim Shukri's Socialist Labor Party won twenty-nine and Kamal Murad's Socialist Liberals won only three seats. Murad himself was defeated. So were many others who had in one way or another criticized Sadat. Khalid Muhi al-Din and his Unionist Progressive Party were entirely eliminated. Mahmud al-Qadi and Ahmad Taha, both of whom had been in every parliament since 1952, also went down to defeat. A number of establishment figures, like Gamal al-'Utaifi and Hilmi

Murad, declined to run (*A*, June 11, 1979; and *TME*, July 1979). The left, the Nasserists, and the religious right as embodied in the Ikhwan were excluded from this forum. By contrast Sadat appointed thirty women and ten Copts to the new legislature.

The only legal force that could trouble the president's arrangements was the Socialist Labor Party and surprisingly it did so. Ibrahim Shukri took his role seriously, and with his long parliamentary and political experience was able for a time to avoid crossing the invisible thresholds of permissible criticism. Like the New Wafd it concentrated on domestic economic policy and the errors of Sadat's approach to Israel and the Palestinians (see for example Hilmi Murad 1980). At first one might have assumed that Sadat was not averse to criticism of the latter kind, for he could use it to show Israel and the US the limits to his room for maneuver. But reality went well beyond this. The unfolding of the Iranian drama in the latter half of 1979 and in 1980 was graphic evidence to Egypt's middle classes of where the combination of sycophancy and megalomania could lead them. The Labor Party and its weekly newspaper *al-Sha'ab* (*The People*) became the symbols of the middle class refusal to abdicate. Shukri's organization became more than irritating; it became threatening. Once again Sadat turned to the referendum to outflank the bourgeoisie with an appeal to the masses. In May of 1980, after castigating the Coptic leadership as noted earlier, Sadat submitted to referendum measures that would allow him to seek reelection as often as he liked, that made the *shari'a* the *sole* source of legislation, that gave approval to setting up a Consultative Council that could foil what little parliamentary opposition Shukri et al. could muster, and that approved a new, sweeping political ethics code called the "Law of Shame" (*qanun al-'aib*). At the same time he took over the prime ministership himself and briefly suspended further negotiations with Israel.[8]

In a remarkable display of middle class and largely civilian protest to these procedures, over seventy prominent Egyptians signed two lengthy denunciations of Sadat's rule by referendum and his policy toward Israel (they were dated May 12 and June 15, 1980). In the first the authors charged:

> . . . we can claim in all honesty that the style in which Egypt is being governed today is not based on any specific form of government. While it is not an outright dictatorship, nazism, or fascism, neither is it a democracy nor even a pseudo-democracy. It has become pointless to discuss any decision, whether it is to support or criticize it, for no sooner is a random decision taken in one direction than it is replaced by another taken in a differrent direction.

[8] According to the Camp David accords, provisions for Palestinian home rule were to have been drawn up by May 26, 1980, but upon reaching that date the two sides were far apart.

Some of the signatories were to be expected, such as leftists like Isma'il Sabri 'Abdullah and Fu'ad Mursi, but the bulk were centrist or nonideological professionals who had in no way suffered under Sadat (e.g., Nur al-Din Tarraf, former minister of tourism, Zaki Hashim, or former Minister of Irrigation 'Abd al-'Azim Abu al-'Atta).[9] The signatories became known as the National Coalition, and from the time of their published denunciations they were marked men and women.

The response of the president was, as usual, on more than one front. Some months after the denunciations, 'Abd al-Salam al-Zayyat, who had stood by Sadat in May 1971, was briefly arrested and a book he had written on parliamentary life under Sadat confiscated and destroyed. The Consultative Assembly was duly appointed as a potential check to the parliament and put under the presidency of another university professor, Subhi 'Abd al-Hakim. The thoroughly docile press tried to impart some legitimacy to this new body. Finally, pressure was brought to bear on the Labor Party itself. In November of 1980 fourteen of the twenty-five Labor MPs were prevailed upon to resign from the party because, they said, it was no longer a constructive opposition. Then the party's newspaper found it increasingly difficult to obtain the newsprint it needed for publication. It appeared that the regime hoped the party would commit hara-kiri like the New Wafd before it.

Agents of Control

Just as the failure of Nasser's socialist mobilization had forced the regime to fall back on control by police, so too Sadat's inability to let liberalization run its course forced him to resort to various means of repression. But it cannot be overstressed that Sadat did not resurrect anything like the police apparatus that characterized Nasserist Egypt in the 1960s. In that sense liberalization was real.

Sadat continued the measures he first took after May 15, 1971. From 1972 on there could be no seizure of fixed or liquid assets without a court order, and the judiciary began to handle all contested sequestration cases. In July 1975 Sadat granted total amnesty to all political prisoners condemned before May 1971, and in 1976 voting rights were restored to some 5,500 citizens in "political isolation." In the ensuing years all those arrested in connection with the May 15 plot were released, culminating with the liberation of 'Ali Sabri in May 1981.

[9] For the record some of the other likely signatories were Kamal al-Din Hussain (RCC), 'Abd al-Latif Baghdadi (RCC), 'Abd al-Salam al-Zayyat, former minister of affairs Mahmud Riad, the leftist lawyer Nabil al-Hilali, Ahmad Taha, Mahmud al-Qadi, Dr. 'Aziz Sidqi, etc. More surprising were the likes of Galal Hamamsi and 'Abd al-Khaliq Shanawi, former minister of irrigation. Abu al-'Atta, be it noted, died a natural death in the fall of 1981.

But running parallel to these measures were others that belied Sadat's overriding concern for control. Membership in parliament, for example, proved to be a very relative kind of protection. Former RCC member Kamal al-Din Hussain, elected to parliament in November 1976, was outspoken in his criticism of Sadat's manipulation of the parliamentary center. Sadat's allies among the MPs censured Hussain and, on February 14, 1977, voted to expel him from parliament. Some weeks later the same majority decided that once expelled, an MP would not have the right to run again. A year later, in March 1978, the Wafdist MP Shaikh 'Ashur Muhammed Nasr was likewise expelled for attacking Sadat personally with regard to soaring food prices. In June of the same year, 'Abd al-Fattah Hassan was expelled because of his alleged links to corrupt elements prior to 1952.

Throughout these years and until 1980 the two-decade-old Emergency Law remained in force. Mamduh Salim (*A*, December 27, 1976) rejected appeals that it be suspended on the grounds that suspension would signify that Egypt had lost its will to resist Israel and that therefore it must remain in force until the final victory or an honorable peace had been achieved. By 1980 Sadat presumably believed that the latter stipulation had been fulfilled and the Emergency Law was suspended. But other laws restraining political life were put in its place.

Laws such as those on national unity or governing the formation of parties are deliberately vague in their wording and scope, leaving to those who apply the law great latitude in interpretation. In that sense the laws are supposed to be a deterrent, promoting self-censorship and prudent behavior before any possible transgression has been committed. In June 1978 the parliament approved a law directed at the opposition parties in parliament and at several journalists who had written or published critical articles abroad. This was the new law on political isolation that led to the self-destruction of the Wafd. One of the clauses of the law laid it down that access to positions of responsibility in the public administration, unions, the public sector, the media, or any other sector that "influences public opinion" would be denied to atheists. The law was an open invitation to a witch hunt.

The array of laws constraining political activity was apparently insufficient, and in May 1980 the Law of Shame was promulgated. The law was to protect the fundamental values of Egyptian society and to punish those who in any way violated them. Some of the offenses included (*Egypt Newsletter*, May 26-June 3, 1980):

Allowing children or youth to go astray by advocating the repudiation of popular religious, moral, or national values or by setting a bad example in public places.

Broadcasting or publishing gross or scurrilous words or pictures which could offend public sensibilities or undermine the dignity of the state or of its constitutional institutions.

All offenses were to be tried before a special Ethics Court and conviction would result in suspension of all political rights, house arrest, travel bans, and suspension of economic activities. Verdicts could not be appealed. The court was to be made up of four members of parliament and three counselors from the Court of Cassation. The first case to be brought before this court involved Sa'ad al-Din Shazli and a dozen other Egyptians who, from Libya, claimed responsibility for Sadat's killing. It was expected that several of those arrested in September 1981, but connected with the bloodshed at Zawia al-Hamra, would likewise be tried under the Law of Shame.

Under Sadat the police and intelligence apparatus erected by Nasser was not dismantled, but it certainly did not occupy center stage. Arbitrary arrests were ended, although persons could be held for up to forty days before formal charges were brought. For the most part the police became visible only at times of civilian unrest or protest, especially when students were involved. While more will be said about this below, the major episodes were in 1971, 1972, 1975, and 1977 and finally 1981. Otherwise the presence of the police was manifested through the prominence of high-ranking officials like Mamduh Salim, variously minister of interior and prime minister, or Hafiz Isma'il, the former head of General Intelligence who, until 1974, was Sadat's chief security advisor. The inability of the police to cope with the riots of January 1977 led to a major effort to improve their training and equipment as well as to increase their numbers.

Sadat's handling of the armed forces was more complicated. From the outset Sadat wanted the military out of politics and as much as possible out of the economy. Two early targets were Generals Fawzi, who sided with the leftists in May 1971, and Sadiq, whose strident denunciations of Soviet military advisors led to his dismissal in 1972. It was not so much the issue itself, for the advisors were sent home in July 1972, but this use of it to rally support within the armed forces that prompted his dismissal.

Sadat sought to enhance the image of the professional soldier. General Sa'ad al-Din Shazli was promoted to chief of staff in 1973 over the heads of thirty more senior officers. His reputation was founded solely on his relatively successful battlefront command in 1967. The October War itself refurbished the image of the armed forces as the defenders of the nation's territory, and the new professionalism was embodied in the person of General 'Abd al-Ghani Gamassi, who succeeded Shazli as chief of staff and eventually became a deputy prime minister and minister of defense.[10]

[10] General Sa'ad al-Din al-Shazli was dismissed as chief of staff in the middle of the October

It is instructive to compare Sadat's accession to the presidency and his showdown with the power centers with that of Husni Mubarak. It is testimony to the space that Sadat created around himself that Mubarak had no institutional satraps to fear. There was no entrenched military leader of the likes of General Fawzi, let alone Hakim 'Amir, who could have stood in Mubarak's path. Sadat had jailed Fawzi, arrested Sadiq, exiled Shazli, and retired Gamassi. A helicopter crash in the spring of 1981 killed Minister of Defense Badawi and a dozen senior officers. Similarly Sadat's National Democratic Party (see following chapter) had no leaders of the caliber nor with the organizational power of 'Ali Sabri. The party secretaries were more ward heelers than political infighters. They lacked all semblance of the organizational power or public image that would have allowed them to make a bid for power. Indeed they could not even aspire to be power brokers. Finally, the cabinet boasted no members who could have blocked Mubarak's path. Mamduh Salim, Isma'il Fahmi, Sayyid Mar'ai, and Ahmad Osman were all distant from the seat of power. When I asked who among the elite (as opposed to the religious fundamentalists) might oppose Mubarak, the only names cited were Ahmad Osman and Jihan Sadat. Mubarak thus reaped the benefits of the process of continuous decapitation that Sadat began in May 1971.

As conventional as the new role of the military may have appeared, Sadat could not ignore the possibility that certain elements might be tempted to seize power. Junior officers had tried to engineer an ill-conceived coup in October 1972, and in 1974, as noted, military cadets conspired with religious extremists to launch another abortive attempt. After the October War the second disengagement agreement with Israel in 1975 sat poorly with many of Egypt's senior officers, and to show them his solicitude, Sadat appointed Husni Mubarak, the commander of the Air Force in 1973, as his vice president. Thus a military man stood in the immediate line of succession.

Despite the return to the barracks, the role of the military in Sadat's Egypt remained ambiguous. Formal peace with Israel left the large Egyptian military machine without an identifiable mission but, as well, without its honor completely restored. Sadat had to make sure that his officers felt they had a meaningful role and the armaments with which to carry it out. The mission became that of policeman in the Red Sea and the Horn of Africa against Soviet and Cuban expansion and the new adversaries became Libya and Ethiopia. With such adversaries it was possible for Egypt to purchase advanced weaponry in the West and to keep the military busy planning for a new kind

---

War. He was later made ambassador to the UK and then to Portugal. In Lisbon, on April 2, 1980, he publicly resigned as ambassador, denounced Sadat for his dictatorial ways, his estrangement from the Soviet Union, and his pseudo-peace with Israel. He then announced the founding of a National Front in exile. While little has come of it to date, it is unlikely that Shazli would have taken this step without some support within the Egyptian armed forces.

of long-distance, highly mobile warfare. Yet two major questions remain and Mubarak must deal with both. First, the uncompleted peace process could drag the military into further confrontation with Israel (e.g., over the annexation of the Golan Heights), and economic circumstances, similar to those in January 1977, could force the military to protect the regime against its own civilians. Either eventually could undo Mubarak's regime.

It remains to consider the place of the administration and the public sector in Sadat's Egypt. Policy was consistent in at least two respects. First, the administration and above all the public sector were seen as useful vehicles for retaining the passive loyalty of a significant portion of the work force. This control would not be lightly traded away in the name of private enterprise or efficiency. Second, there was no effort to reduce the size of the public work force; rather hesitant steps were taken to reduce the rate at which it was growing.

Sadat recognized, however, that the public and civil service sectors had become cumbersome to the point of paralysis. Whether a question of *leger de main* or of a sincere desire to improve performance, there was a mounting effort to decentralize administrative activities, as much as anything to relieve Cairo's growing congestion. Decentralization policies were typically heralded as an "administrative revolution."

This revolution had been regularly proclaimed throughout the years of the republican regime but until 1977 it was more slogan than reality (see *AI*, no. 524, June 15, 1977). Typically the goals have been twofold: first, to disperse service personnel (housing, education, health) among the governorates, reducing the tutelary ministries in Cairo to skeleton crews; and, second, to build up local level planning capabilities and financial resources so that subregions can tailor their own development needs. These goals were pursued erratically. In 1974 Yahia Gamal was appointed to the new Ministry of Administrative Development which was to carry out the revolution. Both the ministry and the minister had disappeared by April 1975, although it was revived in November 1976 with the appointment of a minister of state for administrative development. Yet even that position was abolished as of October 1978.

The other institutional manifestation of administrative reform lay in the Ministerial Committee for Local Government (first presided over by Deputy Prime Minister Hafiz Ghanim in 1976) and the minister of state for local government, Muhammad Mahmud. These grew out of the Local Government Laws 57 of 1971 and 52 of 1975, and were confirmed when President Sadat launched the most recent administrative revolution in May 1977 (see Ayubi 1977). It has been through these institutions that decentralization has been most actively promoted. The effort has been given a considerable boost by USAID and to some extent by the IBRD, which have helped finance banks and funds designed to foster local initiative. All governors have been given ministerial rank and now deal directly with the prime minister. There is no doubt that the governorates have the statutory authority to act independently of Cairo but it is unlikely that they yet have the financial wherewithal to underwrite that independence. Finally, if the past is any indicator, devolution may not curb the growth of the central bureaucracy but will certainly add to the size of local bureaucracies.

Big bureaucracy and the open-door policy have combined to nourish unprecedented amounts of high-level corruption. As under Nasser, tolerance of corrupt practices is both a privilege for and a means of control of the elite. The ever-present threat of exposure encourages political prudence if not servility. Throughout the 1970s accusations of corruption were bandied about and were used by high-powered officials to discredit their rivals. There were attempts to implicate 'Aziz Sidqi through accusations of embezzlement leveled at his clients, especially 'Abdullah Marziban. Hassan Mar'ai, the brother of Sayyid Mar'ai, was, in his capacity as head of the joint Egypt-Iranian Council, implicated in the purchase of overpriced Iranian Mercedes Benz buses. 'Abd al-'Aziz Higazi was dismissed as prime minister in 1975 after the president had made vague reference to high-level malfeasance. On occasion officials were exposed abroad, such as Minister of Energy Ahmad Sultan, who accepted a bribe from Westinghouse, and Arab affairs advisor to the president, Ashraf Marwan, who was named by Jim Hoagland in his series on Arab "money men" in the *Washington Post*.

Ahmad Osman, who had twice had to defend himself in parliament against charges of irregular purchases of construction steel and of nepotism, tried to turn the tables in his autobiography published in 1981. In it he resurrected the allegations that Nasser had illegally appropriated public funds, as well as those against Higazi whom he accused of accepting kickbacks from Kuwaiti investors. The parliament constituted a committee to investigate the charges, and it reported that it could not substantiate either. The president had clearly chosen to rap his most powerful counselor's knuckles, and Osman left his position as advisor to the president on food security.

The malodorous atmosphere around Sadat undoubtedly contributed to his growing estrangement from the Egyptian people in the last year of his incumbency. For example, former Minister of Power Ahmad Sultan was acquitted on a technicality of having accepted a bribe from Westinghouse. Ahmad Osman's attacks on such ill-chosen targets as Nasser's family and 'Abd al-'Aziz Higazi looked like a combination of arrogance and hypocrisy. Sadat's disavowal of the attacks could not mask his friendship for Osman. The last scandal involved an MP. Rashad Osman, a rags-to-riches businessman who had been in partnership with Asmat Sadat, a brother of the president. It became known that Rashad Osman had amassed a colossal fortune, £E 400 million by some accounts (*al-Sharq al-Awsat*, November 28, 1981), mainly in narcotics traffic. While Sadat was alive, Osman was investigated but not charged. After the assassination, however, he was referred to the Values Court that applies the Law of Shame. At the same time Cairo's newspapers began to run stories about shoddy construction in the Canal Zone for which Ahmad Osman was responsible. The newspapers noted that Ahmad Osman had backed Rashad Osman (no relation) for parliament. As Husni Mubarak was to do in other domains, through his actions toward both Osmans he marked his distance from his predecessor.

The Corporatist Alliance under Sadat

Despite high rates of inflation and the deteriorating situation of groups on fixed incomes, it was not the peasants, the workers, or even the civil servants that contested Sadat's policies most strenuously, but rather the students. On specific occasions that we shall examine, other groups, especially the lawyers and the press, made common cause with the students. At the beginning of his incumbency, Sadat was most concerned by leftist and Nasserist student groups that attacked his domestic and foreign policies, and to counter them he allowed Islamic student groups to assert themselves.

President Sadat had declared 1971 to be the decisive year in Egypt's struggle with Israel, but the year came and went without any decisive steps having been taken.[11] In late January 1972 university students in Cairo staged large demonstrations that eventually led to riots that spilled into the streets of the city. Right- and left-wing students denounced Sadat's capitulationist stance, his retreat from Nasserist socialism, and his restriction of political liberties. Mohammed Hassanein Heikal, the powerful editor of *al-Ahram*, and Musa Sabri of *Akhbar* were pilloried for being the propagandists of Sadat's policies and for refusing to publish the students' demands. Some students recognized that the president was able to box them in within the alliance of working forces, and at least one student union, Cairo University's Faculty of Medicine, demanded the repeal of 50 percent representation for workers and peasants so as to "permit the intellectuals to play fully the role that is their due" (Massira 1972, p. 60). The disturbances were put down when security forces occupied the campus of Cairo University.

One year later the scenario was reenacted. In the interim the Soviet military advisors had been expelled from Egypt and General Sadiq fired from the armed forces. Throughout the fall of 1972 student agitation grew at Cairo and 'Ain Shams universities. Sadat warned both the "adventurist left" and

[11] Sadat attributed his inaction to the Indo-Pakistani conflict over Bangladesh, which had drawn international attention away from the Middle East.

the "reactionary right" against further activities, and arrests of student leaders became frequent. Sporadic demonstrations and riots pitted students against police at the end of January and throughout February 1973. In the course of these clashes about 100 students were arrested, and in June 1973, when charges were finally brought against them, it turned out that nearly all were "leftists." Significantly, Salah Gharib, secretary of the General Federation of Labor, issued a statement that endorsed the appeals for greater freedom but emphasized that such appeals must be made through existing channels within the alliance of working forces (*A*, January 4, 1973).

The press gave virtually no coverage to these incidents (Wissa-Wassef 1973b) and this fact prompted several journalists and literary figures to take up the students' cause. On December 17, 1972, the Press Syndicate issued an appeal for the lifting of all press censorship save on matters of military security. Then, early in 1973, over one hundred journalists and writers sent petitions to Sadat not meant for publication in which they defended the legitimacy of some student demands and urged that the press give them some exposure.

The counterattack came on February 1. Because all newspapers were the property of the ASU, it fell to the Discipline Committee of that body to deal with the journalists. The committee included a number of the stalwarts who had rallied to Sadat in May 1971 ('Abd al-Akhir, Dakruri, Mahmud and Muhammed Usman Isma'il), and they eventually suspended the membership of over 100 writers and journalists, depriving them of their right to exercise their profession. Among those targeted were illustrious figures such as Louis Awad, Nagib Mahfuz, Yussef Idris, and Lutfi al-Kholi.[12] Again it was the left that drew disproportionate attention. On the third anniversary of Nasser's death, and just prior to the October War, Sadat reinstated all the writers and journalists in full ASU membership.

For the rest of the decade there were continued skirmishes with students and the press, and on those occasions when these matters reached the courts, with the judiciary as well. In general what Sadat sought to promote with respect to all occupational and interest groups were "honor codes," reflecting in spirit the national codes embodied in the National Unity and Ethics Laws. Each profession would be governed by a supreme council whose membership could be controlled by the president and that would then police its own profession.

In the wake of the 1973 student disturbances an honor code for university students was drawn up emphasizing their duties to society (such as participation in literacy campaigns), to implementing the Plan, and to serving the

---

[12] Many of those suspended were affiliated to *al-Ahram*, and Hassanein Heikal saw to it that they had continued access to their offices and that they received their salaries.

war effort (*Sawt al-Gama'a*, March 19, 1973). The various student unions were placed under the supervision of the ASU secretary for youth (in 1973 Dr. Kamal Abu al-Magd) and the Youth Organization (see for example *A*, July 25, 1973). These measures served for awhile to contain student agitation, but the withering away of the ASU and the growing strength of Islamic groups rendered precarious the regime's grip on the universities by the late 1970s.

Some professional groups proved more difficult to control than others, especially when membership in the ASU was no longer a requirement for union or syndicate office. The engineers never posed any notable problems. In June 1975 a Supreme Council for Engineers was established and Dr. Mustapha Khalil became its secretary (*naqib*). More recently, in 1979, Ahmad Osman became *naqib*, elected to that position by just 7,000 of 103,000 syndicate members. The syndicate deployed most of its efforts in building its financial and commercial assets: in 1980 it founded six companies including a bank, an insurance company, and a brick factory (*AI*, no. 612, October 6, 1980). This syndicate then has simply become an integral part of that symbiosis between the public and private sectors and between foreign and domestic capital.

The lawyers have been somewhat more recalcitrant, and whatever their political hue have unanimously upheld the principle of the independence of the judiciary. In several instances they have refused to do the regime's bidding. For that reason Sadat maintained special "security" tribunals and created ethics courts. But even the security tribunals have not always been cooperative. Nearly 200 people were arrested after the January 1977 riots, and P. M. Mamduh Salim publicly denounced them as saboteurs and foreign agents. Yet when verdicts in their cases were finally handed down in April 1980, 146 were acquitted and twenty were sentenced to jail for one to three years (Christopher Wren, *NYT*, April 20, 1980). After the signing of the Camp David accords, the Lawyers Syndicate refused to issue a formal endorsement of them. Two years later, after the Israeli raid on the Iraqi nuclear reactor, the Syndicate called for the repudiation of the accords.

Sadat could not tolerate such open defiance of his personal policies. On June 26, 1981 lawyers loyal to him packed a session of the Lawyers Syndicate and "voted" out the incumbent leadership. Sadat demanded a parliamentary investigation of this leadership, principally because he was convinced they had defamed Egypt abroad. Unsurprisingly the special parliamentary committee found the incumbent leaders to be disloyal, and the Maglis al-Sha'ab as a whole voted to dissolve the old council of the syndicate and to bring its president (naqib), Ahmad al-Khawaga, before the socialist prosecutor. Gamal al-'Utaifi, to the dismay of many, agreed to head a new provisional council.

Thus Sadat's hope that various professional syndicates would abide by "honor codes" worked out between themselves and the regime (*A*, July 31,

1978) was partially dashed. His long struggle with the journalists was equally unsatisfactory.

After the October War Sadat moved on the press in two directions. The first was to put in place a group of editors upon whom he could rely even in the absence of censorship. On February 1, 1974, Hassanein Heikal, in his weekly column in *al-Ahram*, questioned the good intentions of both Nixon and Kissinger and Egypt's apparent faith in them. This gave Sadat the excuse to remove Heikal from *al-Ahram* (offering him a position as special advisor to the president which Heikal refused) and to put an end to what he later called the last "power center."

With the advent of the *manabir* Sadat placed responsible but credible figures at the head of major publications: Mustapha Amin at *Akhbar al-Yom*, Ahmad Baha al-Din at *al-Ahram*, and 'Abd al-Rahman al-Sharqawi at *Ruz al-Yussef*. He then constituted a Supreme Press Council in May 1975, presided over by Rifa'at Mahgub, secretary of the ASU.[13] The new body got off to a shaky start when 'Abd al-Rahman al-Sharqawi resigned from the council protesting the suspension of the debate between himself and Shaikh 'Abd al-Halim Mahmud, waged in the pages of *Ruz al-Yussef* and *Akhbar al-Yom* (*A*, September 8, 1975).

The next phase comprised the dissolution of the ASU and an effort to exert greater control over the press. The leftist press disappeared almost entirely. The intellectual periodical *al-Katib* was closed down, and Lutfi al-Kholi in 1977 was fired as editor of *al-Tali'a* which, after some months as a scientific journal, ceased publication. The Progressive Unionist Party's newspaper, *al-Ahali*, was seized so often that it went out of business. By 1981 the only remaining publications to the left of the president's center were a cautious *Ruz al-Yussef* and the Socialist Labor Party's *al-Sha'ab*. Through the referendum of May 1978, moreover, the regime was given the mandate to take judicial action against thirty-four Egyptian "Marxist" journalists living abroad and publishing articles hostile to Egypt as well as against another thirty in Egypt accused of the same error. The latter included Hassanein Heikal (*Le Monde*, May 30, 1978). The Ikhwani religious press, however, remained a thorn in Sadat's side.

After the dissolution of the ASU a new ownership formula for the non-partisan press was worked out. The newly created Consultative Council (Maglis al-Shura) would own 51 percent of the newspapers while all those working

---

[13] Besides Mahgub its members were Minister of Information Kamal Abu al-Magd; Deputy Speaker Gamal al-'Utaifi (also legal counsel to *al-Ahram*); 'Abd al-Mun'aim al-Sawi, *naqib* of the journalists' syndicate; Ihsan 'Abd al-Quddus, chairman of *al-Ahram*; Musa Sabri, editor of *Akhbar*; Amin Abu al-'Ainain, editor of the *Egyptian Gazette*; 'Abd al-Rahman al-Sharqawi, chairman of *Ruz al-Yussef*; Professors Suhair Qalamawi and 'Abd al-Malik 'Auda of the College of Communications, and a number of other lesser figures (*A*, May 13, 1975).

for them would own 49 percent. Each newspaper would have a forty-two-member general assembly with twenty-five members from the employees and seventeen from the Consultative Council. Editorial boards would be similarly constituted. All newspapers would be responsible to a Supreme Press Council to include members of the working press, editors, but also eleven appointed opinion leaders and the minister of information (*TME*, January 1980). This panoply of institutions would then govern Egypt's "fourth estate." Within it what can only be called the president's press enjoyed a privileged position. *October* magazine, edited by Anis Mansur, and the weekly newspaper *al-Mayo*, created in 1981, held center stage.

The Style of Containment

Both Sadat and Nasser played the politics of preemption and containment, and the game was founded on their ability to control a large segment of the work force through the state apparatus and state business. Nasser embellished his strategy with moves toward socialist equity monitored by tight police control. Sadat tolerated growing inequalities in wealth while encouraging cosmetic liberalization and more profound steps away from police surveillance. Both men were successful in minimizing internal challenges to their power, although Nasser was in a more vulnerable position vis-à-vis the armed forces than Sadat. The alliance of working forces in both instances proved to be a successful formula for disarming the blue-collar and peasant work force. The alliance of working forces, however, has not been able to contain the reemergence of Muslim organizations. They cut across all the corps of the alliance and possess a legitimacy that made repression an act of desperation.

Sadat, faced with fissures in the social fabric along lines of relative wealth and relative piety, from the outset cast himself in the role of the nation's father. That role, moreover, was openly modeled on the image of the village headman. He frequently proclaimed that the values of village Egypt must be those of all the country, emphasizing patience and hard work (*A*, September 29, 1972):

> It is in the nature of the formation of this people and the source that has influenced it that it is a single family in which each being cares for his brother as it is to this day in our villages. The city can never be an expression of our people; the true expression is the village and so it will ever be.

And Sadat himself was the father or patriarch of that family (*ab al-'a'ila*) to the extent that he addressed MPs as "my son." His close associates adopted the same style. The upper-class Muhammed Mahmud once remarked (*RY*, no. 2593, February 20, 1978):[14] "It's true I'm a lawyer, but also a peasant [*fallah*] and I consider myself in the first analysis someone from the great village that is Egypt."

Sadat Loses his Grip

The evocation of village values and frequent recourse to the role of father of the Egyptian family proved to be puny defenses against a population given over for the most part to cynical indifference, and for a minority to religious indignation. As Egyptians puzzled over the implications of Sadat's death, many were convinced that in some ways he had become unhinged during the summer of 1981. His middle-class critics exasperated him beyond reason, as shown by his thumping of the Lawyers Syndicate. The violence at Zawia al-Hamra and the detailed evidence of an extensive religious conspiracy against him that the Ministry of Interior furnished drove him further into a corner. So threatened did he feel that in one swift move he threw away the last thing that still distinguished him politically from Nasser, i.e., all pretense to political liberalism. Before and after the arrests of September 5 he literally ranted at his real and supposed enemies. In response to a somewhat pointed question from a journalist, he astonished the foreign press corps by replying with a grim smile "In the old days, I could have had you shot for that."

Many observers could and did understand his roundup of religious extremists. But even some of his closest advisors, such as Mansur Hassan, found unwarranted his simultaneous arrest of over one hundred civilian politicians, journalists, and intellectuals.

Many of the personages that have appeared in these pages were swept up on September 5. The full list was published in *A*, September 7, 1981. Among the victims were Fu'ad Serrag al-Din and Hilmi Murad of the New Wafd, Ahmad Zaidan of the Socialist Labor Party, Mahmud al-Qadi (Dr. No), Isma'il Sabri 'Abdullah, Fu'ad Mursi, 'Abd al-Salam al-Zayyat, Milad Hanna, Hassanein Heikal, Fathi Radwan, Kamal Ahmad, Qubari 'Abdullah, etc. There were leftists, Nasserists, rightists, Wafdists, extremists, and gadflies. Anyone, it seemed, who had ever seriously crossed swords with Sadat was picked up.

---

[14] Muhammed Mahmud was secretary general of Sadat's Egypt Party, the predecessor to the NDP. He described the old party thus:

> The Egypt Party emerged from the thought of Sadat as a continuation of the principles of the revolution. This party strikes deep in the history of Sadat's struggle since the dawn of the nationalist movement in the Forties [*sic*], then the July revolution, then as a gift of the May 15 revolution that set the foundations of humanistic, socialist freedom; as it flows from the 10th of Ramadan success (the October War), that glorious date which has covered with honor all the pages of Arabism (*RY*, no. 2618, August 14, 1978).

Some, like Lutfi al-Kholi, Mohammed Sid Ahmad, and Rushdi-Said, owed their liberty only to fortuitous voyages abroad. The randomness and arbitrariness of many of the arrests, and the rather far-fetched accusations brought against some, cast into doubt the legitimacy of the arrests among the extremists that probably were warranted.

Sadat discussed his offensive with three advisors, Husni Mubarak, Nabawi Isma'il, and Mansur Hassan, in the presence of some of the secretaries of the NDP (al-Watan al-'Arabi, no. 242, October 2-8, 1981). It was alleged (but denied to me by one of those present) that Mubarak wanted the president to go even further than he had planned by arresting figures such as Kamal al-Din Hussain, 'Abd al-Latif Baghdadi, 'Aziz Sidqi, and Sidqi Sulaiman, among others. Only Mansur Hassan, it was said, expressed misgivings about the political arrests. This led to Hassan's disgrace and his removal from his position as minister of presidential affairs and of information and culture. Like most Egyptian political stories there was more than one meaning to Mansur Hassan's downfall. Undoubtedly Sadat was piqued at his favorite's foot-dragging and even more at his having contacted members of the National Coalition to try to engineer a reconciliation with Sadat. At the same time part of this rapping of Hassan's knuckles was theater. Sadat was bent on destroying his own loyal opposition, Ibrahim Shukri's Socialist Labor Party. Indeed, publication of the party's newspaper was suspended as of September 5. Sadat would need a new opposition and what better man to run it than Mansur Hassan? But to establish his credentials Hassan would have to do something opposition-like and suffer a brief period in the political wilderness.

In a neat inversion of the stance taken by the National Coalition to prevent Sadat, out of megalomania, from going the way of the shah by crushing his own middle-class opposition, Sadat was convinced that alleged contacts between politicos like Serrag al-Din with the Muslim Brethren and other fundamentalists would lead only to the manipulation of the former by the latter. Sadat saw the equivalent of Bakhtiar, Bani Sadr, and even Barzigan among his secularist opposition, naively falling into the hands of religious fanatics. When the western media, and even the government of François Mitterrand, criticized the September 5 arrests, Sadat is said to have snapped "These imbecilic westerners have not understood that I'm fighting for them. Of what importance is the arrest of Heikal or the removal of the Coptic Pope if these are the means necessary to neutralize our common enemy, the Muslim Brethren?" (as reported by Peroncel-Hugoz, Le Monde, October 6, 1981, roughly similar words were quoted in al-Watan al-Arabi, no. 242, October 2-8, 1981).

Ten days after the arrests, Sadat proceeded to expel the Soviet ambassador to Cairo, Vladimir Polyakov (in the post since 1974) along with six other Soviet diplomats and one thousand technicians still working at Aswan, Helwan, and Nag' Hammadi. Sadat said he had solid evidence that they were part of a conspiracy involving members of the Egyptian left and Muslim extremists to overthrow the regime. The plotters had named their conspiracy "the swamp" (*al-mustanqa'*) and the evidence presented in *al-Mayo* (September 14, 1981) was as murky as the plot's name.

In most respects the evidence was ludicrous. Soviet intentions to sow religious dissension were based on the allegations of collaboration with Egyptians who were in turn charged with inciting such dissension. The evidence against Mahmud al-Qadi is typical:

> Dr. Mahmud al-Qadi was entrusted with contacting the workers, and he began such contacts. His method was to traffic in popular problems, and he began to preach in the *minbars* of mosques in Alexandria in order to light the fires of dissension. He exploited every opportunity to sow discord.

And who was the mastermind of all this, the man who doled out missions to his henchmen? None other than the improbable 'Abd al-Salam al-Zayyat, stalwart supporter of Sadat in 1971, a retiring, aged civilian with a bad heart. His henchmen were as improbable as the plot itself: his sister, Latifa, Fu'ad Mursi, Isma'il Sabri 'Abdullah, Mahmud al-Qadi, Kamal Ahmad, Lutfi al-Kholi and a few others. They had allegedly been hatching their plans with the Soviets for nearly three years. The evidence was laughable and the motive incredible. The accusations made sense only if Sadat were once again displaying his anti-Soviet bona fide for the edification of Reagan and Begin and perhaps to distract the gaze of the Saudis and others from the arrests of the fundamentalists.

Cited as an incriminatory declaration, the words of one of the "plotters," Dr. 'Asmat Saif al-Dawla, purportedly lent the plot its name. Whether real or fabricated they were about the only intelligent words to be flung about in this episode:

> The Egyptian people are like a stagnant swamp of workers and peasants needing to be moved and cleansed in their convictions. It is not enough that there be a coalition among resounding names on the surface, when these names have lost their popularity. Rather what is needed is to plunge into the depths of the swamp and to purify it so that a coalition will occur among the workers and peasants . . . (*al-Mayo*, September 14, 1981).

Nearly every day after the arrests, Sadat made speeches, gave interviews to the foreign press, unburdened himself upon local journalists. His language became more and more intemperate and his appearances so frequent that Egyptians became bored, embarrassed, and irritated. The vituperation culminated in Sadat's long address to the second annual congress of the NDP, on September 30, 1981 (text in *A*, October 1, 1981). No adversary, no matter how obscure or how ancient his offense escaped the president's wrath. The following attack on the opposition is representative of Sadat's rampage:

> In fact we [the NDP?] are the state . . . and those so-called colleagues have not the slightest idea of the state. . . . They want the same as Khomeini. They have no idea about the budget nor of the minister of the treasury, nor of entries and withdrawals, accounting and *diwans* [personnel budgets], and auditing. And when a single piaster is spent outside its place, they start to write and go off to the Maglis al-Sha'ab to complain. . . . We are defending the broad base and we will be very severe in our actions. O.K., so they say this is the liquidation of the opposition after having proclaimed the plurality [of parties] . . . but of course the Communists weren't happy for in their hearts is sickness. But that doesn't concern us in the least. Then in your name I took the necessary measures and went to the people. Eleven million said yes and sixty thousand said no. It is this confidence for which I am responsible before the people. And with this confidence I say that I will never use this delegation (of power) except as you know me, as the head of the Egyptian family. (*A*, October 1, 1981.)

Sadat went on to fulminate against the students and professors whom he threatened with expulsion from the universities if they "stepped outside Egypt's values." He called upon NDP Youth (brown shirts?) to control these destructive elements.

For ten minutes after Sadat's speech, given under the NDP's motto: "National Unity, Democracy, Discipline," the four thousand delegates gave Sadat a standing ovation, chanting "love and loyalty" and singing, as they left the hall, Egypt's unofficial national anthem *biladi, biladi* (my country, my country).

It did not wash. Few believed or even cared about the staging. As one of Sadat's close collaborators remarked to me, "The formation of a terrorist group is one thing. The formation of a larger group to which they can appeal is another. And finally, the creation of a climate in which they can act is the third. While Egypt is not Iran, all three conditions were present. There was an undercurrent building for some time. Sadat exacerbated the situation through the arrests."

It may have been in May 1980 that Sadat first visibly began to lose his grip, when he lashed out at the Copts, and disloyal journalists, and proposed the Law of Shame. For his pains he was sent the denunciatory declaration of the National Coalition. His willingness to swallow humiliation after humiliation at the hands of Begin began to tell on many Egyptians. His one-sided friendship for the US made him look fawning. And corruption continued around him unabated. There was really no one left in Egypt (apparently not even his bodyguard) that was prepared to go to the wall for Sadat.

Epitaph

I do not believe Sadat took the course he did with a light heart nor with much confidence in its wisdom. He may have felt trapped by an uncooperative opposition and the diminishing returns on his own policies. His old nemesis, the British journalist David Hirst, paid what for him was the ultimate tribute (*The Guardian*, October 18, 1981):

> . . . while Sadat put a lot of people in prison he did not torture and execute them en masse. While he reviled Egyptian critics abroad he did not send assassination squads to kill them. While his security forces shot demonstrators they did not bombard whole city quarters with heavy artillery, and while he subverted the judicial process, he did not abolish it wholesale.

Sadat's instincts for political survival, no matter how faulty they proved in the end, outweighed his commitment to liberal principles. His two major policy challenges—peace with Israel and economic reform—had led to stalemate prior to his death. Pending recuperation of the Sinai and satisfactory arrangements for the Palestinians, Sadat put off the economic reforms that had been urged upon him by the international donor community. To contain potential discontent among the bulk of the population, he combined the continuation of gargantuan consumer subsidies with the application of sweeping laws restricting political activity. To avoid economic reform Sadat drew on the bulk of Egypt's hard currency revenues from oil and worker remittances to pay for current consumption. Many observers from the IBRD and the IMF believe these revenues should be used, while they last, to attack the problems of administered pricing, subsidies, and public sector inefficiency. Their voices could not be heeded as long as Sadat had not secured an acceptable peace with Israel. In his dealings with the superpowers and international creditors, Sadat learned that while they may grumble about pouring good money after bad, they did not want to push him to the brink. Both he and Nasser learned to trade Egypt's geopolitical significance against international tolerance of, if not support for, their domestic political and economic experiments.

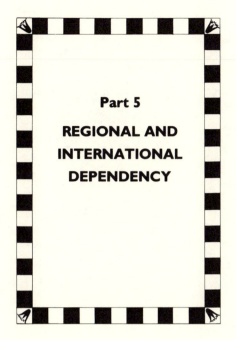

Part 5

**REGIONAL AND
INTERNATIONAL
DEPENDENCY**

Chapter Sixteen

SOCIALIST AND
CAPITALIST DEPENDENCY

We would be in error if we were to expect the great
Western industrial nations and advanced capitalism, that
have combatted our independent national development tenaciously, to change overnight into charitable
organizations whose goal is the happiness of our millions.

[OPNUR 1977, p. 29.]

... The trade balance of the USSR and Eastern Europe
with the West is in deficit while the Comecon countries maintain a positive balance in their relations with
the Third World.... Thus it is that the Eastern countries seek to overcome their deficit with the West by
the transfer of liquid assets earned in their relations
with the Third World, or, when that is difficult, by
selling in the West the raw materials that they are
obliged to accept from the South.

[Samir Amin 1976c, pp. 31-32.]

In examining Egypt's dealings with the superpowers we shall be concerned
primarily with those exchanges that have had a direct impact upon the functioning of the economy and upon the decisions that have determined economic
growth strategies. The two major avenues of great power influence have come
through economic aid and arms sales or transfers. In this light Egypt's experience may well presage that of other LDCs that plunged into an ISI phase
of growth in the 1950s and 1960s, in cooperation with the USSR, only to
move back towards the US and export-led growth in the 1970s and 1980s
(*inter alia*, Indonesia, Sri Lanka, Burma, Sudan, Guinea, Peru, etc.). This
experience has shown that advanced capitalist societies hold no monopoly
over the spread of dependency and that the socialist countries, in light of their
own development needs, have contributed to the same process.

The Political Context of Soviet-Egyptian Relations

It is not my intention to recapitulate the complicated dealings of Egypt with either great power over the last quarter century; rather I want to highlight certain developments that have influenced their aid and armaments programs. These developments with respect to the Soviet Union fall into four distinct periods: 1955-1958, covering the first arms deal and leading to funding of the High Dam; 1959-1967, marking intense economic and military dealings; 1967-1972, during which the USSR was primarily involved in rebuilding the Egyptian armed forces after the June War; and 1972 to the present, characterized by steadily deteriorating relations on all fronts.

The first period, coinciding with the emergence of Khrushchev as leader of the USSR, was characterized by an attempt to coax Third World countries away from Western military alliances by opening up to them an alternative source of arms. At this point Moscow was uncertain about the revolutionary intent of the petit bourgeois regimes with which it had begun to deal. After 1958, however, those in the USSR who argued for the revolutionary potential of national, even military, bourgeoisies, came into favor (Valkenier 1970). Intense economic interaction developed as the USSR encouraged programs of import-substitution oriented toward heavy industrialization. This trend was seen as necessary to the transformation of agrarian societies and the growth of the proletariat. As others have noted the USSR adapted itself to promoting top-down transformation (Keep 1969, p. 29):

> The basic Soviet objective in the Third World is to consolidate and expand the vantage points that have been won by maintaining existing aid programs in all forms: economic, military and political. It is self-evident that this implies revolution "from above" rather than "from below," i.e. the infiltration of key positions rather than the violent overthrow of existing authorities by mass action.

By accepting and encouraging elitist social revolutions the USSR left local communist organizations in disarray; either they struggled on, suffering inevitable repression by the national bourgeoisie while the USSR looked the other way (e.g., Iran), or they threw in their lot with the regime (as in Egypt) where "in conforming to Moscow's line, they deceive the masses, disarm them, and offer them the state capitalist way" (Samir Amin 1976b, p. 75).

In the third period (1967-1972) Soviet influence reached its peak. Moscow held Egypt's military fate in its hands, placed advisors throughout the armed forces, and pursued several of the large industrial projects begun in the 1950s and 1960s. Nasser's fatal illness was well-known to the Kremlin, and it is likely that, following the "key man" strategy, they wished to move 'Ali Sabri into the direct line of succession. To thwart them Nasser first tried to coax 'Abd al-Latif Baghdadi into the vice-presidency, and then turned to Anwar Sadat (Nutting 1972, pp. 447-48).

In earlier chapters it was made clear that many segments of the elite were unhappy with the intensity of Soviet-Egyptian relations, and yet others, like Hakim 'Amir, went along with them because to do so was to their personal advantage. Nasser was frequently on the defensive however. Once in fending off critics of the Soviet presence, he remarked: "We have 3,000 Soviet technicians at Aswan, and as far as I know the Aswanis have not become communists. On the other hand all the Soviet technicians now eat *lib* (roasted pumpkin seeds of which Egyptians are enormously fond).

The fourth period was preceded by ringing affirmations of Soviet-Egyptian friendship. The official completion of the High Dam, for instance, brought Nikolai Podgorny, president of the USSR, to Egypt in January 1971. He was treated to fulsome praise by Sadat (*A*, January 16, 1971):

> For each of America's broken promises, my brethren, there is a Soviet promise fulfilled or on its way to fulfillment; in every sphere of hope and work; in industry, in land reclamation, in electrification, in armaments, in training, in unconditional and unlimited diplomatic support. For the Soviet Union is confident that its stance is one of defense of liberty and defense of peace.

That Podgorny and not First Secretary Brezhnev attended these ceremonies may have indicated that Moscow was not confident of Sadat's real intentions. When he rounded up 'Ali Sabri and other nominally pro-Soviet members of the elite in May 1971, the Kremlin was deeply alarmed. As a token that all was well Podgorny and Sadat signed, on May 27, a fifteen-year treaty of Friendship and Cooperation.

The acid test of friendship as far as Sadat was concerned was the delivery of advanced weaponry and aircraft, and toward that end he visited Moscow in early February 1972. His talks were inconclusive. In the meantime General Sadiq openly criticized the quality of Soviet equipment and the arrogance of Soviet military advisors of whom there may have been 8,000 (Shazli 1980, p. 165 cites 8,000 advisors of which 6,014 were field unit personnel, a much lower figure than the 15,000 frequently cited in the press). One year after the signing of the Friendship Treaty, *al-Ahram* organized a round table, including Soviet experts, to assess Egypto-Soviet relations. Two Egyptian Foreign Ministry representatives, Isma'il Fahmi, later to become foreign minister, and Tahsin Bashir, were especially hard in their judgments (*A*, May 19, 1972). The round table came on the heels of a letter to Sadat calling for a diminished Soviet presence in Egypt and signed by 'Abd al-Latif Baghdadi, Kamal al-Din Hussain, Mustapha Khalil, Ahmad Sharabassi, and others (text in Matar 1972b, p. 189).

Sadat dispatched his prime minister, 'Aziz Sidqi, to Moscow in mid-July to make one last attempt to procure Mig-23s and ground-to-ground missiles. Once again the requests were put off. The president then decided to expel the Soviet military advisors. It was thought he may have wished, in part, to make Richard Nixon a preelection gift, and the fact that he consulted beforehand with the Saudi defense minister, Prince Sultan, who had recently been in the US, lent credence to this view. The USSR may well have suspected Egyptian-US collusion and hence an early breach of the spirit of détente (see R'oi 1975, p. 35; and Sadat's interpretation, *A*, May 15, 1975).

As Egypt prepared for war with Israel it became imperative that military supply channels to the USSR be kept open. In December 1972, as a gesture of good will, Sadat extended the access of Soviet ships to naval facilities at Alexandria and Marsa Matruh, and in February 1973 Moscow agreed to supply Egypt with the SAMs and antitank missiles that were crucial to their success in the October War.[1] During the war itself the Soviets undertook a large airlift to replace Egyptian ground equipment destroyed in the course of the fighting.

The rapprochement between Egypt and the Soviet Union was short-lived. The process of de-Nasserization, and the gradual move toward the open-door policy elicited public condemnation in the Soviet press (*NYT*, March 26, 1974). In particular, the possibility that the public sector might be dismantled worried Soviet leaders. It was when Israel had bombed industrial targets in Egypt in 1970 that the USSR finally agreed to supply Egypt with the SAMs necessary to protect these installations. More than any other aspect of Egypt's socialist experiment, the public industrial sector was seen as the breeding ground of a real proletariat and as a catalyst to further socialist transformation. In 1970 it had to be protected physically and in 1974, it looked as if it were being stripped of its legal defenses. By this time, however, there was no turning back. Sadat was developing his association with the US and Saudi Arabia and little attempt was made to salvage Egypt's links with Moscow. Heikal, who had earlier sought rapprochement with the US, now felt Sadat had gone too far. His disagreement with the president on this issue cost him his position at the head of *al-Ahram*.

On March 15, 1976 Sadat unilaterally abrogated the Friendship Treaty. He was actively seeking Western sources of arms and felt he could forego the Soviet supply. The Saudis, who agreed to pay for much of Egypt's arms,

---

[1] The Kremlin knew in February 1972 that Egypt was going to war. So as to adhere to the letter of détente, the USSR probably told Sadat that it wanted to know no details about his plans; they counseled him against attempting to assault the canal and the Bar Lev Line; they wanted no Soviet involvement in the planning and no Soviet personnel in the hostilities; and they agreed to supply only weapons of a defensive nature. Sadat had said in many interviews from April 1973 on that he was going to war, and the USSR could claim that Washington had been amply warned. See Ro'i 1975 and for a contrasting view Ra'anan 1973.

encouraged Sadat to look for Western sources of supply. Moreover Egypt had been unable to reschedule satisfactorily its sizeable debt to the Soviet Union. The president's explanation of the abrogation was that the USSR had virtually halted sales of military spare parts to Egypt and had forbidden India to sell Egypt Mig engines assembled in India.[2] In August of 1977 Sadat went a step further, suspending all cotton sales to the USSR and Eastern Europe. The suspension effectively ended the bilateral trade protocols between Egypt and these countries.

Relations after 1977 were at best cool and often hostile. The USSR did not welcome the Camp David accords that froze them out of the settlement process, while Soviet support of the Ethiopian government's repression of the secessionist movements in the Ogaden and Eritrea deepened Sadat's fears of communist encirclement. Surprisingly in the midst of this tension the USSR began a cautious resupply of spare parts and Mig engines to the Egyptian air force (*FT*, September 21, 1979 and April 12, 1979). But the Soviet invasion of Afghanistan at the end of 1979 put an end to this tentative warming of relations. Even after the abrogation of the Friendship Treaty something on the order of 1,000 Soviet technicians had stayed on at the Helwan Iron and Steel complex, the High Dam power station and the Nag' Hammadi aluminum smelter. Sadat ordered some of these technicians home because of the Afghan invasion. There was so little substance left to Soviet-Egyptian relations that Sadat's expulsion of the Soviet ambassador, diplomatic officers, and remaining technicians in September 1981 was relatively costless. It is uncertain whether Mubarak will continue his predecessor's confrontationist policies.

Economic Relations and Arms Supply

Egypt greatly reduced its trade dependence on Western markets by shifting a substantial portion of its exports to Eastern Europe and the USSR after 1958. In 1950 11 percent of Egypt's total exports went to these countries which in turn supplied 5 percent of its imports. Twenty years later the respective figures were 61 percent of exports and 34 percent of imports (Hansen and Nashashibi 1975, p. 22). If we look only at trade with the USSR, it increased from 11 percent of Egypt's exports in 1960 to 33 percent in 1973 but declined from 10 percent of Egypt's imports in 1960 to 7 percent in 1973. What is more significant is the nature of Egypt's exports to the USSR. Over the period 1960-1973 83 percent of these exports consisted in raw cotton, cotton yarn, rice, and citrus fruit. Thus primary produce dominated Egypt's exports, and there was very little change in that picture over the thirteen-year

---

[2] A few MPs voted against abrogation, including Sadat's erstwhile ally 'Abd al-Salam al-Zayyat.

period. The few manufactured products that the Soviet Union took consisted in textiles, shoes, beer, cigarettes, and furniture (*AI*, no. 471, April 1, 1975).

In 1975 the Socialist countries still dominated Egypt's foreign trade; 68 percent of all Egypt's exports went to them and 15 percent of all imports came from them. The volume of trade declined rapidly thereafter, falling to 26 percent of exports and 10 percent of imports in 1979. In general the course of Soviet trade with Egypt did little to alter its reliance on raw material exports. On the other hand the USSR did not play a classic colonial role by exporting overpriced manufactured goods to Egypt. To the contrary, the USSR exported primarily unfinished and semi-finished products such as coke, wood pulp, newsprint, lumber, and lubricants.[3] The terms of trade, as we shall see below, were not unfavorable to Egypt. It is equally the case that the socialist countries could not supply Egypt with all its import needs, and therefore Egypt always maintained a large positive trade balance with them. This balance was the major means for Egypt's financing of its external debt to the same countries.

The nonmilitary debt to the socialist countries stood at £E 613 million in 1974 and debt servicing was running at between £E 30 and 40 million per annum. The military, like the civilian debt, owed principally to the USSR, is not exactly known but may have been on the order of $4 billion. Repayment of both civilian and military credits was carried out through annually-negotiated bilateral trade protocols with the socialist partners.

Let us look more closely at the nature of socialist aid to Egypt and the process of servicing the debt. From 1958 to 1977 the USSR committed the equivalent of £E 449 million in nonmilitary aid and disbursed £E 391 million. The other socialist countries disbursed £E 157 million over the same period (Gouda Abdel Khaleq 1982, and Gritli 1974, p. 133).[4] About half of all Soviet aid went into the two phases of constructing the Aswan High Dam. The dam's power station of course fed directly into the industrialization process, and over 80 percent of all other Soviet aid was channeled into manufacturing, especially in iron, steel, and aluminum. The pattern of aid coming from other socialist countries was similar. There can be little doubt that the intent of socialist aid was a thoroughgoing transformation of the Egyptian economy from an agrarian to an industrial base. We have already examined in Part 2 the extent to which that transformation was carried out.

[3] Egypt was the Soviet Union's largest trading partner among the LDCs, accounting for about 11 percent of total trade with LDCs in 1975. At that time about 13 percent of all Soviet trade was with LDCs. The relative dependence of Egypt and the USSR on trade is indicated by the fact that the value of Egypt's external trade in 1976 was equivalent to 49 percent of GNP, while for the Soviet Union the corresponding figure was 11 percent.

[4] Robert Mabro (1975, p. 30) presents substantially different figures, showing a cumulative total of socialist aid to Egypt in 1972 of $2.2 billion. The discrepancy may be accounted for by including nondisbursed aid and an inflated exchange rate.

The terms of socialist aid have been highly favorable. 'Aziz Sidqi, who was mainly responsible for negotiating project aid over the period 1958-1965, claimed that it was these terms rather than socialist affinity that led Egypt into such close cooperation with the USSR. The basic terms were set with the first major technical cooperation agreement in January 1958, worth £E 62 million. Repayment of credits disbursed for specific projects would begin one year after the project had entered into production. The payments then were phased over twelve years at 2.5 percent interest. Egypt was free to market the production of the projects as it saw fit, but the USSR was obligated to buy up to 50 percent of unmarketed production at world prices.

The West could not match these terms. For most of this period the IBRD was reluctant to make loans to public sector enterprise in LDCs. Bilateral sources came with stiff terms. The project to expand the capacity of the Helwan steel plant in 1964 elicited a Western offer that would have required Egypt to pay down 25 percent of the value of the project as well as 6 percent interest on the rest. Sidqi pointed out that some Soviet projects that were suspended as a result of *inkimash* in 1965 were renegotiated with the same terms after 1967 (*al-Tali'a*, July 1975).

Egypt's first debts to the socialist countries were incurred through arms purchases. Exact figures are hard to come by and even more difficult to interpret. Those who have written directly on the subject (e.g., Glassman 1975; and Rubenstein 1977) have failed to go into the terms of the financing of arms deliveries. The general order of magnitude is as follows:

1955	$336 million	
1956-57	170	"
1963	500	"
1965	310	"
1967-1972	2,500	"
1973	1,000(?)	"
Total	4,816	"

There are various opinions on how these arms were paid for. Fu'ad Matar, for example, claims that during Nasser's time payments were 75 percent in Egyptian currency and 25 percent in hard currency. After Nasser's death the formula was changed to 50-50 and then, as de-Nasserization gained momentum, to 25-75 (Matar 1972b, p. 70). General Sa'ad al-Din Shazli, a more authoritative source, described the terms thus (Shazli 1980, pp. 141-42):

Since President Nasser's first arms deal in 1955, Moscow had granted Egypt the most generous terms. We were charged half price. We were loaned the balance at 2 percent interest a year. We could pay off the loan over ten to fifteen years and in nonconvertible currency.

Shazli then explained that in March 1973, after Hafiz Isma'il's successful trip to Moscow in search of arms, the Soviet Union demanded full payment in hard currency. Shazli learned that Sadat had assured the Kremlin that Libya would foot the bill.

The total flow of socialist economic and military resources to Egypt over the twenty years between 1955 and 1975 can thus be roughly calculated at $6.8 billion. It is not known what proportion of this total has been repaid. The IMF put the outstanding civilian debt to socialist countries in 1979 at $724 million.[5] The military debt was unofficially estimated at over $4 billion, which would mean that very little had been paid off.

The process for repaying the debt was incorporated in the annually negotiated trade protocols. The continuous Soviet trade deficit with Egypt was perpetuated by design, the difference between the negotiated value of Soviet imports of Egyptian goods and the value of Soviet exports representing Egypt's annual debt-servicing installment. In December 1975, for example, Egypt's deputy minister of trade and his Soviet counterpart signed a protocol providing for £E 195 million in Egyptian exports and £E 125 million in Soviet exports. The £E 70 million difference constituted Egypt's debt servicing (A, December 13, 1975). It is likely that some portion of the military debt was handled in the same way (Mabro 1975, p. 306). In all it has been estimated that debt servicing averaged £E 50 million per year over the period 1961-1976 (Guwaida 1976c, p. 28).

Because they were both planned economies, the prices and volume of the goods exchanged could be negotiated as well. There was some tendency to overprice Soviet exports but an even more pronounced effort to mark up Egyptian exports well above world market prices. All observers are in accord on that fact (Mabro 1975, p. 229; Gritli 1974, p. 133; E. Montasser 1975). In particular the price of Egyptian rice and cotton exported to the USSR was marked up as much as 40 percent and 20 percent respectively over prices received in other markets. It should be noted that such favorable pricing policies were standard for Moscow's dealings with friendly LDCs.

There is no gainsaying that the terms of credit and trade were in Egypt's favor and, until the mid-1970s, could not be matched by any other source. There is also no question that socialist aid transformed Egypt's industrial and military infrastructure. It even led after 1967 to a resurgence of private sector activity in order to generate more exports to the USSR. But there were undeniable drawbacks as well. It was generally recognized that the quality of Soviet technology and technical assistance was inferior to what could be obtained in the West (although the Aswan High Dam is probably an exception

[5] The IMF figures are lower than many unofficial estimates. *MEED*, February 3, 1977, for example, put the debt to the USSR alone at $8.6 billion, of which was $3.8 billion in trade account and $4.8 billion military.

to that assessment). The quality problem contributed to Egypt's poor performance in export markets and in hostilities with Israel. Second, the USSR was mainly interested in bartering for Egyptian raw materials which on occasion they would then dump, thereby undermining Egypt's position in its traditional export markets.[6] Finally, it was the case that a certain amount of corruption was involved in Soviet-Egyptian trade. Soviet officials apparently insisted on using middlemen to arrange for shipments of goods, and one Egyptian official in the Wadi Agricultural Export Company received £E 1.2 million in commissions over a ten-year period (Guwaida 1976c, p. 152). It is believed that there were side-payments in hard currency made to secret accounts held by Soviet officials abroad.

The Political Context of US-Egyptian Relations

In the early 1950s the US would have dearly loved to step into Great Britain's place as the preeminent power in the Middle East in general and in Egypt in particular. It was the insensitive policy of John Foster Dulles to bludgeon Nasser into some sort of Western military alliance (in the event the Baghdad Pact) to contain the USSR that led to the eclipse of US influence in Egypt. Nasser was unable to obtain arms from Western sources that feared for Israel's security, and he thus turned to the Soviet Union and Czechoslovakia in September 1955. For the next twenty years the US played no role whatsoever in the equipping of Egypt's armed forces. In addition there was little technical or economic assistance to specific projects in Egypt, aside from some early land reclamation programs under the auspices of Point 4. Up to 1967 and the severing of diplomatic links between the two countries, US assistance to Egypt took the form of PL 480 shipments of food grains.

The evolution of US-Egyptian relations in the 1950s and 1960s is well known (*inter alia*, see Badeau 1966; CPSS 1976; Meyer 1980). Qassim's coup in Iraq in 1958 and his suppression with local communist support of pro-Egyptian elements in Iraq led Nasser to crack down on the Egyptian communist movement in January 1959 and to take some distance from the Soviet Union. The election of John Kennedy in 1960 seemed to portend closer relations between the two countries just as Egypt launched its Five-Year Plan. US wheat shipments increased in volume and became a crucial element in keeping Egypt's balance of payments in some semblance of order. The question of arms sales to Israel on the one hand and Egyptian involvement in the Yemen on the other cut this rapprochement short. Kennedy's death brought Lyndon Johnson to the presidency, and it is possible that his friends in the

[6] The complex story of Egyptian cotton exports to the USSR has been best related in Abaza 1981.

oil industry communicated their alarm at the presence of Egyptian troops on the soil of the Arabian peninsula no matter how far from Saudi Arabia's oil fields they may have been. In any event relations between the two countries deteriorated rapidly, leading in 1966 to the suspension of PL 480 grain shipments. Johnson summed up the situation in this manner (Johnson 1971, pp. 289-90):

> Egypt has been trying to dominate the Arab world since Nasser came to leadership in 1954. For a time in the early 1960s, we hoped that he was beginning to concentrate instead on improving the lot of his own people. On this assumption, we gave substantial aid to Egypt, mainly wheat to feed the people in its teeming cities. In the end Nasser persisted in his imperial dreams. While his strained economy slowed down, he sent troops into Yemen to support revolutionaries trying to take over the country. To support his ambitions, he became increasingly dependent on Soviet arms. Nasser's attitude toward the United States grew more and more hostile and his speeches more inflammatory. It became impossible to maintain congressional support for even token assistance to Egypt.[7]

All that prevented a total rupture at this point was Egypt's recognition of the need to resort to some austerity in its development plans and to seek support from the IMF and other Western creditors. The removal of 'Ali Sabri as prime minister and his replacement by Zakaria Muhi al-Din signified Egypt's desire to maintain some sort of dialogue. Whether there was any reasonable hope of that outcome cannot be known, as the June War brought about the severing of diplomatic ties.

Nasser himself, however reluctantly, began the process of bridging the gap between the two countries by his acceptance of the Rogers Plan for a comprehensive settlement with Israel and his agreement to a cease-fire with Israel in the summer of 1970. Sadat simply picked up where his predecessor had left off albeit with greater enthusiasm. He tried to revive the Rogers mission in the spring of 1971, and in an interview with Eric Rouleau (*Le Monde*, October 3-4, 1971) announced that he would negotiate directly with the Israelis if they committed themselves to their pre-1967 frontiers, and that a firm US stance on this issue would be rewarded with the expulsion of Soviet advisors from Egypt.

---

[7] A few comments on this quotation are in order. First, the US had already recognized the so-called "revolutionaries" that established the republican regime in Yemen. Second, the US was twice-miffed that food shipments fed Egyptians while Nasser fought abroad, *and* because they allowed Egypt to export more of its rice to the USSR to pay for its arms. Finally congressional opposition to wheat shipments was led by Phillip Gruening, senator from Alaska, known for his pro-Israeli sentiments.

This bait and the actual expulsion were not enough to move the Nixon Administration, but the October War was. Henry Kissinger's successful shuttle diplomacy brought about an initial Israeli pullback in the Sinai following the hostilities, and diplomatic relations were restored between the two countries. Indeed, they rushed into each other's arms. The US and a pliable IBRD immediately mounted a large aid program, and Egypt reciprocated by legislating the open-door policy. The great event of this honeymoon was Richard Nixon's state visit to Egypt in June 1974, a last and futile effort to save himself from the effects of Watergate. Nixon and Sadat issued a joint communiqué that forecast an era of cooperation and prosperity (*NYT*, June 15, 1974):

> The United States regards with favor and supports the ventures of American enterprises in Egypt. It is noted that such ventures currently being negotiated, are in the field of petrochemicals, transportation, food and agricultural machinery, land development, power, tourism, banking and a host of other economic sectors.
>
> The estimated value of projects under serious consideration exceeds $2 billion.

It was in fact the case, as we know, that very few projects were under serious consideration, and that the $2 billion was arbitrarily fabricated and bore no resemblance to reality. The only American investors interested in Egypt at this point and for some time to come were bankers. But the enormous publicity given to the visit and the communiqué inevitably raised Egyptian expectations.

Sadat's single-minded determination to play the US option fully led him in two mutually supportive directions. First, he eventually abandoned the idea of a comprehensive settlement with Israel and accepted that of a separate deal involving Egypt alone among the Arabs. His trip to Jerusalem in the fall of 1977 and the Camp David accords of March 1979 were the outcome of this policy. Second, to placate his own military and to gain favor in the US Congress he advertised himself as regional policeman in the Red Sea and Horn of Africa and as a first bulwark against Soviet-Cuban expansion in that region. On that basis he could reasonably expect to acquire arms from the US to replace his Soviet source.

For its part, the US tied its economic assistance program to the twin goals of sustaining the peace process and maintaining economic conditions favorable to Sadat's survival. These considerations were explicitly written into requests to Congress for aid appropriations. Both Egypt and Israel in the late 1970s were receiving enormous infusions of aid to further their negotiations. There were some Congressional skeptics, such as Clarence Long of the House Appropriations subcommittee, who asked: "Why should peace cost more than war? . . . All of a sudden we find we have to add greatly to the armaments of both countries . . ." (*NYT*, March 30, 1979).

The negotiations on Palestinian autonomy that were to follow the Camp David accords reached an impasse in 1980 and were for all intents and purposes suspended until after the US and the Israeli elections. This outcome coupled with Egypt's isolation in the Arab world led many Egyptians to question Sadat's reliance on the US. When the question of US access to Egyptian bases for use by the proposed Rapid Deployment Force was raised by Carter and then Reagan, Ibrahim Shukri's Socialist Labor Party took strong exception (*al-Sha'ab*, December 23, 1980), as did the Muslim Brethren. But as Egypt entered the 1980s it had placed itself firmly in the US camp. The style of Egyptian-American cooperation may change under Mubarak, but probably not its substance.

Economic and Military Aid

United States trade was never a negligible factor in Egypt's total trade picture. In 1954 the US accounted for 11 percent of Egypt's imports and took 5 percent of its exports. By 1962 the corresponding figures were 25 percent and 6 percent, and in 1965, even as relations soured, 36 percent and 3 percent (Hansen and Marzouk 1965, p. 185; and *NBE Bulletin* 27, January 1974). This very heavy imbalance in favor of the US consisted mainly in grain sales paid for by Egypt in Egyptian currency and credited to a local US account.

As trade with the socialist countries fell off after 1977, the US picked up some of the slack. By 1980 the US was taking 14 percent of Egypt's exports and supplying over 20 percent of its imports, becoming thereby the country's leading trade partner. This is not however the level of trade concentration that would alarm those concerned about external dependency. Trade concentration with the socialist countries had been much more pronounced in the 1960s.

The heart of Egypt's dependence on the US lay in the food aid program that covered the years 1954 to 1966, and which was renewed in 1974-75. In that first period $643 million in food grains were shipped to Egypt (Wickwar 1965), and the US thus met a substantial portion of Egypt's urban grain consumption. With the renewal of diplomatic relations in 1973 these shipments were resumed and were accompanied by a significant amount of project aid. Initially the US Embassy in Egypt wanted a modest aid program and a skeleton team from USAID to administer it. The first request of the Embassy in 1974 was for $70 million. The State Department replied by asking for a budget on the order of $250 million, and in the following year inflated the Embassy's request for $300 million to $700 million. Since then annual appropriations have been on the order of one billion dollars.

From the outset, then, the aid program was overfinanced and the level of funding was politically determined. It is known that Kissinger promised Sadat that the level of funding to Egypt would always be in rough parity with that of Israel. A chronic problem has been the inability of the Egyptian economy to absorb such high levels of aid. This fact in turn has placed a premium on moving aid funds as rapidly as possible, often at the expense of sound economic analysis or need.

The Aid program in Egypt is financed by the Economic Support Fund, the purpose of which is to channel support to countries that are deemed crucial to US interests for political and strategic reasons. The State Department determines the countries serviced by the Fund and recommends the level of aid. USAID then administers the program on behalf of the State Department. About one-third of all US foreign assistance is channeled through the Fund, and Egypt and Israel receive the bulk of it: $1.5 of $2 billion in 1980.[8]

Through 1979, $3.5 billion had been committed to Egypt: $799 million for capital projects, $1.5 billion for raw materials and equipment, $860 million in food exports, and $433 million in grants. Project aid was directed toward infrastructure, including power stations, storage facilities, housing, irrigation, transportation, and so forth. Assistance in raw materials and equipment ranged from Ward buses for the Cairo Transport Authority to fertilizers, and equipment for a cement factory. Agricultural commodities included mainly wheat, wheat flour, corn, short-staple cotton, and tobacco. In the first year of the program wheat and flour shipments were equivalent to 14 percent of total Egyptian consumption. Since then the US has exported about 1.5 million metric tons to Egypt annually and by 1980 accounted for about 27 percent of national consumption. Finally the terms of payment for all forms of assistance are very easy: all loans incorporate a ten-year grace period after which repayment takes place over forty years at 2 to 3 percent interest.

Since 1973 Congress has directed USAID to orient its programs toward servicing the basic needs of the poorest deciles of the population. Infrastructural projects for the most part meet this criterion as do commodity support programs. A second general directive is to foster private initiative. In this respect, the AID program in Egypt has been quite diligent. In 1976 it became a direct actor in the open-door policy. It promoted the establishment of the Suez Cement Company as a private enterprise under Law 43. It loaned the company $95 million on the same concessionary terms outlined above. What was most unusual about this project was that there were no foreign or Arab investors involved and the Egyptian partners were all public sector cement companies and banks. In order that this company qualify as private under Law 43, the contract stipulated that it would have to make an offering to the

---

[8] Other recipients have been Turkey, Jordan, Spain, Portugal, Zimbabwe, El Salvador, etc.

Egyptian public of 20 percent of its share capital: 10 percent to be subscribed in Egyptian pounds and 10 percent to be bought in dollars by Egyptians living abroad (*A*, April 20, 1976; and *RY*, no. 2649, March 19, 1979).

Another major step in the same direction was taken in 1980 with the establishment of a Special Fund for Private Projects, capitalized at $30 million. The capital was to be deposited in Egypt's four public sector banks. Loans would be for *not less* than $1 million and would be supplemented by loans in local currency from the banks. Parallel to this Fund have been dollar appropriations for Egypt's Development Industrial Bank designed to provide credit to the private industrial sector.

The final rubric to be examined is that of military assistance. With the signing of the Camp David accords, Sadat undertook an intensive lobbying effort to obtain advanced weaponry from the US. Up to that time the US had provided C-130 transport planes. There had been an understanding in 1978 that Saudi Arabia would pay for delivery to Egypt of 50 F5E fighters, but that deal fell through once Egypt signed the Camp David accords. The Carter Administration then put together a $1.5 billion arms package to be phased over three years to provide Egypt with F-16s, personnel carriers, tanks, and twelve Hawk missile batteries. This would be the first installment in a five-year program worth $3 billion (see Burt 1979; and Wren 1980b). The terms of payment for this equipment were not made public.

Conclusion

In the space of five years the US had become Egypt's major trading partner, its single most important source of aid, virtually its sole source of armaments, and the provider of a quarter of its basic grain needs. At the peak of its influence the Soviet Union never had so many points of leverage over Egypt. Although both countries at different periods enjoyed fairly exclusive relations with Egypt, in the 1960s Nasser could still keep open his channels to the US, and presumably Moscow slammed no doors in Sadat's face. In that sense exclusivity did not entail monopoly.

For some years Nasser managed to acquire the patronage of both great powers. Between 1958 and 1966 the USSR helped industrialize Egypt while the US helped feed its work force. It is a curious fact that despite often hostile relations, the value of US aid in those years was superior to that of the Soviet Union, leaving aside the value of arms deliveries. Nasser had succeeded in diversifying his dependency, thereby increasing his room for maneuver.

From 1954 through 1980 the US and the socialist countries committed nearly $13 billion in economic and military assistance to Egypt. Much of this debt has either yet to have been paid or has been forgiven. Nearly all the military and perhaps half of the civilian debt owed the socialist countries is

Table 16.1

US and Socialist Aid to Egypt, 1954-1980

(in billions of US $)

	Economic	Military	Total
US	5.14	1.5	6.64
Socialist Countries	1.24	4.8	6.04
Total	6.38	6.3	12.68

SOURCE: Calculated from figures in the text of this chapter.

still outstanding. About 90 percent of Egypt's obligations to the US have been contracted in the last five or six years and will not fall due for another five. Even at concessionary interest rates, debt servicing on all those obligations, were it to be paid, would exceed $250 million per year.

One may well question whether the $6 billion in arms contributed in any way to Egypt's development or even to its national defense. On the other hand another $6 billion was forthcoming in economic assistance and represents a very sizeable transfer of resources that Egypt will surely never pay for in full. Egypt's dependence on the great powers has allowed it to extract tribute from both.

Chapter Seventeen

THE CLUB OF FRIENDS

> The men who control the Exchequer in more highly
> developed countries are, of course, well aware that it
> is not with statistics, and balance sheets, not with the
> mere paraphernalia of Finance that they are really
> dealing, but with the well-being, the comfort, the hap-
> piness, even the morality of their fellow-citizens.... But
> nowhere in the world is the bearing of the public
> economy upon private welfare either more direct or
> more evident than in Egypt. In other countries it is
> possible to lose sight of it. In Egypt it is always before
> one's eyes. The man must be a fool indeed, who, sit-
> ting in the Finance Office at Cairo, in any position of
> command, is not constantly reflecting upon the condi-
> tion and needs of the people.
> [Milner 1904, p. 173.]

While the superpowers have competed tenaciously to prevent Egypt from
falling irrevocably into the other's camp, lesser creditors have also joined in
the geopolitical game. The IMF and the IBRD, on occasion in apparent
conformity to US policy objectives, have urged upon Egypt economic reform
packages that would foster private enterprise, foreign private investment, and
fiscal responsibility. Implementation of these programs would pull Egypt more
firmly into the Western orbit. Egypt's failure in the last decade to follow their
counsel has not stemmed from ideological resistance but rather from political
expediency. OECD nations have become major creditors, using their aid as
seed money for the development of a potentially large market for their exports,
their technology, and their armaments. Moreover, when Egypt is friendly
with the Arab oil-exporting states, OECD solicitude helps ensure access to
oil supply.

Saudi Arabia, Kuwait, and the Gulf emirates have utilized their surplus oil
earnings to keep Egypt amicable. They cannot afford a neighbor as large and
militarily powerful as Egypt as an adversary. They are also staunchly opposed
to any major Soviet presence in the Arab world and have used their financial

support to lessen Egypt's reliance upon the socialist countries. They share the views of the IMF and the IBRD as to the proper economic strategy for Egypt and have put the same conditions on their credits as these Western financial institutions.

These three constellations of institutional and national actors have come to form Egypt's Club of Friends, the country's major creditors (along with the US) which since 1977 have constituted a Consultative Group on Egypt's economic progress. What first brought them together was the two-edged problem of Egypt's external debt and chronic payments crises. To reduce the first and bring the second into any kind of balance would have necessitated reducing Egypt's domestic consumption and perhaps levels of investment so as to put a cap on the import bill and the need for development loans. To move in this direction would necessitate great hardship for a substantial part of the Egyptian population, and neither the Egyptian government nor its creditors were prepared to exact that price.

Egypt had found itself in similar straits a century before but at that time the response of her creditors was very different. In the 1870s the profligacy of the Khedive Isma'il led Egypt into such overwhelming foreign obligations that European overseers were brought in to impound Egyptian revenues for the purposes of servicing the debt. To pay off the principal and interest on the £E 100 million debt, nearby half of all public revenues went into servicing until 1898, falling to 30 percent up to the First World War, and then tailing off to 10 percent until the abolition of the Caisse de la Dette in 1936 (Crouchley 1938; and Gritli 1974).

In no small measure this crisis in Egypt's external payments led to the occupation of the country by the British in 1881. And the fiscal measures imposed by the experts of the Caisse contributed to the decline in the standard of living that characterized the first half of the twentieth century. For decades Egyptians lived through what would now be called a ''stabilization plan,'' and it was the poor that paid for Egypt's internal austerity and external obligations. Moreover, given England's grip on the country, there was no way that Egypt could wriggle out of its commitments.

The crisis in Egypt's external payments that first made itself felt in 1965-66 took on alarming proportions in 1975-76. In both instances the IMF, the new ''gendarme du grand capital'' (Juruna 1977), tried to establish the terms of meeting debt-servicing obligations and of improving the balance of payments picture. The direct link of such measures to the well-being of average Egyptians was once again made abundantly clear. The first attempts to implement the IMF stabilization program led to the riots of January 1977 (referred to in some circles as the Dickey Riots in honor of Paul Dickey, the IMF representative resident in Cairo). The essential point, however, is that as a fully independent country, Egypt's government is not sufficiently autonomous to impose upon its population the full terms of stabilization, and because of its economic and geopolitical importance its creditors are not willing to exact their due. Egypt's external debt has been constantly refinanced, and in part repudiated (e.g., suspension of payments to the USSR and some Arab creditors), while the reforms its creditors have deemed essential have been watered down or avoided altogether.

In the space of six years, between 1974 and 1980, Egypt was given access to nonmilitary credits and grants worth $17 billion. This included $5.7 billion from the United States, $4 billion from Western Europe and Japan, and $4.5 billion from regional and international banks and funds. Of that total about $10 billion had actually been disbursed (*AI*, no. 625, January 1, 1981). There were in addition lines of credit worth between $2 and $4 billion open for the acquisition of arms (Barkai 1980, p. 130). All of these credits represented something like $75 per capita per year. A substantial proportion went to finance Egypt's growing trade imbalance, and as this was related to the importation of food grains and other basic consumer commodities, the aid in some measure reached the poor. Thus while Egypt's debt remained a matter of international concern in the 1970s, the response of the creditor community was far different than in 1876. This time resources flowed in rather than out, although it may be that the day of reckoning has merely been postponed.

Egypt and the IMF

No other among Egypt's creditors has tried as diligently as the IMF to shape fiscal, trade, and exchange rate policy. But such "interference" is the prescribed role of the IMF. There has been frequent and intense interaction between this Fund and Egypt since 1962, but Egypt has successfully avoided implementing its recommendations fully.

Egypt had run down its sterling balance of £ 425 million accumulated during the Second World War to the point that it was practically exhausted in 1961. Then the failure of the cotton crop (Egypt received £E 16 million in compensatory finance for the cotton losses from the IMF in 1963), compensation payments for nationalized British assets and shares in the Suez Canal Company, and payments to the Sudan for Nubians displaced by the High Dam depleted what little was left. In the same year that Egypt began its socialist transformation, it turned to the IMF for an £E 20 million standby agreement. The conditions were to raise domestic interest rates, reduce government spending, and to devalue the pound. Only this last condition was met, and the pound was devalued from thirty-five to forty-three piastres to the US dollar. There was never any intention on the part of the government, however, to cut down domestic demand or public investment. In addition the outlays for the military expedition in the Yemen were stepped up. "The devaluation of 1962, followed by strongly expansionary domestic demand policies over the next two years, was doomed to be an empty gesture'' (Hansen and Nashashibi 1975, p. 90). A pattern had been set that has yet to be broken. Egypt could always claim that stabilization had not been achieved because the conditions were unrealistic and punitive, while the IMF could plead that the program failed because the conditions had not been met.

Thus, after three years, Egypt faced the next crisis and once again turned to the IMF for help. IMF approval of a reform package would be needed if Egypt was to have any hope of contracting commercial loans from international banks. As early as 1964 Egypt had fallen in arrears in servicing its debts to a number of Western banks and had already arranged for partial rescheduling by selling off part of its gold reserves and by using some of its cotton as collateral for new loans.

These moves bought only a little time. The great powers did nothing to ease the situation. The USSR refused to suspend or reschedule payments on its nonmilitary loans, and the US began to reduce its shipments of PL 480 grain to Egypt. Both countries signaled Egypt that retrenchment was the order of the day, and Prime Minister Zakaria Muhi al-Din negotiated a ''background'' stabilization plan with the IMF toward this end. The conditions included another devaluation of 40 percent, the lowering of consumer subsidies, increased taxes and interest rates, and a reduction in investment. This time Egypt had to comply with a reduction in subsidies simply because its imported grain supply was sharply reduced, and investments were cut back as there was inadequate foreign exchange to cover the importation of raw materials and capital goals. But Nasser was incensed at the idea of further devaluation and refused to comply. Muhi al-Din was replaced as prime minister by Sidqi Sulaiman and no accord was struck with the IMF.

There matters lay until after the October War. Sadat, as we have noted, cited the state of Egypt's balance of payments as one of the causes of the initiation of hostilities. The government of 'Aziz Sidqi in 1972 had attempted with some success to limit luxury imports and with less success to curb government spending. The growing imports of grain at high international prices (because of large Soviet purchases of US grain) pushed Egypt into deep trouble. The country was obliged to resort to short-term commercial loans and suppliers' credits at high rates of interest to cover the import bill. The emergency aid from friendly Arab states in the fall of 1973 allowed Egypt to meet payments on the short-term debt and to continue its grain imports. These stop-gap measures simply postponed the next crisis until 1975.

After the October War Egypt borrowed about $1.5 billion in short-term credits sometimes bearing interest rates of 15-17 percent. These credits were generally rolled over every 90 to 180 days. They contributed to aggregate debt servicing that reached 40 percent of all visible and invisible exports in 1975. In 1976 Egypt fell behind in its payments of short-term debt.

Egypt turned to its Arab neighbors (see below) and to the IMF. Minister of Economy Zaki Shafa'i led the negotiations for a $200 million standby agreement. He summarized the main points of Prime Minister Mamduh Salim's letter of intent to the IMF as follows: trim the government budget by £E 100 to 300 million, curb imports, introduce a float of the Egyptian pound, and reduce subsidies only on semi-luxury goods (*al-Gumhuria*, April 25, 1976). There was little follow-through on the commitments. Arab balance of payments support was not forthcoming on the level expected. Without these resources it would have been difficult to back the proposed commercial exchange rate for the pound. In addition public borrowing and deficit financing actually increased in 1976. 'Abd al-Mun'aim al-Qaissuni's abortive attempt to end a few subsidies triggered the January 1977 riots. Egypt and the IMF were back where they started.

In March after the riots, Qaissuni sent a new letter of intent to Johannes Witteveen, director of the IMF. He promised to introduce a unified exchange rate, to expand the own-exchange system, to curtail bilateral trade agreements, to reduce deficit financing, and to halve commercial borrowing abroad. These points became the basis for protracted negotiations. With $2 billion in support from the Gulf Organization for the Development of Egypt (see below) Egypt was able to pay off a good deal of its short-term debt and to phase its debt servicing over a much longer time period. Nonetheless in 1977 and 1978 debt servicing reached $1 billion and $1.3 billion, representing about 35 percent of all visible export earnings. It was vital to supplement the Arab credits with new infusions of medium and long-term Western capital. To convince political creditors of the soundness of Egypt's economy, the seal of approval of the IMF was sought. This time Egypt requested an "extended facility" of $720 million in three *tranches* over three years (*FT*, May 26, 1978).[1]

In June 1978 an agreement in principle was reached for the three-year facility. This stipulated a unified exchange rate by the beginning of 1979. Six basic commodities—wheat, flour, sugar, tea, fertilizers, and pesticides—were to be imported at the new commercial rate, but they would be sold domestically at subsidized prices. The subsidies were to be financed from a Price Equivalency Fund, set initially at £E 350 million. Also in the first year the government deficit was to be held to £E 850 million (Ghaith 1978b).

Qaissuni must have doubted the feasibility of these pledges for he left the government shortly before the agreement with the IMF was signed. Egypt drew a first *tranche* of $90 million (75 million SDRs) in the summer of 1978, but the second, due in November, was held up when it became apparent that the budget deficit for 1979 would be between £E 1.2 and 1.5 billion (*AI*, no. 561, January 1, 1979). The cutoff of Arab sources of credits after the Camp

[1] Standby agreements are for one year to eighteen months. The extended facility was introduced in 1974 to cover longer time frames and to deal with more embedded problems. The first countries to benefit from this facility were Kenya, the Philippines, and Mexico (see Bhattia and Rothman 1975).

David accords made it look as though Egypt would face yet another severe payments crisis. In that year debt servicing reached an all-time high of 51 percent of all export earnings and 96 percent of visible export earnings. But already the surge in world petroleum prices caused by the cutback in Iranian production, and the growth in worker remittances, had combined to ease Egypt's payments situation. The IMF was reportedly willing to tolerate a budget deficit of £E 2 to 2.5 billion (*MEED*, January 4, 1980). It is astounding to note that between the negotiations for the standby in 1976 and for the second *tranche* of the extended facility in 1979 the tolerable level of deficit financing had increased twentyfold.

The message seemed to be that the best way to deal with tough conditions was to avoid them until the IMF softened them. There has yet to be any compromise on the question of subsidies: the IMF wants them whittled away while Egypt increased the subsidies by large increments in 1980 and 1981. 'Abd al-Razzaq 'Abd al-Magid would have liked to have the Fund's imprimatur on Egyptian finances, but given the country's large foreign exchange reserves there was no longer any sense of urgency in seeking it. For its part the IMF in 1981 had no reason to fear that sticking to its condition would push Egypt into crisis.

When the external debt became a subject of public debate in 1976, Mamduh Salim put it at £E 4.6 billion or about $10.5 billion at the official rate of exchange (*A*, December 12, 1976). Within two years this had risen to $12.8 billion of which $8.3 billion had been disbursed. In mid-1979 the IMF put the total civilian external debt at $15.4 billion of which $11.7 billion had been disbursed. In recent years Egypt has been accepting new obligations at a rate of $2-3 billion per annum while debt servicing has been somewhat less. Thus the external debt was about $17 billion in 1981. While long-term noncommercial loans predominate, it is still the case that commercial loans and suppliers' credits are running at about $1 billion per annum. Thus Egypt faces a very heavy payments schedule in the future. The IBRD projections to the mid-Eighties show a slow increase in payments from $2 billion to $2.5 billion between 1982 and 1986, and an average debt servicing ratio of 19 percent of export earnings. This is a manageable level but one dependent on continued high levels of earnings from petroleum exports and worker remittances. If these sources of revenues falter, Egypt will have to turn once again to the IMF and look austerity squarely in the face.

Egypt and the IBRD

[In 1972] a representative of the World Bank brought
me a letter from my dear friend McNamara. He said
that there were people that Egypt owed money who
wanted the Bank to attest that Egypt was bankrupt. ...

411

> So McNamara asked me, why not put together just $1
> million and send it to me so that I can silence these
> people. ... It took a week to do it, and I sent it to
> him. He gave it to the Bank, and all those people shut
> up.

This, at any rate, is how Sadat remembers his first dealings with the IBRD
(speech to the National Democratic Party, *A*, January 21, 1981). However
apocryphal, there is no doubt that Egypt's relations with the World Bank
since the early 1970s have been cordial. The Bank in fact has acted in two
ways that have had the unintended consequence of undermining the IMF's
push for stabilization and austerity. It has pumped substantial funds into Egypt
regardless of the country's compliance with IMF conditions, and it has been
the organizer of an international Consultative Group that has been a major
conduit for Western credits to Egypt.

It was an IBRD overview of the Egyptian economy in 1974 that set the
stage for an infusion of Western public and private funds. It is likely that the
Bank in this instance reflected the desire of the US to depict Sadat's regime
in the most favorable light possible and to provide Egypt the financial support
that would allow it to pursue economic liberalization and its move away from
the USSR. Between 1974 and 1979 the Bank loaned Egypt $1.2 billion, much
of it on the soft terms provided by the International Development Agency.
This unit of the Bank loans mainly for infrastructural projects, and its credits
are reserved for the poorest LDCs with per capita incomes of $300 or less.
Its loans are for thirty years at .75 percent interest. Some $450 million in
loans for utilities and port improvement have been contracted, along with
$178 million in agriculture (mainly tile drainage) and $229 million for industry
(*AI*, no. 574, July 15, 1979).

In 1980 the Bank's level of funding increased to $575 million: $275 million
from IDA and $300 million in normal bank loans to be repaid over three to
ten years at 8-9 percent interest. But Egypt's per capita income had risen
above $320 and some Bank experts felt the country should no longer qualify
for IDA loans (*A*, December 27, 1980). 'Abd al-Razzaq 'Abd al-Magid
resisted this idea, arguing that Egypt was still very much at the botton end
of the "middle-income" LDCs where per capita income averaged $1,250 per
annum. He received assurances that $119 million in IDA credits would still
be available to Egypt in 1981, and that total Bank lending through 1985 might
reach $1.3 billion (*A*, January 21, 1981).

As important to Egypt's new international standing has been the Bank's
role in organizing its Consultative Group or "Club of Friends" as the Egyptian
press calls it. This group of public and private creditors, including Arab Fund
representatives, was first convened in Paris in May 1977 when Egypt was

mired in the aftermath of the January riots and the continuing payments crisis. The Group was looked to to help reschedule payments and advance new lines of credit. In this respect the Group's role was similar to that performed by the Paris Club for other countries, notably Indonesia in 1965 after the downfall of Sukarno. The Group pledged $3.6 billion in credits at the first meeting, led by the Gulf states and Saudi Arabia which came up with the bulk of the capital.

The next meeting took place in Paris in June 1978 at the same time that the accord with the IMF for the extended facility was signed. The outlook for Egypt's economy had improved greatly. Then the quasi-boycott of Egypt by other Arab states following the Camp David accords threw the Consultative Group into disarray. The third meeting was postponed from June to December 1979 and took place without any representation from Arab funds. Led by the US, which pledged $1.1 billion for 1980, the Western nations and Japan put together a total aid package of $2.5 billion for the same year (*MEED*, January 4, 1980).

This level of credits allowed Egypt to survive the cutoff of Arab funds easily. The following year it was President Sadat and a triumphant 'Abd al-Magid who presided over the fourth meeting of the Consultative Group, held in Aswan in January 1981. The Egyptians wanted to show they were dealing from strength, and despite the fact that the country was practically awash in foreign exchange and unutilized credits, Egypt's friends made pledges totaling $2.9 billion for 1981 (*A*, January 23, 1981). It should be noted that the IBRD stressed to the Egyptians that their comfortable foreign exchange position could be seriously undermined by the mid-1980s unless the public sector were made more efficient and better able to compete in world markets, and unless direct and indirect subsidies, especially of petroleum products, were phased out (see IBRD 1980). Yet in no small measure the Bank's efforts since 1974 had allowed Egypt to avoid the short-term measures advocated by the IMF and the longer-term reforms that it saw as necessary to the future prosperity of the country.

Egypt, Western Europe, and Japan

The EEC is Egypt's major trading partner. In 1978, for example, 42 percent of Egypt's exports went to the EEC and 53 percent of the country's imports came from the same source. If one adds Japan to these figures the totals become 47 percent and 58 percent. It is striking however that the UK, Egypt's former imperial master, provides Egypt only 5 percent of its imports and takes just 4 percent of its exports. In Europe, France, Italy, and the FRG trade more heavily with Egypt than the UK.

In May 1972 the EEC and Egypt signed a preferential trade agreement that provided for tariff reductions up to 55 percent on Egyptian manufactured exports and a range of tariff cuts on agricultural exports. The agreement was renewed in 1978. Although Egyptian exports to the EEC increased substantially between 1972 and 1978, imports from the EEC increased much more rapidly. By 1980 Egypt's trade deficit with the EEC had risen to $1.4 billion.

There are two regions of the world toward which Egypt *must* increase its manufactured exports, the Arab region and Western Europe. The rising protectionism in the EEC, especially against textiles, and the entry of Greece and Spain into full membership mean that countries like Egypt will have an extremely difficult time carving a niche for themselves in European markets.[2] By contrast the large flows of development aid into Egypt have made it an attractive market for European goods and technology. For instance, in 1979 Thomson CSF of France, and Siemens of Austria and the FRG won a $1.8 billion telecommunications project in Egypt. Japan and Western European countries have made credits available for the various stages of widening the Suez Canal, a project that will cost over a billion dollars. However impoverished Egypt may be, it still represents big business.

The Eurodollar market has also opened up to Egypt since 1974. While modest by the standards of Iran or Algeria, Egypt has up to 1980 drawn on nearly $1 billion in Eurodollar loans. Over the same period Egypt's outstanding debt to the governments of Western Europe and Japan rose to $1.2 billion with the FRG being the single largest creditor. At the Aswan meeting of the Consultative Group, Japan, the UK, the FRG, France, Italy, and the EEC itself pledged another $1.2 billion in credits. In essence Europe and Japan have combined to finance Egypt's trade deficit with them. They have used financial assistance in a very successful effort at export promotion.

Arab Brethren

> One must never consider Egypt as an independent entity; it must be seen within the framework of the Arab world, for there is no hope for her to pull through alone.
>
> [Boutros-Ghali 1971, p. 35.]

As Egypt's population has grown to outstrip its agricultural resource base, Boutros-Ghali's caveat has been kept in mind by Egypt's leaders. Egypt needs

---

[2] After the October War the EEC promoted a series of multilateral meetings called the Euro-Arab Dialogue. These were designed to promote greater cooperation and understanding between the EEC and the Arab world. While oil supply was not directly on the agenda, the recycling of petrodollars was. It looked at the outset that, given Egypt's close cooperation with Saudi Arabia and Kuwait, it would be the recipient of Arab capital and European technology. Camp David and Egypt's ostracism in the Arab world brought the Euro-Arab dialogue to a halt.

Arab markets for its migrant labor force and for its manufactured and agricultural exports. It needs Arab finance capital from the oil rich, and it needs to encourage the modernization of agriculture in countries like the Sudan, Iraq, and Morocco so that it can import grain, sugar, and meat from them. Nasser believed that Egypt's military and economic weight in the region entitled it to impose, if need be, its leadership and perhaps its political philosophy on all its neighbors. The long confrontation between Saudi Arabia and Egypt in the Yemen was testimony to this view.

Sadat, prior to the Camp David accords, approached the Arab world in a very different manner. In essence he offered, implicitly, not to throw Egypt's weight around so long as Egypt was compensated for its tolerance by economic and military aid. He accepted a level of dependence upon the rich Arab states that Nasser would not have countenanced. Indeed, such dependence became a source of pride for Sadat. In an address to the ASU Central Committee on July 16, 1977, Sadat announced that Saudi Arabia had agreed to meet all Egypt's defense expenditures for five years. He then pointed out that whereas Nasser had been able to coax only $20 million in military support from the Arab heads of state at the Rabat summit of 1969, he, Sadat, had gotten $500 million from Saudi Arabia in 1973 alone.

Even Nasser, however, had to accept support from his erstwhile enemies. After the debacle of the June War, the Arab heads of state met in Khartoum at the end of August 1967 to set strategy toward Israel. At that meeting Nasser had to kneel before Faisal's financial power. It was estimated that Israeli occupation of the Sinai and the high level of tension in the area would cost Egypt the equivalent in foreign exchange of £E 213 million per year (£E 110 million in canal receipts, £E 60 million in tourist receipts, and £E 43 million in petroleum export earnings). Three conservative, pro-Western oil-exporting nations combined to compensate Egypt partially for this lost revenue. Led by King Faisal, Saudi Arabia pledged to pay £35 million per year, Kuwait £39 million and the Kingdom of Libya £21 million. In the absence of any other significant source of foreign exchange, Nasser had to swallow the fact of dependence upon countries closely allied to the US. He also had to put an end to the Yemeni involvement and to all propaganda campaigns against his new benefactors.

Once again we see that it was Nasser that adopted a policy, as he had done with respect to economic liberalization and the resumption of the dialogue with the US, that Sadat then consolidated and expanded. Just as Sadat came to power, the terms of trade in the international petroleum market began to shift in favor of the producing nations. Nationalizations of foreign-owned operations in Algeria and Libya in 1969 and the unilateral increase of posted prices by OPEC members at Teheran in 1971 presaged an era of masssive capital transfers to oil-exporting states.

Sadat wanted to tap this wealth. He knocked on several doors. The new republic of Libya was his first target. The projected Federation of Arab Republics (Libya, Egypt, the Sudan, and Syria) was inherited from Nasser and pursued by Sadat. After the Sudan dropped out, Libya and Egypt drew up plans for integral union to be effective September 1, 1973. Sadat probably never intended to go through with it. He did not, for instance, inform Qaddafi of his plans to attack the Israelis in the Sinai in October 1973. That slight combined with the fact that Egypt did not press its initial military advantage called forth Qaddafi's wrath. Plans for union were scrapped; Qaddafi labeled Sadat a traitor to the Arab cause; and Libyan payments to Egypt came to an end.

Sadat, however, had been pursuing other initiatives. With the first foreign investment code in November 1971, and the founding of the Arab International Bank under the direction of al-Qaissuni, Egypt tried to attract Arab capital, especially from Saudi Arabia and Kuwait. Well before the codification of *infitah* in Law 43 of 1974, Minister of Finance 'Abd al-'Aziz Higazi actively lobbied for Arab investment in Egypt and put together the $200 million Suez-Mediterranean Pipeline deal financed by Kuwait and Saudi Arabia.

The fallout from the October War raised the financial stakes enormously. Saudi Arabia and all the Gulf emirates were awash in surplus earnings from oil exports. Sadat was not at all reticent in claiming his share. He stressed time and again that had it not been for Egyptian military sacrifice the quantum leap in oil prices declared by OAPEC members would not have been possible. He demanded equitable compensation for this sacrifice, and in no small measure he received it. During the October War itself, Sayyid Mar'ai and Mustapha Khalil toured the Arabian peninsula and came back with pledges of aid totaling $750 million (Saudi Arabia: $400 million, Kuwait: $200 million; Abu Dhabi: $100 million; Qatar: $50 million; see Mar'ai 1979, 3:738-56). At the same time Algeria's president, Houari Boumedienne, flew to Moscow to pay for emergency delivery of weaponry to sustain the Egyptian effort.

More aid followed once the hostilities were over. Grants, loans, and purchases of military equipment poured into Egypt. By the end of 1974 Kuwait had opened credits worth $818 million, Saudi Arabia $661 million, and Iran $480 million, mainly for reconstruction and rehabilitation of the Canal Zone (Waterbury 1978a, p. 229). In all this Sadat heaped praise on his major benefactors and referred to King Faisal as the Commander of the Faithful. Egypt had nicely changed horses, leaving Qaddafi to vituperate, while King Faisal had acquired a very powerful client. In fact Saudi Arabia acquired several clients—Syria, North Yemen, the Sudan, and to some degree the PLO. Sadat added up all the financial and military assets of the Arab states and proclaimed them "the sixth power of the world."

Yet the level of support for Egypt was not enough, especially as the payments crisis of 1975-76 began to deepen. Claiming that in its various confrontations with Israel, Egypt had suffered $12-15 billion in war losses, Sadat called for an "Arab Marshall Plan" to rebuild Egypt.[3] In 1976 Sadat and various of his ministers sought Arab commitments of $10-12 billion in support of Egypt's Five-Year Plan. What Egypt eventually obtained was a commitment of up to $2 billion from the newly constituted Gulf Organization for the Development of Egypt (GODE).

A new wariness had crept into the relations between Egypt and its Arab creditors. On the one hand Saudi Arabia and Kuwait came to the conclusion that what they were providing was essentially balance of payments support to sustain a way of life, based on consumer subsidies, that Egypt could not afford. They were sympathetic to the stabilization packages urged by the IMF and began to advocate similar terms as conditions for further credit. By contrast, resentment of this drift toward "Western" conditionality began to grate on the Egyptians. Ibrahim Nafi'a, the economic editor of *al-Ahram* wrote (*A*, July 24, 1976):

> It is inconceivable that any Arab state—because they too are developing countries whatever the level of their wealth—imposes the same conditions as the great wealthy nations upon the poor countries. For we are all aware of our social and administrative circumstances.

Moreover Egyptians saw their benefactors as niggardly at the same time that they flaunted their wealth. Lutfi al-Kholi echoed the sentiments of many when he wrote of the indifference of those who possessed petrodollars to the plight of those who had shed "petroblood" (*A*, January 30, 1975).

Sadat's trip to Jerusalem in the fall of 1977 accelerated the process of distance-taking, and the Camp David accords caused a near-divorce. A meeting of Arab leaders at Baghdad in March 1979 led to Egypt's expulsion from the Arab League, the suspension of new aid commitments to Egypt, and the initiation of an economic boycott. Sadat immediately shifted ground, stressing that the Arab nations needed Egypt far more than Egypt needed them. On May 1, 1979 Sadat described the Saudi regime as an instrument of Qaddafi, the Syrian 'Alawites (Syria's President, Hafiz al-Assad is an 'Alawite), and the Iraqi Takritis (Saddam Hussain and several other Iraqi elite members are from the town of Takrit).

In a fundamental sense, Sadat was right that the Arabs, or at least moderate, pro-Western Arabs, needed Egypt. For that reason the Saudis had to put up with his barbs. The Soviet invasion of Afghanistan and the turmoil in Iran meant that Saudi Arabia could not afford to alienate its large neighbor to the

---

[3] The most explicit treatment of this appeal is to be found in an interview with Sayyid Mar'ai (*A*, May 22, 1975) and in his book with Sa'ad Hagras (1975, pp. 432-41).

west. The Iraq-Iran war, and Egypt's decision to share in Iraq's resupply, led to closer ties with Saudi Arabia and of course with Iraq itself.

It remains to look in some detail at the evolution of economic exchange between Egypt and the Arab states. These fall under five rubrics: trade, economic aid and credits, investment, military aid, and migrant labor. At the time of the boycott, trade with the Arab world was a small proportion of Egypt's total trade: 12 percent of Egypt's exports went to Arab nations and 4 percent of Egypt's imports came from them ('Issam Rifa'at 1979). Egypt's leaders shortsightedly touted this fact to demonstrate the inconsequential impact the boycott would have. The need to expand Arab markets in the future was simply overlooked.

Arab economic aid to Egypt has been variously estimated, but whatever the level it was substantial. Shortly after the Baghdad summit, the Saudi newspaper *al-Riyadh* asserted that since 1973 Saudi Arabia alone had poured $7 billion into Egypt (*TME*, June 1979). The figure seems very high even if it includes military aid and unpublicized gifts. The IMF estimated that as of September 1977 total Arab credits including interest worth $4.4 billion had been disbursed while another $3.9 billion remained undisbursed. Saudi Arabia and Kuwait were the largest creditors with $1.1 and $1.3 billion respectively in disbursed credits.

In the first years after the October War, most Arab credits were bilateral. But as Egypt's fiscal policy came under closer scrutiny by the Arab countries, a move was made to a multilateral instrument. Matters came to a head in the winter of 1976. Egypt was lagging in its payments of short-term debt, and Sadat felt obliged to go personally to Saudi Arabia and the Emirates to request support. Saudi Arabia reluctantly came up with a $300 million emergency grant, but there was general consensus that Egypt must pay off its short-term debt *and* take those austerity measures that would ensure that it did not fall in that trap once again.

In April, Minister of Finance Ahmad Abu Isma'il made his own tour of the same countries, requesting $10 billion in support of the projected Five-Year Plan. His request was given formal consideration at the Rabat meeting of Arab ministers of finance later in the same month. Four states, Saudi Arabia, Kuwait, Qatar, and the United Arab Emirates announced their intention to set up GODE and to capitalize it at $2 billion over a five-year period.[4] The Egyptians were bitterly disappointed, but the GODE did allow them to overcome their payments crisis. The members of GODE held out the possibility that if Egypt put its economic house in order, the fund would be replenished at higher levels.

---

[4] On March 15, 1976 Sadat abrogated the Soviet-Egyptian Friendship Treaty. He may have thought that this move would have loosened Saudi purse strings.

The GODE's terms of lending were not overly generous. First, it guaranteed two commercial loans of $250 million each, both with three-year grace periods and repayment over seven years at 5 percent in one instance and at a 1 percent premium over the inter-bank lending rate (IBLR) in the other. The GODE itself then lent Egypt $1.475 billion with a three-year grace and repayment over ten years at 5 percent interest (*AI*, no. 547, June 1, 1978). The Central Bank of Egypt guaranteed this latter loan and revenues from the Suez Canal and petroleum exports were used as collateral (*RY*, no. 2491, March 8, 1976). GODE's managers made it clear that any new credits would be contingent upon fulfillment of conditions similar to those set by the IMF in negotiations for the extended facility. Just after the January 1977 riots Sadat secretly visited Saudi Arabia and Kuwait to stress the difficulties involved in implementing any sort of stabilization program. Some Kuwaiti newspapers even suggested that Sadat staged the riots to coax unconditional aid from Saudi Arabia and Kuwait.

By September 1977 Egypt had paid off all arrears on its short-term debt and began to retire a substantial proportion of it. Morgan Stanley & Company, that had been in liaison with the Central Bank of Egypt, the Federal Reserve Board, the Saudi Monetary Agency, and the US Treasury, was brought in to advise the Egyptians on handling the short-term debt.

The GODE loans enabled Egypt to approach the Consultative Group and the IMF with greater confidence in 1978. But the Camp David accords brought about the dissolution of GODE and made Egypt mainly dependent on Western largesse. It is not clear in 1981 whether or not Egypt is servicing its debt to the GODE.

With the demise of the GODE Arab aid to Egypt came to a halt. Multilateral credits from the Arab Fund for Social and Economic Development and the Saudi Development Fund were suspended. More important was the question of long-term, low-interest[5] bank accounts maintained by Saudi Arabia, Kuwait, Libya, and Iraq in Egyptian banks. After the Baghdad summit Egypt froze these accounts, worth $2 billion, anticipating that they might be withdrawn. Under pressure from the IMF Egypt agreed in early 1980 to resume interest payments on them with the understanding that they would not be withdrawn (*MEED*, February 8, 1980).

By the end of 1978 total Arab private investment in Egypt within the framework of Law 43 did not exceed £E 270 million (*AI*, no. 568, April 15, 1979). These investments were concentrated in investment companies (£E 77 million), luxury housing (£E 43 million), and tourist projects (£E 22 million).

[5] *MEED*, January 4, 1980 claimed that *no* interest was paid on these accounts, at least in 1979. *MEED*, February 29, 1980 stated that the interest rate on Kuwait's $937 million deposit had been set at 1 percent below the London Inter-bank Offered Rate (LIBOR).

None of these investments, it appears, was affected by the boycott; in fact new private Arab capital continued to enter Egypt after 1979.

At the peak of fraternal Arab feeling in 1975, Saudi Arabia, Kuwait, Qatar, and the UAE agreed to set up a modern armaments industry in Egypt that would eventually serve the entire Arab region. It was known as the Arab Organization for Military Industrialization, and it was capitalized at $1.04 billion with another $1.5 billion in projected investments. Underway was the manufacture of Jeeps in conjunction with American Motors, and projects were drawn up to assemble Lynx helicopters, and swing-fire antitank missiles from the UK, and Alpha-Jets from France.[6] A major goal of this venture was to wean Egypt and eventually other Arab countries from reliance upon Soviet arms. The Camp David accords led the four founders of the Organization to withdraw their capital from it. In addition Saudi Arabia discontinued its support of Egypt's arms acquisitions including $525 million to purchase fifty F5E jet fighters from the US (*WP*, May 14, 1979).

The final element to be considered is Egyptian labor migration to other Arab states. In the mid-1970s a careful study of this phenomenon put the total number of economically active Egyptian migrants in Arab countries at 368 to 439,000 (Birks and Sinclair 1979, p. 295). Within a few years that figure had to be revised dramatically upwards. Even allowing for the repatriation of some 150,000 of 250,000 Egyptians working in Libya after border clashes in the summer of 1977, there may have been in 1980 1.5 million Egyptian migrants in the Arab world of whom about 1.2 million were economically active. Saudi Arabia hosted the bulk with about 800,000, but Iraq surprisingly may have had as many as 500,000, while Libya still employed 100,000 and Kuwait, Jordan, and the UAE perhaps 50,000 apiece. These figures, which include temporary or undocumented laborers such as pilgrims who stay in Saudi Arabia after the *hajj*, or workers who go first to Kuwait and then to Iraq, must be taken with caution. But it would require migration of this order to generate the $3 billion or more in annual remittances that characterized the early 1980s. Those revenues also appeared to be in jeopardy following the Camp David accords.

In June 1979 seven heads of state of OECD nations, including President Jimmy Carter, met in Tokyo. Sadat sent them a letter appealing for $18.5 billion in aid over five years to offset the anticipated loss of revenue stemming from the boycott. While telling the Arabs how little he needed them, Sadat told the OECD what a crushing financial blow the Arab boycott constituted (*FT*, July 9, 1979). As the recipients of the letter realized, the request had

---

[6] Ashraf Marwan, married to Nasser's daughter, but instrumental in helping Sadat in the May 1971 crisis, was rewarded with the directorship of the Arab Organization for Military Industrialization. Widespread allegations of his personal corruption at its head led to his resignation in 1979.

been grossly inflated, but as we have seen the Consultative Group went on to provide aid to Egypt of $2.5 to 3 billion per annum. If sustained over five years that would work out to between $12 and 15 billion, not far from Sadat's 1979 request. At the same time the boycott has worked imperfectly. Arab bank deposits have been maintained, private investment has increased, trade has not declined, Arab tourists continue to pour into Egypt in the summer, and worker migration (and certainly remittances) has increased. It may be simply a matter of time and patience before full economic relations are restored. Prospects for such restoration have improved substantially with the death of Sadat and the advent of Mubarak.

Conclusion

Egypt's Arab benefactors have found themselves in an unusual posture. Saudi Arabia, Kuwait, and the UAE have in many respects acted as regional executors of policies emanating from the financial bastions of the OECD. They have cooperated closely with private bankers like David Rockefeller and multilateral agencies like the IMF. They have tried to adopt the same conditionality for loans as those employed by the West. At the same time they may be tempted to keep Egypt on the dole, even if Egypt successfully avoids implementing reform programs. The reason is that these small states, but especially Saudi Arabia, may have little interest in a prosperous Egypt, one that can sustain its rate of growth without massive external support. Saudi Arabia wants Egypt as a client not as an independent neighbor that could forego its friendship. The trick is to put enough resources in the Egyptian economy to prevent a major collapse, but not so much as to turn the economy around. This, at any rate, is a possible interpretation of Saudi intentions up to 1979. The Camp David accords forced the Saudis to withdraw their patronage, and one can be sure that that rupture is a source of great concern to Saudi leadership.

Egypt demonstrates that large, geopolitically important LDCs can count on high levels of international capital with relatively mild conditions. There is a kind of implicit blackmail at play: insistence upon austerity and fiscal reform may well destabilize a friendly regime and force the country out of the Western orbit. Some reforms, of course, cannot be avoided, but the lesson to be learned from Egypt is that with each successive crisis, the conditions are increasingly watered down. Moreover there is the unstated expectation that if default on all or part of the debt becomes a likelihood, the Club of Friends will reschedule payments and refinance the debt. In other words, the undeniable dependency bound up in Egypt's debt has not given her creditors as much leverage over economic policy as its sheer size would indicate. It is also the case that creditors have worked at cross-purposes with one another, providing the wherewithal to avoid or delay the very reforms that they urge upon Egypt. Smaller, less strategically placed LDCs cannot count on such lenient treatment by the industrial core and its regional allies, but that does not detract from the fact that Egypt's experience is further proof that dependency need not entail an outflow of resources from the poor country to the rich. Egypt under both Nasser and Sadat has gained more than it has lost in its dealings with its rich friends.

Conclusion

No class in history immediately comprehends the logic
of its own historical situation, in epochs of transition: a
long period of disorientation and confusion may be
necessary for it to learn the necessary rules of its own
sovereignty.

[Anderson 1980, p. 55.]

The period of socialist transformation in Egypt's economy lasted no more
than five years (1961-1966) and that of radical political mobilization at best
two (1965-1967). Both processes were top-down, state-inspired and state-led.
Few observers would deny that Egypt's leaders in the middle 1960s were
able to use the parastatal apparatus effectively as an autonomous instrument
to bring about economic and political change at the expense of existing class
interests. There is less agreement concerning the extent of the changes promoted by the state. A number of students of contemporary Egypt have argued
that all the Nasserist regime did was to undermine the position of the upper
bourgeoisie while bolstering that of the urban and rural petite bourgeoisie
(*inter alia*, Gamal Magdi Hassanain 1979, pp. 111-13). These same students
can argue plausibly that the winding-down of the radical experiments after
1967 represented the final surrender of the regime to its class origins.

Nasser's socialist experiment did come to an end and his successor did
thrust the country into something of a capitalist renaissance. Should we see
this development as the inevitable reassertion of capitalist interests? Did the
relative autonomy of the Nasserist state merely meet a need for the restructuring of relations within the capitalist class and for the acceleration of capitalist accumulation? Throughout the preceding chapters I have argued for the
reality of state autonomy in Egypt and against the proposition that the Nasserist
state wittingly helped ease the transition from one capitalist phase to another.
I want to take up again my basic arguments in this conclusion.

There were three major stages in the process of restructuring capitalist
interests and capitalist accumulation. The first was the 1952 land reform and
the destruction of the material base of Egypt's 2,000 wealthiest landlords. In
other countries such land reforms have been seen as responding to the needs
of an indigenous, entrepreneurial bourgeoisie to expand rural markets. So
long as the countryside is characterized by acute concentration of land own-

423

ership and widespread poverty, the peasant masses will remain marginal to the modern economy. Through exploitation of their labor power they sustain the primary export sector and, for the rest, cultivate only for their own subsistence.

Prior to 1952 there was growing awareness among all civilian politicians that the great landowners in Egypt were an impediment to capitalist economic development. Nothing was done to remove this impediment before the military took power, but within a matter of weeks the RCC drew up the first of three land reform measures. It is important to remember, however, that the primary motive was political; that is, the removal of a powerful class that controlled important resources and could challenge the new regime. By contrast it is hard to find among the officers anyone who conceived of the land reform in its structural economic terms. The only figures that did so were a few civilians associated with the regime, like Rashid al-Barawi and Sayyid Mar'ai.

The second stage of capitalist restructuring involved the Egyptianization of capital, or, put another way, the elimination of foreign ownership, including that of borderline "nationals" such as Jews, Armenians, and Syro-Lebanese. The first major transfer of assets occurred in the wake of the 1956 Suez War, and, as had been the case with land reform, the motive had little to do with the economy. British, French, and somewhat later, Belgian interests were seized as a result of acts of war or diplomatic crises. Moreover, the bulk of the assets seized were kept in the public domain. Only relatively insignificant enterprises were transferred from foreign private owners to Egyptian private owners.

The final stage to be considered here consisted in the nationalizations of 1961. These were the counterpart in the nonagricultural sphere to the land reform of 1952. The state increased its own economic leverage while depriving the entrepreneurial bourgeoisie of the material wherewithal to act as an independent political force. But more importantly Nasser in this instance explicitly cast the state in the role of restructuring the process of capital accumulation and, just as explicitly, in the role of adversary of bourgeois interests. There is, it seems to me, no way in which the July Decrees could be interpreted as resolving contradictions within the dominant capitalist class.

Indeed, there was no dominant class in Egypt at that time nor has one fully taken shape even today. In this respect Egypt was fundamentally different from, say, Mexico or India where powerful private indigenous interests could check the autonomy of the state, although quite similar to Turkey in the 1920s and 1930s at the height of Turkish *étatism*. To the extent Egypt had a dominant class prior to 1961, it was concentrated in the agrarian sector or was made up of non-Egyptians. With the elimination of both class segments between 1952 and 1961, the Egyptian regime encountered no further class opposition from any quarter. One can go a step further: the resurgence of private interests after 1967 had little to do with their own cohesion or influence upon the regime, both of which were minimal, but rather with a complex set of external exigencies with which the regime was grappling.

In several respects the July Decrees were a true test of the autonomy of the Egyptian state. What has been called elsewhere the "popular sector" was in no way mobilized in 1961, and the regime therefore cannot be seen as placating that sector through its confrontation with private capital. By contrast the private sector was at least partially mobilized to resist nationalization. And, within the regime itself, there were very few figures that supported the decrees and several who were probably opposed. Yet despite this opposition, and without the support of credible labor unions or even of Marxists (most of whom were in jail), Nasser implemented the nationalizations without a hitch. The state apparatus performed according to instructions, and those associates of Nasser who were lukewarm or hostile quickly fell into line.

The assertion that the regime was drawn from or acted in the interests of the petite bourgeoisie or of the rural middle class casts little light on the success of the regime in applying the Decrees of 1961. On the other hand, that success can be explained if we conceive of the state apparatus as being in the hands of a group of men whose power and material well-being lay in enhancing its power. It is fallacious to delineate the class background of these men, petty bourgeois or rural middle class though in some instances they may have been, and to conclude that they were captives of their origins. Morroe Berger early on recognized this fundamental distinction between the origins of the military regime and its class interests. "The military regime, it might be more accurate to say, has really been seeking to create a class to represent" (Berger 1957, p. 185 as cited in Abdel-Fadil 1980, p. 109).

Between 1956 and 1966 the regime created that class and handed over to it the management of the state sector. The state bourgeoisie controlled the major means of production in Egypt. It came to make the basic decisions on production and consumption for the entire country. Until the debacle of 1967 this was Egypt's dominant class, but in that capacity it contained within it different strata and interests that were on occasion antagonistic. The core of the state bourgeoisie lay in the public sector companies, General Organizations, and General Authorities, as well as in the ministries directly involved in regulating the economy: Agriculture, Irrigation, Finance, Commerce, Industry, Planning, and Supply. For all intents and purposes the top-level management in all these organizations had a vested interest in expanding state activities. Their internal differences revolved around policy issues: horizontal versus vertical expansion in agriculture, intersectoral investment priorities, competitive public holding companies versus public monopolies, and so forth.

Top personnel in other spheres (Education, Health, Interior, Social Affairs, Foreign Affairs, etc.) shared in the commitment to an expanding state role, but its members were not in the same relation to the means of production and consumption as the core of the state bourgeoisie. In the early 1970s there may have been 50-60,000 officials in the upper echelons of the administration, with 34,000 in the public sector alone. A significant proportion of this upper stratum consisted in the progeny of civil servants and urban professionals. From the pool of 50,000 high-level bureaucrats, a more narrow stratum of top managers and senior civil servants was recruited, numbering about 11,000 in 1972. These Egyptians had the greatest possibilities to influence economic policy, let contracts, and, all too often, to line their own pockets. They were for the most part willing to work with the private sector, particularly through subcontracting arrangements, with the comfortable assurance that the private sector was legally subordinate to and effectively prevented from competing with the public sector. Foreign investment, during these same years in the 1960s was nearly absent from the economy, and multinational companies, such as Pfizer, Fiat, or Hilton, dealt with the state through contracts involving no sale of equity.

Riding the crest of large public investment programs the state bourgeoisie let out business to select private interests that were dependent upon public funds for their survival. These interests were concentrated in the construction sector, textiles, transportation, and wholesaling. But during the 1960s, with the exception of Ahmad Osman, few ever rose to such heights as to form alliances among equals with the public sector managers. It has been only under Sadat and *infitah* that a managerial bourgeoisie, linking public and private figures, has emerged along the lines suggested by Richard Sklar (1979).

The counterpoint to the state bourgeoisie's interaction with the private sector was its dealings with labor and, tangentially, the Arab Socialist Union. As far as one can tell Egypt's economic managers were, to the extent permitted them, profit-maximizers and resisted imposed labor and personnel quotas as well as union demands for higher wages or better working conditions. What benefits labor received were granted not won. Moreover, co-opted union leadership, minority worker representation on management boards, and the corporatist credo of the ASU sapped the labor movement of any effective instruments of pressure or bargaining. Similarly, and despite Sabri's threats, the ASU never penetrated the public sector, organizationally or ideologically.

The period of state expansion came to an end in 1966-67, but not as the result of pressure from the private sector nor of a shift in the ideological predilections of the regime. The balance of payments crisis of 1965-66, itself the result of public sector inefficiency rather than private sector sabotage or external attempts at destabilization, brought about the period of retrenchment. The defeat in the June War left retrenchment as Egypt's only option. In the ensuing seven years of stagnation, the private sector received, by design and by default, new opportunities for growth. The need to increase exports in order to service the debt to the USSR led to a conscious policy of encouraging small-scale private enterprises in leather, artisanal products, furniture, and textiles. Here, for once, the regime catered to the interests of the petite bourgeoisie but for reasons unrelated to pressures from that class. Parallel to this new private sector activity was the exuberant growth of black-market manipulators and smugglers, both private and public, who throve on the acute scarcities that were inherent in retrenchment. An underfinanced state could no longer expand, but an ingenious private sector could. The relative weights of the two shifted modestly but perceptibly, and a more far-reaching symbiosis of public and private interests, often rooted in corrupt practices, ensued. The seeds of *infitah* were planted in those years, but certainly not by design nor as a result of private sector lobbying.

Can a stronger case be made for viewing the Nasserist regime as the representative and instrument of the rural middle class? We saw in Chapter Twelve that only a minority of the Free Officers could be said to have strong roots in this class. Even when we can discern such origins, they tell us little of the attitudes and policy preferences of those concerned. Magdi Hassanain devised the Tahrir Province scheme, so he told me, precisely because he had been raised in the frequently vicious infighting of capitalist farmers among his near relatives. Khalid Muhi al-Din's rural origins made him no more well-disposed toward the kulaks than Magdi Hassanain. Thus, as with the petite bourgeoisie or the private sector writ large, class origins do not necessarily explain the bottom-line interests of any set of individuals.

In some ways, however, I have lent more credence to the proposition that the "revolution" serviced the needs of the RMC than Harik and Zaytoun, although not as much as Binder. I have not accepted Harik's argument that the RMC has been liquidating itself because it had no confidence that the regime had its interests at heart. Presumably the process of selling off rural assets was more pronounced during the Nasser years than under Sadat, who was undeniably friendly to the RMC, but there is no way of knowing for sure. Indeed, there is not even conclusive evidence of the kind of divestiture that Harik reads into data that can be variously interpreted.

The RMC, in my view, *survived* Nasser but was not helped by him. To the contrary, before 1969, various programs involving cooperatives, new communities in the reclaimed areas, the disputes committees, and the Committee to Liquidate Feudalism had as their objective the containment if not the emasculation of the RMC. By 1969, however, the reclaimed lands had failed to fulfill their promise and offered no blueprint for the new rural society. At the same time the ASU, that had taken on the task of engendering new rural political elites to displace RMC local power centers, was restrained at all levels because Nasser no longer needed it to counterbalance the armed forces. Just as the nonagricultural private sector came alive after 1967, so too did the RMC raise its head, but not as a result of its own efforts to bring pressure on the regime.

Under Sadat the RMC gradually asserted its strength and lobbied for policies directly favorable to its rural interests. But it has not yet been able to influence policy-making beyond the agrarian sector. National investment priorities have not been substantially shifted since the 1960s toward the development of the old lands, and what shifts have taken place have been the result as much as anything of external donor pressure. In a broader sense there seems to be some evidence of increasingly high turnover in the RMC, a trend signaled by Binder in his discussions of mixed family-sets, and one that may be accelerating. The question may not be so much one of divestiture as one of occupational migration. The most gifted offspring of the RMC seem to migrate into nonagricultural pursuits: the government and the free professions. The RMC is diversifying its membership, its interests (machine rentals for example), and its sources of revenue. It is no longer clear when the regime is catering to or thwarting its interests.

The autonomy of the Nasserist state was also not constrained by pressures from the "under-classes." The quiesence of private sector labor, organized public sector labor, petty bureaucrats, schoolteachers, tenant farmers, and agricultural labor can only be described as remarkable. Unauthorized strikes of any kind were extremely rare with the one important exception of 1968. There were no land seizures, squatting movements, or crop sabotage. It is hard to explain this quiesence given the legitimacy bestowed upon these masses during the socialist phase of the 1960s. The state of war with Israel could always be invoked to quash any disruption of the home front. Perhaps more important was the long-lasting residual effect from the land reform measures, the employment drive of the 1960s, the reduced work week, social welfare programs, and guaranteed employment for university graduates. These policies were, as usual, granted to the concerned groups. The regime never allowed them to develop the institutional infrastructure and experience that would have enabled them to bargain credibly with the state. The Nasserist state enhanced its autonomy only by denying itself organized popular support.

In the final analysis Nasser balked at some fundamental choices that faced him in the mid-1960s. The choices fell in the political and economic spheres and were closely related. By 1965 there was a savings crisis. The state had run through most of the easy options of once-and-for-all transfers of private assets to public ownership. Further savings could be generated only by extending nationalizations further down into middle and lower-middle class assets by increasing forced savings extracted from fixed-salary employees, and by more manipulation of agricultural prices to favor public revenues at the expense of the peasants. To bring this off would have required a sincere effort at socialist indoctrination and mobilization at all levels, and the creation of an Egyptian "long march" mystique. It would have required in particular the organization and mobilization of the poorest sectors of society to offset efforts by the middle and lower middle income groups to resist the bite the state would have put on them.

Nasser ultimately drew back from both options. He was unwilling to impose the economic sacrifices that the savings crisis demanded and feared the political consequences of mobilizing the masses. In this respect he may have been no more than the "soft" president of yet another "soft state" such as those described by Gunnar Myrdal in *Asian Drama*. We do not know how Nasser read the challenges of the middle 1960s, but we do know that he continued to look toward external assistance to fill the savings gap. It bears reiterating, however, that his hesitancy on the home front was not the product of internal class resistance nor, in any determinant sense, of external pressure. Nor equally, given that he was the man who nationalized the Suez Canal, brutally dismantled the Muslim Brotherhood on two occasions, and went over the brink of war in 1967, can we say that Nasser had some innate fear of conflict *qua* conflict. While not the risk-taker Sadat proved to be, Nasser was prepared to put his survival on the line in certain circumstances. It was just that he *chose* not to do so with respect to national savings.

While the socialist experiment effectively came to an end in 1967-68, no new experiment was begun until Sadat had established his credentials in 1973. Thenceforward Egypt's trajectory was and is much more similar to the evolution of some Latin American countries. There is now in place a resurgent, albeit internally divided, private sector and a growing foreign sector. The public sector and the state bourgeoisie still constitute the center of gravity of the economy and of class formation, but resources and personnel are flowing away from both.

Sadat undermined the two pillars of the Nasserist regime: preemptive corporatism and monopolistic state capitalism. He did not do so consistently or even intentionally. Instead, he groped for formulae to combine the benefits of both with increased political and economic liberalism. By 1981 he had already been obliged to back off from many of the measures of political liberalization, and unless major structural reforms are undertaken in the economy, his sucessor may have to back off from economic liberalism in the middle 1980s. However, before speculating on the future, a summary of the realignment of class interests under Sadat needs to be presented.

By the early 1970s there was a general recognition among Egypt's top policy-makers that something needed to be done to revitalize the public sector and to make it more efficient and capable of competing in international markets. There was also a recognition that the Soviet technology that underlay much public sector activity was of inferior quality and had as a primary effect the locking-in of Egyptian exports to Soviet and Eastern European markets on a barter basis.

The solutions to the problem, which are still being debated today, centered from the outset around reforms that would intensify state capitalism. The essential propositions were to do away with sectoral monopolies, reintroduce market forces at the expense of central planning, and oblige public sector units to compete with one another in terms of cost effectiveness and quality. Finally foreign private investment was to be welcomed in order to upgrade Egypt's technology and managerial skills, to help Egypt invade world markets, and to force public sector firms to compete for local markets.

Sadat's regime did not pursue these goals with single-minded purpose, for each aspect of them was in some way threatening to existing public and private interests. Only the most self-assured and best-trained among the state bourgeoisie could contemplate with equanimity the ending of monopolicy conditions, the application of efficiency criteria in assessing performance, and competing with foreign investors. Similarly Egyptian private sector interests, whether small manufacturers with captive local markets and assured export markets in the socialist countries, or contractors living off of state business, were alarmed at the prospect of foreign private investment in the economy.

Very few influential Egyptians had any incentive to kill off the public sector, and management and labor alike had powerful motives to protect it as much as possible. With over one million people on its various payrolls, the public sector was Sadat's prime instrument of political control. The combination of these forces was sufficient to insure the continued predominance of the state bourgeoisie and the relative autonomy of the state even as the elements of new class interests began to fall into place.

After nearly eight years of *infitah* and the application of Law 43, most public and private Egyptians, let alone foreign investors, are still testing the water. It is difficult at this point to predict the direction in which *infitah* will lead the Egyptian economy. A handful of state technocrats, public bankers, and experienced managers welcomed foreign investment and began to migrate into joint ventures or into the private sector altogether. One suspects however that they have been valuable to foreign investors not so much for their technical expertise but because they are of the elite, they know how the public sector works, they know the language, and they can grease wheels and engineer deals. Joining them are those I have called the *munfatihun*; on the one hand, fixers, brokers, "consultants" and the like who live off of setting up deals, and, on the other, speculators in imported consumer goods and foreign exchange under the new liberalized trade regime. Taken together these groups have no discernible internal cohesion, but they stand to gain the most from *infitah*.

For tens of thousands of public sector managers, however, *infitah* could only be greeted with alarm. Both the new sink-or-swim ethos introduced with the abolition of the General Organizations in 1975, and the advent of foreign partners in joint ventures, presaged an emphasis on accountability, initiative, and technical competence for which most public sector managers were poorly prepared.

For its part, a segment of the industrial labor force stood to gain from the higher salaries paid in *infitah* ventures but at the expense of mandatory profit-sharing and representation on worker-management boards. In general the implications of *infitah* were and are to reduce redundant labor and to link wages to real productivity, practices that had been conspicuously absent at least since 1960. Yet despite these obvious menaces to the public sector status quo, neither labor nor management did much to resist the application of *infitah* policies until about 1979. Then the proposed al-'Amiria textile project seemed to rally the managers of the public textile sector, while workers in several industries protested the virtual sale of their plants to joint ventures that then fell in the private sector. The Law 43 foreign banking sector came under growing criticism from public sector bankers, while prominent figures in industry such as the minister, Taha Zaki, and the head of Nasr Automotive, 'Adil Gazarin, sought protection for their domains.

'Abd al-Razzaq 'Abd al-Magid has tried to come up with the magic formula through the National Investment Bank that will lift state capitalism to new heights while making foreign investment and joint ventures compatible with its success. It is far too early to judge the likely outcome of this approach, but what is essential to keep in mind is that there is nothing inevitable or irreversible in the course Egypt is following.

This is so for the following reasons. The state bourgeoisie has been weakened but it is still the dominant force in the economy. Private sector interests, while growing stronger, are still weak and divided between the *munfatihun* and a struggling manufacturing sector that is threatened by easy imports and the privileges extended to Law 43 enterprises. Parenthetically one may note that if Sadat, or Nasser before him, were truly representatives of the petite bourgeoisie, they would have been much more attentive to these manufacturers than they have been. The real allies over time of this class have rather been the old Wafd, the new Wafd, and perhaps today Ibrahim Shukri's Labor Party. Nasser was far more the champion of the state technocracy and Sadat that of the *munfatihun* than of the petite bourgeoisie. Will Mubarak take up the cause of the latter?

During the 1970s the under-classes did not noticeably increase their organizational autonomy and strength, but it is likely that inflation, the end of the state of war, and the presence of foreign enterprises will lead to increasing labor militancy and an end to Egypt's vaunted social peace. But that day of reckoning may be postponed for two reasons. The first is that substantial external migration has eased the pressure on domestic labor markets while pumping new capital resources into the economy. The second is that skilled labor and craftsmen are benefiting greatly from *infitah* and the unleashing of middle-class consumerism. Egypt can consider itself a developed country at least in the sense that a plumber or a mason now earns more than a university professor. The truly depressed stratum of the under-classes are the 2 million or so civil servants on fixed salaries who are kept afloat only by large annual cost-of-living bonuses and holding down two jobs. Full implementation of an IMF stabilization plan could forge some unity in the ranks of the civil servants.

The upshot of all this is that there is not yet a new dominant class in Egypt. Some amalgam of *munfatihun*, private manufacturers, commercial farmers, and former state capitalists may one day constitute such a class, at which point the state may become its creature. But too much else could intervene before such a class took shape. For instance, a growing foreign presence, ostentatious consumption, and visible corruption could lead to the coalesence of fundamentalist Muslim forces, perhaps in alliance with elements of the armed forces, that could topple the regime. Or a recurrence of the cost-of-living riots of 1977 might this time trigger a direct military takeover and the institution of a BA regime on the same lines as that in Turkey since 1980. Yet again foreign investment may fail to materialize, Western markets may remain closed off to Egypt, and the middle-1980s may witness new balance of payments crises. Such an eventuality might then lead to the resurrection of ISI, a new emphasis on regional integration, and greater warmth toward the USSR. It would also cut the grass from under the feet of the nascent private sector bourgeoisie.

Had Sadat lived and had he studied it (perhaps he had) he would probably have liked Egypt to evolve toward a political and economic system similar to Mexico's. It would be civilian, and his National Democratic Party would occupy the same preponderant position as the PRI. Liberalism could be made manageable by instituting liberal and conservative factions within the ruling party while allowing small parties to function legally on the margins of the political arena. Through the NDP corporate formulas would be maintained through co-opted worker, peasant, business, civil service, and professional unions and syndicates. The public sector would remain the major conduit for investment funds, the single largest employer in the country, and the majority owner of strategic industries. But it would be encouraged to enter into joint ventures with the local and foreign private sectors. These in turn would dominate the high-profit, high-technology sectors. The rural middle class would continue to dominate urban upper-income markets for fresh produce and meat and would pioneer in opening up specialty exports in Europe. These then would be the constituent parts of an Egyptian variant of the *tri-pe*, and it would be underwritten by the control exercised through a dominant civilian political party and a subordinate military establishment.

Does Egypt's external dependency explain any better than class analysis the failure of the country's socialist experiment? I think not, but external pressures *could* have been more powerful than those generated internally, and Nasser may, on occasion, have acted in anticipation of retaliation.

What stands out in Egypt's dealings with the superpowers and the developed countries in general since 1952 is the relative lack of interference and arm-twisting to which the country has been subjected. The two major exceptions were the 1956 Suez War and the suspension of US Food for Peace shipments in 1966. Although Egyptian assets abroad were frozen at the time of the nationalization of the Suez Canal, the attack on Egypt was purely military. It was not the kind of pressure accounted for within the general propositions on the effects of *dependencia*. The suspension of wheat shipments was much more in the vein of economic warfare, but the US made no attempt to rally its allies to similar actions. Negotiations for the resumption of PL 480 sales were already underway when the June War broke out.

Proponents of *dependencia* analysis would expect that when an LDC initiates major changes in growth strategy, core interests that are adversely affected by them will seek to destabilize the regime by denying credits, closing off markets and supplies, divesting, and so forth. Egypt has implemented policy shifts that have been inimical to the interests of both superpowers, yet there is scarcely any evidence that either sought to destabilize Egypt's governing elite. The Socialist Decrees of 1961 were obviously not welcomed in Washington, but their issuance was followed by a period of personal correspondence between Nasser and JFK and by growing US wheat sales to Egypt. Throughout the "socialist" phase, Egypt continued to have access to Western commercial banking credit. The expulsion of the Soviet military advisors, the drift toward the West and private enterprise, and the suspension of payments on Egypt's debt to the USSR, have elicited no retaliatory measures beyond curtailment of the delivery of military spare parts. It was not the United States that brought Egypt's socialist transformation to an end; it was the proven inefficiency of the state sector and the obsolescence of the ASU that did that. Nor was there anything that the USSR could do or chose to do to impede the move away from socialism. Once again I should point out that even until today (1981) the MNCs cannot be given any of the blame or credit for any of the major economic changes that have taken place in Egypt since 1956.

Egypt has had the unusual experience of firmly establishing its external dependency in cooperation with the Soviet Union. Until 1967 the US shared in that relationship through grain shipments, but from 1967-1972 Egypt's dependence upon the USSR was nearly exclusive. Since the Nixon visit of

CONCLUSION

1974 Egypt has found its way back to the West and for a time to the conservative oil-exporting Arab states. None of Egypt's creditors over the last twenty years have ever been fully happy with the country's policies or performance. While conditions have been attached to aid and financial flows, these have never been cut off, and the conditions themselves, as we saw with respect to the IMF, have been constantly redefined and watered down.

In short Egypt has done remarkably well in simple financial terms through its entrenched dependency upon the Eastern and Western core countries. Other LDCs should justifiably be envious. The fault of the core has lain in its leniency, in not insisting on a more efficient utilization of the resources that have been unendingly poured into Egypt. These resources have allowed Egypt to postpone hard decisions about the structural reforms which alone can move it toward real nondependence. Among Egypt's creditors only the Arabs realized the implications of externally financed procrastination and found them good. A prosperous, powerful Egypt is not in their interests.

If the Egyptian *tri-pe* evolves significantly in the coming years, a picture familiar to Latin American *dependistas* could well develop. The MNCs, through their Egyptian affiliates in banking and manufacturing, could infiltrate the Egyptian elite and dominant class and wed them to the interests of the core. And the larger the foreign sector grows, the more likely will there be a net drain of resources abroad through repatriated earnings. The problems of external debt and technological dependency would then be exacerbated. But it is not at all clear that the MNCs are interested in taking over Egypt, although the country may be there for the taking.

The most crucial aspect of Egypt's external dependency is, in my view, its migrant labor force. Egypt is doubly vulnerable on account of these million or so workers. Vulnerable because their earnings maintain a favorable balance of payments situation, and vulnerable because they deprive the domestic labor force of some of its most skilled and enterprising workers. Their presence abroad is thus a mixed and perhaps temporary blessing.

Despite their earnings, despite the returns on oil sales and tourism, the Egyptian economy is all too similar to what it was in 1967. Inflation has blown up aggregate GNP and per capita income figures, but in the same space of time over ten million "real" Egyptians have been born. It may be that because of its geopolitical importance Egypt can live indefinitely on external largesse. At any rate it would have been hard to convince Sadat otherwise given the record of the recent past. But corporate containment, public subsidies, and inefficient state capitalism cannot be expected to paper over the stark realities of limited resources and a growing population. An old Middle Eastern adage is often tossed to Egypt's Cassandras: "The dogs bark but the caravan passes on." I keep that in mind as I talk about severe crisis in a society that has weathered more than any other over the millennia. But I cannot help barking a little.

Bibliography

NOTE: All articles from the following newspapers and periodicals are in Arabic: *al-Ahram (A); al-Ahram al-Iqtisadi (AI); al-Akhbar; al-Akhbar al-Yom (AY); Ruz al-Yussef (RY);* and *al-Tali'a*. Otherwise Arabic sources will be explicitly noted.

Abaza, Shamil. 1981. Concerning Egypt's cotton policy. *AI*, no. 650 (June 29, 1981).

'Abbas, Ra'uf. 1968. *The labour movement in Egypt 1899-1952*. Cairo: Dar al-Kutub al-Arabi lil-Taba'a wal-Nashr. (In Arabic.)

'Abd al-'Azim, Lutfi. 1974. Industry in Egypt. *AI*, no. 462 (November 15, 1974).

————. 1975. The critical state of the general income tax. *AI*, no. 472 (April 15, 1975).

————. 1976. The myth of the increase in industrial exports. *AI*, no. 505 (September 1, 1976).

————. 1977. The relation between export shortfalls and increasing idle capacity. *AI*, no. 527 (August 1, 1977).

'Abd al-Fattah, Fathi. 1973. *The Egyptian village: A study of tenure and relations of production*. Vol. 1. Cairo: Dar al-Thiqafa al-Jadida. (In Arabic.)

————. 1975a. *The contemporary village between reform and revolution*. Vol. 2. Cairo: Dar al-Thiqafa al-Jadida. (In Arabic.)

————. 1975b. *Communists and Nasserists*. Cairo: Ruz al-Yussef Press. (In Arabic.)

'Abd al-Fattah, Hassan. 1974. *Political memoirs*. Cairo: Dar al-Sha'ab. (In Arabic.)

'Abd al-Ghaffar, 'Adil. 1975. The Problems which Fruit-Growers Confront. *A* (June 14, 1975).

'Abd al-Hamid, Fawzi. 1973. *The agricultural question in developing countries and the land reform experiment in Egypt*. Cairo: n.d. (In Arabic.)

'Abd al-Ma'ati, 'Abd al-Basit. 1977. *Class conflict in the Egyptian village*. Cairo: Dar al-Thiqafa al-Jadida. (In Arabic.)

'Abd al-Quddus, Ihsan. 1974. First the Discussion of the Political Order. *A* (September 6, 1974).

'Abd al-Ra'uf, Dr. Muhammed Mahmud. 1973. Vertical Expansion in Agriculture: ARE. Institute of National Planning Memo 1029 (January 1973).

'Abd al-Ra'uf, Dr. Muhammed Mahmud. 1974. Production Co-operatives and the Evolution of Egyptian Agriculture. INP Memo 1069 (July 1974).

'Abd al-Ra'uf, Mahmud. 1974. Agricultural policy and its responsibility for inflation. *al-Tali'a* 10:32-38.

'Abd al-Salam, Muhammed. 1975. *Critical years: Memoirs of a state prosecutor*. Cairo: Dar al-Sharuq. (In Arabic.)

Abdel-Fadil, Mahmoud. 1975. *Development, Income Distribution and Social Change in Rural Egypt 1952-1970*. University of Cambridge Department of Applied Economics Occasional Papers, no. 45. Cambridge: Cambridge University Press.

———. 1980. *The Political Economy of Nasserism*. Cambridge: Cambridge University Press.

Abdel-Khalek, G. and Tignor, R., eds. 1982. *The Political Economy of Income Distribution in Egypt*. New York: Holmes & Meier.

Abdel-Malek, Anouar. 1968. *Egypt: Military Society*. New York: Vintage Books.

Abdel-Rassuf, Ragaa. 1975. Agricultural Sector Planning in a Mixed Economy: The Case of Egypt Examined. Paper read at FAO/SIDA seminar on Agriculture Sector Analysis in the Near East and North Africa, October 20-26, 1975, Cairo.

Abou al-Dahab, Mohammed. 1968. Horizontal Expansion in UAR Agriculture. INP Memo 820 (August 1968).

Abul Fath, Ahmad. 1962. *L'Affaire Nasser*. Paris: Plon.

'Afifi, Sadiq. 1980. Reform of the civil service: Reality and illusion. *AI*, no. 616 (November 3, 1980).

Agwah, A. 1978. Import Substitution, Export Expansion and Consumption Liberalization. *Development and Change* 9:299-329.

Ahwan, 'Abd al-Sahib. 1973. Land Tenure Legislation for Desert Development in the ARE. *EC* 64:98-109.

AI. 1969. Supplement. The Fifty Feddan Law (September 1, 1969).

AI. 1974a. Supplement. *The October Paper* (May 1, 1974).

AI. 1974b. Supplement. *Project Law on Dissolution of Situations Arising from Sequestration* (July 15, 1974).

AI. 1978. Supplement. Egypt 1978: The Plan and Financial Policy (January 1, 1978).

Ajami, Fouad. 1982. Egypt's Retreat from Economic Nationalism. In G. Abdel-Khalek and R. Tignor 1982.

Akeel, H. A. and Moore, C. H. 1977. The Class Origins of Egyptian Engineer-Technocrats. In *Commoners, Climbers and Notables*, ed. C.A.O. Van Neuwenhuijze, pp. 279-92. Leiden: Brill.

Akhavi, Shahrough. 1975. Egypt: Neo-Patrimonial Elite. In *Political Elites and Political Development in the Middle East*, ed. Frank Tachau, pp. 69-113. New York: John Wiley.

'Ali, Shafiq Ahmed. 1977. Fictitious ministers, *RY*, no. 2560 (July 4, 1977).

American University. 1976. *Area Handbook for the ARE (Egypt)*. Washington, D.C.: GPO.

Amin, Galal. 1973. Income Distribution and Economic Development in the Arab World 1950-70. *EC* 64:115-45.

———. 1978. Cost-Benefit Analysis and Income Distribution in Developing Countries: A Symposium. *WD* 6:139-52.

Amin, Mustapha. 1974. *The first year of prison*. Cairo: Modern Egyptian Library. (In Arabic.)

———. 1975. *The second year of prison*. Cairo: Modern Egyptian Library. (In Arabic.)

Amin, Samir. 1970. *L'accumulation à l'échelle mondiale*. Paris: Anthropos.

———. 1973. *Le développement inégal: essai sur les formations sociales du capitalisme periphérique*. Paris: Ed. de Minuit.

———. 1976a. *Unequal Development*. New York: Monthly Review Press.

———. 1976b. *La nation arabe: nationalisme et luttes de classe*. Paris: ed. de Minuit.

———. 1976c. Commentaire sur une critique. *L'Homme et la Société*, nos. 39-40, pp. 29-34.

'Amr, Hassan. 1980. The monopolistic hole in the new import regime. *AI*, no. 597 (June 23, 1980).

'Amr, Ibrahim. 1978a. German car graveyard moves to Egypt. *AI*, no. 537 (January 1, 1978).

———. 1978b. Even medicine is a source of commissions. *AI*, no. 538 (January 15, 1978).

———. 1978c. Deviations of the cooperative federation and setbacks to agricultural cooperatives. *AI*, no. 540 (February 15, 1978).

Anderson, Perry. 1980. *Lineages of the Absolutist State*. London: Verso Editions.

Anis, Muhammed Amin. 1950. A Study of the National Income of Egypt. *EC*, nos. 261-62.

ARE: Maglis al-Sha'ab. 1974. *The Arab and foreign investment law and free zones: Collection of preparatory discussion*. Cairo: ARE. (In Arabic.)

ARE: Ministry of Industry and GOFI. 1974. *Egyptian industry: Its role in the realization of the program of national action 1973-82*. Cairo. (In Arabic.)

ARE: Ministry of Planning. 1975. *Draft plan for economic and social development 1976*. Cairo. (In Arabic.)

———. 1977. *The five-year plan 1978-82*. Vol. IV: *General strategy for agriculture, irrigation and food security*. Cairo. (In Arabic.)

437

BIBLIOGRAPHY

ARE: Presidency, National Specialized Councils. 1974. *Report of the National Council for Education, Scientific Research and Technology*. Cairo. (In Arabic.)

——. 1974-75. *Report of the National Council for Education, Scientific Research and Technology*. Cairo. (In Arabic.)

ARE: Price Planning Board. 1973. Memo no. 18. The distribution of individual incomes. Cairo. (In Arabic.)

ASU, General Secretary. 1962. *Report on the charter*. Report approved June 30, 1962, reissued in 1973. Cairo: Dar al-Ta'awan. (In Arabic.)

ASU. 1973. Documents of the Dialogue. *al-Tali'a* 8:141-46.

Atribi, Muhammed Subhi al-. 1972. Bureaucratic expansion during the last ten years. *al-Tali'a* 8:72-75.

Austin, James E. 1978. Institutional Dimensions of the Malnutrition Problem. In *The Global Political Economy of Food*, ed. R. Hopkins and D. Puchala, pp. 237-62. Madison: University of Wisconsin Press.

Awad, Fouad H. 1973. Industrial Policies in the ARE. *EC* 64:5-54.

Awad, Louis. 1976. *The seven Nasserist convictions (or Veils)*. Beirut: Dar al-Qadaya. (In Arabic.)

——. 1978. Louis Awad's New Year's wishes. *RY* no. 2576 (February 1, 1978).

'Awda, Muhammed. 1976. Nasserism . . . and the reactionary right: Who assesses whom? A reply to Fu'ad Zakaria. *al-Shura* 2:30-69. (In Arabic.)

Ayubi, Nazih. 1977. *The administrative revolution and the crisis of reform in Egypt*. Cairo: CPSS. (In Arabic.)

——. 1980. *Bureaucracy and Politics in Contemporary Egypt*. London: Ithaca Press.

'Azbawi, Hassan Muhammed al-. 1973. Tax evasion and parasitic incomes. *al-Tali'a* 9:101-9.

Badawi, 'Abd al-Salam. 1973. *Administration of the public sector in the Egyptian economy*. Cairo: Anglo-Egyptian Library. (In Arabic.)

Badawi, Gamal. 1980. *Sectarian strife in Egypt: Its roots and causes*. Cairo: Arab Journalism Center. (In Arabic.)

Badeau, John S. 1966. USA and UAR: A Crisis in Confidence. In *Modernization of the Arab World*, ed. J. H. Thompson and R. D. Reischauer, pp. 212-28. Princeton: D. Van Nostrand Co.

Baer, Gabriel. 1962. *A History of Land Ownership in Modern Egypt 1800-1950*. London and New York: Oxford University Press.

——. 1969. *Studies in the Social History of Modern Egypt*. Chicago: Chicago University Press.

Baghdadi, 'Abd al-Latif. 1977. *Memoirs*, Parts I and II. Cairo: Modern Egyptian Library. (In Arabic.)

Baibars, Dia al-Din. 1975. *On the margins of the story of Muhammed Hassanein Heikal*. Beirut: Manshurat al-Maktaba al-'Asria. (In Arabic.)

Baily, Robert. 1980. Egyptian Forces to Get US-Style Facelift. *MEED* (February 29, 1980).

Baker, Raymond. 1978. *Egypt's Uncertain Revolution under Nasser and Sadat*. Cambridge, Mass.: Harvard University Press.

Balba', 'Abd al-Mun'aim. 1977. Egyptian agriculture and the winds of change. *AI*, no. 530 (September 15, 1977).

———. 1978. And so we talk of agricultural development. *AI*, no. 541 (March 1, 1978).

Banna, Ragab al-. 1979. Positive and negative aspects of the public sector. *AI*, no. 572 (June 15, 1979).

Baran, Paul A. 1957. *The Political Economy of Growth*. New York: Monthly Review Press.

Barbour, K. M. 1972. *The Growth, Location, and Structure of Industry in Egypt*. New York: Praeger.

Barkai, Haim. 1980. Egypt's Economic Constraints. *The Jerusalem Quarterly*, no. 14, pp. 122-43.

Basha, Muhammed. 1978. The Suez Canal three years after its reopening. *AI*, no. 548 (June 15, 1978).

Bawwab, Sayyid Ahmad al-. 1977a. Egypt's No. 1 problem—the deficit in the balance of payments. *AI*, no. 516 (February 15, 1977).

———. 1977b. Labour and disguised unemployment in Egypt. *AI*, no. 517 (March 1, 1977).

———. 1980. The extent of national economic benefit from financial institutions benefiting from the investment code. *AI*, no. 601 (July 21, 1980).

Be'eri, Eliezer. 1966. Social Origin and Family Background of the Egyptian Officer Class. *Asian and African Studies* 2:1-40.

———. 1970. *Army Officers in Arab Politics and Society*. London: Praeger-Pall Mall.

Bell, Clive. 1974. Ideology and Economic Interests in Indian Land Reform. In *Peasants, Landlords and Governments: Agrarian Reform in the Third World*, ed. David Lehmann, pp. 190-220. New York: Holmes and Meier.

Benachenou, A. 1973. Forces sociales et accumulation du capital au Maghreb. *Annuaire de l'Afrique du Nord* 12:315-42.

Berger, Morroe. 1957. *Bureaucracy and Society in Modern Egypt*. Princeton: Princeton University Press.

Berque, Jacques. 1957. *Histoire sociale d'un village Egyptien au xxème siècle*. The Hague: Mouton.

Bettelheim, C. 1974. *La lutte des classes en URSS*. Paris: Seuil-Maspéro.

Bhatt, V. V. and Meerman, Jacob. 1978. Resource Mobilization in Developing Countries: Financial Institutions and Policies. *WD* 6:45-64.

Bhattia, R. J. and Rothman, S. L. 1975. Introducing the Extended Fund Facility: The Kenyan Case. *Finance and Development* 12:38-41.

Bienefeld, M. A. 1975. Special Gains from Trade with Socialist Countries: The Case of Tanzania. *WD* 3:247-72.

Bienen, Henry. 1978. *Armies and Parties in Africa.* New York: Holmes and Meier.

Bill, James A. 1972. Class Analysis and the Dialectics of Modernization in the Middle East. *IJMES* 3:417-34.

———— and Leiden, Carl. 1979. *Politics in the Middle East.* Boston: Little, Brown.

Binder, Leonard. 1966. Political Recruitment and Participation in Egypt. In *Political Parties and Political Development*, ed. M. Weiner and J. La-Palombara, pp. 217-40. Princeton: Princeton University Press.

————. 1978. *In a Moment of Enthusiasm: Political Power and the Second Stratum in Egypt.* Chicago: University of Chicago Press.

————et al. 1971. *Crises and Sequences in Political Development.* Princeton: Princeton University Press.

Birks, J. S. and Sinclair, C. A. 1978. *International Migration Project: Country Case Study: Arab Republic of Egypt.* Durham: University of Durham.

————. 1979. Egypt: A Frustrated Labor Exporter? *MEJ* 33:228-303.

Bishri, Tariq al-. 1972. *Political movement in Egypt: 1945-52.* Cairo: General Book Org. (In Arabic.)

————. 1975. *Democracy and Nasserism.* Cairo: Dar al-Thiqafa al-Jadida. (In Arabic.)

Bond, Leslie. 1979. Africa and Eastern Europe: Toward a Political Economy of the Relationship. Senior thesis, Woodrow Wilson School, Princeton University.

Boutros-Ghali, Boutros. 1971. Monde arabe et Tiers Monde. *Eléments*, no. 89, pp. 33-42.

Brahimi, Abdel Hamid. 1977. *Dimensions et perspectives du monde arabe.* Paris: Economica.

Brecher, Michael. 1977. India's Devaluation of 1966: Linkage Politics and Crisis Decision-Making. *British Journal of International Studies* 3:1-25.

Burt, Richard. 1979. US Planning $3 billion for Egypt in Long-term Military Assistance. *NYT* (December 7, 1979).

Buss, Robin. 1970. Wary Partners: The Soviet Union and Arab Socialism. *Adelphi Papers*, no. 73.

Buxton, James. 1978. Egypt Borrows from Arab Monetary Fund. *FT* (August 16, 1978).

————, and Johns, Richard. 1979. Investment Key to Success of Arab Boycott on Egypt. *FT* (April 3, 1979).

BIBLIOGRAPHY

Byres, T. J. 1977. Agrarian Transition and the Agrarian Question. *The Journal of Peasant Studies* 4:258-74.

CAPMAS. 1970. *Statistical indicators*. Cairo: Labor Press. (In Arabic.)

———. 1973. *Population and Development*. Cairo.

———. 1974. *Results of estimation and investigation of employment in the administration of public sector economic activity in the ARE*. Ref. 74/001. Cairo. (In Arabic.)

———. 1976a. The Preliminary Results of General Population and Housing Census, 22-23 November 1976 in Egypt. Translated by AID. Mimeographed.

———. 1976b. Egypt's Population: Results of the general population census 1976. In *AI*, Supplement, May 1, 1977. (In Arabic.)

———. 1978. *General population census of 1976: Detailed results for the entire Republic*. Ref. 93/15111. Cairo. (In Arabic.)

Cardoso, F. H. 1979. On the Characterization of Authoritarian Regimes in Latin America. In *The New Authoritarianism in Latin America*, ed. David Collier, pp. 33-60. Princeton: Princeton University Press.

———. and Faletto, Enzo. 1979. *Dependency and Development in Latin America*. Translated by Marjory Mattingly Urquidi. Berkeley: University of California Press.

Carrière d'Encausse, Hélène. 1975. *La Politique Soviétique au Moyen Orient 1955-1975*. Paris: Presses de la FNSP.

CBE. 1978. *Annual Report 1977*. June 1978.

Chandra, N. K. 1977. USSR and Third World: Unequal Distribution of Gains. *Economic and Political Weekly* 12:349-76. Cited in Bond 1979.

Chase-Dunn, Christopher. 1975. The Effects of International Economic Dependence on Development and Inequality: A Cross-National Study. *American Sociological Review* 40:720-38.

Chernotsky, H. I., Kaufman, R. R., and Geller, D. S. 1975. A Preliminary Test of the Theory of Dependency. *Comparative Politics* 7:303-30.

Chenery, Hollis et al. 1974. *Redistribution with Growth*. New York: Oxford University Press.

Choucri, Nazli and Eckaus, Richard. 1979. Interactions of Economic and Political Change: The Egyptian Case. *WD*. 7:783-97.

Cihat, Iren. 1975. The Growth of the Private Sector in Turkey. Paper read at International Seminar on the Turkish and Other Countries: Experience with a Mixed Economy. October 13-17, 1975, Antalya, Turkey.

Cizanskas, Albert. 1979. International Debt Renegotiations: Lessons from the Past. *WD* 7:199-210.

Clawson, Patrick. 1978. Egypt's Industrialization: A Critique of Dependency Theory. *MERIP Reports N. 72*, 8:17-23.

Cooper, Mark. 1979. Egyptian State Capitalism in Crisis: Economic Policies and Political Interests, 1967-1971. *International Journal of Middle East Studies* 10:481-516.

CPPS. 1976. *Egypt and America*. Cairo: al-Ahram Press. (In Arabic.)

―――. 1977. *Democracy in Egypt*. Cairo: al-Ahram Press. (In Arabic.)

Cross, David. 1972. EEC-Egypt Pact Matches Israel Deal. *The Times* (May 2, 1972).

Crouchley, A. E. 1936. *The Investment of Foreign Capital in Egyptian Companies and Foreign Debt*. Cairo: Government Press.

―――. 1938. *The Economic Development of Modern Egypt*. London.

Cuddihy, William. 1980. *Agricultural Price Management in Egypt*. World Bank Staff Working Paper no. 388. Washington, D.C.: IBRD.

Dassuqi, 'Asim al-. 1975. *Large agricultural landowners and their role in Egyptian society, 1914-52*. Cairo: Dar al-Thiqafa al-Jadida. (In Arabic.)

Da'ud, 'Aziz. 1973. Is there a role for national capitalism? *al-Tali'a* 9:58-75.

Davis, Eric. 1982. Islam and Politics in Modern Egypt. In *Contemporary Social Movements in the Near and Middle East*, edited by Said Arjomand. Albany: SUNY Press.

Dawisha, I. 1975. Intervention in the Yemen: An Analysis of Egyptian Perceptions and Policies. *MEJ* 29:47-63.

Deeb, Marius. 1976. Bank Misr and the Emergence of the Local Bourgeoisie in Egypt. *Middle Eastern Studies* 12:70-86.

De Gré, Gerard. 1974. Realignments of Class Attitudes in the Military and Bourgeoisie in Developing Countries: Egypt, Peru and Cuba. *International Journal of Comparative Sociology* 15:35-46.

Dekmejian, Hrair. 1971. *Egypt under Nasir: A Study in Political Dynamics*. Albany: SUNY Press.

Delcour, Roland. 1972. Quatre-cents magasins vendant des produits étrangers "de luxe" sont fermés. *Le Monde* (April 28, 1972).

Dessouki, Ali E. 1980. The Development of Official Ideology in Egypt: Democracy and Socialism. *Indian Journal of Politics* 14:47-64.

―――, and Labban, Adel al-. 1981. Arms Race, Defense Expenditures and Development: The Egyptian Case 1952-1973. *Journal of South Asian and Middle Eastern Studies* 4:65-77.

Dewidar, M. 1977. An Entry Visa to the Egyptian Village. *EC* 68:85-116. (In Arabic.)

Dib, Muhammed Abu Mandur. 1975. The relation between owner and rentier in Egyptian agriculture. *al-Tali'a* 7:78-83.

―――. 1976. The Role of the Human Factor in Egyptian Agricultural Development. *EC* 67:171-87.

Djilas, Milovan. 1957. *The New Class*. London: Thames and Hudson.

BIBLIOGRAPHY

Dos Santos, Theotonio. 1970. The Structure of Dependence. *American Economic Review* 60:231-36.

Draz, Hamid 'Abd al-Magid. 1976. *Reform of the agricultural tax.* Cairo: Mu'assasa Shabab al-Gama'. (In Arabic.)

Dupuy, Alex, and Truchil, Barry. 1979. Problems in the Theory of State Capitalism. *Theory and Society* 8:1-38.

Eckaus, R. S. et al. 1978. *Multisector General Equilibrium Policy Model for Egypt.* Cairo: Cairo University-DRPTC.

Edel, M. Reda A. el-. 1982. Impact of Taxation on income distribution: An exploratory attempt to estimate tax incidence in Egypt. In G. Abdel-Khalek and R. Tignor, 1982.

Egypt-US Business Council. 1976. *Report on Foreign Investment in Egypt.* N.p.

Emmanuel, Arghiri. 1972. *Unequal Exchange: A Study of the Imperialism of Trade.* New York: Monthly Review Press.

Era 2000 Inc. 1979. *Further Mechanization of Egyptian Agriculture.* Washington, D.C.: ERA 2000 Inc.

Evans, Peter. 1979. *Dependent Development: The Alliance of Multinational State and Local Capital in Brazil.* Princeton: Princeton University Press.

Fakhouri, Hani. 1972. *Kafr el-Elow: An Egyptian Village in Transition.* New York: Holt, Rinehart and Winston.

Fakri, Mustapha, and Fil, Ahmad al-. 1975. Factors responsible for the major proportional decline of rice in Egypt's cropping pattern. *al-Magalla al-Zira'ia* 17:150-60. (In Arabic.)

Faksh, Mahmud A. 1977. The Chimera of Educational Development in Egypt: The Socio-economic Roles of University Graduates. *Middle Eastern Studies* 13:229-40.

FEI. 1976. The private industrial sector and its role in economic development. *Industrial Egypt* 52:1-10. (In Arabic.)

First, Ruth. 1974. *Libya: The Elusive Revolution.* Hammondsworth: Penguin.

Fitch, J. B., Khedr, Hassan, and Whittington, Dale. 1979. The Economic Efficiency of Water Use in Egyptian Agriculture. Draft Paper, 13th International Conference of Agricultural Economists, September 1979, Banff, Canada.

Fitzgerald, E.V.K. 1977. On State Accumulation in Latin America. In *The State and Economic Development in Latin America*, ed. E.V.K. Fitzgerald et al., Occasional Paper 1, Center of Latin American Studies, Cambridge University. Cambridge: Cambridge University Press.

———. 1979. *The Political Economy of Peru, 1956-78.* Cambridge: Cambridge University Press.

Frankel, Francine R. 1978. *India's Political Economy 1947-1977.* Princeton: Princeton University Press.

Fu'ad, Ni'amit. 1978. *The Pyramid Mount Project: The most serious threat to Egypt*. Cairo: 'Alam al-Kutub. (In Arabic.)

Furtado, Celso. 1973. The Concept of External Dependence in the Study of Underdevelopment. In Wilber (1973, pp. 118-123).

Gabali, Mustapha. 1973. Testimony to Maglis al-Sha'ab. *AY* (February 7, 1973).

Gabr, Hatim. 1975. The evolution of the general holding organizations in Egypt. *Administration* 8:19-36. (In Arabic.)

Gall, N. 1971. Peru: The Master is Dead. *Dissent* (June 1971), pp. 281-320.

Gama', Mustapha Gama'. 1973. Organizational structure of cooperatives and the problem of cooperation in the ARE. *EC* 64:188-205. (In Arabic.)

Garrison, Jean L. 1978. Public Assistance in Egypt: An Ideological Analysis. *MEJ* 32:279-90.

Gawhar, Sami. 1975. *The silent speak*. Cairo: Modern Egyptian Library. (In Arabic.)

Gellner, E., and Waterbury, J., eds. 1977. *Patrons and Clients in Mediterranean Societies*. London: Duckworth.

Ghaith, 'Usama. 1977. Inflation: How do we fight it by increasing the deficit? *AI*, no. 528 (August 1977).

―――. 1978a. Customs subsidy to merchants and brokers. *AI*, no. 539 (February 1, 1978).

―――. 1978b. Egypt's negotiations with the IMF. *AI*, no. 548 (June 15, 1978).

Ghamri, Ibrahim al-. 1973. Worker participation in management. *AI*, no. 432 (August 15, 1973).

Ghazzali, 'Abd al-Mun'aim al-. 1973. The July 23 revolution and parasitic capitalism. *al-Tali'a* 9:22-26.

Ghun'aim, 'Adil. [1965]. La révolution de Juillet et le Capitalism. In *La Voie égyptienne vers le socialisme*, pp. 449-73. Cairo: Dar al-Ma'aref.

―――. 1968. Concerning the case of the new class in Egypt. *al-Tali'a* 4:82-93.

Girgis, Malak. 1974. *Egyptian personal psychology and impediments to economic growth*. Cairo: Ruz al-Yussef Press. (In Arabic.)

Giyyar, Mahmud. 1975. Personal Secrets of Gamal 'Abd al-Nasser. *RY*, no. 2476 (November 24, 1975).

Glassman, Jon D. 1975. *Arms for the Arabs: The Soviet Union and War in the Middle East*. Baltimore: Johns Hopkins University Press.

Goldman, Marshal. 1967. The United Arab Republic: Drama, Repayment, and the Bureaucratic Routine. In *Soviet Foreign Aid*, pp. 60-84. New York: Praeger.

Gorman, Stephen. 1978. Peru before the Election. *Government and Opposition* 13:288-307.

Griffin, Keith. 1976. *Land Concentration and Rural Poverty*. London: Macmillan.

———, and Khan, Azizur Rahman. 1978. Poverty in the Third World: Ugly Facts and Fancy Models. *WD* 6:295-304.

Griggs, Lee. 1967. Report from Cairo. *Fortune* (May 1967), pp. 69-75.

Gritli, 'Ali al-. 1947. The Structure of Modern Industry in Egypt. *EC*.

———. 1962. *Population and economic resources in Egypt*. Cairo: Matba' Misr. (In Arabic.)

———. 1974. *The economic history of the revolution: 1952-1965*. Cairo: Dar al-Ma'aref. (In Arabic.)

———. 1975. The Dulles Convention. Interview with Sa'id Sanbal. *AY* (January 4, 1975).

———. 1977. *Twenty-five years: An analytic study of Egypt's economic policies 1952-1977*. Cairo: General Book Organisation. (In Arabic.)

Gumuchian, Hervé. 1975. Les expériences de mise en valeur du désert en République arabe d'Egypte: des projets aux réalisations. *Options méditerranéennes* no. 28, pp. 57-63.

Gunder-Frank, André. 1971. *Lumpen-bourgeoisie et lumpen-développement*. Paris: Maspéro.

Guwaida, Faruq. 1976a. What's the problem with the private sector? *A* (April 5, 1976).

———. 1976b. The story of commissions gained by middlemen with the Eastern Bloc. *A* (August 7, 1976).

———. 1976c. *Egypt's wealth: How does it disappear?* Cairo: al-Ahram Press. (In Arabic.)

Gwertzman, Bernard. 1978. Saudis Call Sadat's Effort for Mideast Peace a Failure. *NYT* (August 3, 1978).

———. 1979. Vance Finds the Mood in Congress is Mixed on Aid to Egypt and Israel. *NYT* (March 29, 1979).

Habashi, Fawzi. 1973. The Extent of parasitic incomes in the contracting sector. *al-Tali'a* 9:27-31.

Hadidi, Gen. Salah al-Din. 1974. *A witness of the '67 war*. Cairo: Dar al-Sharuq. (In Arabic.)

Hafiz, Salah. 1974. The names of the Communists. *RY*, no. 2414 (September 16, 1974).

———. 1978. The historical dilemma of the new government. *RY*, no. 2629 (October 30, 1978).

Halpern, Manfred. 1963. *The Politics of Social Change in the Middle East and North Africa*. Princeton: Princeton University Press.

———. 1977. Toward a Transforming Analysis of Social Classes. In *Commoners, Climbers and Notables*, ed. C.A.O. Van Nieuwenhuizje, pp. 21-53. Leiden: Brill.

Hamamsi, Galal al-Din. 1975. *Dialogue from behind the walls*. Cairo: Modern Egyptian Library. (In Arabic.)

Hamdan, Gamal. 1961. Evolution de l'Agriculture en Egypte. In *A History of Land Use in the Arid Regions*, pp. 133-61. Paris: UNESCO.

———. 1970. *Egypt's personality: A study in local genius*. Cairo: National Egyptian Library. (In Arabic.)

Hamilton, Nora. 1982. *Mexico: The Limits of State Autonomy*. Princeton: Princeton University Press.

Hammouda, Fathi. 1976. Labour Law in Egypt. Mimeographed. Cairo.

Hamrush, Ahmad. *The Story of the July 23 Revolution*. 1974. Pt. I: *Egypt and the Military* (1975) Pt. II: *Nasser's Group*; (1976), Pt. III: *Nasser and the Arabs*; (1977) Pt. IV: *Witnesses of the July Revolution*; 1978. *The Autumn of 'Abd al Nasr*. Beirut: Arab Org. For Studies and Publishing. (In Arabic.)

———. 1975. When the Marshal ruled Egypt. *RY*, no. 2458 (July 21, 1975).

Handleman, Howard. 1980. Peru: The March to Civilian Rule. *AUFS Report*, South America series, 1980, no. 2.

Handoussa, Heba. 1980. The Impact of Economic Liberalization on the Performance of Egypt's Public Sector Industry. Paper read at Second Boston Area Public Enterprise Group Conference, April 2-5, 1980, Boston.

Hanna, Milad. 1978. *I Want a Home: A Problem with a Solution*. Cairo: Ruz al-Yussef Press. (In Arabic.)

———. 1980. *Yes, Copts, but (also) Egyptians*. Cairo: Maktaba Medbuli. (In Arabic.)

Hansen, Bent. 1968. The Distributive Shares in Egyptian Agriculture, 1897-61. *International Economic Review* 9:175-94.

———. 1972. Economic Development of Egypt. In *Economic Development and Population Growth in the Middle East*, ed. Ch. Cooper and Sidney Alexander, pp. 22-91. New York: Elsevier.

———. 1975. Arab Socialism in Egypt. *WD* 3:201-11.

———, and Marzouk, G. 1965. *Development and Economic Policy in the UAR*. Amsterdam: North-Holland Publishing Co.

———, and Nashashibi, Karim. 1975. *Foreign Trade Regimes and Economic Development: Egypt*. Special Conference Series on Foreign Trade Regimes and Economic Development, National Bureau of Economic Research, vol. 4. New York: Columbia University Press.

Hansen, Roger. 1979. *Beyond the North-South Stalemate*. New York: McGraw-Hill.

Harbison, F., and Ibrahim, A. 1958. *Human Resources for Egyptian Enterprise*. New York: McGraw-Hill.

Harik, Ilya. 1971. The Impact of the Domestic Market on Rural-Urban Relations. International Development Research Center, Working Paper, February 2, 1971.

———. 1972. Mobilization Policy and Political Change in Egypt. In *Rural Politics and Social Change in the Middle East*, ed. Harik and Antoun, pp. 287-314. Bloomington: Indiana University Press.

———. 1973. The Single Party as a Subordinate Movement. *World Politics* 26:80-105.

———. 1974. *The Political Mobilization of Peasants: A Study of an Egyptian Community*. Bloomington: Indiana University Press.

———. 1979. *Distribution of Land, Employment and Income in Rural Egypt*. Rural Development Committee, Cornell University.

Hassan, 'Abd al-Fattah. 1974. *Political Memoirs*. Cairo: Dar al-Sha'b. (In Arabic.)

Hassan, Ahmed. 1982. Impact of Agricultural Policies on Income Distribution. In G. Abdel-Khalek and R. Tignor, eds. 1982.

Hassan, Muhammed Muhammed. 1975. Educational and manpower planning: Egypt's experience. *Arab Industrial Development*, October, pp. 34-87. (In Arabic.)

Hassanain, Gamal Magdi. 1979. *The July Revolution and the game of class equilibrium*. Cairo: Dar al-Thiqafa al-Jadida. (In Arabic.)

Hassanain, Magdi. 1975. *The Sahara: Revolution and promise—The story of Tahrir Province*. Cairo: General Book Organisation. (In Arabic.)

Heaphy, James. 1966. The Organization of Egypt: Inadequacies of a Non-Political Model for Nation-building. *World Politics* 18:177-93.

Heikal, Muhammed Hassanein. 1965. Le problème agraire: horizons nouveaux. In *La Voie Egyptienne vers le socialisme* pp. 185-202. Cairo: Dar al-Maaref.

———. 1978. *Sphinx and Commissar*. London: Collins.

Helleiner, G. K. 1979. Relief and Reform in Third World Debt. *WD* 7:113-24.

Heyworth-Dunne, J. 1938. *An Introduction to the History of Education in Modern Egypt*. London: Luzac and Co.

Higazi, 'Abd al-'Aziz. 1973. Dr. Higazi announces the new economic policy. *AI*, no. 432 (August 15, 1973).

Hilal, Ibrahim Hilal. 1976. The phenomenon of embezzlement in the agricultural coop sector. *al-Tali'a* 12:87-92.

Hinnebusch, Raymond. 1981. Egypt under Sadat: Elites, Power Structure, and Political Change in a Post-Populist State. *Social Problems* 28:442-64.

Hirschman, A. O. 1968. The Political Economy of Import-Substituting Industrialization in Latin America. *Quarterly Journal of Economics* 82:1-32.

Hirschman, A. O. 1970. *Exit, Voice and Loyalty: Responses to Declines in Firms, Organizations and States*. Cambridge, Mass.: Harvard University Press.

———. 1973. The Changing Tolerance for Income Inequality in the Course of Economic Development. *Quarterly Journal of Economics* 87:544-66.

———. 1979. The Turn to Authoritarianism in Latin America and the Search for its Economic Determinants. In *The New Authoritarianism in Latin America*, ed. David Collier, pp. 61-98. Princeton: Princeton University Press.

Hoisefield, J. Keith. 1969. *The International Monetary Fund: 1945-1965*. 2 vols. Washington, D.C.: IMF.

Holsen, John. 1979. Notes on the LDC Debt Problem. *WD* 7:145-59.

Holt, P. M., ed. 1968. *Political and Social Change in Modern Egypt*. Oxford: Oxford University Press.

Hopkins, Nicholas. 1980. Notes on the Political Economy of an Upper Egyptian Village. Paper read at MESA meeting, 8 November 1980, Washington, D.C.

Hopkins, R. F., and Puchala, D. J. 1978. *The Global Political Economy of Food*. Madison: University of Wisconsin Press.

Hovey, Graham. 1978. Economists call outlook for Egypt good if it makes hard decisions. *NYT* January 30, 1978.

Huntington, Samuel P. and Nelson, Joan M. 1976. *No Easy Choice: Political Participation in Developing Countries*. Cambridge, Mass.: Harvard University Press.

Hussain, 'Adil. 1975. A critique of the plan and the open door policy. *al-Tali'a* 2:10-23.

———. 1976a. The government and debts, growth and millionaires. *al-Tali'a* 12:52-63.

———. 1976b. The new wave of inflation and the advice of the IMF. *al-Tali'a* 12:13-22.

Hussein, Mahmoud. 1971. *La Lutte de classes en égypte 1945-1970*. Paris: Maspéro.

———. 1975. *L'Egypte II, 1967-1973*, Paris: Maspéro.

Ibrahim, Sa'ad. 1982. Social Mobility and Income Distribution. In G. Abdel-Khaleq and R. Tignor, eds. 1982.

Ibrahim, Youssef A. 1979. Saudis bolstering links with Europe. *NYT* (October 7, 1979).

IBRD, IDF Division. 1977. Review of Small-scale Industry in Egypt. Draft.

———. 1978a. *Arab Republic of Egypt: Economic Management in a Period of Transition*. IBRD. Report No. 1815 EGT. 6 vols. Washington, D.C.

———. 1978b. *World Development Report 1978*. Washington, D.C.: IBRD.

———. 1979a. *State Intervention in the Industrialization of Developing*

Countries: Selected Issues. Staff Working Paper 341. Washington, D.C.: IBRD.

———. 1979b. *Private Direct Investment in Developing Countries.* Staff Working Paper 348. Washington, D.C.: IBRD.

———. 1979c. Meeting Basic Needs in Egypt. EMENA Region, 15 November 1979. Mimeographed.

———. 1980. *ARE: Domestic Resource Mobilization and Growth Prospects for the 1980s.* EMANA Reg. Report #3123 EGT.

I.E.D.E.S. 1960. Pression Démographique et stratification sociale dans les campagnes égyptiennes. *Tiers Monde* 1:313-40.

———. 1961. La societé urbaine égyptienne. *Tiers Monde* 2:183-210.

Ikram, Khalid. 1981. *Egypt: Economic Management in a Period of Transition.* Baltimore: Johns Hopkins University Press.

Imam, 'Abdullah. 1976. *Slaughter of the judiciary.* Cairo: Ruz al-Yussef. (In Arabic.)

Imam, Mustapha. 1981. Where is Egypt's inflation going? *AI*, no. 643 (May 11, 1981).

IMF. 1978. *Arab Republic of Egypt—Recent Economic Developments.* Washington, D.C.: IMF.

———. 1980. *ARAB Republic of Egypt—Recent Economic Developments.* Washington, D.C.:

Isma'il, Muhammed. 1973. The economics of the iron and steel industry in Egypt. *EC* 64:5-43. (In Arabic.)

'Issa, Salah. 1974. The future of democracy in Egypt. *al-Katib*, 14:9-28. (In Arabic.)

Issawi, Charles. 1954. *Egypt at Mid-Century: An Economic Survey.* London: Oxford University Press.

———. 1963. *Egypt in Revolution: An Economic Analysis.* London: Oxford University Press.

Issawy, Ibrahim H. 1982. Interconnections between Income Distribution and Economic Growth in the Context of Egypt's Economic Development. In G. Abdel-Khalek and R. Tignor, eds. 1982.

Jacquemot, Pierre and Raffinot, Marc. 1977. *Le capitalisme d'état algérien.* Paris: Maspéro.

Johnson, Lyndon B. 1971. *The Vantage Point—Perspectives of the Presidency 1963-1969.* New York: Holt, Rinehart and Winston.

Juruna, Julia. 1977. Le gendarme du grand capital. *Le Monde Diplomatique*, October 1977.

Kamil, 'Izz al-Din. 1976. *Mechanized agriculture.* Cairo: Dar al-Thiqafa al-Jadida. (In Arabic.)

Kaufman, Robert. 1979. Industrial Change and Authoritarian Rule in Latin

America. In *The New Authoritarianism in Latin America*, ed. David Collier, pp. 165-254. Princeton: Princeton University Press.

————, Chernotsky, Harry I., and Geller, Daniel S. 1975. A Preliminary Test of the Theory of Dependency. *Comparative Politics* 7:303-330.

Karum, Hassanain. 1975. *'Abd al-Nasser slandered*. Cairo: Madbuli. (In Arabic.)

Keep, John. 1969. The Soviet Union and the Third World. *Survey*, no. 72, pp. 19-38.

Kerr, Malcolm. 1962. The Emergence of a Socialist Ideology in Egypt. *MEJ* 16:127-44.

————. 1963. Arab Radical Notions of Democracy. In *Middle Eastern Affairs*, ed. Albert Hourani, pp. 9-40. St. Anthony's Papers no. 16. London: Chatto and Windus.

————. 1965. Egypt. In *Education and Political Development*, ed. James Coleman, pp. 169-94. Princeton: Princeton University Press.

Khalid, Muhammed. 1975. *The union movement between past and present*. Cairo: Mu'assasa Dar al-Ta'awan lil Tiba'a Wal Nashr. (In Arabic.)

Khalil, Muhammed al-Sawi. 1977. *7000 days in the marketplace: From the memoirs of a public sector board chairman*. Cairo: al-Matba' al-'Alamiya. (In Arabic.)

Kholi, Lutfi al-. 1974. Observations on the "Infitah." *al-Tali'a* 10:5-19.

————. 1975. Petro-dollars and petro-blood. *A* (January 30, 1975).

————. 1975b. These are the *Bayyumiyun*. *al-Tali'a* 11:81-85.

Kholie, Osman al-. 1973. Disparities of Egyptian Personal Income Distribution as Reflected by Family Budget Data. *EC* 64:33-56.

Killick, Tony. 1978. *Development Economics in Action: A Study of Economic Policies in Ghana*. New York: St. Martin's Press.

Korayem, K. 1982. The Agricultural Output Pricing Policy and the Implicit Taxation of Agricultural Income. In G. Abdel-Khalek and R. Tignor, eds. 1982.

Labib, Tewfik. 1974. How the New Investment Law Came About and Procedures for Investing in Egypt. In J. W. Stephens and P. F. Hayek, eds. 1974, pp. 1-14.

La Courture, Jean. 1971. *Nasser*. Paris: Le Seuil.

————, and La Courture, Simone. 1958. *Egypt in Transition*. New York: Criterion Books.

Lall, Sanjaya. 1975. Is "Dependence" a useful concept in analysing Underdevelopment? *WD* 3:799-810.

Landa, R. G. 1966. Again about the Non-Capitalist Path of Development. *Narody Azii Afriki*, no. 6, pp. 30-38.

Lehmann, David, ed. 1974. *Peasants, Landlords and Governments: Agrarian Reform in the Third World*. New York: Holmes and Meier.

Lewis, W. Arthur. 1978. *The Evolution of the International Economic Order*. Princeton: Princeton University Press.

Leys, Colin. 1975. *Underdevelopment in Kenya: The Political Economy of Neo-Colonialism*. Berkeley: University of California Press.

―――. 1978. Capital Accumulation, Class Formation and Dependency— The Significance of the Kenyan Case. Unpublished MS.

Lippmann, Thomas. 1978. Egypt bends Arab boycott rules. *The Guardian* (August 18, 1978).

―――. 1979. Saudis close down Arab Arms Project. *WP* (May 14, 1979).

Lipton, Michael. 1977. *Why Poor People Stay Poor: Urban Bias in World Development*. Cambridge, Mass.: Harvard University Press.

A. D. Little, Inc. 1978. *An Assessment of Egypt's Industrial Sector*.

Lloyd, John. 1978. £1.6bn Egypt telephone deal going to U.S. *FT* (June 2, 1978).

Lotz, Jorgen R. 1966. Taxation in the UAR (Egypt). *IMF Staff Papers* 13:121-53.

Lowenthal, A. F., ed. 1975. *The Peruvian Experiment*. Princeton: Princeton University Press.

Mabro, Robert. 1967. Industrial Growth, Agricultural Under-Employment, and the Lewis Model: The Egyptian Case 1937-65. *The Journal of Development Studies* 3:322-51.

―――. 1974. *The Egyptian Economy: 1952-1972*. Oxford: Clarendon Press.

―――. 1975. Egypt's Economic Relations with the Socialist Countries. *WD* 3:299-314.

―――, and O'Brien, P. 1970. Structural Changes in the Egyptian Economy, 1937-1965. In *Studies in the Economic History of the Middle East*, ed. M. A. Cook, pp. 412-27. London: Oxford University Press.

―――, and Radwan, Samir. 1976. *The Industrialization of Egypt 1939-1973: Policy and Performance*. Oxford: Clarendon Press.

McGowan, P. J. and Smith, D. L. 1978. Economic Dependency in Black Africa: An Analysis of Competing Theories. *International Organisation* 32:179-235.

Mackenzie Wallace, D. 1883. *Egypt and the Egyptian Question*. London: Macmillan.

Mackie, Alan. 1978. Australia bites into the meat and wheat market. *MEED* (September 15, 1978).

―――. 1980a. A Bank to foster small-scale industry, *MEED* (April 18, 1980).

―――. 1980b. Sadat Streamlines Cabinet. *MEED* (May 16, 1980).

―――. 1980c. Arab Banking: Egypt and Sudan. *MEED Special Report* 15 (May 1980):81-84.

Maglis al-Sha'ab. 1973. Plan and Budget Committee Reports of Public Sector Observation, Pts. I and II. Cairo (May 31, 1973). (In Arabic.)

Mahdavy, H. 1970. The Patterns and Problems of Economic Development in Rentier States: The Case of Iran. Studies in the Economic History of the Middle East from the Rise of Islam to the Present Day, ed. M. A. Cook, pp. 428-67. London: Oxford University Press.

Mahfouz, El-Kosheri. 1972. *Socialisme et Pouvoir en Egypt*. Paris: Libraire Générale de Droit et de Jurisprudence.

Maraghi, Mahmud. 1975. Egypt, Moscow and debts. *RY*, no. 2462 (August 18, 1975).

————. 1976a. Has the government agreed to devalue the pound? *RY* (July 5, 1976).

————. 1976b. Arab privileges in Egypt. *RY*, no. 2516 (August 30, 1976).

————. 1978a. Al-Qaissuni and Abu Isma'il face to face. *RY*, no. 2586 (January 2, 1978).

————. 1978b. Interview with Dr. 'Ali al-Salmi: Minister of Administrative Development. *RY*, no. 2592 (February 13, 1978).

————. 1978c. The merchant's four gimmicks. *RY*, no. 2593 (February 20, 1978).

————. 1978d. Will the President use his right of veto against the proposed tax law? *RY*, no. 2596 (March 13, 1978).

————. 1978e. The price game. *RY*, no. 2599 (April 3, 1978).

Mar'ai, Sayyid. 1970. *Agriculture in the era of 'Abd al-Nasr*. Cairo: Dar al-Ta'awan. (In Arabic.)

————. 1975. The Arab project for development: So that we may reap the future. *al-Magalla al-Zira'ia* 17:26-42. (In Arabic.)

————. 1979. *Political papers*: Pt. I, *From the village to reform*; Pt. II, *From the March crisis to the defeat*; Pt. III, *With President Anwar Sadat*. Cairo: al-Ahram Press. (In Arabic.)

————, and Hagras, S. 1975. *If the Arabs will it*. Cairo: Dar al-Ta'awan. (In Arabic.)

Marx, Karl. 1898. *The Eighteenth Brumaire of Louis Bonaparte*. Translated from the German by Daniel de Leon. New York: International Publishing Co.

Massira, al-. 1972. *La Révolte des étudiants égyptiens*. Paris: Maspéro.

Matar, Fu'ad. 1972a. *What has become of Nasser in the Republic of Sadat?* Beirut: Dar al-Nahar lil Nashr. (In Arabic.)

————. 1972b. *Nasserist Russia and Egyptian Egypt*. Beirut: Dar al-Nahar lil Nashr. (In Arabic.)

Matthews, Roger. 1978. IMF and Egypt in talks on $750m credit. *FT* (May 26, 1978).

————. 1979a. Egypt Appeals for $18.5bn to offset Arab Boycott. *FT* (July 9, 1979).

————. 1979b. Egypt receives Soviet military supplies again. *FT* (September 21, 1979).

————. 1979c. Egypt-Moscow relations come in from the cold. *FT* (December 4, 1979).

Mayfield, James B. 1971. *Rural Politics in Nasser's Egypt*. Austin: University of Texas Press.

————. 1974. *Local Institutions and Egyptian Rural Development*. Ithaca: Rural Development Committee, Cornell University.

Mead, Donald C. 1967. *Growth and Structural Change in the Egyptian Economy*. Homewood, Ill.: Richard D. Irwin.

Mendel, Arthur, ed. 1979. *The Essential Works of Marxism*. 15th ed. New York: Bantam.

Meyer, Gail E. 1980. *Egypt and the United States: The Formative Years*. Rutherford, N.J.: Fairleigh Dickinson University Press.

Mikesell, R. F., and Zinser, J. E. 1973. The Nature of the Savings Function in Developing Countries: A Survey of the Theoretical and Empirical Literature. *The Journal of Economic Literature* 11:1-26.

Milner, Alfred. 1904. *England in Egypt*. 11th ed. London: Edward Arnold.

Mirsky, G. I. 1964. Changes in Class Forces and Ideas on Socialism. *Mizan* 6.

Mitchell, Richard P. 1969. *The Society of Muslim Brothers*. London: Oxford University Press.

Mohie Eldine, 'Amr. 1973. The leading role of the public sector in the process of economic growth. *A* (September 28, 1973).

————. 1978. Evaluation of Egypt's Strategy of Industrialization and Future Alternatives. In *The Strategy of Development in Egypt*, ed. Egyptian Association for Political Economy Statistics and Legislation, 2nd Conference of Egyptian Economists, pp. 177-208. Cairo: General Book Organisation. (In Arabic.)

————. 1977. Distributive Effects of Economic Policy. In S. Yassin 1977, pp. 95-105. (In Arabic.)

————. 1982. The Development of the Share of Agricultural Wage Labour in the National Income of Egypt. In G. Abdel-Khalek and R. Tignor, eds. (1982).

Montasser, Adel. 1960-61. La repression anti-démocratique en Egypte. *Les Temps Modernes*. 16:418-42; 17:184-92.

Montasser, Essam. 1974. Egypt's Pattern of Trade and Development: A Model of Import Substitution Growth. *EC* 65:141-246.

————. 1975. Agricultural Prices, Growth, and Sectoral Terms of Trade in

Egypt. *FAO/SIDA SEMINAR in Agriculture Sector Analysis in the Near East and North Africa*. Mimeographed. Cairo.

———. 1976. Egypt's Long-Term Growth: 1976-2000 Preliminary Projections. Paper read at Joint symposium on Long-Range Planning and Regional Integration with Special Reference to the Arab Region CAEU-INP, January 14-21, 1976, Cairo.

Moore, Clement H. 1974. Authoritarian Politics in Unincorporated Society: The Case of Nasser's Egypt. *Comparative Politics* 6:193-218.

———. 1975. Professional Syndicates in Egypt. *American Journal of Arabic Studies* 3:60-82.

———. 1980. *Images of Development: Egyptian Engineers in Search of Industry*. Cambridge, Mass.: MIT Press.

Mungi, 'Abd al-Fattah. 1975. *INP Study to Delimit and Estimate Public Sector Manpower Needs*. Cairo: INP.

Murad, Hilmi. 1974. Slaughter of Judiciary. *AY* (October 19, 1974).

———. 1980. *The other point of view*. Cairo: Dar al-Thiqafa al-Jadida. (In Arabic.)

Murad, Mahmud. 1975. *Who was governing Egypt?* Cairo: al-Ahram Press. (In Arabic.)

Mursi, Fu'ad. 1974. The public sector and private investment. *al-Tali'a* 10:16-23.

———. 1975a. Economic development and foreign investment, *al-Tali'a*, 11:12-27.

———. 1975b. Confronting the resurgence of big capital. *al-Tali'a* 11:12-21.

———. 1975c. The dominance of capitalist production relations. *al-Tali'a* 11:105-25.

———. 1976. *This is the economic open-door policy*. Cairo: Dar al-Thiqafa al-Jadida. (In Arabic.)

Mutwali Mahmud. 1972. The path of Egyptian capitalism after 1961. *al-Katib* 12:31-67. (In Arabic.)

———. 1973a. Characteristics of capitalism in Egyptian economic history. *al-Katib* 13:26-43. (In Arabic.)

———. 1973b. Capitalist personalities in Egypt's economic history. *al-Katib* 13:60-79. (In Arabic.)

———. 1973c. The penetration of foreign capital in Egypt. *al-Katib* 13:26-47, 84-94. (In Arabic.)

Najjar, Fawzi. 1968. Islam and Socialism in the UAR. *Journal of Contemporary History* 3:183-99.

Nasr, Salah. 1975. *Agents of treason and talk of lies*. Beirut: al-Watan al-'Arabi. (In Arabic.)

Nashashibi, Karim. 1970. Foreign Trade and Economic Development in the

UAR: A Case Study. In *Trade Patterns in the Middle East*, by Lee E. Preston and Karim Nashashibi, pp. 73-93. Washington, D.C.: American Enterprise Institute for Public Policy Research.

Nasrat, M. Mohiey, and Goueli, A. Ahmed. 1976. The Productivity of the Human Work Force in Traditional Agriculture with Special Reference to Egypt. In *Proceedings of the World Food Conference of 1976*, pp. 331-37. Ames: Iowa State University Press.

Nassar, Mumtaz. 1975. *The battle for justice in Egypt*. Cairo: Dar al-Sharuq. (In Arabic.)

Nazir, Gamal al-. 1975. Foreign Lessons for Egypt's Growth Path. *AI*, no. 471 (April 1, 1975).

NBE. 1978. The National Economy in 1977. *NBE Economic Bulletin* 31.

Nerfin, Marc. 1974. *Entretiens avec Ahmed ben Salah*. Paris: Maspéro.

Nutting, Anthony. 1972. *Nasser*. London: Constable.

O'Brien, Patrick. 1966. *The Revolution in Egypt's Economic System: From Private Enterprise to Socialism, 1952-1966*. London: Oxford University Press.

—————. 1968. The Long-term Growth of Agricultural Production in Egypt, 1821-1962. In P. M. Holt, ed. 1968, pp. 162-95.

O'Brien, Philip J. 1975. A Critique of Latin American Theories of Dependency. In *Beyond the Sociology of Development*, ed. Ivar Oxaal et al., pp. 7-27. London: Routledge and Kegan Paul.

O'Donnell, Guillermo A. 1973. *Modernization and Bureaucratic Authoritarianism*. Studies in South American Politics, Politics of Modernization Series no. 9. Berkeley: Institute of International Studies.

—————. 1978. Reflections on the Patterns of Change in the Bureaucratic-Authoritarian State. *Latin American Research Review* 13:3-37.

—————. 1979. Tensions in the Bureaucratic-Authoritarian State and the Question of Democracy. In *The New Authoritarianism in Latin America*, ed. David Collier, pp. 285-318. Princeton: Princeton University Press.

Okyar, Osman. 1975. The Mixed Economy in Turkey. Paper read at International Seminar on the Turkish and Other Countries' Experience with a Mixed Economy, October 13-17, 1975, Hacettepe University, Antalya.

OPNUR. 1977. *Observations of the Deputies of OPNUR on the Prime Minister's Declaration and Their Views on (its) Problems*. Cairo: Atlas Printers.

Osman, Osman Ahmad. 1981. *Pages from my experience*. Cairo: Modern Egyptian Library. (In Arabic.)

Owen, E.R.J. 1969. *Cotton and the Egyptian Economy, 1820-1914*. London: Oxford University Press.

Owen, Roger. 1972. Egypt and Europe: From Expedition to British Occupation. In *Studies in the Theory of Imperialism*, ed. Roger Owen and Bob Sutcliffe, pp. 195-209. London: Longman.

Palma, Gabriel. 1978. Dependency: The Formal Theory of Underdevelopment as a Methodology for the Analysis of Concrete Situations of Underdevelopment. *WD* 6:881-924.

Peixoto, Antonio Carlos. 1977. La théorie de la dépendance: bilan critique. *Revue Française de Science Politique* 27:601-29.

Poulantzas, Nicos Ar. 1978. *L'Etat, le pouvoir, le socialisme*. Paris: PUF.

Ra'anan, Uri. 1973. The USSR and the Middle East: Some Reflections on the Soviet Decision-Making Process. *Orbis* 17:946-77.

Radwan, Samir. 1974. *Capital Formation in Egyptian Industry and Agriculture, 1882-1967*. St. Antony's Middle East Monographs, no. 2. London: Ithaca Press.

————. 1977. The Impact of Agrarian Reform on Rural Egypt: 1952-1975. Working Paper 10-6/WP-13, Rural Employment and Policy Research Program, World Employment Programme Research, Geneva.

Ramadan, 'Abd al-'Azim. 1975. *Social and political struggle in Egypt from the July 23 Revolution to the end of the crisis of March 1954*. Cairo: Matba' Madbuli. (In Arabic.)

————. 1976. *'Abd al-Nasser and the March Crisis*. Cairo: Ruz al-Yussef Press. (In Arabic.)

————. 1978a. Pyramid mount between democracy and infitah. *RY*, no. 2608 (June 5, 1978).

————. 1978b. Egypt's capitalists between contraction and exploitation. *RY*, no. 2620 (August 28, 1978).

Rashid, Ahmad. 1970. Bureaucracy in Egypt. *AI* Supplement (April 15, 1970).

RAU. 1968. La Conjoncture économique avant et après, Juin 1967. *L'Ecbnomie et les Finances des Pays Arabes*, no. 129, pp. 61-97, and no. 130, pp. 82-114.

Reid, Donald M. 1974. The Rise of Professions and Professional Organization in Modern Egypt. *Comparative Studies in Society and History* 16:24-57.

Reid, Escott. 1973. *Strengthening the World Bank*. Chicago: Adlai Stevenson Institute.

Riad, Hassan. 1964. *L'Egypte Nassérienne*. Paris: Ed. de. Minuit.

Richards, Alan. 1981. *Egypt's Agricultural Development: Technical and Social Change, 1800-1980*. Boulder, Colo.: Westview Press.

Rifa'at, 'Issam. 1973a. Idle capacity. *AI*, no. 439 (January 12, 1973).

————. 1973b. Have the general organizations achieved what was expected of them? *AI*, no. 431 (August 1, 1973).

————. 1975. Take your hands off the private sector. *AI*, no. 485 (November 1, 1975).

————. 1976. What's happened after the abolition of the general organizations? *AI*, no. 505 (September 1, 1976).

————. 1977a. Danger signals in Egypt's imports. *AI*, no. 527 (August 1, 1977).

————. 1977b. The hidden hands that control the Egyptian market. *AI*, no. 531 (October 1, 1977).

————. 1978a. Archives of a quarter century: Government vehicles. *AI*, no. 539 (February 1978).

————. 1978b. The consumer opening and the productive opening. *AI*, no. 546 (May 15, 1978).

————. 1978c. Raghif al-Khubz: Crisis in production or consumption? *AI*, no. 552 (August 15, 1978).

————. 1979. Arab trade with Egypt. *AI*, no. 568 (April 15, 1979).

Rifa'at, Muhammed 'Ali. 1980. The true picture of the economic open-door policy. *AI*, no. 596 (June 16, 1980), pp. 16-20.

Rivlin, Helen A. 1961. *The Agricultural Policy of Muhammed Ali in Egypt*. Cambridge, Mass.: Harvard University Press.

Riyad, Wagdi. 1979. The end of Cairo's domination of the regions. *AI*, no. 562 (January 15, 1979).

Ro'i, Yaacov. 1975. The USSR and Egypt in the Wake of Sadat's "July Decisions." Russian and East European Research Center, Tel Aviv University, Slavic and Soviet Series, no. 1.

Rouquié, Alain. 1975. L'Hypothèse "Bonapartiste" et l'émergence des systèmes politiques semi-compétitifs. *Revue française de science politique* 25:1077-111.

Roy, Delwin. 1977. Economic Liberalisation and the Private Industry Sector in Egypt. Mimeographed. CIA, Cambridge.

————. 1978. *Private Industry Sector Development in Egypt: An Analysis of Trends*. Draft. Cairo: USAID.

Rubenstein, Alvin. 1977. *Red Star on the Nile*. Princeton: Princeton University Press.

Rushdi, Muhammed. 1972. *The economic evolution of Egypt*. 2 vols. Cairo: Dar al-Ma'arif. (In Arabic.)

Saab, Edouard. 1974. Sadate restitue ce que Nasser a séquestré. *Journal de Genève* (July 9, 1974).

Saab, Gabriel. 1967. *The Egyptian Agrarian Reform 1952-1962*. London: Oxford University Press.

Saaty, Hassan al-. 1977. The New Aristocracized and Bourgeoisized Classes in the Egyptian Application of Socialism. In *Commoners, Climbers, and Notables*, ed. C.A.O. Van Nieuwenhuijze, pp. 196-204. Leiden: Brill.

Sabbagh, Nabil. 1977a. The public budget: Between what is planned and what is needed. *AI*, no. 515 (February 1977).

———. 1977b. Current situation and future of our foreign trade. *AI*, no. 527 (August 1, 1977).

———. 1978. The Deficit in the 1978 budget: What's behind it? *AI*, no. 538 (January 15, 1978).

———. 1979. The evolution of the public sector has begun. *AI*, no. 579 (October 1, 1979).

Sabri, Ibrahim. 1978. Employee's law—What after a quarter century of confusion? *AI*, no. 538 (January 15, 1978).

Sabri, Musa. 1974. *Documents of the October War*. Cairo: Modern Egyptian Library. (In Arabic.)

Sa'dni, 'Izzat. 1974. The indebted Egyptian peasant. *AI*, no. 445 (March 1, 1974).

———. 1975a. The real role of middlemen, black market traders and big landowners. *AI*, no. 480 (August 1975).

———. 1975b. The cotton curse has struck Egypt's peasants. *AI*, no. 486 (November 15, 1975).

———. 1975c. Cotton's bitterness in the cane fields. *AI*, no. 487 (December 1, 1975).

Sa'id, 'Abd al-Mughani. 1974. Questions about infitah . . . to whom and where? *al-Katib* 14:31-38. (In Arabic.)

Sa'id, Muhammed Sayyid. 1976. The commercial market and foreign exchange policy. *AI*, no. 505 (September 1, 1976).

Sa'id, Mustapha al-. 1976. Elections to the people's assembly and new social forces in the village. *A* (November 26, 1976).

———. 1978. Industrial growth in the UAR and the basic needs strategy 1952-1970. In Egyptian Association for Political Economy, Statistics and Legislation. *The Strategy of Development in Egypt*. 2nd Conference of Egyptian Economists. Cairo March 1977, Cairo 1978. (In Arabic.)

Sa'id, Rifa'at. 1972. The middle class and its role in Egyptian society. *al-Tali'a* 8:61-71.

———. 1975. *Nasserist papers*. Cairo: Dar al-Thiqafa al-Jadida. (In Arabic.)

Salacuse, Jeswald. 1975. Egypt's New Law on Foreign Investment: The Framework for Economic Openness. *The International Lawyer* 9:647-60.

———. 1980. Back to Contract: Implications of Peace and Openness for Egypt's Legal System. *American Journal of Comparative Law* vol. 28, 315-33.

———, and Parnall, T. 1978. Foreign Investment and Economic Openness in Egypt: Legal Problems and Legislative Adjustments in the First Three Years. *The International Lawyer* 12:759-77.

Salih, Mahmud 'Ali. 1975. Present Role of the Private Industrial Sector in Egypt's National Plan. Paper read at INP-Ford Foundation: Planning in Mixed Economies, May 10-14, 1975, Cairo.

Salmi, 'Ali al-. 1969. Administrative competence in the public sector. *AI* Supplement (February 15, 1969).

Sanbal, Sa'id. 1977. Infitah . . . and the new class. *AY* (February 5, 1977).

Saqr, Saqr Ahmad. 1978. Savings and Growth Strategy in Egypt. In *The Strategy of Development in Egypt*, Egyptian Assn. for Political Economy, Statistics and Legislation, pp. 295-324. Cairo.

Sayegh, Fayez. 1969. The Theoretical Structure of Nasser's Socialism. In *Arab Socialism*, ed. Sami Hanna and George Gardner, pp. 98-148. Leiden: Brill.

Schmitter, Phillipe C. 1974. Still the Century of Corporatism? *The Review of Politics* 36:85-132.

Scott, James. 1977. Patronage or Exploitation? In E. Gellner and J. Waterbury, eds. 1977, pp. 21-40.

Serrag al-Din, Fu'ad. 1977. *Why the new party?* Cairo: Dar al-Sharuq. (In Arabic.)

Shahat, Mahmud 'Abd al-Hamid, and Nassar, Sa'ad Zaki. 1973a. Evaluation of the performance of agriculture cooperatives in al-Minia governorate. *EC* 64:95-124. (In Arabic.)

———. 1973b. An Economic Analysis of State Farm Credit in Egypt 1960-1970. *EC* 64:93-106.

Shahata, Ibrahim. 1974. On the question of 50 percent representation. *A* (September 20, 1974).

Shalaqany, Ahmad. 1974. Repatriation of Earnings under the Investment Law. In *Investments in Egypt: Law No. 43 and Its Implications for the Transfer of Technology*, ed. John Stephens and P. F. Hayek, pp. 27-38. Cairo: Fund for Multinational Management Education.

Sid Ahmed, Mohammed. 1978. La Securité par le développement des liens économiques? *Le Monde Diplomatique* (January 1978).

Sidqi, Aziz. 1977. Interview. *RY*, no. 2536 (January 17, 1977).

Silberman, Gad S. 1972. National Identity in Nasserist Ideology. *Asian and African Studies* 8:49-86.

Singh, Ajit. 1979. The Basic Needs Approach to Development vs. New International Economic Order: The Significance of Third World Industrialization. *WD* 7:585-606.

Sirfi, 'Atia al-. 1975. *Migrant laborers*. Cairo: Dar al-Thiqafa al-Jadida. (In Arabic.)

Sklar, Richard L. 1979. The Nature of Class Domination in Africa. *The Journal of Modern African Studies* 17:531-52.

Smith, Hedrick. 1974. Cairo under Soviet attack for drift from Socialism. *NYT* (March 26, 1974).

———. 1976. *The Russians*. London: Sphere Books Ltd.

Springborg, Robert. 1975. Patterns of Association in the Egyptian Political Elite. In *Political Elites in the Middle East*, ed. George Lenczowski, pp. 83-108. Washington: American Enterprise Institute for Public Policy Research.

———. 1977. New Patterns of Agrarian Reform in the Middle East and North Africa. *MEJ* 31:127-42.

———. 1978. Professional Syndicates in Egyptian Politics 1952-1970. *IJMES* 9:275-95.

———. 1979. Patrimonialism and Policy-Making in Egypt: Nasser and Sadat and the Tenure Policy for Reclaimed Lands. *Middle East Studies* 15:49-69.

———. 1980. The Political Anthropology of an Egyptian Family: Sayyid Bey Marei. Unpublished MS.

Staats, Steven. 1972. Corruption in the Soviet System. *Problems of Communism* 20:40-47.

Stepan, Alfred. 1978. *The State and Society, Peru in Comparative Perspective*. Princeton: Princeton University Press.

Stephen, J. W. and Hayek, P. F., eds. 1974. *Investments in Egypt: Law 43 and its Implications for the Transfer of Technology*. New York: Fund for Multi-National Management and Education.

Stephens, Robert. 1971. *Nasser: A Political Biography*. London: Allen Lane.

Subhan, Malcolm. 1980. EEC Lends an Ear to Egypt Plaint. *TME* 68:72.

Sultan, Fu'ad. 1973. The free market for foreign exchange. *AI*, no. 432 (August 15, 1973).

Tigarat al-'Arab. 1978. The Merchant's War. *Tigarat al-'Arab* (Cairo) 11:16-22.

Tignor, R. L. 1966. *Modernization and British Colonial Rule in Egypt, 1882-1914*. Princeton: Princeton University Press.

———. 1976. The Egyptian Revolution of 1919: New Directions in the Egyptian Economy. *Middle Eastern Studies* 12:41-67.

———. 1977a. Bank Misr and Foreign Capitalism. *IJMES* 8:161-81.

———. 1977b. Nationalism, Economic Planning, and Development Projects in Interwar Egypt. *International Journal of African Historical Studies* 10:185-208.

———. 1978. The Economic Activities of Foreigners in Egypt 1920-1950: From Millet to Haute Bourgeoisie. Typescript.

———. 1982. Equity in Egypt's Recent Past. In Gouda Abdel-Khalek and R. Tignor, eds. 1982.

Tingay, Michael. 1976. Egypt's Latin American Finances. *FT* (August 26, 1976).

Tinbergen, Jan. 1975. *Income Distribution: Analysis and Policies*. New York: American Elsevier.

Tobgy, H. A. al-. 1976. *Contemporary Egyptian Agriculture*. 2nd ed. Cairo: Ford Foundation.

Tomiche, F. J. 1974. *Syndicalisme et certains aspects du travail en RAU (Egypte) 1900-1967*. Paris: G. P. Maisonneuve et Larose.

Trimberger, Ellen Kay. 1978. *Revolution from Above: Military Bureaucrats and Development in Japan, Turkey, Egypt and Peru*. New Brunswick: Transaction.

UAR Ministry of Industry. 1962. *Industry in Ten Years*. July 1962.

USACDA. 1978. U.S. Arms Control and Disarmament Agency. *World Military Expenditures and Arms Transfers*. Pub. 98, Washington, D.C.

US Department of Agriculture/USAID. 1976. *Egypt: Major Constraints to Increasing Agricultural Productivity*. Foreign Agricultural Economic Report, no. 120, Washington, D.C., June 1976.

USAID. 1976. Ministry of Housing and Reconstruction, Ministry of Planning. *Immediate Action Proposals for Housing in Egypt*, June 1976 (Mona Seragaldin, Appendix I).

USAID. 1977. *Education in Egypt*: A Survey Report, December 30, 1977.

USAID. 1978. *US Economic Assistance to Egypt: A Report of a Special Interagency Task Force*. Washington, D.C.

'Utaifi, Gamal al-. 1969. *The ASU: Political force or state power?* Cairo: ARAC.

———. 1973a. Concerning illegal, parasitic, and smuggled incomes. *A* (June 28, 1973).

———. 1973b. How, when, and under what conditions can we benefit from foreign investments? *A* (August 23, 1973).

———. 1973c. Political variables and their impact. *al-Tali'a* 9:38-50.

———. 1980. *Views on legality and freedom*. Cairo: General Book Organization. (In Arabic.)

Valkenier, Elizabeth. 1970. New Soviet Views on Economic Aid. *Survey*, no. 76, pp. 17-29.

———. 1980. Development Issues in Recent Soviet Scholarship. *World Politics* 32:485-508.

Vatikiotis, P. J. 1961. *The Egyptian Army in Politics*. Bloomington: Indiana University Press.

———. 1978. *Nasser and His Generation*. London: Croom Helm.

Vaucher, Georges. 1959. *Gamal Abdel Nasser et son équipe*. Paris: Juliard.

Vengroff, Richard. 1977. Dependency and Underdevelopment in Black Africa: an Empirical Test. *Journal of Modern African Studies* 15:613-30.

Von Braun, Joachim. 1980. Wirkunger von Nahrungsmittelhilfe in Empfängerhändern vergleichende untersuchung für Ägypten and Bangladesch gö Hingen. Mimeographed. Inst. für Agraïokonmie der Universität Göttingen.

Wakid, Lutfi. 1974. The free officers' movement. *al-Katib* 14:43-52.

Wakin, E. 1963. *A Lonely Minority: the Modern Story of Egypt's Copts*. New York: Morrow.

Wallerstein, Immanuel. 1974. *The Modern World System*. New York: Academic Press.

———. 1976. Semi-peripheral Countries and the Contemporary World Crisis. *Theory and Society* 3:461-84.

———. 1979. *The Capitalist World Economy*. Cambridge: Cambridge University Press.

Warren, Bill. 1973. Imperialism and Capitalist Industrialization. *New Left Review*, no. 81, pp. 3-44.

Waterbury, J. 1976a. Reorganization or Reshuffle of Egypt's Public Sector? *Business International* (January 21, 1976).

———. 1976b. Public vs. Private in the Egyptian Economy. *AUFS Report*, NE Africa Series, vol. 21.

———. 1976c. Corruption, Political Stability and Development: Comparative Evidence from Egypt and Morocco. *Government and Opposition* 11:426-45.

———. 1976d. Egypt: the Wages of Dependency. In *The Middle East: Oil, Conflict and Hope*, ed. A. L. Udovitch, pp. 291-351. Lexington, Mass.: Lexington Books.

———. 1978a. *Egypt: Burdens of the Past, Options for the Future*. Bloomington: Indiana University Press.

———. 1978b. Egyptian Agriculture Adrift. *AUFS Report*, Africa, no. 47.

———. 1979. *Hydropolitics of the Nile Valley*. Syracuse: Syracuse University Press.

———. 1980. The Implications of *Infitah* for U.S. Egyptian Relations. In *The Middle East and the United States*, ed. Haim Shaked and Itamar Rabinovich, pp. 347-68. New Brunswick: Transaction.

———. 1982. Patterns of Urban Growth and Income Distribution in Egypt. In G. Abdel-Khalek and R. Tignor, eds. 1982.

Wheelock, Keith. 1960. *Nasser's New Egypt*. New York: Praeger.

Wiarda, Howard J. 1974. Corporatism and Development in the Iberian-Latin World. *The Review of Politics* 36:3-33.

Wickwar, W. Hardy. 1965. Food and Social Development in the Middle East. *MEJ* 19:177-93.

Wilber, Charles K., ed. 1973. *The Political Economy of Development and Underdevelopment*. New York: Random House.

Wissa-Wassef, Ceres. 1973a. Le prolétariat et le sous-prolétariat industriel et agricole dans la RAU: formation, évolution, rôle politique. In *Social Stratification and Development in the Mediterranean Basin*, ed. Mubeccel B. Kuray, pp. 37-59. The Hague: Mouton.

———. 1973b. Le pouvoir et les étudiants en Egypte. *Maghreb-Machrek*, no. 57, pp. 65-71.

Workers' Educational Association. 1970. *Workers in the UAR: Basic Facts*. Cairo.

Wren, Christopher S. 1978. Sadat Seems Bitter at Arab Moderates. *NYT* (November 20, 1978).

———. 1979. In Egypt, the Ghost of the Tax Man is Suddenly Looking Very Lively. *NYT* (October 21, 1979).

———. 1980a. Egypt's Move to Help Economy Causing Confusion. *NYT* (June 23, 1980).

———. 1980b. Egypt's High Hopes Lock U.S. into Lavish Aid Program. *NYT* (July 27, 1980)..

Wynn, Wilton. 1959. *Nasser of Egypt*. Cambridge, Mass.: Arlington Books.

Yassin, Mohammed Hilmy. 1973. Parasitic incomes in fruit and vegetable trade. *al-Tali'a* 9:35-42.

Yassin, Sayyid al-. 1974. The view of the July Revolution toward social conflict. *al-Katib* 14:54-63.

———, ed. 1977. *The Revolution and Social Change*. Cairo: CPSS, al-Ahram Press. (In Arabic.)

Yussef, Abu Saif. 1973. Dialogue with the dialogue paper. *al-Tali'a* 9:51-71.

Yussef, Yussef Khalil. 1974. A Study on the Relation between Population Growth and the Quantitative Growth of Primary Education in ARE. *Population Studies* (Cairo), no. 10.

Zakaria, Fu'ad. 1974. Commercial relations between the professor and the student. *RY*, no. 2411 (August 25, 1974).

———. 1975a. Was 'Abd al-Nasser above error? *RY*, no. 2444 (April 14, 1975).

———. 1975b. The ugly face of the university. *RY*, no. 2463 (August 25, 1975).

Zaki, Ramzi. 1977. Rescheduling the External Debt and the Future of Economic Growth in Egypt. Paper read at 2nd Annual Conference of Egyptian Economists, March 24-26, 1977, Cairo. (In Arabic.)

Zaldívar, Ramón. 1974. Agrarian Reform and Military Reformism in Peru. In David Lehmann, ed. 1974, pp. 25-70.

Zaydan, Muhammed. 1965. Black market. *RY*, no. 1944 (September 13, 1965).

Zaytoun, Mohaya. 1982. Income Distribution in Egyptian Agriculture and its Main Determinants. In G. Abdel-Khalek and R. Tignor, eds. 1982.

Index

Library of Congress Cataloging in Publication Data

Waterbury, John.
  The Egypt of Nasser and Sadat.

  (Princeton studies on the Near East)
  Bibliography: p.
  Includes index.
  1. Egypt—Economic policy—1952-
2. Egypt—Politics and government—1952-
I. Title.   II. Series.
HC830.W37 1983   338.962   82-61393
ISBN 0-691-07650-2   ISBN 0-691-10147-7 (lim. pbk. ed.)

John Waterbury is Professor of Politics and International Affairs in the Department of Politics at the Woodrow Wilson School, Princeton University. He is the author of *The Hydropolitics of the Nile Valley* (1979), *Egypt: Burdens of the Past, Options for the Future* (1978), and, with Ragai el-Mallakh, *The Middle East in the Coming Decade* (1978).